T0134118

A Guide to the National Initiative for Cybersecurity Education (NICE) Cybersecurity Workforce Framework (2.0)

Internal Audit and IT Audit

Series Editor: Dan Swanson

A Guide to the National Initiative for Cybersecurity Education (NICE) Cybersecurity Workforce Framework (2.0)

Dan Shoemaker • Anne Kohnke • Ken Sigler

CRC Press
Taylor & Francis Group
Boca Raton   London   New York

CRC Press is an imprint of the
Taylor & Francis Group, an **informa** business
AN AUERBACH BOOK

CRC Press
Taylor & Francis Group
6000 Broken Sound Parkway NW, Suite 300
Boca Raton, FL 33487-2742

Printed on acid-free paper
Version Date: 20160121

International Standard Book Number-13: 978-1-4987-3996-2 (Hardback)

Library of Congress Cataloging-in-Publication Data

Names: Shoemaker, Dan, author. | Kohnke, Anne, author. | Sigler, Kenneth, author.
Title: A guide to the National Initiative for Cybersecurity Education (NICE) cybersecurity workforce framework (2.0) / Dan Shoemaker, Anne Kohnke, Ken Sigler.
Description: Boca Raton, FL : CRC Press, [2016] | Series: Internal audit and it audit ; 3 | Includes bibliographical references and index.
Identifiers: LCCN 2016000233 | ISBN 9781498739962 (alk. paper)
Subjects: LCSH: Computer security. | Computer security--United States. | Computer networks--Security measures. | Computer crimes--Prevention.
Classification: LCC QA76.9.A25 S493 2016 | DDC 005.8--dc23
LC record available at http://lccn.loc.gov/2016000233

Visit the Taylor & Francis Web site at
http://www.taylorandfrancis.com

and the CRC Press Web site at
http://www.crcpress.com

Contents

SECTION II   THE NICE CYBERSECURITY WORKFORCE FRAMEWORK AND HOW IT MAPS TO THE CFS FRAMEWORK

Foreword

If you are interested in the field of cybersecurity, it is my personal opinion that you should read this book. Knowing the breadth and depth of the cybersecurity profession is essential in matching your individual talents and desires to efforts that identify threats, defend our national security, protect our national economy, and preserve our way of life.

There are plenty of examples of miscues in our cybersecurity world. Thwarting, guarding, and being a champion requires extensive education, training, and experience. This book, *inter alia*, focuses on each aspect of the cybersecurity profession to provide insight to every reader. It provides an excellent discussion and overview of the National Initiative for Cybersecurity Education (NICE) Cybersecurity Framework (v2.0).

There isn't a version 2.0 without a version 1.0. Stepping back in history just a moment, the Cybersecurity Framework (v1.0), developed under the auspices of the National Institute of Standards and Technology (NIST), was born largely due to the increase in cybersecurity incidents, the need for education and funding, and Congress asking the question "how many cybersecurity professionals do we have in the government?" Until defining what cybersecurity work is, answering with any precision of who was doing cybersecurity work was nigh to impossible! Version 1.0 provided that definition and was the result of a successful concerted effort with (primarily) the government to define the cybersecurity roles.

Even before the Cybersecurity Framework (v1.0) was on the street in 2012 the need to expand the universe of information beyond the government to include industry and academia had become obvious. All aspects of the triumvirate of industry, academia, and government were concerned with the constant and expanding cyber threat to our nation's defense and economic well-being. You name a sector of our society and the cyber threats were (and remain) at the forefront of CEO, CFO, stockholder, and congressional et al. concerns.

To make the NICE Cybersecurity Framework effort truly reflect the national picture, the Framework (v2.0) effort was born. Using Framework (v1.0) as a baseline, planning started in early 2013. By late summer the focus groups started. In the interest of achieving the greatest breadth and depth, the goal for each focus group was to have equal representation from industry, academia, and government (all levels of government). No organization would be represented more than once, and if for some reason an organization attended more than one focus group, the same person did not attend more than once. These focus groups diligently hammered on each Cybersecurity Framework category and specialty area for quality definitions, completeness/sufficiency of substance, and application to their respective disciplines and organizations. Consensus within each focus group was needed and achieved, and the results summarized.

Knowing how absolutely critical the definitions of cybersecurity categories and specialty areas are to every part of our national structure, once the "strawman" Cybersecurity Framework (v2.0) was available, the focus group approach was repeated as a quality review—new focus groups concentrating on what the prior focus groups had developed. The Cybersecurity Framework (v2.0) provides cybersecurity definitions, as well as knowledge, skills, and abilities that are vital to our nation's success now and in the future. The significance of including the most accurate and comprehensive data was paramount.

In late spring of 2014 the Cybersecurity Framework (v2.0) was completed. The cybersecurity profession is not yet stable. It continues to evolve. However, the lessons in this book will be the basis for whatever transpires and their importance cannot be overstated. Successfully thwarting the evolving threats, the defense of our national security, the protection of our national economy, and the preservation of our way of life depend on you!

Roy Burgess
Former Lead, NICE Cybersecurity WorkforceTraining and
Professional Development
Department of Homeland Security

Preface

This book presents a comprehensive discussion of the National Institute of Standards and Technology (NIST), Department of Homeland Security (DHS), and National Initiative for Cybersecurity Education (NICE) Framework (v2.0). The NICE framework was created by the U.S. NIST to delineate the complete spectrum of task, knowledge, skill, and ability (KSA) requirements for the cybersecurity workforce, as well as to provide a common taxonomy and lexicon by which to classify and categorize cybersecurity workers.

The framework is a major national initiative, which is very ambitious in scope. Its elements are intended to communicate a global picture of cybersecurity work, as well as to provide a detailed explication of "how" the relevant aspects of the seven general competency areas of the profession interact in order to ensure suitable performance of that work. The NICE framework can be easily joined with the purpose and intent of another important NIST model, which is the cybersecurity framework (CSF). In that respect, the tasks specified in the NICE model can be factored into the functions specified in the cybersecurity framework. Or in even more practical terms, the NICE model will specify what the particular specialty area of the workforce should be doing in order to ensure that the CSF's identification, protection, defense, response, or recovery functions are being carried out properly. The association between these two highly influential models will be maintained in the discussion of each of the knowledge areas.

The attendant KSA specifications for that specialty area offer elaboration and clarification of the requisite competencies and the actions to be taken to perform the task. Using these two large-scale frameworks it is possible to construct a detailed picture of the proper organization and conduct of a strategic infrastructure security operation. And in that respect, these two frameworks provide the detailed explication of the discipline of cybersecurity as a whole. Thus, as a combination these two models can serve as an explicit definition of the field of cybersecurity.

Why the NICE Initiative Is So Important

The massive scope of the NICE endeavor and the time and effort expended in developing the framework makes NICE the first complete and fully sanctioned definition of the field of cybersecurity. Up to this point, any delineation of this emerging field has been shaped by the background, interests, and biases of the people who are providing the description and therefore cannot be considered authoritative. NICE embodies a carefully researched, all-encompassing presentation of every one of the elements of the profession of cybersecurity. And so, in effect, a full understanding of NICE represents complete mastery of the body of knowledge (BOK) of the field.

The NICE framework is generally considered to be authoritative because it was prepared through a 3-year, highly rigorous process spearheaded by NIST. As a result, NICE "officially" specifies the contents of the field. The ability to put the general shape of the cybersecurity profession into perspective as well as to understand all of its elements is a critical requirement for any professional situation or instructional function that purports to be based on the elements of cybersecurity.

The level of detail provided for each of the specialty areas in NICE makes it possible to structure either a single organizational activity or an entire educational experience based on concrete and officially sanctioned descriptions of KSA competencies. Thus, using the framework managers and educators can be brought to a common understanding of what is required to suitably perform cybersecurity work.

Justification for the NICE Approach

The framework is by necessity vast in concept and therefore the top-level approach that we use in this book is crosscutting. Our aim is to convey the complete contents of the field. In effect, what we are presenting here is an overview explication of the framework, its concepts, the underlying relationships between the areas, and the general content of those areas. In essence, the purpose of the book would be to explain *what* is in the framework and how it relates to the requisite functions in the CSF.

Practically, the textbook can serve as a roadmap of sorts. Because of the scope of the framework, the understanding we are conveying is aimed at Bloom's level two "comprehension" of the total concept and elements of the NICE model. The text serves as the necessary guide to the content areas. The reader can then drill down to whatever level of specificity they desire using other, more focused material. The general goal is to provide comprehensive support for a strategic view of the profession.

In essence, this book will provide a comprehensive roadmap that will allow a person to understand the application and uses of the NICE content. This also holds true for applications of this book in education and training situations. NICE is authoritative, both in job definition and also in terms of defining the work to be done for a particular organizational use. The job-task definition aspect is important because the framework supports the Presidential Job-Driven Training Initiative, which is a recent Presidential Directive (June, 2014).

The NICE initiative has been specifically aligned with the Presidential Job-Driven Training Initiative. As such, NICE will form the core of the comprehensive federal effort to increase the number of workers who complete high-quality cyber training programs and attain skills that are in high demand in the federal and national workforce.

One of the advantages of the NICE approach is that it does not define security as a monolithic field or a single profession. Instead, it provides the complete assortment of required task and KSA competencies for a range of 32 specialty areas and functions. That set can then be tailored and adapted to any relevant situation. Thus, for readers, this book will have a comprehensive description of how to do it right.

In industry, the people who would benefit from this knowledge range from managers through all types of technical workers and specialists. As such, depending on the tailoring it would be possible to make the case that in order to be considered to be performing a function properly that activity should embody some, or all, aspects of the NICE KSAs. The NICE framework applies to anybody who wishes to demonstrate authoritative and standard cybersecurity knowledge and competencies appropriate to their personal, career, or professional area of interest. That would apply from individual tasks all the way up to the strategic planning initiatives that will be required as the profession evolves.

In terms of practical personnel development, the ability to demonstrate standard KSA requirements can be used to validate adequate mastery of the necessary skills for a given workforce role. As a result, the competencies defined for each functional role in the framework ought to eventually become the yardstick to judge whether an employee has the necessary KSAs to do the work.

Unlike any other presently existing books, the value of this book is that it is based around well-accepted standard recommendations rather than presumed expertise. Some of the recommendations presented in this book are brand new; however, the core of the NICE framework has been established and vetted over an almost 4-year period, and its correctness has never been questioned. Therefore, the content of this book would not be a matter of opinion or even a recent fad. It would represent the current best knowledge about the practices to assure an authoritative definition of cybersecurity work. In that respect it is based on a recognized and formally promulgated BOK, which underlies a national level initiative to standardize the profession and which is tied directly to career paths.

That is the key message here. This book is based on a brand-new and unique national level initiative. This is the only book that aligns with and explains the requirements of a national level initiative to standardize the study of information security. Moreover, the knowledge elements contained in the book represent the first fully validated and authoritative BOK in cybersecurity. This book directly relates the requisite security knowledge to specific career tracks and job titles. In addition, it relates this knowledge to the functional requirements of the CSF. Its role-based competencies can be tailored to every level of enterprise and it is likely that commercial certificate authorities will decide to demonstrate that they meet the requirements of the NICE framework. If that is the case, this book will support study to obtain professional level certifications.

Intended Audience

This book is designed to give the reader a comprehensive understanding of cybersecurity work in all of its manifestations. Its recommendations are relevant for a range of professional roles and functions within that profession. The recommended practices for these roles and functions can subsequently be tailored to any relevant application within professional information technology (IT) practice. Thus, the audience could include anyone who wants to gain an understanding of all the KSAs that are appropriate for a particular professional role or academic interest.

The audience in the business world can include everyone from managers and technical workers to specialists such as auditors, testers, and general IT staff. From an organizational standpoint, this book was designed to align with several IT security models, such as the ISO 27000 series and also NIST SP 800-53(4). From the standpoint of higher education, the audience might include students who want to learn how to effectively perform a cybersecurity role and instructors who want to prepare their students for the pragmatic world of cybersecurity work. The tasks and KSA specifications embodied in NICE might also be considered sufficient to satisfy the requirements of commercial certifications for IT security assurance and certification schemes like DoD 8570.

Organization of the Text

The NICE model represents the accepted definition of cybersecurity work. The aim of the NICE workforce model is to provide a comprehensive and detailed set of recommendations about best practice for seven areas of cybersecurity work. The text is organized to help the reader understand how each of these knowledge areas can produce a practical, working cybersecurity solution.

NICE is ideally suited to educators because of its purpose. Unlike other umbrella frameworks, the NICE model was specifically designed to provide detailed task and knowledge requirements for the profession as a whole. Thus, the NICE model is a single authoritative description of the BOK as it applies to every type of professional cybersecurity work.

A comprehensive specification of the requirements for the multitude of roles contained in the model will help an organization tailor best practice to meet its real-world needs. Using a tailoring approach, the organization can create a practical, everyday set of work instructions that are customized to fit its exact needs. More important, the organization can adjust those practices as the situation evolves to ensure a continuing correct response.

This book is divided into two parts. The first part of this book comprises three chapters that give the reader a comprehensive understanding of the structure and intent of how the NICE model, its various elements, and their detailed contents. Chapter 1 introduces the concept of standard definitions of roles within the

32 specialty areas of the framework. This introductory understanding is necessary because the NICE model is descriptive not prescriptive. Therefore, the purposes and intents of the specialty areas have to be fully understood in order to be properly applied. Chapter 2 introduces the explicit tasks and KSAs within each of the specialty areas. Chapter 3 introduces the CSF functions, which define and focus the actual security work within each specialty area.

The second major part of this book, Chapters 4 through 10, introduces each knowledge area individually. Each knowledge area is specifically designed to enable the security goals of a particular aspect of cybersecurity work. The detailed content of the model is presented here. Two of the knowledge areas are combined in Chapter 8. These are the intelligence tradecraft–related parts of the model. The overall objective of this book is to help the reader build a comprehensive understanding of how to organize and execute a cybersecurity workforce definition using standard best practice. To reinforce the reader's understanding of the text and to ensure a successful learning experience, we have provided the following features:

- *Chapter Summary: A bulleted list provides a brief but complete summary of the chapter.*
- *Key Terms: A list of all new terms and their definitions is included in each chapter.*

Acknowledgments

We sincerely thank Dan Swanson who graciously and quickly approved our proposal idea and provided great support throughout the project. We also thank Rich O'Hanley for his support and all of the talented folks at Taylor & Francis who worked very hard to produce what you see.

A book like this expresses the work experiences and education of not only the authors but the team of people who authored the NICE Framework. We are indebted to the team of people who recognized the lack of consistency of how cybersecurity work is defined and the absence of a common language to understand cybersecurity work. It is our hope that our contribution will aid in the NICE Cybersecurity Framework becoming the body of knowledge for the cybersecurity field.

CYBERSECURITY

1

Defining Competencies for the Cybersecurity Workforce and Two Frameworks

Chapter 1

Introduction: Defining the Cybersecurity Workforce

Chapter Objectives

At the conclusion of this chapter, the reader will understand:

- Why security in cyberspace is important
- The issues that have to be overcome in order to ensure cybersecurity
- Two common sense factors that make cybersecurity different
- The general structure and intent of the National Initiative for Cybersecurity Education (NICE) framework
- The general application and justification for the NICE framework
- The elements of the NICE framework

Cybersecurity: Failure Is Not an Option

Computerized systems and the information they process are so tightly bound within the fabric of our society that their reliability and the confidentiality, integrity, and availability of the information that they process must be totally trustworthy in order to enable the fundamental structures of our society.

For instance, one only has to imagine the impact on its customers, if the information that was kept in a bank's databases was corrupted or lost. Or imagine what would happen if national defense information was leaked to our adversaries. Yet the average bank executive or governmental manager has great difficulty appreciating the true value of the systems and information that they manage.

The problem lies in deciding what security is worth to an organization. In a profit-driven world, it is hard for the leaders in the public and private sectors to justify the tangible expense of protecting virtual assets like computers and networks, and their contents. As a result, even though the constituent elements of cyberspace have real value and can directly impact people's lives, it is hard for the people who are putatively responsible for the protection of those contents to understand how the ways that the theft or destruction of a computer or its information might affect them personally.

Equally as important, it is exceedingly difficult and very costly for any organization to ensure reliable and systematic protection for an asset that is as dynamic and abstract as its information technology (IT) systems and information.

The problem lies in the fact that the knowledge that is required to assure reliable and consistent protection of cyber assets changes as rapidly as the technology evolves. As a result, most people view the practices involved in ensuring cybersecurity as an opaque set of activities and requirements that nobody outside the elected few can truly understand or apply.

As a consequence, America's electronic infrastructure is riddled with vulnerabilities that have underwritten an outrageous number of criminal and national security exploits over the past decade. For instance, according to the nonprofit Privacy Rights Clearinghouse we have lost over one *billion* records in the past 10 years. And you should keep in mind that those losses only comprise the outcome of breaches that were *reported*. Since most companies do not like to publicize their security failures that number could be, and probably is, much higher.

The running average of 100 million records reported lost per year has been subject to some variation over time and the source of breach has changed in logical ways. But, the number of reported incidents rose annually from 108 in 2005 to 607 in 2013. And you should still keep in mind that these are only the ones that were reported. So it would be unrealistic to conclude that we have been getting better at protecting information.

Six Blind Men and an Elephant

The problem stems from the fact that the field of cybersecurity suffers from the "Six Blind Men and the Elephant" syndrome. In that old story six blind men are asked to describe an elephant based on what they are touching. So to one, it's a snake, another, a wall, and to another a tree, and so on. In the end, "Though each was partly in the right, all were entirely wrong." (See Figure 1.1.)

We have the same problem with knowing what to do to protect our system and information assets. There are established elements of the field that know how to secure the part of the elephant that they touch. But until we are able to amalgamate that knowledge into a single coordinated solution we cannot realistically say we are protected.

It should be obvious that highly complex problems cannot be solved piecemeal. Effective solutions can only be based on whole system approaches. Or in simple

Figure 1.1 Blind Men and the Elephant syndrome.

terms, "You are not secure if you are not completely secure." Those solutions have to encompass the entire body of knowledge and be taught as a coherent entity, within a disciplinary framework. Needs may vary in their particulars within the overall scope of the problem. But it is important to keep in mind that the elephant is a lot bigger than its individual parts. So you have to understand the entire beast in order to master it.

Cybersecurity: An Emerging Field

The issues associated with cybersecurity can be dated to the advent of the commercial Internet in the mid-1990s. Accordingly, the entire profession has a less than 20-year life span. In that time, cybercrime, cyberespionage, and even cyberwarfare have become visions with real consequences. Consequently, until there is a single commonly accepted definition of the field and the profession it is unrealistic to assume that our way of life is adequately protected.

Yet, even with its newfound national prominence, there is still a lot of disagreement about what legitimately constitutes the right set of actions to prevent harmful or adversarial actions. That disagreement was captured in a 2013 report sponsored by the National Academy of the Sciences (Bishop and Burley, 2013).

The report asserts that cybersecurity is at best an ill-defined field, which is subject to a range of interpretation by numerous special interest groups. Since there has been heretofore no clear definition of the field, the profession and the actual protection of computers and information tend to be characterized by a long track record of hit-and-miss failures (Figure 1.2).

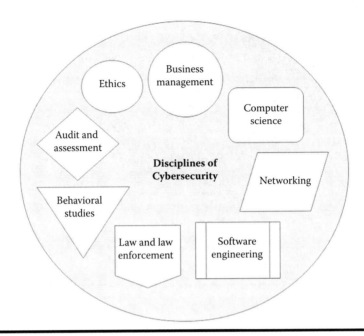

Figure 1.2   The variety of disciplines involved in cybersecurity.

The confusion about what constitutes the proper elements of the field originates in the fact that the profession of cybersecurity could potentially comprise concepts from a number of disciplines. Some content from all of these disciplines might reasonably fall within legitimate boundaries, which includes such diverse areas as the following:

◼ Business management, which contributes concepts like security policy and procedure, continuity planning, personnel management, and contract and regulatory compliance to the cause.

◼ The traditional technical studies of computer security, such as computer science, contribute knowledge about ways to safeguard the processing of information in its electronic form.

◼ Likewise, knowledge from the field of networking adds essential recommendations about how to safeguard the electronic transmission and storage of information.

◼ Software engineering adds the necessary system and software assurance considerations like testing and reviews, configuration management, and life cycle process management.

◼ Law and law enforcement contribute important ideas about such topics as intellectual property rights and copyright protection, privacy legislation, cyber law and cyber litigation, and the investigation and prosecution of computer crimes.

- Behavioral studies address essential human factors like discipline, motivation, training, and certification of knowledge.
- Even the field of ethics, with its consideration of the personal and societal implications of information use and information protection, as well as codes of conduct contributes something to the discussion.

All of these areas could potentially bring something to the overall aim of information protection. As such, it would seem logical to incorporate the principles and methods from each area into the total body of best practice for cybersecurity. Nonetheless, at this point there is still discussion about where the line ought to be drawn or where the focus within those boundaries ought to be, that is, where two simple common sense principles come into play.

Two Common Sense Factors That Make Cybersecurity Different

The factors that make securing systems and their information different from any other form of security endeavor can be summed up by two common sense factors. The first factor is the availability paradox; that is, systems and information have to be optimally available in order to be of any value to their user community. Yet the very requirement for maximum availability makes it difficult to ensure the confidentiality and integrity of that information. In essence, one critical condition, availability, trade off against the other two essential conditions, confidentiality and integrity.

The second factor is more overarching. It is called the "complete protection" principle. In essence, under this rule the system is not secure if any part of it can be exploited. The rule that emerges from the "complete protection" principle is that if a cyber-related situation is to be considered adequately secured, every potential instance of risk and exposure within that system has to be mitigated at all times by a formally defined and maintained protection mechanism.

The real-world condition that makes complete protection hard to sustain is the fact that the availability paradox demands that the information be easily available. In simple terms all protected information has to be obtainable by the user, at the time that they want to use it. This implies that all system and information assets have to be easily accessible while being fully protected.

This is a condition that is very difficult to achieve because important information might exist in three different forms at the same time. In essence, a critical piece of information might exist in a physical form, on paper records for instance, while it is also present in electronic form on servers or even in portable devices like a tablet computer. And even, to stretch the point, that same information might be in the head of an individual.

The problem for security is that every one of those places has to be identified and properly protected in order to ensure that a particular system or information asset of value is actually secure. Otherwise, a compromise of an instance of the item in one location will in essence compromise all other instances of the same item in all other places.

The only way to make certain that a compromise does not occur is to identify all instances of the information and then put technical and/or management controls in place to ensure trusted access. Nonetheless, in order for those controls to be effective, they have to be coordinated. That coordination is normally supplied through a single unified management process. The figurative term for that all-inclusive management process is "information governance."

In its simplest form, information governance ensures that the organization deploys and controls all of its cybersecurity-related functions through a single coordinated means. That specific approach ensures the deployment and subsequent sustainment of a set of mutually supporting controls or countermeasures.

The purpose of a well-defined and formally implemented information governance function is to integrate the requisite set of countermeasures into a coherent operational activity that will theoretically address every known area of potential exploitation. It should be obvious from this requirement that the information governance function has to be adapted, or customized, to meet the needs of each specific situation. Moreover, within that customization process, the designer will have to take into consideration all relevant protection requirements as well as provide the most single effective means of assuring the necessary level of trust.

Instilling Order in a Virtual World

The problem with cybersecurity is that the contents and activities that are done in the virtual world are nothing more than a proxy for human actions in the real world. The value of a piece of information might be derived from the importance of the idea, or the criticality of the decision, or it can represent simple things like doing your taxes or keeping track of your bank balance. Nonetheless, the fact remains that until the tangible outcome and value of that information or programmed action is known and analyzed for inherent risk, it is hard to talk about the concrete mechanisms for protecting it.

So the first problem for cybersecurity professionals is to simply identify and then prioritize those things that are necessary or useful to satisfy the organizational mission. And in conjunction with that they also need to sort out the things that are not. Given the fact that most organizations are awash in digital information and computerized functionality, this is not like finding the proverbial needle in a haystack. It is more like trying to sort out the right needles from a much larger pile of needles. So the first step in any cybersecurity process is to simply get it organized.

That assignment would be relatively easy if you could actually see the information. But since cyber-information is both virtual and easily changed it is essential that the people responsible for assuring trust follow a disciplined and well-defined process. That process has to consistently assure that all organizational systems, and information, of any potential value are identified, assessed, and prioritized. If that identification, assessment, and prioritization activity is comprehensive and accurate, a properly organized cybersecurity process can be created.

Any system or information asset is a potential target for control based on its intrinsic value to the organization. Systems incorporate all of the hardware and system assets, applications, facilities, and personnel that store and process it. Nonetheless, with the exception of hardware, personnel, and facilities, all of these assets are intangible. So, they are not easily accounted for.

It should be clear that in order to have proper security it is important to specifically designate the actual target of control. However in most companies, systems extend everywhere, in some cases globally. And information flows back and forth across organizational boundaries, both virtually and physically.

Worse, the practical business processes of a complex organization can be very diverse, ranging from high finance to shipping and receiving. Moreover, those processes are usually dispersed to a wide range of locations. The need to ensure information in highly diverse and widely dispersed settings gets us back to the problem of intangibility.

It is easy to account for the flow of parts from an inventory or even the physical flow of dollar bills from a teller's till, because these are tangible items that can be seen and accounted for. Actions can be taken based on the ability of the person performing the transaction to actually see and control what has taken place.

Neither systems nor the information they process can be controlled that way, because even though information flows to and from a single point, usually a server, that server can be accessed from an infinite number of locations, thanks to the Internet. Moreover, that access is in the virtual world.

For instance, the whole point of a network is to provide remote access for users. The problem with controlling that access lies in determining who to trust. The responsibility of the cybersecurity process is to ensure that determination is correct. Effective control of access requires the ability to ensure that access is only granted to trusted people.

That implies the need for a formal process that will identify the right individuals and assign the appropriate access privileges. Then, the formal regulation of their access can entail the automated controls and managerial factors, which are integrated into a tangible framework. That framework is operationalized through explicit managerial control objectives and rules, which in their documented form represent the prescribed approach that the organization will use for ensuring trust. The creation of a comprehensive well-coordinated organization-wide set of rules and procedures is the function and purpose of the information governance process.

Combining Effort with Intent in Order to Get a Complete Solution

It goes without saying that, in order for a defense to be effective, all of the requisite countermeasures have to be in place and properly synchronized. This might seem like a self-evident statement, but the fact is that the typical cybersecurity solution will most likely only embody those measures that fall within the specific area of interest and expertise of the people responsible for the approach. Figure 1.3 shows systems, physical space, and stakeholders that together make up a complete solution.

Accordingly, the approach itself is likely to include only those countermeasures that the designers feel are necessary to secure their particular area of responsibility. For instance, if the security of systems and information is seen as a responsibility of the network security people, they are likely to install a firewall and electronic intrusion detection system (IDS). But electronic countermeasures alone will not protect a company from an authorized insider. So a company that relies only on a firewall and IDS solution would be vulnerable to insider theft.

Moreover, a defense that only reflects the focus and interests of a single field will almost certainly have exploitable holes in it. This can be a fatal flaw for any business because any competent attacker will simply scout around for the holes that they know must exist. That is why it is important to involve all of the fields necessary for assurance of that security in the design process, including electronic, personnel, and physical elements. Obviously, if a number of disparate fields are involved it is important to also ensure that the right disciplines are engaged in the overall process by which cybersecurity is both implemented and overseen.

Full involvement of all stakeholders is a very important consideration because of the requirement that no gaps can exist in the defense. For instance, IT installs

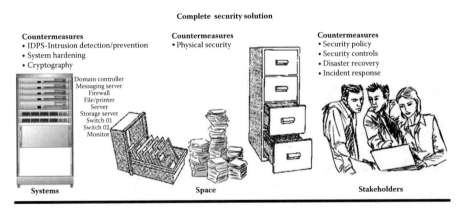

Figure 1.3 Systems, physical space, and stakeholders that together make up a complete solution.

technical countermeasures but it rarely has the responsibility to deploy accompanying physical security controls. Further, while the physical security team might deploy a complete set of physical protection measures, those are rarely coordinated to work in conjunction with the electronic measures utilized by IT to control external user access to their systems.

In fact, in most organizations physical and electronic security involves two entirely separate and independent areas of the company. As a result, gaps in the defense are likely to be created simply because the electronic and physical access control measures are not properly deployed, overseen, and maintained.

Ensuring effective alignment between the countermeasures that have been developed by the various security specialties might be difficult. But, to make matters even worse, most systems and instances of information exist simultaneously in more than one form. For example, customer sales information can be recorded electronically, but the same information can also be written down in a sales book, or just remembered. Therefore, the only way to ensure adequate security is to identify both the critical items of information, as well as all of the places where that information might conceivably be processed and kept.

A reasonably accurate inventory of the important information that the organization has and where it resides is important, because that inventory will allow security designers to establish the right set of procedural, environmental, technical, and human controls to secure its contents. Besides targeting the right information items, these controls also need to ensure that the protection applies to all instances of the information item wherever it is kept across the entire organization.

Finally, any workable solution has to be practical, that is, the overall array of protection measures has to operate within a well-defined and economically feasible management infrastructure. This requirement embodies Saltzer and Schroeder's "Principle Number One, Economy of Mechanism" (Saltzer and Schroeder, 1974). That infrastructure should reflect the assurance needs of the business as well as its business requirements. And the controls themselves must provably address the known threats they are designed to target.

Finally the security scheme itself should be assured to be trustworthy over time. The latter condition just ensures that the protection evolves as the asset base and the threat environment evolve. This is an absolutely necessary consideration because the outrageous evolution of the technology is one of the primary causes of disjointed and therefore easily exploitable security approaches.

Cybersecurity: Finding the Right Set of Activities

As we have seen by example here, cybersecurity, as a basic condition and requirement, is far too broad a concept to be a simple technological concern. Therefore, the cybersecurity process has to be founded on, and sustained by, a well-defined and formally structured organization-wide governance process. The goal of that process is to develop and integrate every requisite technology and management control into a global and sustainable organization-wide system, which is able to meet the assurance needs of each specific threat.

The role of cybersecurity is to ensure that all of the system and information resources necessary to underwrite a particular business strategy are kept robustly, confidential, correct, and available. The process of providing that assurance has to fit within the day-to-day business model and it should always add some value to the enterprise's overall purposes.

One of the common complaints about the everyday actions that are necessary to ensure a safe environment is that those activities slow down, or otherwise adversely impact the business process. Moreover, they are additional overhead so they are seen as costly. Therefore, one of the most important conditions for the development of an effective, comprehensive cybersecurity solution is that the actions involved in ensuring security cannot get in the way of effective and efficient business operation. That requirement is the reason why "Economy of Mechanism" is Saltzer and Schroeder's Principle Number One (Saltzer and Schroeder, 1974).

Thus, the aim of a formal cybersecurity process should always be to maintain an optimum and secure relationship between each of the company's business processes and their respective computerized resources. In that respect, the cybersecurity process needs to create and maintain an optimum set of technical and procedural controls to ensure the protection of all distinct systems and information utilized by each business process.

In practice, cybersecurity develops the specific policies, organizational structures, practices, and procedures needed to achieve effective assurance. Operationally, that involves the definition of explicit procedural and technical controls for any given requirement. These controls should ensure the effective management and operation of all cybersecurity functions.

The comprehensive organizational control structure, which is the operational incarnation of this process, must always be appropriate to the security requirements of the entity being controlled. It must also be consistently executed.

Thus, the control structure itself embodies a carefully designed and explicitly maintained set of electronic and managerial control behaviors, the outcomes of which can be observed and documented. The controls themselves are rarely stand-alone. They are normally integrated along with a range of other types of control to produce a verifiable state of sustainable assurance.

In order to make sustainment practicable, the coordination and management of the cybersecurity function itself should be located at the policy development and enforcement level of the organization. That is normally called the "C" level.

Anchoring the process at that level is necessary because the cybersecurity function itself must always be planned and administered from the organizational level where requirements can be enforced. That level of managerial commitment is essential because the executive-level decision makers are the only people who have the legitimate authority to create and enforce policies and procedures that might be unpopular across the entire organization.

That requirement is reinforced by the fact that cybersecurity is overhead to organization. Therefore, the people at the top have to be actively involved in sponsoring and directly engaged in the development of the strategic plan to ensure the requisite degree of protection for the business. The problem is that most top executives frequently see cybersecurity as a technical exercise. As a result, even though a big enough compromise can literally ruin a company, top-level managers do not think that cybersecurity is their problem. Consequently, they shift that responsibility down to the managers of the functional areas.

This is a mistake because nobody at the managerial level in the next level down has the authority to maintain a given process outside of their own area. And as a consequence, the assurance measures that might be implemented by each given manager in their particular area are likely to be a patchwork of actions. And the piecemeal nature of those activities will create gaps that will be exploitable.

Changing Times, Changing Players: The Stakes Get Higher

In day-to-day practice, the number of defenses that are weak or exploitable have been increasing over the past decade across the spectrum of government, business, and academe (PRC, 2014), because the number and type of attackers is growing in size and sophistication. In the 1990s, a typical attack was something like a criminal trespass, or Web site defacement. The victims tended to be the usual list of suspects, such as government institutions, and attackers themselves were inclined to be counterculture types who worked alone and on the fringes (Schmalleger and Pittaro, 2009).

That situation has changed, as the Internet has become the medium of choice for commerce. Now instead of being inspired by a desire to prove their art, attackers are motivated by financial gain and political ends. As a consequence, the old stereotypical image of the kid living on candy while doing 72-hour hacks out of his mom's basement has been replaced by a much darker and more complex persona, one who is well organized and much more focused on making trouble.

For instance, there are organized groups who perpetrate large-scale raids on financial institutions for the purpose of theft. In fact, the opportunities for financial gain from cybercrime are so great now, that established organized crime syndicates have taken to the business of electronic crime with the same zeal and enthusiasm as they did in the past with traditional physical crimes.

However, this new criminal business does not involve guns and strong-arm tactics. Instead it involves all of the potential ways that information can be obtained and exploited, ranging from sophisticated hacking to dumpster diving.

That range of new exploits raises one final concept, that is, the legal principle of "due care," which is sometimes called "due diligence." Due care is nothing more than the ability to prove that all reasonable precautions were taken to prevent harm resulting from an attack on something that you are legally responsible for. The problem is that, up to this point there has never been a standard definition of what constitutes due diligence in the information protection realm. Now that various models exist as it is possible to judge whether a company has been legally negligent in the way it handles an individual's personal information, that is, where the emerging numbers of best practice standards come into the discussion.

Definitive Step to Ensure Best Practice in Cybersecurity

In simple, operational terms, the cybersecurity process involves nothing more than deploying and then ensuring a coherent set of best practices to protect all assets of value to a particular company. The problem lies in the term "best practice." As we saw with the elephant, everybody has their own definition of what constitutes best practice. So, the actions that one group might view as appropriate to secure an asset may not be seen quite as appropriate to another group.

Therefore, it is essential to adopt a complete and commonly accepted framework of correct practice as a point of reference to guide any actions that an organization might take to protect its assets in the real world. The ideal would be to have that framework authorized and endorsed by a universally recognized and legitimate third party.

In the case of cybersecurity, the best practice framework ought to encompass all of the legitimate actions necessary to ensure a reasonable state of reliable long-term security. Then, with respect to evaluating whether due care has been taken, it can be assumed that, if all of these practices are executed properly then the organization has met its legal and ethical obligations for information protection.

Many other professions, such as the law or medicine, have a commonly agreed on definition of what it takes to meet the minimum standard of due care. Those help set the boundaries of ethical practice as well as guide the correctness of actions within those boundaries. Up to this point however, the problem for cybersecurity professionals is that generally accepted framework did not exist.

So the question became, "what criteria should a model for best practice in IA meet"? Ideally, a model for good cybersecurity practice would be universal in its application. Its correctness would be commonly accepted within the practitioner community. The model's recommendations would embody all of the currently understood correct actions for ensuring the confidentiality, integrity, availability, authentication, and nonrepudiation of information. Moreover, those recommendations would be expressed in a form that would allow a competent practitioner to tailor out a practical and economically feasible system that would protect all of the information of value under their care.

The lack of an acceptable model of the field has been an obvious roadblock to success for a very long time. As a result, the National Institute of Standards and Technology (NIST), which is the standards body for the federal government, was tasked to create a conceptual model that could serve as the single definition of the specialty areas, roles, and job tasks of the field.

During the period 2011 to 2014, the project was authorized and executed as the NICE Initiative. Besides NIST's involvement, the project was staffed and jointly executed by personnel from the Department of Homeland Security (DHS) and the Office of Personnel Management (OPM).

NICE workforce framework defines the complete set of roles that might reasonably be necessary to identify and mitigate all emerging threats in cyberspace. As a whole, the responsibility of those roles is to ensure the most economical and practical level of trust in the integrity and security of information and communication technology (ICT) assets. In essence, the NICE framework defines the field of "cybersecurity."

The structure and content of the NICE framework is generally considered to be the single definition of the field, which had previously been lacking. In that respect, NICE represents the most authoritative picture possible of the whole elephant and therefore it should be considered to be currently definitive. Moreover, due to its role as the definition of the elements of the field a thorough understanding of those elements and the requisite knowledge, skills, and abilities (KSAs) involved in executing them is an essential for any person who desires an in-depth understanding of the field. The aim of this book is to provide that understanding.

National Initiative for Cybersecurity Education Initiative

Cybersecurity is an emerging profession. Fifteen years ago, the notion of a workforce entirely dedicated to the protection of ICT assets would be unheard of. Nonetheless now, especially with the critical role that systems and computerized information plays in every aspect of our lives, a formally defined profession that is dedicated to developing effective ways to assure trust in the confidentiality, integrity, availability, authentication, and nonrepudiation of digital information is right at the forefront of our national priority list.

At present, the actions that we take to ensure cybersecurity are fragmented into a number of camps, all of whom claim that they have the answer. It ought to be obvious from the first sentence that the situation in the second sentence has to be changed if we ever want to be secure. So how do we change it?

The term "holistic" has been used to describe what has to happen in order for the security solution to be complete and correct. But most of the current profession specializes in some vertical aspect of the field. So we will have to reorient our thinking in order to address the problem in its entirety. And we will need a powerful societal force to implement that change.

Fortunately we have society's formal education processes available as a means of effecting change. Throughout time, education has been the mechanism we utilize to shape mass behavior. For that reason, a coordinated program of education can be a powerful public force. And it is education's historical impact on our society that makes it the logical place to start to address the overall problem of cybersecurity.

Nevertheless, there are a number of systemic and cultural challenges that have to be overcome before education can become a practical solution. First, according to a report from the National Academies of Science, cybersecurity is an emerging discipline. Consequently, it is not exactly clear what we ought to teach. Worse, all evidence points to the fact that whatever we should be teaching is cross-cutting. In essence, elements of the discipline of cybersecurity can be taught in places as diverse as engineering, business, medicine, and law.

People who are not academics may not realize the implications of cultural differences in academia. But, the people in those cultures have very different views of what is important and those views tend to be encased in stovepipes. Perhaps more importantly, all of these disciplines compete for students. Thus, their teaching is likely to stress the importance and value of their own content and research agendas to the exclusion of anybody else's.

Cultural differences also raise the question of "to aggregate or not to aggregate." If we leave the teaching of cybersecurity in diverse places on campus, we are not going to get a coherent message, let alone evolve the field into a mature discipline. However, if we pull all of the cybersecurity education into a single place that begs the question of "where should we put it?" since engineers will not play well with law school faculty and vice versa.

It should be obvious that a broad-scale academic strategy has to be based on a comprehensive definition of the field. The federal government has taken the first step in providing that definition with the publication of the NICE National Cybersecurity Workforce Framework (v2.0).

National Cybersecurity Workforce Framework (v2.0)

The DHS's compendium of best practice is titled The National Initiative for Cybersecurity Education National Cybersecurity Workforce Framework (v2.0), and it attempts to satisfy all of those requirements. The NICE framework makes an authoritative, formal statement about what an individual has to know in order to fulfill the requirements of a range of roles in an organization. Figure 1.4 shows the seven general knowledge areas of the NICE Workforce Framework (v2.0).

The framework is a product of the NIST and the Department of Homeland Security National Cyber Security Division (DHS-NCSD). NIST has the advantage of being a federal government entity and so it has the ability to reach across all sectors to assemble a national body of experts. And so given that reach, the experts who worked on NICE were drawn from all of the concerned sectors of our society,

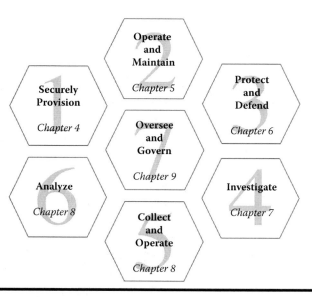

Figure 1.4   The seven general knowledge areas of the NICE Workforce Framework (v2.0).

governmental, business, and academic. That input was then pulled together into a single "national baseline representing the essential knowledge and skills" that all IT security practitioners should possess (NIST, 2014).

The NICE framework is an umbrella framework, in the sense that its intention is to define the complete set of competencies associated with cybersecurity work. However, the NICE model goes a step further in that it also links those competencies to a group of common security roles and a set of functions associated with those roles. That gives individual practitioners a standard set of recommendations about the activities that should be implemented in order to fulfill the requirements of each of those roles.

There have been other attempts to create an inclusive, top-level framework for best practice in cybersecurity. One of the better-known examples of framework models of this type is the International Standards Organization's (ISO) ISO 27000 series of standards. Specifically, ISO 27001/27002 offers a valid model for the definition of an information security management system (ISMS). However, it is not intended as a yardstick to define the common knowledge requirements of a given cybersecurity professional.

There are models that do define personal requirements for practitioners within specific silos of practice. These include the common body of knowledge (CBK) for the Certified Information Systems Security Professional (CISSP) and the Information System Audit and Control Association's (ISACA) Control Objectives for Information and Related Technology (COBIT). Specifically, International Information Systems Security Certification Consortium (ISC2s) CISSP and ISACA's Certified Cybersecurity Manager (CISM) provide a perfectly acceptable

CBK for cybersecurity professionals. However, they are totally different and competing models, in the commercial space, and therefore they cannot be considered to be a commonly accepted basis of the profession.

The aim of the National Cybersecurity Workforce Framework is to "establish the common taxonomy and lexicon to be used to describe all cybersecurity work and workers irrespective of where or for whom the work is performed" (NIST, 2014). The framework is composed of 7 knowledge areas and 32 distinct specialty areas. These knowledge and specialty areas define the range of activities that legitimately comprise the cybersecurity profession. In that respect, NICE has become the first truly holistic definition of the field.

The framework is intended to be applied in the public, private, and academic sectors. Use of the framework does not require that organizations change organizational or occupational structures. In fact, the framework was developed because requiring such changes would be costly, impractical, ineffective, and inefficient. Thus, the framework can be applied to situations across all types of settings and environments.

As depicted in Figure 1.5, the aim of the NICE model is to standardize the concepts and terms of the profession. These are arrayed into seven areas of common practice:

1. Securely provision
2. Operate and maintain
3. Protect and defend
4. Investigate
5. Collect and operate
6. Analyze
7. Oversee and govern

Those seven areas define the entire range of appropriate activities for the assurance of information. The NICE model also factors the activities in these 14 areas into specific professional practice requirements for 65 standard roles in 32 specialty areas.

Those 65 roles range from "chief information officer (CIO)" to "acquisition specialist." In addition to specifying the acceptable actions for each of these professional roles, the NICE model specifies the appropriate KSA requirements for each specialty role. This degree of explicit direction establishes the NICE model as an ideal conceptual framework to base a practical cybersecurity solution on, for any organization.

In order to aid in implementation, the framework contains a catalog of prototypical specialty areas for each of the seven knowledge areas. The knowledge areas themselves are very broad and deep. In essence, they would be considered a "field" in conventional practice. Examples of that are such fields as forensics (investigate), or software engineering (securely provision). Sample job titles that lie within the 32 specialty areas are provided as examples of common work functions that might fall within each specialty area. They are primarily offered as a means of illustrating and ensuring a practical understanding of the application of the framework in real-world settings.

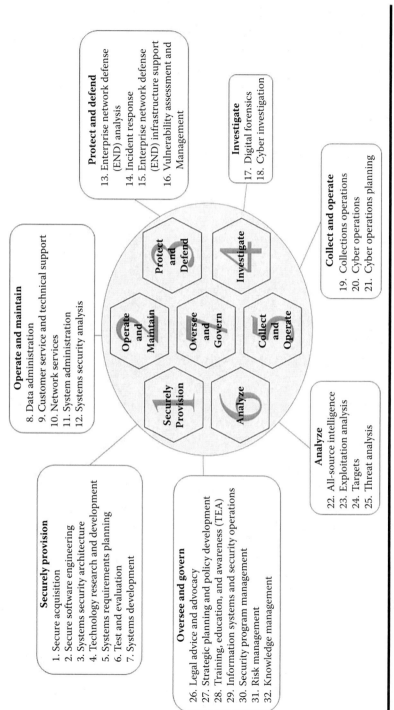

Protect and defend
13. Enterprise network defense (END) analysis
14. Incident response
15. Enterprise network defense (END) infrastructure support
16. Vulnerability assessment and Management

Investigate
17. Digital forensics
18. Cyber investigation

Operate and maintain
8. Data administration
9. Customer service and technical support
10. Network services
11. System administration
12. Systems security analysis

Collect and operate
19. Collections operations
20. Cyber operations
21. Cyber operations planning

Securely provision
1. Secure acquisition
2. Secure software engineering
3. Systems security architecture
4. Technology research and development
5. Systems requirements planning
6. Test and evaluation
7. Systems development

Analyze
22. All-source intelligence
23. Exploitation analysis
24. Targets
25. Threat analysis

Oversee and govern
26. Legal advice and advocacy
27. Strategic planning and policy development
28. Training, education, and awareness (TEA)
29. Information systems and security operations
30. Security program management
31. Risk management
32. Knowledge management

Figure 1.5   Sample job titles that lie within the 32 specialty areas as examples of common work functions.

Knowledge Area 1: Securely Provision

Securely provision encompasses those areas that are responsible for conceptualizing, designing, and building secure IT systems. In essence, these are the workforce roles who are responsible for some aspect of system and software development and maintenance. Securely provision contains seven specialty areas. These areas primarily lie in the academic and professional domain of software and systems engineering. Figure 1.6 shows the relationship between the securely provision general knowledge area, the specialty areas, and their corresponding roles.

The specialty areas that fall within securely provision are not usually considered to be part of traditional information security practice, at least in academe, because the securely provision areas concentrate more on the system itself than the information that it transmits.

Nevertheless, since most exploits target development and maintenance problems, the specialty areas of securely provision are among the most important aspects of the security roles in a modern organization. The specialty areas themselves illustrate the general focus and intent of the knowledge in securely provision. These specialty areas are discussed in the following sections.

Secure acquisition is the first specialty area in the securely provision knowledge area and it is an excellent way of illustrating the difference between the framework and any other model of the field. For the first time a major model of the discipline focuses on the management and support of the acquisition life cycle. Given our dependence on integration as a method of developing systems and the dependence of government and industry on commercial off-the-shelf (COTS) products, acquisition of secure products is a major national security issued.

The elements of acquisition include the necessary project setup and planning; the determination and documentation of the requirements; the selection; and procurement of ICT and cybersecurity products used in the organization's design, development, and maintenance of its infrastructure to minimize potential risks and vulnerabilities.

Acquisition oversees, evaluates, and supports the documentation, specification, contracting and oversight practices necessary to ensure a secure and correct new IT system or software product. It ensures that any purchase meets the organization's information assurance (IA) and security requirement. It ensures appropriate treatment of risk, compliance, and long-term operation of the product. Typical roles in this area include (NIST, 2014):

1. Chief information security officer (CISO)
2. Contracting officer (CO)
3. Contracting officer technical representative (COTR)
4. IT director

Secure software engineering is probably the most clearly recognized specialty area in this group. This is the area where the classic development and maintenance

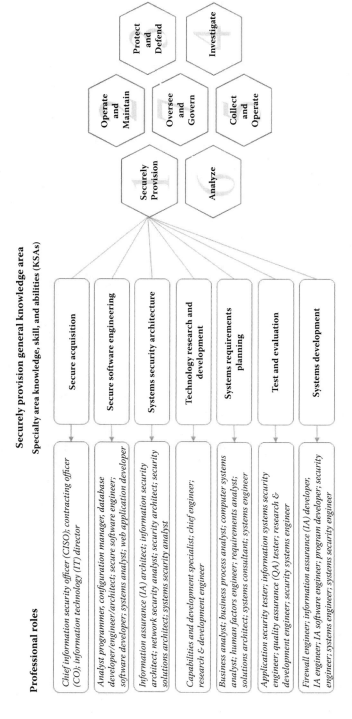

Figure 1.6 **The relationship between the securely provision general knowledge area, the specialty areas, and their corresponding roles.**

professionals work. And elements of this area have been well-recognized industrial roles for at least 50 years.

This is the area, which is primarily responsible for developing and coding new or for modifying existing computer applications, software, or specialized utility programs. Practitioners follow software assurance best practices that have emerged in the field over the past 25 years (NIST, 2014). Typical roles within this category include:

1. Analyst programmer
2. Computer programmer
3. Configuration manager
4. Database developer/engineer/architect
5. IA engineer
6. IA software developer
7. IA software engineer
8. Research & development engineer
9. Secure software engineer
10. Security engineer
11. Software developer
12. Software engineer/architect
13. Systems analyst
14. Web application developer

Systems security architecture is the other traditional area of the field. This specialty area focuses on the first critical stages of the waterfall. The primary focus is at the requirements and design phases of the systems development life cycle. Since these two stages lay down the initial conceptualization of the product, they have a disproportionate degree of influence on the eventual security outcome.

The job roles in this specialty area include researching, defining and capturing, and describing the detailed technological and environmental conditions for eventual incorporation into the system and security designs and processes. Those conditions include incorporating such things as business and legal and regulatory requirements. Typical job roles within this specialty area include:

1. IA architect
2. Information security architect
3. Information systems security engineer
4. Network security analyst
5. Research & development engineer
6. Security architect
7. Security engineer
8. Security solutions architect
9. Systems engineer
10. Systems security analyst

Technology research and development is not the same as testing, which is another specialty area related to assurance. This specialty area is responsible for the development of a meaningfully correct application of the product within the business environment as well as its continuing evolution. As a consequence, the job roles in this specialty area tend to be focused in outwardly facing concept positions, rather than production.

This specialty area does the necessary testing and general assessment of the technology that is required to develop and enhance its capabilities. In that respect, it supports the integration process as well as providing support for the organizations' prototyping capability (NIST, 2014). Typical job titles include:

1. Capabilities and development specialist
2. Chief engineer
3. Research & development engineer

Systems requirements planning is the traditional requirements area of the software engineering body of knowledge (SWEBOK). The requirements and planning process is user oriented in that the focus is on evaluating and documenting the system and/or software functional requirements and the translation of those requirements into technical solutions. This phase drives the design and coding processes that are downstream from it. As such its job roles are normally outwardly focused. Roles in this specialty area include:

1. Business analyst
2. Business process analyst
3. Computer systems analyst
4. Human factors engineer
5. Requirements analyst
6. Solutions architect
7. Systems consultant
8. Systems engineer

Test and evaluation is another traditional area of the SWEBOK. This area does the testing and assurance necessary to ensure a functionally correct and secure product. In that respect, professionals in this area perform formal testing of a system and/or software product with the aim of evaluating its compliance with specifications and requirements.

The focus of the jobs in this role is on the application of classic principles and methods in the planning, evaluating, verifying, and validating of technical, functional, and performance characteristics (including interoperability) of systems or elements of systems incorporating IT (NIST, 2014). Job roles in this category include:

1. Application security tester
2. Information systems security engineer

3. Quality assurance (QA) tester
4. Research & development engineer
5. Research & development research engineer
6. Security systems engineer
7. Software QA engineer
8. Software quality engineer
9. Systems engineer
10. Testing and evaluation specialist

Systems development is the classic development role. The job roles in this category fall within the traditional waterfall life cycle model. And they have been part of formal IT work since the beginning of the field. Within the security universe the focus of the role tends to be on security other than functional assurance. As a result, the roles themselves tend to have titles such as the following:

1. Firewall engineer
2. IA developer
3. IA engineer
4. IA software engineer
5. Information systems security engineer
6. Program developer
7. Security engineer
8. Systems engineer
9. Systems security engineer

Knowledge Area 2: Operate and Maintain

As shown in Figure 1.7, the specialty areas in this domain comprise the traditional areas of IT operation. These specialty areas ensure effectual and capable execution of a conventional IT function. They perform the classic support, administrative, and maintenance activities necessary to ensure correct and effective system performance as well as a sufficient and proper level of security.

In essence, these are the workforce roles that are responsible for the secure day-to-day operation of the IT function. Operate and maintain also has seven specialty areas. These areas primarily lie in the academic and professional domain of system management.

The specialty areas that fall within operate and maintain are at the heart of traditional information security best.

From the beginning the operate and maintain specialty areas have provided the necessary assurance of a desired level of system performance. Thus, the specialty areas of operate and maintain might be considered to be the most visible aspects of cybersecurity in a modern organization. The specialty areas themselves illustrate

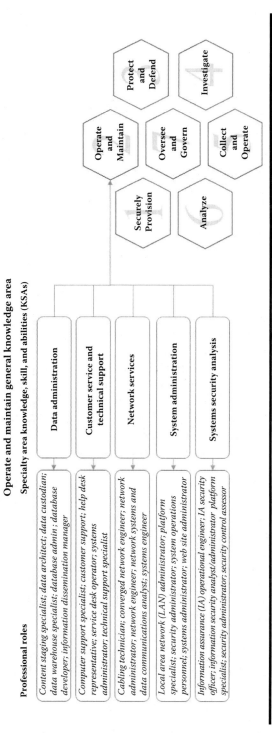

Figure 1.7 The relationship between the operate and maintain general knowledge area, the specialty areas, and their corresponding roles.

the general focus and intent of the knowledge in operate and maintain. These specialty areas are discussed in the following sections.

Data administration. Since information derives from data, this role is essentially the one that ensures the general integrity requirement. This role oversees the organization's databases. It develops and administers those databases and/or the data management systems that allow for the storage, query, and utilization of that data (NIST, 2014). Job roles within this specialty area reflect that development and oversight responsibility:

1. Content staging specialist
2. Data architect
3. Data custodian
4. Data manager
5. Data warehouse specialist
6. Database administrator
7. Database developer
8. Database engineer/architect
9. Information dissemination manager
10. Systems operations personnel

Customer service and technical support. Because user error is one of the primary causes of breach and unauthorized access, this humble area is among the most important and frequently overlooked elements of cybersecurity work. The general activities in this area include troubleshooting of problems as they arise in day-to-day operation. This area also installs, configures, troubleshoots, and provides maintenance of applications with a security requirement or focus. More importantly it is also responsible for executing and (potentially) escalating routine training activities that might arise as a result of routine business operation. Thus, the job roles in this specialty area include such business facing activities as

1. Computer support specialist
2. Customer support
3. Help desk representative
4. Service desk operator
5. Systems administrator
6. Technical support specialist
7. User support specialist

Network services. This specialty area comprises the classic network management function. This is a day-to-day operational, rather than a specific security-oriented function. It performs all of the essential, routine network and firewall installation, configuration, testing, operational, maintenance, and management activities.

That includes responsibility for the hardware and software that allows the sharing and transmission of networked information. The security focus is reflected in the job roles that comprise this specialty area:

1. Cabling technician
2. Converged network engineer
3. Network administrator
4. Network analyst
5. Network designer
6. Network engineer
7. Network systems and data communications
8. Analyst
9. Network systems engineer
10. Systems engineer
11. Telecommunications engineer/personnel/specialist

System administration. This is another one of the classic functions in the cybersecurity universe. Proper system administration ensures the secure operation of the system, its software, and networks. Consequently, the job roles in this specialty area are the ones responsible for the deployment, installation, configuration, and troubleshooting of all of the internal functioning and external communication aspects, both hardware and software, of the information system.

The aim of the job roles in this specialty area is to ensure the confidentiality, integrity, and availability of the data within the system. Job roles in this specialty area manage user accounts, and install and assure operational patches. They are specifically responsible for the classic security functions of access control, password, and account creation and privilege assignment, monitoring, and administration.

1. Local area network (LAN) administrator
2. Platform specialist
3. Security administrator
4. Server administrator
5. System operations personnel
6. Systems administrator
7. Web site administrator

Systems security analysis. This narrowly focused specialty area contains the job roles specifically responsible for ensuring the correctness and integrity of the system and the information it contains and processes. In that respect, the roles in this specialty area encompass the classic areas of traditional information security work.

Thus, the job roles tend to be focused on the integration and testing of new artifacts into the overall system structure along with the day-to-day oversight, analysis, and the maintenance of system integrity and security. Jobs in this specialty area include:

1. IA operational engineer
2. IA security officer
3. Information security analyst/administrator
4. Information security manager
5. Information security specialist
6. Information systems security engineer
7. Information systems security manager (ISSM)
8. Platform specialist
9. Security administrator
10. Security analyst
11. Security control assessor
12. Security engineer

Knowledge Area 3: Protect and Defend

Many people believe that the specialty areas in this domain comprise the entire field of cybersecurity, because the protect and defend knowledge area encompasses all of those specialty areas that ensure effective data transmission, network operations and network security, as shown in Figure 1.8. The job roles within these specialties normally perform the classic network monitoring, administrative, and protection functions required to ensure trusted system and software performance within whatever security parameters the organization sets.

Consequently these are the workforce roles that are responsible for the trusted ongoing functioning and management of the network. The specialty areas within protect and defend are responsible for identification, analysis, and mitigation of all identifiable threats to internal IT systems or networks. Protect and defend has seven specialty areas. These areas primarily lie in the academic and professional domain of network operations/network security.

The specialty areas that fall within protect and defend are the classic information security roles. Those roles have always ensured the organization's desired level of trust in its networks and the information they transmit. Thus, the specialty areas of protect and defend might be considered to be the most commonly understood aspects of cybersecurity among people in general. The specialty areas themselves illustrate the general focus and intent of the knowledge in protect and defend. These specialty areas are discussed in the following sections.

Enterprise network defense (END) analysis. This is the traditional network security specialty area. The job roles within this area are all responsible for some aspect of enterprise-wide network defense. These roles collect information through electronic and behavioral means that will allow the organization to monitor the entire network for incidents, respond appropriately when an incident occurs, and

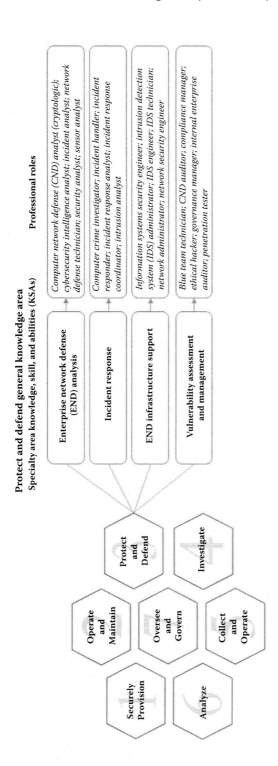

Figure 1.8   The relationship between the protect and defend general knowledge area, the specialty areas, and their corresponding roles.

document the occurrence for further analysis. The aim of all of these roles is to protect some aspect of the organization's information systems and/or their attached networks from threats.

1. Computer network defense (CND) analyst (cryptologic)
2. Cybersecurity intelligence analyst
3. Focused operations analyst
4. Incident analyst
5. Network defense technician
6. Network security engineer
7. Security analyst
8. Security operator
9. Sensor analyst

Incident response. This is perhaps the quintessential information security specialty area. The general aim of the incident response specialty areas is to respond to identified incidents as they occur. The goal is to mitigate any potential harm to the system or its attached networks. Both immediate and potential threats fall within the responsibility of this specialty area.

The job roles in this specialty area investigates and analyzes all relevant response options, prepares, and completes a set of response and recovery alternatives for each foreseeable threat. The aim is to maximize the survival of all systems and networks that fall within the assigned area of responsibility of this domain. Job roles include:

1. Computer crime investigator
2. Incident handler
3. Incident responder
4. Incident response analyst
5. Incident response coordinator
6. Intrusion analyst

END infrastructure support. This is an operational specialty area rather than one oriented specifically to network defense. It primarily monitors network operations in order to actively remediate any unauthorized activities that might be detected.

The job roles within this specialty area are responsible for the testing, implementation, deployment, sustainment, documentation, and management of all hardware and software network and resources that ensure adequate CND. Examples of job roles within this specialty area include:

1. Information systems security engineer
2. IDS administrator
3. IDS engineer
4. IDS technician

5. Network administrator
6. Network analyst
7. Network security engineer
8. Network security specialist
9. Security analyst
10. Security engineer
11. Security specialist
12. Systems security engineer

Vulnerability assessment and management. This is the network security analysis function. The job roles within this specialty area are specifically oriented toward the assessment and analysis of threats and vulnerabilities. The aim of the job roles in this specialty area is to identify and document any nonconformity with acceptable configuration norms or enterprise or local policies. Job roles within this specialty area include such functions as the following:

1. Blue team technician
2. Certified TEMPEST1 professional
3. Certified TEMPEST1 technical authority
4. Close access technician
5. CND auditor
6. Compliance manager
7. Ethical hacker
8. Governance manager
9. Information security engineer
10. Internal enterprise auditor
11. Penetration tester
12. Red team technician
13. Reverse engineer
14. Risk/vulnerability analyst
15. Technical surveillance countermeasures
16. Technician
17. Vulnerability manager

Knowledge Area 4: Investigate

The investigate knowledge area is a narrow aspect of the field that is primarily focused on after-the-fact investigation of incidents and other cyber-related events, such as crimes, intrusions, or harm caused to systems, networks. As the name suggests, the investigate knowledge area, shown in Figure 1.9, contains the job roles that obtain and analyze digital evidence to support evaluations of incidents that have occurred, as well as make recommendations about the ongoing performance of security operations.

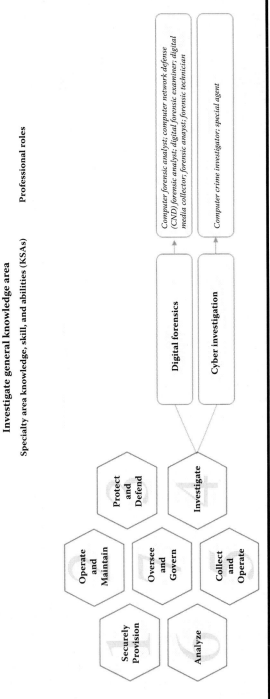

Figure 1.9   The relationship between the investigate general knowledge area, the specialty areas, and their corresponding roles.

The two job roles within this specialty area normally perform the classic forensic functions that are required to ensure trusted system and software performance within whatever parameters the organization sets. Consequently these are the workforce roles that are responsible for the investigation of incidents that have occurred within the domain of the organization's IT function.

The specialty areas within investigate are responsible for the collection, processing, preservation, analysis, and presentation of all evidence that is collected in support of threat and vulnerability mitigation activities of the organization. In addition, investigate may address any system- or information-related attack on the organization's IT systems or networks for law enforcement or counterintelligence purposes. Investigate has two highly focused specialty areas. These areas lie in the academic and professional domain of forensics.

The specialty areas that fall within investigate represent the classic law enforcement and counterintelligence roles of the security services of an organization. In the physical universe, those roles gather forensic data and provide interpretation and analysis in support of classic law enforcement and counterintelligence operation.

Thus, the specialty areas of investigate might be considered to be more in the domain of criminal investigation and counterintelligence work. Nonetheless, it is perfectly appropriate for the investigate specialty areas to focus strictly on detailed threat analysis tasks. The specialty areas themselves illustrate the general focus and intent of the knowledge in investigate. These specialty areas are discussed in the following sections.

Digital forensics is the traditional forensics body of knowledge translated into the digital domain. Specialists in this area obtain electronic clues and other forms of investigative data to support investigations of crime and espionage. As a result, the knowledge base blends superb electronic capabilities with the skills of a good police detective. That includes a profound knowledge of the criminal investigative process including such things as chain-of-custody and police procedure. Typical roles in this specialty area include:

1. Computer forensic analyst
2. CND forensic
3. Analyst
4. Digital forensic examiner
5. Digital media collector
6. Forensic analyst
7. Forensic analyst (cryptologic)
8. Forensic technician
9. Network forensic examiner

Cyber investigation. In many respects this is simply the body of knowledge of detective work. Investigate embodies all of the best-practice police methods and protocols, and criminal investigation procedures that are appropriate for cyberspace. As a result investigate encompasses all of the conventional investigative tools and processes utilized by law enforcement. That includes, interview and interrogation techniques, surveillance, countersurveillance, and surveillance detection methods. The activities in this specialty constitute a hybrid of police investigative and intelligence gathering activities. The job roles in this specialty area reflect that law enforcement focus:

1. Computer crime investigator
2. Special agent

Knowledge Area 5: Collect and Operate

Collect and operate, as shown in Figure 1.10, includes those specialty areas whose primary role is to protect unclassified information that can be used to cause some kind of explicit harm. Collect and operate contains the job roles that are responsible for focused counterespionage and deception operations. It also collects and interprets information that may be used to develop intelligence outcomes. Collect and operate ensures that essential proprietary information cannot be obtained or viewed by an adversary and/or obtains and interprets information from an adversary.

The specialty areas in this domain perform the actions necessary to eliminate or reduce the possibility that critical information can be obtained or interpreted for espionage purposes. This is a hybrid, multidisciplinary information protection function that embodies both electronic and human intelligence (HUMINT) means. In many respects this area overlaps with the role and purposes of the intelligence community. The three job roles within this specialty area typically perform the classic espionage/counterespionage role that is most frequently associated with intelligence work.

The specialty areas within collect and operate are responsible for the collection, processing, analysis, and presentation of information obtained from adversarial sources. The general aim of these roles is to challenge us to look at ourselves through the eyes of anyone who can harm the organization's people, resources, or mission. In essence, the general role of the specialty areas in this domain is to protect an organization's information from unfriendly eyes, which is not simply national defense information. It can include information subject to access by hackers, social engineers, criminals, and industrial espionage.

In many respects, the specialty areas that fall within collect and operate represent the classic intelligence/counterintelligence functions. Thus, the specialty areas of collect and operate might be considered to lie more in the domain of military operations security (OPSEC) and espionage. The specialty areas themselves illustrate the general focus and intent of the knowledge captured in the collect and operate areas. These specialty areas are discussed in the following sections.

Collection operations. This is the classic intelligence gathering function. This is not a linear process. It involves extracting bits of information from diverse sources

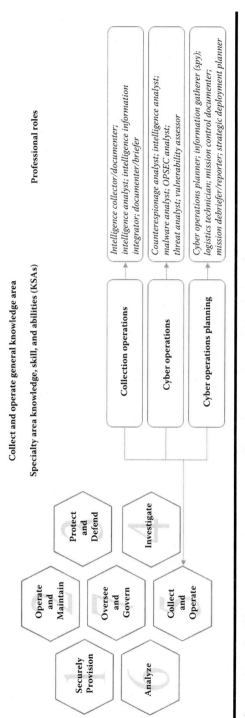

Figure 1.10 The relationship between the collect and operate general knowledge area, the specialty areas, and their corresponding roles.

and then piecing those bits of the puzzle together into a useful picture. It does the actual collecting using whatever common best practice methods appropriate to the organizational entity that sponsors it.

For instance, the approaches to intelligence gathering would be different for the Federal Bureau of Investigation (FBI), Central Intelligence Agency (CIA), and National Security Agency (NSA) even if the intention was similar. The collection would take place within the priorities that are defined by each organization's particular mission. Typical job roles within this area include such classic intelligence functions as

1. Intelligence collector/documenter
2. Intelligence analyst
3. Intelligence information integrator
4. Documenter/briefer

Cyber operations. This is the counterespionage function. Job roles in this category tend to duplicate the OPSEC function of the military. Roles in this specialty area carry out the tasks necessary to gather evidence of criminal or foreign intelligence operations. The long-term goal is to discover and mitigate all threats originating from known adversaries.

This specialty area specifically supports the overall intelligence operation. Its focus is on counterespionage from either electronic or HUMINT sources. In addition, the specialty area focuses on prevention of insider exploits and any form of sabotage or terror activities. The job roles in this specialty area reflect its purpose:

1. Counterespionage analyst
2. Intelligence analyst
3. Malware analyst
4. OPSEC analyst
5. Threat analyst
6. Vulnerability assessor

Cyber operations planning. This is the strategic specialty area for the collect and operate function. This is the specialty area responsible for the performance of in-depth operational planning. It selects the espionage targets and plans the collection operations. This is a pure management specialty. It prepares the operational plans and provides the logistical details. The focus of this specialty area is on a variety of intelligence and counterespionage targets in cyberspace. The job roles that are characteristic of this specialty area illustrate its intent:

1. Cyber operations planner
2. Information gatherer (spy)
3. Logistics technician

4. Mission manager
5. Mission control documenter
6. Mission debriefer/reporter
7. OPSEC planner
8. Strategic deployment planner
9. Quartermaster/provisioner

Knowledge Area 6: Analyze

Analyze focuses on the gathering information to ensure that information assets are fully protected from other people's attempts at attack and exploitation. Analyze does the information gathering and preparatory work that will allow an organization to gain sufficient knowledge of another entity's information and plans in order to ensure that the organization can be made proactively safe from attack. In essence, this knowledge area embraces the various roles of the traditional intelligence function.

Like the classic intelligence function, analyze encompasses those job roles, shown in Figure 1.11, that are responsible for proactive operations against potential adversaries. It collects and interprets information that lets the organization get ahead of potential attacks. Analyze both ensures against future attack. It also puts plans in place to obtain information for use in operations against a given adversary.

The specialty areas in this domain perform the actions required to obtain information about all adversarial targets. Given the understanding of espionage practices required to carry out the work, this knowledge area overlaps with the content of the general intelligence community. The four job roles within this specialty area typically perform the classic intelligence operational roles that are most frequently associated with tradecraft and the spy trade.

The specialty areas within analyze are responsible for learning about the plans and intentions of a given set of adversaries. Since this knowledge area applies to more than just national security settings, adversaries can represent normal organizations that are in competition with the business that supports the analyze function.

The purpose of these roles as a complete set is to ensure that the threat environment is fully understood and that no surprises sneak up on the organization. In essence, the aim of the specialty areas in this domain is to identify and monitor all potential adversaries or sources of harm.

As we said, this is not simply a national defense focus. It can include criminal operations, industrial espionage, asymmetric threats, and threats to business or individuals that originate from nation states.

Thus, the specialty areas that fall within the analyze knowledge area comprise the classic intelligence functions. And therefore, these areas might be considered parts of the cybersecurity workforce that underwrite espionage. The specialty areas

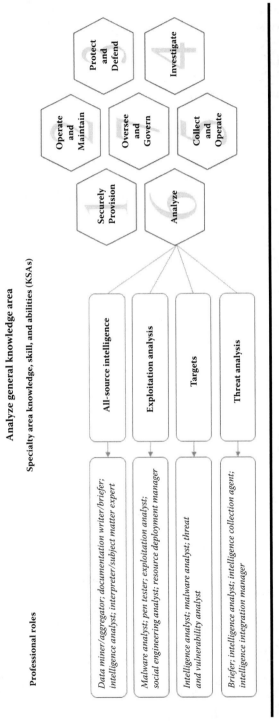

Figure 1.11 The relationship between the analyze general knowledge area, the specialty areas, and their corresponding roles.

themselves illustrate the general focus and intent of the knowledge captured in the analyze knowledge area. These specialty areas are discussed in the following sections.

Threat analysis. This is an omnidirectional sensing role whose purpose is to identify, collect information about, and judge the capabilities of the adversarial spectrum. Targets for analysis include both criminal and nation state operations. Once a threat is identified and fully characterized, the job roles in this specialty area ensure that law enforcement and counterintelligence agencies are kept up-to-date on the activities of the target entity. Job roles in this specialty area include:

1. Briefer
2. Intelligence analyst
3. Intelligence collection agent
4. Intelligence integration manager

All-source intelligence. This is the intelligence amalgamation and oversight specialty area. It does not develop intelligence as much as it manages it. In many respects this is the mirror of the threat analysis area. The purpose of all-source intelligence work is to amalgamate disaggregate threat information from all relevant sources across the intelligence gathering function.

As a consequence, the job roles within this specialty area synthesize outcomes and interpret the results for the purpose of providing an understanding of what the information means in practical terms. The aim is to support decision making regarding next step actions to take. Thus, the job roles in this area tend to reflect the big-picture analytics view:

1. Data miner/aggregator
2. Documentation writer/briefer
3. Intelligence analyst
4. Interpreter/subject matter expert

Exploitation analysis. Analyzes collected information to identify vulnerabilities and potential for exploitation. The tasks and KSAs in this function involve the specific identification of weaknesses and vulnerabilities that are likely targets for exploitation. In effect, this specialty area underwrites the prioritization process that is necessary for good strategic and operational planning.

The aim is to explicitly identify those harmful events that have the greatest likelihood of occurrence as well as potential impact. Job roles in this area characterize the threat as well as understand and document the method of exploitation, which includes:

1. Malware analyst
2. Pen tester
3. Exploitation analyst

4. Social engineering analyst
5. Resource deployment manager

Targets. This is a narrow area because it combines the impact and risk analysis function with the knowledge necessary to understand a particular area of vulnerability in detail. For instance, in order to decide about vulnerabilities the analyst has to have up-to-date knowledge of one or more regions, countries, nonstate entities, and/or technologies.

The aim of the job roles in this area is to gather the necessary information about, and then reliably analyze the significance of, all of the relevant organizational vulnerabilities that might be targets for exploitation. A highly specialized individual is needed to do this successfully. That person must possess intimate knowledge of their area of responsibility along with a wide range of multisource analytic skills. Job roles that fall within these parameters include:

1. Intelligence analyst
2. Malware analyst
3. Threat and vulnerability analyst

Knowledge Area 7: Oversee and Govern

Oversee and govern is a very large knowledge area. As shown in Figure 1.12, it encompasses the more policy/strategic, high-level management functions that are critical to proper information governance. The specialty areas in oversee and govern are all focused on long-term actions that foster organizational leadership, management, policy direction, and/or legal and regulatory compliance. The specialty areas all help create a stable environment where the individuals in an organization can effectively carry out their cybersecurity tasks.

Oversee and govern is by necessity very broad in scope. It encompasses those job roles that provide policy and managerial direction, advance the organization's overall cybersecurity efforts, protect it from external legal and regulatory consequences, and ensure effective and consistent operation of the general cybersecurity effort. Oversee and govern both ensures the trustworthy and reliable operation of the overall cybersecurity effort. It also makes certain that there is coherent and focused policy direction and management of the entire function.

The specialty areas in this domain do all of the things that are essential to overall information security governance. That includes the development of the people who constitute the security resource, the coordination and management of the policy and procedure, and the assurance of legal compliance. The five job roles within this knowledge area typically carry out the classic security policy and management oversight and guidance roles of the organization.

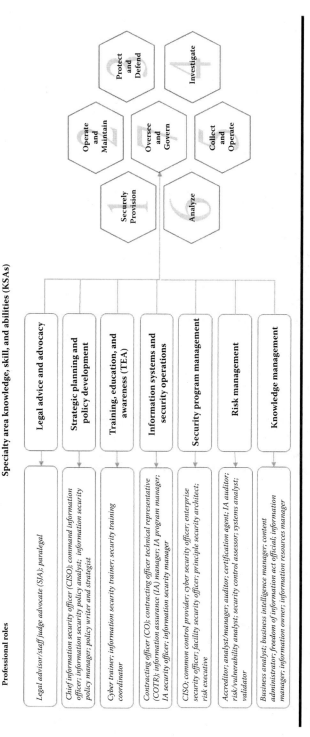

Oversee and govern general knowledge area

Professional roles

Specialty area knowledge, skill, and abilities (KSAs)

Specialty area	Professional roles
Legal advice and advocacy	*Legal advisor/staff judge advocate (SJA); paralegal*
Strategic planning and policy development	*Chief information security officer (CISO); command information officer; information security policy analyst; information security policy manager; policy writer and strategist*
Training, education, and awareness (TEA)	*Cyber trainer; information security trainer; security training coordinator*
Information systems and security operations	*Contracting officer (CO); contracting officer technical representative (COTR); information assurance (IA) manager; IA program manager; IA security officer; information security manager*
Security program management	*CISO; common control provider; cyber security officer; enterprise security officer; facility security officer; principle security architect; risk executive*
Risk management	*Accreditor; analyst/manager; auditor; certification agent; IA auditor; risk/vulnerability analyst; security control assessor; systems analyst; validator*
Knowledge management	*Business analyst; business intelligence manager; content administrator; freedom of information act official; information manager; information owner; information resources manager*

Figure 1.12   The relationship between the oversee and govern general knowledge area, the specialty areas, and their corresponding roles.

The specialty areas within oversee and govern are responsible for a wide range of tasks at a number of levels of the organization. That ranges from the education mandate at lower levels, all the way up to the policy and strategic planning functions at the top.

The purpose of all of these roles is to ensure that the organization's security activities are comprehensively and correctly controlled and governed. In essence, the aim of the specialty areas in this domain is to establish the policy and management aspects of the cybersecurity function. These roles apply in a wide range of settings, from small organizations to the multinationals. But the roles and job tasks are uniformly the same as are the KSA requirements.

Thus, the specialty areas that fall within the oversee and govern knowledge area represent the policy and management requirements of the business. And therefore, these areas might be considered to be the embodiment of the information governance function. The specialty areas themselves illustrate the general focus and intent of the knowledge captured in the oversee and govern knowledge area. These specialty areas are discussed in the following sections.

Legal advice and advocacy. Provides legally sound advice and recommendations to leadership and staff on a variety of relevant topics within the pertinent subject domain. Advocates legal and policy changes and makes a case on behalf of client via a wide range of written and oral work products, including legal briefs and proceedings.

1. Legal advisor/staff judge advocate (SJA)
2. Paralegal

Strategic planning and policy development. Applies knowledge of priorities to define an entity's direction, determine how to allocate resources, and identify programs or infrastructure that are required to achieve desired goals within domain of interest. Develops policy or advocates for changes in policy that will support new initiatives or required changes/enhancements.

1. CIO
2. Command information officer
3. Information security policy analyst
4. Information security policy manager
5. Policy writer and strategist

Education and training. Conducts training of personnel within pertinent subject domain. Develops, plans, coordinates, delivers, and/or evaluates training courses, methods, and techniques as appropriate.

1. Cyber trainer
2. Information security trainer
3. Security training coordinator

Information systems security operations (information systems security officer [ISSO]). Oversees the IA program of an information system in or outside the network environment and may include procurement duties.

1. CO
2. COTR
3. IA manager
4. IA program manager
5. IA security officer
6. Information security program manager
7. ISSM
8. ISSO
9. Information systems security operator

Security program management (CISO). Manages information security implications within the organization, specific program, or other area of responsibility, to include strategic, personnel, infrastructure, policy enforcement, emergency planning, security awareness, and other resources.

1. CISO
2. Common control provider
3. Cybersecurity officer
4. Enterprise security officer
5. Facility security officer
6. ISSM
7. IT director
8. Principal security architect
9. Risk executive
10. Security domain specialist
11. Senior agency information security officer

Risk management. This area focuses entirely on the identification and mitigation of risk. It is a continuous operation in a normal business continuity security function. As the name suggests, risk management workers manage and support the processes necessary to ensure new and existing IT systems meet the organization's IA and security requirements, which is typically an auditing and control responsibility. Risk management deploys the correct countermeasures to assure that all identified risks and monitoring requirements have been met and formally documents that compliance for review by the designated accreting/approving authorities. Job roles may include:

1. Accreditor
2. Analyst/manager
3. Auditor

4. Authorizing official designated representative
5. Certification agent
6. Certifying official
7. Compliance manager
8. Designated accrediting authority
9. IA auditor
10. IA compliance
11. IA manager
12. IA officer
13. Portfolio manager
14. QA specialist
15. Risk/vulnerability analyst
16. Security control assessor
17. Systems analyst
18. Validator

Knowledge management. This specialty area is essentially responsible for intellectual property protection. It oversees and assures the processes and tools that enable the organization to identify, document, and access its intellectual capital and information content. This is a knowledge assurance rather than a knowledge development responsibility. Thus, the job roles in this specialty area reflect the business facing nature of the work involved:

1. Business analyst
2. Business intelligence manager
3. Content administrator
4. Document steward
5. Freedom of Information Act official
6. Information manager
7. Information owner
8. Information resources manager

Chapter Summary

The problem with the current field of cybersecurity is that it is in stovepipes right now; although there are established elements of the field, there is no single coordinated solution. It should be obvious that highly complex problems cannot be solved piecemeal. Effective solutions can only be based on whole system approaches. Or in simple terms, "You are not secure if you are not completely secure."

Those solutions have to encompass the entire body of knowledge and be taught as a coherent entity, within a disciplinary framework. The current situation was captured in the National Academy of the Sciences 2014 report. The report asserts that cybersecurity is at best an ill-defined field, which is subject to a range of interpretation by numerous special interest groups. Since there has been heretofore no clear definition of the field, the profession and the actual protection of computers and information tends to be characterized by a long track record of hit-and-miss failures.

The factors that make securing systems and their information different from any other form of security endeavor can be summed up by two common sense factors. The first factor is the availability paradox, that is, systems and information have to be optimally available in order to be of any value to their user community. The second factor is more overarching. It is called the "complete protection" principle. In essence, under this rule the system is not secure if any part of it can be exploited.

The rule that emerges from the "complete protection" principle is that if a cyber-related situation is to be considered adequately secured, every potential instance of risk and exposure within that system has to be mitigated at all times by a formally defined and maintained protection mechanism. The real-world condition that makes complete protection hard to sustain is the availability paradox. In simple terms, all protected information has to be obtainable by the user, at the time that they want to use it. This implies that all system and information assets have to be easily accessible while being fully protected.

This is a condition that is very difficult to achieve. The only way to make certain that a compromise does not occur is to identify all instances of the information and then put technical and/or management controls in place to ensure trusted access. Nonetheless, in order for those controls to be effective, they have to be coordinated. That coordination is normally supplied through a single unified management process. The figurative term for that all-inclusive management process is "information governance."

The purpose of a well-defined and formally implemented information governance function is to integrate the requisite set of countermeasures into a coherent operational activity that will theoretically address every known area of potential exploitation.

That assignment would be relatively easy if you could actually see the information. But since cyber-information is both virtual and easily changed it is essential that the people responsible for assuring trust follow a disciplined and well-defined process. That process has to consistently assure that all organizational systems, and information, of any potential value are identified, assessed, and prioritized. If that identification, assessment, and prioritization activity is comprehensive and accurate, a properly organized cybersecurity process can be created.

It is easy to account for the flow of parts from an inventory or even the physical flow of dollar bills from a teller's till, because these are tangible items that can be seen and accounted for. Actions can be taken based on the ability of the person performing the transaction to actually see and control what has taken place.

Neither systems nor the information they process can be controlled that way, because even though information flows to and from a single point, usually a server, that server can be accessed from an infinite number of locations, thanks to the Internet. Moreover, that access is in the virtual world. Cybersecurity, as a basic condition and requirement, is far too broad and far too important to be a simple technological concern. Therefore, the cybersecurity process has to be founded on, and sustained by, a well-defined and formally structured organization-wide concept that unifies all necessary processes.

The comprehensive organizational control structure, which is the operational incarnation of this process, must always be appropriate to the security requirements of the entity being controlled. It must also be consistently executed. In simple, operational terms, creating that structure involves nothing more than deploying and then ensuring a coherent set of best practices to protect all assets of value to a particular company.

The problem lies in the term "best practice." As we saw with the elephant, everybody has their own definition of what constitutes best practice. So, the actions that one group might view as appropriate to secure an asset may not be seen quite as appropriate to another group. Therefore, it is essential to adopt a complete and commonly accepted model of correct practice as a point of reference to guide any actions that an organization might take to protect its assets in the real world. The ideal would be to have that framework authorized and endorsed by a universally recognized and legitimate third party.

So the question became, "what criteria should a model for best practice in IA meet"? Ideally, a model for good cybersecurity practice would be universal in its application. Its correctness would be commonly accepted within the practitioner community. The model's recommendations would embody all of the currently understood correct actions for ensuring the confidentiality, integrity, availability, authentication, and nonrepudiation of information. Moreover, those recommendations would be expressed in a form that would allow a competent practitioner to tailor out a practical and economically feasible system that would protect all of the information of value under their care.

During the period 2011 to 2014, the National Institute for Standards and Technology authorized and executed as the NICE Initiative. Besides NIST's involvement, the project was staffed and jointly executed by personnel from the DHS and the OPM.

The NICE workforce framework defines the complete set of roles that might reasonably be necessary to identify and mitigate all emerging threats in cyberspace. The structure and content of the NICE framework is generally considered to be the single definition of the field, which had previously been lacking. In that respect, NICE represents the most authoritative picture possible of the whole elephant and therefore it should be considered to be currently definitive.

The name of this compendium of best practice is the NICE National Cybersecurity Workforce Framework (v2.0), and it attempts to satisfy all of those requirements. The NICE framework makes an authoritative, formal statement about what an individual has to know in order to fulfill the requirements of a range of roles in an organization.

The NICE framework is an umbrella framework, in the sense that its intention is to define the complete set of competencies associated with cybersecurity work. However, the NICE model goes a step further in that it also links those competencies to a group of common security roles and a set of functions associated with those roles. That gives individual practitioners a standard set of recommendations about the activities that should be implemented in order to fulfill the requirements of each of those roles.

"The aim of the National Cybersecurity Workforce Framework is to establish the common taxonomy and lexicon to be used to describe all cybersecurity work and workers irrespective of where or for whom the work is performed" (NIST, 2014). The framework is composed of seven knowledge areas and 32 distinct specialty areas. These knowledge and specialty areas define the range of activities that legitimately comprise the cybersecurity profession. In that respect, NICE has become the first truly holistic definition of the field.

The framework is intended to be applied in the public, private, and academic sectors. Use of the framework does not require that organizations change organizational or occupational structures. In fact, the framework was developed because requiring such changes would be costly, impractical, ineffective, and inefficient. Thus, the framework can be applied to situations across all types of settings and environments.

The aim of the NICE model then was to standardize the concepts and terms of the profession. These are arrayed into seven areas of common practice. Those seven areas define the entire range of appropriate activities for the assurance of information. The NICE model also factors the activities in these 14 areas into specific professional practice requirements for 65 standard roles in 32 specialty areas.

Those 65 roles range from "CIO" to "acquisition specialist." In addition to specifying the acceptable actions for each of these professional roles, the NICE model specifies the appropriate KSA requirements for each specialty role. This degree of explicit direction establishes the NICE model as an ideal conceptual framework to base a practical cybersecurity solution on, for any organization.

In order to aid in implementation, the framework contains a catalog of prototypical specialty areas for each of the seven knowledge areas. The knowledge areas themselves are very broad and deep. In essence, they would be considered a "field" in conventional practice. Sample job titles that lie within the 32 specialty areas are provided as examples of common work functions that might fall within each specialty area. They are primarily offered as a means of illustrating and ensuring a practical understanding of the application of the framework in real-world settings.

Key Concepts

- The cybersecurity (IA) process has many facets.
- Cybersecurity centers on devising tangible means to counter threats.
- Systems and information constitute both an invisible and dynamic resource.
- It is necessary to make inventory and label information in order to make it visible.
- Information is actually a proxy for things that have real-world value.
- The cybersecurity process has to be coordinated to be effective.
- Coordination involves deploying and then maintaining an appropriate set of technical and managerial controls.
- Effective control ensures trusted access to information.
- Cybersecurity requires formal organization and executive sponsorship.
- Adversaries add a new dimension of threat to information.
- Standard models are important roadmaps for organizations to follow.
- The NICE framework is a national level model for cybersecurity.
- The NICE framework outlines the workforce roles for the entire field.

Key Terms

Availability: A state of cybersecurity, where all necessary information is accessible at the time it is needed.

Compromise: A breakdown in organizational control leading to the loss or harm to data.

Confidentiality: A state of cybersecurity, where information is protected from unauthorized access.

Controls: Technical or managerial actions that are put in place to ensure a given and predictable outcome.

Countermeasures: Technical or managerial actions taken to prevent loss of a defined set of information items.

Department of Homeland Security (DHS): Federal agency charged with the overall protection of the national infrastructure.

Information Governance: System and information assets have been identified as needing protection and have been placed within a strategic framework of controls in order to manage and secure them.

Integrity: A state of cybersecurity, where information can be shown to be accurate, correct, and trustworthy.

National Institute of Standards and Technology (NIST): The body responsible for developing and promulgating standards for federal programs and federal government agencies.

Organizational Governance: A condition which ensures that all organizational functions are adequately coordinated and controlled by policy, typically enabled by strategic planning. When applied to information protection, the term is "information governance."

Strategic Planning: The act of translating an organization's intended direction into specific steps along a particular timeline; strategic planning affects the entire organization for a significant period.

Umbrella Framework: A comprehensive set of standard activities intended to explicitly define all required processes, activities, and tasks for a given field or application.

References

Bishop, M. and Burley, D. 2013. *Professionalizing the Nation's Cybersecurity Workforce: Criteria for Decision-Making.* Washington, DC: National Academies of Science.

National Institute of Standards and Technology (NIST). 2014. *NICE Cybersecurity Workforce Framework 2.0.* Gaithersburg, MD: National Institute of Standards and Technology.

Saltzer, J.H. and Schroeder, M.D. 1974. "The Protection of Information in Computer Systems." *Communications of the ACM* 17(7): 388–402.

Schmalleger, F. and Pittaro, M. 2009. *Crimes of the Internet.* Upper Saddle River, NJ: Prentice Hall.

PRC. 2014. "Chronology of Data Breaches Security Breaches 2005–Present." Privacy Rights Clearinghouse, http://www.privacyrights.org/data-breach.

Chapter 2

Creating Standard Competencies for Cybersecurity Work

Chapter Objectives

At the conclusion of this chapter, the reader will understand:

- The knowledge area concepts and justification of the National Initiative for Cybersecurity Education (NICE) workforce model
- The underlying specialty area categories of the NICE workforce model
- The knowledge, skills, and abilities (KSAs) and task structure of the NICE workforce model
- The complete set of task specifications for the NICE workforce model
- The role and justification for all types of planning using the workforce model
- The tailoring of the model to specific applications
- Factors that ensure proper application of the NICE model to a given situation

The NICE Workforce Model

As we saw in the Chapter 1, the field of cybersecurity is currently undefined. That is a serious fundamental problem in the real world. That is because all of the management processes and countermeasures that will eventually comprise the real-world security solution. That solution has to be composed of a single robust set of organizational practices that function together synergistically in common practice. Therefore, organizations have to be able to understand, define, and implement a complete and correct assemblage of activities that provide an adequate and consistent level of assurance.

The problem is that the larger and more complex the organization the more difficult it is to identify and interrelate all of the required elements of the solution into a single cohesive security system. Consequently, some form of standard template is an essential tool that can be used to guide lay managers in the implementation and deployment of a rational real-world approach. That template should constitute a commonly accepted, standardized conceptual model, which embodies all of the required security elements into a single framework of well-defined and highly integrated practices.

The aim of a high-level conceptual model like the NICE framework is to provide a strategic description of all of the elements of the field. NICE specifies all of the commonly agreed on activities and interrelationships associated with good security into a single workforce model. In that respect, the NICE framework stipulates all of the requisite and commonly accepted workforce roles and practices necessary to carry out a complete set of cybersecurity activities. In that respect, by providing a standard definition of the tasks involved in the work to be done the NICE framework comprises a standard definition of the field of cybersecurity.

All of these job roles and their attendant tasks are logically related within the structure of the framework. In that respect then, the framework serves as a template to allow any organization to tailor out its own substantive set of suitable work practices. If the tailoring is done correctly, the assumption is that the resulting practices will, in effect, be correct because they are derived from the commonly accepted correct model of the field, as represented by the NICE framework model. So essentially, the NICE framework provides the standard advice about how to connect the dots in a practical manner between all of the requisite elements of cybersecurity practice. That advice serves as a roadmap to guide an organization in the creation of its own specific security solution.

The purpose of the NICE model is to provide the most comprehensive possible specification of the various specialty areas of the field, their attendant job roles, the practices they should perform and the underlying KSA requirements. Some of these practices are in the traditional areas of information technology (IT), like forensics, network security, and operational security. However, other tasks present a broader view of the information security field, such as secure supply chain management legal and regulatory compliance, and strategic policy. Taken as a whole, the 7 knowledge areas and the 32 specialty areas of the NICE framework comprise a multifaceted array of the things that need to be thought about when building a cyber defense that will address all credible forms of potential attack.

All of the task and KSA behaviors that the creators of the NICE workforce model deemed necessary to ensure fundamentally effective security were assigned to the 32 specialty areas of the model. These specialty areas were created using input from the profession as the point of reference as well as the popular standards in the field. Nonetheless, in order to make the representation of the field of cybersecurity as exhaustive as possible, the recommendations that were built into the model were also filtered through a range of industries and other stakeholders across the spectrum of cybersecurity work.

The work of actually vetting and compiling the competencies was done by a group of subject matter experts (SMEs). That group was formulated under the sponsorship of the Department of Homeland Security's National Cyber Security Division (DHS/NCSD). A range of industry, governmental, and academic participants who had either participated in the formulation of information security standards, or policy, or who had notable efforts in information security, participated in working groups formulated for each knowledge area. These groups produced a 1.0 version of the standard, which was socialized around the various constituent communities, government, industry, and academe for review and revision. The 2.0 version of the NICE workforce model represents the final product of that process and is shown in Figure 2.1.

In essence, each knowledge area represents a broad component of security work. Because these areas are so large they might be considered to be fields in and of themselves. The aim is to capture and incorporate every aspect of cybersecurity work. Then the NICE workforce model specifies a detailed set of specialty areas within each of these broad knowledge areas. These areas comprise the actual areas of practice that can be considered part of the process of achieving each area's basic security purposes. By using the detailed task specifications of the specialty areas, the NICE workforce model provides a comprehensive view of the types of work that legitimately comprise a given aspect of the field of cybersecurity. And a company can customize out its own tangibly correct security infrastructure using the recommendations in that specification. At the same time, the company can assure

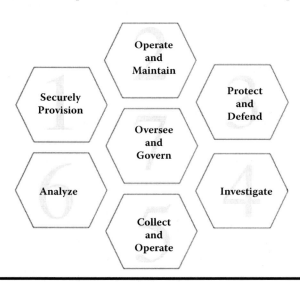

Figure 2.1 **The seven general knowledge areas of the NICE Cybersecurity Workforce Framework (v2.0).**

itself that its tailored approach incorporates commonly accepted best practice, because those practices are recommended and related within the context of the NICE workforce model.

Structure and Intent of the NICE Workforce Framework

As shown in Figure 2.2, the framework is divided into knowledge areas. Each knowledge area is further subdivided into 32 specialty areas. Besides delimiting specific areas of work, these areas also organize the commonly accepted set of requisite tasks, KSAs, and associated competencies into a pragmatic specification of what has to be known and done in order to correctly perform that specific workforce role.

The specialty areas and their associated roles are further elaborated by a constituent set of task specifications and KSA requirements. The KSAs describe the knowledge required to carry out the tasks that fulfill the practical goals of each job role. Those common KSAs and tasks characterize the specific purpose of each specialty area. The use of KSA specifications along with common tasks as a means to organize the specialty areas into functional categories allows the NICE framework to much more precisely define the actual set of discrete behaviors required in that particular aspect of the discipline.

The framework provides communal, standardized terminology, and definitions of terms and concepts. The purpose of this is to provide, "A common understanding of and lexicon for cybersecurity work" (NIST, 2014a). Given the current state of confusion in the field, the standardization of concepts terminology an indispensable step in ensuring that the United States is able to educate, train, and maintain a digitally capable workforce.

The point of the framework is to describe the field of cybersecurity through a common taxonomical listing of its elements. That taxonomy categorizes the various aspects of the process, such as specialty area and job role at the appropriate level of conceptualization and application. And given the disorganized state of the current field, the organization of thinking and perceptions that this enforces can allow the places that adopt the framework to navigate through pitfalls of day-to-day application.

In addition, the common lexicon can be utilized to define all of the diverse aspects of cybersecurity work and its workers, "Irrespective of where or for whom the work is performed" (NIST, 2014a). The framework's taxonomy and lexicon are universal enough in their definition to ensure that target groups will not need to change any of their job titles or organizational structures. Because the aim is collective standardization, the framework is meant to apply to all of the sectors of the economy, both governmental and business as well as in academe. That makes adoption of the framework both an economically feasible proposition as well as an easy to implement process without the usual political considerations of most businesses.

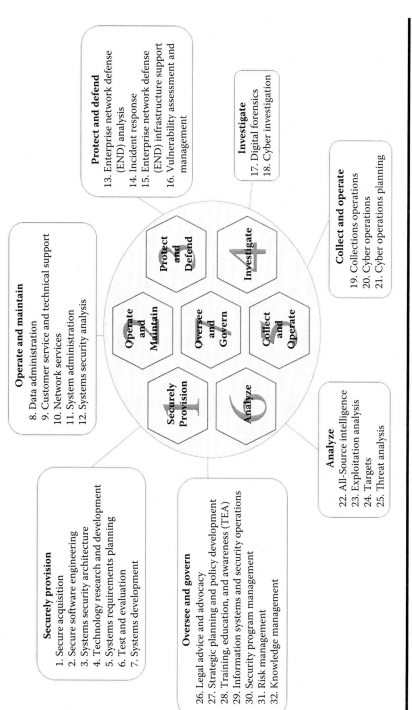

Protect and defend
13. Enterprise network defense (END) analysis
14. Incident response
15. Enterprise network defense (END) infrastructure support
16. Vulnerability assessment and management

Investigate
17. Digital forensics
18. Cyber investigation

Collect and operate
19. Collections operations
20. Cyber operations
21. Cyber operations planning

Operate and maintain
8. Data administration
9. Customer service and technical support
10. Network services
11. System administration
12. Systems security analysis

Analyze
22. All-Source intelligence
23. Exploitation analysis
24. Targets
25. Threat analysis

Securely provision
1. Secure acquisition
2. Secure software engineering
3. Systems security architecture
4. Technology research and development
5. Systems requirements planning
6. Test and evaluation
7. Systems development

Oversee and govern
26. Legal advice and advocacy
27. Strategic planning and policy development
28. Training, education, and awareness (TEA)
29. Information systems and security operations
30. Security program management
31. Risk management
32. Knowledge management

Figure 2.2 **The seven general knowledge areas of the NICE Cybersecurity Workforce Framework and their corresponding 32 specialty areas.**

The framework is also technologically agnostic. It does not assume that a particular technology, or set of technological job requirements underlie its adoption and use. In that respect, it is a top-level, umbrella standard in the sense that its architecture is overarching by design. The framework consists of 32 specialty areas organized into 7 categories. The largest category of things, the knowledge areas, encompass and associate a related set of specialty areas to each other. Therefore, the specialty areas of a given knowledge area can be considered to be logically similar in function. Given that implicit relationship then, each of the specialty areas contain a set of sample task and KSA specifications that elaborate the specific purpose of that specific area.

The framework is very large in concept. That has to be expected given the comprehensiveness of its scope and its detailed definition of terms. The larger policy issue that the consistency and detail of the framework supports will allow any organization to logically understand and rationally explain the real-world influences and underlying forces that affect the workforce and the security requirements of the work being done. All the same, widespread adoption of the framework is expected to allow all organizations to define cybersecurity work and how it relates to their particular workforce to an unprecedented level of consistency, detail, and quality (NIST, 2014a).

This, in turn, supports the concept of capability maturity within the organization. That concept will be much further elaborated by the specifications of the critical infrastructure cybersecurity framework (CSF), which will be introduced in Chapter 3. Combined with the workforce framework, the CSF concepts will ensure that critical strategic and operational workforce issues are properly addressed. At the top of the capability maturity ladder the organization will attain a predictive capability that will support effective identification, defense, protection, response, and recovery (IPDRR) to all reasonable cyber threats.

The framework labels and definitions are meant to be applied flexibly but the true benefit lies in the fact that all of the requisite cybersecurity work, work requirements, and related skills are standardized through the framework's common lexicon. The framework's specific job labels and task and KSA definitions are utilized to leverage the increased organizational capability required in the CSF. The actions that need to be taken in order to move up through the four increasing levels of capability specified there are directly described through the job role definitions of the specialty areas.

The framework is meant to apply, "Across all cybersecurity functions and organizations" (NIST, 2014b). Nevertheless, it does stipulate a specific list of sample job titles for each specialty area. The assumption is that these job titles can help an organizations transition from its current status to on that is much more standardized and communal. It is important to note however that the job title listings in the framework are strictly meant to illustrate rather than constrain the likely set of job titles for a given specialty area function. In actuality, the formal job title should only be made based on a thorough review of the job task requirements of the organization.

Finally, it has to be noted that there are two knowledge areas within the framework, where there are no actual job role titles specified. These are the two areas that generally fall into the category of intelligence work. These do not just apply to the espionage agencies of the federal government. They also apply to the private sector business intelligence areas of a corporation. The standard states that the reason why job titles are not specified is because of the fluid nature of the work, as well as classification issues.

However, the intention of each specialty area within the collect and operate and analyze knowledge areas is clear and common titles can be inferred. Therefore, the organization can still standardize that work at a level of granularity down to the specialties.

The level of detail specified in the framework also makes both the intent and the application of the sample job titles for each specialty area much easier to understand. More importantly, any resultant implementation of those job roles in everyday practice will be better targeted because all of the KSA and task requirements have been specifically detailed.

The NICE Framework Listing of Tasks for Each Specialty Area

In essence, the task listing for each of the specialty areas represents a specification of auditable standard behaviors for that job role grouping. All in all there are 382 tasks specified as appropriate to cybersecurity work. The tasks form a logical set of actions, which are designed to accomplish the purposes of a given area of cybersecurity work. In order to understand the purpose and effect of these specifications it is necessary to see and understand them as a group, underneath the specialty area they are meant to operationalize.

What follows is a comprehensive listing of the tasks that have been specified as appropriate for the field of cybersecurity. This should be considered to be a complete description of the field. These tasks must be seen in their entirety in order to comprehend the wide variety of activities that comprise cybersecurity work.

The complete set of these tasks represents a full explication of the individual specialty area that they lie under. This long list might be difficult to read and comprehend as a whole. But it is essential to see how the model describes the field in total in order to understand the application, design, tailoring, and planning advice that will follow this section (subsequent task listings from NIST, 2014a).

Knowledge Area 1: Securely Provision

As shown in Figure 2.3, secure acquisition oversees, evaluates, and supports the documentation, specification, contracting, and oversight practices necessary to ensure a secure and correct new IT system or software product (NIST, 2014a).

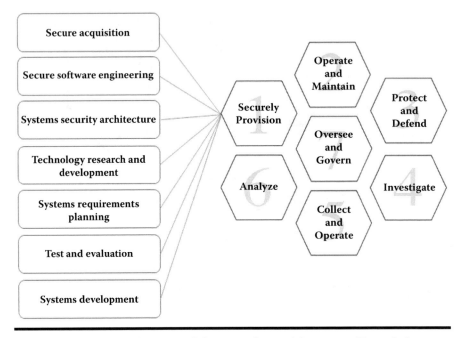

Figure 2.3 The specialty areas of the securely provision general knowledge area.

1. Lead and oversee information security budget, staffing, and contracting.
2. Provide enterprise information assurance (IA) and supply chain risk management guidance for the development of the continuity of operations plans.
3. Draft and publish a supply chain security and risk management policy.
4. Apply defensive functions (e.g., encryption, access control, identity management) to reduce exploitation opportunities of supply chain vulnerabilities.
5. Develop and document supply chain risks for critical system elements, as appropriate.
6. Participate in the acquisition process as necessary, following appropriate supply chain risk management practices.
7. Ensure all acquisitions, procurements, and outsourcing efforts address information security requirements consistent with organization goals.
8. Conduct import/export reviews for acquiring cryptographic systems.
9. Develop contract language to ensure supply chain, system, network, and operational security are met.

Secure software engineering. This is the area that is primarily responsible for developing and coding new, or for modifying existing computer applications, software, or specialized utility programs. The tasks for this area are (NIST, 2014a)

1. Analyze information to determine, recommend, and plan the development of a new application or modification of an existing application.
2. Analyze user needs and software requirements to determine feasibility of design within time and cost constraints.
3. Apply coding and testing standards, security testing tools (including "fuzzing" static analysis code scanning tools), and conduct code reviews.
4. Apply secure code documentation.
5. Capture security controls used during the requirements phase to integrate security within the process, identify key security objectives, and maximize software security while minimizing disruption to plans and schedules.
6. Compile and write documentation of program development and subsequent revisions, inserting comments in the coded instructions so others can understand the program.
7. Conduct trial runs of programs and software applications to ensure the desired information is produced and instructions are correct.
8. Confer with systems analysts, engineers, programmers, and others to design applications and obtain information on project limitations and capabilities, performance requirements, and interfaces.
9. Develop threat model based on customer interviews and requirements.
10. Consult with engineering staff to evaluate interface between hardware and software.
11. Correct errors by making appropriate changes and rechecking the program to ensure desired results are produced.
12. Design, develop, and modify software systems using scientific analysis and mathematical models to predict and measure outcome and consequences of design.
13. Develop and direct software system testing and validation procedures, programming, and documentation.
14. Develop secure code and error messages.
15. Evaluate factors such as reporting formats required, cost constraints, and need for security restrictions to determine hardware configuration.
16. Identify basic common coding flaws at a high level.
17. Identify security implications and apply methodologies within centralized and decentralized environments across the enterprise's computer systems in software development.
18. Identify security issues around steady-state operation and management of software, and incorporate security measures that must be taken when a product reaches the end of its life.
19. Modify existing software to correct errors, adapt it to new hardware or upgrade interfaces, and improve performance.
20. Perform integrated quality assurance testing for security functionality and resiliency attacks.

21. Perform secure programming and identify potential flaws in codes to mitigate vulnerabilities.
22. Perform risk analysis (e.g., threat, vulnerability, and probability of occurrence) whenever an application or system undergoes a major change.
23. Prepare detailed workflow charts and diagrams that describe input, output, and logical operation, and convert them into a series of instructions coded in a computer language.
24. Recognize security implications in the software acceptance phase, including completion criteria, risk acceptance and documentation, common criteria, and methods of independent testing.
25. Translate security requirements into application design elements, including documenting the elements of the software attack surfaces, conducting threat modeling, and defining any specific security criteria.
26. Perform penetration testing as required for new or updated applications.
27. Apply defensive functions (e.g., encryption, access control, identity management) to reduce exploitation opportunities of supply chain vulnerabilities.
28. Design countermeasures and mitigations against potential exploitations of programming language weaknesses and vulnerabilities in system and elements.
29. Determine and document critical numbers of software patches or the extent of releases that would leave software vulnerable.
30. Enable applications with public keying by leveraging existing public key infrastructure (PKI) libraries and incorporating certificate management and encryption functionalities.
31. Identify and leverage the enterprise-wide security services while designing and developing secure applications (e.g., enterprise PKI, federated identity server, enterprise antivirus [AV] solution).
32. Identify and leverage the enterprise-wide version control system while designing and developing secure applications.

Systems security architecture. This area researches, defines, captures, and describes the conditions for eventual incorporation into the system and security designs and processes. The tasks are (NIST, 2014a)

1. Analyze user needs and requirements to plan system architecture.
2. Collaborate with system developers to select appropriate design solutions or ensure the compatibility of system components.
3. Define and prioritize essential system capabilities or business functions required for partial or full system restoration after a catastrophic failure event.
4. Define appropriate levels of system availability based on critical system functions and ensure system requirements identify appropriate disaster recovery and continuity of operations requirements, to include any appropriate

failover/alternate site requirements, backup requirements, and material supportability requirements for system recovery/restoration.

5. Design system architecture or system components required to meet user needs.

6. Develop IA designs for systems and networks with multilevel security requirements or requirements for the processing of multiple classification levels of data (primarily applicable to government organizations).

7. Document and address organization's information security, IA architecture, and systems security engineering requirements throughout the acquisition life cycle.

8. Document design specifications, installation instructions, and other system-related information.

9. Employ secure configuration management processes.

10. Ensure all definition and architecture activities (e.g., system life cycle support plans, concept of operations, operational procedures, and maintenance training materials) are properly documented and updated as necessary.

11. Ensure acquired or developed system(s) and architecture(s) are consistent with organization's IA architecture guidelines.

12. Evaluate current or emerging technologies to consider factors such as cost, security, compatibility, or usability.

13. Evaluate interface between hardware and software and operational and performance requirements of overall system.

14. Identify and prioritize critical business functions in collaboration with organizational stakeholders.

15. Identify the protection needs (i.e., security controls) for information system(s), network(s) and document appropriately.

16. Perform security reviews, identify gaps in security architecture, and develop a security risk management plan.

17. Plan system implementation to ensure that all system components can be integrated and aligned (e.g., procedures, databases, policies, software, hardware).

18. Provide advice on project costs, design concepts, or design changes.

19. Provide input on security requirements to be included in statements of work and other appropriate procurement documents.

20. Provide input to the risk management framework (RMF) process activities and related documentation (e.g., system life cycle support plans, concept of operations, operational procedures, and maintenance training materials).

21. Specify power supply and heating, ventilation, and air conditioning (HVAC) requirements and configuration based on system performance expectations and design specifications.

22. Translate proposed technical solutions into technical specifications.

23. Define and document how the implementation of a new system or new interfaces between systems impacts the security posture of the current environment.

24. Document and manage an enterprise technical risk register prioritizing and managing technical risks throughout the system life cycle.
25. Assess and design key management functions (as related to IA).

Technology research and development. This area tests and assesses the technology, supports the integration process, as well as provides support for the organizations prototyping (NIST, 2014a)

1. Conduct continuous analysis to identify network and system vulnerabilities.
2. Review and validate data mining and data warehousing programs, processes, and requirements.
3. Research current technology to understand capabilities of required system or network.
4. Research and evaluate all available technologies and standards to meet customer requirements.
5. Identify cyber capabilities strategies for custom hardware and software development based on mission requirements.
6. Collaborate with stakeholders to identify and/or develop appropriate solutions technology.
7. Design and develop new tools/technologies as related to IA.
8. Troubleshoot prototype design and process issues throughout the product design, development, and post-launch phases.
9. Identify functional- and security-related features to find opportunities for new capability development to exploit or mitigate cyberspace vulnerabilities.
10. Identify and/or develop reverse engineering tools to detect cyberspace vulnerabilities.
11. Develop and implement credentialing and identity management programs.
12. Develop cloud-based centralized cryptographic key management capability to support mobile workforce.

Systems requirements planning. This area evaluates and documents the system and/or software functional requirements and translates those requirements into technical solutions. The tasks are (NIST, 2014a)

1. Conduct risk analysis, feasibility study, and/or trade-off analysis to develop, document, and refine functional requirements and specifications.
2. Consult with customers to evaluate functional requirements.
3. Coordinate with systems architects and developers, as needed, to provide oversight in the development of design solutions.
4. Define project scope and objectives based on customer requirements.
5. Develop an enterprise system security context, a preliminary system security concept of operations, and define baseline security requirements in accordance with applicable IA requirements.

6. Develop and document requirements, capabilities, and constraints for design procedures and processes.
7. Develop cost estimates for future new or modified system(s).
8. Integrate and align information security and/or IA policies to ensure system analysis meets security requirements.
9. Manage IT projects to ensure that developed solutions meet customer requirements.
10. Oversee and make recommendations regarding configuration management.
11. Perform needs analysis to determine opportunities for new and improved business process solutions.
12. Prepare use cases to justify the need for specific IT solutions.
13. Translate functional requirements into technical solutions.
14. Develop and document supply chain risks for critical system elements, as appropriate.
15. Develop and document user experience (UX) requirements including information architecture and user interface requirements.

Test and evaluation. This area plans, evaluates, verifies, and validates technical, functional, and performance characteristics (including interoperability) of systems or elements of systems incorporating IT. The tasks for this area are (NIST, 2014a)

1. Analyze the results of end-to-end testing.
2. Determine level of assurance of developed capabilities based on test results.
3. Develop test plans to address specifications and requirements.
4. Make recommendations based on test results.
5. Perform conformance testing to assess whether a system complies with defined specifications or standards.
6. Perform developmental testing on systems being concurrently developed.
7. Perform interoperability testing on systems exchanging electronic information with systems of other organizations.
8. Perform operational testing to evaluate systems in an operational environment.
9. Perform validation testing to ensure requirements meet proposed specifications or standards and that correct specifications or standards are available.
10. Develop test bed environment to test and verify hardware and support peripherals to ensure that they meet specifications and requirements by recording and analyzing test data.
11. Determine scope, infrastructure, resources, and data sample size to ensure system requirements are adequately demonstrated.
12. Create auditable evidence of security measures.
13. Conduct and monitor independent validation and verification (IV&V) testing for software applications and systems.

Systems development. This is the classic development role; however, the focus of the role tends to be on security. The tasks for this area are (NIST, 2014a)

1. Analyze design constraints, trade-offs, and detailed system and security designs to identify necessary life cycle support.
2. Apply security policies to applications that interface with one another, such as business-to-business (B2B) applications.
3. Assess the effectiveness of information protection measures utilized by system(s).
4. Assess threats to and vulnerabilities of computer system(s) to develop a security risk profile.
5. Build, test, and modify product prototypes using working models or theoretical models.
6. Conduct privacy impact analysis (PIA) of the applications security design for the appropriate security controls, which protect the confidentiality and integrity of personal identifiable information (PII).
7. Design and develop IA or IA-enabled tools.
8. Design and develop secure interface specifications between interconnected systems.
9. Design, develop, integrate, and update system security measures (including policies and requirements) that provide confidentiality, integrity, availability, authentication, and nonrepudiation.
10. Design hardware, operating systems, and software applications to adequately addresses IA security requirements.
11. Design or integrate appropriate data backup capabilities into overall system designs, and ensure appropriate technical and procedural processes exist for secure system backups and protected storage of backup data.
12. Design systems to the minimum security requirements to ensure requirements are met for all systems and/or applications.
13. Develop and oversee system testing and validation procedures and documentation.
14. Develop architectures or system components consistent with technical specifications.
15. Develop detailed security design documentation for component and interface specifications to support system design and development.
16. Develop disaster recovery and continuity of operations plans for systems under development, and ensure testing prior to systems entering a production environment.
17. Develop risk mitigation strategies to resolve vulnerabilities and recommend security changes to system or system components as needed.
18. Develop specific IA countermeasures and risk mitigation strategies for systems and/or applications.

19. Identifies components or elements, allocate security functions to those elements, and describe the relationships between the elements.
20. Identify and direct the remediation of technical problems encountered during testing and implementation of new systems (e.g., identify and find work-arounds for communication protocols that are not interoperable).
21. Identify and prioritize essential system functions or subsystems, as may be necessary to support essential capabilities or business functions; in the event of system failure or system recovery, observe and adhere to overall system requirements for continuity and availability.
22. Identify, assess, and recommend IA or IA-enabled products for use within a system and ensure recommended products are in compliance with organization's evaluation and validation requirements.
23. Implement security designs for new or existing system(s).
24. Incorporate IA vulnerability solutions into system designs (e.g., IA vulnerability alerts).
25. Perform an information security risk assessment and design security countermeasures to mitigate identified risks.
26. Perform security reviews and identify security gaps in security architecture.
27. Perform risk analysis (e.g., threat, vulnerability, and probability of occurrence) whenever an application or system undergoes a major change.
28. Provide guidelines for implementing developed systems to customers or installation teams.
29. Provide input to implementation plans and standard operating procedures.
30. Provide input to the RMF process activities and related documentation (e.g., system life cycle support plans, concept of operations, operational procedures, and maintenance training materials).
31. Store, retrieve, and manipulate data for analysis of system capabilities and requirements.
32. Provide support to security/certification test and evaluation activities.
33. Trace all system security requirements to design components.
34. Utilize models and simulations to analyze or predict system performance under different operating conditions.
35. Verify stability, interoperability, portability, or scalability of system architecture.
36. Design and develop key management functions to support authentication, encryption, and digital signature capabilities (as related to IA).
37. Analyze user needs and requirements to plan and conduct system security development around UX.
38. Develop IA designs to meet specific operational needs and environmental factors (e.g., access controls, automated applications, networked operations, high integrity and availability requirements, multilevel security/processing of multiple classification levels, and processing sensitive compartmented information [SCI]).

39. Ensure security design and IA development activities are properly documented, providing a functional description of security implementation, and updated as necessary.
40. Implement and integrate system development life cycle (SLDC) methodologies (e.g., IBM Rational Unified Process) into development environment.

Knowledge Area 2: Operate and Maintain

Figure 2.4 shows the key specialty areas for the operate and maintain general knowledge area.

Data administration. This area oversees the organization's databases. It develops and administers those databases and/or the data management systems that allow for the storage, query, and utilization of that data. The tasks for this area are (NIST, 2014a)

1. Analyze and define data requirements and specifications.
2. Analyze and plan for anticipated changes in data capacity requirements.
3. Design and implement database systems.
4. Review and validate data mining and data warehousing programs, processes, and requirements.
5. Develop data standards, policies, and procedures.
6. Install and configure database management systems software.
7. Maintain database management systems software.

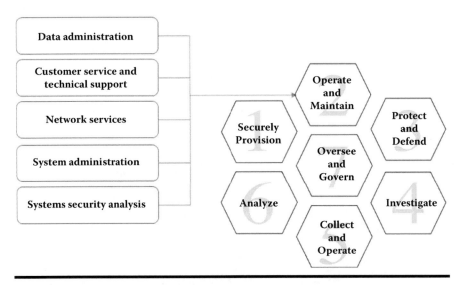

Figure 2.4   Key specialty areas for the operate and maintain general knowledge area.

8. Maintain directory replication services that enable information to replicate automatically from rear servers to forward units via optimized routing.
9. Maintain information exchanges through publish, subscribe, and alert functions that enable users to send and receive critical information as required.
10. Manage the compilation, cataloging, caching, distribution, and retrieval of data.
11. Monitor and maintain databases to ensure optimal performance.
12. Perform backup and recovery of databases to ensure data integrity.
13. Provide a managed flow of relevant information (via Web-based portals or other means) based on mission requirements.
14. Provide recommendations on new database technologies and architectures.
15. Performs configuration management, problem management, capacity management, and financial management for databases and data management systems.
16. Supports incident management, service-level management, change management, release management, continuity management, and availability management for databases and data management systems.

Customer service and technical support. This area installs, configures, troubleshoots, and provides maintenance of applications with a security requirement, or focus. The tasks are (NIST, 2014a)

1. Diagnose and resolve customer-reported system incidents.
2. Assist in the execution of disaster recovery and continuity of operations plans.
3. Identify end-user requirements for software and hardware solutions.
4. Install and configure hardware, software, and peripheral equipment for system users.
5. Manage accounts, network rights, and access to systems and equipment.
6. Manage inventory of IT resources.
7. Monitor client-level computer system performance.
8. Provide recommendations for possible improvements and upgrades.
9. Report emerging trend findings.
10. Test computer system performance.
11. Troubleshoot system hardware and software.

Network services. This area performs routine network and firewall installation, configuration, testing, operational, maintenance, and management activities. The tasks for this area are (NIST, 2014a)

1. Configure and optimize network hubs, routers, and switches.
2. Develop and implement network backup and recovery procedures.
3. Diagnose network connectivity problems.
4. Expand or modify network infrastructure to serve new purposes or improve work flow.

5. Implement new system design procedures, test procedures, and quality standards.
6. Install and maintain network infrastructure device operating system software (e.g., interwork operating system [IOS], firmware).
7. Install or replace network hubs, routers, and switches.
8. Integrate new systems into existing network architecture.
9. Monitor network capacity and performance.
10. Patch network vulnerabilities to ensure information is safeguarded against outside parties.
11. Provide feedback on network requirements, including network architecture and infrastructure.
12. Repair network connectivity problems.
13. Test and maintain network infrastructure including software and hardware devices.

System administration. This area ensures the confidentiality, integrity, and availability of the data within the system. The tasks for this area are (NIST, 2014a)

1. Check server availability, functionality, integrity, and efficiency.
2. Conduct functional and connectivity testing to ensure continuing operability.
3. Conduct periodic server maintenance including cleaning (both physically and electronically), disk checks, routine reboots, data dumps, and testing.
4. Design group policies and access control lists to ensure compatibility with organizational standards, business rules, and needs.
5. Develop and document systems administration standard operating procedures.
6. Develop and implement local network usage policies and procedures.
7. Install server fixes, updates, and enhancements.
8. Maintain baseline system security according to organizational policies.
9. Manage accounts, network rights, and access to systems and equipment.
10. Manage server resources including performance, capacity, availability, serviceability, and recoverability.
11. Monitor and maintain server configuration.
12. Oversee installation, implementation, configuration, and support of network components.
13. Perform repairs on faulty server hardware.
14. Plan and coordinate the installation of new or modified hardware, operating systems, and other baseline software.
15. Plan, execute, and verify data redundancy and system recovery procedures.
16. Provide ongoing optimization and problem solving support.
17. Resolve hardware/software interface and interoperability problems.
18. Install, update, and troubleshoot virtual and remote access servers.

Systems security analysis. This area is responsible for ensuring the correctness and integrity of the system and the information it contains and processes. The tasks for this area are (NIST, 2014a)

1. Apply security policies to applications that interface with one another, such as B2B applications.
2. Apply security policies to meet security objectives of the system.
3. Apply service-oriented architecture security architecture principles to meet organization's confidentiality, integrity, and availability requirements.
4. Develop and test system failover or system operations transfer to an alternate site based on system availability requirements.
5. Discover organizational trends with regard to the security posture of systems.
6. Ensure all systems security operations and maintenance activities are properly documented and updated as necessary.
7. Ensure application of security patches for commercial products integrated into system design meet the timelines dictated by the management authority for the intended operational environment.
8. Ensure IA-enabled products or other compensating security control technologies reduce identified risk to an acceptable level.
9. Establish adequate access controls based on principles of least privilege and need-to-know.
10. Exercise the system disaster recovery and continuity of operations plans.
11. Implement and/or integrate security measures for use in system(s) and ensure that system designs incorporate security configuration guidelines.
12. Implement security designs and approaches to resolve vulnerabilities, mitigate risks, and recommend security changes to system or system components as needed.
13. Implement specific IA countermeasures for systems and/or applications.
14. Implement system security measures that provide confidentiality, integrity, availability, authentication, and nonrepudiation.
15. Integrate and/or implement cross domain solutions (CDS) in a classified environment (primarily applicable to government agencies).
16. Integrate automated capabilities for updating or patching system software where practical, and develop processes and procedures for manual system software updating and patching using current and projected patch timeline requirements for the system's operational environment.
17. Identify and correct security deficiencies discovered during security and certification testing and continuous monitoring, or identify risk acceptance for the appropriate senior leader or authorized representative.
18. Monitor information protection assurance mechanisms related to system implementation and testing practices.
19. Oversee minimum security requirements are in place for all applications.

20. Perform IA testing of developed applications and/or systems to identify security vulnerabilities such as sequel query language (SQL) injection or cross-site scripting.
21. Perform security reviews and identify security gaps in security architecture, resulting in recommendations for the inclusion into the risk mitigation strategy.
22. Plans and recommend modifications or adjustments based on exercise results or system environment.
23. Properly document all systems security implementation, operations, and maintenance activities and updated as necessary.
24. Provide IA guidance to leadership.
25. Provide input to the RMF process activities and related documentation (e.g., system life cycle support plans, concept of operations, operational procedures, and maintenance training materials).
26. Verify and update security documentation reflecting the application/system security design features.
27. Work with others to resolve computer security incidents and vulnerability compliance.
28. Ensure recovery and continuity plans are executable in the system operational environment.

Knowledge Area 3: Protect and Defend

Figure 2.5 shows the key specialty areas for the protect and defend general knowledge area.

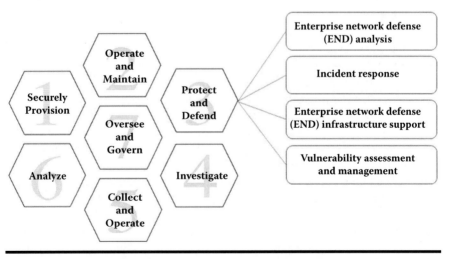

Figure 2.5   Key specialty areas for the protect and defend general knowledge area.

Enterprise network defense (END) analysis. This area collects information through electronic and behavioral means that will allow the organization to monitor the entire network for incidents, respond appropriately when an incident occurs and document the occurrence for further analysis. The tasks for this area are (NIST, 2014a)

1. Develop content for cyber defense tools.
2. Characterize and analyze network traffic to identify anomalous activity and potential threats to network resources.
3. Coordinate with END staff to validate network alerts.
4. Monitor external data sources (e.g., END vendor sites, computer emergency response teams, storage area networks (SANS), security focus) to maintain currency of END threat condition and determine which security issues may have an impact on the enterprise.
5. Document and escalate incidents, including event's history, status, and potential impact for further action, that may cause ongoing and immediate impact to the environment.
6. Perform cyber defense trend analysis and reporting.
7. Perform event correlation using information gathered from a variety of sources within the enterprise to gain situational awareness and determine the effectiveness of an observed attack.
8. Provide daily summary reports of network events and activity relevant to END practices.
9. Receive and analyze network alerts from various sources within the enterprise and determines possible causes of such alerts.
10. Provide timely detection, identification, and alerts of possible attacks/intrusions, anomalous activities, and misuse activities, and distinguish these incidents and events from benign activities.
11. Use cyber defense tools for continual monitoring and analysis of system activity to identify malicious activity.
12. Analyze identified malicious activity to determine weaknesses exploited, exploitation methods, and effects on system and information.
13. Employ approved defense-in-depth principles and practices (e.g., defense-in-multiple places, layered defenses, and security robustness).
14. Determine appropriate course of action in response to identified and analyzed anomalous network activity.
15. Conduct tests of IA safeguards in accordance with established test plans and procedures.
16. Determine tactics, techniques, and procedures (TTPs) for intrusion sets.
17. Examine network topologies to understand data flows through the network.
18. Recommend computing environment vulnerability corrections.
19. Identify and analyze anomalies in network traffic using metadata.
20. Conduct research, analysis, and correlation across a wide variety of all-source datasets.

21. Validate intrusion detection system (IDS) alerts against network traffic using packet analysis.
22. Isolate and remove malware.
23. Identify application and operating systems of a network device based on network traffic.
24. Reconstruct a malicious attack or activity based on network traffic.
25. Identify network mapping and operating system fingerprinting activities.

Incident response. This area responds to identified incidents as they occur. The goal is to mitigate any potential harm to the system or its attached networks. The tasks for this area are (NIST, 2014a)

1. Coordinate and provide expert technical support to enterprise-wide END technicians to resolve cyber defense incidents.
2. Correlate incident data to identify specific vulnerabilities and make recommendations that enable expeditious remediation.
3. Monitor external data sources (e.g., END vendor sites, computer emergency response teams, SANS, security focus) to maintain currency of END threat condition and determine which security issues may have an impact on the enterprise.
4. Perform analysis of log files from a variety of sources (e.g., individual host logs, network traffic logs, firewall logs, and IDS logs) to identify possible threats to network security.
5. Perform command and control functions in response to incidents.
6. Perform END incident triage, to include determining scope, urgency, and potential impact; identifying the specific vulnerability; and making recommendations that enable expeditious remediation.
7. Perform initial, forensically sound collection of images and inspect to discern possible mitigation/remediation on enterprise systems.
8. Perform real-time END incident handling (e.g., forensic collections, intrusion correlation and tracking, threat analysis, and direct system remediation) tasks to support deployable incident response teams (IRTs).
9. Receive and analyze network alerts from various sources within the enterprise and determines possible causes of such alerts.
10. Track and document END incidents from initial detection through final resolution.
11. Write and publish cyber defense techniques, guidance, and reports on incident findings to appropriate constituencies.
12. Employ approved defense-in-depth principles and practices (e.g., defense-in-multiple places, layered defenses, and security robustness).
13. Collect intrusion artifacts (e.g., source code, malware, Trojans) and use discovered data to enable mitigation of potential END incidents within the enterprise.

14. Serve as technical expert and liaison to law enforcement personnel and explain incident details as required.

END infrastructure support. This area monitors network to actively remediate any unauthorized activities that might be detected. The tasks are (NIST, 2014a)

1. Administer END test bed(s), and test and evaluate new cyber defense applications, rules/signatures, access controls, and configurations of platforms managed by service provider(s).
2. Coordinate with END analysts to manage and administer the updating of rules and signatures (e.g., intrusion detection/protection systems, AV, and content blacklists) for specialized cyber defense applications.
3. Create, edit, and manage changes to network access control lists on specialized END systems (e.g., firewalls and intrusion prevention systems).
4. Identify potential conflicts with implementation of any cyber defense tools within the END provider area of responsibility (e.g., tool and signature testing and optimization).
5. Implement RMF/security assessment and authorization (SA&A) requirements for specialized END systems within the enterprise, and document and maintain records for them.
6. Perform system administration on specialized END applications and systems (e.g., AV, audit, and remediation) or virtual private network (VPN) devices, to include installation, configuration, maintenance, backup, and restoration.
7. Assist in identifying, prioritizing, and coordinating the protection of critical END infrastructure and key resources.

Vulnerability assessment and management. This area assesses and analyzes threats and vulnerabilities. The tasks for this area are (NIST, 2014a)

1. Analyze organization's END policies and configurations and evaluate compliance with regulations and organizational directives.
2. Conduct and/or support authorized penetration testing on enterprise network assets.
3. Maintain deployable cyber defense audit toolkit (e.g., specialized cyber defense software and hardware) to support END audit missions.
4. Maintain knowledge of applicable END policies, regulations, and compliance documents specifically related to cyber defense auditing.
5. Prepare audit reports that identify technical and procedural findings, and provide recommended remediation strategies/solutions.
6. Conduct required reviews as appropriate within environment (e.g., technical surveillance, countermeasure [TSCM] reviews, and TEMPEST countermeasure reviews).

7. Perform technical (evaluation of technology) and nontechnical (evaluation of people and operations) risk and vulnerability assessments of relevant technology focus areas (e.g., local computing environment, network and infrastructure, enclave boundary, and supporting infrastructure).
8. Assist with the selection of cost-effective security controls to mitigate risk (e.g., protection of information, systems, and processes).

Knowledge Area 4: Investigate

Figure 2.6 shows the key specialty areas for the investigate general knowledge area.

Digital forensics. This area obtains electronic clues and other forms of investigative data to support investigations of crime and espionage. Task specifications for this area are (NIST, 2014a)

1. Assist in the gathering and preservation of evidence used in the prosecution of computer crimes.
2. Collect and analyze intrusion artifacts (e.g., source code, malware, and Trojans) and use discovered data to enable mitigation of potential END incidents within the enterprise.
3. Conduct analysis of log files, evidence, and other information to determine best methods for identifying the perpetrator(s) of a network intrusion.
4. Confirm what is known about an intrusion and discover new information, if possible, after identifying intrusion via dynamic analysis.
5. Create a forensically sound duplicate of the evidence (i.e., forensic image) that ensures the original evidence is not unintentionally modified, to use for data recovery and analysis processes. This includes, but is not limited to, hard drives,

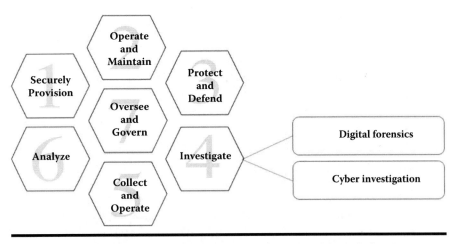

Figure 2.6   Key specialty areas for the investigate general knowledge area.

floppy diskettes, compact discs (CDs), personal digital assistants (PDAs), mobile phones, global positioning satellite devices (GPSs), and all tape formats.

6. Decrypt seized data using technical means.
7. Provide technical summary of findings in accordance with established reporting procedures.
8. Document original condition of digital and/or associated evidence (e.g., via digital photographs, written reports, etc.).
9. Ensure chain of custody is followed for all digital media acquired in accordance with the Federal Rules of Evidence.
10. Examine recovered data for information of relevance to the issue at hand.
11. Employ IT systems and digital storage media to solve and prosecute cybercrimes and fraud committed against people and property.
12. Formulate a strategy to ensure chain of custody is maintained in such a way that the evidence is not altered (e.g., phones/PDAs need a power source, hard drives need protection from shock and strong magnetic fields).
13. Identify digital evidence for examination and analysis in such a way as to avoid unintentional alteration.
14. Perform END incident triage, to include determining scope, urgency, and potential impact; identifying the specific vulnerability; and making recommendations that enable expeditious remediation.
15. Perform dynamic analysis to boot an image of a drive (without necessarily having the original drive) to see the intrusion as the user may have seen it in a native environment.
16. Perform file signature analysis.
17. Perform hash comparison against established database.
18. Perform real-time forensic analysis (e.g., using Helix in conjunction with LiveView).
19. Perform timeline analysis.
20. Perform static media analysis.
21. Perform tier 1, 2, and 3 malware analysis.
22. Prepare digital media for imaging by ensuring data integrity (e.g., write blockers in accordance with standard operating procedures).
23. Provide consultation to investigators and prosecuting attorneys regarding the findings of computer examinations.
24. Provide technical assistance on digital evidence matters to appropriate personnel.
25. Provide testimony related to computer examinations.
26. Recognize and accurately report forensic artifacts indicative of a particular operating system.
27. Review forensic images and other data sources for recovery of potentially relevant information.
28. Serve as technical experts and liaisons to law enforcement personnel and explain incident details, provide testimony, and so on.

29. Extract data using data carving techniques (e.g., Forensic Toolkit [FTK], Foremost).
30. Capture and analyze network traffic associated with malicious activities using network monitoring tools.
31. Use specialized equipment and techniques to catalog, document, extract, collect, package, and preserve digital evidence.
32. Resolve investigations through the use of specialized computer investigative techniques and programs.
33. Write and publish cyber defense techniques, guidance, and reports on incident findings to appropriate constituencies.
34. Conduct cursory binary analysis.
35. Perform virus scanning on digital media.
36. Perform file system forensic analysis.
37. Perform static analysis to mount an "image" of a drive (without necessarily having the original drive).
38. Perform static malware analysis.
39. Utilize deployable Forensics Toolkit to support operations as necessary.

Cyber investigation. This area includes interviews and interrogation techniques, surveillance, countersurveillance, and surveillance detection methods: The tasks for this area are (NIST, 2014a)

1. Analyze computer-generated threats.
2. Assist in the gathering and preservation of evidence used in the prosecution of computer crimes.
3. Conduct analysis of log files, evidence, and other information in order to determine best methods for identifying the perpetrator(s) of a network intrusion.
4. Conduct interviews of victims and witnesses and conduct interviews or interrogations of suspects.
5. Determine and develop leads and identify sources of information in order to identify and prosecute the responsible parties to an intrusion.
6. Develop a plan to investigate alleged crime, violation, or suspicious activity utilizing computers and the Internet.
7. Document original condition of digital and/or associated evidence (e.g., via digital photographs, written reports, etc.).
8. Establish relationships, if applicable, between the IRT and other groups, both internal (e.g., legal department) and external (e.g., law enforcement agencies, vendors, and public relations professionals).
9. Examine recovered data for information of relevance to the issue at hand.
10. Employ IT systems and digital storage media to solve and prosecute cybercrimes and fraud committed against people and property.
11. Fuse computer network attack analyses with criminal and counterintelligence investigations and operations.

12. Identify and/or determine whether a security incident is indicative of a violation of law that requires specific legal action.
13. Identify data or intelligence of evidentiary value to support counterintelligence and criminal investigations.
14. Identify digital evidence for examination and analysis in such a way as to avoid unintentional alteration.
15. Identify elements of proof of the crime.
16. Identify outside attackers accessing the system from Internet or insider attackers (e.g., authorized users attempting to gain and misuse unauthorized privileges).
17. Identify, collect, and seize documentary or physical evidence to include digital media and logs associated with cyber intrusion incidents, investigations, and operations.
18. Conduct large-scale investigations of criminal activities involving complicated computer programs and networks.
19. Prepare reports to document analysis.
20. Process crime scenes.
21. Secure the electronic device or information source.
22. Use specialized equipment and techniques to catalog, document, extract, collect, package, and preserve digital evidence.

Knowledge Area 5: Collect and Operate

Figure 2.7 shows the key specialty areas for the collect and operate general knowledge area.

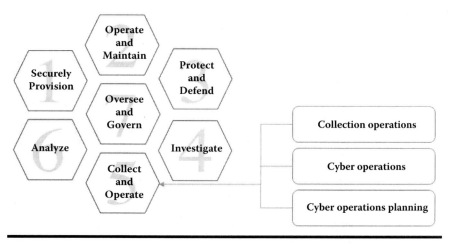

Figure 2.7 Key specialty areas for the collect and operate general knowledge area.

Collection operations. This is the classic intelligence gathering function. It does the actual collecting using whatever common best practice methods appropriate to the organizational entity that sponsors it. Therefore, there are no common best practice recommendations for this specialty area.

Cyber operations. This specialty area specifically supports the overall intelligence operation. Its focus is on counterespionage from either electronic or human intelligence sources. There are no common best practice recommendations in the NICE model for this specialty area.

Cyber operations planning. This is the strategic specialty area for the collect and operate function. This is the specialty area responsible for the performance of in-depth operational planning. The focus of this specialty area is on a variety of intelligence and counterespionage targets in cyberspace. There are no common best practice recommendations in the NICE model for this specialty area.

Knowledge Area 6: Analyze

Figure 2.8 shows the key specialty areas for the analyze general knowledge area.

Threat analysis. The purpose of this function is to identify, collect information about, and judge the capabilities of the adversarial spectrum. There are no common best practice recommendations in the NICE model for this specialty area.

All-source intelligence. This is the intelligence amalgamation and oversight specialty area. The purpose of all-source intelligence work is to amalgamate disaggregate threat information from all relevant sources across the intelligence gathering function. There are no common best practice recommendations in the NICE model for this specialty area.

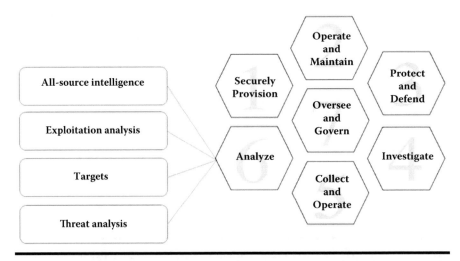

Figure 2.8   Key specialty areas for the analyze general knowledge area.

Exploitation analysis. This analyzes collected information to identify vulnerabilities and potential for exploitation. The tasks and KSAs in this function involve the specific identification of weaknesses and vulnerabilities that are likely targets for exploitation. In effect, this specialty area underwrites the prioritization process that is necessary for good strategic and operational planning. The aim is to explicitly identify those harmful events that have the greatest likelihood of occurrence as well as potential impact. Job roles in this area characterize the threat as well as understand and document the method of exploitation.

Targets. This is a narrow area. Its aim is to gather the necessary information about, and then reliably analyze the significance of, all of the relevant organizational vulnerabilities that might be targets for exploitation. There are no best practice recommendations in the NICE model for this specialty area.

Knowledge Area 7: Oversee and Govern

Figure 2.9 shows the key specialty areas for the oversee and govern general knowledge area.

Legal advice and advocacy. It provides legally sound advice and recommendations to leadership and staff on a variety of relevant topics within the pertinent subject domain. It advocates legal and policy changes and makes a case on behalf

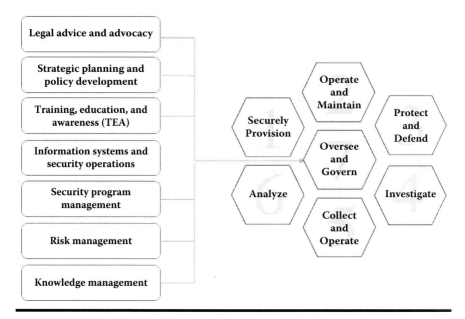

Figure 2.9 Key specialty areas for the oversee and govern general knowledge area.

of client via a wide range of written and oral work products, including legal briefs and proceedings. The tasks for this area are (NIST, 2014a)

1. Acquire and maintain a working knowledge of relevant laws, regulations, policies, standards, or procedures.
2. Advocate organization's official position in legal and legislative proceedings.
3. Conduct framing of allegations to determine proper identification of law, regulatory, or policy/guidance of violation.
4. Develop policy, programs, and guidelines for implementation.
5. Evaluate, monitor, and ensure compliance with information communication technology (ICT) security policies and relevant legal and regulatory requirements.
6. Evaluate contracts to ensure compliance with funding, legal, and program requirements.
7. Evaluate the effectiveness of laws, regulations, policies, standards, or procedures.
8. Evaluate the impact (e.g., costs or benefits) of changes to laws, regulations, policies, standards, or procedures.
9. Explain or provide guidance on laws, regulations, policies, standards, or procedures to management, personnel, or clients.
10. Implement new or revised laws, regulations, executive orders, policies, standards, or procedures.
11. Interpret and apply laws, regulations, policies, standards, or procedures to specific issues.
12. Prepare legal documents.
13. Resolve conflicts in laws, regulations, policies, standards, or procedures.

Strategic planning and policy development. This develops policy that will support new initiatives or required changes/enhancements. The tasks for this area are (NIST, 2014a)

1. Analyze organizational information security policy.
2. Assess policy needs and collaborate with stakeholders to develop policies to govern IT activities.
3. Define current and future business environments.
4. Design a cybersecurity strategy that outlines the vision, mission, and goals that align with the organization's strategic plan.
5. Develop and maintain strategic plans.
6. Develop policy, programs, and guidelines for implementation.
7. Draft and publish security policy.
8. Establish and maintain communication channels with stakeholders.
9. Identify and address IT workforce planning and management issues, such as recruitment, retention, and training.

10. Identify organizational policy stakeholders.
11. Monitor the rigorous application of information security/IA policies, principles, and practices in the delivery of planning and management services.
12. Obtain consensus on proposed policy change from stakeholders.
13. Provide policy guidance to IT management, staff, and users.
14. Review existing and proposed policies with stakeholders.
15. Review or conduct audits of IT programs and projects.
16. Serve on agency and interagency policy boards.
17. Support the chief information officer (CIO) in the formulation of IT-related policies.
18. Write IA policy and instructions.
19. Promote awareness of security issues among management and ensure sound security principles are reflected in the organization's vision and goals.
20. Ensure established cybersecurity strategy is intrinsically linked to organizational mission objectives.
21. Draft and publish a supply chain security and risk management policy.
22. Identify and track the status of protected information assets.
23. Apply knowledge of assessment data of identified threats to decision-making processes.
24. Triage protected assets.
25. Oversee development and implementation of high-level control architectures.
26. Translate applicable laws, statutes, and regulatory documents and integrate into policy.
27. Define and/or implement policies and procedures to ensure the protection of critical infrastructure as appropriate.

Training, education, and awareness (TEA). This conducts training of personnel within pertinent subject domain. It also develops, plans, coordinates, delivers, and/or evaluates training courses, methods, and techniques as appropriate. The tasks for this area are (NIST, 2014a)

1. Conduct interactive training exercises to create an effective learning environment.
2. Correlate business or mission requirements to training.
3. Deliver training courses tailored to the audience and physical environment.
4. Demonstrate concepts, procedures, software, equipment, technology applications to coworkers, subordinates, or others.
5. Design training curriculum and course content.
6. Determine training requirements (e.g., subject matter, format, location).
7. Develop new or identify existing awareness and training materials that are appropriate for intended audiences.
8. Develop the goals and objectives for cybersecurity TEA.

9. Educate customers in established procedures and processes to ensure professional media standards are met.
10. Evaluate the effectiveness and comprehensiveness of existing training programs.
11. Guide employees through relevant development and training choices.
12. Plan classroom techniques and formats (e.g., lectures, demonstrations, interactive exercises, multimedia presentations) for most effective learning environment.
13. Plan non-classroom educational techniques and formats.
14. Review training documentation.
15. Revise curriculum end course content based on feedback from previous training sessions.
16. Serve as an internal consultant and advisor in own area of expertise.
17. Support the design and execution of exercise scenarios.
18. Write instructional materials (e.g., standard operating procedures, production manual) to provide detailed guidance to relevant portion of the workforce.
19. Coordinate with human resources to ensure job announcements are written to reflect required training, education, and/or experience.

Information systems security operations. The information systems security officer (ISSO) oversees the IA program of an information system in or outside the network environ-ment; may include procurement duties. The tasks for this area are (NIST, 2014a)

1. Advise appropriate senior leadership or authorizing official of charges affecting the organization's IA posture.
2. Collect and maintain data needed to meet system IA reporting.
3. Ensure that IA inspections, tests, and reviews are coordinated for the network environment.
4. Ensure that IA requirements are integrated into the continuity planning for that system and/or organization(s).
5. Ensure that protection and detection capabilities are acquired or developed using the information system security engineering approach and are consistent with organization-level IA architecture.
6. Evaluate and approve development efforts to ensure that baseline security safeguards are appropriately installed.
7. Evaluate cost–benefit, economic, and risk analysis in decision-making process.
8. Participate in information security risk assessment during the SA&A process.
9. Participate in the development or modification of the computer environment IA security program plans and requirements.
10. Prepare, distribute, and maintain plans, instructions, guidance, and standard operating procedures concerning the security of network system(s) operations.

11. Provide system-related input on IA security requirements to be included in statements of work and other appropriate procurement documents.
12. Recognize a possible security violation and take appropriate action to report the incident, as required.
13. Recommend resource allocations required to securely operate and maintain an organization's IA requirements.
14. Supervise or manage protective or corrective measures when an IA incident or vulnerability is discovered.
15. Use federal and organization-specific published documents to manage operations of their computing environment system(s).
16. Identify security requirements specific to an IT system in all phases of the system life cycle.
17. Ensure plans of actions and milestones or remediation plans are in place for vulnerabilities identified during risk assessments, audits, inspections, and so on.
18. Assure successful implementation and functionality of security requirements and appropriate IT policies and procedures consistent with the organization's mission and goals.
19. Support necessary compliance activities (e.g., ensure system security configuration guidelines are followed; compliance monitoring occurs).
20. Participate in the acquisition process as necessary, following appropriate supply chain risk management practices.
21. Define and/or implement policies and procedures to ensure protection of critical infrastructure as appropriate.

Security program management. The chief information security officer (CISO) manages information security implications within the organization, specific program, or other area of responsibility, to include strategic, personnel, infrastructure, policy enforcement, emergency planning, security awareness, and other resources. The tasks for this area are (NIST, 2014a)

1. Acquire and manage the necessary resources, including leadership support, financial resources, and key security personnel, to support IT security goals, and reduce overall organizational risk.
2. Acquire necessary resources, including financial resources, to conduct an effective enterprise continuity of operations program.
3. Advise senior management (e.g., CIO) on risk levels and security posture.
4. Advise senior management (e.g., CIO) on cost–benefit analysis of information security programs, policies, processes, systems, and elements.
5. Communicate the value of IT security throughout all levels of the organization's stakeholders.
6. Collaborate with organizational managers to support organizational objectives.
7. Collaborate with stakeholders to establish the enterprise continuity of operations program, strategy, and mission assurance.

8. Ensure security improvement actions are evaluated, validated, and implemented as required.
9. Establish overall enterprise information security architecture (EISA) with the organization's overall security strategy.
10. Evaluate cost–benefit, economic, and risk analyses in decision-making process.
11. Identify alternative information security strategies to address organizational security objective.
12. Identify IT security program implications of new technologies or technology upgrades.
13. Interface and disseminate necessary cyber event information to appropriate external organizations and audiences.
14. Interpret and/or approve security requirements relative to the capabilities of new information technologies.
15. Interpret patterns of noncompliance to determine their impact on the enterprise's levels of risk and/or the IA program's overall effectiveness.
16. Manage alignment of IT security priorities with the organization's security strategy.
17. Lead and oversee information security budget, staffing, and contracting.
18. Manage the monitoring of information security data sources to maintain organizational situational awareness.
19. Publish cyber defense techniques and guidance (e.g., Time Compliance Network Orders [TCNOs], concept of operations, net analyst reports) for the organization.
20. Manage threat or target analysis of adversary's cyber activity information and production of threat information within the enterprise.
21. Monitor and evaluate the effectiveness of the enterprise's IA security safeguards to ensure they provide the intended level of protection.
22. Oversee the IT security training and awareness program.
23. Provide enterprise IA and supply chain risk management guidance for development of the continuity of operations plans.
24. Provide leadership and direction to IT personnel by ensuring that IA security awareness, basics, literacy, and training are provided to operations personnel commensurate with their responsibilities.
25. Provide technical documents, incident reports, and findings from computer examinations, summaries, and other situational awareness information to higher headquarters.
26. Recommend policy and coordinate review and approval.
27. Track audit findings and recommendations to ensure appropriate mitigation actions are taken.
28. Promote awareness of security issues among management and ensure sound security principles are reflected in the organization's vision and goals.
29. Oversee policy standards and implementation strategies to ensure procedures and guidelines comply with cybersecurity policies.

30. Participate in risk governance process to provide security risks, mitigations, and input on other technical risk.
31. Evaluate the effectiveness of procurement function in addressing information security requirements and supply chain risks through procurement activities and recommend improvement.
32. Ensure all acquisitions, procurements, and outsourcing efforts address information security requirements consistent with organization goals.
33. Continuously validate the organization against policies/guidelines/procedures/regulations/laws to ensure compliance.
34. Forecast ongoing service demands and ensure that security assumptions are reviewed as necessary.
35. Define and/or implement policies and procedures to ensure protection of critical infrastructure as appropriate.

Risk management. This area deploys countermeasures to assure that all identified risks and monitoring requirements have been met and formally documents that compliance for review by the designated accrediting/approving authorities. The tasks for this area are (NIST, 2014a)

1. Develop methods to monitor and measure risk, compliance, and assurance efforts.
2. Develop specifications to ensure risk, compliance, and assurance efforts conform to security, resilience, and dependability requirements at the software application, system, and network environment level.
3. Draft statements of preliminary or residual security risks for system operation.
4. Maintain information systems assurance and accreditation materials.
5. Manage and approve accreditation packages (e.g., [ISO/IEC] 15026-2).
6. Monitor and evaluate a system's compliance with IT security, resilience, and dependability requirements.
7. Perform validation steps, comparing actual results with expected results and analyze the differences to identify impact and risks.
8. Plan and conduct security authorization reviews and assurance case development for initial installation of systems and networks.
9. Provide an accurate technical evaluation of the software application, system, or network, documenting the security posture, capabilities, and vulnerabilities against relevant IA compliances.
10. Recommend new or revised security, resilience, and dependability measures based on the results of reviews.
11. Review authorization and assurance documents to confirm that the level of risk is within acceptable limits for each software application, system, and network.
12. Verify that application software/network/system security postures are implemented as stated, document deviations, and recommend required actions to correct those deviations.

13. Verify that the software application/network/system accreditation and assurance documentation are current.
14. Develop security compliance processes and/or audits for external services (e.g., cloud service providers, data centers).
15. Inspect continuous monitoring results to confirm that the level of risk is within acceptable limits for the software application, network, or system.
16. Develop and implement IA-independent audit processes for application software/networks/systems and oversee ongoing independent audits to ensure that operational processes and procedures are in compliance with organizational and mandatory IA requirements and accurately followed by systems administrators and other cybersecurity staff when performing their day-to-day activities.

Knowledge management. This area oversees and assures the processes and tools that enable the organization to identify, document, and access its intellectual capital and information content. Tasks are (NIST, 2014a)

1. Administer the indexing/cataloging, storage, and access of organizational documents.
2. Construct access paths to suites of information (e.g., link pages) to facilitate access by end users.
3. Design, build, implement, and maintain a knowledge management system that provides end users' access to the organization's intellectual capital.
4. Develop an understanding of the needs and requirements of information end users.
5. Develop and implement control procedures into the testing and development of core IT-based knowledge management systems.
6. Monitor and report the usage of knowledge management assets and resources.
7. Plan and manage the delivery of knowledge management projects.
8. Promote knowledge sharing through an organization's operational processes and systems by strengthening links between knowledge sharing and IT systems.
9. Provide recommendations on data structures and databases that ensure correct and quality production of reports/management information.

Implementing the Framework in Practice

The NICE framework specifies a comprehensive set of generic tasks and KSA requirements for cybersecurity. Nonetheless, that comprehensiveness poses both an advantage and a real disadvantage. The advantage of such a broad range of generic practices is that companies whose personnel have been rigorously trained in them can be confident that effective security exists in their organization right down to the level of the individual employee. In addition, because each practice exists within a coherent conceptual framework, the company can also be reasonably certain that all of the practices that are derived from it will be properly coordinated.

Nevertheless, the disadvantage of such a wide-ranging set of practices rests with the level of detail that they are described at. From a usability standpoint, in order to make the NICE framework both coherent and generally applicable the purpose and intent of each of those practices had to be specified at a fairly high level of description. As a result, in order to be put those behavioral practices into effect the contents of the NICE framework have to be taken down to a level of detail that the people responsible for executing those recommendations can understand and execute.

This means that each of the KSA and task specification in each generic specialty area has to be translated into a substantive set of behaviors that will be carried out in order to achieve a given purpose. Likewise, in order for those individuals to execute those behaviors in a way that achieves their intended aims, the specification of the requisite real-world steps has to fit the mind-set of the individuals who are accountable for their performance. Similarly, because the situation or context will vary from situation to situation, it is to be expected that the behaviors that are specified in order to achieve a generic outcome in one situation will look different from the same specifications to achieve the same result in another situation.

The problem of variability has to be resolved if the recommendations of the NICE framework are ever going to be useful in actual practice. Logically, the best way to assure a predictable outcome is to establish a single, design and implementation that will ensure that any action taken to achieve a given security outcome will actually accomplish, and then continue to accomplish, the desired result. In essence, what this means is that a formally delineated and well-documented, organization-wide design and oversight process has to be established in order to ensure that any practical set of standard work instructions, which have been developed to achieve a given security purpose, will reliably achieve that particular purpose in all instances and at all times.

The aim of such a universal design and implementation process is to ensure that an appropriate set of work instructions is created and maintained in a form that is traceable to the generic purposes of the NICE framework element that it is intended to represent. The coordination and control process must maintain the relationship between each individual work instruction in practice and the purposes of the generic recommendation it implements.

Work instructions are expressed at a much greater level of detail than the generic specifications of the NICE framework, which they implement. Nonetheless, it is those work instructions that give the implementation process the required flexibility. Essentially work instructions are developed in order to reasonably achieve some aspect of the assumed purposes of a specialty area. As long as the work instructions achieve that purpose they are correct, no matter how different they might be from one instance of application to another.

From the standpoint of the pragmatic environment, the effectiveness of any individual work instruction has to be able to be evaluated in order to ensure its consistently effective performance. Those criteria should allow managers to judge, by direct observation, whether the actions of the work instruction continue to satisfy the purpose for which it was written. As a result, a substantive set of criteria for evaluation have to be provided with each work instruction. Those criteria have to produce outcomes that can be observed and recorded. Consequently, each work instruction should be documented by describing the following:

1. Behaviors required
2. How each behavior will satisfy the KSA or task it is referenced to
3. Observable outcomes that can be used to evaluate performance
4. Interrelationships with other work instructions that underlie the generic purpose

For example, if there were frequent security errors in the specification of software requirements, the evaluation of those errors should be able to determine the precise steps that would have to be taken to correct the problem, such as static testing of requirements against risk analysis outcomes, or downstream validations of adherence to initial specifications.

The documentation would also describe the behavioral means that would be used to tell whether the recommended corrective actions were successful such as "specification errors will not exceed two per system," or "specifications will be validated at the coding desk checks." Finally, if there are other related work instructions, such as "all acquired elements to be integrated will be checked against specifications," or "all reviews will produce action items for further monitoring," both of which would fall under different specialty areas, the mechanism for coordinating the linkages between related work instructions would also be specified.

Adapting the NICE Framework to an Organization

The NICE framework was developed using the most authoritative sources available. Nonetheless, it was never intended to provide a single monolithic definition of secure practice. Instead, the assumption behind the NICE framework is that its 7 knowledge areas and its 32 roles and associated competencies would provide an across-the-board, coherent baseline representation of the security common body of knowledge as a whole.

Consequently, any behaviors that are tailored out of these basic requirements will by definition be correct if they are expressed correctly. And thus the NICE workforce tasks and KSAs could legitimately serve as a foundation for defining a real-world security response. Therefore, in practical terms, it is understood that the concepts in the NICE framework have to be further elaborated in order to serve as a useful representation of the unique needs of a given situation.

The assumption is that the NICE framework specifies a complete set of correct elements. But the one thing that is certain is that the field will always change and new and unanticipated threats will constantly emerge. Therefore, the ability to add roles and competencies within the organizing structure of the framework makes unique situations easier to adapt to. It also ensures that organizations will always be able to develop and integrate specific responses to meet their security requirements, while still maintaining the logical coherence of the basic structure of the model for coordinated management purposes.

Since the whole point of any security response is to minimize risk, a formal risk identification and risk analysis process is a fundamental precondition of actually implementing the recommendations of the NICE model. In order to plan for their intended security response, a company is obligated to conduct a formal and comprehensive risk analysis.

Once that analysis is complete it is more than likely that the need for additional roles and competencies will be discovered, which do not exist in the basic model. Examples of such needs might be the addition of a lawyer, or paralegal role to satisfy the requirements of the secure acquisition specialty area, or a strategic supply chain management role in the secure acquisition, or even the secure software engineering specialty area. Since the original assumption was that the changing nature of any security situation will require adaptation of the basic recommendations of the NICE framework, the model itself was purposely designed to be easy to expand.

The NICE framework expands in two logical dimensions. First, additional roles could be added to each specialty areas as we did in the example above. This normally happens when new security requirements are identified. For instance, the need for a paralegal role that we just cited in secure acquisition is an example of adding roles. Since contracting is an essential part of the acquisition process, there might be a time when paralegals are needed to review contracts. This role currently exists in the legal advice and advocacy specialty area, although its tasks and KSAs indicate that its function is to assist in compliance rather than contracts. Nevertheless, it is a defined specialty area and the standard security behaviors of a legal advocate exist. So in that case, the structure of the NICE framework makes it easy to simply tailor that standard role into another specialty area.

Also, KSAs and tasks can be added to a role. That would be the case if, for example, the requirements for a unique threat required KSAs from multiple NICE roles. Forensics is a good example of that. It has a well-defined task structure designed to dictate correct behavior in the analysis and documentation of conventional attacks. However, an unexpected threat can emerge in the geopolitical space that will require a range of KSA requirements from the intelligence-related knowledge areas collect and operate and analyze. If that is the case then the specialties from those knowledge areas and their KSAs can be tapped to construct the requisite set of integrated behaviors.

If an organization adopts the NICE framework as its information security model, there are likely to be some specific instances where that model has to be modified to fit that particular organization's operation. Nonetheless, because the NICE framework is built on logical associations between its elements, unless those modifications are done by means of a disciplined and coordinated process, the potential exists to create dysfunctional gaps by installing practices that do not interact correctly with the rest of the elements of the security solution. Therefore the logic of any modification, or change, has to be closely examined.

It is important to continue to understand the purpose and intent of the job titles within the standard role definitions of the NICE framework. NICE roles are generic in nature and by design are broadly defined in order to cover several job titles in different industries. For instance, in the case of a firm with a substantial involvement in integration of components into systems, they may have individuals who are software engineers, whose primary responsibilities include the design, development, and maintenance of the organization's software assets. But they may not be involved in the actual acquisition of those components.

So rather than trying to turn every software engineer into an acquisition specialist, consideration should be given to the actual role that the software engineers in an organization play in acquiring the components that they integrate. If the competencies that are required involve acquisition, than there might be justification for adding a new role, such as supply chain risk manager, to the secure software engineering specialty area. However, if the actual knowledge requirements are more for the development end than in the actual acquisition process, then this particular requirement might be better incorporated under the secure acquisition specialty area and that role would then work in conjunction with the software engineers. In every instance where roles are ambiguous, it is important to first determine whether the competencies that make up that role might actually fit better under an existing specialty area.

Planning: Converting Theory into Practice

The framework underwrites an organization's need to make security a strategic function. In essence, the organization's strategic security process can be put together using the standard components of the framework model. In that respect, the various KSA and task components of the framework can be adapted and tailored into a specific way of conducting a standard security operation. The tailoring is reflected through an organization-wide long-term plan that is normally prepared as part of an overall strategic planning effort.

The strategic plan describes how the organization will conceive, manage, implement, validate, and maintain the desired level of security over a set period. That period is normally anywhere from 1 to 3 years. The organization's strategic security plan is likely to document its planning assumptions in a variety of ways; for instance, text, diagrams, charts, or even programmatic protocols. In practical application, the detailed steps in the overall strategic plan are communicated through a procedure manual or a standard operational protocol that is typically put together to explain how to conduct each job role, or task. The documentation typically contain text descriptions of the sanctioned processes and procedures, along with lists of standard tools, and some form of process diagram to describe the way the organization will perform the plan's requisite activities.

In order to implement a given approach across any organization, the planners have to work from a common inventory of standard behavioral building blocks, or process pieces, along with the necessary support tools. These are then assembled and fitted in a way that will mitigate each specific threat. The organization's approach to security is typically structured by the identification and analysis of threats as they appear. However the overarching architecture of the framework allows the organization to design a comprehensive, and systematic threat response that is based on the body of common best practice for the field.

It takes a great deal of detailed definition in order to establish the necessary behaviors for a company-wide security response, particularly in the case of a large and complex organization. As a result, the overall information security approach is typically developed through three succeedingly more refined organizational planning processes. These processes are designed to ensure that the proper set of carefully thought-through steps are specified at each of the normal levels of organizational functioning:

1. Management plan
2. Design and implementation plan
3. Evaluation plan

The management plan lays out the specialty areas that the organization feels will satisfy the intent of its security requirements. The contents of this plan are shaped by the organization's purpose and mission as well as external factors like the resource and threat environment and the particular business strategy. In other words, the management plan defines the complete set of job roles that the organization plans to deploy and coordinate, in order to ensure that the dictates of best practice are followed. It is assumed that if each relevant NICE framework role executes its intended function within the purposes and intents of the standard model. Then the security aims of the organization will be satisfied.

The design and implementation plan describes the specific behaviors that the organization thinks will satisfy the NICE purpose and intent of the management plan. The design and implementation plan specifies the specific behaviors that the designer consider necessary to achieve the purposes of each functional role. In addition, it specifies how each of those behaviors will be carried out, monitored, and assessed. Because it itemizes the activities that will constitute the day-to-day security system for the organization, the design and implementation plan is really the practical instantiation of the operations manual for the organization's services.

Finally, the evaluation plan documents how the company will assure correct and consistent performance of the behaviors specified in the design and implementation plan. The evaluation plan is written to ensure the reliable execution of any behaviors that are specified as well as how those behaviors might be rationally modified over time based on lessons learned. The evaluation plan also has to specify the provisions that will be taken to assure the continuing trustworthiness of the overall security process. Because the products of this plan involve assessment, the plan also has to specify who will be responsible for doing the actual evaluation and when the evaluation. Finally, the specific measures that will be used to assess performance have to be specified and maintained over time as living specifications.

Mapping the NICE Specialty Areas to Business Purposes

As shown in Figure 2.10, the NICE workforce framework documents 32 specialty areas. These specialty areas are organized in seven knowledge areas. Taken together, the specialty areas constitute an itemized listing of the large functions that a proper security operation would carry out within a given real-world setting.

As a result, a company that can map its particular job titles to the specialty areas of the NICE workforce framework's tasks and associated KSAs can in effect document that it is following a standard definition of correct practice. In actual execution though, that correctness hinges on the ability to document "completeness." Completeness is a relative term. However, with the NICE workforce framework, it means that a company can document that it is able to document that the activities that it performs fit the best practice specifications of the NICE workforce framework's within its current sphere of operation. The simple rule of thumb is that the security can be considered complete if all of the necessary specialty areas that would logically be associated with the tangible security requirements of the organization can be mapped to the appropriate set of NICE workforce framework task and KSA requirements. And that all actual activity required to satisfy a given task and KSA competency can be documented by evidence of performance.

The rationale behind testing for completeness rests with the overall integrative purpose of the NICE workforce framework. In practice, the NICE workforce framework can be used to guide the development and implementation of a competent security solution across a wide spectrum of organizations. That is because, the NICE workforce framework was developed from a broad set of commonly accepted security frameworks, including elements of NIST 800-39, the ISO 27000 series, as well as a whole host of best practices including those promoted by NIST through the 800 Special Publication series of technical publications. Therefore, by distilling and integrating all of the relevant best practices from each of these models, the NICE workforce framework creates a single compendium for defining both effective security practice as well as the complete set of elements of the field of cybersecurity.

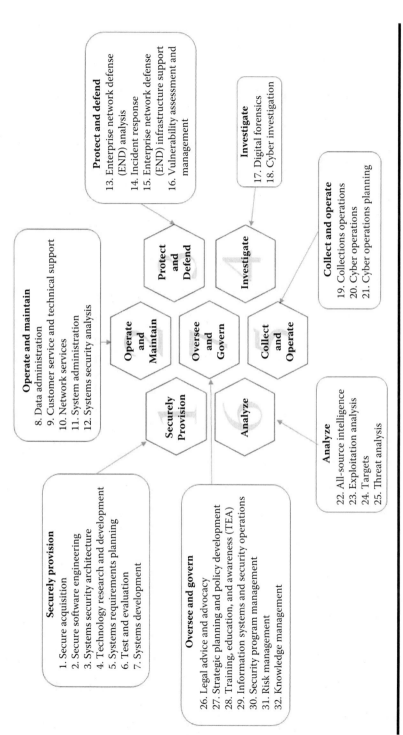

Figure 2.10   The seven general knowledge areas of the NICE Cybersecurity Workforce Framework and their corresponding 32 specialty areas.

Deciding on Which Specialty Area to Employ in a Concrete Solution

Information security work is not homogenous. In fact, the challenges are too big and complex to be solved by a single individual, or even discipline. Thus there are a number of specialty areas that are associated with ensuring an organization. Those areas typically involve a cluster of associated tasks and the attendant KSAs.

The 32 specialty areas that are defined in the NICE workforce framework are the outcome of an exhaustive job/task analysis conducted throughout the federal government. It involved a wide variety of IT job titles and their related security responsibilities. That analysis was initially carried out by the Department of Defense. Ten security specialties were identified in the first study, along with a related set of general competency requirements. Then, in 2010–2011 the Office of Personnel Management (OPM) conducted a similar much broader study, in conjunction with the Department of Homeland Security. The aim of the project s was to identify and then characterize all the forms of IA work that might occur, specifically within the government. As a result, the number of security specialties was expanded to 32, within 7 knowledge areas.

The first thing to note is that the 32 roles in the NICE workforce framework represent job roles rather than job titles. These roles range in a comprehensive spectrum across the IT security workforce. In order to avoid getting caught up in the myriad of job titles that actually exist for equivalent jobs, the NICE workforce framework takes a role-based approach to the definition of the work to be done. It is up to the individual organization then, to assign a job title that is equivalent to the task requirements specified for a given specialty area within the NICE workforce framework. The title is likely to vary across organizations, but the required tasks, competencies, and accountabilities of the KSAs will essentially remain the same.

The standard job roles associated with the specialty areas can be mapped into virtually any organization. However since most organizations have their own titles, the process is not as simple as just dropping the NICE workforce framework KSAs into an existing job description. Instead, the first step in the mapping process is to equate the NICE workforce framework specialty area definition, as described by its constituent tasks, with whatever the organization presently calls the function that performs those tasks. That might require bundling a number of existing job titles into a single NICE workforce framework specialty area. Or it might involve spreading the specialty area requirements across a range of titles.

For instance, as shown in Figure 2.11, the secure software engineering specialty area might encompass a number of existing job titles such as developer or system analyst, malware analyst, or even configuration manager.

Conversely, the mapping might require factoring the activities of an existing job description into more than one specialty area. For instance, some of the tasks and KSAs of the CISO might actually fit better under the risk management specialty, or the activities of the people in the organization's security architecture functions

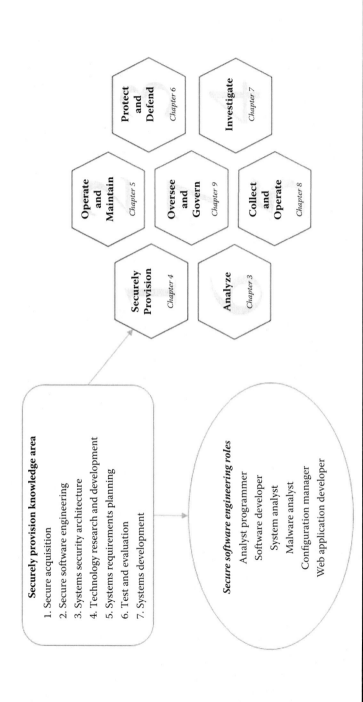

Figure 2.11 Roles for the secure software engineering specialty area.

might be better defined by the tasks and KSAs of both the secure software engineering and the systems security specialty areas.

It is also possible that, in a practical application of the model, focused NICE workforce framework specialties like those in the collect and operate, or the analyze knowledge areas will not have anything mapped to them in the actual operation. This makes sense in the light of the highly concentrated nature of those particular roles. Nonetheless, in the event that there is no analogous job description within the organization, it is important to examine the purposes that are listed for the specialty areas within those knowledge areas. The aim would be to ensure that these specialties are either not required, or are adequately covered by other, successfully mapped organizational job titles.

Whatever the actual situation, the aim of the mapping is to understand how each of the existing job titles in an organization fit within the standard specialty area requirements of the NICE workforce framework. That is because the standard specialty area definitions contribute specific functionality to the overall purpose, which is security. And it is those specialties that form the ultimate basis for every real-world implementation of the model.

Sufficiency of coverage can be ensured by comparing the task and KSA requirements of the role as itemized in the NICE workforce framework with the assigned job responsibilities of a given position. If any meaningful differences are identified in that comparison, then the gaps that exist must be filled by instituting new practices that will ensure the required tasks, KSAs and competencies have been properly institutionalized. This approach is used for all of the existing job titles that fit within the NICE specialty areas.

Tailoring a Solution from the Concept

In order to turn ideal concept into practical reality, the elements that comprise the framework model have to be "tailored" to the specific situation. The term tailoring describes any standard or systematic procedure that the organization uses to convert the general aims of any generic model into a concrete set of actions that will describe how the work is to be done in each instance.

When it comes to their particular security needs, all organizations have unique requirements. The special method of doing business, whether it is in the governmental or the private sector is generally unique. As a result the need for a standard, systematic, top-down plan often gets lost in the development of a set of actions to fit the challenges of a given incident. As we said in the Chapter 1 that focus often translates into ad hoc sometimes conflicting approaches to the same problem in different parts of the organization, which produces ineffective results. It also means that any lessons learned in how to "make the process more effective" get lost in the day-to-day responses to the unrelated incidents that occur within that given organization.

Using a standard set of common elements to guide the design of the across-the-board security response for all instances of a given threat will make the long-term planning and management of the overall security function easier to develop and more effective. That is because knowledge from lessons learned can be adapted from the outcomes of previous responses in order to continuously develop better or more appropriate tools and methods.

The framework specifies the common best practice approach for every security role using a designed set of KSA and task descriptions that are provided for the appropriate specialty area. Thus the tailoring of the concrete response for a given organization starts with the identification of requisite roles for that particular instance.

For example, if the organization does not do software engineering the specialty areas in securely provision might not apply. But the protect and defend specialty areas might. So the approach to tailoring the framework's standard task and KSA specifications to the needs of a specific organization starts with an identification of all relevant roles and knowledge requirements. Then the generic KSA and task recommendations have to be evaluated for relevance and practicality for that particular application.

The applicability of each task and KSA will necessarily vary based on such factors as organizational culture. Nonetheless, in general, the following concepts can be used to think through how to adapt a tailored application from the framework's recommendations. Tailoring the standard framework model to a practical response often requires the following information:

1. Security goals and organizational culture
2. Security technologies and technical work requirements
3. Overall security performance requirements and criteria

This information is combined with the organization's purposes and external factors, such as the following:

1. The organization's business goals
2. The organization's existing security processes and components
3. Standard rules for tailoring the framework to a given application
4. Any external laws, regulations, or standard requirements
5. The organization's overall management philosophy

Every company's approach to tailoring is shaped by its business culture and environment. So in that respect, all tailoring outcomes are implicitly unique. The only rule with tailoring is that the behaviors that are eventually selected are executed as uniformly and systematically as possible within the given situation.

Both management and technology factors are taken into consideration in the tailoring process. As the categorical result of the tailoring process, the explicit day-to-day specifications of the real-world work to be done must mirror the purpose and intent of the behaviors that comprise the specifications of the standard workforce framework. The aim of the tailoring process is to drill-down from the framework's abstract model, in order to define a concrete set of actionable behaviors that align with the needs of the particular situation. That drilling-down process ensures that each individual requirement, which is specified in the framework, is documented in such a way that the behaviors that are necessary to fulfill the purposes of that requirement are embedded within the organization's standard operational practice base.

The company-wide set of uniform security behaviors, which a tailoring process will eventually produce, integrates all of the necessary security knowledge and tasks of all relevant elements of the framework into a single comprehensive day-to-day solution. Each specific work practice that is tailored from the NICE framework is likely to have a set of technical and managerial behaviors associated with it. As a result, the whole specification of all of the technical and managerial behaviors for all relevant NICE framework recommendations can be assumed to represent the formal security approach of that company and that approach is what is specified in the procedure manuals and security protocols. These controls, in essence then, constitute the actions that the organization feels will best achieve its security aims.

Each behavior that is part of the security process has to be individually described and documented in that manual in order to be put successfully into practice. The documentation of all requisite behaviors then serves as the practical handbook for the day-to-day execution of the company's formal cybersecurity process. The one condition that must be satisfied in the tailoring process is that each constituent behavior has to be traceable to the KSA or task recommendation that it implements.

Ensuring traceability validates the correctness of each recommended standard behavior. But more important, it ensures accountability, because it identifies the person responsible for executing that requisite action. Consequently, the documentation has to precisely specify the proper way that each behavior should be carried out, who will carry it out and when it will be executed. Also, in order to ensure proper quantitative management, the documentation for each behavior should also provide a set of well-defined metrics, which will allow the company to verify performance.

Tailoring Specialty Area Tasks to Specific Application

All of the underlying practices that a company institutes as standard operating procedure have to reflect the implementing organization's specific business environment. For instance, common functions like configuration management and network analysis are specified in various places as specialty areas and generic practices in the NICE workforce model. And because, those functions will also likely be a necessary component of every organization's eventual security solution. Their relationship in the overall security process can be understood by referencing the recommendations of the model.

However, the actual tasks and behaviors associated with each of the KSAs in those specialty areas will no doubt be different in a high-security government environment versus a low-tech manufacturing facility. Therefore, the implementation of the concrete solution has to be in the form of a tailoring of the recommendations of NICE to the practical situation. Thus, the NICE framework provides an explicitly defined set of job roles and the attendant KSAs within each specialty area.

The practical task specifications for each specialty area can in effect be turned into an explicit specification of the actual behaviors and outcomes needed to ensure proper performance of that specialty. The experts who formulated the NICE workforce model included the specific knowledge, skill and ability requirements that they deemed necessary to ensure proper execution of the security practices within each specialty area. These behaviors were defined based on a wide range of commonly accepted security standards and best practices. The analysis of those standards produced 65 critical work roles. Each of those roles accomplish some purpose of the specialty area. They are related by the fact that they accomplish one of the intended outcomes of that specialty area.

Because in the real world these workforce roles have a wide range of actual titles, the developers of the NICE model have made it clear that the practical tasks define the explicit purpose of the specialty area rather than the actual job title. In order to differentiate the individual purpose and aims of each of the specialty areas, the framework also provides a precise specification of the necessary KSA requirements for each area. The KSAs describe the actual knowledge skill and ability requirements to perform the required tasks. Those KSA specifications are listed as a next (lower) level hyperlink from the specialty area.

The NICE model also takes the additional step of factoring the specific KSA specifications for each specialty area into a set of highly recognizable competency categories, which are standardized across the field. Those categories include such old warhorses as software quality assurance (SQA) and configuration management as well as new things like acquisition contracting. The competency categories that are associated with each individual KSA are considered to be common to all information security work.

The distilled advice that went into constructing the NICE framework, which was gleaned from all potential sources, essentially guarantees a broad representation of each of the potential elements that might legitimately be considered to be an appropriate component of the field of cybersecurity. And as a result, the NICE model can be considered to represent the most authoritative possible picture of the entire elephant and the terminology, and KSAs associated with the field of cybersecurity.

Three Factors That Ensure Proper Application of the Model

Every individualized security process, which is tailored from a set of standard operating procedures, will be unique by definition. That is because the tailoring process should always reflect three standard considerations, which represent the general factors that influence the form of any concrete security response. These general factors are context, scope, and feasibility. Context dictates the assumptions and underlying conditions that apply to that specific security setting. Scope is derived from context. It defines what will be protected and what will not as well as the priority of the protected items. In that respect, scope serves as the basis for the definition of the defense in depth scheme.

Both context and scope have to be explicitly defined before any consideration can be given to the form of the actual behaviors to be performed. However, once the process of generally defining the desired level and type of response to a given threat has been initiated, the first consideration has to be whether those plans are economically and technically feasible. The fine tuning that must take place, in order to strike a feasible balance between the implementation of the measure and the economic, technical, and social realities of the situation, is what ensures that every security solution will be unique.

Context

The first factor that has to be understood and explicitly dealt with is overall context. That is because it is vital to gain a complete and detailed understanding of the environment that each planned security behavior will operate in prior to its detailed design. In essence, since the security response has to interface with its surroundings the solution has to be fitted to the requirements of those surroundings, not the other way around.

The security response operates day-to-day within the relevant social, economic, and technical variables of the context. Therefore, the first step in the implementation process has to be to discover what operating variables might influence that functioning. For instance, a very rigorous system of controls that are best suited to a high security context would most likely be counterproductive if it were imposed on a typically low-tech manufacturing context. The opposite would also be true. Thus, for the sake of ensuring an effective fit between the security response and its setting it is necessary to identify and document all of the concrete requirements of that environment.

Context is a critical first step in tailoring. That requirement is often overlooked because the participants in the planning are likely to assume that all of the members of the organization have the same motivation and commitment to security that they do. Consequently, during the process of developing that security response, implicit, and often incorrect, assumptions may never be made explicit. The result is that important behavioral considerations, which could have a critical impact on the success, or failure of the overall security system, might never be identified, or factored into the eventual set of required security practices.

A simple example of that might be a solution that requires extremely complex passwords, which would better ensure security, but which would be extremely aggravating to the individual user because they would be difficult to remember. The inevitable consequence of hard to remember passwords in conventional businesses would be that individual users would write them down and leave them in handy places, simply because they needed the memory boost. Of course, leaving a record of your password in an easily accessible place also defeats the intent of a strong password system. Therefore, behavioral factors such as that should be factored into the design of any security system.

Scope

The next step involves the specific actions that are taken to establish the security perimeter. It is important to unambiguously define where the security scheme will apply because whatever countermeasures to be deployed will demand resources. And so, the greater the extent of the protected space that is defined, the greater the resource requirements. Documenting the scope of the protected space involves clarifying such practical issues as detailing the specific aspects of the operation that will be secured, who should be responsible for carrying out each of the security functions within the protection scheme, what reporting lines will be followed, and who will eventually be accountable for the overall success of the process.

The detailed definition of the organizational boundaries of protected space is an essential step in the proper management of the system, which will eventually be implemented. That is because it dictates the resource requirements. Because the decisions about what will reside in the protected space can be political as much as they are rational, that definition has to be the result of a formal organizational definition process. That process should be supported by and referenced to any relevant commonly accepted authorities such as standards, regulations, or even internal policies. Moreover in order to ensure that the currently defined scope continues to remain effective, an appropriate set of measures to assess and judge the performance of the security system should also be provided.

Even though this part of the process sounds more like a conceptual exercise than a concrete activity, unique and meaningful secure boundaries have to be established for each processing, communications, storage, and information resource component that will have to be protected and those interrelationships have to be made explicit. A thorough and precise mapping of the protected items in secured space is required, because it is necessary to ensure that all relevant functions that ensure security are actually being carried out.

In practice for all protected items, there is rarely a one-to-one match between a specification of the generic KSA requirements that a document like the NICE framework provides, and the actual work responsibilities that might fall under a given job title in the real world. So the overall aim of the process should be to determine whether all of the generic security requirements, which have been derived from the NICE framework, have been satisfied by real-world job titles and their attendance behaviors. The amount of documentation required to ensure the relationship between an ideal model and the realities of its implementation is extensive. So for the sake of efficient tracking, it is helpful to keep a comprehensive definition of the behaviors that the organization should expect to see within the scope of its intended security solution under rigorous configuration control.

Availability of Resources

Once all required components have been identified, it is then necessary to estimate whether what has been proposed can be implemented within the real-world resources that the organization has allocated for that solution. A lot of security solutions fail because they are not feasible within the resources available to execute them, or are just technically infeasible.

Consequently, the viability of the solution within resource constraints has to be confirmed. That requires the company to estimate all of the resources required in order to both establish as well as maintain the desired level of security. It also requires planners to look at how the technology is progressing, in order to ensure that whatever technologies will be required in the future will be available.

Chapter Summary

The aim of a high-level conceptual model like the NICE framework is to provide a strategic description of all of the elements of the field. NICE specifies all of the commonly agreed on activities and interrelationships associated with good security into a single workforce model. In that respect, the NICE framework stipulates all of the requisite and commonly accepted workforce roles and practices necessary to carry out a complete set of cybersecurity activities. In that respect, by providing a standard definition of the tasks involved in the work to be done the NICE framework comprises a standard definition of the field of cybersecurity.

In that respect, then the framework serve as a template to allow any organization to tailor out its own substantive set of suitable work practices. If the tailoring is done correctly, the assumption is that the resulting practices will, in effect, be correct because they are derived from the commonly accepted correct model of the field, as represented by the NICE framework model. So essentially, the NICE framework provides the standard advice about how to connect the dots in a practical manner between all of the requisite elements of cybersecurity practice. That advice serves as a roadmap to guide an organization in the creation of its own specific security solution.

Information security work is not homogenous though. In fact the challenges are too big and complex to be solved by a single individual, or even discipline. Thus there are a number of specialty areas that are associated with ensuring an organization. Those areas typically involve a cluster of associated tasks and the attendant KSAs. The KSAs describe the knowledge required to carry out the tasks that fulfill the practical goals of each job role. Those common KSAs and tasks characterize the specific purpose of each specialty area. The use of KSA specifications along with common tasks as a means to organize the specialty areas into functional categories allows the NICE framework to much more precisely define the actual set of discrete behaviors required in that particular aspect of the discipline.

The framework underwrites an organization's need to make security a strategic function. In essence, the organization's strategic security process can be put together using the standard components of the framework model. In that respect, the various KSA and task components of the framework can be adapted and tailored into a specific way of conducting a standard security operation. The tailoring is reflected through an organization-wide long-term plan that is normally prepared as part of an overall strategic planning effort.

Obviously in order to implement a given approach across any organization, the planners have to work from a common inventory of standard behavioral building blocks, or process pieces, along with the necessary support tools. These are then assembled and fitted in a way that will mitigate each specific threat.

Nevertheless, in order to turn ideal concept into practical reality the elements that comprise the framework model have to be "tailored" to the specific situation. The framework specifies the common best practice approach for every security role using a designed set of KSA and task descriptions that are provided for the appropriate specialty area. The aim of the tailoring process is to drill down from the framework's abstract model, in order to define a concrete set of actionable behaviors that align with the needs of the particular situation. That drilling-down process ensures that each individual requirement, which is specified in the framework, is documented in such a way that the behaviors that are necessary to fulfill the purposes of that requirement are embedded within the organization's standard operational practice base.

The company-wide set of uniform security behaviors, which a tailoring process will eventually produce, integrates all of the necessary security knowledge and tasks of all relevant elements of the framework into a single comprehensive day-to-day solution. Each specific work practice that is tailored from the NICE framework is likely to have a set of technical and managerial behaviors associated with it. As a result, the whole specification of all of the technical and managerial behaviors for all relevant NICE framework recommendations can be assumed to represent the formal security approach of that company and that approach is what is specified in the procedure manuals and security protocols. These controls, in essence then, constitute the actions that the organization feels will best achieve its security aims.

Every individualized security process, which is tailored from a set of standard operating procedures will be unique by definition. That is because the tailoring process should always reflect three standard considerations, which represent the general factors that influence the form of any concrete security response. These general factors are context, scope, and feasibility. Context dictates the assumptions and underlying conditions that apply to that specific security setting. Scope is derived from context. It defines what will be protected and what will not as well as the priority of the protected items. In that respect, scope serves as the basis for the definition of the defense in depth scheme.

In order to be put those behavioral practices into effect the contents of the NICE framework have to be taken down to a level of detail that the people responsible for executing those recommendations can understand and execute. This means that each of the KSA and task specification in each generic specialty area has to be translated into a substantive set of behaviors that will be carried out in order to achieve a given purpose. Likewise, in order for those individuals to execute those behaviors in a way that achieves their intended aims, the specification of the requisite real-world steps has to fit the mind-set of the individuals who are accountable for their performance. Similarly, because the situation or context will vary from situation to situation, it is to be expected that the behaviors that are specified in order to achieve a generic outcome in one situation will look different from the same specifications to achieve the same result in another situation.

The aim of a universal design and implementation process is to ensure that an appropriate set of work instruction is created and maintained in a form that is traceable to the generic purposes of the NICE framework element that it is intended to represent. The coordination and control process must maintain the relationship between each individual work instruction in practice and the purposes of the generic recommendation it implements.

If an organization adopts the NICE framework as its information security model, there are likely to be some specific instances where that model has to be modified to fit that particular organization's operation. Nonetheless, because the NICE framework is built on logical associations between its elements, unless those modifications are done by means of a disciplined and coordinated process, the potential exists to create dysfunctional gaps by installing practices that do not interact correctly with the rest of the elements of the security solution. Therefore the logic of any modification, or change, has to be closely examined.

Key Terms

CISO Function: Usually the highest level administrative position in the information security hierarchy, responsible for overall policy development and leadership of the IT security operation.

Data Security: A specialty area of the NICE framework related to ensuring the confidentiality, integrity, and availability of enterprise data.

Digital Forensics: A specialized competency area of the NICE framework focused on the evidence gathering function, specifically targeted toward the collection of electronic evidence.

Enterprise Security: A competency area of the NICE framework related to ensuring the continuing survival of the business and that its data assets will be preserved in the event of a disaster.

Incident Management: A dimension of the NICE framework focused on the specific steps designed to deal with a known event, typically supported by risk assessment and planning.

IT Security Competency: A specific area of knowledge and skill commonly associated with a specific need or function that is a necessary aspect of ensuring the security of information.

IT Security Architect: A NICE framework role primarily responsible for the development of EISAs.

IT Security Training and Awareness: A dimension of the NICE framework focused on ensuring that the workforce has adequate skills to perform assigned security functions.

Job Title: A specific title used by an organization to describe a standard function carried out by an assigned person.

Model: A comprehensive conceptual framework used to describe the elements of a generic process or entity.

Operate and Maintain Professional: A knowledge area of the NICE framework devoted to ensuring the proper day-to-day functioning of an established security system.

Acquisition: A dimension of the NICE framework focused on ensuring that products and services acquired by the organization are secure.

Legal Compliance: A dimension of the NICE framework focused on ensuring that the organization complies with all relevant laws, directives, regulations, and standards.

Role: A generic area of security work, delineated by a common set of skills and functional purposes.

Risk Management: A dimension of the NICE framework focused on the identification, analysis, and mitigation of risks.

Security Solution: A specific architecture of controls designed to mitigate a given set of risks within a particular organizational context.

Software Development: The life cycle process devoted to the creation of software typically involves specification, design, code, test, and acceptance of software products.

Strategic Security Planning: A function focused on the development of strategies and policies to govern organizational directions for some defined period.

References

National Institute of Standards and Technology (NIST). 2014a. *The NICE Cybersecurity Workforce Framework 2.0*. Gaithersburg, MD: National Institute of Standards and Technology.

National Institute of Standards and Technology (NIST). 2014b. *Framework for Improving Critical Infrastructure Cybersecurity (CSF)*. Gaithersburg, MD: National Institute of Standards and Technology.

Chapter 3

Implementing Standard Cybersecurity

Chapter Objectives

At the conclusion of this chapter, the reader will:

- Have an overview understanding of the Framework for Improving Critical Infrastructure Cybersecurity including its history, purpose, and benefits
- Be able to identify and describe each component of the framework core
- Understand the implementation tier model of the framework and be able to compare that model to similar models used in the information and communication technology (ICT) industry
- Understand how the framework uses profiles to aid organizations in creating and assessing their cybersecurity program
- Be able to develop a plan for implementing the framework

Why It Is Difficult to Protect Our Critical Information Infrastructure

The need for rigorous protection of our critical infrastructure should be self-evident in a world where the exchange of computerized information underwrites global commerce. Nevertheless, that goal has always been like one of the Ten Commandments, commendable but rather hard to put into day-to-day practice. It is unfortunate because it is also probably true that the fastest and easiest way to bring a postindustrial era society to its knees is to destroy its information infrastructure.

One part of the problem stems from how we understand, or perhaps the correct term is misunderstand, the concept of information. Generally speaking, when companies undertake to secure their information resources they apply a very narrow and potentially disastrous definition to the actual asset. Specifically, typical information security protection schemes are exclusively aimed at assuring the resources maintained in the corporation's electronic repositories. Whereas common sense alone should dictate that any tangible information that adds value to the business should be protected.

Accordingly an effective information security scheme needs to assure the integrity of anything of value that is written, formally communicated, or kept in any format. For example, it is a fact (PRC, 2014) that 71% of the breaches of information security in the year 2013 resulted from physical theft and personnel breakdowns, which illustrates that no matter how many double lock boxes the electronic encryption scheme implements there is no practical assurance unless the workers understand what constitutes an organizational information asset as well as experience the consequences of a security violation.

The second aspect of the problem lies in the fact that although everybody agrees that information protection is a good thing, nobody has the slightest idea what it encompasses. The chief executive officers (CEOs) of every information-intensive organization in the world should be able to assure themselves that they are fully protected against every conceivable source of mischief to their information resource, which is not the case in most instances, since the actual mechanisms for security are deployed in an undisciplined and totally unsystematic way. Or in practical terms, information security is neither well defined, nor is it well documented. There are a lot of nuances involved in securing the information resource and failure to embody a coherent defense in any of those cases can open the door to unthinkable disaster.

Plus if these defenses have been prepared by the information technology (IT) department, one can practically guarantee that there are going to be significant holes in the protection related to the business function. Simply put, IT managers are experts in technology concerns not business security and most business security experts are specialists in physical security, which means that they are as clueless about the fundamentals of assuring virtual IT functioning as IT managers are about enabling business security.

Thus, there is almost always a serious disconnect between the three functional areas of the organization represented by its virtual information, its physical IT assets—for example, those aspects of IT work that are tangible such as the personnel, the workspace, the machinery, and the actual program inventory and the general business operation itself. Obviously any security arrangement that does not provide a concrete solution for every aspect of the unique concerns that each of these areas raise is going to be incomplete and by implication ineffective. Thus, an itemization of the security requirements for all three legs of the stool is a necessary adjunct to establishing complete security protection for the organization.

To confound this problem further, the responsibility for information assurance is located in an understandable but totally dysfunctional place in the organization, which Figure 3.1 illustrates.

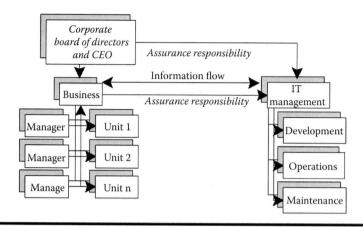

Figure 3.1 Flow of responsibility for information assurance.

Essentially, the units responsible for achieving the purposes of the business use the corporate information resources to attain those goals. These units in turn are overseen and directed by the board of directors and executive officers of the company. The IT function supports this through its standard development, operations and maintenance functions. The flow of information is back and forth from the working units to the IT function as information resources are developed and utilized.

However, the problem lies in the direction of the assignment of responsibility for the assurance of the fundamental resource. If the purpose of corporate information is to accomplish the ends of the business, then the responsibility for protecting that asset lies at least with the functional unit managers who use it and by implication with the board, not with the management of the IT function.

At a minimum the consequence of this illogical placement is that the responsibility for assuring the basis on which the sheer survival of the corporation might rest lies with the group that by definition is the most disconnected from its generation and use. Furthermore, this is a technical group, not one either well versed or interested in the nuances of the business operation. The outcome is inevitably and quite understandably going to be a narrow technical solution, which will not come close to confronting all the myriad of threats faced by a modern, multinational corporation.

The final unique assurance problem stems from the basic purpose of IT itself, which is to enhance communication. In the world of physical security it is easy to account for assets because they are tangible and can be kept in an identified place. The problem with IT assets is that they have to be dispersed as part of their basic function; that is, the whole point of the Internet is to provide remote access from a myriad of sources. So in order to be useful IT assets are by definition difficult to secure. For example, candidates for security control include such asset categories as hardware and system software, applications, information and data, and organizational interfaces. None of these is easily controlled because they are either intangible or dynamic. The fact is that organizations can rarely account for the exact status of their system and applications software, information and data assets, or events occurring on the organizational interfaces (think Internet transactions for instance). Yet, all of these constitute the asset base that must be accounted for.

Thus, a precondition to the establishment of security assurance is the existence of an explicit mechanism, which can serve as the basis for making virtual assets concrete by labeling them. In addition, there must be a formal device that allows for the specification of the rules for control as well as how the ongoing assessment of status will be conducted. And since security involves coordinating a range of functions as well as communication and cooperation among and between organizations it would also be helpful if that framework was commonly understood and accepted. Simply put, it would be nice if a company could find a way to underwrite worldwide trust in their integrity on a standard basis. Obviously, what is required is a good old-fashioned standard, which will dictate the right set of best practices in sufficient detail to give everybody involved confidence that they are doing the right thing.

Background: A System of Best Practices

That is where the National Institute of Standards and Technology (NIST), "Framework for Improving Critical Infrastructure Cybersecurity, Version 1.0" (cybersecurity framework [CSF]), comes in. This standard provides the exact specification of the basic functions necessary to implement a complete infrastructure protection system for cybersecurity, which is a particularly useful thing if, for example, a company is doing business on the Internet. This standard, shown in Figure 3.2, is new but it is already recognized by the federal government as the mechanism for establishing expert best practice safeguards for information and computer assets.

The concept of a common framework, which allows practitioners to communicate and embody every element of best practice protection in their security assurance system, is a logical evolutionary next step. The CSF provides such a structure. In that respect it represents a true lingua franca for the industry. The standard covers the full range of cybersecurity protection. In addition, it provides an explicit basis for controlling and improving practices in each of those areas.

Distinction between This and Other Standards

This standard is groundbreaking, because it is not just a "silver bullet," meaning it is not a narrow technological solution nor does it simply focus on assuring the technology itself. Instead it creates a comprehensive and persistent top-down management infrastructure that will allow an organization to maintain effective security over all aspects of its work. As we have seen, completeness is a critical condition of success.

Cybersecurity framework (CSF) core			
Functions	Categories	Subcategories	Informative references
Identify			
Protect			
Detect			
Respond			
Recover			

Figure 3.2   The CSF, Cybersecurity Framework core.

In that respect, the standard's concentration on establishing a complete cyber-security protection framework is an important practical distinction between it and the technology-based approaches that have been employed to this point. It moves security responsibility into the realm of strategic governance rather than the IT shop and makes it understandable and acceptable to conventional managers.

That fact alone might be one of its more important attributes since, as we have seen, these people have always tended to view technology solutions as either out of their area of responsibility or inappropriate to their role. Thus, there has been little interest or real initiative to install information security controls on the business side of the enterprise, which leaves those businesses vulnerable to any malicious individual, either external or internal, who might be interested in breaching their thin or nonexistent defenses.

One only has to think about the total dependence that sectors like banking and finance have on their electronic records to understand the magnitude of the havoc that a concerted attack could wreak. And the fact is that, beyond trifles like passwords, most corporations are not only vulnerable, but they are also completely undefended.

Moreover, the consequences of such a security breach can be disastrous. At the least, lost or stolen data are expensive to replace and at the worst, the loss of the organization's information can lead to total business collapse. For instance, the financial impacts of security breakdowns are serious and growing. A national survey conducted by McAfee estimates that $600 billion was lost to cybercrime in the year 2013 (Kirk, 2014).

Furthermore, "serious" breaches occur a lot more frequently than one might think. Overall, 90% of the responding companies acknowledged some form of loss due to a computer breach. And three quarters of those reported that these were from the inside, as well as the outside. Surveys in the United Kingdom, which were conducted by their cabinet level Department of Trade and Industry (DTI) indicate that more than 60% of the organizations in that country had suffered some sort of information security breach in the last 2 years and 75% of those reported a "serious" breach. Worse, three quarters of the organizations in that set had no disaster plan in place to deal with the consequences.

Benefits

The purpose of the CSF is to provide a common model for cybersecurity best practice. It is designed to enable managers and corporate end users to leverage their levels of security assurance to higher states. It allows companies to identify gaps in their security management infrastructure. It also allows companies of all sizes to demonstrate the effectiveness of their information security management to prospective trading partners. The standard provides common ground for companies wishing to trade with each other, assuring them that they are operating at a common level of computer security.

Besides this functional advantage the standard has many practical and even legal benefits. Where they exist at all, IT security operations tend to be tactical and reactive by nature, passively waiting for the bad guys to show up to rob the bank. On the other hand, if information security is based on the deterrent principles defined by industry best practice, it can be strategy driven, that is, organizations can initiate a full-scale set of proactive measures that will prevent rather than react to security threats.

As we said earlier, this is a comprehensive organizational governance model rather than a technical solution. The design of a formal infrastructure is the quintessential first step in enacting rational management over any aspect of IT, which just makes good common sense, since it is particularly difficult to establish and maintain organizational control over an activity that is basically conceptual and abstract by nature. The alternative to a technology-based solution is a formally engineered process architecture tailored to fit the specific requirements of a given situation.

Relationship between the CSF and the NICE Framework

From the discussions in Chapters 1 and 2, you have learned that the National Initiative for Cybersecurity Education (NICE) framework provides a strategic description of all of the elements of the cybersecurity field. It specifies all of the commonly agreed on activities and interrelationships associated with good security into a single workforce model. Moreover, the NICE framework stipulates all of the requisite and commonly accepted workforce roles and practices necessary to carry out a complete set of cybersecurity activities. However, with cyber threats changing on nearly a daily basis and with them, an organization's business environment and ability to meet new changing requirements, the ability to apply new risk strategies is also critical. Well-planned, developed, and documented strategies are applied to the vast array of levels of security needed in order to evolve and support business operations and risk, not simply as an effort in compliance of local, state, and federal regulations.

The framework for improving critical infrastructure cybersecurity (CSF) is a set of guidelines and practices also created by NIST, which provides government and nongovernment organizations a vital first step toward managing cybersecurity risk. Moving forward, organizations need solutions that not only satisfy the NIST CSF at the time of deployment but that also enable continued security as threats and business needs change and evolve. That said, the conclusion can be made that the combination of the CSF and NICE framework provide the "complete package" in managing cybersecurity risk. The CSF provides a categorized set of cybersecurity outcomes and recommended controls for their achievement, while the NICE framework defines the tasks required to accomplish the control activities, in addition to defining the knowledge and skills sets necessary to perform those activities (identified in the form of knowledge, skills, and abilities [KSAs]).

It is noteworthy to mention that, at the time of this writing, the implementation of the NIST CSF is voluntary. However, while some organizations and government agencies may feel that the framework does not constitute a foolproof formula for cybersecurity, its benefits may be missed by those who choose to skip or postpone implementation of the guideline, in part or in whole, because the framework comprises best practices from various standards bodies that have proved to be successful when implemented, and it also may deliver regulatory and legal advantages that extend well beyond improved cybersecurity for organizations that adopt it early. In reality, while the framework targets organizations that own or operate critical infrastructure, adoption may prove advantageous for businesses across virtually all industries.

The NIST CSF, which was drafted by the Commerce Department's NIST, contains no surprises. The majority of what is presented in common sense material. Bob Gourley states in his article "Initial Assessment on NIST Coordinated Framework for Improving Critical Infrastructure" that, "… experienced cyber security professionals will find this framework is very basic. Think of it as a high school level introduction to cyber security challenges" (Gourley, 2015). However, what is not mentioned in his article is that the framework does not introduce new standards or concepts, rather it leverages and integrates industry-leading cybersecurity practices that have been developed by organizations like NIST and the International

Standardization Organization (ISO). The framework is basic. If not presented at a basic level, the framework risked the likelihood that it would not gain the attention of the ICT industry. As mentioned above, the framework is not intended to be an all-in-one guide. Therefore, ICT managers need to be familiar with the standards the framework references, in order to implement the cybersecurity practices defined within each category.

Standard Practice Approach to Implementation

Formal standards are meant to embody the model for the "common body of knowledge and accepted state of industry best practice" (NIST CSF and NICE framework). Logic should support the correctness of that assumption without much additional proof, as it would be impossible to build a common cybersecurity process supported with individuals with the knowledge and skills to support that process without adopting some sort of standard accepted model. Given the amount of activities embodied in ICT work, such a model has to be broad and comprehensive. As a result, such all-embracing models are commonly called umbrella frameworks. Recall we have already used that term to describe the NICE framework in earlier chapters.

It is important to reiterate that umbrella frameworks are named after their intent, which is to cover the entire scope of ICT that they define. In that respect, umbrella frameworks specify an ideal model at a level sufficient to allow any organization to tailor processes to fit within its structure. Theoretically a single umbrella framework, or a combination of two as we describe in this book, can define a competent technology or management process in any level of detail.

Many of the umbrella frameworks utilized in the ICT industry provide specifications for the activities performed in software and system life cycle processes. Noticeably absent in those frameworks are specifications for activities related to cybersecurity processes. You will learn in the next several chapters that, as much as there is a life cycle for activities performed to develop ICT systems and software, there exists an umbrella framework providing specifications for cybersecurity life cycle processes and the knowledge needed to perform activities within those processes. Further, you will learn that many of the defined cybersecurity activities can and should be performed in parallel with the activities of the other industry frameworks.

Nonetheless, you should keep two important caveats in mind when considering the application of umbrella frameworks. First, no two organizations operate in the same way, so each individual cybersecurity life cycle process has to be considered differently in terms of its particulars. These differences may be large or small, but because they exist, every organization must decide how to explicitly array the definitions it prescribes within the larger concepts and principles of a cybersecurity life cycle model represented by an umbrella framework. In other words, although organizations can use the CSF and NICE framework in combination to guide the creation of a coherent set of defined processes and knowledge areas, they must tailor the implementation in a way that makes the most sense for them.

Second, an organization should not rely on just the definitions of the umbrella framework. All umbrella frameworks reference, in one way or another, other industry standards to further define the activities and documentation required. Our discussion of the framework for improving critical infrastructure cybersecurity, for example, is no different. This framework provides the foundation for the definition of cybersecurity life cycle processes and relies on Control Objectives for Information and Related Technology (COBIT 5), Council on Cybersecurity (CCS) Top 20 Critical Security Controls (CSCs), ANSI/ISA-62443-2-1 (99.02.01)-2009 Security for Industrial Automation and Control Systems: Establishing an Industrial Automation and Control Systems Security Program, ANSI/ISA-62443-3-3 (99.03.03)-2013 Security for Industrial Automation and Control Systems: System Security Requirements and Security Levels, ISO/IEC 27001, Information technology—Security techniques—Information security management systems—Requirements, and NIST Special Publication 800-53 Revision 4: *Security and Privacy Controls for Federal Information Systems and Organizations* to further define each activity.

Overview of the NIST Framework for Improving Critical Infrastructure Cybersecurity

The framework is the result of a February 2013 Executive Order titled *Improving Critical Infrastructure Cybersecurity*. The order emphasized that "[i]t is the Policy of the United States to enhance the security and resilience of the Nation's critical infrastructure and to maintain a cyber-environment that encourages efficiency, innovation, and economic prosperity while promoting safety, security, business confidentiality, privacy, and civil liberties" (Executive Order no. 13636, 2013). That order resulted in 10 months of collaborative discussions with more than 3000 security professionals to develop a risk-based compilation of guidelines that can help organizations identify, implement, and improve cybersecurity practices, and create a common language for internal and external communication of cybersecurity issues.

The Executive Order defines critical infrastructure as "systems and assets, whether physical or virtual, so vital to the United States that the incapacity or destruction of such systems and assets would have a debilitating impact on security, national economic security, national public health or safety, or any combination of those matters" (Executive Order no. 13636, 2013). The key point to be made is that cybersecurity external and internal threats to the private and public sector are on the rise. It is becoming increasingly important for organizations and federal agencies responsible for critical infrastructure to have a defined reiterative approach to identifying, assessing, and managing cybersecurity risk.

The resulting CSF is a reiterative process designed to evolve in sync with changes in cybersecurity threats, processes, and technologies. At the time of this writing the framework was in its inaugural version. It will be revised periodically to incorporate lessons learned and industry feedback. In effect, the framework envisions effective cybersecurity as a dynamic, continuous loop of response to both threats and solutions.

The framework provides an assessment mechanism that enables organizations to determine their current cybersecurity capabilities, set individual goals for a target state, and establish a plan for improving and maintaining cybersecurity programs. It comprises three primary components: core, profile, and implementation tiers.

"The Core presents industry standards, guidelines, and practices in a manner that allows for communication of cybersecurity activities and outcomes across the organization from the executive level to the implementation/operations level." (NIST, 2014). The core is a hierarchical structure, which consists of five cybersecurity risk functions. Each function is further broken down into categories and subcategories. These categories include processes, procedures, and technologies such as asset management, alignment with business strategy, risk assessment, access control, employee training, data security, event logging and analysis, and incident response plans. Together, they provide ICT management a high-level strategic view of the activities performed in life cycle cybersecurity risk management. Each subcategory is further matched to information resources. The information resources are industry standards and guidelines, which, in combination provide a set of cybersecurity risk management best practices.

The profile component gives organizations the ability to align and improve cybersecurity practices based on their individual business needs, tolerance to risk, and resource availability. To do so, organizations create a current profile by measuring their existing programs against the recommended practices in the framework core.

To identify a target profile, organizations employ the same core criteria to determine the outcomes necessary to improve their overall cybersecurity program. Unique requirements by industry, customers, and business partners can be factored into the target profile. Once completed, a comparison of the current and target profiles will identify the gaps that should be closed to enhance cybersecurity and provide the basis for a prioritized roadmap to help make improvements.

Implementation tiers help create a context that enables organizations to understand how their current cybersecurity risk management capabilities rate against the characteristics described by the framework. Tiers range from Partial (Tier 1) to Adaptive (Tier 4). NIST recommends that organizations seeking to achieve an effective, defensible cybersecurity program progress to Tier 3 or Tier 4. Figure 3.3 shows the implementation tiers.

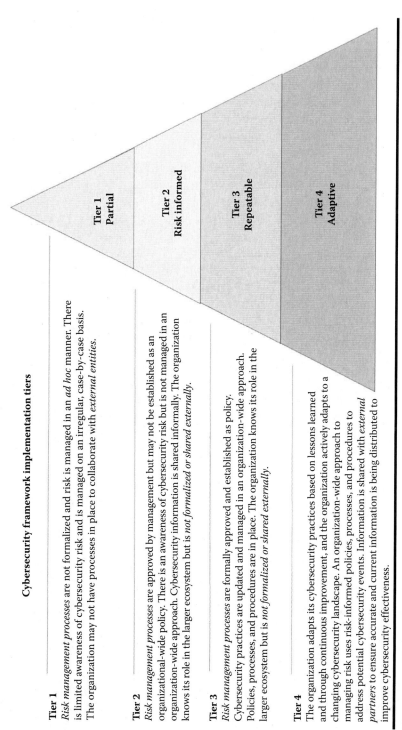

Cybersecurity framework implementation tiers

Tier 1

Risk management processes are not formalized and risk is managed in an *ad hoc* manner. There is limited awareness of cybersecurity risk and is managed on an irregular, case-by-case basis. The organization may not have processes in place to collaborate with *external entities*.

Tier 2

Risk management processes are approved by management but may not be established as an organizational-wide policy. There is an awareness of cybersecurity risk but is not managed in an organization-wide approach. Cybersecurity information is shared informally. The organization knows its role in the larger ecosystem but is *not formalized or shared externally*.

Tier 3

Risk management processes are formally approved and established as policy. Cybersecurity practices are updated and managed in an organization-wide approach. Policies, processes, and procedures are in place. The organization knows its role in the larger ecosystem but is *not formalized or shared externally*.

Tier 4

The organization adapts its cybersecurity practices based on lessons learned and through continuous improvement, and the organization actively adapts to a changing cybersecurity landscape. An organization-wide approach to managing risk uses risk-informed policies, processes, and procedures to address potential cybersecurity events. Information is shared with *external partners* to ensure accurate and current information is being distributed to improve cybersecurity effectiveness.

Tier 1
Partial

Tier 2
Risk informed

Tier 3
Repeatable

Tier 4
Adaptive

Figure 3.3   The implementation tiers.

Benefits of Adopting the Cybersecurity Framework

For many organizations, regardless if they are owners, operators, or suppliers for critical infrastructure, the NIST CSF may be well worth adopting merely for its stated goal of improving risk-based security. But it also can provide additional benefits that include effective collaboration and communication of security initiatives with upper-level management and industry organizations, as well as potential future improvements in legal implications and even assistance with regulatory compliance.

An important goal in the development of the framework was collaboration to share information and improve cybersecurity practices and threat intelligence within and between industry organizations.

Effective collaboration is dependent upon open and meaningful discussions. To that extent, the framework has created a common language to facilitate conversation about cybersecurity processes, policies, and technologies, both internally and with external entities such as third-party service providers and partners. The federal government, though NIST, encourages organizations to share current intelligence on vulnerabilities, threat information, and response strategies. The potential benefits of a common language and definition of life cycle cybersecurity activities together with increased collaboration are abundant. If, for example, an organization's entire supply chain adopts the framework, risks to the supply chain can be better communicated, understood, and potentially lessened.

It's important to note that the framework presents the discussion of cybersecurity in the vocabulary of risk management. With good reason: executive leaders and board members typically are well-versed in risk management, and framing cybersecurity in this context will enable security leaders to more effectively articulate the importance and goals of cybersecurity. It can also help organizations prioritize and validate investments based on risk management.

A common framework for cybersecurity will also enable ICT managers to effectively communicate practices, goals, and compliance requirements with third-party partners, service providers, and regulators. In particular, there should be a more meaningful, structured dialog of cybersecurity priorities with third parties.

The Cybersecurity Framework Core

The main thrust of the framework is described in the "framework core," which describes a set of activities and references that are outcome-based and focused on specific actions at all levels of the organization. These functions and categories are not new, but instead have roots in existing information security standards. In this section, you will learn about the underlying structure of the framework, how it defines each of its functions, the categories within each Function, and the standard information resources used to match each subcategory. Figure 3.1 depicts the hierarchical structure of the framework core.

Functions

Five separate functions organize cybersecurity activities at their highest level. The framework functions include the following:

1. *Identify*: Activities that provide an understanding of how to manage cybersecurity risks to systems, assets, data, and capabilities
2. *Protect*: The controls and safeguards necessary to protect or deter cybersecurity threats
3. *Detect*: Continuous monitoring to provide proactive and real-time alerts of cybersecurity-related events
4. *Respond*: Incident response activities
5. *Recover*: Business continuity plans to maintain resilience and recover capabilities after a cyberattack

The functions provide the mechanism for ICT management to organize cybersecurity risk information. Through an organized approach supported by appropriate internal and external data and information, the organization is in a better position to make risk management decisions, address cybersecurity threats, and provides the resources necessary for process improvement. The functions also align with existing methodologies for incident management and help show the impact of investments in cybersecurity. Within the framework core, each function can easily be mapped to individual categories and subcategories by using the functions unique identifier. Figure 3.4 shows the list of the identifiers and their associated function.

Function unique identifier	Function
ID	Identify
PR	Protect
DE	Detect
RS	Respond
RC	Recover

Figure 3.4   The list of the identifiers and their associated function.

Categories

At the next level of the hierarchy, the framework core identifies a desired set of common outcomes for each function. In every area of business, organizations need a clear set of agreed upon goals to help drive the decisions that managers make on a day-to-day basis. Likewise, goals need to be established to help measure the quality and completeness of each of the activities performed within each business area. The framework core provides leverage for each organization to determine how to perform the cybersecurity activities within each function. To that extent, it provides a clear set of outcomes for each function at a lower level of abstraction in order to present a clear set of criteria that can easily be managed and measured. The framework takes a unique approach in defining the outcomes. At the category level, each function is broken into three to six general categories that define outcomes for that function. As will be explained in the next section, those categories are further broken down into subcategories that provide greater support for cybersecurity managerial decision making and process improvement. Similar to functions, each category can be mapped back to its associated functions and activities using a unique identifier containing the function identifier and an alphabetic code classifying each category. Figure 3.5 provides a list of the category identifiers and categories for each function.

Subcategories

The framework core further divides each category into three to six subcategories that provide specific outcomes of technical and/or management activities. Mapping through the framework core is again extended into each subcategory, each containing a label that includes the category identifier combined with a successive numbering sequence. It is important to note that the framework uses the term "results" to describe what is provided by each subcategory. Remember that the key to effective management decision making and process quality measurement are accomplished through assessment of the provided results.

Caution should be taken that the subcategories define what the activities of that category should accomplish. They do not, however, provide detail about how they should be completed. The decision of how activities are completed is largely dependent upon an organization's environment. To that extent, the framework provides information resources for each subcategory that an organization can use to further define how an activity should be performed.

Information Resources

The framework does not create anything new; it draws from other existing industry best practices that can be applied to facilitate behavioral changes in an organization. At the lowest level of abstraction in the framework core are the information

Function unique identifier	Function	Category unique identifier	Category
ID	Identify	ID.AM	Asset management
		ID.BE	Business management
		ID.GV	Governance
		ID.RA	Risk assessment
		ID.RM	Risk management strategy
PR	Protect	PR.AC	Access control
		PR.AT	Awareness and training
		PR.DS	Data security
		PR.IP	Information protection processes and procedures
		PR.MA	Maintenance
		PR.PT	Protective technology
DE	Detect	DE.AE	Anomalies and events
		DE.CM	Security continuous monitoring
		DE.DP	Detection processes
RS	Respond	RS.RP	Response planning
		RS.CO	Communications
		RS.AN	Analysis
		RS.MI	Mitigation
		RS.IM	Improvements
RC	Recover	RC.RP	Recovery planning
		RC.IM	Improvements
		RC.CO	Communications

Figure 3.5   A list of the category identifiers and categories for each function.

resources. Each subcategory is mapped to specific sections of standards and guidelines. When a subcategory is mapped to a particular resource, defined process tasks are provided that illustrates a method to achieve the outcomes associated with that subcategory.

It is through the selection of which information resource is used by the organization that flexibility in process implementation is achieved. For example, an organization may already have businesses processes standardized based on COBIT 5. As such, they choose to implement the processes that achieve the framework subcategory outcomes strictly through the use of that standard.

A scenario such as that would not be atypical. However, caution must be taken, in that case, regarding the coverage COBIT 5 provides for the entire scope of the framework core. Some subcategories do not map to all of the information resources referenced by the framework. The best course is to evaluate all of the resources for each subcategory, after which a decision can be made relative to the combination of resources that come closest to the existing business environment. The information resources referenced by the framework include:

■ *COBIT 5*: COBIT is a framework for developing, implementing, monitoring, and improving IT governance and management practices.

■ The COBIT 5 framework is published by the IT Governance Institute and the Information Systems Audit and Control Association (ISACA). The goal of the framework is to provide a common language for business executives to communicate with each other about goals, objectives, and results.

■ COBIT 5 is based on five key principles for governance and management of enterprise IT:
Principle 1: Meeting stakeholder needs
Principle 2: Covering the enterprise end-to-end
Principle 3: Applying a single, integrated framework
Principle 4: Enabling a holistic approach
Principle 5: Separating governance from management

■ *Council on Cybersecurity Top 20 Critical Security Controls (CCS CSCs)*: The "Top 20" CSCs (20 CSCs—also known as the Consensus Audit Guidelines [CAGs] and formerly referred to as the SANS 20 CSCs) have emerged as a de facto yardstick from which cybersecurity programs can be measured. They are a recommended set of actions for cyber defense that provide specific ways in which organizations can stop cybersecurity attacks. They were developed and are maintained by a consortium of hundreds of security experts from across the public and private sectors.

■ The 20 CSCs are now governed by the CCS, an independent, expert, not-for-profit organization with a global scope.

■ *ANSI/ISA-62443-2-1 (99.02.01)-2009, Security for Industrial Automation and Control Systems: Establishing an Industrial Automation and Control Systems Security Program*: This standard is part of a multipart ISA 62443 series that addresses the issue of security for industrial automation and control systems (IACSs). This part, in particular, what the standard refers to as "elements" related to cybersecurity management for use in the IACSs environment provides guidance on how to meet the requirements described for each element.

■ *ANSI/ISA-62443-3-3 (99.03.03)-2013, Security for Industrial Automation and Control Systems: System Security Requirements and Security Levels*: This standard is also part of a multipart ISA 62443 series. This part of

the ISA-62443 series provides detailed technical control system requirements (SRs) associated with seven foundational requirements (FRs) that
are described in ISA-62443-1-1 (99.01.01) including defining the requirements for control system capability security levels, SL C (control system).
These requirements would be used by various members of the IACS community along with what the standard refers to as "the defined zones and
conduits" for the system under consideration (SuC) while developing the
appropriate control system target SL, SL-T (control system), for a specific
asset.

■ *ISO/IEC 27001, Information technology—Security techniques—Information
security management systems—Requirements*: This document has quickly
become the de facto international standard for information security management. The purpose of ISO IEC 27001 is to help organizations to establish and maintain an information security management system (ISMS).
An ISMS is a set of interrelated elements that organizations use to manage and control information security risks and to protect and preserve the
confidentiality, integrity, and availability of information. These elements
include all of the policies, procedures, processes, plans, practices, roles,
responsibilities, resources, and structures that are used to manage security
risks and to protect information.

■ *NIST Special Publication 800-53 Revision 4,* Security and Privacy Controls
for Federal Information Systems and Organizations: This NIST Special
Publication (SP) provides guidance for the selection of security and privacy controls for federal information systems and organizations. Revision
4 is the most comprehensive update since the initial publication. The primary goal of this update was to provide coverage of an expanding threat
space and increasing sophistication of cyberattacks. This publication provides a full examination of how the NIST changes impact organizations,
why privileged accounts are continually targeted by cyberattackers in
advanced persistent threats (APTs), and how the proper implementation
of privileged account controls can lessen the attack surface of advanced
threats.

"The Informative References presented in the Framework Core are illustrative
and not exhaustive. They are based upon cross-sector guidance most frequently
referenced during the Framework development process" (NIST, 2014).

Many industries are driven by a set or sets of defined best practices. While
the resources referenced in the framework provide coverage of all subcategory outcomes, care should be taken to also refer to the standards and guidelines that define
processes of the industry from which the organization belongs.

The Cybersecurity Framework Implementation Tiers

For many years, ICT managers have been examining software life cycle processes in terms of the level of quality provided through each of the process activities and degree of process improvement is evident through management practices performed throughout the life cycle. In the mid-1980s a gentleman by the name of Watts Humphrey, from the Carnegie Mellon Software Engineering Institute, developed a model called the Capability Maturity Model (CMM) and described it in the 1989 book *Managing the Software Process*. The CMM was originally intended as a tool to evaluate the ability of government contractors to perform a contracted software project. Though it comes from the area of software development, it can be, has been, and continues to be widely applied as a general model of the maturity of ICT life cycle processes.

To that extent CMM has evolved into a new model called the Capability Maturity Model Integration (CMMI). The model identifies five levels of process maturity for an organization. Within each of these maturity levels are key process areas (KPAs), which characterize that level. The five maturity levels include the following:

1. *Initial*: Processes are usually in chaos and the organization usually does not provide a stable environment.
2. *Repeatable*: Software development successes are repeatable. The processes may not repeat for all the projects in the organization. The organization may use some basic project management to track cost and schedule.
3. *Defined*: The organization's set of standard processes, which is the basis for level 3, is established and improved over time. These standard processes are used to establish consistency across the organization.
4. *Managed*: Precise measurements and metrics are used so that management can effectively control the software development effort.
5. *Optimizing*: Focusing on continually improving process performance through both incremental and innovative technological improvements. Quantitative process-improvement objectives for the organization are established, continually revised to reflect changing business objectives, and used as criteria in managing process improvement.

With the help of standards and defined software frameworks, organizations can implement process improvement mechanisms necessary to gradually progress to their desired level of process maturity.

The CSF provides a similar process improvement mechanism through a tiered structure that measures an organization's ability to implement risk management activities. Tiers do not represent maturity levels, however. "Progression to higher Tiers is encouraged when such a change would reduce cybersecurity risk and be cost effective. Successful implementation of the Framework is based upon achievement of the outcomes described in the organization's Target Profile(s) and not upon Tier determination" (NIST, 2014).

The implementation tiers serve as a method to describe how well organizations have incorporated cybersecurity risk management into the environment throughout the organization. In using this technique, organizations can measure the consistency and complexity of the risk management program and how well cybersecurity information flows and influences decisions throughout the organization.

However, it should not necessarily be thought of as a maturity level for a security program. Individual requirements and risk tolerance should be the driving force that guides organizations to work toward a predetermined target implementation tier. The framework describes each tier from three different perspectives: risk management process, integrated risk management program, and external participation. Table 3.1 lists each tier and a general description of the risk management characteristics evident at each tier.

Too frequently cybersecurity is erroneously thought of as an ICT problem. Realistically however, security efforts exist only to support business operations, and when not properly aligned they can potentially be ineffective, inefficient, and could even impede on organizational progress.

The need for aligning cybersecurity efforts with business processes is one of the main objectives of the CSF. It is also the reason that the framework cannot be excessively prescriptive with defining controls that should be implemented by every organization. Although cohesions exist, especially in related sectors, each organization's structure, goals, risk tolerance, culture, and system design will vary and should be assessed individually to determine adequate levels of protection.

Using business requirements as a driving factor in determining security efforts assists in understanding the possible business impacts for information security inadequacies and helps to prioritize defensive determinations and resource allocation toward the most important security activities. Important to note, by communicating to cybersecurity personnel the business context will help them to precisely

Table 3.1 Framework Implementation Tiers

Tier 1	Partial	Risk management is chaotic, with limited awareness of risks and no collaboration with others
Tier 2	Risk informed	Risk management processes and programs are in place but are not integrated enterprise wide; collaboration is understood but organization lacks formal capabilities
Tier 3	Repeatable	Formal policies for risk management processes and programs are in place enterprise wide, with partial external collaboration
Tier 4	Adaptive	Risk management processes and programs are based on lessons learned and embedded in culture, with proactive collaboration

design controls that follow critical security principles and helps them to determine a baseline for the norms and identify the anomalous.

Therefore, to begin developing an understanding of cybersecurity requirements for an organization is to have a definitive and documented understanding of the organization itself and have well-written documentation of how the organization's missions and goals flow down to business processes supported by security programs. To that extent, cybersecurity planning and implementation efforts must extend beyond security and ICT personal to include all stakeholders such as business process owners, executive management, and audit and accountability personnel.

Just as important as other business life cycles, feedback loops must also be created to ensure that all appropriate stakeholders are informed about the performance of the security program since the programs failure could have an effect to the organization.

The framework is not meant to provide solutions for all cybersecurity-related issues or even tell an organization exactly what it must do. It does, however, provide a common body of knowledge that organizations can use to assess and streamline their own security programs. It can also be used to disseminate best practices and standards across related sectors and industries. When used in combination with critical business process re-engineering efforts, best practices, security assessments, and audit from governance security program, it can help organizations to significantly reduce cybersecurity risk, better detect and respond to security breaches, and successfully recover from significant cybersecurity-related events.

The Framework Profile

The framework profile is a selection or set of security activities (categories and subcategories) from the framework core. Profiles have several important purposes. Recall from a discussion earlier in this chapter that each organization performs an initial baseline activity in an effort to assess its current security capabilities and organize them into a current profile. The framework then recommends that the organization create a target profile consisting of desired security capabilities, perform a gap analysis between the current and target profiles, and develop and implementation action plan for addressing the gap.

Profiles are also a valuable tool for sharing best practices or establishing industry standards. As previously mentioned, the security activities from the framework core are not designed to be either a minimum standard or the target profile for the organization. Rather, business decisions must drive the selection of control activities. Industry partners, regulating bodies, security consultants, not-for-profits, and others may use the common structure and body of knowledge of the CSF to create minimum recommended standards in the form of a profile. Establishment, dissemination, and coordination of these common profiles is required in addition to the criteria already defined in the framework to establish specific actions that should be considered minimum "cyber due care" standards for organizations.

The profiles schema that organization leadership agree upon should mirror the functions, categories, and subcategories from the framework core but may also include additional security activities, which are not currently found in the core but that would help to address specific security requirements.

As an example of using framework profiles to share best practices, the CSC has used its list of CSCs to develop a profile to help organizations focus on the most beneficial activities first. The CSC framework profile provides organizations with common set of prioritized, detailed, and actionable measures, which should be implemented as a first step by any organization that is concerned with defending its systems and information against cyber threats. The CSC profile can act as a roadmap and starting point for organizations that are looking to develop their own profiles based on their specific security requirements. Target profiles can and should be created as a baseline for industry-specific regulatory compliance requirements, which can then be easily shared.

The Cybersecurity Framework Is Descriptive and Not Prescriptive

It is noteworthy to reiterate that the CSF is not an all-in-one guide for organizations to use in developing their cybersecurity risk management programs; every organization is unique in terms of its environment, business relationships with industry partners and stakeholders, as well as its culture. The framework is descriptive, not prescriptive and should be used as a standard set of best practices used to meet the individual needs of the organization.

Section 3 of the framework, titled "How to Use the Framework" provides some high-level guidelines that organizations can use to get started. The section includes an introduction to cybersecurity and risk management, very similar to the discussion that we had in Chapter 1 of this book. Attention should be drawn to Section 3.2, however, in which the framework provides guidelines for establishing a new or improving an existing cybersecurity program.

Section 3.2 "Establishing and Improving a Cybersecurity Program" provides a set of illustrative steps that show organizations how the framework can be used to establish a security program. Further, by consistently repeating the same steps, the organization can interject continuous improvement into the program. Following are the steps that the framework recommends for establishing and improving their cybersecurity program (Figure 3.6):

Step 1: Prioritize and scope. The organization identifies its business/mission objectives and high-level organizational priorities. With this information, the organization makes strategic decisions regarding cybersecurity implementations and determines the scope of systems and assets that support the selected business line or process. The framework can be adapted to support the different

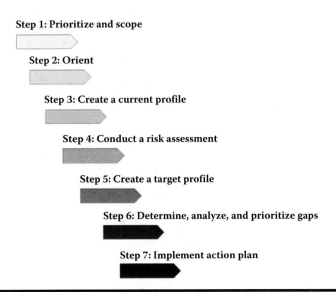

Figure 3.6   Seven steps to establish and improve a cybersecurity program.

business lines or processes within an organization, which may have different business needs and associated risk tolerance.

Step 2: Orient. Once the scope of the cybersecurity program has been determined for the business line or process, the organization identifies related systems and assets, regulatory requirements, and overall risk approach. The organization then identifies threats to, and vulnerabilities of, those systems and assets.

Step 3: Create a current profile. The organization develops a current profile by indicating which category and subcategory outcomes from the framework core are currently being achieved.

Step 4: Conduct a risk assessment. This assessment could be guided by the organization's overall risk management process or previous risk assessment activities. The organization analyzes the operational environment in order to discern the likelihood of a cybersecurity event and the impact that the event could have on the organization. It is important that organizations seek to incorporate emerging risks and threat and vulnerability data to facilitate a robust understanding of the likelihood and impact of cybersecurity events.

Step 5: Create a target profile. The organization creates a target profile that focuses on the assessment of the framework categories and subcategories describing the organization's desired cybersecurity outcomes. Organizations also may develop their own additional categories and subcategories to account for unique organizational risks. The organization may also consider influences and requirements of external stakeholders such as sector entities, customers, and business partners when creating a target profile.

Step 6: Determine, analyze, and prioritize gaps. The organization compares the current profile and the target profile to determine gaps. Next, it creates a prioritized action plan to address those gaps that draws upon mission drivers, a cost/benefit analysis, and understanding of risk to achieve the outcomes in the target profile. The organization then determines resources necessary to address the gaps. Using profiles in this manner enables the organization to make informed decisions about cybersecurity activities, supports risk management, and enables the organization to perform cost-effective, targeted improvements.

Step 7: Implement action plan. The organization determines which actions to take in regards to the gaps, if any, identified in the previous step. It then monitors its current cybersecurity practices against the target profile. For further guidance, the framework identifies example informative references regarding the categories and subcategories, but organizations should determine which standards, guidelines, and practices, including those that are sector specific, work best for their needs (NIST, 2014).

The rate at which these steps are repeated is determined by the organization in terms of the speed at which continuous improvement should take place. Management can also use the feedback loop created through the completion of each step to continuously update the current profile and complete that to their target profile.

Structure of the Book's Presentation of the NICE and Cybersecurity Framework

With an understanding of the introductory material provided in this and the preceding two chapters, a more detailed view of the NICE framework can take place. Each of the seven categories of the NICE framework will be explored in greater detail in its own individual chapter, while mapping each specialty area of that category back to each CSF core outcome.

Depending on specific need, some readers may find it helpful to read individual chapters as they apply to their organizations' implementation of cybersecurity workforce development and/or a cybersecurity risk management program. Each NICE category is so unique in terms of KSA tasks and mapping back to the CSF that each chapter can be understood without having read the others. Still, other readers will find benefit in reading each of the next seven chapters in sequence.

At relevant points in the discussion we will discuss the intersection between these two models. The NICE framework can be easily joined with the purpose and intent of the CSF at the task level. In essence, the tasks specified in the NICE model can be factored into the functions specified in the CSF. Or in even more practical terms, the NICE model will specify the particular specialty area of the workforce who should be doing a certain identification, protection, defense, response, or recovery function.

Then the attendant KSA specifications for that specialty area will provide elaboration and clarification of the requisite competencies and the actions to be taken to perform the task. Using these two large-scale frameworks it is possible to construct a detailed picture of the proper organization and conduct of a strategic infrastructure security operation. And in that respect these two frameworks provide the detailed explication of the discipline of cybersecurity as a whole. Thus, as a combination these two models can serve as an explicit definition of the field of cybersecurity.

Chapter Summary

- The CSF is the result of a Presidential Executive Order that emphasized that the Policy of the United States is improve the security and flexibility of the nation's critical infrastructure and to maintain a cyber-environment that promotes efficiency, innovation, and economic prosperity while also promoting safety, security, business confidentiality, privacy, and civil liberties.
- The framework provides a way for organizations to assess their current cybersecurity program, set goals for maintaining cybersecurity processes already in place, and develop plans for continuous improvement of their cybersecurity efforts.
- The framework core is made up of functions, categories, and subcategories presented in different levels of abstraction in order to provide details of necessary outcomes of a cybersecurity program. The categories and subcategories are matched to industry standards that can be used to guide organizations in how to achieve the outcomes.
- The implementation tiers make up a model that the framework uses to give organizations perspective on how their cybersecurity program ranks against an accepted set of best practice criteria.
- Framework profiles are used to help the organization understand what framework outcomes currently exist within their cybersecurity program, and to determine where they want their cybersecurity program to be in terms of implementation of process activities that achieve framework outcomes to a greater extent.

Key Terms

Core: A set of cybersecurity outcomes and associated control resources categorized to assist organizations in establishing a risk management-based cybersecurity program.

Critical Infrastructure: The basic systems necessary for survival of an organization or nation. The US government states that the country's critical infrastructure is the "infrastructure and assets vital to national security, governance, public health and safety, economy, and public confidence."

Detect: Function within the CSF containing outcomes pertaining to detection of cyber threats.

Identify: Function within the CSF containing outcomes that establish an understanding of how to manage cybersecurity risks to systems, assets, data, and capabilities.

Implementation Tiers: Help create a context that enables organizations to understand how their current cybersecurity risk management capabilities stack up against the characteristics described by the CSF.

Life Cycle Model: Defines, maintains, and assesses life cycle processes, policies, and procedures consistent with and organizations' objectives.

Profile: Component within the CSF that enables organizations to align and improve cybersecurity practices based on their individual business needs, tolerance for risk, and available resources.

Protect: Function within the CSF containing outcomes that establish safeguards necessary to protect or deter cybersecurity threats.

Recover: Function within the CSF containing outcomes that establish business continuity plans to maintain resilience and recover capabilities after a cyber breach.

Respond: Function within the CSF with outcomes aimed at performing Incident Response activities.

Risk: A given threat with a known likelihood of impact.

Risk Assessment: The evaluation of the likelihood and impact of a given threat.

References

Executive Order no. 13636. 2013. *Improving Critical Infrastructure Cybersecurity.* DCPD-201300091, February 12.

Gourley, Bob. 2015. "Initial Assessment on NIST Coordinated Framework for Improving Critical Infrastructure Cybersecurity." February 14. Accessed January 1, 2015. https://ctovision.com/.

Kirk, Jeremy. 2014. "Cybercrime Losses Top $400 Billion Worldwide," IDG News Service, June 9, 2014.

National Institute of Standards and Technology (NIST). 2014. *Framework for Improving Critical Infrastructure Cybersecurity.* Gaithersburg, MD: National Institute of Standards and Technology.

Privacy Rights Clearinghouse (PRC). 2014. *Chronology of Data Breaches Security Breaches 2005–Present.* San Diego, CA: Privacy Rights Clearinghouse.

THE NICE CYBERSECURITY WORKFORCE FRAMEWORK AND HOW IT MAPS TO THE CFS FRAMEWORK

II

Chapter 4

Securely Provision

Chapter Objectives

At the conclusion of this chapter, the reader will understand:

- The justification and contents of the securely provision domains
- The focus and purpose of the securely provision specialty areas
- The focus and purpose of the securely provision knowledge area
- The relationship between the securely provision specialty areas and the National Institute of Standards and Technology (NIST) cybersecurity framework (CSF)

Chapters 5 through 10 of this book present a detailed examination of the knowledge areas that make up the National Initiative for Cybersecurity Education (NICE) framework. Each chapter explains each required knowledge, skill, and ability (KSA) task within the specialty areas of the knowledge area discussed in that chapter, and leverage those areas to the organization, or individual's capacity to apply their knowledge to practical situations. The overall aim of the discussion is to increase your understanding about how substantive information and communication technology (ICT) work can be done using the guidelines recommended in the NICE framework.

Twenty years ago, corporate and national information infrastructures were separate and distinct. Today they are one and the same. The federal government depends on the same computer networks and networking equipment to fight against terrorist attacks, whereas the private sector depends upon the same to conduct business. Moreover, there is likely no argument that one of the key factors in keeping public and private sector ICT systems free from exploitations begins with a secure system engineering process and individuals working within the system engineering life cycle process with adequate knowledge of appropriate security policies, procedures, and controls.

Before being able to design secure systems, ICT professionals must thoroughly understand the means, motives, and opportunities of potential attackers. First, the ICT professional derives the list of possible attackers determined by who stands to profit in exploiting the system. Next, they characterize attackers in terms of their available resources, access to the targeted system, and risk tolerance. Then, maps are created to show how information flows throughout the system. Studying the information flow allows the ICT professionals to discover all the critical components and procedures. Components are vulnerable during design, implementation, distribution, maintenance, use, and retirement. Each step of every function within the ICT life cycle must be scrutinized. The ICT professional determines when and how an attacker can gain access at each point in time. For each access point, there must be considerations into what an attacker could accomplish, within the bounds of their resources and objectives.

Securely Provision Category Overview

Consideration of security in the system development life cycle (SDLC) is essential to implementing and integrating a comprehensive ICT strategy. However, determining the appropriate level of security for systems is difficult. The decision depends on many factors, including the trust level of the operating environment, the security levels of the systems it will connect to, who will be using the system, the sensitivity of the data, how critical the functions are to the business, and how costly it will be to apply optimal security measures. The knowledge of the process and economics of system development is essential to understanding why few systems in production used today can be considered sufficiently secure.

The benefit of building secure systems is a trade-off between the security and the functionality that system is intended to provide. Every dollar that goes into protecting a system is a dollar that would not be put toward building a more functional, usable system. However, as hackers, criminals, and terrorists become more sophisticated in their methods, organizations are obligated to look for new ways to reveal system vulnerabilities that result from uncommon conditions. Securely built systems depend on our ability to elevate the visibility and priority of security throughout each phase of the life cycle process. Even as early as project initiation, we can begin formulating the security goal based on organizational goals, risks, and monetary constraints. Throughout the requirements and design phase, functional and architectural flaws that compromise security can systematically be revealed. Inspection and automation methods can be applied during construction and testing to identify flaws in coding that make the system vulnerable to security attacks. Every decision made during the development process should consider the risk the organization is willing to accept as a trade-off for lower development costs, time to market, increased functionality, or usability. In using defined system development process models and by applying rigorous change control methods, we can be sure the system will meet both user needs and organizational security standards.

There are many SDLC methodologies that have been used by organizations to effectively develop an ICT system. The traditional waterfall SDLC, a linear sequential model, assumes that the system will be delivered in its final stages of the development life cycle. Another SDLC method uses the prototyping model, which is often used to develop an understanding of system requirements without actually developing a final operational system. More complex systems may require more iterative development models. More complex models have been developed and successfully used to address the evolving complexity of advanced and sometimes large ICT system designs. Examples of these more complex models are the rapid application development (RAD) model, the joint application development (JAD) model, the prototyping model, the spiral model, and the agile model. The expected size and complexity of the system, development schedule, and length of a systems life will affect the choice of which SDLC model to use. In that regard, many organizations use a variety of process models rather than choosing a single model that provides best practices for secure system development.

Because many systems can be built from a single correct process model, the creation of an enterprise-wide architecture from an ideal model of overall best practice is likely to resolve many problems associated with building secure systems with an unstructured ICT process. In that respect, the International Organization for Standardization (ISO) 12207-2008: *Systems and Software Engineering— Software Life Cycle Processes* standard provides the generic model that defines the ideal structure of the ICT process as a whole (ISO, 2008). It serves as a stable basis for defining a secure life cycle process that it is applicable to any form of ICT operation. In addition, ISO 12207 provides a commonly recognized, worldwide basis for standardizing terminology and processes to effectively manage any software or ICT development, sustainment, or acquisition process.

The specialty areas of the NICE framework securely provision knowledge area are "responsible for conceptualizing, designing, and building secure information technology (IT) systems (i.e., responsible for some aspect of systems development)" (NIST, 2013). As each of the specialty areas are discussed, ISO 12207 will be referenced as a process model that can be used to implement each of the tasks. Figure 4.1 provides an overview and brief description of each of the seven specialty areas in this category.

Specialty Area 1: Secure Acquisition

ICT products (e.g., hardware, software, or entire information systems) are developed through a global supply chain. Supply chains are not different from any other organizational function in that they are intended to accomplish a specific purpose. The purpose of all supply chains is to provide a product or service through coordinated work that involves several organizations. The process of managing supply chains is through the acquisition life cycle.

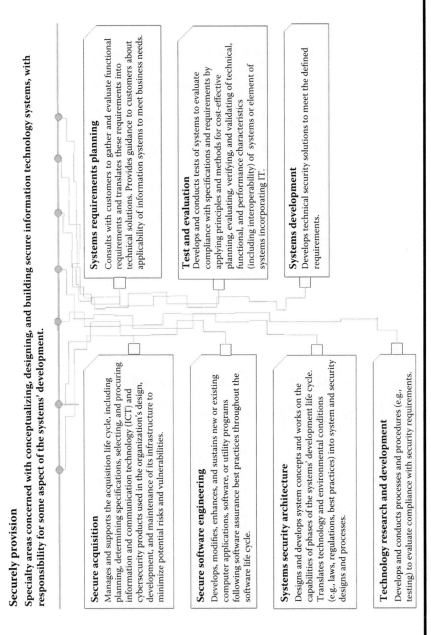

Securely provision

Specialty areas concerned with conceptualizing, designing, and building secure information technology systems, with responsibility for some aspect of the systems' development.

Systems requirements planning

Consults with customers to gather and evaluate functional requirements and translates these requirements into technical solutions. Provides guidance to customers about applicability of information systems to meet business needs.

Test and evaluation

Develops and conducts tests of systems to evaluate compliance with specifications and requirements by applying principles and methods for cost-effective planning, evaluating, verifying, and validating of technical, functional, and performance characteristics (including interoperability) of systems or element of systems incorporating IT.

Systems development

Develops technical security solutions to meet the defined requirements.

Secure acquisition

Manages and supports the acquisition life cycle, including planning, determining specifications, selecting, and procuring information and communication technology (ICT) and cybersecurity products used in the organization's design, development, and maintenance of its infrastructure to minimize potential risks and vulnerabilities.

Secure software engineering

Develops, modifies, enhances, and sustains new or existing computer applications, software, or utility programs following software assurance best practices throughout the software life cycle.

Systems security architecture

Designs and develops system concepts and works on the capabilities of phases of the systems' development life cycle. Translates technology and environmental conditions (e.g., laws, regulations, best practices) into system and security designs and processes.

Technology research and development

Develops and conducts processes and procedures (e.g., testing) to evaluate compliance with security requirements.

Figure 4.1   Securely provision specialty area overview.

The acquisition life cycle consists of the customer's role in procurement activities. The activities specified for acquisition are intended to convey the work that must be done when an organization procures an ICT product or service. Acquisition always operates in conjunction with the supply process, which delineates a supplier's obligations in providing that product or service. The standard activities of the acquisition life cycle describe an ideal way to deal with a supplier. Similarly, supply dictates the ideal way to deliver a product or service. These two processes together are the basis for formulating an ICT service delivery or system purchase contract.

The activities that must be managed in the acquisition life cycle convey the ideal steps that an organization would take to acquire an ICT system or service product. The goal of the acquisition life cycle is to purchase fundamentally correct ICT products. The process begins with the identification of customer needs and ends with acceptance of the product or service as defined in the contract. The acquisition life cycle itself is a strategic function that is established and maintained through formal planning. Planning for each acquisition project takes place within the framework of practices established in the overall strategic planning activity.

The primary function of the acquisition life cycle is to ensure that the right vendor is chosen. Because vendors supply a product or service, an organization must know the precise requirements for that purchase to make an intelligent decision. Therefore, the first priority of the acquisition life cycle is to define and document all relevant products' functional and security requirements, along with the criteria for judging whether those requirements were met. The outcome of this generic requirements definition activity is that a legal contract is written, which designates all required roles, responsibilities, and obligations of the supplier and customer.

The contract also establishes the appropriate monitoring and control mechanisms needed to ensure that the supplier satisfies the terms and conditions of the contract. Once the contractual terms have been satisfied, the acquisition life cycle then ensures an efficient transfer of the product from the vendor to the customer.

Once all elements that are part of the operating environment are understood and all risks have been investigated, an organization must plan a risk management approach and then put the plan in place. The plan itemizes the details for managing risk, including the risk assessment mechanism that will be used, the method for designing and deploying risk mitigations, monitoring activities for risk mitigation, and how these activities will be adjusted to changing conditions.

The approach to risk must be fully documented in a project life cycle risk management plan. This plan should include an estimate of the cost of risk management over the entire life cycle, and it should describe all project life cycle actions for risk management. Those actions are determined by the importance and sensitivity of information processed by the proposed ICT product as well as the current vulnerability and threat status. The plan documents a concrete set of activities for mitigating risk, including a description of how each activity will be monitored for acceptable performance.

Supply Chain Risk Management Implications

The management, assessment, and mitigation of risks to ICT systems are a fundamental component of every organization's information assurance and cybersecurity program. An effective risk management process enables an organization to protect its information assets and supports its ability to carry out its mission successfully.

The following activities compose the risk management framework. These activities are fundamental to the management of organizational risk and can be applied to both new and legacy information systems within the context of the SDLC:

1. Categorize information systems
2. Select security controls
3. Implement security controls
4. Access security controls
5. Authorize information systems
6. Monitor security control

Security categorization standards for information and ICT systems provide a common framework and understanding for documenting the potential impact to organizations or individuals should there be a breach of security (e.g., a loss of confidentiality, integrity, possession, utility authenticity, or availability) to information or the information system. Federal Information Processing Standard (FIPS) 199, *Standards for Security Categorization of Federal Information and Information Systems*, can assist government agencies and organizations in determining the security category of data and ICT systems. The categorization process also promotes effective management of ICT systems and consistent reporting.

To address minimum security requirements, organizations make use of security controls from guidelines such as "NIST Special Publication 800-53, *Recommended Security Controls for Federal Information Systems*." This publication provides a catalog of controls that organizations can select to protect their ICT systems in accordance with their missions and business requirements. An initial baseline set of security controls is determined based on the impact analysis conducted under the provisions of FIPS standards. Organizations can then tailor and supplement the selection of baseline security controls based on their assessment of risks.

There are numerous guides that provide assistance in implementation of security controls. One guide in particular, which deserves mention is the NIST Special Publication Checklists for IT Products. Checklists of security settings are useful tools that have been developed to guide ICT managers and security personnel in selecting effective security settings that will reduce the risks and protect systems from attacks. A checklist, sometimes called a security configuration guide, lockdown guide, hardening guide, security technical implementation guide, or benchmark, is a series of instructions for configuring an ICT product to an operational environment. Checklists can be effective in reducing vulnerabilities to systems, especially for small organizations with limited resources. ICT vendors often create checklists for their own products, but other organizations such as consortia, academic groups, and government agencies have also developed them.

Assess the security controls using appropriate methods and procedures is provided through a risk management process in order to determine the extent in which the controls are implemented correctly, operating as intended, and producing the desired outcome with respect to meeting the security requirements for the system. The information assurance compliance professionals have the responsibility to provide certification services to assist business functions in meeting assessment requirements.

The authorize information system operation is based on a determination of the risk to organizational operations, organizational assets, or to individuals resulting from the operation of the information system and the determination that this risk is acceptable. NIST SP 800-37, *Guide for the Security Certification and Accreditation of Federal Information Systems*, discusses the steps leading to a decision by a senior management to authorize operation of an information system, accepting the risks to agency operations, agency assets, or individuals based on the implementation of an agreed-upon set of security controls.

The final activity is to monitor selected security controls in the ICT system on a continuous basis including documenting changes to the system, conducting security impact analyses of the changes, and reporting the security status of the system to appropriate organization leaders on a regular basis.

Proper supply chain risk management (SCRM) lessens security concerns by providing a consistent, disciplined environment for developing the product, assessing what could go wrong in the process (i.e., assessing risks), determining which risks to address (i.e., setting priorities), and implementing appropriate activities that address high-priority risks. Typically, supply chains are hierarchical, with the primary supplier forming the root of several levels of parent–child relationships. From an assurance standpoint, what this implies is that every individual product of each individual node in that hierarchy has to be correct as well as correctly integrated with all other components up and down the production ladder. Because the product development process is distributed across a supply chain, maintaining the integrity of the products that are moving within that process is the critical concern. Responsibilities associated with maintaining integrity are managed and implemented within the acquisition life cycle.

Factoring Secure Acquisition Workforce Tasks into the Cybersecurity Framework Functions

The previous discussion characterized system acquisition as the conceptualization, initiation, design, development, test, contracting, production, deployment, logistic support, modification, and disposal of systems, supplies, products, or services (including construction) to satisfy agency/department needs intended for use in or in support of that organization's mission. Generally it is a management function that takes place at the stage of the life cycle after requirements have been identified and agreed upon.

Factoring cybersecurity into the supply chain practices, the NICE framework identifies 10 distinct secure acquisition tasks that primarily focus on the strategizing, planning, and managing risk implications created through contracting with third-party vendors.

Historically, risk management focused more on management elements, such as schedule and cost, and less on technical risks for well-defined or smaller projects. However, larger and more complex projects and environments have increased the uncertainty for the technical aspects of many projects. Although the entire Federal CyberSecurity Framework (CSF) is based on risk management to increase the likelihood of successful project and program outcomes, the CSF recommends that risk strategies and plans be created and executed early in the project life cycle and addresses those outcomes in the identify function. Each of the categories within that function (asset management, business environment, governance, risk assessment, and risk management strategy) contains at least one subcategory that addresses interaction with third parties. The controls implemented to satisfy those subcategory outcomes adequately define the activities necessary to ensure the planning, policy development, and risk management guidelines associated with secure acquisition.

There is a clear distinction between providing the documentation, plans, and guidelines associated with ensuring risk management strategies in secure acquisition and performing the steps to acquire ICT components according to that documentation, plans, and guidelines. The NICE framework defines three such tasks, within the secure acquisition specialty area that define the need to budget, staff, and contract, apply defense functions, and participate in any facet of the acquisition process. On the basis of the premise that secure acquisition is intended to contribute to the underlying scope of information protection processes, a case can be made that those three tasks are aligned more definitively with the protect function of the CSF. Figure 4.2 shows the mapping of the NICE framework secure acquisition tasks to the CSF.

Underlying Knowledge, Skill, and Ability Requirements for Secure Acquisition

The responsibility of secure acquisition is normally performed by the combined efforts of the chief information security officer (CISO), contracting officer (CO), contracting officer technical representative (COTR), and information technology (IT) director. Individuals at that level have likely spent many years working in most facets of the system life cycle and have gained skill in project management, analysis, development, and telecommunications. Through their experience they have gained knowledge of security measures that must be implemented to mitigate risk within the process.

In addition to risk awareness skills gained through experience, managers with acquisition responsibility must also be able to understand risk management and supply chain management to the extent that organizational risk strategies can be effectively aligned with those of stakeholders throughout the entire supply

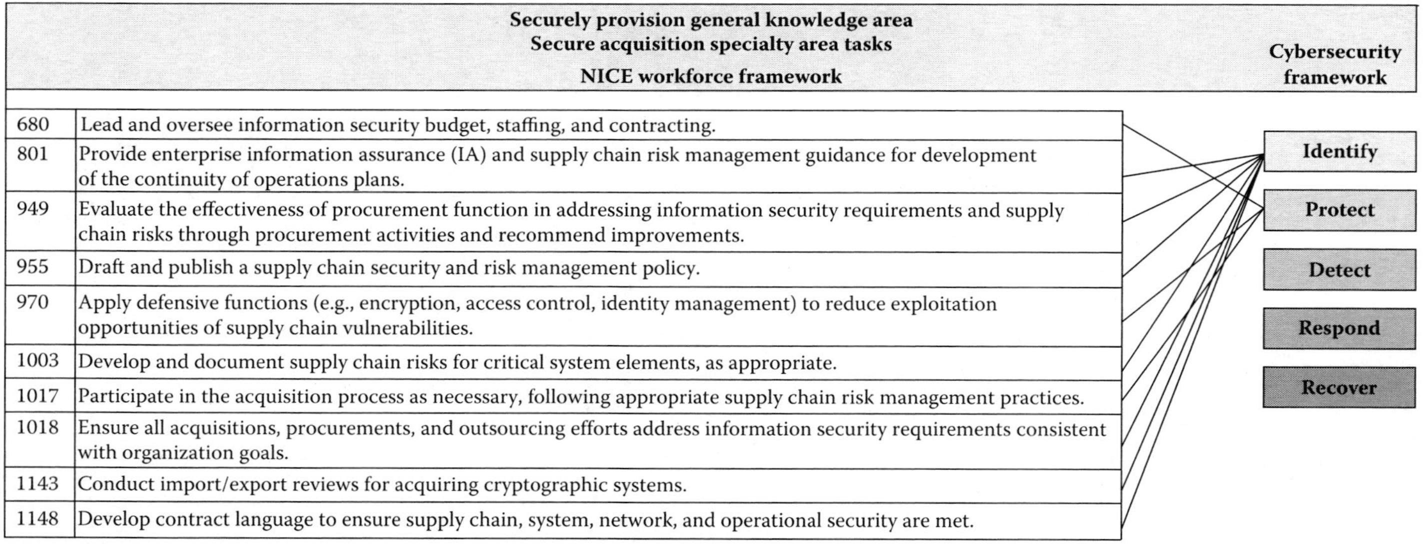

	Securely provision general knowledge area Secure acquisition specialty area tasks **NICE workforce framework**	Cybersecurity framework
		Identify
		Protect
		Detect
		Respond
		Recover
680	Lead and oversee information security budget, staffing, and contracting.	
801	Provide enterprise information assurance (IA) and supply chain risk management guidance for development of the continuity of operations plans.	
949	Evaluate the effectiveness of procurement function in addressing information security requirements and supply chain risks through procurement activities and recommend improvements.	
955	Draft and publish a supply chain security and risk management policy.	
970	Apply defensive functions (e.g., encryption, access control, identity management) to reduce exploitation opportunities of supply chain vulnerabilities.	
1003	Develop and document supply chain risks for critical system elements, as appropriate.	
1017	Participate in the acquisition process as necessary, following appropriate supply chain risk management practices.	
1018	Ensure all acquisitions, procurements, and outsourcing efforts address information security requirements consistent with organization goals.	
1143	Conduct import/export reviews for acquiring cryptographic systems.	
1148	Develop contract language to ensure supply chain, system, network, and operational security are met.	

Figure 4.2   Secure acquisition specialty area tasks mapped to the cybersecurity framework (CSF).

chain. In most cases, this can be accomplished through effectively managing the implementation of controls, such as those defined in NIST SP 800-53.

Table 4.1 displays the entire set of general and specialty KSA requirements for the secure acquisition specialty area as well as the associated competency areas (all within the NICE framework).

Specialty Area 2: Secure Software Engineering

Simply put, secure software engineering (SSE) is not necessarily engineering security software. SSE seeks to apply processes, principles, and methods to build vulnerability free software, software that remains in a secure state under attack and continues to provide service to authorized users. The key questions normally asked are the following:

- Isn't security something handled by network administrators?
- How does the software we are developing open vulnerabilities?
- Aren't there already solutions we can add on to provide the needed protections?

As stated above, SSE is not necessarily engineering security software. SSE can certainly be applied to build security software, but SSE techniques can be applied to building any type of software. Furthermore, it is becoming increasingly important to look at applying SSE techniques to application software throughout the entire life cycle. There is a tendency among many software developers to view computer and network security as an operational subject that the ICT department or network administrators handle. In the ICT context, security assurance is obtained by installing/configuring firewalls, keeping virus definitions up to date, and applying the latest patches. The correct context to address the root cause of most computer security failures is through software development in which process activities provide accommodations for obtaining software assurance.

When the topic of security is raised in the development context, an almost reflexive reaction is to think about specialized security features such as cryptography, authentication, and copy protection, and how the development team might add on or integrate software components providing these security features. However, the development team must realize that such add-on components are not a security solution. Software assurance cannot be achieved by simply "plugging in" security software. The requirements, design, code, and selected implementation language may all impact security. SSE is concerned with engineering software (all types) such that the end product provides some level of software assurance. SSE is predicated on the fact that attackers frequently exploit vulnerabilities originating within the software development life cycle (SDLC) during requirements, design, implementation, or are missed during verification.

Table 4.1 Secure Acquisition Specialty Area Knowledge, Skill, and Abilities (KSAs)

Item ID	KSA	Statement	Competency
107	KSA	Knowledge of resource management principles and techniques	Project management
296	KSA	Knowledge of how information needs and collection requirements are translated, tracked, and prioritized across the extended enterprise	Telecommunications
325	KSA	Knowledge of secure acquisitions (e.g., relevant contracting officer's technical representative [COTR] duties, secure procurement, supply chain risk management)	Contracting/procurement
954	KSA	Knowledge of import/export control regulations and responsible agencies for the purposes of reducing supply chain risk	Contracting/procurement
979	KSA	Knowledge of supply chain risk management standards, processes, and practices	Risk management
1004	KSA	Knowledge of critical information technology (IT) procurement requirements	Contracting/procurement
1005	KSA	Knowledge of functionality, quality, and security requirements and how these will apply to specific items of supply (i.e., elements and processes)	Contracting/procurement
1021	KSA	Knowledge of risk threat assessment	Risk management
1037	KSA	Knowledge of IT supply chain security and risk management policies, requirements, and procedures	Risk management
1039	KSA	Skill in evaluating the trustworthiness of the supplier and/or product	Contracting/procurement
1061	KSA	Knowledge of the life cycle process	Systems life cycle
1122	KSA	Ability to apply supply chain risk management standards	Computer network defense
1127	KSA	Knowledge of import/export regulations related to cryptography and other security technologies	Legal, government, and jurisprudence

So, then the question is, what is software assurance? It is the level of confidence that software functions in the intended manner and is free from vulnerabilities, whether they are designed into the software or accidentally inserted during its life cycle. Once an organization decides to meet software assurance goals, the next step is to assess its current development and procurement activities and practices. Such an analysis requires at least two things: a repeatable and objective assessment process and a clear benchmark or target that represents a suitable level of risk management given the nature of the organization and the software's mission. Performing this assessment periodically helps an organization to understand the maturity of its software assurance capabilities.

The general perception is that while software engineering is about ensuring that certain things happen, security is about ensuring that they do not. Requirements definition is much more complex. Security requirements differ greatly from one system to another. One typically needs some combination of user authentication, transaction integrity and accountability, fault tolerance, message secrecy, and covertness. But many systems fail because their designers protect the wrong things or protect the right things but in the wrong way.

Therefore, getting protection right depends on several different types of process. Organizations determine what needs protecting, and how to protect it. You also need to ensure that the people who will guard the system and maintain it are properly motivated.

Choosing a methodology for appraising the ability to meet software assurance and SSE goals may seem overwhelming because several models are available, each with its own focus and level of granularity. An organization that is new to the two disciplines might find it challenging simply to find good sources of guidance, much less understand which parts of each model are best suited to its environment and supply chain. However, organizations should not wait for a software assurance and security program to be mandated through, for example, a quality audit/review process. Such mandates are typically "one size fits all" and offer limited flexibility. Organizations are best served by tailoring a software assurance strategy to their own supply chains.

There are three underlying functions of software assurance and SSE: construction, verification, and deployment. Activities within each function play a vital role in ensuring delivery of software products free from security threat and vulnerability. Each of the tasks defined by the NICE framework SSE specialty area is contained in one or more of the three functions.

Construction

In general, construction can be characterized as "the processes and activities related to how an organization defines goals and creates software within development projects. In general, this will include product management, requirements gathering, high-level architecture specification, detailed design, and implementation" (Chandra, 2009).

This aspect of software engineering encompasses processes and activities related to how an organization defines goals and creates software within development projects consistent with the actions identified in the preceding definition of software assurance. The security practices applied at this level include the following:

- *Threat assessment.* Identifies potential attacks against the organization's software to help it better understand the risks and improve the ability to manage them
- *Security requirements.* Enforces the practice of including security requirements during the software development process
- *Secure architecture.* Improves the software design process by promoting secure-by-default designs and greater control over the technologies and processes from which the software is built

Threat assessment helps an organization identify and understand project-level risks based on the functionality of the software being designed and developed, and on the characteristics of the software's operating environment. A key requirement for achieving the goals of this practice is a detailed understanding about the attacks that could take place and the likelihood that they could affect the success of the project. With this understanding, the organization can operate more effectively by making better decisions about how to prioritize security initiatives. By starting with simple threat models and then gradually developing more detailed methods of threat analysis and measurement, an organization can progressively improve its knowledge of threats and security mechanisms.

Just as an organization should identify its software requirements from a physical and logical perspective, it should identify the software's expected behavior with respect to security. The security requirements tasks provide activities that focus on identifying and documenting software security requirements. By adding analysis activities at the project level, security requirements are initially gathered based on the high-level business purpose of the software. As an organization advances, it can use more advanced techniques such as access control specifications to discover new security requirements that may not have been obvious during initial development.

A significant requirement of this practice is that an organization must map its security requirements into its relationships with suppliers and then perform audits on each project to ensure that all are following specified security requirements.

Tasks associated with secure architecture define the roles of an organization that strives to design and build secure software as part of its standard development process. By integrating reusable components and services into the software design process, many of the normal security risks that arise during software development can be dramatically reduced and sometimes eliminated.

An organization does not have to overwhelm its design process with this integration from the start. By beginning with simple implementations of software frameworks, such as ISO 12207, and clear consideration of secure design principles, an organization will naturally evolve toward consistent use of design patterns for its security functions. This group of tasks also encourages project teams to take advantage of centralized security services and infrastructure. They serve as frameworks upon which developers can build custom software with less risk of vulnerabilities.

Verification

Verification is frequently mischaracterized as the practice of testing software as part of the larger software implementation process. However, most standard bodies and frameworks define verification as "confirmation, through the provision of objective evidence, that specified requirements have been fulfilled" (ISO 9000, 2005). This definition suggests that the purpose of verification is to determine whether the products of a software activity fulfill the requirements or conditions imposed on them in the previous activity of the life cycle model used for that project. For example, you might verify that an item's software design meets the requirements for that item. Important to note, verification typically includes quality assurance work such as testing, but it can also include other review and evaluation activities.

The preceding definition suggests that many standards and frameworks broaden the scope of verification to include aspects of both verification and validation (often referred to as V&V). You can see evidence of this suggestion in the tasks identified within this area of the NICE framework. The security verification practices defined at this level of the framework are as follows:

- *Design review.* Entails a thorough assessment of the specifications created during the design process to ensure consistency with the organization's security expectations
- *Code review.* Involves the inspection of source code to identify possible vulnerabilities and to provide a baseline for the organization's secure coding protocol
- *Security testing.* Entails testing software in a runtime environment to further identify vulnerabilities and establish standards for software reuse

Design review defines activities that aim to identify and assess software design and architecture for security problems. Work within the software process has a tendency to slow at a specific point to allow rework to be completed for a previous stage of the life cycle. The activities defined for this practice allow an organization to detect architecture-level issues early in software development and thereby avoid potentially large costs from revisiting earlier life cycle processes because of security concerns.

Code review focuses on activities that are normally performed by the programmer of a project team. In general, this practice stresses the requirement for software inspection at the source code level to find security vulnerabilities. Code-level vulnerabilities are typically found through unit testing; they are generally simple to understand, but even the best coders can make mistakes that leave software open to potential compromise.

To begin this practice, an organization uses checklists that correspond to previously developed and documented test cases. For efficiency, the organization inspects only the most critical software modules. However, as the organization continues to mature, it can integrate techniques that take advantage of automation technology in an effort to improve coverage and efficacy of code review activities.

While code review attempts to identify and remedy security flaws through unit testing as each piece of software is built, security testing focuses on inspecting software in the runtime environment to find security problems. The activities within this practice are normally performed through penetration testing and high-level test cases. These testing activities strengthen the assurance case for software by checking it under real-world conditions, which draws attention to mistakes in business logic that are difficult to find otherwise. As a security program strengthens, most organizations transitioned to using security testing automation to cover the wide variety of test cases that might demonstrate vulnerability in the system.

Deployment

Software systems are no longer stand-alone applications. Increasingly, software systems are the sum of many integrated components, both executable and data, that can be dispersed over numerous networks. Consider the relatively simple case of mobile handsets, which are shells into which a variety of document viewers, collaboration tools, and other operations can be fit to create the effect of an integrated system. Such "systems of systems" integrate components from different organizations that have different release schedules and goals.

Software developers in this context no longer distribute complete systems. They must therefore find a way to deal with greater uncertainty in their operating environments. For example, before they can guarantee a successful installation, developers must be able to determine which components will be used to integrate the software, the configuration of those components, and the internal and external security vulnerabilities that may exist in the operating environment. Also, because the components are produced by multiple organizations, developers must be able to anticipate or react to updated components that are not under their control. These issues are magnified when companies integrate their software with the Internet, given the vast numbers of developers and consumers as well as the great distances involved.

Clearly, software deployment is a large and complex task that creates new challenges in the areas of release, installation, activation, deactivation, updates, and removal of components. The growing complexity of software systems mandates that software deployment activities receive more attention. Much of this attention, particularly as it applies to software assurance, can be provided through the following security practices with associated tasks defined within this area of the NICE framework:

- *Vulnerability management.* Enhances the software assurance program by establishing managerial processes for reporting internal and external vulnerabilities

- *Environment hardening.* Establishes and implements controls within the software's operating environment to strengthen its security
- *Operational enablement.* Makes system operators aware of relevant security information so they can properly configure, deploy, and run the software application

Vulnerability management focuses on the activities of an organization with respect to handling vulnerability reports and security incidents. By having this framework in place, an organization can run its projects more consistently and handle security events with increased efficiency. More formally stated, vulnerability management is the "thorough dissecting of incidents and vulnerability reports to collect detailed metrics and other root-cause information to feed back into the organization's downstream behavior" (Chandra, 2009).

The environment hardening tasks help an organization build assurance for its software's operating environment. Over the past decade, changes to these environments have evolved quickly and increased the difficulty of assessing their assurance needs. No longer do COBOL programs run on large mainframes in remote data centers and serve as the basis for business information processing. Not only must organizations consider assurance procedures that they can apply to client/server infrastructures, they must also now face a new obstacle in building assurance into "as-a-service" architectures that have become popular with the emergence of cloud computing solutions. Such implementations create security concerns that are beyond the control of the organization that deploys the software. Because an application's security can be deteriorated by problems in external components, hardening the underlying environment directly improves the overall security of the software.

Because an operating environment can change so rapidly, the best starting point for hardening the environment is to track and distribute information to keep development teams informed. An organization can then evolve to use scalable methods for deploying security patches and early-warning detectors to protect against potential security damage.

Keeping the software's users and operators informed is the focus of the practices of operational enablement. Gathering critical security information from the project team's software and communicating it to users and operators is vital to the deployment process. You may think you have developed very secure software, but without the information gained from this practice, even the most securely designed software carries undue risks because users and operators will not know about important security characteristics and choices.

Distribution of the security information does not have to be elaborate. Avoid overwritten documentation with a lot of technical jargon; it would not be understood and as a consequence will not be read. By starting with simple documentation to capture the most important details for users and operators, an organization evolves toward building complete security guides that are delivered with each release.

Factoring Secure Software Engineering Workforce Tasks into the Cybersecurity Framework Functions

The CSF was conceptually written from the ICT system perspective. The outcomes of each of the five functions address the risk management practices that should be implemented to protect ICT assets at the system/network level, with little mention of risk implications associated with software usage or software engineering activities that may make an organization vulnerable to cyberattack. As shown in Figure 4.3, only two outcomes of the framework (ID.AM.2 and ID.AM.5) even make reference to software. That is not to say that it does not fit within the scope of the criteria many of the other outcomes, however. In particular, two of the software engineering tasks provide alignment of several outcomes defined in the CSF identify function, while the remainder of the tasks within this specialty area aligns to many outcomes of the protect function.

Identify/Asset Management

According to the CSF, in achieving the outcome of the asset management category, "the data, personnel, devices, systems, and facilities that enable the organization to achieve business purposes are identified and managed consistent with their relative importance to business objectives and the organization's risk strategy" (NIST, 2014b). This outcome can be realized through hardware asset management (HAM) and software asset management (SAM).

HAM is the process of tracking and managing the physical components of computers and computer networks from acquisition through disposal. The goals of HAM are to account for all hardware assets on the ICT infrastructure to provide comprehensive inventory visibility in order to better assess risk.

While the argument can be made that HAM has little to do with software engineering, with the increased organization-wide emphasis on cybersecurity, SAM has become not just an activity within the life cycle; rather, it is vital to an organization's ability to assess risk from the software perspective. Similar to HAM, SAM focuses on software assets, including licenses, versions, and installed endpoints. The underlying goal of SAM is to reduce ICT costs and limit business, legal and security risks related to the ownership and use of computer software, while maximizing ICT responsiveness and end-user productivity.

Identify/Business Environment

Most security professionals agree that, along with a strong background in technology, a thorough understanding of the business is of paramount importance when it comes to creating secure solutions for that business. From the software engineering perspective, understanding the business can help in the identification of regulatory and compliance requirements, applicable risk, architectures to be used, technical controls to be incorporated, and the users to be trained or educated. For example, a financial institution that chooses to allow transactions over the Internet will

	Securely provision general knowledge area Secure software engineering specialty area tasks NICE workforce framework	Cybersecurity framework
		Identify / Protect / Detect / Respond / Recover
408	Analyze information to determine, recommend, and plan the development of a new application or modification of an existing application.	
414	Analyze user needs and software requirements to determine feasibility of design within time and cost constraints.	
417	Apply coding and testing standards, security testing tools (including "fuzzing" static-analysis code scanning tools), and conduct code reviews.	
418	Apply secure code documentation.	
432	Capture security controls used during the requirements phase to integrate security within the process, identify key security objectives, and maximize software security while minimizing disruption to plans and schedules.	
446	Compile and write documentation of program development and subsequent revisions, inserting comments in the coded instructions so others can understand the program.	
459	Conduct trial runs of programs and software applications to ensure the desired information is produced and are correct.	
461	Confer with systems analysts, engineers, programmers, and others to design applications and obtain information on project limitations and capabilities, performance requirements, and interfaces.	
465	Develop threat model based on customer interviews and requirements.	
467	Consult with engineering staff to evaluate interface between hardware and software.	
477	Correct errors by making appropriate changes and rechecking the program to ensure desired results are produced.	
506	Design, develop, and modify software systems using scientific analysis and mathematical models to predict and measure outcome and consequences of design.	
515	Develop and direct software system testing and validation procedures, programming, and documentation.	
543	Develop secure code and error messages.	
602	Evaluate factors such as reporting formats required, cost constraints, and need for security restrictions to determine hardware configuration.	
634	Identify basic common coding flaws at a high level.	
644	Identify security implications and apply methodologies within centralized and decentralized environments across the enterprise's computer systems in software development.	

Figure 4.3   Secure software engineering (SSE) specialty area tasks mapped to the CSF.   *(Continued)*

	Cybersecurity framework
	Identify
	Protect
	Detect
	Respond
	Recover

Securely provision general knowledge area
Secure software engineering specialty area tasks
NICE workforce framework

#	Task
645	Identify security issues around steady state operation and management of software, and incorporate security measures that must be taken when a product reaches the end of its life.
709	Modify existing software to correct errors, adapt it to new hardware or upgrade interfaces, and improve performance.
756	Perform integrated quality assurance testing for security functionality and resiliency attacks.
764	Perform secure programming and identify potential flaws in codes to mitigate vulnerabilities.
770	Perform risk analysis (e.g., threat, vulnerability, and probability of occurrence) whenever an application or system undergoes a major change.
785	Prepare detailed workflow charts and diagrams that describe input, output, and logical operation, and convert them into a series of instructions coded in a computer language.
826	Recognize security implications in the software acceptance phase, including completion criteria, risk acceptance and documentation, common criteria, and methods of independent testing.
865	Translate security requirements into application design elements, including documenting the elements of the software attack surfaces, conducting threat modeling, and defining any specific security criteria.
969	Perform penetration testing as required for new or updated applications.
970	Apply defensive functions (e.g., encryption, access control, identity management) to reduce exploitation opportunities of supply chain vulnerabilities.
971	Design countermeasures and mitigations against potential exploitations of programming language weaknesses and vulnerabilities in system and elements.
972	Determine and document critical numbers of software patches or the extent of releases that would leave software vulnerable.
1149	Enable applications with public keying by leveraging existing public key infrastructure (PKI) libraries and incorporating certificate management and encryption functionalities.
1150	Identify and leverage the enterprise-wide security services while designing and developing secure applications (e.g. enterprise PKI, federated identity server, enterprise AV solution).
1151	Identify and leverage the enterprise-wide version control system while designing and developing secure applications.

Figure 4.3 (*Continued*) Secure software engineering (SSE) specialty area tasks mapped to the CSF.

need to integrate into their software processes with regulatory requirements such as financial privacy, safeguards, and pretexting rules as part of its compliance with the Gramm Leach Bliley Act (GLBA). Since the early 2000s, medical organizations have been mandated to provide the software assurance that all processes address the risk of disclosure of personally identifiable and medical information.

It is through the achievement of the business environment outcomes that software engineers are able to more accurately understand the current information flows through an organization's existing value chain and identify new required flows that should be developed and implemented within new applications, consistent with time and cost constraints.

Identify/Governance

Policies, standards, and procedures should be formulated to address software development methodology and establish practical built-in security features. The policies should not just be documented but enforced, tested, and measured. In addition to internal policies that govern software assurance, external regulatory, legal, privacy, and compliance requirements should be factored into the software security requirements. Some examples appropriate to software assurance include identification and authentication policy, remote access policy, use of company resources policy, software security standards, data classification standards, encryption standards, logging and monitoring standards, and disaster recovery and business continuity standards.

Identify/Risk Assessment

Software risk assessment and formal risk management are disciplines that are essential to the application development process and a vital component to overall understanding of software engineering. In the context of software, risk management is the vehicle used to identify software project risk factors using empirical data (or the lack of empirical data) to quantify factors that could cause a software project to fail. Important to note is that risk is not entirely bad. Every major work effort involves risk. However, with risk comes knowledge and opportunity—the opportunity for planning to overcome potential threats to software project success. Every project is at risk to fail. The opportunity comes with the project team's knowledge and understanding of the risk factors and the inclusion of software implications within the risk management plan to mitigate the risk.

Protect

In addition to ensuring that the hardware and telecommunications of an ICT system is protected, it is essential that any sensitive information processed by software be protected as well. Sensitive information refers to any information that the organization considers valuable. This is the information that is not in the public domain and would result in loss, damage, or even business collapse should the information be lost, stolen, corrupted, or in any way compromised. Sensitive information may be personal, health, financial, or any other information that can affect the competitive edge of an organization.

While it is easy to identify some sensitive data elements such as medical records or credit card information, other elements may not be that evident. Software engineers can determine what is sensitive and what is not by performing data classification activities, with the business stakeholders involved in this process. Software that either transports, processes, or stores sensitive information must build in necessary security controls to protect this information.

A software engineer must be familiar with the process of data classification and protection mechanisms against data disclosure. In general, data classification is the deliberate decision to assign a level of sensitivity to data as it is being created, amended, stored, transmitted, or enhanced. The classification level of that data should then determine the extent to which the data needs to be controlled/secured.

Underlying Knowledge, Skill, and Ability Requirements for Secure Software Engineering

The work of SSE is primarily performed by information security engineers. These individuals apply security principles to all stages of the software engineering life cycle, from requirements analysis through development and on to deployment and beyond.

As a software engineer, you may be responsible for selecting or creating software security systems. Establishing linkages between software and firewalls is a relatively common job expectation. Other necessary skills include the ability to perform software risk assessment, software configuration, and identification of vulnerabilities within software.

Some employers may ask software engineers to model security threats. You could even be expected to try to hack the software yourself. Moreover, there is an expectancy that software engineers have the skills necessary to respond to incidents and provide the related documentation.

Most software engineering bachelor degree programs provide knowledge and skills related to all aspects of the software life cycle. One common misconception is that a software engineer is merely responsible for application coding and testing. That is no longer the case. Organizations expect professionals working within the software engineering life cycle to have skills in coding applications of the most popular language (such as Java and Visual Basic) in addition to knowledge in areas such as project management, requirements analysis, design, and maintenance. Furthermore, the NICE framework acknowledges the need for software engineers to also have security background (i.e., information assurance, vulnerability assessment, network security, incident management, and risk management) in order to effectively understand the risks associated with the applications under development, and implement the necessary software mechanisms to protect, detect, and respond to cybersecurity incidents.

Table 4.2 displays the entire set of specialty KSA requirements and associated competencies for the SSE specialty area (all from the NICE framework).

Table 4.2   SSE Specialty Area KSAs

Item ID	KSA	Statement	Competency
3	KSA	Skill in conducting vulnerability scans and recognizing vulnerabilities in security systems.	Vulnerabilities assessment
20	KSA	Knowledge of complex data structures.	Object technology
23	KSA	Knowledge of computer programming principles such as object-oriented design.	Object technology
38	KSA	Knowledge of organization's enterprise information security architecture system.	Information assurance
40	KSA	Knowledge of organization's evaluation and validation requirements.	Systems testing and evaluation
43	KSA	Knowledge of embedded systems and Internet of things.	Embedded computers
56	KSA	Knowledge of information assurance (IA) principles and methods that apply to software development.	Information assurance
63	KSA	Knowledge of IA principles and organizational requirements to protect confidentiality, integrity, availability, authenticity, and non-repudiation of information and data.	Information assurance
74	KSA	Knowledge of low-level computer languages (e.g., assembly languages).	Computer languages
81	KSA	Knowledge of network protocols (e.g., Transmission Critical Protocol/Internet Protocol [TCP/IP], Dynamic Host Configuration Protocol [DHCP]), and directory services (e.g., Domain Name System [DNS]).	Infrastructure design
90	KSA	Knowledge of operating systems.	Operating systems

(Continued)

Table 4.2 (Continued)   SSE Specialty Area KSAs

Item ID	KSA	Statement	Competency
95	KSA	Knowledge of penetration testing principles, tools, and techniques (e.g., metasploit, neosploit).	Vulnerabilities assessment
100	KSA	Knowledge of privacy impact assessments (PIA).	Personnel safety and security
102	KSA	Knowledge of programming language structures and logic.	Computer languages
109	KSA	Knowledge of secure configuration management techniques.	Configuration management
116	KSA	Knowledge of software debugging principles.	Software development
117	KSA	Knowledge of software design tools, methods, and techniques.	Software development
118	KSA	Knowledge of software development models (e.g., waterfall model, spiral model, agile model).	Software engineering
119	KSA	Knowledge of software engineering.	Software Engineering
121	KSA	Knowledge of structured analysis principles and methods.	Logical systems design
123	KSA	Knowledge of system and application security threats and vulnerabilities.	Vulnerabilities assessment
124	KSA	Knowledge of system design tools, methods, and techniques, including automated systems analysis and design tools.	Logical systems design
149	KSA	Knowledge of web services, including service oriented architecture. Simple Object Access Protocol (SOAP), and web service description language.	Web technology
168	KSA	Skill in conducting software debugging.	Software development
172	KSA	Skill in creating and utilizing mathematical or statistical models.	Modeling and simulation

(Continued)

Table 4.2 (Continued)   SSE Specialty Area KSAs

Item ID	KSA	Statement	Competency
174	KSA	Skill in creating programs that validate and process multiple inputs, including command line arguments, environmental variables, and input streams.	Software testing and evaluation
177	KSA	Skill in designing countermeasures to identified security risks.	Vulnerabilities assessment
185	KSA	Skill in developing applications that can log errors, exceptions, and application faults.	Software development
191	KSA	Skill in developing and applying security system access controls.	Identity management
197	KSA	Skill in discerning the protection needs (i.e., security controls) of information systems and networks.	Information systems/network security
238	KSA	Skill in writing code that is compatible with legacy code (e.g., Common Business-Oriented Language [COBOL], FORTRAN IV) in a modern programming language (e.g., Java, C++).	Computer languages
904	KSA	Knowledge of interpreted and compiled computer languages.	Computer languages
905	KSA	Knowledge of secure coding techniques.	Computer languages
968	KSA	Knowledge of software-related information technology (IT) security principles and methods (e.g., modularization, layering, abstraction, data hiding, simplicity/minimization).	Information systems/network security
973	KSA	Skill in using code analysis tools to eradicate bugs.	Software development
974	KSA	Ability to tailor code analysis for application-specific concerns.	Software testing and evaluation

(Continued)

Table 4.2 (Continued)   SSE Specialty Area KSAs

Item ID	KSA	Statement	Competency
975	KSA	Skill in integrating black box security testing tools into quality assurance process of software releases.	Quality assurance
976	KSA	Knowledge of software quality assurance process.	Software engineering
978	KSA	Knowledge of root cause analysis for incidents.	Incident management
979	KSA	Knowledge of supply chain risk management standards, processes, and practices.	Risk management
980	KSA	Skill in performing root cause analysis for incidents.	Incident management
1020	KSA	Skill in secure test plan design (i.e., unit, integration, system, acceptance).	Systems testing and evaluation
1034	KSA	Knowledge of personally identifiable information (PII) and payment card industry (PCI) data security standards.	Security
1037	KSA	Knowledge of information technology (IT) supply chain security and risk management policies, requirements, and procedures.	Risk management
1038	KSA	Knowledge of local specialized system requirements (e.g., critical infrastructure systems that may not use standard IT) for safety, performance, and reliability.	Infrastructure design
1071	KSA	Knowledge of secure software deployment methodologies, tools, and practices.	Software engineering
1072	KSA	Knowledge of network security architecture concepts, including topology, protocols, components, and principles (e.g., application of defense-in-depth).	Information systems/network security

(Continued)

Table 4.2 (Continued)   SSE Specialty Area KSAs

Item ID	KSA	Statement	Competency
1131	KSA	Knowledge of security architecture concepts and enterprise architecture reference models (e.g., Zackman, federal enterprise architecture [FEA]).	Enterprise architecture
1135	KSA	Knowledge of the application firewall concepts and functions (e.g., single point of authentication/audit/policy enforcement, message scanning for malicious content, data anonymization for PCI and PII compliance, data loss	Computer network defense
1137	KSA	Skill in deploying Service Gateway at the network edge as the first point of contact or proxy into enterprise infrastructure handling layer 7 protocols (e.g., web, XML SOAP, REST, or legacy protocols [EDI]).	Infrastructure design
1140	KSA	Skill in using public-key infrastructure (PKI) software development kit (SDK) to add encryption and digital signature capabilities into applications (e.g., S/MIME email, SSL traffic).	Encryption

Specialty Area 3: Systems Security Architecture

The architecture function has been around for some time in the building of towns and cities, and the term is not uncommon. So, it makes sense to begin this section by examining the meaning of "architecture" in this traditional context. Architecture is a set of rules and conventions used to create buildings that serve a variety of purposes, both functionally and aesthetically. The general premise of the word is one that it supports our need to live, to work, to do business, to travel, to socialize, and to pursue leisure activities. The complex interaction of these various activities must be supported, and this includes the relationship between the activities themselves and their integration into a whole lifestyle. Architecture is founded upon an understanding of the needs that it must fulfill. These needs are expressed in terms of function, aesthetics, culture, government policies, and civil priorities. They take into account how we feel about ourselves and about our neighbors and how they feel about us. In these various ways, architecture must serve all those who will experience it in any way. Architecture is also both driven and constrained by a number of specific factors. These include the materials available within the locale that can be used for construction; the terrain, the climate; the technology; and the engineering skills of the people.

The concept of architecture has been adapted to areas of life other than the building of towns and cities. For example, a naval architect is someone that designs and supervises the construction of ships. In more recent times, the term has been adopted in the context of designing and building ICT systems, and so the concept of information systems architecture developed. In the same way that conventional architecture defines the rules and standards for the design and construction of buildings, information systems architecture addresses these same issues for the design and construction of computers, communications networks, and the distributed ICT systems that are implemented using these technologies. As with the conventional architecture of buildings, towns, and cities, information systems architecture must, therefore, take account of

- The goals that we want to achieve through the systems.
- The environment in which the systems will be built and used.
- The technical capabilities needed to construct and operate the systems and their component subsystems.

By accepting this analysis, you are well on the way to recognizing that information systems architecture is concerned with much more than just technical factors. It is concerned with what the enterprise wants to achieve and with the environmental factors that will influence those achievements. In some organizations, this broad view of information systems architecture is not well understood. Technical factors are often the main ones that influence the architecture, and under these conditions the architecture can fail to deliver what the business expects and needs. The tasks defined in the systems security architecture specialty area of the NICE framework take into consideration each of the information systems architecture characteristics mentioned above. It should be noted that for each form of architecture we are describing, the premise remains the same. The role of performing architecture in each context is just slightly modified to be consistent with each specialization.

One of the key functions of architecture is to provide a framework within which complexity can be successfully managed. Small projects do not necessarily need architecture, because of their lack of complexity. The developer can normally manage the overall design on their own. However, as the size and complexity of a project grows, more developers are needed, all working as a team to create something that has the appearance of being developed by a single individual.

Furthermore, if an individual project is intended to fit harmoniously within a much wider, highly complex set of other projects, then an architecture is needed to act as a "road map" within which all of these projects can be brought together into a seamless structure. This applies whether the individual projects are developed simultaneously, or whether they are developed independently over an extended period. As complexity increases, a framework is needed from which each developer can work in contributing to the overall intended result. Each development team member must also be confident that his or her work will be in harmony with that of team members and that the overall integrity of the resulting product will not be threatened by the work being split across a large development team. The role of architecture is to provide the framework that breaks down complexity into apparent simplicity. This is achieved by layering techniques—focusing attention on specific conceptual levels of thinking, and by modularization—breaking the overall system/software design into manageable pieces that have defined functionality and interfaces. If this latter point sounds familiar, that is because this process is also known as systems engineering, which was discussed from the security perspective in the last section of this chapter.

It is common in many organizations that information security solutions are often designed, acquired, and installed on a tactical basis. A requirement is identified, a specification is developed, and a solution is developed and implemented to meet that situation. In this process, there is no opportunity to consider the strategic objectives, and the result is that the organization builds up a mixture of technical solutions on an ad hoc basis, each independently developed with no guarantee that they will be compatible and interoperable. There is often no analysis of the long-term costs, especially the operational costs that make up a large proportion of the total cost of ownership, and there is no strategy that can logically be aligned with the goals of the organization. An approach that avoids these piecemeal problems is the development of a security architecture, which is business driven and describes a structured interrelationship between the technical and procedural solutions to support the long-term needs of the organization. If the architecture is to be successful, then it must provide a rational framework within which decisions can be made upon the selection of security solutions. The decision criteria should be derived from a thorough understanding of the business requirements, including the need for cost reduction, modularity, scalability, ease of component reuse, operability, usability, interoperability both internally and externally, and integration with the overall ICT architecture and its legacy systems.

Moreover, ICT systems security is only a small part of the overall scope. Information assurance, software assurance, and information risk management need also be considered. Through addressing all three aspects, the scope broadens to overall security of the entire organization. Organizational operations security embraces three major areas: information security, business continuity, and physical and environmental security. Broader still is the view that organizational operations security is concerned with all aspects of operational risk management. Only through an integrated approach to these broad aspects of business security will it be possible for the organization to make the most cost-effective and beneficial decisions with regard to the management of operational risk. The NICE framework recommends that the systems security architecture and the security management process embrace all of these areas.

There are several models and frameworks that organizations can follow to place emphasis on security architecture within their ICT function. Any one of those can be a generic starting point for an organization, but by going through the process of analysis and decision making implied by its structure, the output becomes specific to the organization, and is finally highly customized to a unique business model. As such, it is central to the success of the strategies of ICT security management within the organization.

The tasks defined within the NICE framework can be appropriately categorized into a layered model that looks at the role of systems security architecture from four separate levels of abstraction: the business view (contextual security architecture), the architect view (conceptual security architecture), the designer view (logical security architecture), and the builder view (physical security architecture). It should be noted, that in addition to identifying the tasks being performed related to systems security architecture, the NICE framework emphasizes the importance of documentation through specification and code comments.

Contextual Security Architecture

Any attempt to define an architecture that avoids this step is likely to be unsuccessful. Moreover, many organizations performing architectural work do not take this stage seriously. It is very common for systems architecture work to begin from a technical perspective, looking at technologies and solutions while ignoring the requirements.

The net result of skipping requirements definition stages of an architecture development are abundantly clear. An observation of many large organizations and their ICT systems infrastructure managers or applications teams shows that the relationship with the business community is often strained. One likely reason is that ICT vendor interests and technical innovations often drive business systems development strategy, rather than it being driven by business needs. Those with responsibility for architecture and technical strategy often fail to understand the business requirements because they do not know how to do otherwise. Ignorance of architectural principles is often the devil's advocate.

Within this layered approach, the contextual architecture is concerned with the following:

■ The business, its assets to be protected (brand, reputation, etc.) and the business needs for information security (security as a business enabler, secure electronic business, operational continuity and stability, compliance with the law, etc.). In terms of the highest level of information architecture, this is expressed as "business decisions," along with business goals and objectives.

■ The business risks expressed in terms of business opportunities and the threats to business assets. These business risks drive the need for business security (enabling eBusiness, brand enhancement and protection, fraud prevention, loss prevention, fulfilling legal obligations, achieving business continuity, etc.).

■ The business processes that require security (business interactions and transactions, business communications, etc.).

■ The organizational aspects of business security (governance and management structures, supply chain structures, outsourcing relationships, and strategic partnerships).

■ The business geography and location-related aspects of business security (the global village market place, distributed corporate sites, remote working, jurisdictions, etc.).

■ The business time dependencies and time-related aspects of business security in terms of both performance and sequence (business transaction throughput, lifetimes and deadlines, just-in-time operations, time to market, etc.).

Conceptual Security Architecture

A security architect is a creative person with a grand vision. Architects thrive on challenging business requirements. They use their skill, experience, and expertise to create a picture of what the secure ICT system will look like. They create rough diagrams and high-level descriptions. They prepare the way for more detailed work in later stages, when other people with different types of expertise and skill will fill in the gaps.

The architect's view is the overall concept by which the business requirements of the organization can be met. Therefore, this layer is referred to as the conceptual security architecture. It defines principles and fundamental concepts that guide the selection and organization of the logical and physical elements at the lower layers of abstraction.

In describing the systems security architecture, the tasks at this layer describe the security concepts and principles that will be used, which include:

■ What you want to protect, in terms of information assets. Once these are identified, risk assessment is carried out.

- Why the protection is important, in terms of control and enablement objectives. Control and enablement objectives are derived directly from an analysis of business operational risks (this risk assessment being made based on the identification of information assets) and are a conceptualization of business motivation for security.
- How the organization wants to achieve the protection, in terms of high-level technical and management security strategies and a process-mapping framework through which to describe business processes. These strategies set out the conceptual layered framework for integrating individual tactical elements at the lower levels, ensuring that these fit together in a meaningful way to fulfill the overall strategic goals of the business. Such strategies may include the strategy for applications security, the network security strategy, the public key infrastructure (PKI) strategy, the role-based access control (RBAC) strategy, and so on. For every major area of the business requirements identified in the contextual security architecture, there will be a security strategy (or group of strategies) that supports it.
- Who is involved in security management, in terms of roles and responsibilities and the type of business trust that exists between the parties, including asset owners, custodians and users, and service providers and service customers. The trust concepts are concerned with the various policy authorities that govern trust within a domain, the policies that they set to govern behavior of entities in each of those domains, and the interdomain trust relationships.
- Where the organization wants to achieve the protection conceptualized in terms of a security domains framework. The concepts here are security domains (both logical and physical), domain boundaries, and security associations.
- When the protection is relevant, expressed in terms of a business time management framework. The important concept is the through-life risk management framework.

Logical Security Architecture

Once the architect has completed their work, the designer takes over. The designer has to interpret the architect's conceptual vision and turn it into a logical structure that can be engineered to create a secure product. The architect can be analogized as an artist and visionary, while the engineer as a designer.

In addition to the NICE framework tasks identified in each of the previous sections of this chapter, this design process is completed by the system security engineer. It involves the identification and specification of the logical architectural elements of an overall system. This view models the entire organization as a system with system components that are themselves subsystems. It shows the major architectural security elements in terms of logical security services and describes the logical flow of control and the relationships between these logical elements.

In terms of architectural decomposition down through the layers, the logical security architecture should reflect and represent all of the major security strategies in the conceptual security architecture. At this logical level, everything from the higher layers is transformed into a series of logical abstractions. The logical security architecture is concerned with the following:

■ Information and its logical representation within the organization. It is this information that needs to be secured.
■ Specifying the security and risk management policy requirements (high-level security policy, registration authority policy, certification authority policy, physical domain policies, logical domain policies, etc.) for securing information.
■ Specifying the logical security services (entity authentication, confidentiality protection, integrity protection, nonrepudiation, system assurance, etc.) and how they fit together as common reusable building blocks into a complex security system that meets the overall business requirements. The logical flow of security services is also specified in terms of process maps, and a functional specification describes the required functionality.
■ Specifying the entities (users, security administrators, auditors, etc.) and their interrelationships, attributes, authorized roles and privilege profiles in the form of a schema, and the trust that exists between them in the form of a trust framework.
■ Specifying the security domains and interdomain relationships (logical security domains, physical security domains, and security associations).
■ Specifying the security-related calendar and timetable in terms of start times, deadlines, and lifetimes (such as for registration, certification, login, session management, etc.).

Physical Security Architecture

Once logical design is complete, the lowest layer involves the individuals who design the physical aspects of the ICT system. In general, this is normally done by coders, testers, and other members of the implementation team. These individuals take the logical descriptions and drawings and turn them into a physical security architecture that describes the actual technology model and specifies the detailed design of the various system components. The logical security services are now expressed in terms of the physical security mechanisms and servers that will be used to deliver these services. The physical security architecture is concerned with the following:

■ Specifying the business data model and the security-related data structures (tables, messages, pointers, certificates, signatures, etc.)
■ Specifying rules that drive logical decision making within the system (conditions, practices, procedures, and actions)

- Specifying security mechanisms (encryption, access control, digital signatures, virus scanning, etc.) and the physical applications, middleware, and servers upon which these mechanisms will be hosted
- Specifying the people dependency in the form of the human interface (screen formats and user interactions) and the access control systems
- Specifying security technology infrastructure in the form of the host platforms and the networks (physical layout of the hardware, software, and communications lines)
- Specifying the physical time management in terms of the timing and sequencing of processes and sessions (sequences, events, lifetimes, and time intervals)

Factoring Systems Security Architecture Workforce Tasks into the Cybersecurity Framework Functions

In short, the primary reason for the development of the CSF was to support the risk-based security implications of system architecture. Understanding, prioritizing, and cataloging of those implications are clearly addressed within the identify function. Therefore, it makes sense that all but two of the NICE framework tasks defined within the systems security architecture specialty area align to that function.

Recall from the previous discussion that systems security architecture embodies all of the system life cycle processes from inception to retirement. Most organizations implement those processes by following the definitions of international standards such as ISO 15288 or ISO/IEC/IEEE 12207. However, such standards fall short in the definition of tasks associated with providing the process mechanisms necessary for securing such systems. A quick glance at the tasks that the NICE framework defines for this specialty area shows the tasks typically defined in the international standards in addition to the security-related tasks that lack those standards.

An interpretation of the CSF may steer you into the direction that the CSF should be viewed as a risk-based security umbrella to all of the processes associated with system architecture. Put differently, an individual working within the scope of system architecture would be expected to be efficient in implementing the controls associated with identifying system assets, protecting the assets based on predetermined risk priorities, monitoring the system, responding to system attacks, and performing recovery procedures necessary to make the system functional after an attack. However, from a life cycle perspective, consideration has to be made that the tasks of the systems security architecture specialty area would have been completed before the implementation of the controls associated with the CSF protect, detect, respond, and recover functions. Figure 4.4 shows the mapping between the systems security architecture tasks and the CSF.

Underlying Knowledge, Skill, and Ability Requirements for Systems Security Architecture

A systems security architect should have at least 10 years' experience in information security and system life cycle processes, and at one point in his/her career should have had hands on technical experience in anything from help desk support to being a UNIX or database administrator. This person should have extensive knowledge of security platforms; has managed acquisition efforts; identity access management, cyberwarfare, and governance as it is translated from security standards and policies into an operational technical environment that is aligned with the core business processes whether they are financial institutions like Bank of America or ecommerce companies like Amazon or Netflix. This person should have played major roles in protecting the organization on the front lines of cyberbattles such as the popular NIMDA worm infestation or experience in Advanced Persistence Testing (APT). Optimally, the person should be Information Technology Infrastructure Library (ITIL), Certified Information System Security Professional—Information System Security Architecture Professional (CISSP-ISSAP), or Certified Secure Software Life Cycle Professional (CSSLP) certified, have a cybersecurity or computer science degree, be a visionary, and understand security supports business objectives. The NICE framework KSAs for this specialty area paint the picture that, ultimately, the systems security architect is a perfect blend of a highly skilled security engineer, a governance and policy expert, an enterprise architect, an information system engineer, and a business savvy professional with a warrior spirit.

Table 4.3 displays the entire set of specialty KSA requirements and associated competencies for the systems security architecture specialty area (all from the NICE framework).

Specialty Area 4: Technology Research and Development

In building strategies for organization implementation and support of ICT infrastructures, there is a tendency to focus more attention on the software implications. A thoughtful technology strategy can also have a meaningful impact on an organization's success. Having a disciplined process that manages demand for technology resources, vendor selection, implementation, and support will help a firm limit mistakes that lead to disappointing results. With the increasing reliance upon technology and the high level of regulatory scrutiny over an organization's control of their market access, financial advisors, and customer-facing technologies, it is imperative that technology is well managed and controlled. The NICE framework provides tasks in the technology research and development specialty area that provides the means for such a strategy that impacts the technological security of each system life cycle process.

The key word is "research." Organizations must have individuals on their ICT team who spend a significant amount of time researching current and new trends

Securely provision general knowledge area
Systems security architecture specialty area tasks

	NICE workforce framework	Cybersecurity framework
		Identify / Protect / Detect / Respond / Recover
413	Analyze user needs and requirements to plan system architecture.	
437	Collaborate with system developers to select appropriate design solutions or ensure the compatibility of system components.	
483	Define and prioritize essential system capabilities or business functions required for partial or full system restoration after a catastrophic failure event.	
484	Define appropriate levels of system availability based on critical system functions and ensure system requirements identify appropriate disaster recovery and continuity of operations requirements, to include any appropriate failover/alternate site requirements, backup requirements, and material supportability requirements for system recovery/restoration.	
502	Design system architecture or system components required to meet user needs.	
534	Develop information assurance (IA) designs for systems and networks with multilevel security requirements or requirements for the processing of multiple classification levels of data (primarily applicable to government organizations).	
561	Document and address organization's information security, IA architecture, and systems security engineering requirements throughout the acquisition life cycle.	
563	Document design specifications, installation instructions, and other system-related information.	
568	Employ secure configuration management processes.	
569	Ensure all definition and architecture activities (e.g., system life cycle support plans, concept of operations, operational procedures and maintenance training materials) are properly documented and updated as necessary.	
579	Ensure acquired or developed system(s) and architecture(s) are consistent with organization's IA architecture guidelines.	

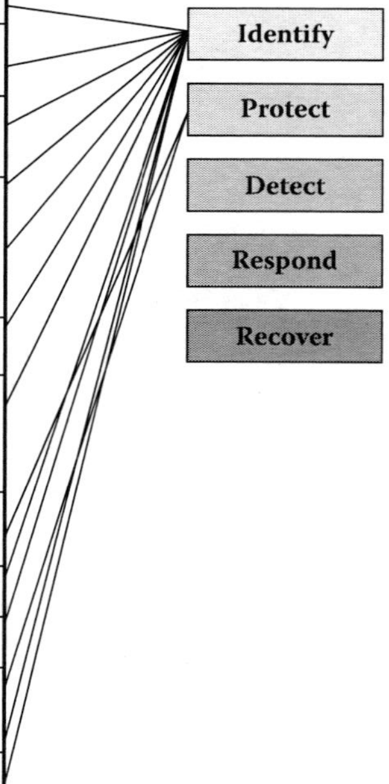

Figure 4.4   Systems security architecture specialty area tasks mapped to the CSF.

(*Continued*)

Securely provision general knowledge area — Systems security architecture specialty area tasks — NICE workforce framework	Cybersecurity framework
	Identify
	Protect
	Detect
	Respond
	Recover
601 Evaluate current or emerging technologies to consider factors such as cost, security, compatibility, or usability.	
603 Evaluate interface between hardware and software and operational and performance requirements of overall system.	
631 Identify and prioritize critical business functions in collaboration with organizational stakeholders.	
646 Identify the protection needs (i.e., security controls) for information system(s), network(s), and document appropriately.	
765 Perform security reviews, identify gaps in security architecture, and develop a security risk management plan.	
780 Plan system implementation to ensure that all system components can be integrated and aligned (e.g., procedures, databases, policies, software, hardware).	
797 Provide advice on project costs, design concepts, or design changes.	
807 Provide input on security requirements to be included in statements of work and other appropriate procurement documents.	
809 Provide input to the risk management framework (RMF) process activities and related documentation (e.g., system life cycle support plans, concept of operations, operational procedures, and maintenance training materials).	
849 Specify power supply and heating, ventilation, and air conditioning (HVAC) requirements and configuration based on system performance expectations and design specifications.	
864 Translate proposed technical solutions into technical specifications.	
994 Define and document how the implementation of a new system or new interfaces between systems impacts the security posture of the current environment.	
995 Document and manage an enterprise technical risk register prioritizing and managing technical risks throughout the system life cycle.	
996 Assess and design key management functions (as related to information assurance [IA]).	

Figure 4.4 (Continued)   Systems security architecture specialty area tasks mapped to the CSF.

Table 4.3   Systems Security Architecture Specialty Area KSAs

Item ID	KSA	Statement	Competency
8	KSA	Knowledge of authentication, authorization, and access control methods.	Identity management
21	KSA	Knowledge of computer algorithms.	Mathematical reasoning
25	KSA	Knowledge of encryption algorithms (e.g., Internet Protocol Security [IPSEC], Advanced Encryption Standard [AES], Generic Routing Encapsulation [GRE], Internet Key Exchange [IKE], Message Digest Algorithm [MD5], Secure Hash Algorithm [SHA], Triple Data Encryption Standard [3DES]).	Cryptography
27	KSA	Knowledge of cryptography and cryptographic key management concepts.	Cryptography
34	KSA	Knowledge of database systems.	Database management systems
38	KSA	Knowledge of organization's enterprise information security architecture system.	Information assurance
40	KSA	Knowledge of organization's evaluation and validation requirements.	Systems testing and evaluation
43	KSA	Knowledge of embedded systems and Internet of things.	Embedded computers
46	KSA	Knowledge of fault tolerance.	Information assurance
51	KSA	Knowledge of how system components are installed, integrated, and optimized.	Systems integration
52	KSA	Knowledge of human-computer interaction principles.	Human factors
53	KSA	Knowledge of the Security Assessment and Authorization (SA&A) process.	Information assurance

(Continued)

Table 4.3 (Continued)   Systems Security Architecture Specialty Area KSAs

Item ID	KSA	Statement	Competency
62	KSA	Knowledge of industry-standard and organizationally accepted analysis principles and methods.	Logical systems design
63	KSA	Knowledge of information assurance (IA) principles and organizational requirements to protect confidentiality, integrity, availability, authenticity, and non-repudiation of information and data.	Information assurance
65	KSA	Knowledge of information theory, including source coding, channel coding, algorithm complexity theory, and data compression.	Mathematical reasoning
68	KSA	Knowledge of information technology IT architectural concepts and frameworks.	Information technology architecture
70	KSA	Knowledge of IT security principles and methods (e.g., firewalls, demilitarized zones, encryption).	Information systems/network security
78	KSA	Knowledge of microprocessors.	Computers and electronics
79	KSA	Knowledge of network access, identity, and access management (e.g., public key infrastructure [PKI]).	Identity management
81	KSA	Knowledge of network protocols (e.g, Transmission Critical Protocol/ Internet Protocol [TCP/IP], Dynamic Host Configuration Protocol [DHCP]), and directory services (e.g., Domain Name System [DNS]).	Infrastructure design
82	KSA	Knowledge of network design processes, including security objectives, operational objectives, and tradeoffs.	Infrastructure design
90	KSA	Knowledge of operating systems.	Operating systems

(Continued)

Table 4.3 (Continued)   Systems Security Architecture Specialty Area KSAs

Item ID	KSA	Statement	Competency
92	KSA	Knowledge of how traffic flows across the network (e.g., Transmission Control Protocol and Internet Protocol [TCP/IP], Open System Interconnection model [OSI]).	Infrastructure design
94	KSA	Knowledge of parallel and distributed computing concepts.	Information assurance
109	KSA	Knowledge of secure configuration management techniques.	Configuration management
110	KSA	Knowledge of key concepts in security management (e.g., release management, patch management).	Information assurance
111	KSA	Knowledge of security system design tools, methods, and techniques.	Information systems/network security
113	KSA	Knowledge of server and client operating systems.	Operating systems
119	KSA	Knowledge of software engineering.	Software engineering
124	KSA	Knowledge of system design tools, methods, and techniques, including automated systems analysis and design tools.	Logical systems design
130	KSA	Knowledge of systems testing and evaluation methods.	Systems testing and evaluation
132	KSA	Knowledge of technology integration processes.	Systems integration
133	KSA	Knowledge of key telecommunication concepts (e.g., routing algorithms, fiber optics systems link budgeting, add/drop multiplexers).	Telecommunications
141	KSA	Knowledge of the enterprise information technology (IT) architecture.	Information technology architecture
143	KSA	Knowledge of the organization's enterprise information technology (IT) goals and objectives.	Enterprise architecture

(Continued)

Table 4.3 (Continued)   Systems Security Architecture Specialty Area KSAs

Item ID	KSA	Statement	Competency
144	KSA	Knowledge of the systems engineering process.	Systems life cycle
155	KSA	Skill in applying and incorporating information technologies into proposed solutions.	Technology awareness
180	KSA	Skill in designing the integration of hardware and software solutions.	Systems integration
183	KSA	Skill in determining how a security system should work, including its resilience and dependability capabilities, and how changes in conditions, operations, or the environment will affect these outcomes.	Information assurance
197	KSA	Skill in discerning the protection needs (i.e., security controls) of information systems and networks.	Information systems/network security
224	KSA	Skill in design modeling and building use cases (e.g., unified modeling language).	Modeling and simulation
904	KSA	Knowledge of interpreted and compiled computer languages.	Computer languages
993	KSA	Knowledge of the methods, standards, and approaches for describing, analyzing, and documenting an organization's enterprise information technology (IT) architecture (e.g., Open Group Architecture Framework [TOGAF], Department of Defense Architecture Framework [DODAF], Federal Enterprise Architecture Framework [FEAF]).	Enterprise architecture
1034	KSA	Knowledge of personally identifiable information (PII) and payment card industry (PCI) data security standards.	Security
1037	KSA	Knowledge of information technology IT supply chain security and risk management policies, requirements, and procedures.	Risk management

(Continued)

Table 4.3 (Continued) Systems Security Architecture Specialty Area KSAs

Item ID	KSA	Statement	Competency
1038	KSA	Knowledge of local specialized system requirements (e.g., critical infrastructure systems that may not use standard IT) for safety, performance, and reliability.	Infrastructure design
1072	KSA	Knowledge of network security architecture concepts, including topology, protocols, components, and principles (e.g., application of defense-in-depth).	Information systems/network security
1073	KSA	Knowledge of network systems management principles, models, methods (e.g., end-to-end systems performance monitoring), and tools.	Network management
1130	KSA	Knowledge of organizational process improvement concepts and process maturity models (e.g., Capability Maturity Model Integration (CMMI) for development, CMMI for services, and CMMI for acquisitions).	Process control
1133	KSA	Knowledge of service management concepts for networks and related standards (e.g., Information Technology Infrastructure Library, v3 [ITIL]).	Network management
1141	KSA	Knowledge of an organization's information classification program and procedures for level information loss.	Information management
1142	KSA	Knowledge of security models (e.g., Bell-LaPadula model, Biba integrity model, Clark-Wilson integrity model).	Enterprise architecture

in computer technology. Moreover, during feasibility analysis and systems requirements planning, those individuals use their knowledge of security risk management, information/network security, and vulnerability assessment to assist the organization in determining if desired or required technology provides the appropriate support for a given project at the level of security prioritized by the risk management plan.

Once the appropriate technology is selected and vendors chosen, it must be integrated into telecommunication, network, and operating and application systems during the development process. For example, a development team implementing an infrastructure as a service (IaaS) solution depends on individuals with knowledge of service-oriented architecture (SOA) to properly configure the operating system and application software. Similarly, the organization depends upon those same individuals to implement the necessary security controls that minimize the likelihood of exploitation, based on their knowledge of that technology.

Factoring Technology Research and Development Workforce Tasks into the Cybersecurity Framework Functions

The CSF defines critical infrastructure as "systems and assets, whether physical or virtual, so vital to the United States that the incapacity or destruction of such systems and assets would have a debilitating impact on security, national economic security, national public health or safety, or any combination of those matters" (NIST, 2014b). Using that definition as a basis, it is easy to see how the tasks associated with technology research and development are associated with the outcomes specified in the identify and detect functions. Without an adequate understanding of the technology implemented within an organization's ICT system, it is impossible to identify all of the vulnerabilities that come from its use. Further, the organization must have knowledge of appropriate technologies that can be used to protect the system and act as a monitor for potential attacks. Nevertheless, the CSF does have one technology-related outcome that stands out from the rest.

The protective technology category, or technical security architecture, as it is often referred, focuses on the mapping between the control architecture and the protection processes, life cycle issues, and contextual drivers; it typically defines controls for protection settings that can be implemented by technical mechanisms and identifies what is commonly called technical security policy, as opposed to enterprise policy. The interaction between other elements is the prime focus of technical security architecture, but it commonly encompasses the elements of context more than any other area. These are the who, what, where, why, when, and how of the protect function. The CSF describes this category as the controls in which "technical security solutions are managed to ensure the security and resilience of systems and assets, consistent with related policies, procedures, and agreements" (NIST, 2014b). Figure 4.5 shows the mapping between the technology research and development tasks to the CSF.

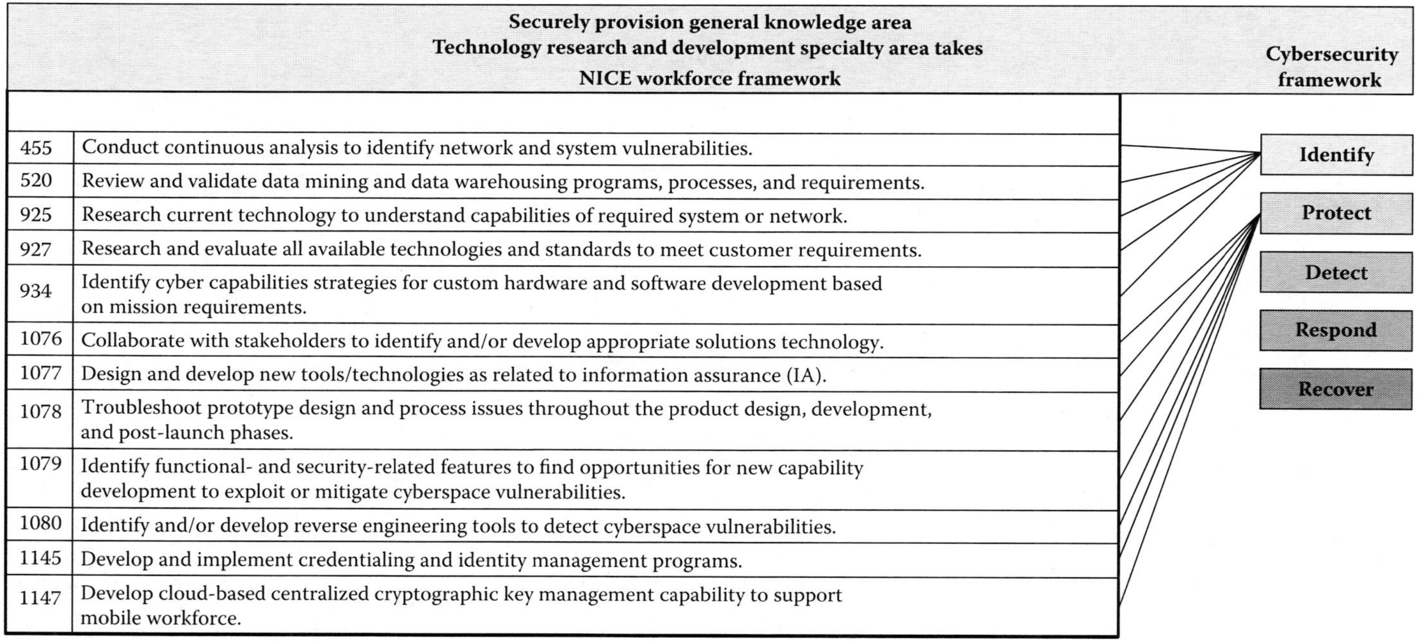

	Securely provision general knowledge area Technology research and development specialty area takes NICE workforce framework	Cybersecurity framework
		Identify · **Protect** · **Detect** · **Respond** · **Recover**
455	Conduct continuous analysis to identify network and system vulnerabilities.	
520	Review and validate data mining and data warehousing programs, processes, and requirements.	
925	Research current technology to understand capabilities of required system or network.	
927	Research and evaluate all available technologies and standards to meet customer requirements.	
934	Identify cyber capabilities strategies for custom hardware and software development based on mission requirements.	
1076	Collaborate with stakeholders to identify and/or develop appropriate solutions technology.	
1077	Design and develop new tools/technologies as related to information assurance (IA).	
1078	Troubleshoot prototype design and process issues throughout the product design, development, and post-launch phases.	
1079	Identify functional- and security-related features to find opportunities for new capability development to exploit or mitigate cyberspace vulnerabilities.	
1080	Identify and/or develop reverse engineering tools to detect cyberspace vulnerabilities.	
1145	Develop and implement credentialing and identity management programs.	
1147	Develop cloud-based centralized cryptographic key management capability to support mobile workforce.	

Figure 4.5 Technology research and development specialty area tasks mapped to the CSF.

Underlying Knowledge, Skill, and Ability Requirements for Technology Research and Development

Vital to the success of any cybersecurity program are individuals with strong technical aptitude in all aspects of the secure system life cycle. The NICE framework provides a set of KSAs that, at first glance, may appear that they belong in the combination of systems security architecture and systems development specialty areas. Further insight shows that the KSAs have a stronger technical focus than those included in the other areas.

In particular, attention should be drawn to the KSA that NICE defines as: "skill in applying and incorporating information technologies into proposed solutions" (NIST, 2013). An organization's ability to build secure ICT solutions is largely dependent upon individuals with knowledge of current and future trends in technology. That knowledge comes from persistent research into what technology is currently available, what has worked in terms of securing systems for other organizations, and what technological trends are predicted in the future. Moreover, those individuals must have the required skill sets necessary to lead the organization in the secure development and implementation of that technology when required as a component of a secure ICT solution. Put differently, an organization is dependent on individuals who are participants in technology circles and can use their knowledge in, for example, vulnerability assessment, risk management, hardware engineering, system life cycles, computer programming, and cryptography, to apply those skills to whatever technology the solution requires.

Table 4.4 displays the entire set of specialty KSA requirements and associated competencies for the technology research and development specialty area (all from the NICE framework).

Specialty Area 5: Systems Requirements Planning

The NICE framework summarizes the tasks of systems requirements planning suggesting that the individual working within this phase of the system life cycle "consults with customers to gather and evaluate functional requirements and translates these requirements into technical solutions. Provides guidance to customers about applicability of information systems to meet business needs" (NIST, 2013). This general description provides significant alignment to the ISO 12207 standard. Stakeholder Requirements Definition activities and System Requirements Analysis activities are defined by the ISO 12207 Technical Process. Moreover, this specialty area highlights the necessity for configuration management (CM), which is an ISO 12207 Supporting Process. Furthermore, the framework defines the task associated with developing a security context, a preliminary security concept of operations, and development of baseline security requirements that are in alignment with information assurance requirements. NIST SP 800-53 provides excellent guidelines for performing those activities.

Table 4.4 Technology Research and Development Specialty Area KSAs

Item ID	KSA	Statement	Competency
3	KSA	Skill in conducting vulnerability scans and recognizing vulnerabilities in security systems.	Vulnerabilities assessment
4	KSA	Ability to identify systemic security issues based on the analysis of vulnerability and configuration data.	Vulnerabilities assessment
10	KSA	Knowledge of application vulnerabilities.	Vulnerabilities assessment
15	KSA	Knowledge of capabilities and applications of network equipment including hubs, routers, switches, bridges, servers, transmission media, and related hardware.	Hardware
27	KSA	Knowledge of cryptography and cryptographic key management concepts.	Cryptography
42	KSA	Knowledge of electrical engineering as applied to computer architecture, including circuit boards, processors, chips, and associated computer hardware.	Hardware engineering
88	KSA	Knowledge of new and emerging information technology (IT) and cybersecurity technologies.	Technology awareness
95	KSA	Knowledge of penetration testing principles, tools, and techniques (e.g., metasploit, neosploit).	Vulnerabilities assessment
129	KSA	Knowledge of system life cycle management principles, including software security and usability.	Systems life cycle
132	KSA	Knowledge of technology integration processes.	Systems integration

(Continued)

Table 4.4 (Continued) Technology Research and Development Specialty Area KSAs

Item ID	KSA	Statement	Competency
133	KSA	Knowledge of key telecommunication concepts (e.g., routing algorithms, fiber optics systems link budgeting, add/drop multiplexers).	Telecommunications
144	KSA	Knowledge of the systems engineering process.	Systems life cycle
155	KSA	Skill in applying and incorporating information technologies into proposed solutions.	Technology awareness
172	KSA	Skill in creating and utilizing mathematical or statistical models.	Modeling and simulation
180	KSA	Skill in designing the integration of hardware and software solutions.	Systems integration
238	KSA	Skill in writing code that is compatible with legacy code (e.g., Common Business-Oriented Language [COBOL], FORTRAN IV) in a modern programming language (e.g., Java, C++).	Computer languages
321	KSA	Knowledge of products and nomenclature of major vendors (e.g., security suites: Trend Micro, Symantec, McAfee, Outpost, Panda, Kaspersky, etc.) and how differences affect exploitation/vulnerabilities.	Technology awareness
371	KSA	Skill in reading, interpreting, writing, modifying, and executing simple scripts (e.g., PERL, Visual Basic Scripting [VBS]) on Windows and Unix systems (e.g., tasks such as parsing large data files, automating manual tasks, fetching/processing remote data).	Operating systems

(Continued)

Table 4.4 (Continued) Technology Research and Development Specialty Area KSAs

Item ID	KSA	Statement	Competency
905	KSA	Knowledge of secure coding technologies.	Computer languages
1037	KSA	Knowledge of information technology (IT) supply chain security and risk management policies, requirements, and procedures.	Risk management
1038	KSA	Knowledge of local specialized system requirements (e.g., critical infrastructure systems that may not use standard IT) for safety, performance, and reliability.	Infrastructure design
1040	KSA	Knowledge of relevant laws, policies, procedures, or governance related to work impacting critical infrastructure.	Criminal law
1042	KSA	Ability to apply network programming toward client/server model.	Requirements analysis
1044	KSA	Skill in identifying forensic footprints.	Computer forensics
1047	KSA	Skill in writing kernel level applications.	Software development
1052	KSA	Knowledge of global systems for mobile communications (GSM) architecture.	Telecommunications
1054	KSA	Knowledge of hardware reverse engineering techniques.	Vulnerabilities assessment
1055	KSA	Knowledge of middleware (e.g., enterprise service bus and message queuing).	Software development
1056	KSA	Knowledge of operations security.	Public safety and security
1059	KSA	Knowledge of networking protocols.	Infrastructure design

(Continued)

Table 4.4 (Continued) Technology Research and Development Specialty Area KSAs

Item ID	KSA	Statement	Competency
1061	KSA	Knowledge of the life cycle process.	Systems life cycle
1062	KSA	Knowledge of software reverse engineering techniques.	Vulnerabilities assessment
1063	KSA	Knowledge of Unix/Linux operating system structure and internals (e.g., process management, directory structure, installed applications).	Operating systems
1064	KSA	Knowledge of Extensible Markup Language (XML) schemas.	Infrastructure design
1066	KSA	Skill in utilizing exploitation tools (e.g., Foundstone, fuzzers, packet sniffers, debug) to identify system/software vulnerabilities (e.g., penetration and testing).	Vulnerabilities assessment
1067	KSA	Skill in utilizing network analysis tools to identify software communications vulnerabilities.	Vulnerabilities assessment
1072	KSA	Knowledge of network security architecture concepts, including topology, protocols, components, and principles (e.g., application of defense-in-depth).	Information systems/network security
1135	KSA	Knowledge of the application firewall concepts and functions (e.g., single point of authentication/audit/policy enforcement, message scanning for malicious content, data anonymization for PCI and PII compliance, data loss protection scanning, accelerated cryptographic operations, SSL security, REST/JSON processing).	Computer network defense
1142	KSA	Knowledge of security models (e.g., Bell-LaPadula model, Biba integrity model, Clark-Wilson integrity model).	Enterprise architecture

Stakeholder Requirements Definition

The purpose of stakeholder requirements definition is to describe the functions and security mechanisms that the user wants the ICT system to perform. The stakeholder requirements process describes how the system will interact with its operating environment. That description then provides a reference against which the system's actual ability to satisfy stakeholder needs will be validated. Thus, in order to make that judgment, the definition of requirements must be accompanied by description of all of the stakeholders who will use the system. The information that the stakeholder requirements definition has developed will then be analyzed and transformed into a description of the common set of stakeholder requirements.

Stakeholder input is important to the overall success of the system life cycle because that input helps developers understand how the specific performance of a function will be carried out by a particular audience. In order to communicate that performance with the maximum degree of accuracy and security, the stakeholder requirements process needs to describe how the user community intends to use the system. It must also describe all of the constraints on the system. Furthermore, in order to determine whether stakeholder needs have been satisfied, the process must be able to establish traceability between documented requirements and the stakeholders who expressed them. This process establishes the basis for validating that the system conforms to its requirements and provides the basis for negotiating and agreeing to its eventual delivery. The first step in this process is to identify the stakeholder community.

Stakeholder identification is an important step because in order to be useful the system must meet the requirements of an explicit set of users. Therefore, those requirements must be captured and accurately portrayed. The list of stakeholder needs and constraints that are the outcome of this documentation and analysis process can then be formulated into formal stakeholder requirements.

Stakeholder requirements communicate what the system must do to meet the demands of its users within the operating environment. The requirements of those stakeholders then provide the point of reference that will guide the system development process throughout its life cycle. It also serves as the means to determine whether the system has fulfilled its contractual requirements. The deliverable that emerges from the stakeholder identification process has to fully describe all of the characteristics and operating context of the user community as well as the general assumptions that underlie the system definition.

The complete description of system requirements, assumptions, and constraints will then serve as the foundation for validating the system as built, and will also provide the basis for negotiating the contract to provide the system or service. Later in the process, an organization must be able to demonstrate that all stakeholder requirements can be directly traceable to the individual stakeholders who defined them. In addition to confirming the satisfaction of all stakeholder requirements, the process must also confirm that the operational constraints that might influence the system are explicitly tied to the requirements they affect.

Once stakeholders have been identified and described, the next step in the process is to elicit their requirements. Ideally, those requirements should fully describe the system's functions and operations that will satisfy the stakeholders. These requirements are typically captured in a formal document that describes the system's scope and purpose and the specific behaviors required to achieve that purpose. The document is typically called a requirements specification, and it includes a complete listing of the functions required for the system as well as a full description of the system's environmental constraints.

Environmental constraints are particularly critical because they itemize the influences on the system's construction. When citing constraints, it is important to document their sources, justifications, or rationales and any underlying assumptions of stakeholders. Constraints fall into several possible categories, ranging from large-scale issues such as the communal needs the system has to satisfy to detailed concerns such as contractual constraints imposed by the customer. In general, constraints are dictated by the capabilities and operating characteristics of the customer. It is likely that several constraints will be identified as users and other stakeholders interact with a system during its life cycle. The capabilities and skill limitations of the ICT system team are important considerations in constraint identification because they help set the usability requirements. In addition, the system will probably be influenced by existing agreements, management decisions, and technical decisions. Specific measures of effectiveness should be specified in all cases because some form of concrete assessment is needed in order to determine whether a given requirement has been satisfied.

Health, safety, and security concerns encompass one of the greatest areas of focus for system definition. These concerns can be categorized as environmental- or stakeholder-driven issues. Typical areas of concern include the safety or security risks that are associated with the various methods of operation or support for the system. In addition, there are threats to intellectual property and environmental influences that might affect the system.

Project teams have to be able to identify functions that could have an effect on the security of their system or its users. Potential areas of concern include anything that might enable unauthorized access or cause harm to any personnel, property, or information that falls within the system's scope. Areas of concern could also include functions that might compromise sensitive information or deny the right of entry of individuals to property and information they have been authorized to access. The impacts of these concerns need to be identified and specified. Any additional security functions that need to be implemented in the system, including planned mitigations and containment measures, need to be made clear.

System Requirements Analysis

The purpose of the system requirements analysis is to transform the stakeholder requirements into a set of technical specifications that will guide system design. This process is critical because the end result is the formal specification of product requirements.

ISO 12207 and the NICE framework are aligned in an itemized set of criteria that must be met before the specification can be confirmed as correct. Because these criteria also define the components of the system specification, the list can serve as a general table of contents for the deliverable. Therefore, the requirements specification must describe a valid set of functional and qualitative requirements. Qualitative requirements are also known as nonfunctional requirements, and they cover such important intangibles as product security and quality.

The tasks associated with system requirements analysis require a fundamental inventory of system requirements, in addition to a separate listing of all operational, physical, and environmental influences on each of the components that have been specified. The requirements analysis process also includes an explicit representation of all internal, embedded, and external interfaces, and it provides a set of qualification criteria for each item specified.

In the more specific areas of safety and security, the specification should also stipulate that those factors consider methods of operation and maintenance, environmental influences, and potentials for personnel injury relating to each software item, as well as items related to compromise of sensitive information. The specification should also consider a range of ergonomic elements, including aspects of manual operations, human/machine interactions, constraints on personnel, and areas needing concentrated human attention, that are sensitive to human errors and training.

The specification of requirements should also consider all user documentation and all aspects of anticipated operation, maintenance, and execution. A key point is that the specification must be documented, traceable, testable, feasible, and consistent with the needs of the acquiring organization. Moreover, to ensure the ability to confirm the compliance of the finished system specification, the developer should conduct a joint review in order to generate consistent understanding of the requirements. Upon successful completion of the review, the formal requirements document becomes the basis for the CM baseline and the systems explicit model for the rest of the development process.

Configuration Management

CM defines and enforces control over an organization's assets. The type of CM described in the systems requirements planning specialty area is meant to be the formal mechanism for managing change to any facet of the ICT system under development. The CM process is essential for monitoring and controlling all forms of development activity. CM specifies the methods for controlling changes to assets throughout their useful life cycle.

CM refers to the understanding and maintenance of information about the status of a system, software item, or service. Its objective is to control changes to those items in a way that preserves their integrity. CM provides two primary advantages: it maintains the integrity of configurations and allows changes to be evaluated and made rationally. CM also gives the company's top managers and policy makers direct input into the evolution of a company's ICT asset base. It does this by ensuring managers are involved in decisions about the form of the controlled asset. CM provides the basis to measure quality, security, improve the software development and maintenance cycle, make testing and QA easier, remove error-prone steps from product releases, provide traceability of related components, and dramatically ease problems with change management and problem tracking.

CM involves three major elements in the system life cycle:

1. Development, which supports the identification process
2. Maintenance, which supports authorization and configuration control
3. Assurance, which supports verification

The latter two functions are cornerstones of the process because they ensure correct configuration of all of the systems under configuration control.

The three roles that are involved in CM are those of the customer, the producer (which can be the supplier or the developer), and any associated subcontractors. The producer establishes a CM plan with the customer and then ensures that it is understood, properly set up, and maintained at all levels of the organization. The producer appoints configuration managers who have defined responsibilities for ensuring that requirements are properly executed and maintained. The producer must also be able to assure product quality by performing occasional inspections independent of developer activity.

The customer assigns a representative who has the proper authority to resolve all pending issues between his company and the producer. This representative has the responsibility for approving proposals and concluding agreements with the producer and for ensuring that his own organization observes all agreements. The producer's configuration manager is generally responsible for ensuring each subcontractor's participation as contracted. All aspects of the agreement between the producer and customer generally apply to the subcontractor and are included in the CM plan.

CM incorporates the two processes, configuration control and verification control, which are implemented through three interdependent management activities that must be fitted to the needs of each project. The three activities are change process management, which is made up of change authorization, verification control, and release processing; baseline control, which is composed of change accounting and library management; and configuration verification, which includes status accounting to verify compliance with specifications.

Security Control Formulation and Implementation

The challenge in formulating and implementing security controls is identifying the right set of controls to address the situation. Given the complexity of most organizations, it is a significant challenge to ensure that an exactly correct set controls are in place to address an organization's unique requirements. For that reason, the concept of using a standard baseline of "must address" controls as a starting point is very helpful to the implementation process. These standard baselines represent best practice as understood by the experts at NIST, "The baselines alleviate a considerable amount of inertia when setting up a security control system by jump-starting the organization to create an initial version" (NIST, 2014a).

According to the standard, the baseline controls comprise the minimum set of security behaviors needed to achieve the requisite level of assurance. For conventional organizations, these assurance requirements would probably be established based on a comprehensive threat analysis. For government organizations, the requirements are dictated by the formal security categorizations and associated baseline controls. However, regardless of which source is used to dictate the requirements, NIST SP 800-53 can be a handy place to begin formulating controls.

NIST SP 800-53 specifies three sets of minimum security baseline controls that correspond to the low-, moderate-, and high-impact levels. Each of the three baselines provides a set of minimum security controls for a particular impact level associated with a security category. "The baseline controls specified for the security categories provide a point of reference for the organization to select and install necessary countermeasures to achieve the security goals for a system's impact level" (NIST, 2014a).

The minimum assurance requirements for the controls in the NIST SP 800-53 security control catalog are stipulated in a set of three formal baselines. These baselines specify the behaviors and activities that the organization must deploy to achieve the minimum degree of compliance with a given security category. The organization then implements the controls and monitors them to provide continual assurance that they were implemented correctly, are operating as designed, and are producing the desired security outcomes.

The NIST SP 800-53 control activities are applied as one control at a time. However, to keep the complete set of control measures at a consistent level of application, the controls are grouped by security control baseline. The baselines are homogenous in that each control within the baseline relates to a set of logically associated security requirements.

Factoring Systems Requirements Planning Workforce Tasks into the Cybersecurity Framework Functions

Before we begin a discussion about the association of the system requirements process to the CSF, we should make an important point. One logical interpretation of the outcomes and referenced controls iterates that the CSF was written from the perspective that an ICT system already exists. In that context, the framework thus provides the outcomes and controls necessary to implement cybersecurity into that critical infrastructure. It is from that interpretation, there are few obvious and direct relations between the CSF outcomes and tasks within the system requirements process of the system life cycle. However, we suggest that there are some indirect relations between the CSF and system requirements that require consideration and further discussion.

The classic view of the systems requirements process is that business needs are matched with business objects, and through feasibility and system analysis techniques requirements for an ICT solution are identified and documented. Many of the tasks defined within the systems requirements planning specialty area of the NICE framework are consistent with that view. However, organizations are now faced with the reality that cybersecurity is now a business need high on the priority list. Moreover, organizations are now faced with making cybersecurity a key component of their business objectives. It is through this sense of reality that cybersecurity needs to be built into the requirements of ICT solutions. Similarly, one should begin to see associations between system requirements tasks and several outcomes of the identify function of the CSF as shown in Figure 4.6.

We said a moment ago that requirements are identified based on feasibility studies performed. Traditionally technology, cost, time, and human resources were the primary focus of those studies consisted of considerations. Today, organizations are faced with another aspect of feasibility, and that is risk management. In addition to identification of resilience requirements, all identified system requirements must be assessed in terms of the cybersecurity risk that requirement imposes. In addition, there must exist alignment between each requirement and established organizational security governance policies, risk management, business continuity, response, and recovery plans.

Underlying Knowledge, Skill, and Ability Requirements for Systems Requirements Planning

Since the early days of SDLC processes (which dates back to the early 1960s), the belief was that in order to adequately perform the tasks associated with system requirements knowledge and skills in the competency areas of requirements analysis, systems integration, logical systems design, mathematical reasoning, information technology infrastructure, modeling, contracting, and procurement were a necessity. The same beliefs exist today. So much that the NICE framework identifies many KSAs in the systems requirements specialty area that attain those competencies. However, recall from our previous discussion that organizations must now build security implications into their system requirements.

Noteworthy is the degree to which the framework requires understanding of security implications to system requirements. Most of the security-related KSAs defined for this specialty area require knowledge of the competency area. That said, the framework suggests that to perform the tasks associated with system requirements an individual must have enough knowledge of the security implications in order to determine the degree to which each aspect of security affects the defined requirement. The only "security-related" skills that the framework requires is the ability to apply confidentiality, integrity, and availability principles, in addition to the need for skills in using incident handling methodologies.

Table 4.5 displays the entire set of specialty KSA requirements and associated competencies for the systems requirements planning specialty area (all from NICE, 2014).

Securely provision general knowledge area
Systems requirements planing specialty area tasks
NICE workforce framework

Cybersecurity framework

Identify
Protect
Detect
Respond
Recover

	Task
458	Conduct risk analysis, feasibility study, and/or trade-off analysis to develop, document, and refine functional requirements and specifications.
466	Consult with customers to evaluate functional requirements.
476	Coordinate with systems architects and developers, as needed, to provide oversight in the development of design solutions.
487	Define project scope and objectives based on customer requirements.
511	Develop an enterprise system security context, a preliminary system security concept of operations, and define baseline security requirements in accordance with applicable information assurance (IA) requirements.
517	Develop and document requirements, capabilities, and constraints for design procedures and processes.
528	Develop cost estimates for future new or modified system(s).
669	Integrate and align information security and/or IA policies to ensure system analysis meets security requirements.
700	Manage information technology (IT) projects to ensure that developed solutions meet customer requirements.
726	Oversee and make recommendations regarding configuration management.
760	Perform needs analysis to determine opportunities for new and improved business process solutions.
789	Prepare use cases to justify the need for specific IT solutions.
863	Translate functional requirements into technical solutions.
1003	Develop and document supply chain risks for critical system elements, as appropriate.
1144	Develop and document user experience (UX) requirements including information architecture and user interface requirements.

Figure 4.6 Systems requirements planning specialty area tasks mapped to the CSF.

Table 4.5 Systems Requirements Planning Specialty Area KSAs

Item ID		Statement	Competency
9	KSA	Knowledge of applicable business processes and operations of customer organizations.	Requirements analysis
16	KSA	Knowledge of capabilities and requirements analysis.	Requirements analysis
25	KSA	Knowledge of encryption algorithms (e.g., Internet Protocol Security [IPSEC], Advanced Encryption Standard [AES], Generic Routing Encapsulation [GRE], Internet Key Exchange [IKE], Message Digest Algorithm [MD5], Secure Hash Algorithm [SHA], Triple Data Encryption Standard [3DES]).	Cryptography
27	KSA	Knowledge of cryptography and cryptographic key management concepts.	Cryptography
46	KSA	Knowledge of fault tolerance.	Information assurance
51	KSA	Knowledge of how system components are installed, integrated, and optimized.	Systems integration
53	KSA	Knowledge of the security assessment and authorization (SA&A) process.	Information assurance
55	KSA	Knowledge of information assurance (IA) principles used to manage risks related to the use, processing, storage, and transmission of information or data.	Information assurance
62	KSA	Knowledge of industry-standard and organizationally accepted analysis principles and methods.	Logical systems design
63	KSA	Knowledge of information assurance (IA) principles and organizational requirements to protect confidentiality, integrity, availability, authenticity, and non-repudiation of information and data.	Information assurance
64	KSA	Knowledge of information security systems engineering principles.	Information systems/ network security

(Continued)

Table 4.5 (Continued)   Systems Requirements Planning Specialty Area KSAs

Item ID	KSA	Statement	Competency
65	KSA	Knowledge of information theory, including source coding, channel coding, algorithm complexity theory, and data compression.	Mathematical reasoning
68	KSA	Knowledge of information technology (IT) architectural concepts and frameworks.	Information technology architecture
78	KSA	Knowledge of microprocessors.	Computers and electronics
79	KSA	Knowledge of network access, identity, and access management (e.g., public key infrastructure [PKI]).	Identity management
81	KSA	Knowledge of network protocols (e.g., Transmission Critical Protocol/Internet Protocol [TCP/IP], Dynamic Host Configuration Protocol [DHCP]), and directory services (e.g., Domain Name System [DNS]).	Infrastructure design
82	KSA	Knowledge of network design processes, including security objectives, operational objectives, and tradeoffs.	Infrastructure design
88	KSA	Knowledge of new and emerging information technology (IT) and cyber security technologies.	Technology awareness
90	KSA	Knowledge of operating systems.	Operating systems
92	KSA	Knowledge of how traffic flows across the network (e.g., Transmission Control Protocol and Internet Protocol [TCP/IP], Open System Interconnection model [OSI]).	Infrastructure design
94	KSA	Knowledge of parallel and distributed computing concepts.	Information assurance
100	KSA	Knowledge of privacy impact assessments (PIA).	Personnel safety and security

(Continued)

Table 4.5 (Continued) Systems Requirements Planning Specialty Area KSAs

Item ID	KSA	Statement	Competency
101	KSA	Knowledge of process engineering concepts.	Logical systems design
110	KSA	Knowledge of key concepts in security management (e.g., release management, patch management).	Information assurance
124	KSA	Knowledge of system design tools, methods, and techniques, including automated systems analysis and design tools.	Logical systems design
126	KSA	Knowledge of system software and organizational design standards, policies, and authorized approaches (e.g., International Organization for Standardization [ISO] guidelines) relating to system design.	Requirements analysis
129	KSA	Knowledge of system life cycle management principles, including software security and usability.	Systems life cycle
130	KSA	Knowledge of systems testing and evaluation methods.	Systems testing and evaluation
133	KSA	Knowledge of key telecommunication concepts (e.g., routing algorithms, fiber optics systems link budgeting, add/drop multiplexers).	Telecommunications
143	KSA	Knowledge of the organization's enterprise information technology (IT) goals and objectives.	Enterprise architecture
144	KSA	Knowledge of the systems engineering process.	Systems life cycle
155	KSA	Skill in applying and incorporating information technologies into proposed solutions.	Technology awareness
156	KSA	Skill in applying confidentiality, integrity, and availability principles.	Information assurance

(Continued)

Table 4.5 (Continued) Systems Requirements Planning Specialty Area KSAs

Item ID	KSA	Statement	Competency
158	KSA	Skill in applying organization-specific systems analysis principles and techniques.	Systems testing and evaluation
162	KSA	Skill in conducting capabilities and requirements analysis.	Requirements analysis
224	KSA	Skill in design modeling and building use cases (e.g., unified modeling language).	Modeling and simulation
229	KSA	Skill in using incident handling methodologies.	Incident management
911	KSA	Ability to interpret and translate customer requirements into operational cyber actions.	Requirements analysis
1002	KSA	Skill in conducting audits or reviews of technical systems.	Information technology Performance assessment
1004	KSA	Knowledge of critical IT procurement requirements.	Contracting/procurement
1005	KSA	Knowledge of functionality, quality, and security requirements and how these will apply to specific items of supply (i.e., elements and processes).	Contracting/procurement
1036	KSA	Knowledge of applicable laws (e.g., Electronic Communications Privacy Act, Foreign Intelligence Surveillance Act, Protect America Act, search and seizure laws, civil liberties and privacy laws), US Statutes (e.g., Titles 10,18, 32, 50 in US Code), Presidential Directives, executive branch guidelines, and/or administrative/criminal legal guidelines and procedures relevant to work performed.	Criminal law
1037	KSA	Knowledge of information technology (IT) supply chain security and risk management policies, requirements, and procedures.	Risk management

(Continued)

Table 4.5 (Continued) Systems Requirements Planning Specialty Area KSAs

Item ID	KSA	Statement	Competency
1038	KSA	Knowledge of local specialized system requirements (e.g., critical infrastructure systems that may not use standard IT) for safety, performance, and reliability.	Infrastructure design
1039	KSA	Skill in evaluating the trustworthiness of the supplier and/or product.	Contracting/procurement
1040	KSA	Knowledge of relevant laws, policies, procedures, or governance related to work impacting critical infrastructure.	Criminal law
1073	KSA	Knowledge of network systems management principles, models, methods (e.g., end-to-end systems performance monitoring), and tools.	Network management
1133	KSA	Knowledge of service management concepts for networks and related standards (e.g., Information Technology Infrastructure Library, v3 [ITIL]).	Network management
1141	KSA	Knowledge of an organization's information classification program and procedures for level information loss.	Information management

Specialty Area 6: Test and Evaluation

Before beginning this discussion, it should be noted that testing is done throughout the entire system development and deployment process. Unit testing is completed by coders who are responsible for programming the software artifacts. Integration testing is completed by the development team to measure for compatibility at the point that all components of the systems are developed. Acceptance testing (sometimes called beta testing) is performed by a sample of the customer base, just before system deployment. The NICE framework describes this specialty area suggesting that the development team "Develops and conducts tests of systems to evaluate compliance with specifications and requirements by applying principles and methods for cost-effective planning, evaluating, verifying, and validating of technical, functional, and performance characteristics (including interoperability) of systems or elements of systems incorporating information technology (IT)" (NIST, 2013). This definition most closely relates to the activities associated with integration testing.

Test Readiness

Because the integration activity incorporates the fundamental software and hardware components of the product into a finished system, each of these items must be tested against their expressed requirements. The framework requires a documented set of test results for each qualification requirement of the system. Therefore, the developer must produce and document a set of tests and test procedures for conducting system qualification testing and must ensure that the integrated system is ready for the testing.

For each qualification requirement, the developer prepares and documents a set of tests, test cases (inputs, outputs, and test criteria), and test procedures for conducting qualification testing of the product. This process includes the development of a regression strategy that will be applied if retesting is required. The developer then ensures that the integrated system is ready for system qualification testing. The integrated system is evaluated for test readiness based on the degree of test coverage, appropriateness of test methods and standards, conformance to expected results, and feasibility of system qualification testing, preparation, and maintenance.

Functional and Security Testing

It is common knowledge that any ICT systems being developed or undergoing software, hardware, and/or communication modification must be tested and evaluated before being implemented. That activity is contained within any life cycle methodology that an organization adopts. The objective of the test and evaluation process is to validate that the developed ICT system is consistent with functional and security requirements defined in the requirements specifications.

All testing is completed based on a text of test plans containing test cases for each function or security requirement. The test case provides scenarios describing how the system will be used. Testing is performed by applying each scenario to the system in order to verify accuracy of response. In general the test cases should aim to ensure specificity, repeatability, and iteration. In the case of specificity, test results should indicate that relevant security requirements are developed as intended for use in their environment. For repeatability, the testing results should show that the test are capable of execution a series of times against an ICT system and yield similar results each time. Iteration testing requires that each system execute functional tests in whole or in part several times in order to achieve the level of compliance defined in the test plan. To this end, the test case results are published to ensure that the test process is repeatable and iterative. Any security functionality not tested during the functional or automated testing are examined to ensure compliance with the requirements during the explicit security control test and evaluation.

Important to note, only test data should be used during system development. Absolutely no operational, security-relevant, or personally identifiable information should be used in any system or software during development.

Qualification Testing

The purpose of systems qualification testing is to ensure that the implementation of each system requirement is certified compliant and that the system is ready for delivery. This process determines whether the end product has met the qualification criteria expressed in the design. Thus, the process must be rigorous to ensure that the function of each requirement is fully tested and documented.

While performing these tests, the developer must evaluate the design, code, tests, test results, and user documentation using traceability, external and internal consistency, appropriateness of the methodology and standards employed, and feasibility as criteria. As a result of the testing, a set of criteria is developed for evaluating compliance with the system requirements, and the integrated system is tested using the defined criteria. The test results are recorded, and the readiness of the system is assured. In conjunction with this activity, the developer is required to support and document any audits that might be required at this point.

If the end product of the development process is a system rather than software, the finished system must undergo qualification testing based on a set of system qualification requirements. Each deliverable system component is evaluated to assess compliance with the original requirements, and the system is evaluated to determine whether it is ready for delivery. Final decisions are generally based on traceability, external and internal consistency, appropriateness of the methodology and standards employed, and practical feasibility.

The testing results are documented for all stakeholders. The success of qualification testing is usually judged based on the demonstrated degree of test coverage of the system requirements, the subsequent conformance to expected results, and the product's feasibility of operation and maintenance, including readiness for delivery. To support this evaluation, the developer must conduct joint reviews and must audit any configuration items that had not been audited previously. The developer has to support these audit(s).

To support long-term CM, the developer has to establish a formal release baseline. That baseline records the approved design and code elements of each component as a single coherent entity. The standard stipulates that qualification testing may be only a verification or validation process. This provision is a practical concession to variability in the product delivery process. If all system elements pass their audits, the developer can begin the installation stage.

Factoring Test and Evaluation Workforce Tasks into the Cybersecurity Framework Functions

The case can be made, in addition to testing the functionality, validation, and verification of an ICT artifact. Testing procedures must be followed to ensure the security of the product under development. As important as the need that testing produces the assurance that the product meets the specified requirements, it is the responsibility of the quality assurance team to ensure that test cases are performed that lead to the conclusion that protocols established in the organizations risk management, continuity, response, and security plans are being met. This need for security qualification is clearly established within the outcomes and supporting controls of the CSF identify and protect functions. Interesting to note, however, there is only one task within the test and evaluation specialty area of the NICE framework that directly addresses the need for providing evidence that security measures are met. Although the level of abstraction at which NICE addresses testing for security is quite high, two forms of testing that the CSF puts significant emphasis, penetration testing and testing of system monitoring and monitoring tools, should be discussed.

Penetration Testing

Put simply, penetration testing is ethical hacking. If an organization has computers, with e-mail and Internet connections, their network is exposed. An organization's network can be self-contained or connected to other networks across the supply chain. All a hacker needs is an open window, in computer terms, a "port," which computers use to communicate. Hackers find weaknesses and try to exploit them. Penetration testing is just that—finding holes in an organization's network or communication with other networks and trying to exploit them. The only difference is intent. Hackers have malicious intentions. Penetration testers intend to find weaknesses and help get them fixed. Penetration testing is the process of testing whether the tools and technologies that ICT teams have purchased and put in place are actually working correctly to keep networks secure.

Penetration testing is a requirement of many regulatory bodies and established within the controls supporting identify, protect, and detect outcomes of the CSF. But the real value of penetration testing is to reduce risk. Consider the following benefits:

- It can help justify technical security expenditures being requested.
- It tests existing security controls.
- It tests existing incident detection and response procedures.
- It assesses whether sound practices exist.
- It meets compliance requirements (SOX recommendations, PCI requirements, etc.).
- It is a critical component to a data breach–prevention program.

System Monitoring Tool Testing

System monitoring is the means by which cybersecurity attacks are detected and response initiated in the most efficient manner. This is achieved through a variety of tools and techniques, for example, intrusion detection systems, intrusion prevention systems, malicious code protection software, audit record monitoring software, and network monitoring software. Organizations strategically place monitoring devices within the ICT system to capture important information about potential attacks and security changes within the system. The type and amount of the information collected is determined by the organization based on its risk management objectives.

NIST SP 800-53 states that "testing intrusion-monitoring tools is necessary to ensure that the tools are operating correctly and continue to meet the monitoring objectives of organizations. The frequency of testing depends on the types of tools used by organizations and methods of deployment" (NIST, 2014a). Figure 4.7 shows the test and evaluation specialty area mapped to the CSF.

Underlying Knowledge, Skill, and Ability Requirements for Test and Evaluation

The NICE framework provides a set of KSAs that you would expect of any quality assurance professional. These individuals must have knowledge and skills in creating and executing test plans that define procedures for assurance at the infrastructure, hardware, operating system, and software level. This includes the capability to perform a variety of tasks related to unit, integration system testing. In addition, the framework provides a greater degree of support then we saw of the tasks in our discussions in the previous section for the knowledge and skills necessary to provide security assurance to the ICT artifacts under development.

In order to test an artifact for security assurance, an individual must have adequate knowledge in the conceptual principles of information security/network

Securely provision general knowledge area Test and evaluation specialty area tasks NICE workforce framework	Cybersecurity framework
	Identify
	Protect
	Detect
	Respond
	Recover
412	Analyze the results of end-to-end testing (e.g., software, hardware, transport, seams, interfaces).
508	Determine level of assurance of developed capabilities based on test results.
550	Develop test plans to address specifications and requirements.
649	Make recommendations based on test results.
747	Perform conformance testing to assess whether a system complies with defined specifications or standards.
748	Perform developmental testing on systems being concurrently developed.
757	Perform interoperability testing on systems exchanging electronic information with systems of other organizations.
761	Perform operational testing to evaluate systems in an operational environment.
773	Perform validation testing to ensure requirements meet proposed specifications or standards and that correct specifications or standards are available.
858	Develop test bed environment to test and verify hardware and support peripherals to ensure that they meet specifications and requirements by recording and analyzing test data.
951	Determine scope, infrastructure, resources, and data sample size to ensure system requirements are adequately demonstrated.
1006	Create auditable evidence of security measures.
1156	Conduct and monitor independent validation and verification (IV&V) testing for software applications and systems.

Figure 4.7   Testing and evaluation specialty area tasks mapped to the CSF.

security and risk management. In addition to understanding confidentiality, integrity, and availability as they relates to ICT system, success in security assurance requires technical aptitude necessary to test capabilities of network topologies, implementation of proper secure networking protocols, and technical capabilities of a variety of other network components.

To state that an individual with responsibility in assuring the security of ICT artifacts need only knowledge and skills learned in an educational setting, may be cutting ourselves short. Granted, information system and information assurance knowledge is important. However, the individual with this responsibility must also have adequate knowledge of the risk management, business continuity, and response policies of the organization, in addition to an in-depth understanding of the system requirements in order to test the artifact for assurance that it meets the standards established by the organization and satisfies the requirements defined in the system specifications. Table 4.6 displays the entire set of specialty KSA requirements and associated competencies for the test and evaluation specialty area (all from the NICE framework).

Specialty Area 7: Systems Development

Systems development is probably the process that is most commonly associated with the discipline of software engineering because the formal description methodologies that are used to create the system are typically utilized by software engineers. In this phase, the developer produces the technical design for each component itemized in the architectural design and ensures that all requirements are directly traceable to a component that is being built at this stage. This activity is iterative; the depiction of all system components is successively refined, so they can be represented at the coding and testing stage.

The requirement for constructing the external and internal interfaces is the same for the implementation phase as it is for the architectural design. The developer creates and documents an explicit design for all external and internal interfaces, including those between the components themselves. A quirk in the typical system development process should probably be explained here. In the conventional manufacturing model for the ICT components, the person or team that is responsible for the technical design will probably not do the coding. Therefore, the technical design should be as self-sustaining as possible and should not require continuous "walking back and forth" between teams that could even be located on different continents. Therefore the design should be unambiguously understandable to all participants.

As in the architectural design phase, the developer also produces a technical design for the database and updates the user documentation as necessary. At this point, the developer needs to define and document the testing milestones and requirements for each component in the technical design. Once these review points

Table 4.6   Test and Evaluation Specialty Area KSAs

Item ID	KSA	Statement	Competency
38	KSA	Knowledge of organization's enterprise information security architecture system.	Information assurance
40	KSA	Knowledge of agency evaluation and validation requirements.	Systems testing and evaluation
53	KSA	Knowledge of the security assessment and authorization (SA&A) process.	Information assurance
63	KSA	Knowledge of information assurance (IA) principles and organizational requirements to protect confidentiality, integrity, availability, authenticity, and non-repudiation of information and data.	Information assurance
81	KSA	Knowledge of network protocols (e.g., Transmission Critical Protocol/Internet Protocol [TCP/IP], Dynamic Host Configuration Protocol [DHCP]), and directory services (e.g., Domain Name System [DNS]).	Infrastructure design
83	KSA	Knowledge of network hardware devices and functions.	Hardware
127	KSA	Knowledge of systems administration concepts.	Operating systems
144	KSA	Knowledge of the systems engineering process.	Systems life cycle
169	KSA	Skill in conducting test events.	Systems testing and evaluation
176	KSA	Skill in designing a data analysis structure (i.e., the types of data your test must generate and how to analyze those data).	Systems testing and evaluation
182	KSA	Skill in determining an appropriate level of test rigor for a given system.	Systems testing and evaluation
190	KSA	Skill in developing operations-based testing scenarios.	Systems testing and evaluation

(Continued)

Table 4.6 **(Continued) Test and Evaluation Specialty Area KSAs**

Item ID	KSA	Statement	Competency
220	KSA	Skill in systems integration testing.	Systems testing and evaluation
239	KSA	Skill in writing test plans.	Systems testing and evaluation
904	KSA	Knowledge of interpreted and compiled computer languages.	Computer languages
950	KSA	Skill in evaluating test plans for applicability and completeness.	Systems testing and evaluation
1034	KSA	Knowledge of personally identifiable information (PII) and payment card industry (PCI) data security standards.	Security
1037	KSA	Knowledge of information technology (IT) supply chain security and risk management policies, requirements, and procedures.	Risk management
1038	KSA	Knowledge of local specialized system requirements (e.g., critical infrastructure systems that may not use standard IT) for safety, performance, and reliability.	Infrastructure design
1072	KSA	Knowledge of network security architecture concepts, including topology, protocols, components, and principles (e.g., application of defense-in-depth).	Information systems/network security

are known, a reasonable schedule for testing each component can be defined. Ultimately, all deliverables in this phase should be evaluated based on the common criteria of traceability, external and internal consistency, appropriateness of the methodology and standards employed, and feasibility.

Once the technical design is confirmed to be correct, it is turned over to the people who do the actual construction. System construction is where the coders get involved in the development process. The developer builds the component or writes the code for each required component and then creates a full set of documentation for each item. Then, the test procedures that were defined in both the architectural and detail design phases are conducted, and the data from each test is recorded. Once development is complete, the developer conducts joint reviews among stakeholders to validate the build. Next, the developer again updates the user documentation, updates the test requirements if necessary, and schedules the necessary integration.

In the systems development specialty area, the NICE framework defines tasks associated with the discussion above. However, the framework puts emphasis on integrating security into standard system development activities. A handy resource for understanding the security implications of the development process is NIST SP 800-64, *Security Considerations in the System Development Life Cycle*. The main security tasks defined by the framework for this specialty area are

- Conduct the risk assessment and use the results to supplement the baseline security controls identified in the requirements phase.
- Analyze security requirements and design the appropriate artifacts that meet those requirements.
- Perform functional and security testing.
- Prepare documents supporting the security design and information assurance activities.
- Design security architecture.

The order in which these and other security-related activities are performed during development is not fixed. Security analysis of complex systems is an iterative process and continues indefinitely, or until consistency and completeness is achieved.

Risk Assessment

The objective of a risk assessment is to evaluate what is currently known of the system's design, documented functional requirements, and documented security requirements resulting from the security categorization process to determine their ability to minimize risk. The outcomes of this process should be able to show that defined security controls put into place can provide the necessary protection or highlight areas where further consideration is needed. The key to success of the assessment process includes stakeholders with knowledge in each of the area of the system domain (e.g., users, technology experts, operations experts). Risk assessment should always be done before the design specifications are approved. This allows for the possibility of additional specifications. Similarly, organizations should take into account how system will affect other systems that are connected to it. This may lead to the identification of inherited common controls or identify other risks that need consideration.

Considering all of the types of risk, internal threats remain the highest probability. Exploitation by employees, who are also privileged users of the system, is a real threat. Security policy within the organization should include independent audits of the system and its supporting processes. Continuously monitoring internal activities and using integrity tools to ensure configuration audit and control are one way of providing an automated central audit log collection, correlation, and analysis tool.

Another consideration should be risks resulting from systems with multiple owners. It is important to identify and address shared and inherited risks. Depending on the amount of security necessary the complexity of the system, it may also be beneficial to follow the data flow/information sharing beyond the first interface. Not doing so may result in inheriting unknown risks. Other inherited risks may be evaluated through the supply chains. Supply chain risk should be understood and evaluated to minimize potential use of fraudulent, pirated, unlicensed, or intentionally compromised material.

Selection and Documentation of Security Controls

The selection and documentation of security controls should be consistent with the organization's risk management plan. The selection of security controls consists of three activities:

1. Selection baseline security controls
2. Application of security controls providing the capability to adjust the initial security control baseline
3. Implementation of alternatives of the defined baseline with additional controls based on risk assessment and local conditions

Important to note, complete organization-wide "buy-in" is vital in the selection of security controls. This common view will ultimately ensure that risk minimization is achieved throughout all business processes and ICT systems supporting those business processes.

The security control selection process should include consideration of laws and regulations in which the organization must abide, such as FISMA, HIPPA, industry-specific governance regulations, or FIPS and other legislation and federal regulations that define applicable specifics to the security controls selected.

Common sense security planning suggests that the goal should be cost-effective implementation that meets the requirements for protection of an organization's information assets. In each situation, a balance should exist between the benefits of the security control and the risks associated with operation of the system.

The security controls protecting each individual ICT system must be documented in the system security plan. Security plan provides a single source of the security requirements for the ICT systems within an organization and describes the security controls implemented or currently being planned. The plan provides rationale for security categorization, application, and supplemental activities, in how each individual control is implemented within the organization's operational environment, and the defined restrictions on ICT systems as a result of risky situations. Security plans are useful for management in that they document the decisions taken during the security control selection process and the rationale for those decisions. They are approved by appropriate authorizing officials within the organization and provide one of the key documents in security accreditation influential in authorization decisions.

Security Architecture Design

With cloud computing and shared services on the rise, the movement toward centralizing key security controls within organizations is increasing. Further, it is becoming more important to plan such services and understand how they will be integrated in existing ICT systems.

Organization-wide alignment of ICT system must ensure that the systems continue to support the organization's long-term plans and does not create unnecessary duplication of controls. Moreover, as the complexity of the systems evolve and decisions made regarding the services provided, the architecture should also evolve to gain optimal integration.

From the system perspective, security should be architected and then engineered into the design of the system. Security designing takes into consideration services provided external to the organization, planned system integration, and the wide variation of users of the system (e.g., accounting versus ICT administrators).

A system auditing strategy should be developed to accurately trace or reconstruct priority and high-risk work flows. Included within the audit strategy should be audit records from various system components such as Web applications, databases, legacy systems, and Web servers. The thrust should be to gain as much audit information as possible but to retrieve only what is needed to provide enough information for investigation of potential security breaches and system failures.

Supporting Document

Perhaps the most important document, at least from the security perspective, is the system security plan. However, there are several other documents that support it, including:

- CM plan
- Contingency plan

- Continuous monitoring plan
- Security awareness, training, and education plan
- Incident response plan
- Privacy impact assessment

It is essential that each of these documents take into consideration all of the security controls being implemented. In some cases, these documents will provide details related to known requirements, common controls, and templates, thus leaving gaps that must be filled as early as possible during the project.

Through the documentation, the key is to affirm the security approach, the scope by which security controls are implemented, and an understanding of roles and responsibilities. The process of documentation, however, should not be left until the development phase of the life cycle. Providing the appropriate plans and documentation as the system development progresses can provide cost savings and enhance decision-making capabilities through a comprehensive approach that allows early detection of error, risks, or constraints.

Factoring Systems Development Workforce Tasks into the Cybersecurity Framework Functions

In consideration of the high level of abstraction at which the CSF is written, combined with frequent reference to organization level processes, a common misconception is that much of the work in implementing controls that satisfy the outcomes is primarily performed at some level of management. To the contrary, in most organizations management merely provides the oversight for security planning and implementation. The majority of the control implementation is performed by individuals directly working within each life cycle process. It is for that reason there is such as strong relationship between many of the outcomes defined by the CSF protect function and tasks identified by the systems development specialty area of the NICE framework.

There is just one task of this specialty area that is an exception to what was stated above. Building from the assumption that an organization already has security policies, a risk management plan, business continuity plan, and response plan in place, we need to consider that ICT products evolve over time. As such the NICE framework aligns with the identify function in defining a task that addresses the need for system developers to identify design constraints, trade-offs, along with system and security designs to identify the needed life cycle support.

According to NICE, the system developer is then responsible for performing risk assessment activities including threat and vulnerability identification and risk prioritization. Once risk assessment is performed, the developer is responsible for assisting management in updating the risk management plan and security policies that support new risks resulting from the development and implementation of new ICT artifacts.

On the basis of the understanding of the threats and vulnerabilities identified of the new ICT solution, the developer must implement protective mechanisms based on established organizational security plans and standards to protect the system from those risks. For example, the NICE framework states that the system developer must "Develop information assurance (IA) designs to meet specific operational needs and environmental factors (e.g., access controls, automated applications, networked operations, high integrity and availability requirements, multilevel security/processing of multiple classification levels, and processing Sensitive Compartmented Information [SCI])" (NIST, 2013). Once those protective mechanisms are in place, the developer must update and test response and recovery plans, in addition to updating configuration baselines.

Most organizations purchase "off-the-shelf" security incident detection system (IDS). However, the NICE framework recognizes that once an IDS is purchased, system developers are responsible for customizing the detection system to meet the needs of the organization based on identified threats and vulnerabilities. In some cases, the organization cannot afford or chooses not to purchase an IDS. As such, it is the system developer's responsibility to design and develop the appropriate system monitoring tools that adequately detect potential system exploitation. Figure 4.8 shows the systems development specialty area mapped to the CSF.

Underlying Knowledge, Skill, and Ability Requirements for Systems Development

Considering the discussions we have had in each of the previous sections of the NICE systems development specialty area, a somewhat humorous conclusion that can be made is that a developer must have the knowledge and skills of a "Jack of all trades." Based on the KSAs defined for this specialty area and the realities that exist in industry, that characterization is not too far-fetched.

Important to note, with the exception of testing and evaluation, systems development tasks pick up where system requirement leaves off (though they are both part of the SDLC) and carry the process forward to system realization. As such, the system developer must have hardware, software, telecommunications, and technology skills necessary to perform any of the development tasks. In addition, the developer must have the knowledge of information assurance/cybersecurity and their organization's priorities related to information assurance and cybersecurity to the extent that they can design and develop security mechanisms to support those organizational objectives. Similarly, the developer must be familiar with the risk management plans and security policies of the organization in order to update those plans as new development takes place. Table 4.7 displays the entire set of

Cybersecurity framework

Identify
Protect
Detect
Respond
Recover

Securely provision general knowledge area
Systems development specialty area tasks
NICE workforce framework

#	Task
416	Analyzes design constraints, trade-offs, and detailed system and security designs to identify necessary life cycle support.
419	Apply security policies to applications that interface with one another, such as business-to-business (B2B) applications.
425	Assess the effectiveness of information protection measures utilized by system(s).
426	Assess threats to and vulnerabilities of computer system(s) to develop a security risk profile.
431	Build, test, and modify product prototypes using working models or theoretical models.
457	Conduct privacy impact analysis (PIA) of the applications security design for the appropriate security controls, which protect the confidentiality and integrity of personal identifiable information (PII).
494	Design and develop information assurance (IA) or IA-enabled tools.
495	Design and develop secure interface specifications between interconnected systems.
496	Design, develop, integrate, and update system security measures (including policies and requirements) that provide confidentiality, integrity, availability, authentication, and nonrepudiation.
500	Design hardware, operating systems, and software applications to adequately addresses IA security requirements.
501	Design or integrate appropriate data backup capabilities into overall system designs, and ensure appropriate technical and procedural processes exist for secure system backups and protected storage of backup data.
503	Design systems to the minimum security requirements to ensure requirements are met for all systems and/or applications.
516	Develop and oversee system testing and validation procedures and documentation.

Figure 4.8 Systems development specialty area tasks mapped to the CSF.

Securely provision general knowledge area
Systems development specialty area tasks
NICE workforce framework

Cybersecurity framework

| Identify |
| Protect |
| Detect |
| Respond |
| Recover |

#	Task
527	Develop architectures or system components consistent with technical specifications.
530	Develop detailed security design documentation for component and interface specifications to support system design and development
531	Develop disaster recovery and continuity of operations plans for systems under development, and ensure testing prior to systems entering a production environment.
542	Develop risk mitigation strategies to resolve vulnerabilities and recommend security changes to system or system components as needed.
547	Develop specific information assurance (IA) countermeasures and risk mitigation strategies for systems and/or applications.
626	Identify components or elements, allocate security functions to those elements, and describe the relationships between the elements.
630	Identify and direct the remediation of technical problems encountered during testing and implementation of new systems (e.g., identify and find workarounds for communication protocols that are not interoperable).
632	Identify and prioritize essential system functions or subsystems, as may be necessary to support essential capabilities or business functions; in the event of system failure or system recovery, observe, and adhere to overall system requirements for continuity and availability.
648	Identify, assess, and recommend IA or IA-enabled products for use within a system and ensure recommended products are in compliance with organization's evaluation and validation requirements.
659	Implement security designs for new or existing system(s).
662	Incorporate information assurance IA vulnerability solutions into system designs (e.g., IA vulnerability alerts).
737	Perform an information security risk assessment and design security countermeasures to mitigate identified risks.
766	Perform security reviews and identify security gaps in security architecture.
770	Perform risk analysis (e.g., threat, vulnerability, and probability of occurrence) whenever an application or system undergoes a major change.
803	Provide guidelines for implementing developed systems to customers or installation teams.

Figure 4.8 (*Continued*) Systems development specialty area tasks mapped to the CSF.

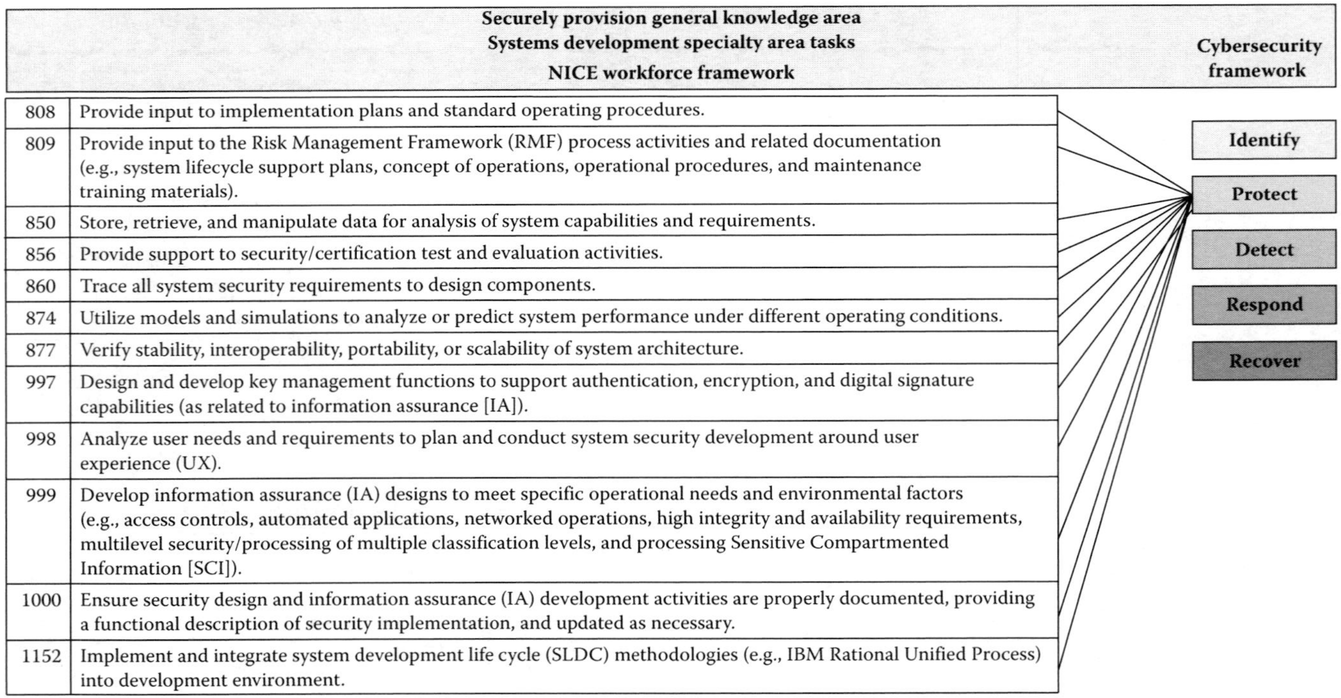

	Securely provision general knowledge area Systems development specialty area tasks NICE workforce framework	Cybersecurity framework Identify / Protect / Detect / Respond / Recover
808	Provide input to implementation plans and standard operating procedures.	
809	Provide input to the Risk Management Framework (RMF) process activities and related documentation (e.g., system lifecycle support plans, concept of operations, operational procedures, and maintenance training materials).	
850	Store, retrieve, and manipulate data for analysis of system capabilities and requirements.	
856	Provide support to security/certification test and evaluation activities.	
860	Trace all system security requirements to design components.	
874	Utilize models and simulations to analyze or predict system performance under different operating conditions.	
877	Verify stability, interoperability, portability, or scalability of system architecture.	
997	Design and develop key management functions to support authentication, encryption, and digital signature capabilities (as related to information assurance [IA]).	
998	Analyze user needs and requirements to plan and conduct system security development around user experience (UX).	
999	Develop information assurance (IA) designs to meet specific operational needs and environmental factors (e.g., access controls, automated applications, networked operations, high integrity and availability requirements, multilevel security/processing of multiple classification levels, and processing Sensitive Compartmented Information [SCI]).	
1000	Ensure security design and information assurance (IA) development activities are properly documented, providing a functional description of security implementation, and updated as necessary.	
1152	Implement and integrate system development life cycle (SLDC) methodologies (e.g., IBM Rational Unified Process) into development environment.	

Figure 4.8 (*Continued*) Systems development specialty area tasks mapped to the CSF.

Table 4.7   Systems Development Specialty Area KSAs

Item ID	KSA	Statement	Competency
3	KSA	Skill in conducting vulnerability scans and recognizing vulnerabilities in security systems.	Vulnerabilities assessment
8	KSA	Knowledge of authentication, authorization, and access control methods.	Identity management
21	KSA	Knowledge of computer algorithms.	Mathematical reasoning
25	KSA	Knowledge of encryption algorithms (e.g., Internet Protocol Security [IPSEC], Advanced Encryption Standard [AES], Generic Routing Encapsulation [GRE], Internet Key Exchange [IKE], Message Digest Algorithm [MD5], Secure Hash Algorithm [SHA], Triple Data Encryption Standard [3DES]).	Cryptography
27	KSA	Knowledge of cryptography and cryptographic key management concepts.	Cryptography
34	KSA	Knowledge of database systems.	Database management systems
38	KSA	Knowledge of organization's enterprise information security architecture system.	Information assurance
40	KSA	Knowledge of organization's evaluation and validation requirements.	Systems testing and evaluation
42	KSA	Knowledge of electrical engineering as applied to computer architecture, including circuit boards, processors, chips, and associated computer hardware.	Hardware engineering
43	KSA	Knowledge of embedded systems and Internet of things.	Embedded computers
46	KSA	Knowledge of fault tolerance.	Information assurance

(Continued)

Table 4.7 (Continued) Systems Development Specialty Area KSAs

Item ID	KSA	Statement	Competency
51	KSA	Knowledge of how system components are installed, integrated, and optimized.	Systems integration
52	KSA	Knowledge of human-computer interaction principles.	Human factors
63	KSA	Knowledge of information assurance (IA) principles and organizational requirements to protect confidentiality, integrity, availability, authenticity, and non-repudiation of information and data.	Information assurance
64	KSA	Knowledge of information security systems engineering principles.	Information systems/network security
65	KSA	Knowledge of information theory, including source coding, channel coding, algorithm complexity theory, and data compression.	Mathematical reasoning
70	KSA	Knowledge of information technology (IT) security principles and methods (e.g., firewalls, demilitarized zones, encryption).	Information systems/network security
72	KSA	Knowledge of local area network (LAN) and wide area network (WAN) principles and concepts, including bandwidth management.	Infrastructure design
75	KSA	Knowledge of mathematics, including logarithms, trigonometry, linear algebra, calculus, and statistics.	Mathematical reasoning
78	KSA	Knowledge of microprocessors.	Computers and electronics
79	KSA	Knowledge of network access, identity, and access management (e.g., public key infrastructure [PKI]).	Identity management

(Continued)

Table 4.7 (Continued) Systems Development Specialty Area KSAs

Item ID	KSA	Statement	Competency
81	KSA	Knowledge of network protocols (e.g., Transmission Critical Protocol/Internet Protocol [TCP/IP], Dynamic Host Configuration Protocol [DHCP]), and directory services (e.g., Domain Name System [DNS]).	Infrastructure design
82	KSA	Knowledge of network design processes, including security objectives, operational objectives, and trade-offs.	Infrastructure design
90	KSA	Knowledge of operating systems.	Operating systems
92	KSA	Knowledge of how traffic flows across the network (e.g., Transmission Control Protocol and Internet Protocol [TCP/IP], Open System Interconnection model [OSI]).	Infrastructure design
94	KSA	Knowledge of parallel and distributed computing concepts.	Information assurance
98	KSA	Knowledge of policy-based and risk-adaptive access controls.	Identity management
100	KSA	Knowledge of privacy impact assessments (PIA).	Personnel safety and security
101	KSA	Knowledge of process engineering concepts.	Logical systems design
109	KSA	Knowledge of secure configuration management techniques.	Configuration management
110	KSA	Knowledge of key concepts in security management (e.g., release management, patch management).	Information assurance
118	KSA	Knowledge of software development models (e.g., Waterfall Model, Spiral Model, Agile Model).	Software engineering
119	KSA	Knowledge of software engineering.	Software engineering
121	KSA	Knowledge of structured analysis principles and methods.	Logical systems design
124	KSA	Knowledge of system design tools, methods, and techniques, including automated systems analysis and design tools.	Logical systems design

(Continued)

Table 4.7 (Continued)   Systems Development Specialty Area KSAs

Item ID	KSA	Statement	Competency
126	KSA	Knowledge of system software and organizational design standards, policies, and authorized approaches (e.g., International Organization for Standardization [ISO] guidelines) relating to system design.	Requirements analysis
129	KSA	Knowledge of system life cycle management principles, including software security and usability.	Systems life cycle
130	KSA	Knowledge of systems testing and evaluation methods.	Systems testing and evaluation
133	KSA	Knowledge of key telecommunication concepts (e.g., routing algorithms, fiber optics systems link budgeting, add/drop multiplexers).	Telecommunications
144	KSA	Knowledge of the systems engineering process.	Systems life cycle
173	KSA	Skill in creating policies that reflect system security objectives.	Information systems security certification
177	KSA	Skill in designing countermeasures to identified security risks.	Vulnerabilities assessment
179	KSA	Skill in designing security controls based on information assurance (IA) principles and tenets.	Information assurance
180	KSA	Skill in designing the integration of hardware and software solutions.	Systems integration
191	KSA	Skill in developing and applying security system access controls.	Identity management
197	KSA	Skill in discerning the protection needs (i.e., security controls) of information systems and networks.	Information systems/network security
199	KSA	Skill in evaluating the adequacy of security designs.	Vulnerabilities assessment
224	KSA	Skill in design modeling and building use cases (e.g., unified modeling language).	Modeling and simulation

(Continued)

Table 4.7 (Continued) Systems Development Specialty Area KSAs

Item ID	KSA	Statement	Competency
904	KSA	Knowledge of interpreted and compiled computer languages.	Computer languages
1002	KSA	Skill in conducting audits or reviews of technical systems.	Information technology performance assessment
1034	KSA	Knowledge of personally identifiable information (PII) and payment card industry (PCI) data security standards.	Security
1037	KSA	Knowledge of information technology (IT) supply chain security and risk management policies, requirements, and procedures.	Risk management
1038	KSA	Knowledge of local specialized system requirements (e.g., critical infrastructure systems that may not use standard IT) for safety, performance, and reliability.	Infrastructure design
1072	KSA	Knowledge of network security architecture concepts, including topology, protocols, components, and principles (e.g., application of defense-in-depth).	Information systems/network security
1073	KSA	Knowledge of network systems management principles, models, methods (e.g., end-to-end systems performance monitoring), and tools.	Network management
1133	KSA	Knowledge of service management concepts for networks and related standards (e.g., Information Technology Infrastructure Library, v3 [ITIL]).	Network management
1141	KSA	Knowledge of an organization's information classification program and procedures for level information loss.	Information management
1142	KSA	Knowledge of security models (e.g., Bell-LaPadula model, Biba integrity model, Clark-Wilson integrity model).	Enterprise architecture

(Continued)

specialty KSA requirements and associated competencies for the systems development specialty area (all from the NICE framework).

Chapter Summary

There are many system/software methodologies that have been used by organizations to effectively design and develop entire ICT systems and system artifacts. Regardless of the method used, processes related to secure acquisition, SSE, systems security architecture, technology research and development, systems requirements planning, test and evaluation, and systems development are vital to success of any ICT project. The securely provision knowledge area of NICE framework provides the tasks that should be performed within each process in addition to the knowledge and skills necessary to perform the process tasks in order to produce a secure system that meets organizational security standards.

The secure acquisition specialty area provides the tasks and KSAs that provide the management and support of the system acquisition life cycle, including planning, determining specifications, selecting, and procuring ICT and cybersecurity products used in the organization's design, development, and maintenance of its infrastructure to minimize potential risks and vulnerabilities. Such risks and vulnerabilities cannot be considered in isolation. Consideration must be taken into how the acquired artifact will affect the risk implications of the entire supply chain.

Within the software engineering specialty area, the framework provides tasks and activities that follow software assurance best practices throughout the software life cycle. This includes the development, modification, enhancements, and sustainment of new or existing computer applications, software or utility programs. Tasks and knowledge related to the design and development system concepts are the focus of the framework system development specialty area. Most of the tasks and KSAs are directly aligned with the capability phases of the systems development life cycle. In addition, the framework emphasizes the necessity for the ability to translate technology and environmental conditions (e.g., laws, regulations, best practices) into system and security designs and processes.

The NICE framework provides tasks in the technology research and development specialty area that provides the means for such a strategy that impacts the technological security of each system life cycle process. To that end, the tasks and KSAs not only focus on the ability to provide IT solutions that take advantage of the newest trends in technology, but also address the need for adequate security protection provided by that technology. Organizations must employ individuals who provide the aptitude for researching technological trends and providing decision makers the information they need to ensure that the technology used will provide the level of security that meets established organizational standards.

Systems requirements planning involves tasks associated with consulting with customers to gather and evaluate functional requirements and translates these requirements into technical solutions. In addition, individuals working within this life cycle process must have the skills necessary to provide guidance to customers about applicability of information systems to meet business needs from a functional and security perspective.

The test and evaluation specialty area of the NICE framework defines the tasks and KSAs necessary to develop and conduct tests of systems to evaluate compliance with specifications and requirements by applying principles and methods for cost-effective planning; evaluating; verifying; and validating technical, functional, and performance characteristics (including interoperability) of systems or elements of systems incorporating ICT. In addition to the testing of systems, tasks within this specialty area also address the need for testing the plans that the organization enforces to implement risk management and security control mechanisms.

Systems development is much more than programming (as many lacking knowledge of ICT believe). With the exception of test and evaluation, this specialty area defines the tasks and KSAs related to all life cycle processes from the point that requirements are identified and documented to ICT solution realization. In particular, the focus of this area of the framework is on the design and development of technical security solutions to meet the defined requirements.

Key Terms

Acquisition Life Cycle: Process in which systems and software are contracted and acquired from the supplier.

Authentication: Security mechanism that verifies system user access privileges.

Availability: One of three core system security objectives, in which assurance is provided that the system or software can be accessed.

Business Continuity Plan: Policies and procedures that define steps taken to keep the business operational in the face of security attack.

Confidentiality: One of three core system security objectives, in which assurance is provided that the data and information processed and stored by the system will be kept private.

Cryptography: Security methodology that serves to preserve confidentiality of data by using algorithms and binary keys to put the data into an undecipherable format during transmission.

IaaS: One form of service-oriented architecture in which infrastructure is provided on demand.

Integrity: One of three core system security objectives, in which assurance is provided that data and information processed and stored by the system will not be tampered and/or modified.

Public Key Infrastructure: Most widely used method of encrypting data by using binary algorithms.

Recovery Plan: A documented set of processes and procedures that guide an organization toward recuperation from the effects of a security incident.

Response Plan: A documented set of processes and procedures that guide an organization in acting upon the report of a security incident.

Risk Management Plan: A document providing guidelines that assist an organization in the process of identifying, assessing, and responding to risk.

Risk Mitigation: The understanding of risks that can impact the objectives of the organization and taking the appropriate steps to reduce the risks to an acceptable level.

Role-Based Access Control: A method of regulating access to computer or network resources based on the roles of individual users within an enterprise.

Service-Oriented Architecture: An approach used to create a system architecture based on the use of services. The services carry out some small functions, such as producing data, validating a customer, or providing simple analytical services.

Software Assurance: The level of confidence that software is free from vulnerabilities, either intentionally designed into the software or accidentally inserted at any time during its life cycle, and that the software functions in the intended manner.

Stakeholder: Any individual or business that has a monetary or functional interest in the security of an ICT system.

Supply Chains: All parties involved, directly or indirectly, in fulfilling a customer request. The supply chain not only includes the manufacturer and suppliers, but also transporters, warehouses, retailers, and customers themselves.

Supply Chain Risk Management: The practice of collaborating with partners in a supply chain in an effort to apply risk management process tools to deal with risks and uncertainties caused by identified threats and vulnerabilities.

System Development Life Cycle: The sequence of processes in the development of an information communication technology system or individual application, which requires mutual effort on the part of both the user and technical staff.

Threat: Anything or anyone capable of causing harm, through exploitation, to an ICT system.

Threat Assessment: The process in which threats are identified, categorized, and prioritized in terms of the potential harm they can cause to an ICT system.

Vulnerability: A weakness within the ICT system that allows an attacker to access and cause harm.

References

Chandra, Pravir. 2009. *Software Assurance Maturity Model.* Version 1.0.

International Organization for Standardization (ISO). 2005. ANSI/ISO/ASQ Q9000-2005: *Quality Management Systems—Fundamentals and Vocabulary*, Geneva, Switzerland: International Organization for Standardization.

International Organization for Standardization (ISO). 2008. ISO/IEC 12207:2008 *Systems and Software Engineering—Software Life Cycle Processes.* Geneva, Switzerland: International Organization for Standardization.

National Institute of Standards and Technology (NIST). 2013. *National Initiative for Cybersecurity Education Framework.* Gaithersburg, MD: National Institute of Standards and Technology.

National Institute for Standards and Technology (NIST). 2014a. NIST SP 800-53 Rev 4: *Security and Privacy Controls for Federal Information Systems and Organizations.* Gaithersburg, MD: National Institute of Standards and Technology.

National Institute of Standards and Technology (NIST). 2014b. *Framework for Improving Critical Infrastructure Cybersecurity.* Gaithersburg, MD: National Institute of Standards and Technology.

Chapter 5

Operate and Maintain

Chapter Ojectives

At the conclusion of this chapter, the reader will understand:

- The justification and contents of the operation and maintenance domains
- The focus and purpose of the operate and maintain specialty areas
- The focus and purpose of the operate and maintain knowledge area
- The relationship between the operate and maintain specialty areas and the National Institute of Standards and Technology (NIST) cybersecurity framework (CSF)

Around the world, many countries are experiencing severe infrastructure needs, owing to growing populations, economic growth, increasing urbanization, and aging legacy assets. While demands are skyrocketing, supply is impeded by various factors, resulting in a global investment gap of about $1 trillion per year.

To bridge the gap, most governments and industries emphasize constructing new assets, but this strategy is not a "silver-bullet" solution; after all, public-budget constraints exist, as do multiple difficulties in getting projects from idea to implementation in a reasonable time frame. A complementary and potentially more cost-effective approach is to improve the utilization, efficiency, and longevity of the existing infrastructure stock—in short, to make the most of existing assets by means of optimal operations and maintenance. To do so, however, requires individuals with the knowledge and skills that can adequately perform the roles of operations and maintenance while providing support for the organizations risk management strategies through the implementation of cybersecurity controls and frameworks.

Recall from the discussions of the National Initiative for Cybersecurity Education (NICE) framework securely provision knowledge area introduced in Chapter 4, the specialty areas conform to the supply, acquisition, requirements analysis, design, and development tasks of the system development life cycle (SDLC). This chapter can be articulated as picking up where Chapter 4 leaves off, by providing discussions of the last two phases (operations and maintenance) of the life cycle.

Operate and Maintain Knowledge Area Overview

The purpose of the system operation process is to maintain the required level of performance of the information and communication technology (ICT) product during its life cycle execution. That execution always takes place in the intended environment. In addition, the operations process provides ongoing support to customers of the product. That support takes place after the product is implemented in its environment.

The organization or functional area responsible for that operation will define a strategy and criteria for evaluating whether that actual performance of the operations process is sufficient to achieve the acquiring organization's purposes. The systems that are actually being operated in conventional use are also tested from time-to-time in order to determine whether they are operating correctly and whether proper operation can be sustained in the planned environment. Assistance and consultation are also provided to customers in accordance with the operational plan.

Because of its everyday focus, operations are probably the most overlooked and underestimated process in an ICT organization. Yet, because it specifies the steps necessary to perform "the operation of the software product and operational support to users" (International Standards Organization, 2008), it is generally the most prominent process in users' everyday lives, one of the most pivotal processes affecting an organizations fight against cybersecurity threats and vulnerabilities, and arguably one of the most expensive in the long-term ICT budget. Because the operations process almost always involves hardware, its activities apply both to hardware and software. It is for that reason, the NICE framework specialty areas within the operate and maintain category contain a strong mix of technical and software roles and knowledge, skill, and abilities (KSAs).

The operations process begins with a plan, but it also includes a requirement to designate an appropriate set of explicit standards to guide the work. The overall goal of this portion of the process is to define a stable set of guidelines from which a given system, software product, or software service can be effectively ensured, operated, and maintained. Operation does not imply construction; thus, the product being operated must come from an external source.

From the point when the system is placed into use, the activities in the operations process are characterized by ongoing execution of the system's operational steps, which could include a range of routine user support activities, database administration, system and network administration, as well as change management and problem resolution.

The system maintenance process does modifications and support for the product, such as training or operating a help desk. Just as acquisition is the necessary counterpart of supply, maintenance goes hand in hand with operation. For that reason, the NICE framework combined the two processes into the same knowledge area.

The goal of maintenance is to change an existing ICT product while preserving its integrity and security. It is a formal process built around management of change. The maintenance process identifies the impact(s) of proposed changes to the system and the organization obtains approval for the change and then ensures that the change is properly executed. Maintenance then updates the affected documentation as needed.

The maintenance process uses testing to demonstrate that system requirements are not compromised. In addition, product upgrades are sent to the customer and the modifications are communicated to all affected parties. Maintenance is an important function in an ICT organization because it can curtail the natural tendency toward chaos that occurs in most complex organizations.

Maintenance normally comes into play when a product requires modifications to supporting technology, code, or associated documentation. Such changes are usually a consequence of a reported problem or a request for a change or refinement. Normally the process begins through the roles of customer service or technical support by the initiation of a problem report passed to maintenance through the operations process. Maintenance responsibilities also include tasks for migrating and retiring the software product. In general, maintenance is composed of planning, control, assurance, and communication activities.

The maintenance process usually starts with a user request to modify or enhance an existing system, software product, or service. The goal of maintenance is to control changes to an organization's systems or products in a way that preserves their integrity, while providing a basis for measuring their security and quality. In practice, the process focuses on the consistent labeling and tracking of information about the system, product, or service. In conjunction with the routine practices of upkeep, the maintainer may also be required to perform activities that would normally be associated with development, such as design and testing.

The specialty areas of the NICE framework operate and maintain knowledge area are "responsible for providing the support, administration, and maintenance necessary to ensure effective and efficient information technology (IT) system performance and security" (NIST, 2015). Figure 5.1 provides a list and brief description of each of the five specialty areas in this category.

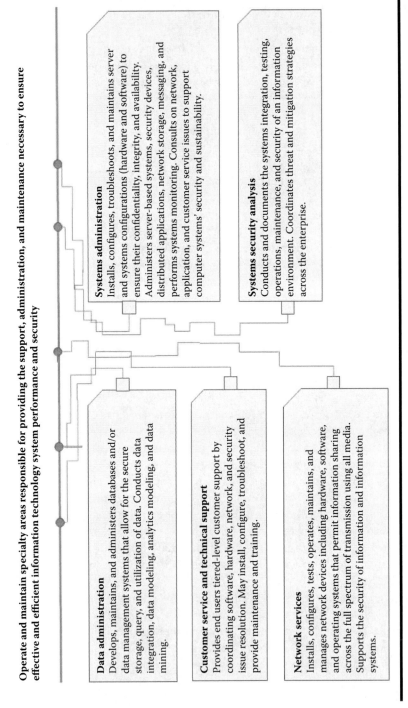

Operate and maintain specialty areas responsible for providing the support, administration, and maintenance necessary to ensure effective and efficient information technology system performance and security

Systems administration

Installs, configures, troubleshoots, and maintains server and systems configurations (hardware and software) to ensure their confidentiality, integrity, and availability. Administers server-based systems, security devices, distributed applications, network storage, messaging, and performs systems monitoring. Consults on network, application, and customer service issues to support computer systems' security and sustainability.

Systems security analysis

Conducts and documents the systems integration, testing, operations, maintenance, and security of an information environment. Coordinates threat and mitigation strategies across the enterprise.

Data administration

Develops, maintains, and administers databases and/or data management systems that allow for the secure storage, query, and utilization of data. Conducts data integration, data modeling, analytics modeling, and data mining.

Customer service and technical support

Provides end users tiered-level customer support by coordinating software, hardware, network, and security issue resolution. May install, configure, troubleshoot, and provide maintenance and training.

Network services

Installs, configures, tests, operates, maintains, and manages network devices including hardware, software, and operating systems that permit information sharing across the full spectrum of transmission using all media. Supports the security of information and information systems.

Figure 5.1   Operate and maintain specialty areas.

Specialty Area 1: Data Administration

An observation that should be made at the outset of our discussion of this specialty area is that the NICE framework gives it the name "data administration" and states that the individual serving in this capacity of ICT operations and maintenance "Develops, maintains, and administers databases and/or data management systems that allow for the secure storage, query, and utilization of data. Conducts data integration, data modeling, analytics modeling, and data mining" (NIST, 2015). What the framework describes as data administration is more closely aligned with the roles performed by the database administrator (DBA). In general, the DBA uses their technical expertise to more effectively design and develop databases using their knowledge of database management systems. On the other hand, a data administer (DA) has a greater aptitude toward business management and separates the business aspects of data resource management from the technology used to manage data. When the DA function exists in an organization it is more closely aligned with the actual business users of data. The DA is responsible for understanding the business lexicon and translating it into a logical data model. The DA is involved more in the requirements gathering, analysis, and design phases; DBA in the design, development, testing, and operational phases. It is for this reason that we will use both job titles in our discussion of the data administration specialty area.

The size and role of the DBA function varies from organization to organization, as does its placement within the organizational structure. On the organizational chart, the DBA function might be defined as either a staff or line position. In a staff position, the DBA often takes on a consulting role; the DBA can devise the data administration strategy but does not have the authority to enforce it or resolve possible conflicts. In a line position, the DBA has both the responsibility and authority to plan, define, implement, and enforce the policies, standards, and procedures used in data administration.

There is no standard for how the DBA function fits in an organization's structure, partly because the function itself is probably the most dynamic of any in an organization. In fact, the fast-paced changes in database management systems (DBMS) technology dictate changing organizational styles. For example:

- The development of distributed databases can force an organization to decentralize data administration further. The distributed database requires the system DBA to define and delegate the responsibilities of each local DBA, thus imposing new and more complex coordinating activities on the system DBA.
- The growing use of Internet-accessible data and the growing number of data warehousing applications are likely to expand the DBA's data modeling and design activities.
- The increasing sophistication and power of personal computer-based DBMS packages provide an easy platform for developing user friendly, cost-effective, and efficient solutions. However, such an environment also invites data

duplication, not to mention the problems created by people who lack the technical qualifications to produce good database designs. In short, the new computing environment requires the DBA to develop a new set of technical and managerial skills.

■ The increasing use of cloud data services is pushing many database platforms and infrastructures into the cloud. This can free the DBA from many lower-level technology oriented tasks, allowing DBAs to focus on higher value strategic issues. In such environments, the DBA becomes a data use service provider and advisor for the organization.

■ Conversely, the growing use of big data in organizations can force the DBA to become more technology oriented. Ongoing efforts to integrate Hadoop storage systems with both NoSQL and relational databases require DBAs to be familiar with the lower-level storage and access issues that are still dominant in those emerging disciplines.

DBA roles are commonly defined and divided according to the phases of the system life cycle (SLC). If that approach is used, the DBA function requires personnel to cover the following activities:

■ Database planning, including the definition of standards, procedures, and enforcement
■ Database requirements gathering and conceptual design
■ Database logical and transaction design
■ Database physical design and implementation
■ Database testing and debugging
■ Database operations and maintenance, including installation, conversion, and migration
■ Database training and support
■ Data quality monitoring and management

Keep in mind that an organization might have several incompatible DBMSs installed to support different operations. For example, some organizations have a hierarchical DBMS to support daily transactions at the operational level and a relational database to support middle and top management's ad hoc information needs. A variety of personal computer DBMSs might be installed in different departments. In such an environment, the company might have one DBA assigned for each DBMS. The general coordination of all DBAs is sometimes one of the responsibilities of the system administrator (discussed later in this chapter).

There is a growing trend toward specialization in data management and that is where data administration comes in. The DA, also sometimes known as the information resource manager (IRM), usually reports directly to top management and is given a higher degree of responsibility and authority than the DBA, although the two roles can overlap.

The DA is responsible for controlling the overall corporate data resources, both computerized and manual. Thus, the DA's job covers more operations than the DBA's because the DA controls data outside the scope of the DBMS in addition to computerized data. Depending on an organization's structure, the DBA might report to the DA, the IRM, the IS manager, or directly to the company's chief executive officer (CEO).

Factoring Data Administration Workforce Tasks into the Cybersecurity Framework Functions

Without data, an organization has no record of transactions, its ability to serve its customer, and ability to make managerial decisions. Today, every organization within every private or public sector relies on ICT systems, and those systems rely on data to produce the information necessary to operate effectively. Therefore, data security is a critical aspect of cybersecurity. The majority of tasks defined within the data administration specialty area of the NICE framework have a direct correlation to the outcomes and associated controls specified within the data security category of the critical framework for improving critical infrastructure cybersecurity (CSF) protect function as shown in Figure 5.2.

Put simply, data security can be defined as the policies and procedures associated with protecting data in transmission, in processing, and at rest (storage). The CSF defines it as: "Information and records (data) are managed consistent with the organization's risk strategy to protect the confidentiality, integrity, and availability of information" (NIST, 2014). The value that organizations have on data is what motivates attackers to steal or corrupt it. An effective security program will protect the integrity and value of an organization's data. In considering the implications risk management has on the underlying activities associated with data security, the case can be made that tasks related to analyzing data requirements and specifications, anticipating changing requirements of data capacity, development of data standards and policies, and providing recommendations for database technology and architecture specified by the NICE framework data administration specialty area align to the identity function. Thus, recommendations, standards, policies, and procedures cannot come to realization until assets are identified, the business environment is understood, and organization-wide risk management strategies and objectives are developed and communicated.

Much of the critical data that organizations store is accessible through DBMS managed by a DA. The process of maintaining the confidentiality, integrity, and availability of the data managed by a DBMS is known as database security. Database security is accomplished by the DA applying a wide range of managerial, physical, and technical controls consistent with the priorities defined in the risk management plan. Managerial controls include policies, procedures, and governance. Technical controls include access control and authentication, auditing, application security, backup and recovery, encryption, and integrity processes.

	Operate and maintain general knowledge area **Data administration specialty area tasks** **NICE workforce framework**
400	Analyze and define data requirements and specifications.
401	Analyze and plan for anticipated changes in data capacity requirements.
498	Design and implement database systems.
520	Review and validate data mining and data warehousing programs, processes, and requirements.
529	Develop data standards, policies, and procedures.
664	Install and configure database management systems software.
684	Maintain database management systems software.
688	Maintain directory replication services that enable information to replicate automatically from rear servers to forward units via optimized routing.
690	Maintain information exchanges through publish, subscribe, and alert functions that enable users to send and receive critical information as required.
702	Manage the compilation, cataloging, caching, distribution, and retrieval of data.
712	Monitor and maintain databases to ensure optimal performance.
740	Perform backup and recovery of databases to ensure data integrity.
796	Provide a managed flow of relevant information (via web-based portals or other means) based on mission requirements.
815	Provide recommendations on new database technologies and architectures.
1154	Perform configuration management, problem management, capacity management, and financial management for databases and data management systems.
1155	Support incident management, service level management, change management, release management, continuity management, and availability management for databases and data management systems.

Cybersecurity framework

Identify

Protect

Detect

Respond

Recover

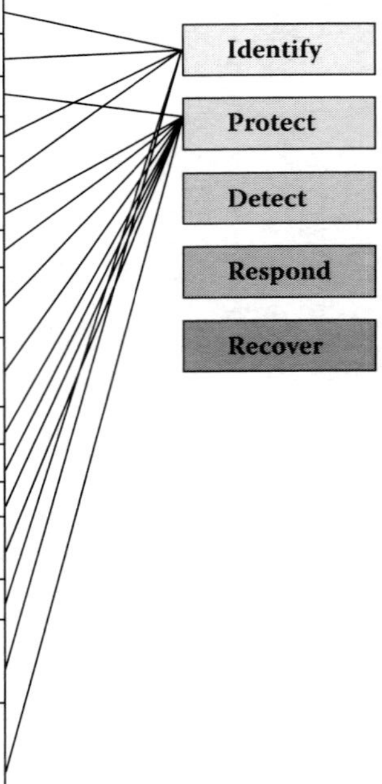

Figure 5.2   Data administration specialty area tasks mapped to the cybersecurity framework (CSF).

Underlying Knowledge, Skill, and Ability Requirements for Data Administration

In order to implement secure data administration appropriately and effectively careful thought and planning is required on the part of the organization. At the core of that thought and planning process is a capable DA. The following is a list of core knowledge and skills that an individual working in that capacity should possess in order to provide sufficient contributions to securing the data within ICT systems:

1. *General database management*: The DA is the central source of database knowledge in the organization. Therefore, they must understand the basic concepts of database technology and be able to accurately communicate them to others.
2. *Database schema creation and management*: A DA must be able to translate a data model or logical database design into an actual physical database implementation and securely manage that database once it has been implemented.
3. *Ensuring data integrity*: A DA must be able to design databases so that only accurate, secure, and appropriate data are entered and maintained. To do so, the DA can deploy multiple types of database integrity including entity integrity, referential integrity, check constraints, and database triggers. Moreover, the DA must ensure the structural integrity of the database.
4. *Backup and recovery*: Implementing secure backup and recovery procedures is the insurance policy of the DA. They must implement an appropriate database backup and recovery strategy based on data volatility and application availability requirements.
5. *Data modeling and database design*: The DA must possess the ability to create an efficient physical database design from a logical data model and application specifications. If the data resource management discipline has not been created, the DA also must be responsible for data modeling, normalization, and conceptual and logical design.
6. *Ensuring availability*: Applications and data increasingly are required to be up and available 24×7. The DA must be able to ensure data availability using nondisruptive administration tactics.
7. *Procedural skills*: Modern databases manage more than merely data. The DA must possess procedural skills to help design, debug, implement, and maintain stored procedures, triggers, and user-defined functions that are stored in the DBMS.
8. *Performance management and tuning*: Dealing with performance problems is usually the biggest postimplementation nightmare faced by DAs. As such, the DA must be able to proactively monitor the database environment and to make changes to data structures, Structured Query Language (SQL), application logic, or the DBMS subsystem to optimize performance.

9. *SQL code reviews and walkthrus*: Although application programmers usually write SQL, DAs usually are blamed for poor performance and lack of security measures. Therefore, DAs must possess in-depth SQL knowledge so they can understand and review SQL and host language programs and to recommend changes for optimization.

10. *Data security*: The DA is charged with the responsibility to ensure that only authorized users have access to data. This requires the implementation of a rigorous security infrastructure for production and test databases; in addition to a database auditing capability to document compliance.

11. *Security policy compliance*: The DA is responsible for being familiar with the organization's cybersecurity policies as defined in the risk management plan. The individual in this capacity must also have thorough understanding of the organization's position on the prioritization of identified threats and vulnerabilities in order to implement the appropriate data security controls.

12. *General systems management and networking skills*: Because once databases are implemented they are accessed throughout the organization and the organization's supply chain, as well as interact with other technologies, the DA must be a jack of all trades. Doing so requires the ability to integrate data administration requirements and tasks with general systems management requirements and tasks (like job scheduling, network management, transaction processing, etc.).

13. *Capacity planning*: As data consumption and usage continue to grow, the DA must be prepared to support more data, more users, and more connections. The ability to predict growth based on application and data usage patterns and to implement the necessary database changes to accommodate the growth is a core capability of the DA.

14. *Enterprise resource planning and business knowledge*: For businesses doing ERP, the DA must understand the requirements of the application users and be able to administer their databases to avoid interruption of business. Most ERP applications (SAP, PeopleSoft, Oracle, etc.) use databases differently than homegrown applications. DAs require an understanding of how the ERP packaged applications impact the business and how the databases used by those packages differ from traditional relational databases.

15. *Storage management techniques*: The data stored in every database reside on disk somewhere (unless it is stored on one of the new main memory DBMS products). DAs must understand the storage hardware and software, including how it interacts with the DBMS.

Table 5.1 displays the entire set of general and specialty KSA requirements for the data administration specialty area as well as the associated competency areas (all from the NICE framework).

Table 5.1 Data Administration Specialty Area Knowledge, Skill, and Abilities

Item ID	KSA	Statement	Competency
28	KSA	Knowledge of data administration and data standardization policies and standards.	Data management
29	KSA	Knowledge of data backup, types of backups (e.g., full, incremental), and recovery concepts and tools.	Computer forensics
31	KSA	Knowledge of data mining and data warehousing principles.	Data management
32	KSA	Knowledge of database management systems, query languages, table relationships, and views.	Database management systems
35	KSA	Knowledge of digital rights management.	Encryption
44	KSA	Knowledge of enterprise messaging systems and associated software.	Enterprise architecture
79	KSA	Knowledge of network access, identity, and access management (e.g., public key infrastructure [PKI]).	Identity management
90	KSA	Knowledge of operating systems.	Operating systems
98	KSA	Knowledge of policy-based and risk-adaptive access controls.	Identity management
104	KSA	Knowledge of query languages such as structured query language (SQL).	Database management systems
120	KSA	Knowledge of sources, characteristics, and uses of the organization's data assets.	Data management
137	KSA	Knowledge of the characteristics of physical and virtual data storage media.	Data management
152	KSA	Skill in allocating storage capacity in the design of data management systems.	Database administration

(Continued)

Table 5.1 (Continued) Data Administration Specialty Area Knowledge, Skill, and Abilities

Item ID	KSA	Statement	Competency
166	KSA	Skill in conducting queries and developing algorithms to analyze data structures.	Database management systems
178	KSA	Skill in designing databases.	Database administration
186	KSA	Skill in developing data dictionaries.	Data management
187	KSA	Skill in developing data models.	Modeling and simulation
188	KSA	Skill in developing data repositories.	Data management
201	KSA	Skill in generating queries and reports.	Database management systems
208	KSA	Skill in maintaining databases.	Database management systems
213	KSA	Skill in optimizing database performance.	Database administration
910	KSA	Knowledge of database theory.	Data management
1034	KSA	Knowledge of personally identifiable information (PII) and payment card industry (PCI) data security standards.	Security
1123	KSA	Knowledge of advanced data encryption (e.g., column and tablespace encryption) security features in databases, including built-in cryptographic key management features.	Database management systems
1124	KSA	Knowledge of advanced data remediation security features in databases.	Database administration
1128	KSA	Knowledge of Java-based database access application programming interface (API) (e.g., Java Database Connectivity [JDBC]).	Database management systems
1141	KSA	Knowledge of an organization's information classification program and procedures for level information loss.	Information management

Specialty Area 2: Customer Service and Technical Support

The question we should begin with is ... Are the tasks associated with customer service and those of technical support one in the same? The correct answer is no, but individuals performing those tasks work very closely together.

A customer service representative (CSR) interacts with an organization's customers to provide them with information to address inquiries regarding products and services. In addition, they deal with and help to resolve any customer complaints. For instance, a CSR may assist you in opening an account or help you to resolve a problem if you cannot access your account or if your order never arrived. Within ICT organizations the CSR handles calls as the first contact with the user, registers and categorizes calls, determines supportability, and dispatches calls to the appropriate functional area, technical support for example.

Technical support functions within an ICT organization to ensure that the proper technical expertise is available to ensure delivery of the intended services of the ICT system. This functional area maintains an appropriate number of individuals who serve in the capacity of providing technical information, guidance, and resources for deployment activities and all aspects of maintaining ICT infrastructure. Thus, individuals working within this function will be the first technical point of contact when cybersecurity events occur.

Oxford Dictionary defines technical support as "a service provided by a hardware or software company that provides registered users with help and advice about their products" (Oxford Dictionaries, n.d.). That definition compliments the NICE framework's description in which it states that individuals working within this specialty area "provide end users tiered-level customer support by coordinating software, hardware, network, and security issue resolution. May install, configure, troubleshoot, and provide maintenance and training" (NIST, 2015).

The range of tasks performed by technical support is both broad and diverse and includes but is not limited to:

- Research and development associated with new trends in technology
- Third-line technical support, normally initiated by incidents reported by the help desk and general problem resolution
- Advisor to suppliers, in providing expertise in relation to the procurement of ICT components
- Liaison to ICT design and planning activities, particularly with regard to technical documentation
- Liaison with deployment during the release and operational acceptance processes
- Tactical implementation of overall improvements to the quality of ICT services

- Assistance in the execution of cybersecurity disaster recovery and business continuity plans
- As indicated above, technical support plays a vital role in capacity management, design, planning, deployment, and operations. It should be noted that support is not only provided for business and technology changes, such as to ensure smooth operation of ICT system, it also provides guidance for systems that directly impact continuous improvement of development and production of services provided by the organization.

Factoring Customer Service and Technical Support Workforce Tasks into the Cybersecurity Framework Functions

Considering the roles defined of the customer service and technical support specialty area of the NICE framework, it is clear that the functions performed largely correlate to the responsibilities of liaison between the ICT capacity of the organization (be it outsourced or in-house) and the individual users. In the case of cybersecurity in which the event is detected by the user, the individuals working within the customer service/technical support capacity must be able to adequately assess the circumstances, determine if cybersecurity event did occur, provide the appropriate event information within an event report, and pass that information to the appropriate ICT personnel (usually the cybersecurity incident response team [CSIRT]). From this descriptive series of responsibilities, you may be quick to associate the roles that NICE defines of this specialty area to just the response planning and communications outcomes specified within the respond function of the CSF. The CSF defines the outcomes of the two categories as "response processes and procedures are executed and maintained, to ensure timely response to detected cybersecurity events" and "response activities are coordinated with internal and external stakeholders, as appropriate, to include external support from law enforcement agencies" respectively (NIST, 2014). However, we need to further explore the context of the word "user."

A common misconception is to simply associate ICT users as an organization's customers or individuals using the system to perform tasks within many of the organization's business processes. While that interpretation is partially correct, these days users of the system may also include other organizations within the supply chain. Further, though a little bit far-fetched, the individuals who manage, develop, operate, and maintain the ICT system are also considered being users. To that extent, a case can be made that the roles defined within this specialty area of the NICE framework also align with outcomes specified within the categories of the identify and protect functions of the CSF as shown in Figure 5.3.

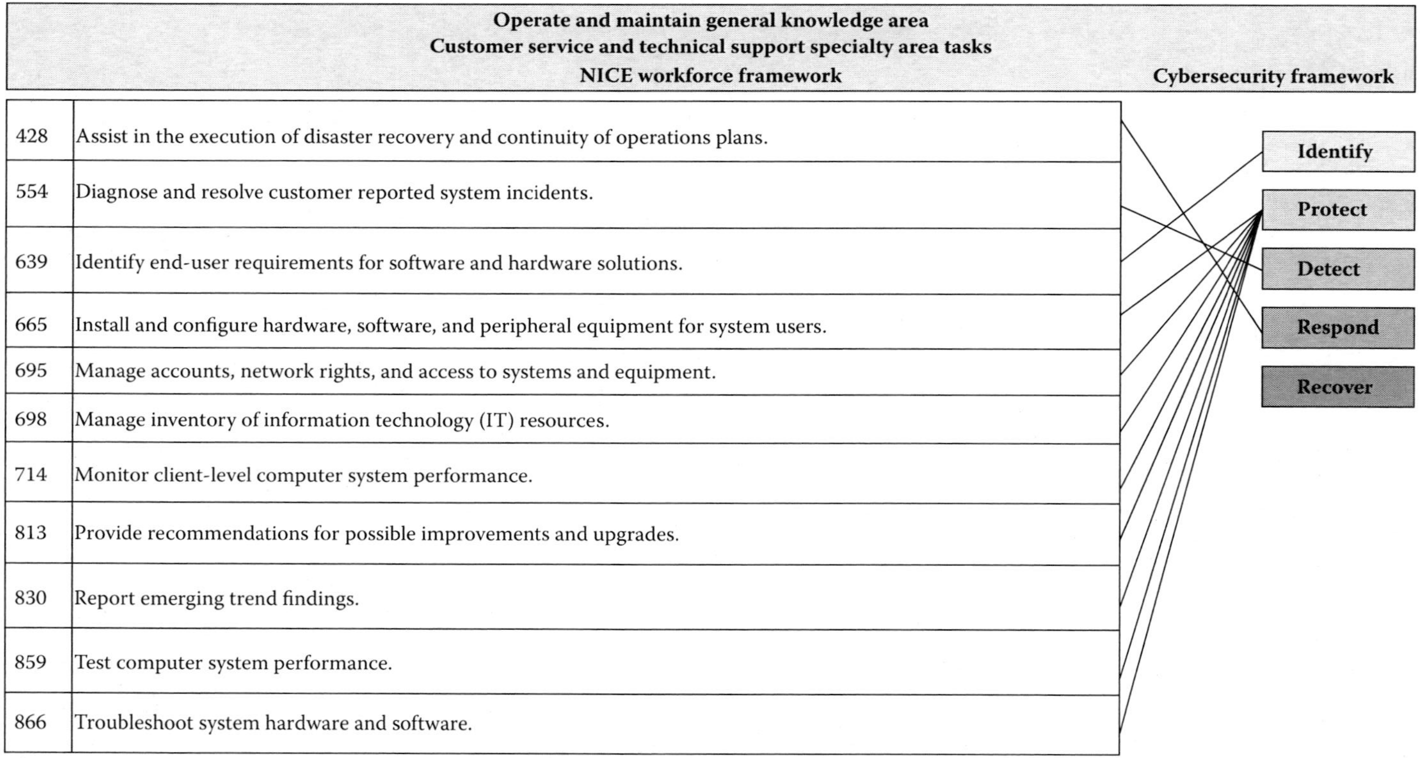

	Operate and maintain general knowledge area Customer service and technical support specialty area tasks NICE workforce framework	Cybersecurity framework
428	Assist in the execution of disaster recovery and continuity of operations plans.	Identify
554	Diagnose and resolve customer reported system incidents.	Protect
639	Identify end-user requirements for software and hardware solutions.	Detect
665	Install and configure hardware, software, and peripheral equipment for system users.	Respond
695	Manage accounts, network rights, and access to systems and equipment.	Recover
698	Manage inventory of information technology (IT) resources.	
714	Monitor client-level computer system performance.	
813	Provide recommendations for possible improvements and upgrades.	
830	Report emerging trend findings.	
859	Test computer system performance.	
866	Troubleshoot system hardware and software.	

Figure 5.3   Customer service and technical support specialty area mapped to the CSF framework.

Identify

Successful performance of many cybersecurity-related roles completed by customer service and technical support depends on knowledge of the organization's roles within the supply chain, the organization's position within the critical infrastructure and industry sector, and cybersecurity priorities as they align with organizational mission and objectives. Given their position as a legitimate first point of contact in incident response circumstances, such information becomes invaluable in assessing the event in terms of its impact to the organization. For example, a tier-one supplier of a major automotive company may experience a cybersecurity attack. Through their own response procedures, the supplier notifies the technical support department of the automotive company. With the knowledge technical support has regarding the integration of ICT assets with that tier-one supplier, appropriate measures can be taken to investigate the impact of the event or protect integrated ICT components. The business environment category of the CSF addresses this need for communication of integration and prioritization in its outcome stating, "The organization's mission, objectives, stakeholders, and activities are understood and prioritized; this information is used to inform cybersecurity roles, responsibilities, and risk management decisions" (NIST, 2014).

Furthermore, the subcategories of CSF risk assessment and risk management categories provide outcomes addressing the need for the organization to identify and document cybersecurity risks, in terms of threats and vulnerabilities, while determining the impact of those risks to ICT components. Individuals performing roles within the customer service and technical support capacity are dependent on the accuracy of the risk assessment documentation and risk management plans in order to appropriately determine the severity of a potential cybersecurity incident.

Protect

One of the roles that the NICE framework defines for these specialty areas is that customer service and technical support "manage accounts, network rights, and access to systems and equipment" (NIST, 2015). In this capacity, the assumption is that access to accounts and equipment is through the privileges provided into networks, operating systems, and miscellaneous software components. The access control category outcome of the CSF states that "Access to assets and associated facilities is limited to authorized users, processes, or devices, and to authorized activities and transactions" (NIST, 2014).

Underlying Knowledge, Skill, and Ability Requirements for Customer Service and Technical Support

Depending upon the organization, individuals in the technical support role can be one or more of several hats. It might be easiest to understand the KSAs of this specialty area by addressing two competencies that must exist within this capacity in *any* organization: incident response and knowledge management.

Recall from our previous discussion that the individuals working within the technical support capacity are normally the point-of-contact between the end user and ICT function. The technical support representative must have basic networking, operating system, software, and hardware KSAs in order to troubleshoot the problem and, if necessary, forward the issue to the appropriate ICT professional for follow-up. In many cases the user simply has an access authentication issue. To that extent the technical support representative needs to have knowledge of personal identification industry standards.

Now consider the case in which the user is calling to report a possible cybersecurity attack. Technical support must have the capability of isolating the issue to the extent that an attack did take place. Further, they must have knowledge of the risk management priorities of the organization, incident response plans, and business continuity plans in order to activate the appropriate reporting mechanisms and perform other security response measures as necessary.

Anybody that has worked or studied ICT technologies for a period of time, knows that almost as quickly as new trends evolve new trends to take their place and make them obsolete are already being explored through research and development. Similarly, software continuously evolves through updates, and patches that may be intended to fix potential security issues. Individuals working in the technical support capacity must constantly browse the Internet reading articles and participating in discussion forums, for example, in order to stay abreast of changing technologies and pending software releases. That knowledge will further assist them in advising the user and achieving problem resolution in an expeditious manner. Likewise, individuals working within the technical support capacity should be comfortable searching knowledge bases for resolutions to issues that are unfamiliar.

Table 5.2 displays the entire set of specialty KSA requirements, and associated competencies for the customer service and technical support specialty area (all from the NICE framework).

Specialty Area 3: Network Services

Care must be taken into what context the term network services is used. The technical definition articulates the term in relationship between the protocols of layers 4 and 7 of the Open Systems Interconnection (OSI) model. Other definitions conceptualize it as the activities performed related to installing, configuring, and managing the networks that support the data communications of an ICT infrastructure. The NICE framework uses the later interpretation in which an individual working within this specialty area "installs, configures, tests, operates, maintains, and manages network devices including hardware, software, and operating systems that permit information sharing across the full spectrum of transmission using

Table 5.2 Customer Service and Technical Support Specialty Area KSAs

Item ID	KSA	Statement	Competency
7	KSA	Knowledge of knowledge-based capabilities for identifying the solutions to less common and more complex system problems.	Knowledge management
33	KSA	Knowledge of database procedures used for documenting and querying reported incidents.	Incident management
37	KSA	Knowledge of disaster recovery and continuity of operations plans.	Incident management
76	KSA	Knowledge of measures or indicators of system performance and availability.	Information technology performance assessment
127	KSA	Knowledge of systems administration concepts.	Operating systems
142	KSA	Knowledge of the operations and processes for diagnosing common or recurring system problems.	Systems life cycle
145	KSA	Knowledge of the type and frequency of routine maintenance needed to keep equipment functioning properly.	Systems life cycle
165	KSA	Skill in conducting open source research for troubleshooting novel client-level problems (e.g., online development communities, system security blogging sites).	Knowledge management
204	KSA	Skill in identifying possible causes of degradation of system performance or availability and initiating actions needed to mitigate this degradation.	Systems life cycle
221	KSA	Skill in testing and configuring network workstations and peripherals.	Network management

(Continued)

Table 5.2 (Continued)   Customer Service and Technical Support Specialty Area KSAs

Item ID	KSA	Statement	Competency
222	KSA	Skill in the basic operation of computers.	Computer skills
235	KSA	Skill in using the appropriate tools for repairing software, hardware, and peripheral equipment of a system.	Computers and electronics
264	KSA	Knowledge of basic physical computer components and architectures, including the functions of various components and peripherals (e.g., central processing units [CPUs], network interface cards [NICs], data storage).	Computers and electronics
281	KSA	Knowledge of electronic devices (e.g., computer systems/components, access control devices, digital cameras, electronic organizers, hard drives, memory cards, modems, network components, printers, removable storage devices, scanners, telephones, copiers, credit card skimmers, facsimile machines, global positioning systems [GPSs]).	Hardware
1034	KSA	Knowledge of personally identifiable information (PII) and payment card industry (PCI) data security standards.	Security
1072	KSA	Knowledge of network security architecture concepts, including topology, protocols, components, and principles (e.g., application of defense-in-depth).	Information systems/ network security
1141	KSA	Knowledge of an organization's information classification program and procedures for level information loss.	Information management

all media. Supports the security of information and information systems" (NIST, 2015). In general, an organization will seek the expertise of a network engineer to perform these tasks.

Network engineers can be thought of as the architects of a network supporting an organization's ICT system. This is the reason why they are also known as network architects. They see to it that the network infrastructure is available to all the organization's users. They ensure that the company's computers, voice, and firewall systems are functioning as they should for the firm's staff, customers, clients, and others who may need to use the system for business purposes. Network engineers are different from system administrators (described later in this chapter) because the latter are concerned with providing daily support to the computer's network and servers. Meanwhile, network engineers are concerned with planning and implementation at the highest levels.

Depending on the size of the organization, the network engineer may be in charge of a single part of the entire system or they may take on the responsibility of the entire network. They may also work with different types of networks such as local area networks (LANs), metropolitan area networks (MANs), wide area networks (WANs), wireless local area network (WLANs), or voice over Internet protocol networks (VoIP).

Network engineers configure the system, install it, and define and stipulating the standards it should follow. After they have established the organization's networking environment, they continue to work to improve it and make it more durable. They constantly monitor the network's performance and respond to network problems, troubleshooting when needed. They also take care of upgrading the network so that it becomes more resilient.

One of the most important tasks of network engineers occurs during the installation phase. Since the network equipment can be installed outside the company's headquarters, they provide remote support for the engineers and users who are on-site. If there are problems during the initial installation, they also give the support that they need remotely. They continue to work with and communicate with the project management team and other engineers regularly.

As far as cybersecurity is concerned, network engineers establish and enforce regulations as to who can access the network. They support and administer firewalls following IT security protocol. If there are issues with the network's security, they gather information from various sources to determine the cause. They then constantly report to the organization's management on the network's operational status based on the information they have gathered.

From a process perspective, the tasks performed by the network engineer and defined within the NICE framework network service can logically fit within four distinct categories: design, network technologies, operational engineering, and maintenance and troubleshooting.

Design

Network engineers establish plans to connect LANs within buildings and WANs between buildings. In the design role, they determine cable requirements to connect computers to the network communication equipment. The engineer is essentially designing a virtual post office. When you drop an envelope into a mailbox, the post office utilizes established routes to deliver it to its destination. Similarly, the network engineer establishes all the cabling and equipment needed to route data to a designated destination.

Network Technologies

Network engineers work with the hardware devices connecting an organization's ICT infrastructure services, including switches and routers. While switches connect printers and computers in a LAN over physical cabling, routers connect LANs to WANs. The engineer configures routers to direct the flow of data from the source to the destination location. Routers will need to be reconfigured to accommodate changes in traffic loads, capacity upgrades, and any changes in available routes. Adjustments will also be needed to reroute traffic during maintenance activities.

Operational Engineering

Once the equipment is up and running, network engineers use applications to monitor the network. A good analogy for this activity is air traffic control. Instead of monitoring airplanes, the network engineer monitors the flow of data through hardware devices and over physical cabling. Monitoring applications provide a visual representation of the network, enabling the engineer to see failed hardware components or areas of congestion that may slow down performance. Operational monitoring allows the engineer to view the daily health of a network and make adjustments to ensure optimal performance.

Maintenance and Troubleshooting

Network engineers will not always work 9-to-5. Installs and maintenance activities are often scheduled after business hours to avoid impacting the user community. Some on-call work can also be expected. When problems arise, an engineer will be counted upon to resolve them. Analytical and troubleshooting skills are essential to solve network and equipment problems quickly and effectively. Predictive analytical skills are also vital to enable the engineer to predict the effects of configuration changes before deciding which actions to take.

Embracing the Value of Outsourcing Network Services Tasks

Many organizations find it expensive to keep up with new ICT technologies or simply prefer to devote their limited ICT resources to the core business, rather than routine ongoing network management.

Managed network services can enable an organization to evolve, by giving decision makers access to network technologies and management expertise without requiring high initial capital expenditures or ongoing investments in technology upgrades.

When an organization subscribes to a managed service, a service provider manages the network equipment and applications on the organizations premises according to the terms of a service-level agreement (SLA) established to meet the organizations unique business needs.

Some managed services are also hosted, meaning that the service provider hosts the equipment in its facility instead of the organizations, and delivers services to employees over the WAN to wherever they are physically located.

Factoring Network Services Workforce Tasks into the Cybersecurity Framework Functions

The roles defined by the NICE framework for the network services specialty area center on two underlying principles: network connectivity and the management of data flows within and between networks. Another term for the latter is "data communications." The practices associated with network connections and data communications are not new. Network engineers have been assuming such responsibilities since the days when mainframes and minicomputer-based infrastructures served as basis from which large corporate ICT functions were built. Nevertheless, what is new since the turn of the century is the increase of integrated networks connecting ICT infrastructures up and down the supply chain; moreover, the increased need to implement measures to adequately secure the network connections and the data flows between them.

Characteristic to what can be said about many other specialty areas of the NICE framework, significant parallels exist between the roles of network services and the outcomes of the functions defined in the CSF. For example, subcategories IM.AM-1, IM.AM-2, IM.AM-4, and IM.AM-5 of the asset management category provide outcomes necessitating the network engineer identify and catalog physical network devices, communication data flows, integration with external networks, and categorize network hardware, software, and data based on its criticality to business objectives. Individuals performing the roles of network services also assist in accomplishment of the CSF risk assessment category outcomes by identifying potential threats and vulnerabilities that may exist through network connections and data communications. Nevertheless, there are four outcomes of the CSF directly impacting the work of network services that deem individualized attention. Those include the following: network integrity protection through access control, protective technology outcomes related to communication and control network protection, establishment of a baseline of network operations and expected data flows for the purposes of anomaly and event detection, and continuous security monitoring. Figure 5.4 shows the network services specialty area mapped to the CSF.

Network Integrity Protection

The objective of the CSF protect function category PR.AC-5 is "to ensure the protection of information in networks and its supporting information processing" and "to maintain the security of information transferred within an organization and with any external entity" (ISO/IEC, 2013). What this outcome is really defining, is the requirement for network security management.

Network security management entails monitoring and implementing necessary security controls related to all communications that take place on internal networks in addition to communications between internal networks and external interfaces. One of the most widely implemented techniques of securing information flows within an organization in addition to network within an organization and external interfaces is through network segregation. This process can be complex, but the basics are straightforward. Simply put, it is the process of logically grouping network assets, resources, and applications together into compartmentalized areas that have no trust of each other. The topic of network segregation is beyond the scope of this book. However, there are some key requirements to take into consideration when segregating networks:

1. Gain visibility of traffic, users, and assets
2. Protect communications and resources on both inbound and outbound requests
3. Implement granular controls on traffic, users, and assets
4. Set a default deny policy on all intersegment connections

Regardless of the network segmentation approach, each of those four requirements should be considered while focusing on only a single segment at a time. Begin with areas that are simpler to segment away from the wider network, such as development or test areas. Pick the lowest hanging fruit first and learn lessons on the way to the more complex areas.

Communication and Control Network Protection

Communication and control network protection practices have not changed significantly in the last decade. Most perimeters rely for protection on stateful inspection firewalls with "holes" liberally poked through them, backed up by noisy and largely ignored intrusion prevention or detection systems. Although communication

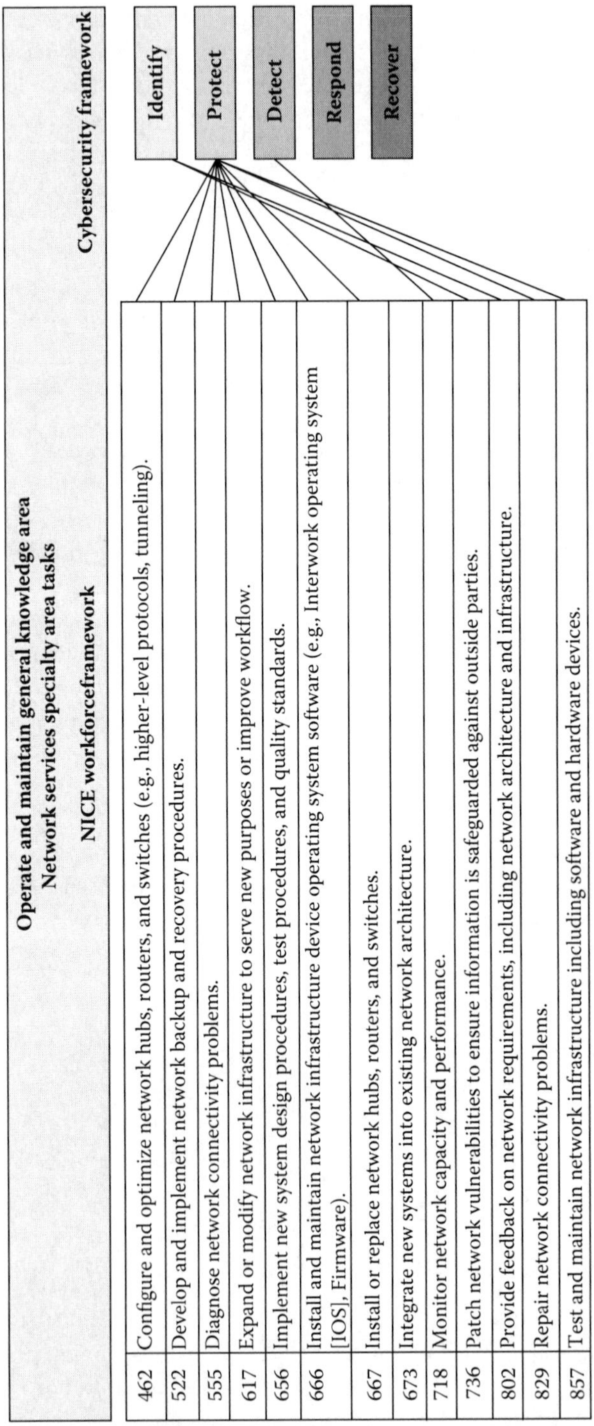

	Operate and maintain general knowledge area Network services specialty area tasks	Cybersecurity framework
	NICE workforceframework	Identify / Protect / Detect / Respond / Recover
462	Configure and optimize network hubs, routers, and switches (e.g., higher-level protocols, tunneling).	
522	Develop and implement network backup and recovery procedures.	
555	Diagnose network connectivity problems.	
617	Expand or modify network infrastructure to serve new purposes or improve workflow.	
656	Implement new system design procedures, test procedures, and quality standards.	
666	Install and maintain network infrastructure device operating system software (e.g., Interwork operating system [IOS], Firmware).	
667	Install or replace network hubs, routers, and switches.	
673	Integrate new systems into existing network architecture.	
718	Monitor network capacity and performance.	
736	Patch network vulnerabilities to ensure information is safeguarded against outside parties.	
802	Provide feedback on network requirements, including network architecture and infrastructure.	
829	Repair network connectivity problems.	
857	Test and maintain network infrastructure including software and hardware devices.	

Figure 5.4 Network services specialty area mapped to the CSF.

protections have not changed, business and collaboration requirements have driven the use of Internet applications and interorganization connectivity skyward. As such, the roles of network services require implementation and monitoring of the new connectivity requirements. These services, located in the demilitarized zone at the perimeter of the control network, often traverse the perimeter with little to no oversight or control. Regulatory compliance has mandated many ICT teams "bolt on" certain controls such as data loss prevention and encryption. From "encrypt everything" strategies to "check box" implementations of these solutions, many organizations are still left blind to what gets through the network perimeter. Therefore, network engineers continue to investigate new and improved encryption strategies to meet the regulatory compliance standards and overarching cybersecurity strategies of the organization.

An effective communication and control network architecture enhances the organization's security posture, as well as its visibility. Instead of a hodgepodge of point products that keep critical threat intelligence in silos, the effective security measures will build an accountable and complete picture of communications that permits the organization to easily, effectively, and securely manage traffic flow.

Establishment of a Baseline Network Operations and Data Flows

Generally, a lot of time in network security is spent discussing the discovery of anomalies that can indicate attack, one thing that sometimes gets forgotten, however, is how fundamental it is to first understand what "normal" looks like. Establishing baseline data for normal traffic activity and standard configuration for network devices can go a long way toward helping security analysts spot potential problems and is a key responsibility of those working in roles associated with network services. There are so many different activities in ICT networks with a high amount of variance that it is extremely difficult to discover security issues without understanding what normal looks like. When a network engineer establishes baseline data, it makes it easier to track deviations from that baseline.

However, simply understanding normal can be a challenging task. Baselining activities can mean tracking many different attributes across multiple dimensions, which means understanding normal host behavior, network behavior, user behavior, and application behavior, along with other internal information, such as the function and vulnerability state of the host is a vital knowledge capacity within network services. Additionally, external context, such as reputation of IP, plays a factor.

When the network engineers have identified the appropriate parameters needed to classify traffic from the "unknown" to the "known bad" column, it is important to share that information, first internally to control the security of the network, and then more widely, so others might learn how they can detect anything similar on their own networks.

Continuous Security Monitoring

As data breaches become a more frequent and damaging occurrence, organizations are being forced to focus on analyzing every possible way that a malicious attacker is able to breach their ICT systems. While it is important to know where vulnerabilities lie, large organizations including the US government are still experiencing devastating cyberattacks after analyzing their systems' weaknesses.

The intrusions suffered by these groups exploited not only the complexity of modern ICT systems but also human nature. Some organizations become vulnerable by their use of interconnected systems, while others are victims of sophisticated spear phishing schemes. With so many places to gain entry and a wide variety of methods to attack, data breaches are all but guaranteed to happen to an organization. With this in mind, organizations need to move away from trying to prevent cyberattacks altogether and instead focus on mitigating the associated risks.

Network engineers need to understand how to proceed after different types of assets have been compromised. If financial data are exploited, or intellectual property is stolen, what are the backup plans in place to make the fallout as minimal as possible? Once those processes are put in place, risk management teams should develop strategies to detect breaches as soon as possible, since mitigation efforts will not mean anything if the company does not know it is been infiltrated.

With a network monitoring solution implemented through network services, organizations receive continuous surveillance of systems in order to identify malicious activity as soon as possible. Network monitoring refers to the practice of overseeing the operation of a computer network using specialized management software tools. Network monitoring systems are used to ensure availability and overall performance of host computers and network services. These systems are typically employed on larger scale corporate and university IT networks.

Underlying Knowledge, Skill, and Ability Requirements for Network Services

Network engineers need to have a solid and in-depth knowledge of how to set up, maintain, and secure computer networks of all sizes and types. They also will need to understand how to install, uninstall, update, and configure software; know how to set up computer servers; and have an above-average knowledge of how to configure hardware. The latter is necessary for the integrative responsibilities that the engineers perform in collaboration with the organizations' system administrators.

Network engineers are generally responsible for the nonsecurity and security aspects of networking systems. In essence, they must ensure that networking systems can withstand or, in the event of mishaps, quickly recover from problems caused by hacker attacks, natural disasters, or other means.

Network engineers should have a multipronged background that includes information technology, information security, networking and engineering. In addition to having the right educational training providing the appropriate skill set, network engineers should also consider certifications such as Certified Information System Security Professional (CISSP) and Cisco Certified Network Associate (CCNA). Moreover, the importance of having hard skills in areas like client/desktop support, programming and network protocols and maintenance, and soft skills in areas like communicating with coworkers and management, problem solving, and decision making cannot be overestimated. Network engineers should also strive for lifelong learning. This includes keeping abreast of new networking and security trends, combing networking and security publications to stay in the loop, and taking advantage of opportunities either to pick up new skills or to improve the ones already acquired.

While no two organizational network infrastructures alike, there are some specific skills that will help network engineers face the various challenges they will encounter on a daily basis. What follows are just a handful of specific skills required for network security engineers:

1. *Assess network security needs*: Network engineers need to consider things like firewall setup, antispam, antivirus, Web content filtering, backups, password policy, antimalware, and antiphishing. After conducting a thorough assessment of enterprise-class networks, they need to be able to suggest mitigation strategies and work alongside relevant parties to redesign the network if needed. Having an in-depth knowledge of Web security gateways, perimeter security, network access control, end point security, perimeter incident detection system/intrusion prevention system (IDS/IPS) is important. Likewise, it also would not hurt to be well-versed in routing protocols such as Multiprotocol Label Switching (MPLS), High Assurance Internet Protocol Encryptor (HAIPE/IP), Quality of Service (QoS), and Wide Area Network (WAN).

2. *Establish network security policies*: Network engineers need to have the knowledge and skills necessary to assist in devising comprehensive network security policies. This will include ascertaining security issues that need to be addressed, identifying security strategies needed to deal with the risks, putting in place policies for allocating administrative tasks, keeping on top of audit logs to flag suspicious activity, and devising network password procedures.

3. *Work on business continuity/disaster recovery strategy*: Network engineers must have the ability to take a leading role in putting together business continuity/disaster recovery plans. This will include dialoging with corporate stakeholders to keep business continuity/disaster recover documentation up to date. They should also have skills in conducting disaster recovery tests routinely.

4. *Test solutions prior to implementation*: Network engineers need to know how to test new computers, software, switch hardware, and routers before implementation. Doing so will help to maintain the integrity of corporate networks.

5. *Fix problems on-site and off-site*: Network engineers need to be able to examine, troubleshoot, and fix network irregularities both at the facility and remotely. They should have expertise in providing end users, application developers, and operational personnel with network services support. They also need to be able to fix client business network issues through network management support, network installation and customization, and network administration.

Table 5.3 displays the entire set of specialty KSA requirements and associated competencies for the network service specialty area (all from the NICE framework).

Specialty Area 4: System Administration

Both network engineering (which we introduced in a previous section) and system administration are a branch of engineering that concerns the operational management of human–computer systems. They are unusual as an engineering discipline in that they address both the technology of computer systems and the users of the technology on an equal basis. It is about putting together a network of computers (the role of network engineers), and getting them running and then keeping them running in spite of the activities of users who tend to cause the systems to fail (the role of system administrators). The NICE framework defines the role more specifically by stating that a system administrator "installs, configures, troubleshoots, and maintains server and systems configurations (hardware and software) to ensure their confidentiality, integrity, and availability. Administers server-based systems, security devices, distributed applications, network storage, messaging, and performs systems monitoring. Consults on network, application, and customer service issues to support computer systems' security and sustainability" (NIST, 2015).

A system administrator works for users, so that they can use the system to produce work. However, a system administrator should not just cater for one or two selfish needs, but also work for the benefit of a whole community. Today, that community is a global entity of computer servers and organizations, which spans every niche of human society and culture, thanks to the Internet. It is often a difficult balancing act to determine the best policy, which accounts for the different needs of everyone with a stake in a system. Once a computer is attached to the Internet, we have to consider the consequences of being directly connected to all the other computers in the world.

In the future, the widespread growth of cloud-based service architectures and other improvements in technology might render system administration a somewhat easier task—one of pure resource administration—but, today, system administration is not just an administrative job, it is an extremely demanding engineer's job. It's about hardware, software, user support, diagnosis, repair and prevention. System administrators need to know a bit of everything: the required skills to

Table 5.3   Network Service Specialty Area KSAs

Item ID	KSA	Statement	Competency
12	KSA	Knowledge of communication methods, principles, and concepts (e.g., encoding, signaling, multiplexing) that supports the network infrastructure.	Infrastructure design
15	KSA	Knowledge of capabilities and applications of network equipment including hubs, routers, switches, bridges, servers, transmission media, and related hardware.	Hardware
27	KSA	Knowledge of cryptography and cryptographic key management concepts.	Cryptography
41	KSA	Knowledge of organization's local area network (LAN)/wide area network (WAN) pathways.	Infrastructure design
55	KSA	Knowledge of information assurance (IA) principles used to manage risks related to the use, processing, storage, and transmission of information or data.	Information assurance
70	KSA	Knowledge of information technology (IT) security principles and methods (e.g., firewalls, demilitarized zones, encryption).	Information systems/network security
72	KSA	Knowledge of local area network (LAN) and wide area network (WAN) principles and concepts, including bandwidth management.	Infrastructure design
76	KSA	Knowledge of measures or indicators of system performance and availability.	Information technology performance assessment

(Continued)

Table 5.3 (Continued)   Network Service Specialty Area KSAs

Item ID	KSA	Statement	Competency
81	KSA	Knowledge of network protocols (e.g., Transmission Critical Protocol/ Internet Protocol [TCP/IP], Dynamic Host Configuration Protocol [DHCP]), and directory services (e.g., Domain Name System [DNS]).	Infrastructure design
92	KSA	Knowledge of how traffic flows across the network (e.g., Transmission Control Protocol and Internet Protocol [TCP/IP], Open System Interconnection model [OSI]).	Infrastructure design
106	KSA	Knowledge of remote access technology concepts.	Information technology architecture
112	KSA	Knowledge of server administration and systems engineering theories, concepts, and methods.	Systems life cycle
133	KSA	Knowledge of key telecommunication concepts (e.g., Routing Algorithms, Fiber Optics Systems Link Budgeting, Add/Drop Multiplexers).	Telecommunications
148	KSA	Knowledge of virtual private network (VPN) security.	Encryption
154	KSA	Skill in analyzing network traffic capacity and performance characteristics.	Capacity management
193	KSA	Skill in developing, testing, and implementing network infrastructure contingency and recovery plans.	Information assurance
198	KSA	Skill in establishing a routing schema.	Infrastructure design
205	KSA	Skill in implementing, maintaining, and improving established security practices.	Information systems/ network security

(Continued)

Table 5.3 (Continued) Network Service Specialty Area KSAs

Item ID	KSA	Statement	Competency
207	KSA	Skill in installing, configuring, and troubleshooting local area network (LAN) and wide area network (WAN).	Infrastructure design
231	KSA	Skill in using network management tools to analyze network traffic patterns (e.g., simple network management protocol).	Network management
234	KSA	Skill in using subnetting tools.	Infrastructure design
261	KSA	Knowledge of basic concepts, terminology, and operations of a wide range of communications media (e.g., computer and telephone networks, satellite, fiber, wireless).	Telecommunications
271	KSA	Knowledge of common network tools (e.g., ping, traceroute, nslookup) and interpret the information results.	Infrastructure design
278	KSA	Knowledge of different types of network communication (e.g., local area network [LAN], wide area network [WAN], metropolitan area network [MAN], wireless local area network [WLAN], wireless wide area network [WWAN]).	Telecommunications
347	KSA	Knowledge of Windows command line (e.g., ipconfig, netstat, dir, nbtstat).	Operating systems
891	KSA	Skill in configuring and utilizing hardware-based computer protection components (e.g., hardware firewalls, servers, routers).	Configuration management
893	KSA	Skill in securing network communications.	Information assurance
896	KSA	Skill in protecting a network against malware.	Computer network defense

(Continued)

Table 5.3 (Continued) Network Service Specialty Area KSAs

Item ID	KSA	Statement	Competency
900	KSA	Knowledge of web filtering technologies.	Web technology
901	KSA	Knowledge of the capabilities of different electronic communication systems and methods (e.g., e-mail, Voice over Internet Protocol [VoIP], Instant Messenger [IM], web forums, direct video broadcasts).	Network management
902	KSA	Knowledge of the range of existing networks (e.g., private branching exchange [PBX], local area networks [LANs], wide area networks [WANs], wireless fidelity [WI-FI]).	Network management
903	KSA	Knowledge of wireless fidelity (WI-FI).	Network management
985	KSA	Skill in configuring and utilizing network protection components (e.g., firewalls, virtual private networks [VPNs], network intrusion detection systems [IDSs]).	Configuration management
989	KSA	Knowledge of Voice over Internet Protocol (VoIP).	Telecommunications
990	KSA	Knowledge of common attack vectors on the network layer.	Computer network defense
1034	KSA	Knowledge of personally identifiable information (PII) and payment card industry (PCI) data security standards.	Security
1072	KSA	Knowledge of network security architecture concepts, including topology, protocols, components, and principles (e.g., application of defense-in-depth).	Information systems/network security

(Continued)

Table 5.3 (Continued)   Network Service Specialty Area KSAs

Item ID	KSA	Statement	Competency
1073	KSA	Knowledge of network systems management principles, models, methods (e.g., end-to-end systems performance monitoring), and tools.	Network management
1074	KSA	Knowledge of transmission records (e.g., Bluetooth, radio frequency identification [RFID], infrared networking [IR], wireless fidelity [Wi-Fi], paging, cellular, satellite dishes), and jamming techniques that enable transmission of undesirable information, or prevent installed systems from operating correctly.	Web technology
1133	KSA	Knowledge of service management concepts for networks and related standards (e.g., Information Technology Infrastructure Library, v3 [ITIL]).	Network management
1134	KSA	Knowledge of symmetric key rotation techniques and concepts.	Encryption
1141	KSA	Knowledge of an organization's information classification program and procedures for level information loss.	Information management
1142	KSA	Knowledge of security models (e.g., Bell–LaPadula model, Biba integrity model, Clark–Wilson integrity model).	Enterprise architecture

successfully accomplish system administration tasks are technical, administrative, and sociopsychological.

A key task of system administration is to build server configurations, another is to configure software systems; such as operating system installation and the management of access privileges. Both of these tasks are performed for users. Each of these tasks presents its own challenges, but neither can be viewed in isolation. Hardware has to conform to the constraints of the physical world; it requires power, a temperate (usually indoor) climate, and a conformance to basic standards in order to work systematically. The type of hardware limits the kind of software that can run on it. Software requires hardware, a basic operating system infrastructure and a conformance to regulatory and organization standards, but is not necessarily limited by physical concerns as long as it has hardware to run on.

Modern software, in the context of a global network, needs to interoperate and survive the possibility of cyberattacks or hostilities of incompatible or inhospitable competitors. Today the complexity of multiple software systems sharing a common Internet space reaches almost the level of the biological. In older days, it was normal to find proprietary solutions, whose strategy was to lock users into one organizations products. Today that strategy is less dominant, and even untenable, thanks to networking. Today, there is not only a physical environment but a technological one, with a diversity that is constantly changing. Part of the challenge is to knit apparently disparate pieces of this community into a harmonious whole.

We apply technology in such an environment for a purpose (running a business or other practice), and that purpose guides our actions and decisions, but it is usually insufficient to provide all the answers. Software creates abstractions that change the basic world view of administrators. The software domain .com does not have any fixed geographical location, but neither do the domains .uk or .no. Servers belonging to these software domains can be located anywhere in the world. It is not uncommon to find foreign embassies with domain names inside their country of origin, despite being located around the world. We are thus forced to think globally.

The global view, presented to us by information and communication technology means that those performing the tasks of system administration have to think penetratingly about the systems that are deployed. The extensive filaments of our internetworked systems are exposed to attack, both accidental and malicious ignore the environment and the organization exposes itself to unnecessary risk.

Factoring System Administration Workforce Tasks into the Cybersecurity Framework Functions

Given the similarities of the tasks performed by network services and those of system administration, a case can be made that the alignment we established in a previous section of this chapter between the CSF and network services can also be applied to the system administration. Recall that network services deals with internetwork and extranet connectivity and communication protocols. This area is also responsible for facilitation of data flows within and between networks. The tasks associated with system administration are much more routine and are focused around the ongoing hardware and software installation, configuration, operation, and maintenance of the servers and other ICT components that make up the organizations networking system. To that extent the network engineer and system administrator work very closely together to provide the level of security defined by organizational standards and industry regulations.

Nevertheless, the system administrators role of facilitating the functionality of network servers puts them in closer proximity to the users; perhaps, most notably in terms of granting and managing user access privileges to servers and other ICT components. The PR.AC-1, PR.AC-2, PR.AC-3, and PR.AC-4 protect function subcategories of the CSF address that need by providing outcomes that require management of credentials for authorized devices and users, managing access to physical assets (servers and other networking equipment), managing remote access to servers, and managing server access privileges according to the principles of least privilege and separation of duties, respectively.

Albeit a stretch to establish this mapping alignment, so much so that we did not include it in the accompanying figure for this specialty area, the system administrator also provides significant contribution to the implementation of controls that satisfy the outcomes of the CSF response and recovery functions. Many organizations include that individual on the CSIRT fur the insight they bring into the investigation of detection systems during incident response process. In many cases, they are the lead in the recovery project that is engaged in the aftermath of a cybersecurity event. To that extent, the system administrators familiarity with the organizations incident response plan, recover plan, and risk management strategies is imperative to their ability to function in their capacity of protecting the organizations critical infrastructure. Figure 5.5 shows the mapping between the system administration specialty area and the CSF.

Underlying Knowledge, Skill, and Ability Requirements for System Administration

A system administrator is responsible for the operation, maintenance, and security of servers that make up the ICT system and must possess a wide variety of skills. An extensive knowledge of computer operating systems and applications as well as hardware and software is required to properly support the organizations ICT system in this capacity. This individual must have the skills needed to troubleshoot and repair server and network connectivity issues, as well as implement all necessary security measures. In addition to these technical skills, a system administrator

Securely provision general knowledge area
System administration specialty area tasks

NICE workforce framework

Cybersecurity framework

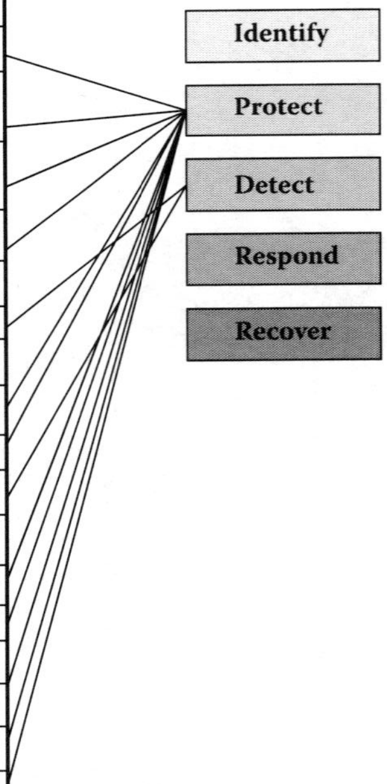

Identify | Protect | Detect | Respond | Recover

ID	Task
434	Check server availability, functionality, integrity, and efficiency.
452	Conduct functional and connectivity testing to ensure continuing operability.
456	Conduct periodic server maintenance including cleaning (both physically and electronically), disk checks, routine reboots, data dumps, and testing.
499	Design group policies and access control lists to ensure compatibility with organizational standards, business rules, and needs.
518	Develop and document systems administration standard operating procedures.
521	Develop and implement local network usage policies and procedures.
668	Install server fixes, updates, and enhancements.
683	Maintain baseline system security according to organizational policies.
695	Manage accounts, network rights, and access to systems and equipment.
701	Manage server resources including performance, capacity, availability, serviceability, and recoverability.
713	Monitor and maintain server configuration.
728	Oversee installation, implementation, configuration, and support of network components.
763	Perform repairs on faulty server hardware.
776	Plan and coordinate the installation of new or modified hardware, operating systems, and other baseline software.
781	Plan, execute, and verify data redundancy and system recovery procedures.
811	Provide ongoing optimization and problem solving support.
835	Resolve hardware/software interface and interoperability problems.
1153	Install, update, and troubleshoot virtual and remote access servers.

Figure 5.5 System administration specialty area mapped to the CSF.

must be able to communicate effectively with other ICT professionals. The system administrator is required to hold an array of professional certifications and participate in continuing education programs to keep up with changing technology.

An extensive working knowledge of computer operating systems, and the protocols associated with them, is one of the most important skills needed for a system administrator. This individual must fully understand the abilities and limitations of various operating systems to keep equipment running smoothly at all times. These individuals should also be skilled in the use of different computer applications operating on the servers that they maintain, in order to ensure functionality and security. Moreover, they must be very familiar with the actual hardware used in ICT system component in order to provide up-to-date, efficient operation. A broad knowledge of various types of software is also needed to choose programs that are suited for specific business operations.

Another essential skill needed within the system administration capacity is to have the ability to quickly identify and repair common problems. These individuals are frequently called upon by the technical support staff to identify and correct various issues such as error messages and software conflicts. System administrators must be able to act quickly to keep business services operational and prevent the loss of important data. In that regard and as we discussed in the previous section, they play a significant role in the processes associated with cybersecurity disaster response and recovery. As such, these individuals are required to have up-to-date knowledge of the various security measures available to prevent data theft and other computer system intrusions, and should also possess the skills needed to identify, repair, and assess the damage caused by a cybersecurity attack.

Table 5.4 displays the entire set of KSA requirements and associated competencies for the system administration specialty area (all from the NICE framework).

Specialty Area 5: Systems Security Analysis

A word of caution … Do not let the title of this specialty area confuse the need for functional security and system security requirements analysis that is logically addressed within the systems requirements planning specialty area of the securely provision category. Our discussion, here, centers on the overarching security implications of the operations and maintenance phases of the SDLC. In that regard, the NICE framework summarizes the tasks of systems security analysis suggesting that the individual working within this phase of the SLC "conducts and documents the systems integration, testing, operations, maintenance, and security of an information environment. Coordinates threat and mitigation strategies across the enterprise" (NIST, 2015).

Prior to the events of 9/11, the tasks performed within the operations phase of the SDLC consisted of network engineers, system administrators, and computer operators performing activities aimed at keeping the systems operational and backed up. Operation manuals and guidelines were provided, but little documentation of securing the system was provided. Maintenance was typically performed

Table 5.4 System Administration Specialty Area KSAs

Item ID	KSA	Statement	Competency
70	KSA	Knowledge of information technology (IT) security principles and methods (e.g., firewalls, demilitarized zones, encryption).	Information systems/ network security
72	KSA	Knowledge of local area network (LAN) and wide area network (WAN) principles and concepts, including bandwidth management.	Infrastructure design
76	KSA	Knowledge of measures or indicators of system performance and availability.	Information technology performance assessment
81	KSA	Knowledge of network protocols (e.g., Transmission Critical Protocol/Internet Protocol [TCP/IP], Dynamic Host Configuration Protocol [DHCP]), and directory services (e.g., Domain Name System [DNS]).	Infrastructure design
89	KSA	Knowledge of new technological developments in server administration.	Technology awareness
96	KSA	Knowledge of performance tuning tools and techniques.	Information technology performance assessment
99	KSA	Knowledge of principles and methods for integrating server components.	Systems integration
112	KSA	Knowledge of server administration and systems engineering theories, concepts, and methods.	Systems life cycle
113	KSA	Knowledge of server and client operating systems.	Operating systems
114	KSA	Knowledge of server diagnostic tools and fault identification techniques.	Computer forensics
127	KSA	Knowledge of systems administration concepts.	Operating systems

(Continued)

Table 5.4 (Continued) System Administration Specialty Area KSAs

Item ID	KSA	Statement	Competency
141	KSA	Knowledge of the enterprise IT architecture.	Information technology architecture
145	KSA	Knowledge of the type and frequency of routine maintenance needed to keep equipment functioning properly.	Systems life cycle
148	KSA	Knowledge of virtual private network (VPN) security.	Encryption
167	KSA	Skill in conducting server planning, management, and maintenance.	Network management
170	KSA	Skill in configuring and optimizing software.	Software engineering
171	KSA	Skill in correcting physical and technical problems that impact server performance.	Network management
194	KSA	Skill in diagnosing connectivity problems.	Network management
195	KSA	Skill in diagnosing failed servers.	Network management
202	KSA	Skill in identifying and anticipating server performance, availability, capacity, or configuration problems.	Information technology performance assessment
206	KSA	Skill in installing computer and server upgrades.	Systems life cycle
209	KSA	Skill in maintaining directory services.	Identity management
211	KSA	Skill in monitoring and optimizing server performance.	Information technology performance assessment
216	KSA	Skill in recovering failed servers.	Incident management
219	KSA	Skill in system administration for Unix/Linux operating systems.	Operating systems

(Continued)

Table 5.4 (Continued)   System Administration Specialty Area KSAs

Item ID	KSA	Statement	Competency
286	KSA	Knowledge of file extensions (e.g., .dll, .bat, .zip, .pcap, .gzip).	Operating systems
287	KSA	Knowledge of file system implementations (e.g., New Technology File System [NTFS], File Allocation Table [FAT], File Extension [EXT]).	Operating systems
342	KSA	Knowledge of Unix command line (e.g., mkdir, mv, ls, passwd, grep).	Computer languages
344	KSA	Knowledge of virtualization technologies and virtual machine development and maintenance.	Operating systems
386	KSA	Skill in using virtual machines.	Operating systems
892	KSA	Skill in configuring and utilizing software-based computer protection tools (e.g., software firewalls, antivirus software, antispyware).	Configuration management
986	KSA	Knowledge of organizational IT user security policies (e.g., account creation, password rules, access control).	Identity management
1033	KSA	Knowledge of basic system administration, network, and operating system hardening techniques.	Information systems/network security
1034	KSA	Knowledge of personally identifiable information (PII) and payment card industry (PCI) data security standards.	Security
1072	KSA	Knowledge of network security architecture concepts, including topology, protocols, components, and principles (e.g., application of defense-in-depth).	Information systems/network security
1074	KSA	Knowledge of transmission records (e.g., Bluetooth, radio frequency identification [RFID], infrared networking [IR], wireless fidelity [Wi-Fi], paging, cellular, satellite dishes) and jamming techniques that enable transmission of undesirable information, or prevent installed systems from operating correctly.	Web technology

by individuals in several job classifications within the ICT function. The tasks were performed based on established maintenance plans based on standards such as IEEE 1219–1993 *Standard for Software Maintenance*. Again, very little documentation or procedures existed to provide security of the software or the entire ICT system during maintenance. Likewise, operations and maintenance was typically performed in-house with little consideration needing to be given to integration between ICT system components within the supply chain.

Today, the scope of operations and maintenance is much different than the early 2000s. Organizations now have risk management plans, business continuity plans, disaster recovery plans, incident response plans, and other cybersecurity policies in place. They expect the individuals working within the operations and maintenance phases to be familiar with, and execute those plans based on knowledge of information assurance (IA) principles. Moreover, with the availability of Internet technologies, there is a greater degree of business-to-business (B2B) integration that affects the organization's ability to operate their systems at a desired level that maintains the level of confidentiality, integrity, and availability of their ICT systems.

Worthy of mention is that the NICE framework assumes the organization has already established all relevant cybersecurity plans and policies. Therefore, the tasks within the systems security analysis specialty area specify the execution and update of those plans and policies as deemed necessary. Further, the tasks associated with systems security analysis cannot be tied to any one job classification. However, management oversight is normally in place to ensure cybersecurity plans and policies are properly executed and updated within the operations and maintenance phases. For this reason, it is important for joint reviews to be performed on a predefined regular basis.

Factoring Systems Security Analysis Workforce Tasks into the Cybersecurity Framework Functions

Recall from the previous section that the NICE framework includes the systems security analysis specialty area that includes an all-inclusive group of tasks and KSAs pertaining to securing critical infrastructures during operations and maintenance, which do not necessarily fit within the definition of the other four specialty areas (data administration, customer service and technical support, network services, and system administration). Moreover, the roles defined for this specialty area largely pertain to security responsibilities below the level of what might be expected of ICT management. To that extent, the roles could easily be associated with the function of IA. IA is defined by Department of Defense Instruction (DoDI) 8500.01E as "measures that protect and defend information and information systems by ensuring their availability, integrity, authentication, confidentiality, and non-repudiation." Therefore, it is not an overexaggeration to conclude that, with the exception of governance and risk management outcomes defined within the identify function, the roles defined by the NICE framework for the systems security analysis specialty area align with all outcomes defined by the CSF as shown in Figure 5.6.

Underlying Knowledge, Skill, and Ability Requirements for Systems Security Analysis

Good systems security analysts are hard to find. Numerous articles and other periodicals that you read agree that, in the United States, there are just a handful of truly recognized experts. By the word "experts" we mean, those with the right technical knowledge and skills, practical experience within a single organization to have knowledge of ICT supply chain security and risk management policies, requirements, and procedures, knowledge of defined local specialized system requirements, knowledge of relevant laws, policies, procedures, or governance related to work impacting critical infrastructure of the organization, and the underlying mind-set to practice effective cybersecurity along with the curiosity and passion of an accomplished hacker.

Perhaps the "silver-bullet" in finding the systems security analyst that will most effectively provide the level of cybersecurity organizations desire is to locate a hacker … an individual who has a hacker's passion and mentality. Ideally, these systems security analysts must be able to think like a cracker. Only then can they strategically and tactically compete against crackers in order to defend against an attack; you have to understand what it takes to create an attack, recognize and exploit vulnerabilities, and provide the necessary security to protect ICT systems based on the knowledge of those vulnerabilities. These are the people that like to take things apart, be it hardware, software or really anything. They like to figure out how they work, identify their weaknesses and then create solutions to make them better.

Other abilities that are vital of the systems security analyst, though harder to quantify, come from the individual's soft skills. Good analysts have an aptitude for games of strategy like chess, poker, and risk, for example. This usually allows them the ability to see patterns of behavior in an opponent's moves. Though skills like these and other soft skills cannot necessarily be taught, they have been found to be evident in cybersecurity analysts who are considered true experts in the field.

Moreover, the ideal experts have both hands-on technical skill and the ability to lead other technical people. They have a view of the big picture and how security impacts the business and its customers. In his article "Cybersecurity: How to be Truly Great," Emmett O'Ryan provides the following list of some of the vital technical skills necessary for success in systems security analysis:

■ Examine security from a holistic view, including threat modeling, specifications, implementation, testing, and vulnerability assessment

	Operate and maintain general knowledge area System security analysis specialty area tasks NICE workforce framework	Cybersecurity framework
		Identify
		Protect
		Detect
		Respond
		Recover
419	Apply security policies to applications that interface with one another, such as Business-to-Business (B2B) applications.	
420	Apply security policies to meet security objectives of the system.	
421	Apply service-oriented architecture security architecture principles to meet organization's confidentiality, integrity, and availability requirements.	
525	Develop and test system fail-over or system operations transfer to an alternate site based on system availability requirements.	
559	Discover organizational trends with regard to the security posture of systems.	
571	Ensure all systems security operations and maintenance activities are properly documented and updated as necessary.	
572	Ensure application of security patches for commercial products integrated into system design meet the timelines dictated by the management authority for the intended operational environment.	
576	Ensure information assurance-enabled products or other compensating security control technologies reduce identified risk to an acceptable level.	
593	Establish adequate access controls based on principles of least privilege and need-to-know.	
616	Exercise the system disaster recovery and continuity of operations plans.	
652	Implement and/or integrate security measures for use in system(s) and ensure that system designs incorporate security configuration guidelines.	
653	Implement security designs and approaches to resolve vulnerabilities, mitigate risks, and recommend security changes to system or system components as needed.	
660	Implement specific information assurance (IA) countermeasures for systems and/or applications.	
661	Implement system security measures that provide confidentiality, integrity, availability, authentication, and nonrepudiation.	

Figure 5.6 Systems security analysis specialty area mapped to the CSF.

	Operate and maintain general knowledge area System security analysis specialty area tasks NICE workforce framework	Cybersecurity framework
		Identify / Protect / Detect / Respond / Recover
670	Integrate and/or implement cross domain solutions (CDS) in a classified environment (primarily applicable to government agencies).	
671	Integrate automated capabilities for updating or patching system software where practical, and develop processes and procedures for manual system software updating and patching using current and projected patch timeline requirements for the system's operational environment.	
708	Identify and correct security deficiencies discovered during security and certification testing and continuous monitoring, or identify risk acceptance for the appropriate senior leader or authorized representative.	
717	Monitor information protection assurance mechanisms related to system implementation and testing practices.	
729	Oversee minimum security requirements are in place for all applications.	
754	Perform information assurance (IA) testing of developed applications and/or systems to identify security vulnerabilities such as SQL injection or cross-site scripting.	
767	Perform security reviews and identify security gaps in security architecture, resulting in recommendations for the inclusion into the risk mitigation strategy.	
782	Plan and recommend modifications or adjustments based on exercise results or system environment.	
795	Properly document all systems security implementation, operations and maintenance activities and update as necessary.	
806	Provide guidance to leadership.	
809	Provide input to the risk management framework (RMF) process activities and related documentation (e.g. system lifecycle support plans, concept of operations, operational procedures, and maintenance training materials).	
876	Verify and update security documentation reflecting the application/system security design features.	
880	Work with others to resolve computer security incidents and vulnerability compliance.	
938	Ensure recovery and continuity plans are executable in the system operational environment.	

Figure 5.6 (Continued)   Systems security analysis specialty area mapped to the CSF.

- Understand security issues associated with operating systems, networking, and virtualization software
- Understand Web application security concepts and practices
- Understand the architecture of systems and network including identifying the security controls in place and how they are used
- Understand database weaknesses and security best practices
- Advanced understanding of general information security concepts and principles, system architectures and development
- Expert knowledge of software development security principles, concepts, and best practices
- Ability to write tools to automate certain security tasks
- Ability to do systems and network hardening
- Organize and coordinate technical vulnerability assessments including systems and network vulnerability assessments, penetration testing, Web application assessments, social engineering assessments, physical security assessments, wireless security assessments, and implementing secure infrastructure solutions
- Recommend and set the technical direction for managing security incidents
- Maintain the integrity of process and approach, as well as controls, for the whole incident management process including the ability to coordinate and manage major/highly sensitive investigations with potential for business wide impact/reputational damage
- Be able to understand and forensically show how attacks from the Internet are done (O'Ryan, 2012).

Table 5.5 displays the entire set of specialty KSA requirements and associated competencies for the systems security analysis specialty area (all from the NICE framework).

Chapter Summary

As a consequence to the routine nature of the tasks associated with operations, it is perhaps the most overlooked phase of the ICT process. To the contrary, operations is perhaps the most prominent process in terms of the tasks performed, having a significant effect on the "everyday" lives of the system users. Likewise, it is also the most critical process affecting an organizations efforts toward identifying and protecting and ICT system against cybersecurity threats and vulnerabilities. Although, it is also one of the most expensive in the long-term ICT budget due to the constant need for hardware and software purchases.

The system maintenance process does modifications and support for the product with an underlying goal to change an existing ICT product while preserving

Table 5.5 Systems Security Analysis Specialty Area KSAs

Item ID	KSA	Statement	Competency
3	KSA	Skill in conducting vulnerability scans and recognizing vulnerabilities in security systems.	Vulnerabilities assessment
18	KSA	Knowledge of circuit analysis.	Computers and electronics
25	KSA	Knowledge of encryption algorithms (e.g., Internet Protocol Security [IPSEC], Advanced Encryption Standard [AES], Generic Routing Encapsulation [GRE], Internet Key Exchange [IKE], Message Digest Algorithm [MD5], Secure Hash Algorithm [SHA], Triple Data Encryption Standard [3DES]).	Cryptography
27	KSA	Knowledge of cryptography and cryptographic key management concepts.	Cryptography
34	KSA	Knowledge of database systems.	Database management systems
42	KSA	Knowledge of electrical engineering as applied to computer architecture, including circuit boards, processors, chips, and associated computer hardware.	Hardware engineering
43	KSA	Knowledge of embedded systems and internet of things.	Embedded computers
46	KSA	Knowledge of fault tolerance.	Information assurance
51	KSA	Knowledge of how system components are installed, integrated, and optimized.	Systems integration

(Continued)

Table 5.5 (Continued)   Systems Security Analysis Specialty Area KSAs

Item ID	KSA	Statement	Competency
52	KSA	Knowledge of human-computer interaction principles.	Human factors
58	KSA	Knowledge of known vulnerabilities from alerts, advisories, errata, and bulletins.	Information systems/network security
63	KSA	Knowledge of information assurance (IA) principles and organizational requirements to protect confidentiality, integrity, availability, authenticity, and nonrepudiation of information and data.	Information assurance
65	KSA	Knowledge of information theory, including source coding, channel coding, algorithm complexity theory, and data compression.	Mathematical reasoning
70	KSA	Knowledge of information technology (IT) security principles and methods (e.g., firewalls, demilitarized zones, encryption).	Information systems/network security
75	KSA	Knowledge of mathematics, including logarithms, trigonometry, linear algebra, calculus, and statistics.	Mathematical reasoning
78	KSA	Knowledge of microprocessors.	Computers and electronics
79	KSA	Knowledge of network access, identity, and access management (e.g., public key infrastructure [PKI]).	Identity management
82	KSA	Knowledge of network design processes, including security objectives, operational objectives, and tradeoffs.	Infrastructure design
90	KSA	Knowledge of operating systems.	Operating systems

(Continued)

Table 5.5 (Continued) Systems Security Analysis Specialty Area KSAs

Item ID	KSA	Statement	Competency
92	KSA	Knowledge of how traffic flows across the network (e.g., Transmission Control Protocol and Internet Protocol [TCP/IP], Open System Interconnection model [OSI]).	Infrastructure design
94	KSA	Knowledge of parallel and distributed computing concepts.	Information assurance
109	KSA	Knowledge of secure configuration management techniques.	Configuration management
110	KSA	Knowledge of key concepts in security management (e.g., Release Management, Patch Management).	Information assurance
111	KSA	Knowledge of security system design tools, methods, and techniques.	Information systems/network security
119	KSA	Knowledge of software engineering.	Software engineering
130	KSA	Knowledge of systems testing and evaluation methods.	Systems testing and evaluation
133	KSA	Knowledge of key telecommunication concepts (e.g., Routing Algorithms, Fiber Optics Systems Link Budgeting, Add/Drop Multiplexers).	Telecommunications
144	KSA	Knowledge of the systems engineering process.	Systems life cycle
160	KSA	Skill in assessing the robustness of security systems and designs.	Vulnerabilities assessment
177	KSA	Skill in designing countermeasures to identified security risks.	Vulnerabilities assessment

(Continued)

Table 5.5 (Continued) Systems Security Analysis Specialty Area KSAs

Item ID	KSA	Statement	Competency
179	KSA	Skill in designing security controls based on IA principles and tenets.	Information assurance
183	KSA	Skill in determining how a security system should work, including its resilience and dependability capabilities, and how changes in conditions, operations, or the environment will affect these outcomes.	Information assurance
191	KSA	Skill in developing and applying security system access controls.	Identity management
199	KSA	Skill in evaluating the adequacy of security designs.	Vulnerabilities assessment
904	KSA	Knowledge of interpreted and compiled computer languages.	Computer languages
922	KSA	Skill in using network analysis tools to identify vulnerabilities.	Vulnerabilities assessment
1034	KSA	Knowledge of personally identifiable information (PII) and payment card industry (PCI) data security standards.	Security
1037	KSA	Knowledge of IT supply chain security and risk management policies, requirements, and procedures.	Risk management
1038	KSA	Knowledge of local specialized system requirements (e.g., critical infrastructure systems that may not use IT) for safety, performance, and reliability).	Infrastructure design
1039	KSA	Skill in evaluating the trustworthiness of the supplier and/or product.	Contracting/procurement

(Continued)

Table 5.5 (Continued)   Systems Security Analysis Specialty Area KSAs

Item ID	KSA	Statement	Competency
1040	KSA	Knowledge of relevant laws, policies, procedures, or governance related to work impacting critical infrastructure.	Criminal law
1072	KSA	Knowledge of network security architecture concepts, including topology, protocols, components, and principles (e.g., application of defense-in-depth).	Information systems/network security
1073	KSA	Knowledge of network systems management principles, models, methods (e.g., end-to-end systems performance monitoring), and tools.	Network management
1132	KSA	Knowledge of service catalogues and service management standards (e.g., Information Technology Infrastructure Library, v3 [ITIL]).	Operations support
1133	KSA	Knowledge of service management concepts for networks and related standards (e.g., Information Technology Infrastructure Library, v3 [ITIL]).	Network management
1138	KSA	Skill in developing and applying user credential management system.	Identity management
1139	KSA	Skill in implementing enterprise key escrow systems to support data-at-rest encryption.	Infrastructure design
1141	KSA	Knowledge of an organization's information classification program and procedures for level information loss.	Information management
1142	KSA	Knowledge of security models (e.g., Bell-LaPadula model, Biba integrity model, Clark–Wilson integrity model).	Enterprise architecture

its integrity and security. Maintenance starts with a plan that defines priorities and processes used to support the ICT system and is the process in which many of the cybersecurity protection tasks are initiated. Some of those protection tasks will require supplemental transversal through the entire SLC, while others can be performed consistent with established, risk management, disaster recovery, and business continuity plans.

The NICE framework defines five specialty areas that support operations and maintenance:

1. Data administration tasks and KSAs focus on the development, maintenance, and administration of databases and data management systems that adequately facilitate secure storage, query, and utilization of data. NICE framework tasks also address the DA roles associated with performing data integration, data modeling, analytics modeling, and data mining.

2. The tasks and KSAs defined within the customer service and technical support specialty area adequately serve the ICT system user customer support needs by providing software, hardware, network, and security issue resolution. Individuals working within this specialty area also serve in the capacity of providing installation, configuration, troubleshooting, maintenance, and training.

3. The NICE framework defines a network services specialty area in which tasks and KSAs are specified for individuals working as network engineers. These individuals support operations and maintenance by installing, configuring, testing, operating, maintaining, and managing network devices including hardware, software, and operating systems that support data communications across all networks within the organization. Additionally tasks are defined that support facilitation of network connections across the entire supply chain using all forms media.

4. System administration tasks and KSAs defined by the NICE framework establish a capacity of individuals working closely with network engineers, and specifically install, configure, troubleshoot, and maintain server and systems configurations (hardware and software) to ensure their confidentiality, integrity, and availability.

5. The NICE framework defines the tasks and KSAs associated with systems security analysis such that individuals working in this capacity must be able to adequately conduct and document the systems integration, testing, operations, maintenance, and security of the ICT system. Likewise, they also coordinate threat and mitigation strategies across the organization.

Key Terms

Big Data: Datasets with volumes so huge that they are beyond the scope of a standard relational database system to capture store and analyze.

Data Integration: Generally implemented by data warehouses, it supports the analytical processing of large datasets by aligning, combining, and presenting each dataset from organizational departments and external remote sources to fulfill integrator objectives.

Data Mining: Analysis of large pools of data to find patterns and rules that can be used to guide decision making and predict future behavior.

Data Modeling: The formalization and documentation of existing processes and events that occur during application software design and development. Such techniques and tools capture and translate complex system designs into easily understood representations of the data flows and processes, creating a blueprint for construction and/or reengineering.

Open Systems Interconnection (OSI) Model: A reference model for how applications can communicate over a network.

Predictive Analytics Modeling: Predictive modeling is a process used in predictive analytics to create a statistical model of future behavior. Predictive analytics is the area of data mining concerned with forecasting probabilities and trends.

Service-Level Agreement: A contract between a service provider and its internal or external customers who documents what services the provider will furnish.

References

International Standards Organization. 2008. *ISO/IEC 12207:2008 Systems and Software Engineering-Software Life Cycle Processes.* Switzerland, Geneva: ISO.

ISO/IEC. 2013. *ISO/IEC 27001 Information Technology—Security Techniques—Information Security Management Systems—Requirements.* Switzerland, Geneva: ISO.

National Institute of Standards and Technology (NIST). 2014. *Framework for Improving Critical Infrastructure Cybersecurity.* Gaithersburg, MD: NIST.

National Institute of Standards and Technology (NIST). 2015. *National Initiative for Cybersecurity Education Framework.* Gaithersburg, MD: NIST.

O'Ryan, Emmett R. 2012. "Cybersecurity: How to be Truly Great." Accessed May 22, 2015. http://insights.dice.com/2012/03/02/cybersecurity/.

Oxford Dictionaries. n.d. "Technical Support." Accessed May 7, 2015. https://www.oxforddictionaries.com/us/definition/american_english/technical-support.

Chapter 6

Protect and Defend: Description of Standard Roles and KSAs

Chapter Objectives

At the conclusion of this chapter, the reader will understand:

- The justification and contents of the protect and defend domains
- The focus and purpose of the four protect and defend specialty areas
- The underlying tasks of each specialty area within the oversee and govern general knowledge area (GKA)
- The relationship between the four protect and defend specialty areas and the national cybersecurity framework (CSF)

Introduction to the Protect and Defend General Knowledge Area

The need for a high degree of interconnectivity poses many challenges to organizations to adequately protect and defend their infrastructure from sophisticated cyberattacks. External and internal attackers have caused substantial losses to organizations, not only in reputations. They employ a variety of techniques and strategies to steal financial data, intellectual property, and expose sensitive information. Hackers and cyber-adversaries are motivated, persistent, and highly capable of compromising systems and disrupting services. They range from individual attackers, to activist groups, to teams of well-funded criminal enterprises, to full-time attackers employed on behalf of nation–states.

As shown in Figure 6.1, the protect and defend GKA (GKA 3) comprises four specialty areas that focus on the defense, assessment, and management of the critical infrastructure and systems.

These areas are responsible for identifying, analyzing, and mitigating threats to internal information technology (IT) systems or networks (National Institute of Standards in Technology [NIST], 2014). The following job roles have been identified and included in the National Initiative for Cybersecurity Education (NICE) framework:

For specialty area 1: Enterprise network defense (END) analysis, the job roles and sample job titles that perform the identification, analysis, and reporting of events that may or actually occur within the enterprise network in order to protect information are network security engineer, security analyst, cybersecurity intelligence analyst, END analyst, and incident analyst.

For specialty area 2: Incident response, the job roles and sample job titles that respond to disruptions to mitigate immediate and potential threats are computer crime investigator, incident handler, incident responder, incident response analyst or coordinator, and intrusion analyst.

For specialty area 3: END infrastructure support, the job roles and sample job titles that test, implement, deploys, maintains, reviews, and administers the infrastructure hardware, software, and documentation are information systems security engineer, intrusion detection system (IDS) administrator, IDS engineer, IDS technician, network administrator, network security engineer, security analyst, security engineer, and systems security engineer.

For specialty area 4: Vulnerability assessment and management—the job roles and sample job titles that conduct threat and vulnerability assessments are blue team technician, ethical hacker, compliance manager, computer network defense (CND) auditor, governance manager, information security engineer, internal enterprise auditor, network security engineer, red team technician, penetration tester, reverse engineer, risk/vulnerability analyst, technical surveillance countermeasures technician, and vulnerability manager.

Specialty Area 1: Enterprise Network Defense Analysis

The specialty area END analysis "uses defense measures and information collected from a variety of sources to identify, analyze, and report events that occur or might occur within the enterprise network in order to protect information, information systems, and networks from threats" (NIST, 2014). Of all the commodities that have been developed and marketed, the value of information and the importance of it in our daily lives has escalated information to the top of the list. As a society, we have become accustomed to creating and receiving information about everything and everyone as it becomes available. New industries and business models have emerged due to the proliferation of information and its access.

The capability to process, store, and transmit timely and relevant information that supports business objectives and functions has driven increasingly complex IT

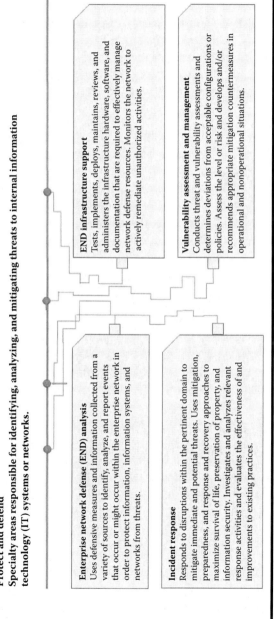

Protect and defend
Specialty areas responsible for identifying, analyzing, and mitigating threats to internal information technology (IT) systems or networks.

Enterprise network defense (END) analysis
Uses defensive measures and information collected from a variety of sources to identify, analyze, and report events that occur or might occur within the enterprise network in order to protect information, information systems, and networks from threats.

Incident response
Responds to disruptions within the pertinent domain to mitigate immediate and potential threats. Uses mitigation, preparedness, and response and recovery approaches to maximize survival of life, preservation of property, and information security. Investigates and analyzes relevant response activities and evaluates the effectiveness of and improvements to existing practices.

END infrastructure support
Tests, implements, deploys, maintains, reviews, and administers the infrastructure hardware, software, and documentation that are required to effectively manage network defense resources. Monitors the network to actively remediate unauthorized activities.

Vulnerability assessment and management
Conducts threat and vulnerability assessments and determines deviations from acceptable configurations or policies. Assess the level or risk and develops and/or recommends appropriate mitigation countermeasures in operational and nonoperational situations.

Figure 6.1   Protect and defend general specialty area overview.

infrastructures that must be secured. Organizations must vigorously protect their mission critical assets, network infrastructure, and information from a variety of internal and external threats. If the network has already been compromised, it is imperative that the organization have the talent and tools to detect and prevent further attack activities.

To protect and defend against attack activities, network security engineers and security analysts must be proficient in footprinting and reconnaissance; gathering information to search for vulnerabilities; conducting vulnerability analyses; planning and scheduling penetration testing; conducting external and internal penetration testing; monitoring firewall and intrusion detection and protection systems (IDPSs), structured query language (SQL), and Web application penetration testing; network enumeration; password cracking; Transmission Critical Protocol/Internet Protocol (TCP/IP) packet analysis; best practices in circumventing social engineering attacks; conduct continuous monitoring; and current knowledge of malware attacks and the variety of tools to mitigate such attacks.

If an organization does not have policies and security controls in place to handle threats, they will pay the price in costly data breaches and inevitable legal issues. Resources must be allocated to develop and implement a robust IT security operational plan that includes a risk assessment, vulnerability and threat assessment, implementation of appropriate security controls and countermeasures, testing and evaluation of those controls, continuous monitoring, data collection, and plans to address any deficiencies. More information about the IT security operation plan can be found in Chapter 9, Specialty Area 4: Information Systems and Security Operations.

As shown in Figure 6.2, the NICE framework specifies 25 potential tasks for the analysis, protection, and defense of the enterprise network. The effect of these 25 activities is to ensure that the process of monitoring, analyzing, mitigation, and reporting on the variety of threats is properly handled. The tasks for this specialty area aligns with the protect, defend, and recover functions of the CSF.

Factoring Enterprise Network Defense Analysis Workforce Tasks into the Cybersecurity Framework Functions

IT networks supporting multiple hardware platforms, operating systems, software applications, and sensitive data all have to be secured and continuously monitored. As part of a risk assessment, the identification of threats and vulnerabilities to organizational assets is a fundamental exercise an organization must conduct. This information along with the level of acceptable risk and the boundaries of the systems to include in the scope of protection will not only drive what security controls are implemented but also how systems are monitored and how events are categorized.

Every organization must examine the possible threats to their network infrastructure and information security based on their unique circumstances. Identifying potential sources of harm (threats) to information assets and evaluating the probability and impact (outcomes or consequences) are the basic elements of threat

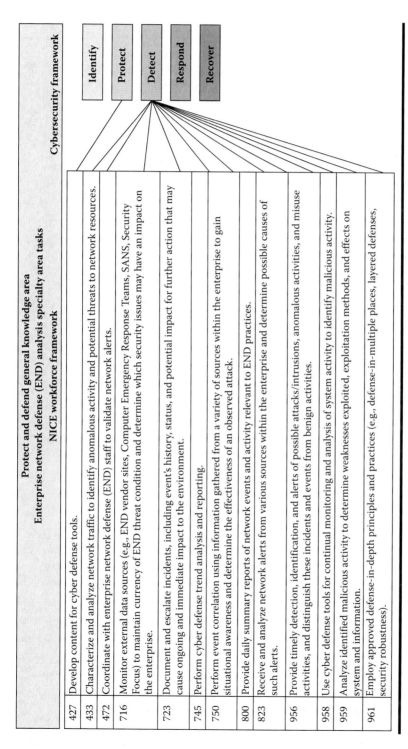

Protect and defend general knowledge area
Enterprise network defense (END) analysis specialty area tasks
NICE workforce framework

Cybersecurity framework

		Identify
		Protect
		Detect
		Respond
		Recover

427	Develop content for cyber defense tools.
433	Characterize and analyze network traffic to identify anomalous activity and potential threats to network resources.
472	Coordinate with enterprise network defense (END) staff to validate network alerts.
716	Monitor external data sources (e.g., END vendor sites, Computer Emergency Response Teams, SANS, Security Focus) to maintain currency of END threat condition and determine which security issues may have an impact on the enterprise.
723	Document and escalate incidents, including event's history, status, and potential impact for further action that may cause ongoing and immediate impact to the environment.
745	Perform cyber defense trend analysis and reporting.
750	Perform event correlation using information gathered from a variety of sources within the enterprise to gain situational awareness and determine the effectiveness of an observed attack.
800	Provide daily summary reports of network events and activity relevant to END practices.
823	Receive and analyze network alerts from various sources within the enterprise and determine possible causes of such alerts.
956	Provide timely detection, identification, and alerts of possible attacks/intrusions, anomalous activities, and misuse activities, and distinguish these incidents and events from benign activities.
958	Use cyber defense tools for continual monitoring and analysis of system activity to identify malicious activity.
959	Analyze identified malicious activity to determine weaknesses exploited, exploitation methods, and effects on system and information.
961	Employ approved defense-in-depth principles and practices (e.g., defense-in-multiple places, layered defenses, security robustness).

Figure 6.2 Enterprise network defense (END) analysis tasks mapped to the cybersecurity framework (CSF) functions.

(Continued)

	Protect and defend general knowledge area NICE workforce framework	Cybersecurity framework
		Identify
		Protect
		Detect
		Respond
		Recover
1010	Determine appropriate course of action in response to identified and analyzed anomalous network activity.	
1102	Conduct tests of information assurance (IA) safeguards in accordance with established test plans and procedures.	
1103	Determine tactics, techniques, and procedures (TTPs) for intrusion sets.	
1104	Examine network topologies to understand data flows through the network.	
1105	Recommend computing environment vulnerability corrections.	
1107	Identify and analyze anomalies in network traffic using metadata.	
1108	Conduct research, analysis, and correlation across a wide variety of all source dataset (e.g., indications and warnings).	
1109	Validate intrusion detection system (IDS) alerts against network traffic using packet analysis tools.	
1110	Isolate and remove malware.	
1111	Identify application and operating systems of a network device based on network traffic.	
1112	Reconstruct a malicious attack or activity based on network traffic.	
1113	Identify network mapping and operating system fingerprinting activities.	

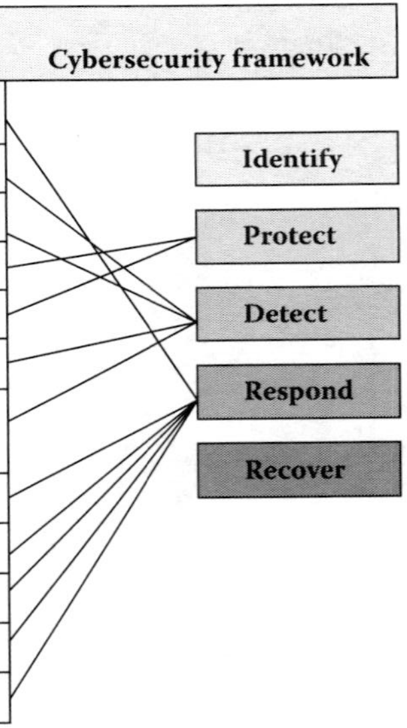

Figure 6.2 (Continued)   Enterprise network defense (END) analysis tasks mapped to the cybersecurity framework (CSF) functions.

assessment. In order for a risk to be identified, a threat source must act on an existing vulnerability. That is why it is important to analyze both internal and external threats and vulnerabilities in order to understand the possible consequences that may occur. Unless an analysis of threats, vulnerabilities, and possible outcomes is conducted, the organization has no idea of their overall risk to their information and systems.

Threats can be categorized into three levels:

1. Man-made such as insiders to include employees, consultants, or contractors; hackers; hacktivists; crackers; strategic business partners; competitors; and terrorists
2. Natural disasters that include fires, floods, earthquakes, tornadoes, hurricanes, and severe storms
3. A blend of both human and non-human involvement to include malicious code (created by a human) that once installed on internal systems, morphs and replicates itself to cause severe damage that is frequently impossible to fully remove (Trojan horses, viruses, and worms)

Table 6.1 shows the threat categories that can be used as a basis to determine potential sources. Once the threat sources have been identified, the next step in the process is to determine the likelihood and possible consequences if the threat materialized. These three elements: threat sources, likelihood, and consequences define the overall risk to information and the infrastructure.

To effectively address threats and vulnerabilities, the organization must:

■ Develop and maintain an understanding of threats and threat activities
■ Characterize and analyze network traffic to identify anomalous activity and potential threats
■ Employ approved defense-in-depth principles and practices (e.g., defense-in-multiple places, layered defenses, and security robustness)
■ Assess all countermeasures and security controls
■ Collect, research, correlate, and analyze all source datasets
■ Perform cyber defense trend analysis and reporting
■ Isolate and remove malware, document and escalate incidents as appropriate
■ Document and communicate security status to all appropriate stakeholders

Continuous Monitoring to Protect and Detect

Ever-changing threats and new ways of exploitation increase the challenges of anticipating new threats and proactively responding. Maintaining real-time views of information security risks across the enterprise is a multifaceted responsibility and include asset management, configuration management, network management, vulnerability management, patch management, malware detection, event management, incident management, license management, and information management and aligns

Table 6.1   Threat Categories/Sources

Threat Categories	
Insider (employee, consultant, contractor, former insiders)	*Negligence, failure, sabotage, harassment, bribery, extortion, identity theft, data corruption, unauthorized access, abuse of confidential information, loss of reputation*
Hackers/crackers/ hacktivists	*Unauthorized access, intrusion, data theft, defacement, identity theft, fraud, bribery, extortion, spoofing, social engineering*
Malicious code	*Loss of data, noncompliance of governmental regulatory agencies, denial or disruption of service, damage to systems, loss of reputation*
Strategic business partners	*Theft of trade secrets, sabotage, abuse of confidential information, loss of reputation, noncompliance of governmental regulatory agencies*
Competitors	*Theft of trade secrets, sabotage, abuse of confidential information, loss of reputation, noncompliance of governmental regulatory agencies*
Terrorists	*Theft of trade secrets, sabotage, abuse of confidential information, loss of reputation, noncompliance of governmental regulatory agencies*
Natural disasters	*Denial or disruption of service, corruption of data, loss of data, harm to staff, damage to facilities, lack of access to facilities*

with the detect function of the CSF. Data within all of these areas must be continuously monitored and collected, correlated, analyzed, and reported in order to fully understand the security status of the organization. The implementation of a continuous monitoring strategy allows an organization to maintain ongoing control of an organization's security posture while taking into consideration the security risk tolerances that senior leaders establish. Continuous monitoring strategies may evolve over time as risk-based decision making and requirements for information change. A continuous monitoring strategy encompasses security status monitoring, the continual assessment of implemented security control effectiveness, and processes for incident handling that are in alignment with risk tolerances. It is important to note that knowledgeable network security engineers, security analysts, and administrators are required to implement, operate, and maintain the tools and technologies used to execute a continuous monitoring strategy. Additionally, effectively implemented security controls and countermeasures are required to ensure the validity of the data that is being continuously monitored and captured.

Given the substantial volumes of data that many organizations have, it is impractical and cost-prohibitive to collect and assess every aspect of every security control deployed across the organization at any given time. Reasonable assessment frequencies (e.g., daily, weekly, monthly, quarterly) for collecting critical information should be established. An alternative to attempting to assess all security controls is to take a sampling of the data. Careful consideration must be taken to ensure that the sample size methodology is sufficient to capture the variations that would be obtained if the full population were assessed.

Automated tools to streamline processes can also be valuable in identifying patterns and relationships in large volumes of data that would not otherwise be found by human analysts. Automating certain repetitive tasks such as scanning for vulnerabilities and automatically applying appropriate patches can reduce the amount of time a security professional would otherwise spend on those tasks and allow them to focus on higher level analysis that requires human interpretation of findings. When analyzing security-related information, there are several things network security engineers and security analysts need to take into consideration such as

- The organizational risk tolerance
- The potential impact that the vulnerabilities may have on critical assets, business processes, and the organization as a whole
- The potential impact of the mitigation strategies that may be employed
- Evolving threat and vulnerability data

Cost-effectiveness or return on investment of a mitigation strategy may heavily influence the determination whether to share/transfer, avoid/reject, or accept the risk. Responses to findings may also result in changes to security policies and IT governance and the policies and plans should be updated accordingly. Going forward, any modifications, enhancements, or additions to existing security controls need to be assessed to ensure the revised controls are effective in their implementations.

The responsibility for this job function should be clearly assigned so that all relevant individuals are aware of who is regularly reviewing the logs and audits. Due to the variety of systems, such as firewalls, Web servers, e-mail servers, database servers, the organization may assign the monitoring to a team of IT professionals.

Intrusion Detection and Prevention Technologies

Network security engineers and security analysts are tasked with gathering information about the organization and network activities to identify all network assets and aligned with the detect function of the CSF. The process of footprinting identifies network assets and activities and allows administrators to understand their computing environments. Footprinting reveals information a hacker would also try to ascertain such as public information about the domain name using a "whois" lookup; domain name system (DNS) tables using "nslookup" or "dig" to find the names of machines, network blocks, IP addresses, networking protocols used, telephone numbers, access control lists, and IDPS deployed (if any). Fingerprinting activities can then be used to identify the specific services offered on those active network assets and in turn be used to determine the tactics, techniques, and procedures to secure those assets.

Violations of security controls and practices can come from either internal or external attackers and have many causes such as intentional malicious malware or nonintentional errors and simple negligence caused by careless employees. Attackers gaining unauthorized access or internal authorized users, who misuse their privileges to gain access to systems in which they are not authorized, are incidents that can be continuously monitored and reported by an IDPS. IDPSs are valuable in performing packet sniffing and network traffic analysis to record observed events, block suspicious activity, provide notifications to network and security analysts, and produce reports in which an organization can use to understand the frequency and characteristics of detected threats to their systems. This information can be used to identify the appropriate countermeasures that should be implemented to protect the information assets. Often, internal employees will take shortcuts to existing security policies if those policies increase their workload. By implementing an IDPS system and notifying all employees that their network traffic is being monitored, employees who know they are being monitored may be less likely to violate security policies.

Many software companies combine detection and prevention capabilities; however, they are two separate technologies. IDS software automates the process of detecting events occurring on the network or computer systems to determine whether an incident or intrusion is in progress. Intrusion protection system (IPS) software builds on the IDS capabilities and is designed to prevent or halt possible incidents.

There are several types of IDPS technologies that network security engineers and security analysts need to know and are generally categorized into the following four groups.

1. Network-based IDPS (NIDPS) systems are installed on a computer or appliance programmed to monitor traffic and recognize attacks on a segment of an organization's network. The NIDPS examines data packets and looks for patterns that indicate an intrusion event is about to begin or already underway. This device can be installed on the inside of an edge router or firewall so that it can monitor traffic going in and out of a specific network. Inline sensors can be deployed on the inside of a firewall so that all traffic it is monitoring must pass through it and report back to the NIDPS. If malicious traffic is detected, the NIDPS can terminate the traffic passing through the inline sensor and protect all downstream assets. Passive sensors can be deployed that monitor a copy of the actual network traffic at key locations such as activity on a demilitarized zone (DMZ) subnet.

2. Host-based IDPS (HIDPS) systems are deployed on a specific computer or server, known as the host, and monitors activity only on that system. These types of systems are also known as system integrity verifiers as they monitor the status of key system files and detect when an attacker creates, modifies, or deletes files being monitored. HIDPS maintain their own log files and

provide an independent audit trail so as to prevent successful hackers from covering their tracks by deleting their activities.

3. Application-based IDPS (AppIDPS) systems examine an application for abnormal events by looking at the files created by the application and looking for occurrences such as invalid file executions and users exceeding their authorization. AppIDPS systems monitor and track interactions between the users, the application, and the data and is able to trace specific activity back to the individual user level. Encrypted data being decrypted by the application can be viewed and examined to identify any potential anomalies in user access or how the data are handled.

4. Wireless IDPS systems monitors and analyzes traffic running across the wireless network to identify suspicious activity involving the Layer 2 and Layer 3 (Open Systems Interconnection [OSI] model) wireless protocols (IEEE 802.11a, b, g, n, ac, and ad). These systems are not designed to identify suspicious activity at the application level or communications at higher levels such as IP addresses, Transmission Control Protocol (TPC), and User Datagram Protocol (UPD). Typical events captured by wireless IDPS systems are poorly secured wireless local area network (WLAN) devices, wireless network scanners, denial of service (DoS) attacks, unusual usage patterns such as failed attempts and higher than usual traffic between a device, spoofing (man-in-the-middle attacks), and unauthorized WLAN devices. By using the strength of an attacker's signal, a WLAN is able to calculate the physical location of the threat by approximating the distance from multiple sensors. This can be very beneficial in that physical security staff can then be sent to catch the attacker.

The network security engineer or security analyst determines what type of IDPS system is most appropriate for the organization's network security. A common practice is to implement a blended solution and use host and application based systems on mission critical assets and a robust NIDPS for global infrastructure protection.

Intrusion Detection and Protection Methodologies

In addition to the types of IDPS technologies that can be deployed, IDPS systems use three common methodologies or approaches to detect incidents. They are called signature-based, anomaly/behavior-based, and stateful protocol analysis. A signature-based detection approach examines traffic in search of preconfigured and predetermined attack patterns that match known signatures. Examples of distinct signatures are DoS and distributed DoS (DDoS) attacks and known forms of malware sent via e-mail such as fake 30-day-free trials of McAfee VirusScan (FakeAV) and Trojan ZipCard posing as a "new greeting" from a family member with the malicious attachment called Greeting_Card.zip. For known threats, signature-based detection is very effective. However, a slight modification of a malicious filename or a new threat will go undetected. The signature database must be kept up-to-date in order for it to be effective.

An anomaly-based detection approach focuses on the frequency of network activity and compares observed events to recognized definitions of what activity is considered normal network activity. A baseline of network performance must be established first and becomes the definition of normal activity on the network. Once the baseline is established, periodic samples of network activity are captured and compared to the baseline. Statistical methods are used to determine if the data collected falls outside of the baseline parameters and if so, will trigger notifications to the administrator. One advantage to this approach is that it can detect new threats because it is looking for any type of abnormal activity.

A stateful protocol analysis approach uses protocol models to identify deviations between observed events and predetermined profiles of benign activity. The protocol models are based on standards established by entities such as the Internet Engineering Task Force (IETF) and software vendors. Universal profiles of the protocol models are developed and specify how the network, transport, and application protocols should be used. One downside is that vendors may add proprietary features to a protocol and without complete details of how this protocol should be used, the IDPS will not perform well or provide an accurate analysis. As the IDPS tracks the various states in which activities occur, it can detect suspicious activity based on expected sequences of commands. For example, if a user is trying to log in to a system and has not successfully completed the authentication process, they are in an unauthenticated state. The IDPS system knows that there are very few commands that can be performed in this state. However, once the user successfully authenticates, the session changes to the authenticated state and the commands expected to be performed in this state are different. Stateful protocol analysis identifies unexpected sequences of commands for each state and individual commands. Due to the processing requirements of tracking so many simultaneous sessions and the complexity of the continuous analysis, this approach is very resource intensive.

Network Alerts

During the risk assessment process, the network security engineer or security analyst needs to determine what gets logged, what kinds of events kick off alerts, and what actions are required if an alert is generated. Whenever suspicious behavior is detected or a critical event occurs, an alert from the IDPS is generated and must be acted upon. It is important to configure IDPS systems so that excessive notification alerts and false positives (identifying benign activity as malicious) from IDPS systems does not increase the noise level to the degree where it becomes almost impossible to differentiate important alert signals from less significant events. Analysis and fine tuning of the rules to reduce the false-positive noise and filtering the alerts by level of confidence may be useful so that the administrator can determine relevant notifications. Many security engineers configure the IDPS notifications to decrease false negatives (failing to detect malicious activity), which has the consequence of increasing false-positive detection that requires more analysis to differentiate benign events from truly malicious activity.

Malware

Malware remains a significant threat causing widespread damage and disruption to organizations. Spyware, intended to violate a user's privacy, is just another form of malware and has recently become widespread. As nearly every malware incident requires some kind of containment action, the security analysts should have strategies and procedures in place for making decisions that are in alignment with the acceptable risk levels established by the organization. At a minimum, the organization should establish a malware prevention policy and user awareness program that explains acceptable and proper rules of behavior, social engineering tricks, and proper use of the organization's IT assets. All users should be aware of the risks that malware presents, the way in which malware spreads, and their role in preventing a malware attack. This policy should include all internal users, users working remotely, and address contractors, business partners, and mobile devices.

Security analysts must analyze all identified malicious activity to determine the weaknesses exploited, the exploited methods, and the effects on the system and information. With this analysis, security analysts should also consider the following to prevent malware-related events:

- Deploy and configure both network and host-based IPS to detect and stop known and unknown threats
- Require authentication before allowing access to a network service
- Restrict the use of removal media (USB drives) on systems that are high risk such as publicly accessible kiosks and computers
- Restrict the use of mobile devices on trusted network or adopt a rigorous "bring your own device" (BYOD) policy and use container technology to control devices that are lost or stolen
- Require all software application changes, firewall and router configurations, and database changes on production systems to be approved through a formal change control process
- Keep systems up-to-date with operating system, application upgrades, and patches—implement a patch management policy
- Restrict the use of administrator-level privileges by users
- Employ the principle of least privilege allowing the minimum rights to the appropriate users, processes, and hosts
- Disable or remove unneeded services, particularly network services
- Deploy and manage an antivirus software program
- Restrict the use of user-installed applications, such as instant messaging, peer-to-peer file sharing, and so on, that are often used to transfer malware

- Require the scanning of all e-mail attachments and .zip files before they are opened
- Deploy spyware detection and removal utilities
- Only permit access to other networks using organization-approved and secured mechanisms
- Configure application settings to increase security such as restricting macro use, preventing automatic loading of e-mail images, preventing software installation within Web browsers, restricting Web browsing cookies, blocking suspicious e-mail attachments, filtering spam, blocking pop-up windows, and limiting mobile code execution
- Disable automatic execution of binaries and scripts

Underlying Knowledge, Skill, and Ability Requirements for Enterprise Network Defense Analysis

Along with a detailed set of tasks, the NICE Workforce Framework (v2.0) also provides a distinctive set of knowledge, skill, and ability (KSA) specifications for each specialty area. The major competencies for this specialty area include the following:

- *CND.* This includes a team of IT professionals to identify network vulnerabilities and threats, continuously monitor and analyze the network and systems for suspicious activity, and defend the network by applying best practices and countermeasures.
- *Information systems/network security.* This includes a team who provides secure daily operating management of network access, firewall access and admissions control administration, network intrusion detection and prevention monitoring, vulnerability scanning and reports, baseline configuration standards, patch management, user ID/password verification, and enforcement of security policies.
- *Vulnerabilities assessment.* Conducted as part of an overall risk assessment process.
- *Risk and incident management.* Ongoing management of incident handling procedures and processes.

Table 6.2 displays the specialty area KSA requirements for the END analysis specialty area as well as the associated competency areas (NIST, 2014).

END analysis work requires a broad range of technical and behavioral capabilities. Knowledge of cyber defense mitigations techniques and vulnerability assessment tools, including open source tools, and their capabilities is required. Vulnerability scanning tools are designed to identify hosts and what is running on them such as operating systems, software applications, and open ports. Vulnerability scanning can identify missing patches, misconfigurations, identify open ports, outdated software versions, and validate compliance or deviations of the organization's IT security policy. Like virus scanners and IDPS systems, vulnerability scanners rely on a repository of signatures and require updates in order to identify the most current vulnerabilities.

Table 6.2   END Analysis Specialty Area Knowledge, Skills, and Abilities (KSAs)

Item ID	KSA	Statement	Competency
3	KSA	Skill in conducting vulnerability scans and recognizing vulnerabilities in security systems	Vulnerabilities assessment
19	KSA	Knowledge of cyber defense mitigation techniques and vulnerability assessment tools, including open-source tools and their capabilities	Computer network defense
27	KSA	Knowledge of cryptography and cryptographic key management concepts	Cryptography
29	KSA	Knowledge of data backup, types of backups (e.g., full, incremental), and recovery concepts and tools	Computer forensics
49	KSA	Knowledge of host and network access control mechanisms (e.g., access control list)	Information systems/Network security
59	KSA	Knowledge of intrusion detection system (IDS) tools and applications	Computer network defense
61	KSA	Knowledge of incident response and handling methodologies	Incident management
63	KSA	Knowledge of information assurance (IA) principles and organizational requirements to protect confidentiality, integrity, availability, authenticity, and nonrepudiation of information and data	Information assurance

(Continued)

Table 6.2 (Continued)   END Analysis Specialty Area Knowledge, Skills, and Abilities (KSAs)

Item ID	KSA	Statement	Competency
66	KSA	Knowledge of intrusion detection methodologies and techniques for detecting host- and network-based intrusions via intrusion detection technologies	Computer network defense
81	KSA	Knowledge of network protocols (e.g., Transmission Critical Protocol/Internet Protocol [TCP/IP], Dynamic Host Configuration Protocol [DHCP]), and directory services (e.g., Domain Name System [DNS])	Infrastructure design
87	KSA	Knowledge of network traffic analysis methods	Information systems/Network security
88	KSA	Knowledge of new and emerging information technology (IT) and cyber security technologies	Technology awareness
92	KSA	Knowledge of how traffic flows across the network (e.g., TCP/IP, Open System Interconnection model [OSI])	Infrastructure design
95	KSA	Knowledge of penetration testing principles, tools, and techniques (e.g., metasploit, neosploit)	Vulnerabilities assessment
98	KSA	Knowledge of policy-based and risk-adaptive access controls	Identity management
102	KSA	Knowledge of programming language structures and logic	Computer languages

(Continued)

Table 6.2 (Continued)   END Analysis Specialty Area Knowledge, Skills, and Abilities (KSAs)

Item ID	KSA	Statement	Competency
105	KSA	Knowledge of system and application security threats and vulnerabilities (e.g., buffer overflow, mobile code, cross-site scripting, Procedural Language/Structured Query Language [PL/SQL] and injections, race conditions, covert channel, replay, return-oriented attacks, malicious code)	Vulnerabilities assessment
110	KSA	Knowledge of key concepts in security management (e.g., release management, patch management)	Information assurance
115	KSA	Knowledge of content development	Computer network defense
138	KSA	Knowledge of the enterprise network defense (END) provider reporting structure and processes within one's own organization	Information systems/Network security
148	KSA	Knowledge of virtual private network (VPN) security	Encryption
150	KSA	Knowledge of what constitutes a network attack and the relationship to both threats and vulnerabilities	Information systems/Network security
165	KSA	Skill in conducting open source research for troubleshooting novel client-level problems (e.g., online development communities, system security blogging sites)	Knowledge management
175	KSA	Skill in developing and deploying signatures	Information systems/Network security

(Continued)

Table 6.2 (Continued)   END Analysis Specialty Area Knowledge, Skills, and Abilities (KSAs)

Item ID	KSA	Statement	Competency
181	KSA	Skill in detecting host and network based intrusions via intrusion detection technologies (e.g., Snort)	Computer network defense
212	KSA	Skill in network mapping and recreating network topologies	Infrastructure design
214	KSA	Skill in performing packet-level analysis using appropriate tools (e.g., Wireshark, tcpdump)	Vulnerabilities assessment
229	KSA	Skill in using incident handling methodologies	Incident management
233	KSA	Skill in using protocol analyzers	Vulnerabilities assessment
234	KSA	Skill in using sub-netting tools	Infrastructure design
270	KSA	Knowledge of common adversary tactics, techniques, and procedures (TTPs) in assigned area of responsibility (e.g., historical country-specific TTPs, emerging capabilities)	Computer network defense
271	KSA	Knowledge of common network tools (e.g., ping, traceroute, nslookup) and interpret the information results	Infrastructure design
277	KSA	Knowledge of defense-in-depth principles and network security architecture	Computer network defense

(Continued)

Table 6.2 (Continued) END Analysis Specialty Area Knowledge, Skills, and Abilities (KSAs)

Item ID	KSA	Statement	Competency
278	KSA	Knowledge of different types of network communication (e.g., local area network [LAN], wide area network [WAN], metropolitan area network [MAN], wireless local area network [WLAN], wireless wide area network [WWAN])	Telecommunications
286	KSA	Knowledge of file extensions (e.g., .dll, .bat, .zip, .pcap, .gzip)	Operating systems
342	KSA	Knowledge of Unix command line (e.g., mkdir, mv, ls, passwd, grep)	Computer languages
347	KSA	Knowledge of Windows command line (e.g., ipconfig, netstat, dir, nbtstat)	Operating systems
353	KSA	Skill in collecting data from a variety of cyber defense resources	Computer network defense
895	KSA	Skill in recognizing and categorizing types of vulnerabilities and associated attacks	Information assurance
912	KSA	Knowledge of collection management processes, capabilities, and limitations	Configuration management
915	KSA	Knowledge of front-end collection systems, including network traffic collection, filtering, and selection	Information systems/Network security
922	KSA	Skill in using network analysis tools to identify vulnerabilities	Vulnerabilities assessment

(Continued)

Table 6.2 (Continued) END Analysis Specialty Area Knowledge, Skills, and Abilities (KSAs)

Item ID	KSA	Statement	Competency
965	KSA	Knowledge of organization's risk tolerance and/or risk management approach	Risk management
984	KSA	Knowledge of cyber defense policies, procedures, and regulations	Computer network defense
985	KSA	Skill in configuring and utilizing network protection components (e.g., firewalls, VPNs, network IDSs)	Configuration management
990	KSA	Knowledge of common attack vectors on the network layer	Computer network defense
991	KSA	Knowledge of different classes of attacks (e.g., passive, active, insider, close-in, distribution)	Computer network defense
992	KSA	Knowledge of different operational threat environments (e.g., first generation [script kiddies], second generation [non-nation state sponsored], and third generation [nation state sponsored])	Computer network defense
1007	KSA	Skills in data reduction	Data management
1008	KSA	Knowledge of how to troubleshoot basic systems and identify operating systems-related issues	Operating systems
1021	KSA	Knowledge of threat assessment	Risk management

(Continued)

Table 6.2 (Continued)   END Analysis Specialty Area Knowledge, Skills, and Abilities (KSAs)

Item ID	KSA	Statement	Competency
1033	KSA	Knowledge of basic system administration, network, and operating system hardening techniques	Information systems/network security
1036	KSA	Knowledge of applicable laws (e.g., Electronic Communications Privacy Act, Foreign Intelligence Surveillance Act, Protect America Act, search and seizure laws, civil liberties and privacy laws), US Statutes (e.g., Titles 10, 18, 32, 50 in US Code), Presidential Directives, executive branch guidelines, and/or administrative/criminal legal guidelines and procedures relevant to work performed	Criminal law
1069	KSA	Knowledge of general attack stages (e.g., footprinting and scanning, enumeration, gaining access, escalation or privileges, maintaining access, network exploitation, covering tracks)	Computer network defense
1072	KSA	Knowledge of network security architecture concepts, including topology, protocols, components, and principles (e.g., application of defense-in-depth)	Information systems/Network security
1114	KSA	Knowledge of encryption methodologies	Cryptography
1115	KSA	Skill in reading hexadecimal data	Computer languages

(Continued)

Table 6.2 (Continued)   END Analysis Specialty Area Knowledge, Skills, and Abilities (KSAs)

Item ID	KSA	Statement	Competency
1116	KSA	Skill in identifying common encoding techniques (e.g., Exclusive Disjunction [XOR], American Standard Code for Information Interchange [ASCII], Unicode, Base64, Uuencode, Uniform Resource Locator [URL] encode)	Computer languages
1117	KSA	Skill in utilizing virtual networks for testing	Operating systems
1118	KSA	Skill in reading and interpreting signatures (e.g., Snort)	Information systems/Network security
1119	KSA	Knowledge of signature implementation impact	Information systems/Network security
1120	KSA	Ability to interpret and incorporate data from multiple tool sources	Data management
1121	KSA	Knowledge of Windows and Unix ports and services	Operating systems
1133	KSA	Knowledge of service management concepts for networks and related standards (e.g., Information Technology Infrastructure Library, v3 [ITIL])	Network management

Vulnerability scanners can be run on a local host or from the network. Network-based scanning is primarily used for network discovery of active systems and to identify open ports and vulnerabilities. Host-based local scanning is conducted primarily to identify the host operating system and any application misconfigurations and vulnerabilities. Host-based scanning requires a root-level administrative account and can provide a higher level of detail. Although vulnerability scanning can disrupt network operations by taking up bandwidth and slowing down response times, the output of vulnerability scanners are very useful in providing information on systems in which a penetration test can then be run. The outcome of a thorough vulnerability scan includes a prioritized list of vulnerabilities in which the security engineer and security analyst can determine how to remediate.

Ethical Hacking: Hardening Checks and Penetration Testing

Ethical hacking is often conducted by the network security engineer or network administrator to attack the system on behalf of the organization with the goal to uncover vulnerabilities in which a malicious hacker could exploit. There are two separate tests an ethical hacker performs: a hardening check and a penetration test. For each piece of internal equipment, especially new network components, a hardening check will uncover any bad system configurations or operational weaknesses such as checking that daemons are switched off, firewalls are deployed, default login account are not in use, and that all patches are up-to-date.

A penetration test checks for vulnerabilities on the outside of the infrastructure components. At the point the network security engineer believes the network is at the desired security posture, penetration tests are recommended. Penetration tests mimic real-world attacks with the goal of identifying techniques and methods of bypassing the security features that were put in place to protect the network, application, or system. Penetration tests report how security was breached so that the security engineer and analysts can determine how to remediate. Popular penetration tools are Wireshark, metasploit, and Nmap security scanner. Penetration tests can be very helpful in determining how capable the network security engineer and security analysts are able to detect the attacks and respond appropriately. During a penetration security test, combinations of vulnerabilities (rummaging through trashcans, social engineering, and network scanning) are often identified and exploited, with no knowledge or consent of the targets, in order to gain unauthorized access. Usually only the chief executive officer (CEO), board members, and executive management are aware beforehand of a full ethical penetration test. This type of security testing should be done after careful planning and requires expertise to minimize the risk to targeted systems as significant damage can be done in the course of the test.

Penetration tests are designed to exploit the vulnerabilities that have been identified during the vulnerability scan, thus confirming their existence. These types of tests can be run on routers, firewalls, internal networks, IDS, Web applications, and database servers. Common types of vulnerabilities exploited by penetration tests include the following:

- Injection flaws (such as OS commands, XML parsers, lightweight directory access protocol [LDAP], and SQL) occur when untrusted data are sent to an interpreter as part of a command or query. An injection can result in data loss, corruption, denial of access, and sometimes complete host takeover.
- Flawed authentication and session management—examples such as sending passwords and session IDs over unencrypted without hashing or encryption, exposing session IDs in the URL, and not rotating session IDs after successful login can all cause vulnerabilities.
- Cross-site scripting (XSS) flaws are the most prevalent Web application security flaws and occur when an app uses user supplied data in a page sent to the browser without properly validating the content. Attackers can execute scripts to hijack user's browser sessions, deface Web sites, and insert malware.
- Insecure direct object references—applications frequently use the actual name or key of an object when generating Web pages and do not always verify if the user is authorized for the target object. Unless object references are unpredictable, an attacker can access all available data referenced by the parameter.
- Misconfigured security settings such as out-of-date software, operating systems, and code libraries; unnecessary features enabled such as ports, services, and accounts; default accounts and their passwords are still enabled and unchanged. With these types of settings misconfigured, attackers can access the systems undetected and steal or modify data over time.
- Incorrect file and directory permissions assigned to users and/or processes.
- Kernel flaws—as the core of an operating system, any flaw in the kernel code puts the entire system in danger.
- Buffer overflows. A buffer overflow occurs when a program or process tries to store more data in a buffer than what was intended to store. The overflow of data can allow attackers to modify and add code to the overflow data to trigger specific actions such as changing data, exposing confidential information, and damaging user's files.

Other nontechnical types of penetration tests include methods of attack such as physical security breaches and the use of social engineering to gain unauthorized access. The use of social engineering is rapidly increasing and reveals weaknesses in users failing to follow standard security procedures and processes. One example of social engineering, called phishing, involves sending carefully designed e-mails to look exactly like a particular financial institution in order to steal information such as account numbers, user IDs, passwords, and ideally social security numbers. Social engineering may be used to target high profile or executives by hacking into their e-mail and sending bogus instructions to accounts payable to ship money via electronic transfers on their behalf. Other phishing attacks include individuals posing as helpdesk agents calling to notify users that their systems are reporting issues and to install unknown malware. These types of attacks are getting more sophisticated and requires organizations to train their workforce on how to handle these types of attacks.

Technical Tools

Network security engineers and security analysts should have a core set of tools that are used to conduct the various network testing and to keep skills up-to-date. Tools should be obtain from trusted sources and can be a combination of freeware tools, commercial off-the-shelf (COTS), open-source tools, or developed in-house. Many tools require specific operating systems to run and are often installed using virtual machine (VM) technology versus dual-boot systems. Multiple VMs can run on a single host and be configured to run different operating systems. The ability to run several operating systems allows security professionals to use a wider variety of tools and run simultaneous tests without having to reboot the system to toggle over to another operating system. Security engineers and analysts should be knowledgeable and comfortable using all operating systems as well as using VM technology. Table 6.3 shows the variety of tools available for the various security testing techniques.

Specialty Area 2: Incident Response

The specialty area of incident response "responds to disruptions within the pertinent domain to mitigate immediate and potential threats. Uses mitigation, preparedness, and response and recovery approaches to maximize survival of life, preservation of property, and information security. Investigates and analyses relevant response activities and evaluates the effectiveness of an improvements to existing practices" (NIST, 2014). Cyberattacks have not only become more widespread and sophisticated but also more damaging and disruptive. Having IDPS systems in place and continually monitoring the network for potential attacks is essential. New types of malware and attack strategies emerge daily and preventative countermeasures can help reduce the number of incidents. Incident response is an organized approach to addressing security breaches and managing the negative consequences. As not all incidents can be prevented, risks to infrastructure, people, and information assets can be planned for and anticipated during a risk assessment process.

One of the most challenging parts of the incident response process is detecting possible security incidents and determining the magnitude of the problem. A computer security incident can mean a lot of different things which is why it is important to establish a common lexicon of what it means to have detected an event or an incident. Events are any observable occurrence in a system or network; however, not all events are or will have a negative impact on the system or network. If an event becomes a genuine threat to the organization and violates established policy, it immediately becomes an incident. Establishing clear processes and procedures to handle incidents is critical.

Table 6.3 Security Testing Techniques and Security Testing Tools

Security Testing Technique	Security Testing Tool
Network sniffing	Wireshark, Cain and Abel, tcpdump, dSniff, Ettercap, Kismet, snoop, Scapy, SkyGrabber, CommView, Lanmeter, Ntop, P0f, NetworkMiner, EtherApe, Ngrep, inSSIDer, and KisMAC
Network discovery	Nmap Security Scanner, Kismet, Ettercap, Network Stumbler, Aerosol, AirMagnet, MacStumbler, WiStumbler, AiroPeek, Airscanner, AP Scanner, dstumbler, and Sniffer Wireless
File integrity checking	iScanner, Autopsy, Tripwire, AlienVault, and AIDE
Application security testing	W3af, OWASP Zed Attack Proxy (ZAP), OWASP CAL9000, SPIKE, skipfish, Burp Suite, WebScarab, sqlninja, and Wfuzz
Network port and service identification	Nmap Security Scanner, Unicornscan, Angry IP Scanner, Superscan, and NetScan Tools
Wireless scanning	Aircrack, Kismet, NetStumbler, AirSnort, WEPcrack, inSSIDer, and KisMAC
Vulnerability scanning	Nessus, Metasploit, w3af, GFI LanGuard, Core Impact, Snort, Canvas, Netsparker, Social Engineer Toolkit, and sqlmap
Penetration testing	Wireshark, Metasploit, Nmap Security Scanner, and Yersinia
Traffic monitoring tools	Ettercap, Splunk, Nagios, Ntop, Argus, Wireshark, tcpdump, WinDump, and P0f
Password cracking	John the Ripper, Cain and Abel, Aircrack, THC Hydra, ophcrack, Medusa, Brutus, Wfuzz, SolarWinds, RainbowCrack, and fgdump
Digital forensics	Digital Forensics Framework (DFF), Kali Linux, Helix, Maltego, Foremost, EnCase, PTK Forensics, The Sleuth Kit, and Hashkeeper
Rootkit detectors	Sysinternals, Tripwire, DumpSec, HijackThis, and AIDE

The function of incident response can require substantial planning and resources and include a wide range of stakeholders. Starting with executive management, this level of management needs to understand what the computer security incident response team (CSIRT) does and who is on the team. Executive management must give the CSIRT team authorization to carry out its functions with all levels of the business functions of the organization in the event a security breach has occurred. IT managers need to understand and plan for the demand on resources that will directly impact the IT security professional staff and the potential impact an incident will have on existing networks, systems, and components. Anticipation and preapproval of certain CSIRT actions to significant events must be obtained in the planning process for successful incident handling. Computer crime investigators and forensic analysts are required to collect and preserve data so that it can be used in a court of law. Data collection techniques are critical and procedures must be implemented to preserve the integrity of the artifacts that legal chain of custody is maintained. The legal department or outside counsel should review the procedures and documentation of the CSIRT team to ensure processes and procedures will be performed in alignment with legal and ethical guidelines. Service-level agreements and nondisclosure agreements will need to be run through the legal department. The human resources (HR) department can assist organizations who require outside help in responding to security incidents. If the organization does not have adequate technical staff, the HR department can assist in hiring and staffing the CSIRT team. Public relations must ensure that the proper amount of information is disclosed to the public as well as to appropriate agencies, law enforcement, and the media. Additional stakeholders include physical security, insurance organizations, and key business partners such as contractors, consultants, suppliers, and vendors.

Given the challenges to ensure all stakeholders are informed with the appropriate information at any given time, a communication plan is a critical part of the incident response plan.

Factoring Incident Response Workforce Tasks into the Cybersecurity Framework Functions

Table 6.4 shows the tasks for the incident response specialty area mapped to the CSF functions. Once an event has been detected and categorized as an Incident, the entirety of the tasks for this specialty area map to the respond function of the CSF.

Organizing an effective incident response program involves many decisions and activities. The following outlines the major activities:

■ Organize the appropriate individuals to staff the CSIRT
■ Develop a common definition for what an incident is and establish a scope of what services the incident response team should provide
■ Develop an incident response policy and incident response plan
■ Develop policies and procedures for the detection and analysis of incidents and reporting
■ Develop procedures for incident documentation

Table 6.4   Incident Response Specialty Area Mapped to the CSF Functions

Item ID	KSA	Statement	Competency
29	KSA	Knowledge of data backup, types of backups (e.g., full, incremental), and recovery concepts and tools.	Computer forensics
50	KSA	Knowledge of how network services and protocols interact to provide network communications.	Infrastructure design
60	KSA	Knowledge of incident categories, incident responses, and timelines for responses.	Incident management
61	KSA	Knowledge of incident response and handling methodologies.	Incident management
66	KSA	Knowledge of intrusion detection methodologies and techniques for detecting host- and network-based intrusions via intrusion detection technologies.	Computer network defense
81	KSA	Knowledge of network protocols (e.g., Transmission Critical Protocol/Internet Protocol [TCP/IP], Dynamic Host Configuration Protocol [DHCP]), and directory services (e.g., Domain Name System [DNS]).	Infrastructure design
87	KSA	Knowledge of network traffic analysis methods.	Information systems/Network security
93	KSA	Knowledge of packet-level analysis.	Vulnerabilities assessment
105	KSA	Knowledge of system and application security threats and vulnerabilities (e.g., buffer overflow, mobile code, cross-site scripting, procedural language/structured query language [PL/SQL] and injections, race conditions, covert channel, replay, return-oriented attacks, malicious code).	Vulnerabilities assessment

(Continued)

Table 6.4 (Continued)   Incident Response Specialty Area Mapped to the CSF Functions

Item ID	KSA	Statement	Competency
150	KSA	Knowledge of what constitutes a network attack and the relationship to both threats and vulnerabilities.	Information systems/Network security
153	KSA	Skill of identifying capturing, containing, and reporting malware.	Computer network defense
217	KSA	Skill in preserving evidence integrity according to standard operating procedures or national standards.	Computer forensics
893	KSA	Skill in securing network communications.	Information assurance
895	KSA	Skill in recognizing and categorizing types of vulnerabilities and associated attacks.	Information assurance
896	KSA	Skill in protecting a network against malware.	Computer network defense
897	KSA	Skill in performing damage assessments.	Information assurance
923	KSA	Knowledge of security event correlation tools.	Information systems/Network security
984	KSA	Knowledge of cyber defense policies, procedures, and regulations.	Computer network defense
991	KSA	Knowledge of different classes of attacks (e.g., passive, active, insider, close-in, distribution).	Computer network defense

- Develop plans for the training of CSIRT team members and awareness for all organizational members
- Develop testing plans for the incident response plan and conduct period testing
- Develop an incident prioritization scheme
- Develop a communication plan that includes incident notification, an escalation process, guidelines and procedures for handling communication with outside entities regarding incidents
- Develop procedures for containment, eradication, and recovery
- Develop processes and procedures for evidence gathering and handling
- Develop evidence retention guidelines
- Develop guidelines for information sharing
- Develop a process and guidelines for after-action reviews

The incident response life cycle can be organized into 10 phases. Figure 6.3 shows a 10-phase incident response life cycle.

Building the Team

The CSIRT may be an informally recognized group of individuals with the technical skills to respond to a cyberattack or a more formal implementation. Larger organizations generally appoint the chief information security officer (CISO) to select members from the organization's department managers and the IT security professionals to staff the CSIRT team who will develop and execute the incident response plans. An important determination that the CISO must make is whether they have the expertise in-house to staff the CSIRT team or require outside help. Conducting a gap analysis of the skills necessary to successfully implement an incident response plan is essential. A typical CSIRT needs knowledge and skills in capturing, containing, and reporting malware; network administration, intrusion detection methodologies; firewall and system administration; packet-level analysis; data storage and recovery; and cryptography, data collection, and artifact preservation. Organizations may choose to hire additional employees to close the skills gap or outsource some portion of the duties of the incident response.

Often members of the CSIRT team are expected to rotate or be on-call 24/7 and in the event of an incident, required to be available on-site at a moment's notice. Continuous monitoring and incident response work can be demanding and time consuming and being on-call 24/7 can eventually wear down a CSIRT team. To help prevent this, one prevalent outsourcing arrangement is 24/7 continuous monitoring of intrusion detection sensors and firewalls to an off-site-managed security services provider. If the outsourced provider identifies any suspicious activity, they report it to an internal IT security team to handle and remediate. This arrangement may help in balancing the workload and still keep internal IT security professionals engaged in the process.

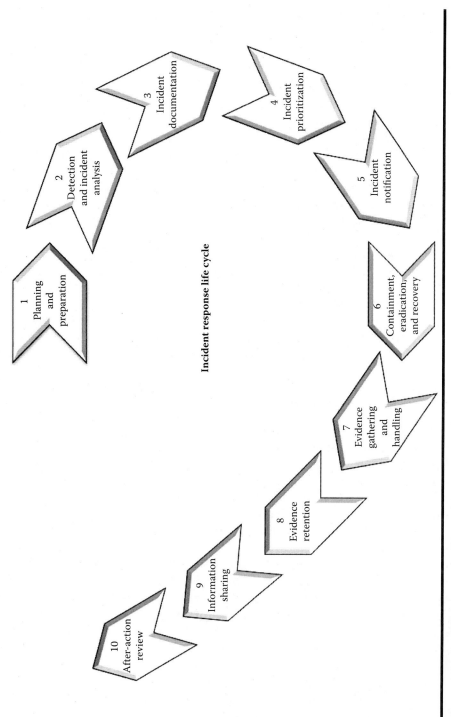

Figure 6.3 Incident response life cycle.

If the organization is geographically dispersed, multiple CIRTs with the responsibility for handling incidents specific to their location is often effective for large organizations. However, the teams should be part of a centralized structure so that information can be shared and that policies and procedures are consistently handled across the enterprise.

Incident Response Policy

It is neither realistic nor advisable to attempt to develop policies and procedures for handling every conceivable incident, especially as new ones are generated so often. However, the incident response team should be prepared to handle incidents from known common methods of attack such as through Web-based applications; USB flash drives; e-mail; social engineering; equipment theft; and improper use of systems by internal and external users. One of the first deliverables of the CSIRT is an incident response policy document. It is important to gain the full support of executive management and that the policy is clearly understood by all stakeholders. The incident response policy document defines the roles and responsibilities of the CSIRT and provides clarity for the authority level the CSIRT has to confiscate, monitor, or disable any equipment in the event of a breach. The policy document also provides definitions of known computer security incidents and how security incidents will be prioritized. It also includes performance measures and how the team will report ongoing activities.

Incident Response Plan

Organizations have unique requirements and require plans that are in alignment with the organization's mission, size, structure, and functions. The incident response plan is a roadmap and provides a detailed set of processes and procedures that kicks into immediate effect once an incident is detected or reported. From a process standpoint, it is advisable that organizations provide a centralized team, which is the focal point for reporting any suspicious activity. This team is often the helpdesk, which has a published contact number which users are often familiar with and is often staffed 24/7. The incident response plan should include a statement that discusses management support as many members of the CSIRT often have full-time positions in addition to the incident response duties. For significant breaches, these employees may be away from their regular positions for an extended time as they work to resolve any incidents and department managers need to understand the level of support for the CSIRT at the highest levels of the organization. The incident response plan should include the following elements:

- Mission, strategies, and goals
- Senior management approval
- The organization approach to incident response

- Instructions on incident notification to include contact information for CSIRT members, backup contacts, how to notify appropriate entities such as the system owner; HR; law enforcement; legal; public affairs; local, state, or federal governmental agencies
- Description of the overall process of incident response from reporting to after-action reviews
- Documented incident handling procedures for every potential attack scenario—sometimes called an incident plan
- Documentation instructions to include use of logbooks, audio recordings, and digital cameras
- Instructions on evidence gathering and handling
- Post-incident activities to include after-action reviews
- Evidence retention policy
- Information sharing and reporting requirements—write and publish cyber defense techniques, guidance, and reports on incident findings to appropriate constituencies

Preparing to Handle Incidents

The prevention of threats and attacks is the responsibility of the network security engineers and security analysts. Incident response activities are reactionary measures and are not considered preventative. It is only after an event has been analyzed and categorized as an incident that the CSIRT is alerted and called to action. However, before any engagement of the CSIRT, it is helpful to have tools and resources in place to aid in the organization and handling of any incident. The following is a list of items that should be considered before and not during an incident:

- A contact list that includes primary and backup contacts that will be distributed internally and to external entities such as law enforcement. Instructions for verifying the contact's identity should also be included.
- Escalation procedures and on-call schedules if team members rotate when they are available.
- Issue tracking system that collects detailed information about each reported incident.
- Smartphones issued to each CSIRT member with preloaded contacts of all other relevant entities.
- A common meeting area for all members to gather to discuss incidents and one in which sensitive information being discussed remains private.
- Evidence-gathering materials such as digital cameras, audio recorders, notebooks, chain of custody forms, evidence storage bags, tape, and tags to ensure integrity and preserve for possible admittance as evidence in a court of law.
- Digital forensic workstations/laptops, cables, blank removable media, backup devices, portable printer, and preloaded digital forensic software

to analyze disk images, preserve log files, disk images, and all relevant incident data.

■ Packet sniffers, protocol analyzers, and encryption software.
■ Spare networking equipment to reconstruct and analyze malicious attacks or activity.
■ Network diagrams and documentation of all critical assets and databases.
■ A list of all commonly used ports and Trojan horse ports and cryptographic hashes of critical files.
■ Current baselines of expected network, systems, and application activity.

Incident Detection and Analysis

As mentioned earlier, incident detection may be the most difficult task. Many times, incidents are false positives from IDPS systems or are reported through the helpdesk with ambiguous, incomplete, or contradictory information. Although IDPS, antivirus software, file integrity checking, and third-party monitoring services can create alerts and notifications, it takes skilled and experienced IT security professionals to effectively and efficiently analyze the events and take appropriate actions.

Once an incident has been reported, the CSIRT is responsible to perform analysis of the incident and provide updates to management. In general, analysis attempts to answer the following questions:

■ How did this incident occur in the first place?
■ What systems were compromised, and what is the extent of the damage?
■ Was anything stolen? Was anything changed?
■ How do we prevent this incident from occurring in the future?

Depending upon the extent of the incident, the analysis process can take a day, week, or even months to complete. For example, investigation into the extent of a malware attack through e-mail attachment may be handled by the IT security team with CSIRT oversight. On the other hand, response to identity theft potentially caused by database tampering can take much longer.

Incident Documentation

From the time an incident is detected, every step taken should be tracked and documented to include date and timestamps. Documentation can include audio recordings, log files, images, e-mails, and handwritten or typed field notes. It is important that there is a secure repository for this type of information as it will contain sensitive information. A software application such as an incident tracking system that can capture the pertinent information about each incident is highly recommended. If legal action is taken at a later date, these documents will be considered and possibly used as evidence in a court of law.

Incident Prioritization

Incidents should not be managed on a first-come, first-served basis but on a prioritized basis that takes into consideration the following:

- *The business impact of the incident.* The functionality of the IT systems that were compromised and the impact on the system users.
- *The impact of the incident on information.* The confidentiality, integrity, and availability of the organization's information.
- *The scope and the efforts required to recover from the incident.* An incident may require more resources to recover from than the value of the asset. Critical judgment of recovery efforts must be weighed against the value and cost of the effort.

Prioritizing detected incidents is one of the most critical aspects in the incident detection and analysis process. It is imperative that the incident responders have the knowledge and experience to act swiftly to analyze suspicious activity in order to understand the magnitude of the breach. For each incident, the IT security and incident response team members should consider the impact on the business and the estimated efforts required to recover from the incident as the basis for deciding the response prioritization. Incidents with low efforts for recovery but are highly impactful on the functionality of the IT systems are ideal candidates to consider as high priority. The CSIRT should also consider ranking each prioritized incident for the purpose of helping management and others outside of the technical team understand the magnitude of the incident and possible duration for recovery. Senior management may only want to be notified for incidents that reach a certain level of impact to the business, users, and information.

Incident Notification

After an incident is prioritized, the response team notifies all appropriate stakeholders. The incident response policy and plan should state the following:

- *Who is to be notified.* CEO, chief information officer, CISO, IT security manager, HR, public affairs, legal department, and any outside agencies.
- *What method.* In-person, telephone, e-mail, Web portal, voicemail, flyers on bulletin boards and on doors in heavy traffic areas.
- *How often.* Some managers want regular updates every 15 or 30 minutes for severe incidents. Each organization needs to determine who and how often regular updates should occur.
- *What information.* Specific information should be gathered for each incident as part of the notification process. Examples include severity level of incident; current status such as new, in-progress, resolved; a summary; actions taken

by all incident handlers; impact assessment; contact information of system owners, administrators, managers; next steps to be taken in the process of resolving the incident.

Containment Strategies

Depending upon the incident, containment strategies will vary and should be determined and documented for each type of potential incident. The criteria for determining a containment strategy may include the following:

- Availability of services such as network connectivity, fileserver access to include mission critical software applications and databases
- Severity of the impact, potential damage, or theft of information
- Knowledge and resources needed (both human and equipment) to resolve the incident
- Time needed to implement emergency workaround, temporary solution, or permanent solution

The CSIRT should determine acceptable levels of risk and plan containment activities in advance. Some decisions to contain an incident may include disabling certain functionality, disconnecting a system from the network, or shutting it down altogether. It is important that the managers of every department be notified in advance that containment strategies and procedures may include shut down and data loss from the time of backups.

During eradication, it is important to identify all systems that have been impacted and to notify the system owners. The elimination of malware may require unplanned downtime, new hardware, and a restoration to a point before data was backed up. Managers need to have processes and procedures in place to be able to temporarily function without the use of automated systems. Recovery may involve rebuilding systems from scratch, installing patches, changing passwords, restoring systems from clean backups, changes in firewall rulesets, and router access control lists. Often attackers who were successful will brag on blogs, which increases the likelihood that either they or one of the blog readers will attack again. An analysis of the exploited vulnerabilities to prevent future attacks is often a part of the recovery process.

Evidence Collection and Retention

In responding to incidents, many decisions and activities occur in rapid succession. During containment activities when the IT security team is working to resolve an incident, it is also important to gather evidence that may be needed for legal proceedings. It is important to discuss how evidence collection and handling will occur when the tendency to focus on restoring mission critical systems takes priority. From an evidentiary standpoint, it is better to get a snapshot of the system at the onset of a detected incident rather than trying to backtrack after others have made alterations to the systems. Forensic computer crime investigators must be able to work in tandem with the IT network security engineers to both resolve incidents and properly collect and handle any critical evidence.

Many organizations have a data retention policy that states how long specific data will be kept to meet legal and business data archival requirements. Depending upon the industry and governmental regulatory requirements, the laws and statues will dictate how long certain data should be kept and different types of data require different lengths of retention. Retained data must be able to identify the source and destination of a communication; the data, time, and duration; as well as the type of communication. Other aspects to consider regarding a data retention policy is the ongoing identification of data that is no longer needed; the access and search capabilities of the archived data; the security and encryption policy for transmitted and data at rest; the permanent deletion of retained data; deletion of the encryption key after the retention period; and effectively deleting data that resides locally, at an off-site data center or at a cloud storage provider. If the organization is operating in different parts of the world, it is important that the CSIRT know the data retention laws of each country.

Information Sharing

The goal of sharing threat, attack, and vulnerability mitigation strategies with stakeholders and outside entities is to expand knowledge in order to prevent future attacks and more effectively handle exploits to existing vulnerabilities. However, sharing incident information across the organization, with peers, and strategic business partners can be a double-edged sword. On one hand, sharing information may help security engineers and analysts in effectively resolving incidents or prevent malware from spreading to connected networks and systems. On the other hand, sharing too much information or preliminary information that turns out to be wrong can set off a chain reaction and negatively impact the reputation, market value, and bring potential legal actions against the organization.

Before sharing information with external organizations, it is advisable to first consult with the legal department. A policy that balances the benefits of sharing incident information with protecting sensitive information with the appropriate individuals is required as part of the incident response plan. It is important to identify which individuals both internal and external to the organization should be receiving information and what kinds of business and technical information.

After-Action Reviews

As soon as an incident is resolved, a detailed examination of the events from first detection to final recovery should commence. After-action reviews are an essential part of incident response and provide an opportunity for the key CSIRT members to discuss the events, review their actions and documentation, and analyze areas where the incident response plan worked and what did not work so well. The information gathered during these meetings should be used to improve and update the incident response policies and procedures moving forward. Ideally, the after-action review meetings will be recorded and used for training future CSIRT members.

How these meetings are conducted can have a significant impact on the organizational culture and must be handled in a way that encourages openness and honesty with the goal of learning and improving versus blame. These are perfect opportunities for management to recognize and reward outstanding dedication for those members who worked to contain and resolve incidents under high stress conditions.

Underlying Knowledge, Skill, and Ability Requirements for Incident Response

Along with a detailed set of tasks, the NICE Workforce Framework (v2.0) also provides a distinctive set of KSA specifications for each specialty area. The major competencies for this specialty area include the following:

- *CND.* This includes a team of IT professionals to identify network vulnerabilities and threats, continuously monitor and analyze the network and systems for suspicious activity, and defend the network by applying best practices and countermeasures.
- *Information systems/network security.* This includes a team who provides secure daily operating management of network access; firewall access and admissions control administration; network intrusion detection and prevention monitoring; vulnerability scanning and reports; baseline configuration standards; patch management; user ID/password verification; and enforcement of security policies.
- *Information assurance.* This includes skill in recognizing and categorizing types of vulnerabilities, associated tasks; performing damage assessments; and security network communications.
- *Vulnerabilities assessment.* Conducted as part of an overall risk assessment process.
- *Incident management.* Knowledge of incident response and handling methodologies is critical for all members of the CSIRT as they will be responsible for establishing the processes and procedures and carrying out incident responses.
- *Infrastructure design.* Knowledge of network protocols, Dynamic Host Configuration Protocol (DHCP), and directory services such as Domain Name Service is required to understand how network services and protocols interact to provide network communications. Skill in this area will aid in the detection and analysis of events using packet sniffing and protocol analysis technology.

Table 6.5 displays KSAs for the incident response specialty area.

Table 6.5   Incident Response Specialty Area KSAs

Item ID	KSA	Statement	Competency
29	KSA	Knowledge of data backup, types of backups (e.g., full, incremental), and recovery concepts and tools.	Computer forensics
50	KSA	Knowledge of how network services and protocols interact to provide network communications.	Infrastructure design
60	KSA	Knowledge of incident categories, incident responses, and timelines for responses.	Incident management
61	KSA	Knowledge of incident response and handling methodologies.	Incident management
66	KSA	Knowledge of intrusion detection methodologies and techniques for detecting host- and network-based intrusions via intrusion detection technologies.	Computer network defense
81	KSA	Knowledge of network protocols (e.g., Transmission Critical Protocol/Internet Protocol [TCP/IP], Dynamic Host Configuration Protocol [DHCP]), and directory services (e.g., Domain Name System [DNS]).	Infrastructure design
87	KSA	Knowledge of network traffic analysis methods.	Information systems/network security
93	KSA	Knowledge of packet-level analysis.	Vulnerabilities assessment

(Continued)

Table 6.5 (Continued) Incident Response Specialty Area KSAs

Item ID	KSA	Statement	Competency
105	KSA	Knowledge of system and application security threats and vulnerabilities (e.g., buffer overflow, mobile code, cross-site scripting, procedural language/structured query language [PL/SQL] and injections, race conditions, covert channel, replay, return-oriented attacks, malicious code).	Vulnerabilities assessment
150	KSA	Knowledge of what constitutes a network attack and the relationship to both threats and vulnerabilities.	Information systems/Network security
153	KSA	Skill of identifying capturing, containing, and reporting malware.	Computer network defense
217	KSA	Skill in preserving evidence integrity according to standard operating procedures or national standards.	Computer forensics
893	KSA	Skill in securing network communications.	Information assurance
895	KSA	Skill in recognizing and categorizing types of vulnerabilities and associated attacks.	Information assurance
896	KSA	Skill in protecting a network against malware.	Computer network defense
897	KSA	Skill in performing damage assessments.	Information assurance
923	KSA	Knowledge of security event correlation tools.	Information systems/Network security
984	KSA	Knowledge of cyber defense policies, procedures, and regulations.	Computer network defense

(Continued)

Table 6.5 (Continued) Incident Response Specialty Area KSAs

Item ID	KSA	Statement	Competency
991	KSA	Knowledge of different classes of attacks (e.g., passive, active, insider, close-in, distribution).	Computer network defense
992	KSA	Knowledge of different operational threat environments (e.g., first generation [script kiddies], second generation [non-nation state sponsored], and third generation [nation state sponsored]).	Computer network defense
1029	KSA	Knowledge of malware analysis concepts and methodology.	Computer network defense
1033	KSA	Knowledge of basic system administration, network, and operating system hardening techniques.	Information systems/Network security
1069	KSA	Knowledge of general attack stages (e.g., foot printing and scanning, enumeration, gaining access, escalation or privileges, maintaining access, network exploitation, covering tracks).	Computer network defense
1072	KSA	Knowledge of network security architecture concepts, including topology, protocols, components, and principles (e.g., application of defense-in-depth).	Information systems/Network security
1141	KSA	Knowledge of an organization's information classification program and procedures for level information loss.	Information management

Specialty Area 3: Enterprise Network Defense Infrastructure Support

The END infrastructure support specialty area "tests, implements, deploys, maintains, reviews, and administers the infrastructure hardware, software, and documentation that are required to effectively manage network defense resources. Monitors the network to actively remediate unauthorized activities" (NICE, 2014). In the early years of computing, most network infrastructures were relatively simple. As applications advanced in functionality and complexity such as Web-based ecommerce systems, enterprise resource planning systems, data warehousing, and cloud computing, the demand for 24/7 availability and global reach has necessitated some sophisticated network infrastructure designs. Mergers and acquisitions add to the complexity as organizations face the challenges of trying to integrate and consolidate infrastructure components that are incompatible. The continual changing of the structure of the network as organizations develop new products, merge or acquire other organizations, and grow into new geographical territories create challenges for enterprise network security engineers and analysts.

Factoring Enterprise Network Defense Infrastructure Support Workforce Tasks into the Cybersecurity Framework Functions

Figure 6.4 shows the END infrastructure support mapped to the CSF. The seven tasks in this specialty area all map to the protect function of the CSF. The protect function consists of activities such as creating a baseline configuration of the control systems, access control, backups, data security, protective technology, and maintenance of organizational assets. These activities are in alignment with what network security engineers and network administrators perform and manage on a daily basis.

The variety of end-user devices, software applications, database servers, operating systems, storage networks, technologies such as virtualization, and network components such as routers, switches, firewalls, some of which may be proprietary, require IT security engineers and administrators to keep continually up-to-date and secure. In addition to ethical hacking, there are two additional security strategies that network security engineers and administrators use to secure the infrastructure. They are layered security and separation of duties. A layered security strategy, also known as defense-in-depth strategy, utilizes a variety of technologies in order to make it more difficult for hackers to break through the barriers. Each layer can be integrated with an IDPS to detect breaches. The strategy of deploying multiple layers of protection is that if one layer is bypassed unnoticed, there are other layers in place to prevent a breach. Layers can consist of firewalls, IDPS systems, surveillance cameras, badge access systems, authentication tokens, smart cards, biometric recognition systems, antivirus software programs, security policies, and security awareness training programs. One disadvantage to the design of layered security is

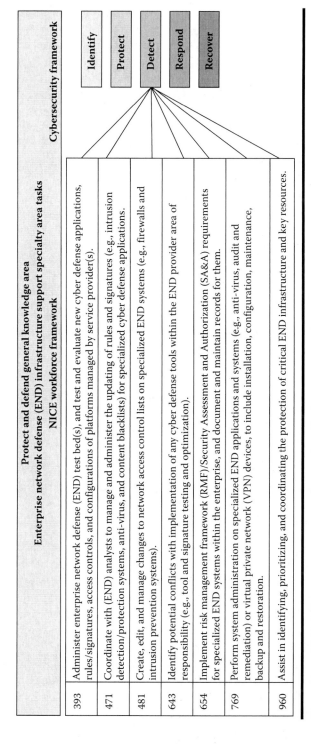

	Protect and defend general knowledge area Enterprise network defense (END) infrastructure support specialty area tasks NICE workforce framework	Cybersecurity framework
393	Administer enterprise network defense (END) test bed(s), and test and evaluate new cyber defense applications, rules/signatures, access controls, and configurations of platforms managed by service provider(s).	Identify
471	Coordinate with (END) analysts to manage and administer the updating of rules and signatures (e.g., intrusion detection/protection systems, anti-virus, and content blacklists) for specialized cyber defense applications.	Protect
481	Create, edit, and manage changes to network access control lists on specialized END systems (e.g., firewalls and intrusion prevention systems).	Detect
643	Identify potential conflicts with implementation of any cyber defense tools within the END provider area of responsibility (e.g., tool and signature testing and optimization).	Respond
654	Implement risk management framework (RMF)/Security Assessment and Authorization (SA&A) requirements for specialized END systems within the enterprise, and document and maintain records for them.	Recover
769	Perform system administration on specialized END applications and systems (e.g., anti-virus, audit and remediation) or virtual private network (VPN) devices, to include installation, configuration, maintenance, backup and restoration.	
960	Assist in identifying, prioritizing, and coordinating the protection of critical END infrastructure and key resources.	

Figure 6.4   END infrastructure support mapped to the CSF.

that it increases complexity and users may circumvent layers due to the perception of inconvenience or layers adding to their workloads.

Separation of duties is another strategy that assigns parts of tasks to different job roles within the IT department. By dividing up or separating the duties of engineers, analysts, administrators such as database and network, and other IT professionals, no single person would have the system permissions to compromise the infrastructure. The policy of least privilege is related in that users are given the lowest level of system access and privileges necessary to perform their job functions.

Recent trends such as BYOD have created additional challenges as the conflicting interests of system managers who want full control of the network and owners of the devices want full freedom have created clashes. Recent technology called "containerization" create isolated "containers" on employee's personal devices, separating business data from personal data. This allows network security engineers and administrators to control and provide a secure environment of corporate data. IT policy and management applies to the container contents and if the device is lost or stolen, the network administrators can wipe the containers without impacting the personal information.

Cloud computing as a business model has also introduced additional security concerns. The variety of services, whether it be software (SaaS), platform (PaaS), or infrastructure as a service (IaaS) can be beneficial in managing costs; however, the absolute security of hypervisor operation and VM operations is still to be proved. Cloud technology also routinely makes copies of data to prevent loss due to server failure; however, the more copies that are made, the more exposure an organization has to breaches. And if encryption keys are not managed well, encrypted data can be lost if the encryption key is lost.

Underlying Knowledge, Skill, and Ability Requirements for Enterprise Network Defense Infrastructure Support

The major competencies for this specialty area include the following:

- *CND.* This includes IT professionals who are knowledgeable about IDS tools and applications, know the types of IDS systems and optimal hardware configurations. Skill in tuning sensors; protecting the network against malware; and knowledge of cyber defense policies, procedures, and regulations. Skills in using virtual private network (VPN) devices and encryption.
- *Information systems/network security.* This includes a team who is knowledgeable about network traffic analysis methods, administers host and network access control mechanisms, is knowledgeable of what constitutes a network attach and the relationship to both threats and vulnerabilities, and is knowledgeable of network security architecture concepts including topology, protocols, components, and principles.

- *Information assurance.* This includes skill in recognizing and categorizing types of vulnerabilities, associated tasks; performing damage assessments; and security network communications.
- *Vulnerabilities assessment.* Knowledge of packet-level analysis and knowledge of system and application security threats and vulnerabilities, such as buffer overflow, mobile code, XSS, race conditions, and SQL injections.
- *Incident management.* Knowledge of incident response and handling methodologies is critical for all members of the CSIRT as they will be responsible for establishing the processes and procedures and carrying out incident responses.
- *Infrastructure design.* Knowledge of network protocols, DHCP, and directory services such as Domain Name Service is required to understand how network services and protocols interact to provide network communications. Skill in this area will aid in the detection and analysis of events using packet sniffing and protocol analysis technology.
- *Web technology.* Knowledge of transmission records such as Bluetooth, radio frequency identification (RFID), infrared (IR) networking, wireless fidelity (Wi-Fi), paging, cellular, and satellite dishes. Knowledge of jamming techniques that enable transmission of undesirable information or prevent systems from operating correctly.

Table 6.6 displays the KSAs for the incident response specialty area.

Specialty Area 4: Vulnerability Assessment and Management

The vulnerability assessment specialty area "conducts threat and vulnerability assessments and determines deviations from acceptable configurations or policies. Assess the level of risk and develops and/or recommends appropriate mitigation countermeasures in operational and non-operational situations" (NIST, 2014). The process of risk management and conducting risk assessments are not a one-time activity but should be conducted on an ongoing basis. Risk management involves protecting assets by identifying, understanding, and mitigating threats and vulnerabilities while considering cost, resources, and the potential likelihood of the vulnerability being exploited. Vulnerabilities are not limited to information systems hardware and the enterprise infrastructure. Viewing organizational vulnerabilities in a broader context, they also include weaknesses in internal controls, business processes, systems development life cycle processes, supply chain activities, facilities, lack of effective risk management strategies, poorly implemented security policies and procedures, poor communication, misalignment of enterprise architecture to support mission/business activities, and external service providers.

Table 6.6   END Infrastructure Support Specialty Area KSAs

Item ID	KSA	Statement	Competency
29	KSA	Knowledge of data backup, types of backups (e.g., full, incremental), and recovery concepts and tools.	Computer forensics
49	KSA	Knowledge of host and network access control mechanisms (e.g., access control list).	Information systems/Network security
59	KSA	Knowledge of intrusion detection system (IDS) tools and applications.	Computer network defense
61	KSA	Knowledge of incident response and handling methodologies.	Incident management
63	KSA	Knowledge of information assurance (IA) principles and organizational requirements to protect confidentiality, integrity, availability, authenticity, and non-repudiation of information and data.	Information assurance
81	KSA	Knowledge of network protocols (e.g., Transmission Critical Protocol/Internet Protocol [TCP/IP], Dynamic Host Configuration Protocol [DHCP]), and directory services (e.g., Domain Name System [DNS]).	Infrastructure design
87	KSA	Knowledge of network traffic analysis methods.	Information systems/Network security
92	KSA	Knowledge of how traffic flows across the network (e.g., Transmission Control Protocol and Internet Protocol [TCP/IP], Open System Interconnection model [OSI]).	Infrastructure design
93	KSA	Knowledge of packet-level analysis.	Vulnerabilities assessment

(Continued)

Table 6.6 (Continued)   END Infrastructure Support Specialty Area KSAs

Item ID	KSA	Statement	Competency
105	KSA	Knowledge of system and application security threats and vulnerabilities (e.g., buffer overflow, mobile code, cross-site scripting, procedural language/structured query language [PL/SQL] and injections, race conditions, covert channel, replay, return-oriented attacks, malicious code).	Vulnerabilities assessment
146	KSA	Knowledge of the types of IDS hardware and software.	Computer network defense
148	KSA	Knowledge of virtual private network (VPN) security.	Encryption
150	KSA	Knowledge of what constitutes a network attack and the relationship to both threats and vulnerabilities.	Information systems/Network security
157	KSA	Skill in applying host/network access controls (e.g., access control list).	Network management
227	KSA	Skill in tuning sensors.	Computer network defense
229	KSA	Skill in using incident handling methodologies.	Incident management
237	KSA	Skill in using VPN devices and encryption.	Encryption
893	KSA	Skill in securing network communications.	Information assurance
896	KSA	Skill in protecting a network against malware.	Computer network defense
900	KSA	Knowledge of web filtering technologies.	Web technology
984	KSA	Knowledge of cyber defense policies, procedures, and regulations.	Computer network defense

(Continued)

Table 6.6 (Continued)   END Infrastructure Support Specialty Area KSAs

Item ID	KSA	Statement	Competency
989	KSA	Knowledge of voice over internet protocol (VoIP).	Telecommunications
1011	KSA	Knowledge of processes for reporting network security-related incidents.	Security
1012	KSA	Knowledge of Capabilities and Maturity Model Integration (CMMI) at all five levels.	Internal controls
1072	KSA	Knowledge of network security architecture concepts, including topology, protocols, components, and principles (e.g., application of defense-in-depth).	Information systems/Network security
1074	KSA	Knowledge of transmission records (e.g., Bluetooth, radio frequency identification [RFID], infrared networking [IR], wireless fidelity [Wi-Fi], paging, cellular, satellite dishes), and jamming techniques that enable transmission of undesirable information, or prevent installed systems from operating correctly.	Web technology
1131	KSA	Knowledge of security architecture concepts and enterprise architecture reference models (e.g., Zackman, federal enterprise architecture [FEA]).	Enterprise architecture

The organization culture, resource limitations, risk tolerance, and ever-changing security threats collectively challenge compliance managers, auditors, security engineers, and analysts to continuously assess and manage any vulnerability the organization may face. Hackers are aware of commonly known vulnerabilities and use a variety of tools to exploit them. An example of this is when operating system and software vendors quickly create fixes or patches as vulnerabilities are reported to them. However, when an attacker exploits a vulnerability before the vendor releases a patch or bug fix, it is known as a zero-day attack. Surprisingly, a most precarious period usually comes immediately after a fix is released by the vendor as attackers work to reverse engineer the fix to discover more about the vulnerability. Sometimes it only takes hours for an attacker to reverse engineer the fix and launch another attempt to exploit the vulnerability.

Factoring Vulnerability Assessment and Management Workforce Tasks into the Cybersecurity Framework Functions

Figure 6.5 shows the vulnerability assessment and management specialty area tasks mapped to the CSF. There are eight tasks in this specialty area; four of the tasks map to the identify function of the CSF (risk assessment ID.RA category) and the other four map to the protect function (information protection processes and procedures PR.IP category).

As a subset of the overall risk management process, vulnerability assessment and management involves evaluating the critical technical assets (software applications and enterprise infrastructure components) and the nontechnical (security policies, procedures, operations, and people) to identify security weaknesses based on a given set of threats. This includes the areas of focus such as the local computing environment, network infrastructure, enclave boundary, and supporting infrastructure). The vulnerability assessment provides a basis for determining what security policies and countermeasures to implement in order to protect and defend the critical assets.

The outcome of the vulnerability and threat assessments should answer the following questions:

- What are the consequences should an exposed system be exploited?
- What is the likelihood that the vulnerability will be exploited and fail?
- What is an acceptable level of risk the organization is willing to tolerate?

Most information system vulnerabilities can be associated with security controls that have been either poorly implemented or intentionally not implemented as opposed to emergent vulnerabilities that arise over time as new technologies proliferate and new threats emerge. In the context of such change, existing security controls that are not periodically assessed and updated become inadequate. As mentioned earlier, it is critical for organizations to conduct continuous monitoring

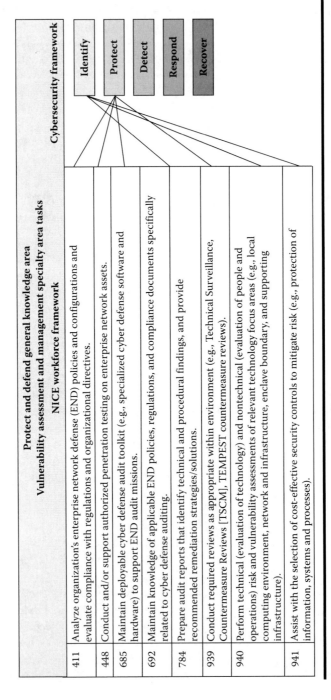

	Protect and defend general knowledge area Vulnerability assessment and management specialty area tasks NICE workforce framework	Cybersecurity framework
		Identify
		Protect
		Detect
		Respond
		Recover
411	Analyze organization's enterprise network defense (END) policies and configurations and evaluate compliance with regulations and organizational directives.	
448	Conduct and/or support authorized penetration testing on enterprise network assets.	
685	Maintain deployable cyber defense audit toolkit (e.g., specialized cyber defense software and hardware) to support END audit missions.	
692	Maintain knowledge of applicable END policies, regulations, and compliance documents specifically related to cyber defense auditing.	
784	Prepare audit reports that identify technical and procedural findings, and provide recommended remediation strategies/solutions.	
939	Conduct required reviews as appropriate within environment (e.g., Technical Surveillance, Countermeasure Reviews [TSCM], TEMPEST countermeasure reviews).	
940	Perform technical (evaluation of technology) and nontechnical (evaluation of people and operations) risk and vulnerability assessments of relevant technology focus areas (e.g., local computing environment, network and infrastructure, enclave boundary, and supporting infrastructure).	
941	Assist with the selection of cost-effective security controls to mitigate risk (e.g., protection of information, systems and processes).	

Figure 6.5   Vulnerability assessment and management specialty area mapped to the CSF.

processes that include system, network, and organization-wide risk assessment, auditing, and authorized penetration testing on enterprise network assets to maintain situational awareness of the organizational security posture. In order to perform the threat and vulnerability assessments, the security assessors must maintain deployable cyber defense audit toolkits (e.g., specialized cyber defense software and hardware) to support END audit missions.

Increasingly organizations are being held legally responsible to prevent attacks to their information assets so that the resources hacked cannot be used to attack strategic business partner information assets. With information security being such a critical function and covering a wide area of risk and responsibility, areas of knowledge and specialties within IT security are emerging to manage the risk. Ethical hacking, also referred to as white-hat hackers and red teaming, is a process designed to detect network and system vulnerabilities by simulating an attacker-like approach to organizational assets. The goal of red teaming is to exploit existing vulnerabilities with the purpose of evaluating the overall security posture and put in place the necessary countermeasures and policies to mitigate the vulnerabilities. Blue teaming functions as a defender with the same goals of identifying and implementing strategies to mitigate the vulnerabilities.

Underlying Knowledge, Skill, and Ability Requirements for Vulnerability Assessment and Management

The major competencies for this specialty area include the following:

- *Vulnerabilities assessment.* This includes knowledge and skill in conducting vulnerability scans and recognizing vulnerabilities in security systems; the ability to identify systemic security issues based on the analysis of vulnerability and configuration data; knowledge of application security threats and vulnerabilities such as buffer overflow, mobile code, XSS, race conditions, and SQL injections; knowledge of penetration testing principles, tools, and techniques; skill in performing packet-level analysis using appropriate tools (e.g., Wireshark, tcpdump); and skills in using network analysis tools to identify vulnerabilities.
- *CND.* This includes IT professionals who are knowledgeable about IDS tools and applications; know the types of IDS systems and optimal hardware configurations; possess skill in detecting host- and network-based intrusions; skill in mimicking threat behaviors; knowledge of different classes of attacks (e.g., passive, active, insider, close-in, distribution); and knowledge of general attack stages (e.g., foot printing and scanning, enumeration, gaining access, escalation or privileges, maintain access, network exploitation, and covering tracks).

- *Infrastructure design.* Knowledge of network protocols and how traffic flows across the network, DHCP, and directory services such as Domain Name Service is required to understand how network services and protocols interact to provide network communications. Skill in this area will aid in the detection and analysis of events using packet sniffing and protocol analysis technology.
- *Information systems/network security.* This includes a team who is knowledgeable about network traffic analysis methods, administers host and network access control mechanisms, is knowledgeable of what constitutes a network attach and the relationship to both threats and vulnerabilities, and knowledge of network security architecture concepts including topology, protocols, components, and principles.
- *Information assurance.* This includes skill in recognizing and categorizing types of vulnerabilities, associated tasks; performing damage assessments; and security network communications.

Table 6.7 displays the KSAs for the incident response specialty area.

Chapter Summary

The protect and defend GKA contains four specialty areas. They are END analysis, incident response, END infrastructure, and vulnerability assessment and management. All are focused on protecting and defending the organization's critical technical assets (network infrastructure, software applications, information) and nontechnical assets (security policies, procedures, operations, physical environment, and people) from both external and internal attacks.

The END analysis team focuses on defense measures and information collected to identify, analyze, and report events that may occur or have occurred within the enterprise network in order to protect information, systems, and the network from threats. This is accomplished in several ways such as footprinting and reconnaissance to gather information to search for vulnerabilities; conducting vulnerability analyses; planning, scheduling, and conducting both internal and external penetration testing; monitoring firewalls and IDPS; analyzing software applications; conducting TCP/IP packet analysis; implementing best practices to circumvent social engineering attacks; and keeping current knowledge on the various tools to mitigate malware attacks.

END analysts must be knowledgeable in conducting threat and vulnerability assessments and to understand the overall risk to the systems and applications they support. Threats can be categorized into the following three levels: man-made, natural disasters, or a blend of both. Once the threat sources have been identified, the next step in the process is to determine the likelihood and possible consequences if the threat materialized. The three elements: threat sources, likelihood,

Table 6.7 Vulnerability Assessment and Management Specialty Area KSAs

Item ID	KSA	Statement	Competency
3	KSA	Skill in conducting vulnerability scans and recognizing vulnerabilities in security systems.	Vulnerabilities assessment
4	KSA	Ability to identify systemic security issues based on the analysis of vulnerability and configuration data.	Vulnerabilities assessment
10	KSA	Knowledge of application vulnerabilities.	Vulnerabilities assessment
27	KSA	Knowledge of cryptography and cryptographic key management concepts.	Cryptography
29	KSA	Knowledge of data backup, types of backups (e.g., full, incremental), and recovery concepts and tools.	Computer forensics
63	KSA	Knowledge of information assurance (IA) principles and organizational requirements to protect confidentiality, integrity, availability, authenticity, and nonrepudiation of information and data.	Information assurance
79	KSA	Knowledge of network access, identity, and access management (e.g., public key infrastructure [PKI]).	Identity management
81	KSA	Knowledge of network protocols (e.g., Transmission Critical Protocol/Internet Protocol [TCP/IP], Dynamic Host Configuration Protocol [DHCP]), and directory services (e.g., Domain Name System [DNS]).	Infrastructure design

(Continued)

Table 6.7 (Continued) Vulnerability Assessment and Management Specialty Area KSAs

Item ID	KSA	Statement	Competency
92	KSA	Knowledge of how traffic flows across the network (e.g., Transmission Control Protocol and Internet Protocol [TCP/IP], Open System Interconnection model [OSI]).	Infrastructure design
95	KSA	Knowledge of penetration testing principles, tools, and techniques (e.g., metasploit, neosploit).	Vulnerabilities assessment
102	KSA	Knowledge of programming language structures and logic.	Computer languages
105	KSA	Knowledge of system and application security threats and vulnerabilities (e.g., buffer overflow, mobile code, cross-site scripting, Procedural Language/Structured Query Language [PL/SQL] and injections, race conditions, covert channel, replay, return-oriented attacks, malicious code).	Vulnerabilities assessment
115	KSA	Knowledge of content development	Computer network defense
123	KSA	Knowledge of system and application security threats and vulnerabilities.	Vulnerabilities assessment
128	KSA	Knowledge of system diagnostic tools and fault identification techniques.	Systems testing and evaluation
150	KSA	Knowledge of what constitutes a network attack and the relationship to both threats and vulnerabilities.	Information systems/network security
157	KSA	Skill in applying host/network access controls (e.g., access control list).	Network management

(Continued)

Table 6.7 (Continued) Vulnerability Assessment and Management Specialty Area KSAs

Item ID	KSA	Statement	Competency
160	KSA	Skill in assessing the robustness of security systems and designs.	Vulnerabilities assessment
181	KSA	Skill in detecting host and network-based intrusions via intrusion detection technologies (e.g., Snort).	Computer network defense
210	KSA	Skill in mimicking threat behaviors.	Computer network defense
214	KSA	Skill in performing packet-level analysis using appropriate tools (e.g., Wireshark, tcpdump).	Vulnerabilities assessment
225	KSA	Skill in the use of penetration testing tools and techniques.	Vulnerabilities assessment
226	KSA	Skill in the use of social engineering techniques.	Human factors
897	KSA	Skill in performing damage assessments.	Information assurance
904	KSA	Knowledge of interpreted and compiled computer languages.	Computer languages
922	KSA	Skill in using network analysis tools to identify vulnerabilities.	Vulnerabilities assessment
991	KSA	Knowledge of different classes of attacks (e.g., passive, active, insider, close-in, distribution).	Computer network defense
992	KSA	Knowledge of different operational threat environments (e.g., first generation [script kiddies], second generation [non-nation state sponsored], and third generation [nation state sponsored]).	Computer network defense

(Continued)

Table 6.7 (Continued) Vulnerability Assessment and Management Specialty Area KSAs

Item ID	KSA	Statement	Competency
1038	KSA	Knowledge of local specialized system requirements (e.g., critical infrastructure systems that may not use standard information technology [IT]) for safety, performance, and reliability.	Infrastructure design
1039	KSA	Skill in evaluating the trustworthiness of the supplier and/or product.	Contracting/procurement
1040	KSA	Knowledge of relevant laws, policies, procedures, or governance related to work impacting critical infrastructure.	Criminal law
1069	KSA	Knowledge of general attack stages (e.g., footprinting and scanning, enumeration, gaining access, escalation or privileges, maintaining access, network exploitation, covering tracks).	Computer network defense
1072	KSA	Knowledge of network security architecture concepts, including topology, protocols, components, and principles (e.g., application of defense-in-depth).	Information systems/network security
1141	KSA	Knowledge of an organization's information classification program and procedures for level information loss.	Information management
1142	KSA	Knowledge of security models (e.g., Bell-LaPadula model, Biba integrity model, Clark-Wilson integrity model).	Enterprise architecture

and consequences define the overall risk to information infrastructure. A threat category graphic was provided to assist in identifying the possible threats to the organization and categories. This graphic can be used to then determine and record the likelihood of the threat and then to prioritize the threats in order to implement countermeasures and policies to mitigate the threats.

Continuous monitoring is a critical job function of security network engineers and security analysts. Automated tools to streamline the process of continuous monitoring are valuable in identifying patterns and relations in large volumes of data that would not otherwise be found by human analysts. When analyzing security relation information, the following things are considered: the organizational risk tolerance; the potential impact the vulnerabilities may have on critical assets; the potential impact of the mitigation strategies that may be employed; and evolving threat and vulnerability data. Cost-effectiveness of a mitigation strategy may heavily influence the determination whether to share/transfer, avoid/reject, or accept the risk. The implementation and periodic evaluation of sound security control policies are essential to good IT governance.

Violations of security controls and practices can come from either internal or external attackers and have many causes such as intentional malicious malware or nonintentional errors and simple negligence caused by careless employees. IDPSs are valuable in performing packet sniffing and network traffic analysis to record observed events, block suspicious activity, provide notifications to network and security analysts, and produce reports in which an organization can use to understand the frequency and characteristics of detected threats to their systems. This information can be used to identify the appropriate countermeasures that should be implemented to protect the information assets. There are four types of IDPS technologies that network security engineers and security analysts need to know: network-based, host-based, application-based, and wireless IDPS. The network security engineer or security analyst determines what type of IDPS system is most appropriate for the organization's network security. A common practice is to implement a blended solution and use host- and application-based systems on mission critical assets and a robust NIDPS for global infrastructure protection.

In addition to the types of IDPS technologies that can be deployed, IDPS systems use three common methodologies or approaches to detect incidents. They are called signature-based, anomaly/behavior-based, and stateful protocol analysis. During the risk assessment process, the network security engineer or security analyst needs to determine what gets logged, what kinds of events kick off alerts, and what actions are required if an alert is generated. Whenever suspicious behavior is detected or a critical event occurs, an alert from the IDPS is generated and must be acted upon.

Malware remains a significant threat causing widespread damage and disruption to organizations. At a minimum, the organization should establish a malware prevention policy and user awareness program that explains acceptable and proper rules of behavior, social engineering tricks, and proper use of the organization's IT assets. All users should be aware of the risks that malware presents, the way in which malware spreads, and their role in preventing a malware attack.

END analysis work requires a broad range of technical and behavioral capabilities. Knowledge of cyber defense mitigations techniques and vulnerability assessment tools, including open-source tools and their capabilities is required. Ethical hacking is often conducted by the network security engineer or network administrator to attack the system on behalf of the organization with the goal to uncover vulnerabilities in which a malicious hacker could exploit. There are two separate tests an ethical hacker performs: a hardening check and a penetration test. For each piece of internal equipment, especially new network components, a hardening check will uncover any bad system configurations or operational weaknesses such as checking that daemons are switched off, firewalls are deployed, default login account are not in use, and that all patches are up-to-date. A penetration test checks for vulnerabilities on the outside of the infrastructure components and mimic real-world attacks with the goal of identifying techniques and methods of bypassing the security features that were put in place to protect the network, application, or system. Penetration tests are designed to exploit the vulnerabilities that have been identified during the vulnerability scan, thus confirming their existence. Penetration tests report how security was breached so that the security engineer and analysts can determine how to remediate. Other nontechnical types of penetration tests include methods of attack such as physical security breaches and the use of social engineering to gain unauthorized access. The use of social engineering is rapidly increasing and reveals weaknesses in users failing to follow standard security procedures and processes.

Network security engineers and security analysts should have a core set of tools that are used to conduct the various network testing and to keep skills up-to-date. Tools should be obtained from trusted sources and can be a combination of freeware tools, COTS, open-source tools, or developed in-house. Many tools require specific operating systems to run and are often installed using VM technology versus dual-boot systems. Security engineers and analysts should be knowledgeable and comfortable using all operating systems as well as using VM technology. A figure was provided that shows the variety of tools available for the various security testing techniques.

The specialty area of incident response responds to disruptions within the pertinent domain to mitigate immediate and potential threats. One of the most challenging parts of the incident response process is detecting possible security incidents and determining the magnitude of the problem. A computer security incident can mean a lot of different things which is why it is important to establish a common lexicon of what it means to have detected an event or an incident. The function of incident response can require substantial planning and resources and include a wide range of stakeholders. Given the challenges to ensure all stakeholders are informed with the appropriate information at any given time, a communication plan is a critical part of the incident response plan.

The CSIRT may be an informally recognized group of individuals with the technical skills to respond to a cyberattack or a more formal implementation. Larger organizations generally appoint the CISO to select members from the organization's department managers and the IT security professionals to staff the CSIRT team who will develop and execute the incident response plans. An important determination that the CISO must make is whether they have the expertise in-house to staff the CSIRT team or require outside help. Conducting a gap analysis of the skills necessary to successfully implement an incident response plan is essential.

One of the first deliverables of the CSIRT is an incident response policy document. It is important to gain the full support of executive management and that the policy is clearly understood by all stakeholders. The incident response policy document defines the roles and responsibilities of the CSIRT and provides clarity for the authority level the CSIRT has to confiscate, monitor, or disable any equipment in the event of a breach. The policy document also provides definitions of known computer security incidents and how security incidents will be prioritized. It also includes performance measures and how the team will report ongoing activities.

Organizations have unique requirements and require plans that are in alignment with the organization's mission, size, structure, and functions. The incident response plan is a roadmap and provides a detailed set of processes and procedures that kicks into immediate effect once an incident is detected or reported. The prevention of threats and attacks is the responsibility of the network security engineers and security analysts. Incident response activities are reactionary measures and are not considered preventative. It is only after an event has been analyzed and categorized as an incident that the CSIRT is alerted and called to action. Once an incident has been reported, the CSIRT is responsible to perform analysis of the incident and provide updates to management.

From the time an incident is detected, every step taken should be tracked and documented to include date and timestamps. Documentation can include audio recordings, log files, images, e-mails, and handwritten or typed field notes. It is important that there is a secure repository for this type of information as it will contain sensitive information.

Prioritizing detected incidents is one of the most critical aspects in the incident detection and analysis process. It is imperative that the incident responders have the knowledge and experience to act swiftly to analyze suspicious activity in order to understand the magnitude of the breach. For each incident, the IT security and incident response team members should consider the impact on the business and the estimated efforts required to recover from the incident as the basis for deciding the response prioritization.

Depending upon the incident, containment strategies will vary and should be determined and documented for each type of potential incident. The CSIRT should determine acceptable levels of risk and plan containment activities in advance. Some decisions to contain an incident may include disabling certain functionality, disconnecting a system from the network, or shutting it down altogether.

It is important that the managers of every department be notified in advance that containment strategies and procedures may include shut down and data loss from the time of backups.

In responding to incidents, many decisions and activities occur in rapid succession. During containment activities when the IT security team is working to resolve an incident, it is also important to gather evidence that may be needed for legal proceedings. It is important to discuss how evidence collection and handling will occur when the tendency to focus on restoring mission critical systems takes priority.

The goal of sharing threat, attack, and vulnerability mitigation strategies with stakeholders and outside entities is to expand knowledge in order to prevent future attacks and more effectively handle exploits to existing vulnerabilities. Before sharing information with external organizations, it is advisable to first consult with the legal department. A policy that balances the benefits of sharing incident information with protecting sensitive information with the appropriate individuals is required as part of the incident response plan.

As soon as an incident is resolved, a detailed examination of the events from first detection to final recovery should commence. After-action reviews are an essential part of incident response and provide an opportunity for the key CSIRT members to discuss the events, review their actions and documentation, and analyze areas where the incident response plan worked and what did not work so well. The information gathered during these meetings should be used to improve and update the incident response policies and procedures moving forward.

The END infrastructure support specialty area "tests, implements, deploys, maintains, reviews, and administers the infrastructure hardware, software, and documentation that are required to effectively manage network defense resources. Monitors the network to actively remediate unauthorized activities" (NICE, 2014). The continual changing of the structure of the network as organizations develop new products, merge or acquire other organizations, and grow into new geographical territories create challenges for enterprise network security engineers and analysts. The variety of end-user devices, software applications, database servers, operating systems, storage networks, technologies such as virtualization, and network components such as routers, switches, firewalls, some of which may be proprietary, require IT security engineers and administrators to keep continually up-to-date and secure.

Recent trends such as BYOD have created additional challenges as the conflicting interests of system managers who want full control of the network and owners of the devices want full freedom have created clashes. Cloud computing as a business model has also introduced additional security concerns. The variety of services, whether it be SaaS, PaaS, or IaaS can be beneficial in managing costs; however, the absolute security of hypervisor operation and VM operations is still to be proved. Cloud technology also routinely makes copies of data to prevent loss due to server failure; however, the more copies that are made, the more exposure an organization has to breaches. And if encryption keys are not managed well, encrypted data can be lost if the encryption key is lost.

The vulnerability assessment specialty area "conducts threat and vulnerability assessments and determines deviations from acceptable configurations or policies. Assess the level of risk and develops and/or recommends appropriate mitigation countermeasures in operational and non-operational situations" (NIST, 2014). The process of risk management and conducting risk assessments are not a one-time activity but should be conducted on an ongoing basis. Risk management involves protecting assets by identifying, understanding, and mitigating threats and vulnerabilities while considering cost, resources, and the potential likelihood of the vulnerability being exploited. The organization culture, resource limitations, risk tolerance, and ever-changing security threats collectively challenge compliance managers, auditors, security engineers, and analysts to continuously assess and manage any vulnerability the organization may face.

Key Terms

Antivirus Software: A malicious program that monitors a computer or network to identify all types of malware and prevent or contain malware incidents.

Buffer Overflow: A buffer overflow occurs when a program or process tries to store more data in a buffer than what was intended to store.

Cross-Site Scripting (XSS): Flaws are the most prevalent Web application security flaws and occur when an app uses user supplied data in a page sent to the browser without properly validating the content.

False Negative: When no alarm or notification is sent when an attack has taken place.

False Positive: An alert that incorrectly indicates that a vulnerability is present.

File Integrity Checking: Software that generates, stores, and compares message digests for files to detect changes made to the files.

Fingerprinting: Used to identify the specific services offered on active network assets and in turn be used to determine the tactics, techniques, and procedures to secure those assets.

Footprinting: Identifies network assets and activities and allows administrators to understand their computing environments.

Injection Flaw: Occurs when untrusted data are sent to an interpreter as part of a command or query.

Kernel Flaws: As the core of an operating system, any flaw in the kernel code puts the entire system in danger.

Malware: A program that is inserted into a system with the intent of compromising the confidentiality, integrity, or availability of the victim's data, applications, or operating system.

Network Discovery: The process of discovering active and responding hosts on a network, identifying weaknesses, and learning how the network operates.

Network Sniffing: A passive technique that monitors network communication, decodes protocols, and examines headers and payloads for targeted information.

Password Cracking: The process of recovering secret passwords stored in a computer system or transmitted over a network.

Penetration Testing: Security testing, which mimics real-world attacks.

Phishing: A digital form of social engineering that uses bogus but authentic-looking e-mails to acquire information from users or direct them to a fake Web site that solicits information.

Port Scanner: A program that can remotely determine which ports of a system are open and allow connections.

Social Engineering: The process of attempting to trick someone into revealing information that can be used in an attack.

Virtual Machine: Software that is designed to allow a single host to run multiple guest operating systems.

Vulnerability: A weakness in an IT system, policy, procedure, or operations that can be exploited by an attacker.

Vulnerability Scanning: A technique used to identify hosts and their attributes and associated vulnerabilities.

Reference

NIST. 2014. *NICE Cybersecurity Workforce Framework 2.0.* Gaithersburg, MD: National Institute of Standards in Technology.

Chapter 7

Investigate

Chapter Objectives

At the conclusion of this chapter, the reader will understand:

- The specialty areas of the investigate knowledge area
- The underlying tasks of the digital forensics specialty area
- The underlying knowledge, skill, and abilities (KSAs) of the digital forensics specialty area
- The relationship between the digital forensics specialty area and the cybersecurity framework (CSF)
- The underlying tasks of the cyber investigation specialty area
- The underlying KSAs of the cyber investigation specialty area
- The relationship between the cyber investigation specialty area and the CSF

The investigate knowledge area contains two specialty areas as shown in Figure 7.1. These are digital forensics and cyber investigation. Both are focused on investigating and characterizing any form of adverse activity performed by, or recorded on, a digital device. Since the primary purpose of this knowledge area is data recovery and subsequent investigation, its focus is after-the-fact. The incidents that it addresses are cyber-related events, such as crimes, intrusions, or harm caused to systems, networks.

As the name suggests, the investigate knowledge area encompasses the particular job roles that acquire, examine, and act on digital evidence. Its primary purpose is to support the understanding of electronic anomalies, or adverse occurrences, as well as make recommendations about the necessary operational response.

The two job roles within this specialty area normally perform the classic forensic and investigative functions required to ensure trustworthy cyber operation. This takes place within whatever parameters the organization sets. For that reason, these jobs are the workforce roles that are responsible for the investigation of electronic incidents.

Investigate

Specialty responsible for investigating cyber events or crimes related to information technology systems, networks, and digital evidence.

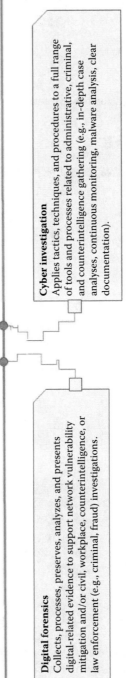

Cyber investigation

Applies tactics, techniques, and procedures to a full range of tools and processes related to administrative, criminal, and counterintelligence gathering (e.g., in-depth case analyses, continuous monitoring, malware analysis, clear documentation).

Digital forensics

Collects, processes, preserves, analyzes, and presents digital-related evidence to support network vulnerability mitigation and/or civil, workplace, counterintelligence, or law enforcement (e.g., criminal, fraud) investigations.

Figure 7.1 Investigate specialty areas.

Investigate has two highly focused specialty areas. These areas lie in the academic and professional domain of computer forensics and criminal justice. The specialty areas within investigate—collect, process, preserve, study, and document electronic evidence gathered in support of the organization's threat and vulnerability mitigation activities. In addition, the two specialty areas in investigate may address any averse system- or information-related incidents that occur within the organization's information technology (IT) or networks infrastructure. This work can be for internal security operations purposes, law enforcement, and even counterintelligence reasons.

Specialty Area 1: Digital Forensics

The specialty area called digital forensics encompasses the classic evidence gathering, analysis, and documentation tasks that are normally associated with law enforcement. In the physical universe, these roles gather material data at a crime scene and provide understanding of that evidence in support of basic criminal and civil actions.

Because of its classic fact-finding focus, the digital forensics specialty area might be considered to be more suitably a part of the discipline of criminal justice rather than computing. Nonetheless, it is perfectly appropriate for the forensics process to focus strictly on data collection and analysis of electronic threat and intrusion events, rather than the physical aspects of criminal activity. The detailed task specifications of the digital forensics specialty area illustrates the focus and intent of each this area.

In its raw electronic form, forensic evidence is very difficult to read or understand, so the task of forensic discovery in the cyber universe is a highly involved process. The main problem is that virtual space requires totally different methods for evidence gathering. For instance, it is possible to commit a crime that could be described in no other terms as a "bank robbery" from a location 6000 miles from the actual scene of the crime.

The virtuality of cyberspace permits the sort of "uninvolved criminality" and it also imposes unique complications of access and timing on the gathering and recording of forensic evidence. Moreover, a lot of forensic evidence exists as binary information within a computer system.

Because of the dynamic nature of the internal representation process for such information, it is far too easy for the forensic investigator to take actions during the data gathering process that can irreversibly damage the evidence or violate legal rules of procedure. Therefore, proper management and planning for the process itself helps to ensure that the organization will not unintentionally violate the integrity of the forensic process.

The National Initiative for Cybersecurity Education (NICE) framework specifies 39 potential tasks for the execution of digital forensics. The effect of these

39 activities is to ensure that the digital forensics process is properly executed. As we said earlier, much of the focus of the digital forensics process is in the recovery, interpretation, and handling of evidence.

Organizing the Tasks of Digital Forensics Using Cybersecurity Framework Functions

As we said in Chapter 3, the National Institute of Standards and Technology (NIST) CSF provides a "prioritized, flexible, repeatable, performance-based, and cost-effective approach" to manage cybersecurity risk for those processes, information, and systems directly involved in the delivery of critical infrastructure services (NIST, 2014b).

The framework consists of three parts: the framework core, the framework profile, and the framework implementation tiers. The framework core specifies a set of activities designed to achieve specific cybersecurity outcomes identified by industry as helpful in managing cybersecurity risk (NIST, 2014b).

The aim of the core is to specify the elements of cybersecurity risk management at their highest level. To review, these functions are identify, protect, detect, respond, and recover (IPDRR). The IPDRR functions are meant to be performed concurrently and continuously to form an operational culture that addresses cybersecurity risk:

1. *Identify*: Develop the organizational understanding to manage cybersecurity risk to systems, assets, data, and capabilities
2. *Protect*: Develop and implement the appropriate safeguards to ensure delivery of critical infrastructure services
3. *Detect*: Develop and implement the appropriate activities to identify the occurrence of a cybersecurity event
4. *Respond*: Develop and implement the appropriate activities to take action regarding a detected cybersecurity event
5. *Recover*: Develop and implement the appropriate activities to maintain plans for resilience and to restore any capabilities or services that were impaired due to a cybersecurity event

Factoring Workforce Tasks into the Cybersecurity Framework Categories

Forensics is almost always associated with law enforcement. So the most fundamental purpose of the digital forensics process is to assist in gathering and preserving evidence that is used in the prosecution of computer crimes. In doing this, the forensic examiner collects and analyzes any evidence that is generated by the actual cyber exploit. That might include such artifacts as source code, malware, and

Trojans. One aspect of that activity is to support criminal investigation. However, another important aspect is the potential use of forensic data to support the organizations own organized cyber defense operations.

The evidence itself is digital and so its footprint is found in electronic sources such as computer log files, reference monitor files, and other hidden sources of information. The subsequent analysis supports decisions about the best means of identifying the source and reasons for an unauthorized access. That can include such evidence gathering methods as dynamic and static analysis.

Dynamic analysis tests a program by executing it in real time using a dataset explicitly designed to identify the type and sources of a cyberattack or intrusion. The other primary methodology is static analysis. In that process, the examiner directly reviews the code without executing it. Because such techniques require tool support the forensic examiner also has to know how to utilize a Forensic Toolkit (FTK).

The process itself mainly involves evidence gathering. Once there is an indication of a breach or other form of cyber exploit the examiner creates a forensically sound duplicate of the target of the attack. This duplicate is called a "forensic image." The purpose of the image is to protect the integrity of the original crime scene by creating a duplicate to use for the subsequent data recovery and analysis procedures.

Artifacts that might be imaged include, but are not limited to, hard drives, floppy diskettes, compact discs (CDs), personal digital assistants (PDAs), mobile phones, global positioning satellite devices (GPSs), and all tape formats (NIST 2014a). If any of the data that is part of the examination is encrypted, the forensic examiner also decrypts it using tools. In that respect the forensic examiner must also be knowledgeable in cracking encryptions using tool support. The examiner then provides a technical summary of the findings in accordance with the organization's established reporting procedures. Figure 7.2 shows the digital forensics specialty area tasks mapped to the CSF functions.

Identification/Analysis Tasks

As might be expected from an activity that is mainly concentrated on gathering and interpreting evidence, the majority of the digital forensics tasks that are specified by the NICE framework lie in the CSF area of "identify." Nevertheless, because subsequent interpretation can lead to additional actions in defense of the organization, digital forensics also supports the creation of better protection schemes, which is in the bailiwick of "protect." And the ability to reconstruct evidence also supports the goals of "recover." Thus, the digital forensics process can truly be seen as extending throughout the infrastructure protection process.

The first step in a digital forensics investigation is to gather all of the disparate evidence of an attack or intrusion. During this first part of the process, the examiner documents the original condition of all digital and any associated physical

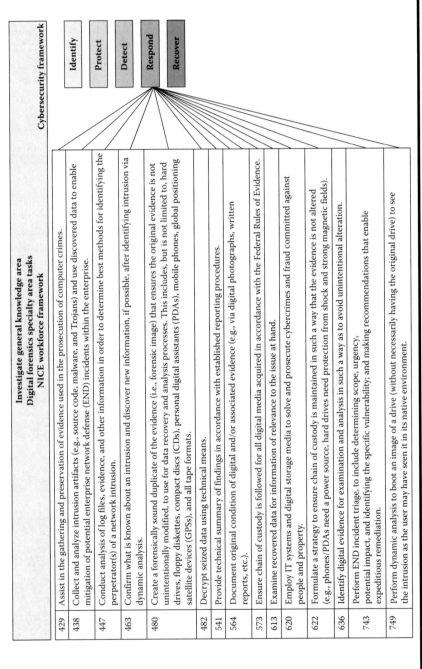

	Investigate general knowledge area Digital forensics specialty area tasks NICE workforce framework	Cybersecurity framework
		Identify
		Protect
		Detect
		Respond
		Recover
429	Assist in the gathering and preservation of evidence used in the prosecution of computer crimes.	
438	Collect and analyze intrusion artifacts (e.g., source code, malware, and Trojans) and use discovered data to enable mitigation of potential enterprise network defense (END) incidents within the enterprise.	
447	Conduct analysis of log files, evidence, and other information in order to determine best methods for identifying the perpetrator(s) of a network intrusion.	
463	Confirm what is known about an intrusion and discover new information, if possible, after identifying intrusion via dynamic analysis.	
480	Create a forensically sound duplicate of the evidence (i.e., forensic image) that ensures the original evidence is not unintentionally modified, to use for data recovery and analysis processes. This includes, but is not limited to, hard drives, floppy diskettes, compact discs (CDs), personal digital assistants (PDAs), mobile phones, global positioning satellite devices (GPSs), and all tape formats.	
482	Decrypt seized data using technical means.	
541	Provide technical summary of findings in accordance with established reporting procedures.	
564	Document original condition of digital and/or associated evidence (e.g., via digital photographs, written reports, etc.).	
573	Ensure chain of custody is followed for all digital media acquired in accordance with the Federal Rules of Evidence.	
613	Examine recovered data for information of relevance to the issue at hand.	
620	Employ IT systems and digital storage media to solve and prosecute cybercrimes and fraud committed against people and property.	
622	Formulate a strategy to ensure chain of custody is maintained in such a way that the evidence is not altered (e.g., phones/PDAs need a power source, hard drives need protection from shock and strong magnetic fields).	
636	Identify digital evidence for examination and analysis in such a way as to avoid unintentional alteration.	
743	Perform END incident triage, to include determining scope, urgency, potential impact, and identifying the specific vulnerability; and making recommendations that enable expeditious remediation.	
749	Perform dynamic analysis to boot an image of a drive (without necessarily having the original drive) to see the intrusion as the user may have seen it in its native environment.	

Figure 7.2   Digital forensics specialty area tasks mapped to the cybersecurity framework (CSF) functions.   *(Continued)*

	Investigate general knowledge area NICE workforce framework	Cybersecurity framework
		Identify
		Protect
		Detect
		Respond
		Recover
752	Perform file signature analysis.	
753	Perform hash comparison against established database.	
758	Perform real-time forensic analysis (e.g., using helix in conjunction with live view).	
759	Perform timeline analysis.	
768	Perform static media analysis.	
771	Perform tier 1, 2, and 3 malware analysis.	
786	Prepare digital media for imaging by ensuring data integrity (e.g., write blockers in accordance with standard operating procedures).	
799	Provide consultation to investigators and prosecuting attorneys regarding the findings of computer examinations.	
817	Provide technical assistance on digital evidence matters to appropriate personnel.	
819	Provide testimony related to computer examinations.	
825	Recognize and accurately report forensic artifacts indicative of a particular operating system.	
839	Review forensic images and other data sources for recovery of potentially relevant information.	
846	Serve as technical experts and liaisons to law enforcement personnel and explain incident details, provide testimony, and so on.	
868	Extract data using data carving techniques (e.g., forensic Toolkit [FTK], Foremost).	
870	Capture and analyze network traffic associated with malicious activities using network monitoring tools.	
871	Use specialized equipment and techniques to catalog, document, extract, collect, package, and preserve digital evidence.	
872	Resolve investigations through the use of specialized computer investigative techniques and programs.	
882	Write and publish cyber defense techniques, guidance, and reports on incident findings to appropriate constituencies.	

Figure 7.2 (Continued)   Digital forensics specialty area tasks mapped to the cybersecurity framework (CSF) functions.   (Continued)

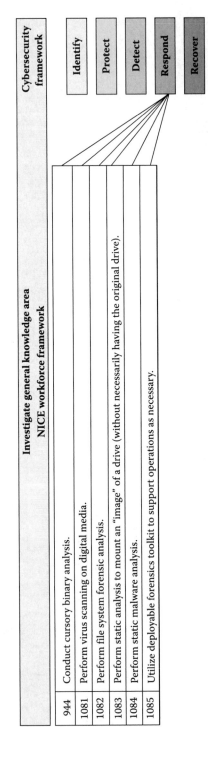

Figure 7.2 (Continued) Digital forensics specialty area tasks mapped to the cybersecurity framework (CSF) functions.

evidence, for instance photographs or written reports. This essentially preserves the crime scene.

The examiner also formulates a strategy to ensure that legal chain of custody is maintained. This strategy must provide legally supportable documentation that the evidence has not been altered in any way. That includes assurance that chain of custody is followed in accordance with the Federal Rules of Evidence for all digital media acquired.

To begin with, in order to ensure the integrity of the actual analysis the examiner must identify and label the digital evidence in such a way that it can be established that it has not been intentionally or unintentionally altered. Electronic information is invisible and highly dynamic. This step is necessary in order to ensure that the investigation does not inadvertently destroy or alter evidence during the investigative process. The forensic examiner then analyzes the recovered data in order to document its relevance to the issue at hand.

The general aim of the forensics process is to investigate any violation of computer or digital media for the purpose of prosecuting instances of cybercrime or fraud committed against people and property. Nonetheless, another purpose besides the criminal investigation and prosecution mandate is the development of all of the information necessary to ensure that the enterprise's networks and systems are fully and properly defended against any form of intrusion. This is done by fully scrutinizing the immediate environment in order to determine incident scope, urgency, and potential impact.

Following that, the forensics process identifies the specific vulnerability that was targeted and makes the recommendations necessary to ensure fast and efficient patching or repair. It should be stressed that forensics does not do the repair. It simply provides the necessary information to support the restoration process.

In order to do this the forensic examiner performs the necessary dynamic analysis. The aim is to fully understand the nature of the intrusion from the standpoint of its original point of origin. The file signature in the message header and a hashkeeper analysis are used to weed out any suspect files.

The hash values of known and innocuous objects are kept in a database of such files at a number of places on the Internet. The real-time viewing and analysis process are then undertaken using a forensically sound imaging tool such as Helix. The critical goal is to not alter the image by use of the tool. An event or timeline analysis is done.

This is followed by the performance of a static malware analysis. A static analysis is aimed at identifying known indicators of malicious activity. Dynamic analysis demonstrates the behavior of the object. Static analysis seeks to explain its behavior. As a result, it is possible to understand the operation of the code from both perspectives.

Static analysis has the benefit of helping the analyst to understand the behavior of the code because all of the elements of the program are under scrutiny, not just the executables. In order to do a proper analysis it is necessary to utilize tools such as source code analyzers, disassemblers, and even decompilers. Using those tools, the examiner can conduct a cursory binary analysis, do virus scanning on the media, perform file system analysis, as well as examine the "image" of the drive without necessarily having the original drive present to examine.

At the same time that the static analysis is undertaken, the forensic examiner may also perform a malware analysis focused at various levels of scrutiny. This is normally done by disassembling, decompiling, or reverse engineering the code blocks in order to detect malicious code elements such as backdoors, which have been inserted at the source code and machine language level. This is done using both static and dynamic analytic techniques. That includes ensuring target program and data integrity by the creation of partitioning and confinement measures such as virtual machine and secure firewall partitioning techniques.

The aim is to resolve each investigation through the use of specialized computer investigative techniques and programs. That may lead the examiner to utilize deployable forensics toolkit to support operations as necessary. In a detailed sense that might include characterizing and accurately reporting the forensic artifacts that are indicative of the existence, or use of a particular operating system, the review of forensic images and other data sources for recovery of potentially relevant information, and the provision of technical expertise and liaison to law enforcement personnel in order to explain incident details and prepare testimony.

The detailed work can entail a number of methods that are specifically designed to isolate the evidence to be analyzed and presented. In that respect, the examiner uses specialized equipment and techniques to catalog, document, extract, collect, package, and preserve digital evidence.

For example, because the environment of the investigation will be primarily composed of irrelevant material the forensic examiner needs to extract the relevant artifacts and data from the surrounding code using such data carving techniques as FTK. The examiner also has to capture and analyze the network traffic that is associated with the malicious activities using network monitoring tools.

Protection and Recovery Tasks

The chief role of the forensic examiner is to provide technical assistance in the identification and analysis of digital evidence. However, there is also a protection and recovery component in digital forensics work.

Once the evidence has been collected and analyzed it is reported to the appropriate organizational personnel for remedial action. Mostly this entails providing consultation to investigators and prosecuting attorneys regarding the findings of the digital examination. The investigator is also likely to provide testimony related to that examination in legal proceedings if that is required.

However, because forensic evidence is an excellent source of lessons learned, the forensic examination often leads to reports on incident findings that lead to improvements in the protection scheme of the organization. The writing and publication of new cyber defense techniques, guidance, and other advice is an essential by-product of the digital forensics process.

Besides the advice that digital forensics offers in the form of findings about prior adverse actions on the system, forensics can also serve as a basis for restoration of a system that has been harmed as a result of an accident or attack. The same methods, tools, and techniques that are employed to identify evidence of an attack can be used to rebuild and repair a system to its desired restoration point. In essence, the forensics process can also serve as a baseline point of reference for bringing the system back to its former level of operations following an attack.

Underlying Knowledge, Skill, and Ability Requirements for Digital Forensics

Along with a detailed set of tasks, the NICE workforce also provides a distinctive set of KSA specifications for each specialty area. These KSAs offer much clearer elaboration and characterization of the activities that underlie each task and also help the educational community to understand the precise knowledge requirements to be used in the design of targeted training and education programs in that specific specialty area.

The knowledge and specialty area categories are the central organizing basis for the framework. In essence, specialty areas in a given category are typically more similar to one another than to specialty areas in other categories. The authors of the model clustered related types of work together into categories. These categories serve as the unifying mechanism that allows the reader to understand the specific nature of the work involved.

A good forensics investigator has to have technical capabilities that are sufficient to allow them to work comfortably at the level of binary representation and transmission for a wide range of technical media and processes. On the other end of the spectrum, the forensics investigator also has to have a good working knowledge of the rules of criminal and civil procedure as they apply to the gathering and preservation of legal evidence. Finally, forensic investigators have to have the kind of investigative skills that are normally found in people like police detectives.

It is hard for an organization to assure that its forensic investigators will have all of these capabilities without the presence of a formal training process, which has been carefully designed and developed to produce a very well-defined skill set. Obviously those skills have to be built into each forensics investigator and so the essential first step in creating a sustainable forensics process is to document the KSA requirements necessary to ensure an acceptable level of capability.

That specification of requirements is the purpose of the KSAs enumerated by the NICE workforce model. Typical tasks and KSAs are specified within each specialty area. Each KSA has exactly one competency associated with it. Each KSA defines a specific KSA requirement. In application these requirements may be assigned to one or more specialty areas within the model.

Table 7.1 displays the specialty KSA requirements for the digital forensics specialty area as well as the associated competency areas (NIST 2014a).

Table 7.1 Digital Forensics Specialty Area Knowledge, Skill, and Abilities (KSAs)

Item ID	KSA	Statement	Competency
24	KSA	Knowledge of concepts and practices of processing digital forensic data.	Data management
25	KSA	Knowledge of encryption algorithms (e.g., Internet Protocol Security [IPSEC], Advanced Encryption Standard [AES], Generic Routing Encapsulation [GRE], Internet Key Exchange [IKE], Message Digest Algorithm [MD5], Secure Hash Algorithm [SHA], Triple Data Encryption Standard [3DES]).	Cryptography
29	KSA	Knowledge of data backup, types of backups (e.g., full, incremental), and recovery concepts and tools.	Computer forensics
61	KSA	Knowledge of incident response and handling methodologies.	Incident management
90	KSA	Knowledge of operating systems.	Operating systems
105	KSA	Knowledge of system and application security threats and vulnerabilities (e.g., buffer overflow, mobile code, cross-site scripting, procedural language/structured query language [PL/SQL] and injections, race conditions, covert channel, replay, return-oriented attacks, malicious code).	Vulnerabilities assessment
113	KSA	Knowledge of server and client operating systems.	Operating systems
114	KSA	Knowledge of server diagnostic tools and fault identification techniques.	Computer forensics
139	KSA	Knowledge of common networking protocols (e.g., Transmission Control Protocol and Internet Protocol [TCP/IP]) and services (e.g., web, mail, Domain Name System [DNS]) and how they interact to provide network communications.	Infrastructure design

(Continued)

Table 7.1 (Continued) Digital Forensics Specialty Area Knowledge, Skill, and Abilities (KSAs)

Item ID	KSA	Statement	Competency
193	KSA	Skill in developing, testing, and implementing network infrastructure contingency and recovery plans.	Information assurance
214	KSA	Skill in performing packet-level analysis using appropriate tools (e.g., Wireshark, tcpdump).	Vulnerabilities assessment
217	KSA	Skill in preserving evidence integrity according to standard operating procedures or national standards.	Computer forensics
264	KSA	Knowledge of basic physical computer components and architectures, including the functions of various components and peripherals (e.g., central processing units [CPUs], network interface cards [NICs], data storage).	Computers and electronics
287	KSA	Knowledge of file system implementations (e.g., New Technology File System [NTFS], file allocation table [FAT], file extension [EXT]).	Operating systems
290	KSA	Knowledge of processes for seizing and preserving digital evidence (e.g., chain of custody).	Forensics
294	KSA	Knowledge of hacking methodologies in Windows or Unix/Linux environment.	Surveillance
302	KSA	Knowledge of investigative implications of hardware, operating systems, and network technologies.	Computer forensics
310	KSA	Knowledge of legal governance related to admissibility (e.g., Federal Rules of Evidence).	Criminal law

(Continued)

Table 7.1 (Continued)   Digital Forensics Specialty Area Knowledge, Skill, and Abilities (KSAs)

Item ID	KSA	Statement	Competency
316	KSA	Knowledge of processes for collecting, packaging, transporting, and storing electronic evidence to avoid alteration, loss, physical damage, or destruction of data.	Criminal law
340	KSA	Knowledge of types and collection of persistent data.	Computer forensics
345	KSA	Knowledge of webmail collection, searching/analyzing techniques, tools, and cookies.	Web technology
346	KSA	Knowledge of which system files (e.g., log files, registry files, configuration files) contain relevant information and where to find those system files.	Computer forensics
350	KSA	Skill in analyzing memory dumps to extract information.	Reasoning
360	KSA	Skill in identifying and extracting data of forensic interest in diverse media (i.e., media forensics).	Computer forensics
364	KSA	Skill in identifying, modifying, and manipulating applicable system components within Windows, Unix, or Linux (e.g., passwords, user accounts, files).	Operating systems
369	KSA	Skill in collecting, processing, packaging, transporting, and storing electronic evidence to avoid alteration, loss, physical damage, or destruction of data.	Forensics
374	KSA	Skill in setting up a forensic workstation.	Forensics
381	KSA	Skill in using forensic tool suites (e.g., EnCase, Sleuthkit, Forensic Toolkit [FTK]).	Computer forensics
386	KSA	Skill in using virtual machines.	Operating systems

(Continued)

Table 7.1 (Continued) Digital Forensics Specialty Area Knowledge, Skill, and Abilities (KSAs)

Item ID	KSA	Statement	Competency
389	KSA	Skill in physically disassembling personal computers (PCs).	Computers and electronics
888	KSA	Knowledge of types of digital forensics data and how to recognize them.	Computer forensics
889	KSA	Knowledge of deployable forensics.	Computer forensics
890	KSA	Skill in conducting forensic analyses in multiple operating system environments (e.g., mobile device systems).	Computer forensics
908	KSA	Ability to decrypt digital data collections.	Computer forensics
923	KSA	Knowledge of security event correlation tools.	Information systems/ Network security
982	KSA	Knowledge of electronic evidence law.	Criminal law
983	KSA	Knowledge of legal rules of evidence and court procedure.	Criminal law
1033	KSA	Knowledge of basic system administration, network, and operating system hardening techniques.	Information systems/ Network security
1036	KSA	Knowledge of applicable laws (e.g., Electronic Communications Privacy Act, Foreign Intelligence Surveillance Act, Protect America Act, search and seizure laws, civil liberties and privacy laws), US Statutes (e.g., Titles 10, 18, 32, 50 in US Code), Presidential Directives, executive branch guidelines, and/or administrative/criminal legal guidelines and procedures relevant to work performed.	Criminal law

(Continued)

Table 7.1 (Continued)   Digital Forensics Specialty Area Knowledge, Skill, and Abilities (KSAs)

Item ID	KSA	Statement	Competency
1072	KSA	Knowledge of network security architecture concepts, including topology, protocols, components, and principles (e.g., application of defense-in-depth).	Information systems/Network security
1086	KSA	Knowledge of data carving tools and techniques (e.g., Foremost).	Computer forensics
1087	KSA	Skill in deep analysis of captured malicious code (e.g., malware forensics).	Computer network defense
1088	KSA	Skill in using binary analysis tools (e.g., Hexedit, command code xxd, hexdump).	Computer languages
1089	KSA	Knowledge of reverse engineering concepts.	Vulnerabilities assessment
1091	KSA	Skill in one way hash functions (e.g., Secure Hash Algorithm [SHA], Message Direct Algorithm [MD5]).	Data management
1092	KSA	Knowledge of antiforensics tactics, techniques, and procedures (TTPs).	Computer forensics
1093	KSA	Knowledge of common forensic tool configuration and support applications (e.g., VMware, Wireshark).	Computer forensics
1094	KSA	Knowledge of debugging procedures and tools.	Software development
1095	KSA	Knowledge of how different file types can be used for anomalous behavior.	Vulnerabilities assessment

(Continued)

Table 7.1 (Continued) Digital Forensics Specialty Area Knowledge, Skill, and Abilities (KSAs)

Item ID	KSA	Statement	Competency
1096	KSA	Knowledge of malware analysis tools (e.g., Oily Debug, Ida Pro).	Computer network defense
1097	KSA	Knowledge of virtual machine aware malware, debugger aware malware, and packing.	Computer network defense
1098	KSA	Skill in analyzing anomalous code as malicious or benign.	Computer network defense
1099	KSA	Skill in analyzing volatile data.	Computer forensics
1100	KSA	Skill in identifying obfuscation techniques.	Computer network defense
1101	KSA	Skill in interpreting results of debugger to ascertain TTP.	Computer network defense

Digital Forensics KSAs

The majority of the KSA requirements for the forensics specialty area can be factored into four distinct areas of standard application.

1. *Information systems/network security* is a classic area of cybersecurity protection.
2. *Infrastructure design* is an area, whose decision making is supported by forensics.
3. *Vulnerability assessment and risk management* is the classic risk component.
4. *Legal, government, and jurisprudence* entails the rules of evidence.

Each of these elements is required in order to ensure that the forensics process is both trustworthy and sustainable. Forensics work requires a broad range of technical and behavioral capabilities. Many of those capabilities are typically not found in conjunction with each other.

Forensics activities require intimate knowledge of the inner workings of the machine. That knowledge is always obtained by use of specialized tools and equipment. These tools are utilized to ensure that every aspect of the collection and handling of virtual evidence is documented in such a way that the absolute integrity of the chain of custody is provably maintained. Also, because of the nature of digital evidence it is almost impossible to collect and preserve it without tool support.

The second requirement in the establishment of a digital forensics process is to define the specific reporting lines and oversight that the forensics process will function in. Because of the wide range of organizations that might be involved and their diverse ways of doing business, this is not a simple matter of dropping a stock business framework down into the target organization. The assurance of a properly resourced array of reporting lines requires a well-designed policy level planning process.

The outcome of that process should be a defined set of decision criteria that establish the exact nature, type, scope, and depth of the information to be provided to each legitimate decision maker. That planning process also requires the organization to ensure the precise authorizations to guarantee that the right information is available to the right people as needed. Finally, the interface between the forensic process and the overall IT operation has to be established. In essence, the condition has to be assured where conventional IT processes will enable all necessary activities of the digital forensic process.

The impact and reach of digital forensics can be widespread and this may result in a lot of systems being examined for forensic implication. Since that is the case, it is highly likely that policies and procedures will need to be created in advance or modified to ensure that forensic workers have the knowledge and the access necessary to do their job. There are two general types of policies required to ensure alignment between normal IT and digital forensic work. The first type of policy dictates the procedures to ensure that forensics work is properly synchronized with the activities of the overall IT operation. For instance, existing data classification policies that define data types and access to data based on position, data sensitivity, and need to know may have to be modified to permit forensic personnel to access the code in the course of their assigned duties.

In addition to the organizational issues, there is also a need for explicit policy and procedure framework to ensure standard execution of the electronic evidence/ data recovery and analysis process. In addition, the reporting and archival requirements of examined material have to be aligned with relevant standards, procedures, directives, policies, regulations, and laws. Along with standard operating rules, there also has to be policies and procedures for the actual imaging and duplication of the electronic media. Since the actual examination process requires tangible equipment, the standardized requirements for hardware and software to support the digital forensic program have to be specified along with the hardware and software requirements and configuration of the forensic laboratory and mobile toolkit.

Since the aim of forensics is to gather evidence, there have to be explicit policies and procedures for the preservation of electronic evidence, data recovery and analysis, and the reporting and archival requirements of examined material. These have to ensure proper chain of custody assurance in accordance with all relevant standards; procedures; legal directives; national, state, and local regulations; and laws.

In addition to the assurance of the verity of the evidence, there also has to be a standard set of qualification requirements for guaranteeing the capabilities of the forensics examiners including a system for maintaining competencies over time. Thus, periodic competency testing has to be planned prior to granting the examiner investigative privileges along with periodic proficiency testing and certification as a basis for the requirement for ongoing continuing education.

The justification for the forensic process lies in its ability to identify and truly understand latent vulnerabilities in information systems and programs. This ability is the initial step in the formal risk management process, which is so vital to the success of any information security effort. Risk management's general goal is to ensure that adverse occurrences do not impact the business or its goals. Thus, effective risk management requires that all relevant risks are identified, assessed, and prioritized. Following that, the organization will take a set of planned and systematic steps to mitigate the likelihood of occurrence and impact of each relevant instance of the risk.

The problem with risk to computers is that the kind of threats that are the most destructive—back doors, Trojan horses, logic bombs, and other kinds of malware—tend to hide in the code that executes all of the desired functions of the program. Thus, in order to truly mitigate the threat it is necessary to understand it and that is very difficult when the risk is 10 lines of binary hidden in 100,000 lines of code. Accordingly, the only possible way to reach the necessary level of knowledge is through the kind of analysis represented by the digital forensics KSAs. As a result, the KSA specifications of the NICE model in the areas of vulnerability and risk management represent the only viable avenue to a successful threat and risk mitigation effort at the code level.

The KSAs related to jurisprudence and the general rules of evidence are an especially insightful element of the NICE framework. Digital forensics evidence is like no other form of legally actionable evidence in that it is virtual. Thus, the collection, preservation, and presentation processes are not the same as it would be for physical evidence. Legally, evidence must be verified as correct, relevant, and in the same state as it was when it was gathered. This is easy to do with physical crime scene artifacts in that it is visible and protocols can be followed to ensure its continuing integrity. Digital evidence is primarily binary representation. It is both invisible and highly dynamic. Thus, the assurance of correctness is difficult to maintain.

Nonetheless, without absolute proof that the chain of custody has been maintained and that the evidence remains untainted by subsequent change, it is impossible for it to be admissible in a legal proceeding. However, up to this point there has been no consideration of the special circumstances for digital evidence. That is because the only people capable of obtaining and preserving digital evidence are computer professionals, not lawyers. Thus, the NICE KSAs related to maintaining legal admissibility are extremely useful in the overall understanding of the skill set required for a digital forensics professional.

Application: Organizing a Digital Forensics Function Based on the CSF

As illustrated here, the process by which an organization implements and performs routine digital forensics involves a mix of management and technical KSAs. As a group, the general role of these tasks is to ensure that the digital forensics function is seamlessly embedded in the ongoing operation of the organization. Thirteen specific tasks from this list can be associated directly with the CSF:

1. Assist in collecting and preserving evidence in accordance with established procedures, plans, policies, and best practices (*identification*)
2. Perform forensic analysis on networks and computer systems, and make recommendations for remediation (*identification and protection*)
3. Apply and maintain intrusion detection systems; intrusion prevention systems; network mapping software; monitoring and logging systems; and analyze results to protect, detect, and correct information security-related vulnerabilities and events (*identification and defense*)
4. Follow proper chain-of-custody best practices in accordance with standards, procedures, directives, policies, regulations, and laws (*identification*)
5. Collect and retain audit data to support technical analysis relating to misuse, penetration, reconstruction, or other investigations (*identification*)
6. Provide audit data to appropriate law enforcement or other investigating agencies, to include corporate security elements (*identification and protection*)
7. Assess and extract relevant pieces of information from collected data (*identification*)

8. Report complete and accurate findings, and result of the analysis of digital evidence, to appropriate resources (*identification, protection, recovery*)
9. Coordinate dissemination of forensic analysis findings to appropriate resources (*identification, protection, recovery*)
10. Provide training as appropriate on using forensic analysis equipment, technologies, and procedures—such as the installation of forensic hardware and software components (*defend*)
11. Advise on the suitability of Standard Operating Environment's (SOE) baseline standard for forensic analysis (*identification, protection, recovery*)
12. Coordinate applicable legal and regulatory compliance requirements (*protection*)
13. Coordinate, interface, and work under the direction of appropriate corporate entities (e.g., corporate legal, corporate investigations) regarding investigations or other legal requirements—including investigations that involve external governmental entities (*identification, protection, recovery*)

As we have seen, at its root, digital forensics work is a personal exercise that requires a mix of KSAs. On the surface, these skills do not intuitively relate to each other. Intimate knowledge of how electronic data are represented and manipulated is required. However, it is also essential to have a lawyer's command of legal procedure and the investigative skills of a trained police detective. Moreover, strict deterministic rules do not apply to the collection of evidence because that evidence resides in a diverse and highly dynamic virtual environment. So in most cases, the individual skills of the practitioner and the appropriate use of tools are the factors that determine the success of a forensic exercise.

Nevertheless, there are some basic principles that can be universally assumed. These, in effect, define the elements and sequence of a digital forensics process. Similarly they can also be used to both structure and run a digital forensics operation. In order to implement a digital forensic function, three sequential activities have to be performed: data collection, data recovery and analysis, and reporting. These relate to three of the core function requirements of the CSF. Data collection, recovery, and analysis aid identification, whereas reporting supports both protection and recovery.

Identification: Ensuring an Accurate Picture

The process of creating the accurate picture of any type of incident typically involves the generation of a forensically sound copy of the evidence. This is done for the purpose of analysis. Since that evidence usually resides in a number of diverse places, the collection process always originates with a thorough survey and identification of all of the locations where instances of relevant data might exist. This is basically a tool supported inventory process.

Nonetheless, it is critically important to implement and follow a formal standard protocol to ensure that the forensic agent has looked in all of the places that have to be searched. Besides being kept in diverse places, that information can be stored in a number of ways. That includes archived and existing active files, files that are protected either by encryption or passwords or even in latent form such as deleted or partially overwritten sectors. There are also files that are only used by the system and hidden files. In most cases, none of that information is viewable. So the specific skills and tools have to be specified and put in place to allow the organization to obtain whatever forensic evidence is required for its purposes.

Because that evidence is usually electronic, the forensic collection process has to be ensured to be technically correct and the data have to be proven empirically sound. That assurance is necessary to guarantee beyond a shadow of doubt that all of the evidence that is collected and analyzed will be a true and accurate reflection of the facts of the matter, at a given point in time.

Ensuring legally correct evidence is a tricky proposition. It relies on the proper use of tools. These tools and their accompanying data collection and analysis methods are utilized in a stock fashion in order to ensure that all relevant evidence has been obtained. Appropriate use of tools implies the need for a specification of a fundamental set of technical capabilities for the examiner. In essence, these capabilities represent the required skill set for the forensics professional in each organization. Likewise, as tools and methods change over time it is also important that the organization ensures that its forensics professionals keep abreast of those changes. The KSA requirements of the NICE framework make this clear.

In addition, the organization has to ensure that their forensics professionals have a good working knowledge of all relevant rules of civil and criminal procedure. Most importantly, the organization has to have mechanisms in place to guarantee the integrity of the chain of custody. In its simplest form chain of custody requires the documentation of each step of the process as it occurred. Because the forensics professional is typically working at the level of internal representation of electronic data, the forensic process needs to utilize a set of dedicated tools to record as well as continuously authenticate the precise status of the evidence at any point in the process.

Electronic evidence is basically intangible. Therefore, in the case of litigation that relies on electronic evidence, it is critical that the organization is able to certify that whatever evidence they bring to court has been obtained in a correct fashion and has not been tampered with. Consequently, a formal protocol has to be utilized in order to ensure integrity of the process of data collection. That has to be spelled out in any plan to establish a forensics process.

Basically, the plan that establishes any forensic process ought to ensure strict control over the access of any individual to the forensic data that are collected during the collection and analysis phases. The plan should also ensure that the integrity of the data can be confirmed by empirical means both before and after each access. This level of absolute control is particularly essential in a Court of Law due to the unique volatility of electronic data and its ease of alteration. Accordingly, if the protocols that underlie the organization's chain of custody arrangements cannot be documented then the data might be legally suspect. The fear of having an iron clad case thrown out of court because the chain of custody has been broken is the reason why the NICE model takes such pains in the definition of the requisite KSAs for preservation of evidence for the digital forensics professional.

Chain of custody is a highly detail oriented protocol that traces its origins back to English Common Law. Since it is such a well-established concept, it entails a very explicit set of practices that are designed to ensure maximum integrity in the collection and preservation of evidence. Therefore, one of the most important requirements for a general forensics plan is that it is built around an unambiguous set of KSA specifications. Those specifications have to be capable of assuring that critical forensic functions, such as data collection in criminal matters, data collection in response to civil proceedings, and data collection in response to internal investigations are carried out in a standard and competent way by the practitioner. The NICE model provides such assurance in its standard competency requirements.

Each KSA item has to have an attendant set of real world practices developed from it. The assurance of correctness of those practices is an important part of successful implementation. In order to be trustworthy, the practices that are derived from the standard tasks and KSAs need to be documented and tested for effectiveness. More important, the forensic examiners have to be provably capable of executing them properly. That level of proven capability is an essential element of the process of creating a forensics competency. Finally, because of the highly technical nature of forensic investigations, the work is often outsourced to specialty practitioners. Even in the case of outsourced work, the capabilities that are required to carry out the forensics examiner role have to be documented, unambiguously clear, and enforced for all outsourced work.

Identification: Analyzing Data and Recording Results for Future Reference

Along with capture, the forensics process also involves the steps that are taken for the analysis of data once they have been collected. It is almost impossible to stipulate a standard operating procedure for an analytic process. That is because the process itself involves so many unknown variables. Most of those are situational. For instance, the analysis activity will be different depending on whether it is in support of litigation in civil or criminal matters. It is also going to be different if it is part of a post incident analysis, since the aim there is to determine the nature of an attack and how to better defend, respond, and recover from it rather than to support litigation. Forensic analysis methodologies and tools might even apply to the recovery of data after a hardware or software failure.

However, some general organizational requirements are always part of the analysis process. First the analysis has to be duplicable and repeatable. That is necessary to ensure empirical correctness and impartiality. It is critical in a legal proceeding for opposing experts to be able to validate a given set of findings by duplicating the process. Otherwise the evidence would likely be inadmissible in court.

In that respect, the forensic analysis process should be structured to address four basic conditions. The first and most obvious condition is that sufficient evidence has to be obtained to support legal action. Accordingly, there are two related questions involved with the evidence gathering process. The first is whether all existing evidence has been identified and collected. The second is whether that collection process satisfies all of the requirements of the court rules of procedure.

Outside of the considerations related to evidence there are two procedural ones. The first has to do with whether the forensic analysis is being used to reconstruct an electronic crime. The reason for differentiating an analysis done to investigate a crime from the one done to investigate civil or noncriminal issues is that aim of the former is prosecution, while the other is oriented more toward learning about a specific event that has occurred in order to make a decision about redress.

Finally, forensic analysis can be used to determine what was accessed, taken, or harmed. This final application is a particularly unique condition of digital information. That is because digital information is one of the few things that can be taken or tampered with without any physical sign that anything has actually occurred. In effect, things are undoubtedly being stolen after a robbery in the physical world. That is because they can be seen to be missing. However, digital information can be taken without any obvious sign that it has ever been accessed. Since it is hard to even tell what items have been affected, the exact focus of the investigation has to be specified in advance in order to narrow down the items that have to be considered. This rule is primarily intended to ensure that resources are utilized efficiently.

Protect and Recover: Writing a Forensic Recovery and Analysis Plan

There are two primary constituents of the forensic analysis and recovery process. First and most obvious is the protection and subsequent recovery of the computer itself. While at the same time there is the equally important issue of the protection and recovery of the network. Network incidents are also subject to the same kind of analysis, but the network does not have the same issues as the computer.

In the case of the computer, the forensics professional has to be able to assemble all of the evidence that was obtained in the collection process from a properly identified, given device. That can include everything from the date and time that the evidence was gathered, through notes about the techniques that were used to collect the evidence as well as any tool use. These findings are typically summarized in the working notes that the analyst will later turn into the final report. The method for doing this should be repeatable and therefore the forensics process itself should be built around a precise protocol that the organization follows in a disciplined and repeatable process.

For instance, the analyst will generally work the indecent analysis from the outside in. This means that the analyst will first process any external media like thumb drives or CDs. Then they will move on to the internal circuitry for the purpose of mapping all relevant sources of forensic evidence. Once that is done, the analyst uses the appropriate tool to identify, obtain, catalog, and analyze all relevant data from both external media and also internal circuitry. There are far too many tools on the market to list here; however, some of the products that are the most popular at the present time are NCASE, Access Data's FTK, and Paraben Software's P2 suite. On the open-source side two popular tools are Sleuth Kit and E-fense's Helix. The details of both the method and the tool support have to be specified in the forensics recovery plan.

The network requires a different approach. Forensic analysis of network traffic can also provide considerable supporting evidence about breaches and violations if the right reconstructive methods and tools are used. The forensic analysis of a network can be conducted both from a retrospective point of view, as a means of preventing the reoccurrence of an event. That analysis satisfies the CSF functional goals of "protect."

However, the network analysis can also be from a prospective direction, in the sense that the discovery that an event has occurred on a given network can lead to a much broader analysis of the circumstances and context that motivated and enabled that event. Network analyses are also tool supported. Nevertheless, because networks have different requirements and conditions than computers, the scope of the forensic examination process, as it applies to networks, has to be stated in the plan.

The specification of the precise scope of the forensics examination is particularly important in the case of network oriented forensics. That is because all of the capture and analysis tools have to be in place prior to the occurrence of the event. Forensic analysis of networks is typically based on the logging of traffic and that information can only be obtained if a sensor is in place prior to the incident that is being studied. Because of the use of similar traffic monitoring tools for incident detection systems (IDS), there is some debate about where to draw the line between monitoring for forensics purposes versus incident response. That is the reason why, no matter what tool used, the extent of network monitoring for forensics purposes has to be spelled out in detail.

Protecting and Recovering: Setting Up an Effective Communication Process

The design of the protection scheme and any subsequent recovery plan is best supported by exact information about a given threat. That requires an effective, standardized and highly organized communication process. There are several critical elements involved in ensuring a successful communication process. The first of these elements is planning.

Prospective incident planning is critical to the success of a forensic examination. Done right the plan will reduce the risk of errors, incorrect reporting lines, or omissions in reporting the results of a forensics investigation. Most importantly, the plan should ensure that the actions utilized to obtain the results are reproducible, clear, and understandable. Reproducibility ensures the acceptability of the evidence in all legal proceedings. Thus, reproducibility simply means that the same actions performed by different people would still produce the same results.

The forensics examination plan also has to include the formal provisions for communicating the results of the process to the protection planning and recovery phase. That includes all relevant decision makers as well as any attorneys. In operational terms this means that, any procedures for communication have to ensure that all parties will fully understand and work with other parties. The most important people in the process are probably the security professionals responsible for developing mitigations or changing the security scheme after breach. However, there are a number of other people who need to be informed of forensics results such as the CEO, financial officers, and probably also public relations and marketing.

Equally important to the specification of the actors in the process and their proper lines of communication is the requirement that any findings involved in any form of litigation adhere to all court rules of procedure for forensic evidence. That includes the findings that support affidavits and expert testimony. Finally it must be ensured that all communications in a legal proceeding are expressed in a way that can be easily understood and acted on by jurors. Given the legal implications of most forensic evidence the communication process and the method of documenting outcomes has to be both well-defined in the plan and then rigorously adhered to.

The communication plan also has to ensure that the findings contained in the report document any expert conclusions drawn from the evidence. In general, these conclusions should only be statements of fact about questions that have been raised by decision makers or participants in the litigation. For instance, the report could state that the evidence supports the contention that a certain event occurred at a certain time. If there are specific laws, policies, or standards involved in guiding the analysis the plan should ensure that these are clearly stated. In addition, the protocol must be unambiguous that ensures that the evidence is directly mapped to the requirements of those regulations.

From a process standpoint, because forensics reporting is meant to support decision making about protection, it should generally be reviewed and discussed as part of the overall strategic plan for the organization. The forensic examiner who has been assigned the case is normally responsible for preparing the actual report. The forensic examiner sends the report to the appropriate upper level manager and that manager is then responsible for distribution to the right people for action. Depending on circumstances, the report might also be given to the corporate attorney, opposing attorneys, or other interested parties. There has to be a single manager who is solely accountable for initiating whatever actions implied by the findings. The plan should always ensure proper procedure is followed in these areas.

Recovery: Reconstructing Events

The simplest requirement for forensic evidence is that it is accurate and actionable. Therefore, the forensics process has to produce objective evidence that is obtained by an empirical process. Because credibility is such an important factor in the forensics process it is necessary to have a reliable set of standard tasks and KSAs to ensure that the discovery and processing of that evidence is always done correctly.

Specifically, these tasks and KSAs have to spell out and ensure that forensics professionals adhere to a trusted protocol in performing their investigation. That protocol involves everything from procedures for identifying what data to collect to the identification of the sources that it will be obtained from. In that respect then, data collection is an important element in the overall identification and recovery process. That is because that data comprise the record of the desired state of things in the system. Thus, the tasks and KSAs that are adopted by the organization have to guarantee that the data are acquired and accurately preserved in accordance with all of the dictates of standard best practice as outlined in the NICE model.

Characterizing the Incident

The actual requirements for each forensics examination are derived from the type of incident that is being investigated. Therefore, the specific aim of the process is to understand the precise nature of the incident. That understanding is necessary because the nature of the incident will define the scope of the analysis. It will also dictate how the actual investigation will be conducted. For instance, there would be considerable difference in the actions that are taken to collect and analyze a simple criminal trespass versus an industrial espionage episode or a bank robbery exploit.

Consequently, the first necessity in the forensic identification effort is to characterize all of the implications and potential outcomes of the incident under study. That determination process is not as simple as it might sound. That is because most of the impacts of a cyber event are in the virtual world and therefore they cannot be observed or characterized in physical terms. To illustrate this, if an earthquake occurs it is easy to survey the damage to the surrounding houses. However, an all-out cyberattack that could conceivably cause equivalent damage in the virtual world would leave no observable results.

Thus, the first step in the forensic examination process involves identifying and surveying any of the known, or assumed, areas of impact in order to characterize the underlying harm that has occurred. This first step is not very much different from initial crime scene surveys that detectives do in the physical world. The first aim is to define what happened and who the victims were. If all of that is understood then the exact nature of the event will point to the places that have to be investigated. This step essentially narrows the sources of evidence down to a workable set.

Identifying the Sources of Data

The next substantive stage in the forensic examination is the identification of the precise sources of data to support the investigation. This is not as simple a process as it might sound, since there are always bewildering arrays of potential data sources in the electronic universe. Any one of these sources could be tapped to reconstruct a misuse, penetration, reconstruction, or other investigative event. Consequently, the first step in establishing the investigation is to identify only those sources that are likely to be relevant to the incident at hand. In general, that data can usually be found in two places.

System Logs

The first source of forensic data is usually the electronic logs that are kept by the system. The electronic log information is generated as part of the normal operation of most computer systems. As a consequence, it can be one of the likeliest sources for investigative data. Those logs constantly document what happened in various parts of the system. For instance, firewall logs, intrusion detection/prevention system logs, and access control logs all contain entries that provide step by step descriptions of the events that took place during a computer incident. In essence, the logs contain the detailed record of what transpired.

Nonetheless, those logs are not created and configured by chance. They require careful and detailed human intervention in order to be set up and maintained. Therefore, one important early aspect of the implementation process for forensic discovery is to ensure that all of the electronic record keeping logs that record system activity exist and are collecting reliable data about system events.

Physical Media

The other source of evidence is the actual media on which the digital record is kept. This can include all internal storage sources such as static memory as well as disks and other forms of storage. There are also a range of external media on which a record of system events might be kept. That includes thumb drives, CDs, and other forms of external storage such as tape. Any one of these artifacts could provide meaningful evidence to support the investigation.

Nevertheless, because that evidence exists in digital form it can be obtained through the use of electronic supporting tools such as unerase and undelete software and tools, which are designed to read data represented at the binary level. All of these tools do their work below the end user, at the system operation level. They are designed to allow the analyst to both see and subsequently evaluate the evidence at hand. However, the actual interpretation of what evidence is meaningful versus data that is irrelevant in a court of law has to be done by a human being.

Evidence-Handling Protocols

Evidence-handling protocols are generally dictated by what that evidence will subsequently be used for. More specifically, if the evidence has to be available for use in court, strict chain of custody procedures must be clearly documented and adopted from the outset in order to ensure trust.

Trusted procedure is critical in the case of chain of custody because any perceived deviation from the specified protocols for the process will generally lead to the evidence being rendered inadmissible in court. Furthermore, because of the legal concept of "the fruit of the poisoned tree" it is possible that one questionable item of evidence can also eliminate other forms of evidence that might be derived from that item.

That principle applies in both criminal and civil cases. Therefore, the assurance of the integrity of the chain of custody is a critical part of setting up and executing the discovery process. Therefore, it is essential that chain-of-custody protocols exist that comply all relevant standards, procedures, directives, policies, regulations, and laws are documented and enforced.

Analysis and Reporting Phases

After collecting all of the relevant evidence, investigators analyze the data in order to establish the constituent events. Based on the results of the analysis process, conclusions can be drawn about the actions that are needed to correct, remediate, or report a happening. If the decision involves reporting the incident to law enforcement, or engaging law enforcement in the subsequent investigation, then procedures will also have to be presented to allow the evidence to be shared with the appropriate authorities.

Operationally, this sharing will require the organization to provide the appropriate pieces of evidence and to respond to requests from law enforcement or other investigating agencies. A similar situation occurs in legal discovery events that are brought in the form of a subpoena. Preplanning and preparation is essential to success here, as time is usually a factor when evidence sharing is done under a court order.

The final element of the forensics process is the dissemination of the findings. Dissemination is typically done in the form of a report. That report distributes the results of the forensic analysis to the appropriate authorities and acts as a historical record. The principal feature of the final report is always the recommendation about the root cause of the incident. This is provided where available. Where the root cause is known, the necessary steps to prevent a reoccurrence of event at a future point in time are also provided.

Practical Management Considerations

It is prudent for most large organizations to maintain a digital forensics capability because of today's litigious environment. Creating that capability requires developing a precise set of operational responsibilities for leadership and management of the digital forensics process. It also includes more humble, practical considerations such as workspace, tools, personnel, and reporting chains. The planning work that underlies the creation of the digital forensics process typically determines the standard set of identification, protection/mitigation, and recovery actions required to control and limit adverse effects. These reactions can range from procedures for the simple rebuilding of a single machine to shifting to a backup site while a large portion of the enterprise is rebuilt.

Nonetheless, forensics work can be time consuming and expensive. So depending upon the size of the firm, it may be advantageous to maintain a group of in-house trained forensic personnel, along with tools and a workspace. On the other hand, depending on the situation it may also make sense to outsource the forensic work to an outside contractor. Determining the best approach and then organizing and communicating the strategy to the rest of the firm is part of the overall digital forensics strategic management process.

Ensuring a Capable Workforce

Finally, even if the forensics process is properly defined and the staffing is correct, the workforce still has to be capable of performing all of the requisite forensic tasks. Therefore, the forensics process entails its own set of formal training procedures. The purpose of these procedures is to ensure that the workforce is capable of performing all of their necessary duties. This particular necessity is one of the primary justifications and advantages of the NICE workforce model and its explicit task and KSA specifications.

A very important aspect of the universality of the NICE framework is the fact that most forensics examinations are done for a third party. And third party requirements are likely to have conditions built into them that might not be familiar to a given forensics staff.

Consequently, there have to be provisions built into any workforce capability development plan, which will ensure that the particular workers on a given project are sufficiently trained and knowledgeable to meet the specific requirements of that project. The use of a standard framework and nomenclature immeasurably aids this process.

Moreover, as forensics investigations progress it is frequently necessary to coordinate, interface with, or work under the direction of other appropriate organizational entities, such as corporate legal counsel or even the physical security operation. That requirement for cooperation can also include external governmental entities at the local, state, national, and even international level. Therefore, it is important to have the necessary situational awareness and the ability to facilitate intergroup work into the skill set for forensics professionals. The commonality of the NICE model and its customizability ensures that standard training and awareness programs can be developed for diverse settings.

Ensuring Correctness through Routine Evaluations

The aim of the evaluation function is to ensure that the management controls that have been instituted to ensure the quality and disciplined performance of the forensics process do not erode over time. Without constant oversight the performance of the forensic process can become slipshod and undisciplined. This erosion is particularly dangerous in a precise process like forensics where serious vulnerabilities in the operation can occur and not be identified if the process is not handled correctly.

Therefore, it is essential that the forensics processes and its performance is regularly assessed, tested, and verified as being accurate, appropriate, and up to date. A routine review process can also produce timely information that managers can use to fine-tune the forensics operation so that it is always functioning at optimum capability.

There are nine evaluation criteria that should be considered when evaluating the general performance of a forensics process. These are all primarily management in orientation.

1. Ensure the effectiveness of forensic processes and accuracy of forensic tools used by digital forensic examiners, and implement changes as required
2. Review all documentation associated with forensic processes or results for accuracy, applicability, and completeness
3. Assess the effectiveness, accuracy, and appropriateness of testing processes and procedures followed by the forensic laboratories and teams, and suggest changes where appropriate
4. Assess the digital forensic staff to ensure they have the appropriate KSA to perform forensic activities
5. Validate the effectiveness of the analysis and reporting process, and implement changes where appropriate
6. Review and recommend standard validated forensic tools
7. Assess the digital forensic laboratory quality assurance program, peer review process, and audit proficiency testing procedures, and implement changes where appropriate
8. Examine penetration testing and vulnerability analysis results to identify risks and implement patch management
9. Identify improvement actions based on the results of validation, assessment, and review

There are several strategies that can be adopted to carry out the actual reviews of the forensics process. One is based on routine assessments. At regular intervals, such as quarterly or semiannually, all relevant forensics procedures, protocols, and technologies are reviewed to ensure their effectiveness against corporate goals.

A second method is to institute rigorous change management control over the forensic process itself. In that respect, reviews and tests are initially done as part of the evaluation of the correctness of the forensics process. Then the process itself is maintained in alignment with any changes in the systems it is meant to address. This latter approach eliminates any time lag that might take place between significant system changes and updates to the forensic process and it ensures that forensics practices and technologies always remain up-to-date and valid.

Both of these approaches will serve to validate the correctness of the forensics process; however, the practical solution is usually a combination of these two. Some elements, particularly those that are part of the technology, are best included into the change process itself. That ensures the technology that underlies the forensic capability is always in-step with the enterprise as it changes. Nonetheless, policy and procedure and other high level functions are not usually subject to change management. Therefore, they need a higher level review process involving inspections and audits.

Inspections, audits, and other types of human-powered reviews are much more resource intensive so they are normally done on a routine periodic basis. The target of these kinds of inspections is usually the forensics policy, protocols and procedures, and other activities that are not subject to empirical tests.

The overall plan that establishes the forensics operation should be used to design and schedule these types of evaluations. The aim is to ensure that all aspects of the program receive periodic review, whether change is a factor or not. The evaluation of policies procedures, protocols, and training creates a series of baselines that can be used to actually understand the organization's forensic capability. Moreover, as the various requirements for the process change, these baselines can be adjusted to meet the new situation. That is the reason why evaluation is a necessary and important aspect of the forensic process.

Specialty Area 2: Cyber Investigation

As we said in the first chapter, in many respects cyber investigation is simply the body of knowledge of criminal justice. The cyber investigation specialty area embodies all of the best practice police methods and protocols, and criminal investigation procedures that are appropriate for cyberspace. As a result, cyber investigation encompasses all of the conventional investigative tools and processes utilized by law enforcement. The activities in this specialty area constitute a hybrid of police investigative and intelligence gathering activities.

Cyber investigation techniques normally entail interview and interrogation techniques, surveillance, countersurveillance, and surveillance detection methods. These techniques are designed to analyze and better understand computer-generated threats. Since cyber investigation particularly targets the criminal aspects of the investigate knowledge area, it is aimed at assisting in the gathering and preservation of evidence used in the prosecution of computer crimes.

The practical tasks involve analyzing log files and cataloging and analyzing evidence and other information. The purpose of this is to determine the best way to identify the perpetrators of an intrusion, either at the computer or network level. Therefore, it is appropriate that the cyber investigator conducts interviews of victims and witnesses and conduct interviews or interrogations of suspects in a manner similar to conventional police detectives.

And just as a normal police detective does, the cyber investigator determines and develops leads and identifies sources of information in order to find and prosecute the responsible parties for that intrusion. Nevertheless, the focus of the cyber investigator is on the conduct of a formal process to investigate the alleged crime, violation, or suspicious activity by utilizing computers and the Internet.

Just as a normal police detective would do, the cyber investigator documents the original condition of the digital and/or associated evidence. That can include everything from digital photographs to stored files containing reports. If an incident significant enough to affect the entire organization is involved, the cyber investigator will also establish the requisite coordination between the incident response team and other groups such as the legal and forensics staff and external agencies such as law enforcement, vendors, and public relations professionals.

The cyber investigator might not do the forensics examination but like a physical detective they will examine all of the recovered data for information of relevance to the issue at hand. This is likely to involve an examination of the effected systems and digital storage media. The aim is to solve and prosecute cybercrimes and fraud committed against people and property using those systems. In that respect, the cyber investigator fuses computer network attack analyses with criminal investigations and operations in order to identify and/or determine whether a security incident is a violation of the law and requires specific legal action by police agencies. If that is the case then the cyber investigator identifies digital evidence that might constitute the proof of a crime. In all respects that examination and analysis are done in such a way as to avoid unintentional alteration.

Besides the police, the cyber investigator is also likely to encounter situations where data or intelligence might be pertinent to the purposes of counterintelligence. In both cases, the cyber investigator identifies and investigates all pertinent outside attackers and any insiders who might be perpetrating an unauthorized use or an attempt to gain and misuse nonauthorized privileges. Most investigations involve the identification, collection, and seizure of documentary or physical evidence to support the investigation. This might include digital media and logs associated with cyber intrusion incidents, investigations, and operations.

The cyber investigator conducts large-scale investigations of criminal activities involving complicated computer programs and networks. The investigator processes crime scenes, secures the electronic device or information source, uses specialized equipment and techniques to catalog, document, extract, collect, package, and preserve digital evidence and prepares reports to document the analysis.

Application: Organizing a Digital Forensics Function Based on the CSF

As illustrated here, the process by which an organization implements and performs routine cyber investigations involves a mix of management and technical KSAs. As a group, the general role of these tasks is to ensure that the cyber investigation function is effectively a part of the ongoing operation of the organization. Figure 7.3 shows the cyber investigation specialty area tasks mapped to the CSF functions.

Seven specific tasks from this list can be associated directly with the CSF:

1. Interview and interrogation, surveillance, countersurveillance, and surveillance detection—*identify*
2. Analyze and better understand computer-generated threats—*identify/protect*
3. Identify the perpetrators of an intrusion—*identify/defend*
4. Documents the original condition of the digital and/or associated evidence—*identify*
5. Solve and prosecute cybercrimes and fraud committed against people and property—*identify/defend*
6. Conduct large-scale investigations of criminal activities, process crime scenes, secure the electronic device or information source, use specialized equipment and techniques to catalog, document, extract, collect, package, and preserve digital evidence—*identify/respond*
7. Prepare reports to document the analysis—*identify*

This all requires specialized KSA. Table 7.2 displays the specialty KSA requirements for the cyber investigation specialty area as well as the associated competency areas (NIST, 2014a).

The majority of the KSA requirements for the forensics specialty area can be factored into five distinct areas of standard application.

1. *Information systems/network security* is a classic area of cybersecurity protection.
2. *Hardware and forensics* is a necessary element of investigation.
3. *Infrastructure design* is an area whose decision making is supported by forensics.
4. *Vulnerability assessment and risk management* is the classic risk component.
5. *Legal, government, and jurisprudence* entails the legal process.

Each of these elements is required in order to ensure that the cyber investigation process is both effective and sustainable. Cyber investigation work requires a broad range of technical and behavioral capabilities. Many of those capabilities are typically not found in conjunction with each other, especially the legal and investigative skills in conjunction with technical knowledge and ability.

	Investigate general knowledge area Digital forensics specialty area tasks NICE workforce framework	Cybersecurity framework
		Identify
		Protect
		Detect
		Respond
		Recover
402	Analyze computer-generated threats.	
429	Assist in the gathering and preservation of evidence used in the prosecution of computer crimes.	
447	Conduct analysis of log files, evidence, and other information in order to determine best methods for identifying the perpetrator(s) of a network intrusion.	
454	Conduct interviews of victims and witnesses and conduct interviews or interrogations of suspects.	
507	Determine and develop leads and identify sources of information in order to identify and prosecute the responsible parties to an intrusion.	
512	Develop a plan to investigate alleged crime, violation, or suspicious activity utilizing computers and the Internet.	
564	Document original condition of digital and/or associated evidence (e.g., via digital photographs, written reports, etc.).	
597	Establish relationships, if applicable, between the incident response team and other groups, both internal (e.g., legal department) and external (e.g., law enforcement agencies, vendors, and public relations professionals).	
613	Examine recovered data for information of relevance to the issue at hand.	
620	Employ information technology (IT) systems and digital storage media to solve and prosecute cybercrimes and fraud committed against people and property.	
623	Fuse computer network attack analyses with criminal and counterintelligence investigations and operations.	
633	Identify and/or determine whether a security incident is indicative of a violation of law that requires specific legal action.	
635	Identify data or intelligence of evidentiary value to support counterintelligence and criminal investigations.	

Figure 7.3   Cyber investigation specialty area tasks mapped to the CSF functions.   (*Continued*)

	Investigate general knowledge area NICE workforce framework	Cybersecurity framework
		Identify
		Protect
		Detect
		Respond
		Recover
636	Identify digital evidence for examination and analysis in such a way as to avoid unintentional alteration.	
637	Identify elements of proof of the crime.	
642	Identify outside attackers accessing the system from Internet or insider attackers (e.g., authorized users attempting to gain and misuse nonauthorized privileges).	
649	Identify, collect, and seize documentary or physical evidence to include digital media and logs associated with cyber intrusion incidents, investigations, and operations.	
663	Conduct large-scale investigations of criminal activities involving complicated computer programs and networks.	
788	Prepare reports to document analysis.	
792	Process crime scenes.	
843	Secure the electronic device or information source.	
871	Use specialized equipment and techniques to catalog, document, extract, collect, package, and preserve digital evidence.	

Figure 7.3 (Continued) Cyber investigation specialty area tasks mapped to the CSF functions.

Table 7.2 Cyber Investigation Specialty Area Knowledge, Skill, and Abilities (KSAs)

Item ID	KSA	Statement	Competency
105	KSA	Knowledge of system and application security threats and vulnerabilities (e.g., buffer overflow, mobile code, cross-site scripting, procedural language/structured query language [PL/SQL] and injections, race conditions, covert channel, replay, return-oriented attacks, malicious code).	Vulnerabilities assessment
217	KSA	Skill in preserving evidence integrity according to standard operating procedures or national standards.	Computer forensics
281	KSA	Knowledge of electronic devices (e.g., computer systems/components, access control devices, digital cameras, electronic organizers, hard drives, memory cards, modems, network components, printers, removable storage devices, scanners, telephones, copiers, credit card skimmers, facsimile machines, global positioning systems [GPSs]).	Hardware
290	KSA	Knowledge of processes for seizing and preserving digital evidence (e.g., chain of custody).	Forensics
310	KSA	Knowledge of legal governance related to admissibility (e.g., Federal Rules of Evidence).	Criminal law
316	KSA	Knowledge of processes for collecting, packaging, transporting, and storing electronic evidence to avoid alteration, loss, physical damage, or destruction of data.	Criminal law

(Continued)

Table 7.2 (Continued)   Cyber Investigation Specialty Area Knowledge, Skill, and Abilities (KSAs)

Item ID	KSA	Statement	Competency
340	KSA	Knowledge of types and collection of persistent data.	Computer forensics
369	KSA	Skill in collecting, processing, packaging, transporting, and storing electronic evidence to avoid alteration, loss, physical damage, or destruction of data.	Forensics
383	KSA	Skill in using scientific rules and methods to solve problems.	Reasoning
917	KSA	Knowledge of social dynamics of computer attackers in a global context.	External awareness
1036	KSA	Knowledge of applicable laws (e.g., Electronic Communications Privacy Act, Foreign Intelligence Surveillance Act, Protect America Act, search and seizure laws, civil liberties and privacy laws), US Statutes (e.g., Titles 10, 18, 32, 50 in US Code), Presidential Directives, executive branch guidelines, and/or administrative/criminal legal guidelines and procedures relevant to work performed.	Criminal law
1039	KSA	Skill in evaluating the trustworthiness of the supplier and/or product.	Contracting/procurement

Cyber investigation activities require intimate knowledge of the inner workings of the machine. That knowledge is always obtained by use of specialized tools and equipment. These tools are utilized to ensure that every aspect of the collection and handling of virtual evidence is documented in such a way that the absolute integrity of the chain of custody is provably maintained. Also, because of the nature of digital evidence, it is almost impossible to collect and preserve it without tool support.

Chapter Summary

The investigate knowledge area contains two specialty areas. These are digital forensics and cyber investigation. Both are focused on investigating and characterizing any form of adverse activity performed by, or recorded on, a digital device. Since the primary purpose of this knowledge area is data recovery and subsequent investigation, its focus is after-the-fact. The incidents that it addresses are cyber-related events, such as crimes, intrusions, or harm caused to systems networks.

As the name suggests, the investigate knowledge area encompasses the particular job roles that acquire, examine, and act on digital evidence. Its primary purpose is to support the understanding of electronic anomalies, or adverse occurrences, as well as make recommendations about the necessary operational response.

The two job roles within this specialty area normally perform the classic forensic and investigative functions required to ensure trustworthy cyber operation. This takes place within whatever parameters the organization sets. For that reason, these jobs are the workforce roles that are responsible for the investigation of electronic incidents.

The specialty area called digital forensics encompasses the classic evidence gathering, analysis, and documentation tasks that are normally associated with law enforcement. In the physical universe, these roles gather material data at a crime scene and provide understanding of that evidence in support of basic criminal and civil actions.

Because of its classic fact-finding focus, the digital forensics specialty area might be considered to be more suitably a part of the discipline of criminal justice rather than computing. Nonetheless, it is perfectly appropriate for the forensics process to focus strictly on data collection and analysis of electronic threat and intrusion events, rather than the physical aspects of criminal activity. The detailed task specifications of the digital forensics specialty area illustrate the focus and intent of each of this area.

Forensics is almost always associated with law enforcement. So the most fundamental purpose of the digital forensics process is to assist in gathering and preserving evidence that is used in the prosecution of computer crimes. In doing this, the forensic examiner collects and analyzes any evidence that is generated by the actual cyber exploit.

The evidence itself is digital and so its footprint is found in electronic sources such as computer log files, reference monitor files, and other hidden sources of information. The subsequent analysis supports decisions about the best means of identifying the source and reasons for an unauthorized access. That can include such evidence gathering methods as dynamic and static analysis.

Along with a detailed set of tasks, the NICE workforce also provides a distinctive set of KSA specifications for each specialty area. These KSAs offer much clearer elaboration and characterization of the activities that underlie each task and also help the educational community to understand the precise knowledge requirements to be used in the design of targeted training and education programs in that specific specialty area.

The knowledge and specialty area categories are the central organizing basis for the framework. In essence, specialty areas in a given category are typically more similar to one another than to specialty areas in other categories. The authors of the model clustered related types of work together into categories. These categories serve as the unifying mechanism that allows the reader to understand the specific nature of the work involved.

That specification of requirements is the purpose of the KSAs enumerated by the NICE workforce model. Typical tasks and KSAs are specified within each specialty area. Each KSA has exactly one competency associated with it. Each KSA defines a specific KSA requirement. In application, these requirements may be assigned to one or more specialty areas within the model.

Each of these elements is required in order to ensure that the forensics process is both trustworthy and sustainable. Forensics work requires a broad range of technical and behavioral capabilities. Many of those capabilities are typically not found in conjunction with each other.

Forensics activities require intimate knowledge of the inner workings of the machine. That knowledge is always obtained by use of specialized tools and equipment. These tools are utilized to ensure that every aspect of the collection and handling of virtual evidence is documented in such a way that the absolute integrity of the chain of custody is provably maintained. Also, because of the nature of digital evidence it is almost impossible to collect and preserve it without tool support.

The second requirement in the establishment of a digital forensics process is to define the specific reporting lines and oversight that the forensics process will function in. Because of the wide range of organizations that might be involved and their diverse ways of doing business, this is not a simple matter of dropping a stock business framework down into the target organization. The assurance of a properly resourced array of reporting lines requires a well-designed, policy level planning process.

Finally, even if the forensics process is properly defined and the staffing is correct, the workforce still has to be capable of performing all of the requisite forensic tasks. Therefore, the forensics process entails its own set of formal training procedures. The purpose of these procedures is to ensure that the workforce is capable of performing all of their necessary duties. This particular necessity is one of the primary justifications and advantages of the NICE workforce model and its explicit task and KSA specifications.

In many respects, cyber investigation is simply the body of knowledge of criminal justice. The cyber investigation specialty area embodies all of the best practice police methods and protocols, and criminal investigation procedures that are appropriate for cyberspace. As a result, cyber investigation encompasses all of the conventional investigative tools and processes utilized by law enforcement. That includes interview and interrogation techniques, surveillance, countersurveillance, and surveillance detection methods. The activities in this specialty area constitute a hybrid of police investigative and intelligence gathering activities.

Cyber investigation techniques normally entail interview and interrogation techniques, surveillance, countersurveillance, and surveillance detection methods. These techniques are designed to analyze and better understand computer-generated threats. Since cyber investigation particularly targets the criminal aspects of the investigate knowledge area, it is aimed at assisting in the gathering and preservation of evidence used in the prosecution of computer crimes.

Each of these elements is required in order to ensure that the cyber investigation process is both effective and sustainable. Cyber investigation work requires a broad range of technical and behavioral capabilities. Many of those capabilities are typically not found in conjunction with each other, especially the legal and investigative skills in conjunction with technical knowledge and ability.

Cyber investigation activities require intimate knowledge of the inner workings of the machine. That knowledge is always obtained by use of specialized tools and equipment. These tools are utilized to ensure that every aspect of the collection and handling of virtual evidence is documented in such a way that the absolute integrity of the chain of custody is provably maintained. Also, because of the nature of digital evidence it is almost impossible to collect and preserve it without tool support.

Key Terms

Binary: The representation of computerized information in machine readable form—the native state of all computer information often represented as hexadecimal values.

Cyber Investigation Professional: A specialized area of work devoted to identification and prosecution of perpetrators and explanation of cyber events.

Competency: Achievement of a desired outcome based on a given expectation regarding the result.

Data: Discrete values that can be specifically associated with an event or action and which provide insight into that event or action.

Digital Forensics: A specialized competency area of the NICE framework focused on the evidence gathering function, specifically targeted toward the collection of electronic evidence.

Digital Forensics Professional: A specialized area of work devoted to evidence gathering and analysis of cyber events.

Evidence: Tangible artifacts or electronic indicators that document the actions of a specific, usually criminal, activity.

Forensic Tools: Hardware and software specifically dedicated to the gathering of evidence and the assurance of its continuing state of accuracy and integrity.

Incident Management: Specific steps designed to deal with a known event, typically supported by risk assessment and planning.

IT Security: A specific state commonly associated with a given need or function that is a necessary aspect of ensuring the protection of information.

IT Security Architecture: A purposely built framework primarily responsible for the provision of comprehensive enterprise information protection.

Investigation: A protocol or action adopted to discover the cause and effect behind a given set of facts or evidence.

KSA: A single specific element of KSA that allows the individual possessing it to reliably perform a desired action or task.

Legal Rules of Evidence: The legal requirement that all evidence gathered and utilized in an investigation remains in the state it was at when it was gathered.

Model: A comprehensive conceptual framework used to describe the elements of a generic process or entity.

Risk Management: A dimension of the NICE framework focused on the identification, analysis, and mitigation of risks.

Role: A generic area of security work, delineated by a common set of skills and functional purposes.

Strategic Planning: A function focused on the development of strategies and policies to govern organizational directions for some defined period.

References

National Institute of Standards and Technology (NIST). 2014a. *National Cybersecurity Workforce Framework.* Gaithersburg, MD: NIST.

National Institute of Standards and Technology (NIST). 2014b. *Framework for Improving Critical Infrastructure Cybersecurity (CSF).* Gaithersburg, MD: NIST.

Chapter 8

Collect and Operate and Analyze General Knowledge Areas

Chapter Objectives

At the conclusion of this chapter, the reader will understand:

- The justification and contents of the collect and operate and analyze domains
- The focus and purpose of the collect and operate specialty areas
- The focus and purpose of the analyze knowledge areas
- The relationship between these two knowledge areas in national security work
- The contents and recommendations of the Central Intelligence Agency (CIA) Analytic Tradecraft Notes
- The elements of intelligence analysis assessment and management

Introduction to the Knowledge Areas of the Intelligence Community

Unlike the rest of this book, this chapter combines two domains, knowledge area 5—collect and operate and knowledge area 6—analyze as shown in Figures 8.1 and 8.2.

This arrangement is necessary because unlike the other five areas of the National Initiative for Cybersecurity Education (NICE) framework, the collect and operate and the analyze knowledge areas, the job roles, tasks, and knowledge, skill, and abilities (KSAs) for those areas have not been explicitly defined, because these areas comprise the elements of intelligence work.

Collect and operate
Specialty areas responsible for specialized denial and deception operations and collection of cybersecurity information that may be used to develop intelligence.

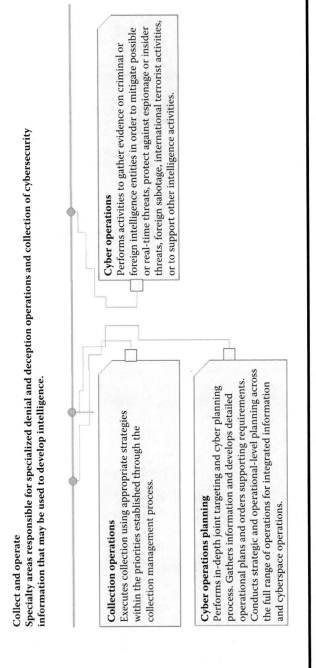

Cyber operations
Performs activities to gather evidence on criminal or foreign intelligence entities in order to mitigate possible or real-time threats, protect against espionage or insider threats, foreign sabotage, international terrorist activities, or to support other intelligence activities.

Collection operations
Executes collection using appropriate strategies within the priorities established through the collection management process.

Cyber operations planning
Performs in-depth joint targeting and cyber planning process. Gathers information and develops detailed operational plans and orders supporting requirements. Conducts strategic and operational-level planning across the full range of operations for integrated information and cyberspace operations.

Figure 8.1   Collect and operate general knowledge area overview.

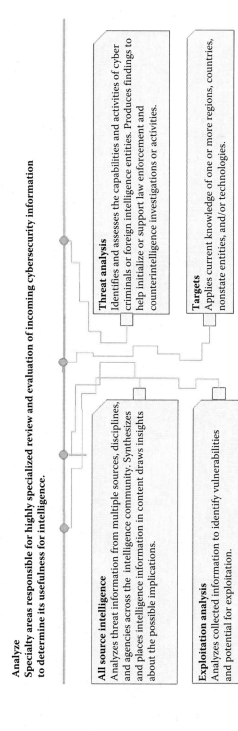

Analyze
Specialty areas responsible for highly specialized review and evaluation of incoming cybersecurity information to determine its usefulness for intelligence.

All source intelligence
Analyzes threat information from multiple sources, disciplines, and agencies across the intelligence community. Synthesizes and places intelligence information in content draws insights about the possible implications.

Exploitation analysis
Analyzes collected information to identify vulnerabilities and potential for exploitation.

Threat analysis
Identifies and assesses the capabilities and activities of cyber criminals or foreign intelligence entities. Produces findings to help initialize or support law enforcement and counterintelligence investigations or activities.

Targets
Applies current knowledge of one or more regions, countries, nonstate entities, and/or technologies.

Figure 8.2   Analyze general knowledge area overview.

The contents of all of the other five areas can obviously be factored into the generic roles and responsibilities of the information technology (IT) function. The contents of these two areas are most closely associated with espionage and counterintelligence. As a consequence, these two knowledge areas do not have explicit task and KSA definitions associated with them, because the work in those areas is generally considered to be too "unique and highly specialized" to be described in a common-use framework standard like the NICE model. Another explanation for the lack of detailed explication is that most of this work is tradecraft, which is highly secretive and involves classified material.

The collect and operate knowledge area (KA 5) comprises those specialty areas whose primary mission is to protect the organization and its information from covert electronic attacks. Collect and operate ensures that valuable intellectual property and information cannot be obtained or viewed by an adversary. This area also obtains and interprets information from an adversary National Institute of Standards and Technology (NIST, 2014).

As a consequence, the collect and operate knowledge area entails job roles that perform any type of formally defined work designed to inhibit or prevent an act of electronic espionage. Specialty areas in the domain also carry out deception operations aimed at giving an adversary false information that might fool them into drawing incorrect conclusions, or prevent them from taking adverse actions against an organization's information using misinformation. In generic circles, this type of activity is normally termed "counterintelligence." While at the same time, operate and maintain collects and interprets all-source electronic information that can be utilized to produce a desired intelligence outcomes.

The specialty areas in this domain seek to create an accurate picture of the actual intelligence collection capabilities of every potential adversary. Thus, the actions taken within this area typically fall into two logical categories: defensive intelligence and offensive intelligence. The former category seeks to prevent organized intelligence gathering and the latter seeks to generate intelligence knowledge of an adversary's activities.

Because these dual purposes to some extent conflict collect and operate fuses task and knowledge requirements into a set of multidisciplinary protection activities that involve both electronic and human intelligence (HUMINT) elements. So in many respects, this area overlaps with the role and purposes of the actual national intelligence community. However, most countries separate their counterintelligence and intelligence functions into separate organizational entities and that is reflected in the way the NICE framework organizes the job role requirements.

The three job roles within the collect and operate specialty area typically perform the classic spy versus spy role that is most frequently associated with counterintelligence work. Thus, the specialty areas within collect and operate—collect, process, analyze, and present to decision makers all relevant information obtained from adversarial sources.

The aim of these roles is to be proactive as much as reactive. The intelligence work itself is designed to ensure that no harm can come to the organization's people, resources, or mission. In essence, the overall goal of the specialty areas within this domain is to ensure that our adversaries are unable to read our mail, which is not simply a national defense objective. It can also embrace any item of information in any business that might be subject to attack by hackers, criminals, saboteurs, and industrial spies. In a national security/military sense, the specialty areas that fall within the collect and operate domain represent the classic operations security (OPSEC) function for the military establishment. The specialty areas themselves illustrate the general focus and intent of the proactive/reactive protection mandate.

Domain 6, analyze, focuses on classic intelligence work and in that respect its appearance in a cybersecurity body of knowledge reflects the growing role of intelligence in the global fight to keep our systems secure. This area seeks to gather the intelligence information required to ensure against attack or exploitation by any foreign or domestic adversary.

It is the emphasis on active gathering of any pertinent information that might be useful against an adversary in any form that primarily differentiates analyze from collect and operate. Fundamentally, analyze does the information gathering and preparatory work that lets an organization connect-the-dots to understand another entity's secrets and plans. The general aim is to ensure that the organization takes the necessary steps to make itself safe from attack. In essence, the analyze knowledge area embraces all of the various roles of the traditional intelligence function. The actions that these roles perform come under the generic description of "tradecraft."

Like the classic intelligence gathering and analysis function, the analyze knowledge area encompasses those job roles that are responsible for direct, usually covert operations against potential adversaries. It collects and interprets information that lets the organization anticipate and get in front of potential attacks. Analyze ensures against future attack. It also puts plans in place to obtain information for use in operations against all relevant adversaries.

The specialty areas in this domain perform all of the activities necessary to obtain actionable intelligence about all relevant adversarial targets. This knowledge area directly corresponds with the general body of knowledge of the intelligence community. Given that the methods and techniques that are required to carry out the necessary espionage practices that are needed to carry out the work. The four job roles within this specialty area typically execute the classic intelligence roles that are most frequently associated with operational tradecraft and the spy trade.

The specialty areas within analyze are responsible for discovering everything useful about the plans and intentions of a given set of adversaries. And then making the necessary assumptions, inferences, and deductions to turn that information into actionable intelligence. Since this knowledge area applies to situations other than just national security settings, target adversaries can represent conventional competitors who are in competition with the business that supports the analyze function.

The purpose of each of these roles is to ensure that the detailed elements of the threat environment are fully understood and that no surprises sneak up on the organization. In essence, the aim of the specialty areas in this domain is to identify and monitor all potential adversaries, or sources of harm for any new, or suspicious activity. As we said, this is not simply a national defense focus. It can include criminal intelligence operations, every aspect of industrial espionage and competitive analysis, it can also address asymmetric threats and threats to business or individuals that originate from single individuals, competitors, or nation states.

Specialty Areas: Collect and Operate and Analyze

The specialty areas that fall within the collect and operate and the analyze knowledge areas encompass classic intelligence work. The specialty areas themselves illustrate the general focus and intent of the actions required to perform the collect and operate and analyze knowledge area requirements.

Collect and Operate

As we saw in the Chapter 1, there are three specialty areas in the collect and operate areas. These specialty areas are:

Collection Operations

This is classic tradecraft. It is a creative process rather than a linear process. It involves the integration of pieces of information that are collected from diverse sources. And then piecing those bits of the puzzle together into an actionable picture.

The collection of information involves a set of common best practice methods that are appropriate to the organization that uses the intelligence. For instance, the approaches to intelligence gathering would be different for Federal Bureau of Investigation (FBI), CIA, and National Security Agency (NSA) even if the intention was similar. The collection would take place within the priorities that are defined by each organization's particular mission.

Cyber Operations

This is counterespionage tradecraft. This category also explicitly embraces the actions associated with cyberwarfare. This specialty area specifically supports the overall intelligence operation. Its focus is on counterespionage from either electronic or human intelligence sources. In addition, the specialty area focuses on prevention of insider exploits and any form of sabotage or terror activities. This area is frequently called OPSEC in the military. Roles in this specialty area gather evidence of criminal or foreign intelligence operations. The long-term goal is to discover and mitigate all threats originating from known adversaries.

Cyber Operations Planning

This is the long-term strategy area for the collect and operate knowledge area. This specialty area performs all of the detailed strategic planning for the cyber operations function. It selects the targets for the collection operation and plans the overall proactive and collective defense operations. As a result, this embodies a strategic set of job roles.

Cyber operations planning prepares the strategic plans and defines the operational details. The focus of this specialty area is on any appropriate adversarial target in cyberspace. However, the cyber operations specialty area has been explicitly linked to cyberwar through its association with US Cybercommand. Accordingly, the tradecraft in this area is based around five common principles:

1. Cyberspace is an appropriate domain for warfare
2. Active defense
3. Critical infrastructure protection
4. Collective defense
5. Technological evolution

Analyze

As we saw in the Chapter 1, there are four specialty areas in the analyze knowledge area. These specialty areas are:

Threat Analysis

All intelligence is based around threat detection. This specialty area fulfills that function. Its general purpose is to identify all meaningful threats, collect the information required in order to be able to judge the capabilities of the relevant threats in the adversarial spectrum. Targets might include every type of threat from local criminal to nation state operations.

Once a threat has been detected and fully analyzed and described, the duty of the roles in this area is to ensure that all appropriate law enforcement and counterintelligence agencies are kept up-to-date on how the threat is evolving and any potential points of attack or areas of vulnerability.

All-Source Intelligence

The purpose of the all-source intelligence specialty area is to amalgamate disaggregated threat information from all relevant sources across the intelligence gathering function.

This area is often operationalized by the "fusion center" concept. A fusion center is a place that manages and integrates intelligence that is collected by all valid entities from all legitimate sources. The aim of the fusion center is to collect and combine all available information for analysis. That information can be collected from any appropriate entity including the intelligence community, law enforcement, or the private sector. All of these sources can provide raw information for the analysis function.

As can be seen, this area does not develop intelligence as much as it manages it. So in many respects this specialty area is the driver for all threat analysis work. Workers within this specialty area synthesize outcomes and interpret the results for the purpose of providing an understanding of what the information means in practical terms. The aim is to support decision making regarding next step actions to take. Thus, the job roles in this area tend to reflect the big-picture analytics view.

Exploitation Analysis

This professional area is sometimes called "pen-testing." The exploitation ana-lyst collects all information necessary to identify vulnerabilities and potential for exploitation. The tasks and KSAs in this function involve the specific identification of weaknesses and vulnerabilities that are likely targets for exploitation. In effect, this specialty area underwrites the prioritization process that is necessary for good strategic and operational planning.

The aim is to explicitly identify those harmful events that have the greatest poten-tial for occurrence as well as potential for harm. Then once a priority list is compiled the exploitation analyst has to identify the precise attack method and any relevant mitiga-tions for such an attack. This can involve considerable technical detail where malware and other kinds of hacking exploits are involved. It can also require good understand-ing of behavioral factors since social engineering exploits also fall into this category.

Targets

This is a diffuse area because it amalgamates the knowledge gained from the impact and risk analysis with the knowledge that is required to understand in detail the nuances of a particular area under scrutiny, or of an adversary of inter-est. For instance, in order to decide about potential targets for proactive action in some part of the world the analyst has to have up-to-date knowledge of the region and the countries, non-state entities, and/or technologies that reside there.

The aim of the tasks in this area is to gather the necessary information about, and then reliably prioritize and target any action needed in order to mitigate all relevant vulnerabilities, which might be sources of exploitation. A very broad-minded indi-vidual is needed to do this successfully. That person must possess intimate knowledge of their area of responsibility along with a wide range of multisource analytic skills.

Body of Knowledge for Collect and Operate and Analyze

The NICE framework defines nothing below the specialty areas for these two areas. Therefore, it is necessary to turn to other sources to more completely understand the body of knowledge for this area. Fortunately such a body of knowledge is avail-able in the Tradecraft Notes prepared by the CIA (1997, 2009).

In many respects, there are three authoritative documents that provide an authori-tative source of knowledge to fill in the task and KSA specification of these two NICE areas. Because we owe the reader a complete explication of all of the knowledge areas, we are going to adopt these notes as the basis for the body of knowledge (BOK) of this chapter. However, the reader should note that that none of what will follow is derived from the NICE workforce framework. These serve as the basis for the discussion.

Essentially, the tasks and KSAs in this area can be boiled down into three types of general activity, information acquisition, information analysis, and general knowledge management and reporting. There are 10 general principles that under-lie and guide these activities (all from CIA, 1997).

Addressing US Interests in Assessments

This first principle makes the essential link between intelligence work and policy making. In essence, it ensures proper focus of the effort. It also directly states that the intelligence community is guided by an agenda set at the policy level, not vice versa. Table 8.1 displays the tasks for principle 1.

Access and Credibility

This second principle highlights the need for access, credibility, and trust between the intelligence worker and key consumers as shown in Table 8.2. It is the principle that demands that close attention must be paid to validating facts and sourcing of intelligence as well as the assumptions that underlie the work. The aim is to main-tain credibility in an environment of uncertainty.

Articulation of Assumptions

This third principle simply states that critical thinking is required. In essence, all underlying assumptions about the intelligence mission must be clarified prior to doing the work. That includes the necessity to identify, challenge, and justify all of the key variables involved and think through all of the assumptions that underlie those drivers. Table 8.3 shows the key tasks for this principle.

Outlook

This fourth principle requires a little fortune telling. The worker must lay out the probable development and outcomes of the mission going forward. The likeliest courses as well as any probable alternative outcomes all have to be considered in doing the intelligence work. The aim is to have contingency plans in place for all reasonable alternatives. Their likelihood can range from plausible to remote pos-sibilities. Table 8.4 shows the key tasks for this principle.

Facts and Sourcing

This fifth principle is the meat and potatoes of intelligence work. Being able to concretely establish the facts and their basis is central to the credibility of the intel-ligence mission. There are three general criteria here (CIA, 1997):

1. Be precise about what is known
2. Distinguish between reported information and analyst judgment
3. Take account of the possibility of deception

Table 8.5 shows the key tasks for this principle.

Table 8.1   Principle 1: Addressing US Interests in Assessments Tasks

Item ID	KSA	Statement
1	KSA	Evaluate dangers for US interests, especially unexpected developments that may require reaction.
2	KSA	Evaluate motives, objectives, strengths, and vulnerabilities of adversaries, allies, and other actors.
3	KSA	Evaluate direct and indirect sources of leverage on foreign players and issues.
4	KSA	Evaluate tactical alternatives for advancing stated policy goals.
5	KSA	Obtain information regarding goals and motives as well as the strengths and weaknesses of target.
6	KSA	Convert substantive expertise into action-support analysis before conveying it to consumers.
7	KSA	Study how customers absorb information and reach judgments, as well as current priorities.
8	KSA	Target the policymakers' specific interest in a substantive issue.
9	KSA	Be aware that consumers' needs may change as the policymaking process evolves.
10	KSA	Support policymaking without engaging in it. Use probabilities rather than recommendations.
11	KSA	Concentrate on how and why an event might come about, including leverage for enforcing action.
12	KSA	Identify and clarify the vulnerabilities of adversaries sources leverage.
13	KSA	Deliver, intelligence updates and other analytic support in a timely fashion to meet decision deadlines.
14	KSA	Convert issues into policy questions.
15	KSA	Use the "so-what" test in reviewing a first draft.
16	KSA	Evaluate whether draft effectively address what key policymakers need to know to get their jobs done?

Table 8.2   Principle 2: Access and Credibility Tasks

Item ID	KSA	Statement
1	KSA	Present objective analysis to counter conflicting information and views.
2	KSA	Structure assessments to address implications, dangers, and opportunities.
3	KSA	Convey analyst's distinctive expertise on an issue.
4	KSA	Make appropriate use of unique, information that provides insights not otherwise available.
5	KSA	Convey the distinctive issues in the prescribed space make recommendations "actionable."
6	KSA	Make explicit what is known with confidence to warrant reliance in planning and execution.
7	KSA	Also address what analysts do not know that could have significant consequences.
8	KSA	Make explicit information sources of information.
9	KSA	Differentiate direct evidence from testimonial evidence.
10	KSA	Make explicit the level of confidence in the evidence.
11	KSA	Itemize findings from hard evidence as trends, patterns, and precedents.
12	KSA	Spell out how facts have been extended to actionable conclusions.
13	KSA	Clarify premises, suppositions, and other elements that support critical thinking.
14	KSA	Clarify not only degree of confidence but also level of criticality.
15	KSA	Identify the dynamics that will have the greatest impact on subsequent developments.
16	KSA	Identify factors that could lead to unexpected developments.
17	KSA	Engage in contingency planning.
18	KSA	Address all factors that could influence subsequent events.
19	KSA	Rank factors relative importance.
20	KSA	Relate factors to a range of plausible outcomes.

Table 8.3   Principle 3: Articulation of Assumptions Tasks

Item ID	KSA	Statement
1	KSA	Communicate an intelligence assessment in support of the bottom-line judgments.
2	KSA	Make logical soundly reasoned assumptions.
3	KSA	Make precise clearly stated assumptions.
4	KSA	Make realistic assumptions attuned to the hazards of forecasting error.
5	KSA	Identify drivers or key variables most likely to determine outcome.
6	KSA	Define premises that hold the argument together and warrant the validity of the conclusion.
7	KSA	Be able to defend judgments by marshaling supporting evidence and reasoning.
8	KSA	Identify inherent uncertainty.
9	KSA	Identify plausible alternative courses of development
10	KSA	The more complex the issue, the more the analysts should explain the reasoning.
11	KSA	Organize the assessment to display critical thinking.
12	KSA	Set aside any drivers obtained from a prior exercise.
13	KSA	Focus initially on the range and alignment of assumptions.
14	KSA	Generate a list of all important factors that cannot be known with certainty.
15	KSA	Assess the relationships among these variables.

(Continued)

Table 8.3 (Continued)   Principle 3: Articulation of Assumptions Tasks

Item ID	KSA	Statement
16	KSA	Search for hierarchies of importance and other linkages in variables.
17	KSA	Construct competing cases for selecting the drivers from among the host of variables.
18	KSA	Identify factors would have to change to change the expected outcome.
19	KSA	Assess the quality of the evidence.
20	KSA	Test the soundness of the supporting line of reasoning (e.g., subordinate assumptions).
21	KSA	Test key assumptions against any contrary judgments held by other informed observers.
22	KSA	Determine whether a decision maker could summarize the assessment's reasoning.
23	KSA	Determine whether hard evidence adequately explains linchpin assumptions.
24	KSA	Determine whether assumptions adequately defend the bottom-line conclusions.

Table 8.4   Principle 4: Outlook Tasks

Item ID	KSA	Statement
1	KSA	Address the most likely course of development but also important alternative outcomes.
2	KSA	Acquire an understanding of unlikely developments to prepare contingency plans.
3	KSA	Prepare arguments to justify a selected outlook.
4	KSA	Judge likely outcomes based on evidence and articulation of assumptions.
5	KSA	Ensure that drivers and linchpin assumptions are precisely stated and well defended.
6	KSA	Identify plausible alternative outcomes.
7	KSA	Provide understanding of alternatives to determine whether to review contingency plans.
8	KSA	Identify the factors at play that could lead to unexpected developments.
9	KSA	Identify the key variables that could drive the outcome in a different direction.
10	KSA	Identify what plausible reversal of linchpin assumptions could turn things around.
11	KSA	Identify signposts or indicators of change.
12	KSA	Identify intermediate developments that might indicate events may not work as expected.
13	KSA	Identify events that could trigger a major shift in direction.
14	KSA	Identify any essentially unpredictable events that could precipitate an unexpected outcome.
15	KSA	Help policymakers and warfighters engage in contingency planning by.

(Continued)

Table 8.4 (Continued)   Principle 4: Outlook Tasks

Item ID	KSA	Statement
16	KSA	Address all important factors at play that could influence subsequent events.
17	KSA	Rank the relative importance of all important factors at play.
18	KSA	Relate all important factors at play to a range of plausible outcomes.
19	KSA	Identify alternatives analysts deem to be remote possibilities.
20	KSA	Avoid unrealistic precision in citing odds.
21	KSA	Avoid phrases that compound unavoidable uncertainty with unnecessary confusion.
22	KSA	Use constructions that tie the outcome to the driver and linchpin assumptions.
23	KSA	When making important judgments, combine probabilistic phrases and rough numerical odds.
24	KSA	Understand the confusion that long odds cause decision makers.
25	KSA	Switch focus from whether something will happen to how it could happen.
26	KSA	Generate lists of the key individual and group players that can determine the outcome of an issue.
27	KSA	Start with the assumption that the targeted danger or opportunity has occurred.
28	KSA	List assumptions that fell by the wayside in reaching the bottom line.

Table 8.5   Principle 5: Facts and Sourcing Tasks

Item ID	KSA	Statement
1	KSA	Ensure verified information, something known to exist or to have happened.
2	KSA	Reduce uncertainty.
3	KSA	Identify direct information.
4	KSA	Identify indirect information
5	KSA	Depict the manner in which information was obtained.
6	KSA	Identify information that increases the likelihood that a matter under scrutiny is factual.
7	KSA	Be precise about what is known.
8	KSA	Identify precisely what the all-source analysts know and how they know it.
9	KSA	Never exaggerate what is known.
10	KSA	Report any important gaps.
11	KSA	Distinguish carefully between information and fact.
12	KSA	Distinguish carefully between information and estimative judgment.
13	KSA	Judgments cannot rely solely on reported opinions of foreign players or clandestine sources.
14	KSA	Judgements must be argued in terms of the entire body of available information.
15	KSA	Take care to avoid confusion over an estimative judgment or an opinion.
16	KSA	Take account of substantive complexity.
17	KSA	Take account of policy sensitivity. The burden of proof is high on controversial matters.
18	KSA	Take account of the possibility of deception.
19	KSA	Determine whether all the sources and collection platforms have reported.
20	KSA	Determine whether involved intelligence services have a record of perpetrating deceptions.
21	KSA	Use the term "evidence" sparingly to reduce uncertainty surrounding a specific matter.
22	KSA	The special character of the subject matter, the delivery vehicle, or the audience can require exceptions.

Analytic Expertise

This sixth principle is the other side of facts and sourcing. It is also a critical requirement. It simply states that the analysts must have sufficient knowledge and capability to address the issue under examination. This includes (CIA, 1997) the following:

1. In-depth substantive knowledge needed to clarify complex issues
2. Skill in interpreting unique intelligence information
3. The ability to efficiently organize data in support of findings and judgments
4. Credibility with an understanding of decision-making processes of officials

Table 8.6 shows the key tasks for this principle.

Effective Summary

This seventh principle highlights the need to be able to create an efficient and clear summary of findings for actionable purposes. An effective summary has to convey evidence of the underlying analysis as well as key findings and judgments.

Table 8.7 shows the key tasks for this principle.

Implementation Analysis

This eighth principle is practical. It requires the intelligence worker to prepare an assessment of tactical alternatives to that decision makers can adopt to address a given threat or weakness. Table 8.8 shows the key tasks for this principle.

Conclusions

This ninth principle goes hand-in-hand with the effective summary principle. It requires the intelligence worker to provide an estimate of their level of trust in their conclusions. Intelligence work is by definition speculative. However, there are differing degrees of confidence associated with the information that is gathered and analyzed. Thus, the completeness and correctness of that information and the degree to which the analysis produces hard conclusions has to be explicitly described. Table 8.9 shows the key tasks for this principle.

Tradecraft and Counterintelligence

This tenth principle has to do with the fact that adversaries utilize deception in their own tradecraft. Thus, the information contained in the facts and sourcing and conclusions areas has to be examined in order to test for deception or other forms of tradecraft on the adversary's part. Thus, analysts have to express a level of confidence that they are not being deceived. Table 8.10 shows the key tasks for this principle.

Table 8.6   Principle 6: Analytic Expertise Tasks

Item ID	KSA	Statement
1	KSA	Demonstrate expertise in intelligence assessments in order to gain access to and credibility.
2	KSA	Tailor demonstration of expertise to the circumstances of each assignment.
3	KSA	Deliver assessments to stand out from intelligence providers, journalists, and scholars.
4	KSA	Demonstrate in-depth substantive knowledge to establish credentials for an assessment.
5	KSA	Demonstrate skill in accessing and interpreting clandestine and technically collected information.
6	KSA	Demonstrate deft organization of data in support of findings and judgments.
7	KSA	Deal effectively with longshot contingencies and with uncertainty generally.
8	KSA	Demonstrate insight into the decision-making processes of intelligence customers.
9	KSA	Demonstrate breadth and depth of analytic expertise.
10	KSA	Show in-depth knowledge of subject history, culture, and general context.
11	KSA	Where possible demonstrate experience-based insights.
12	KSA	Bring to bear all disciplines that define the issue, political, economic, and military.
13	KSA	Bring to bear all-source information.
14	KSA	Reflect sensitivity to the timeline, decision points, and underlying tensions.
15	KSA	Demonstrate an effective method or structure for arraying information and reducing uncertainty.

(Continued)

Table 8.6 (Continued)   Principle 6: Analytic Expertise Tasks

Item ID	KSA	Statement
16	KSA	Make key assumptions clear and deal rigorously with alternative interpretations and outcomes.
17	KSA	Utilize research papers.
18	KSA	Cite evidence of previous research.
19	KSA	Demonstrate evidence of scholarship.
20	KSA	Utilize databases.
21	KSA	Cite or utilize evidence of direct on-site experience.
22	KSA	Provide evidence of teamwork.
23	KSA	Provide in depth analysis of target issue leadership individuals.
24	KSA	Convey understanding of sensitive information from clandestine and technical sources.
25	KSA	Demonstrate skill in dealing with uncertainty.
26	KSA	Demonstrate awareness of all policy timelines and key matters under debate.
27	KSA	Demonstrate particular knowledge of consumer capabilities and their decision cycle.
28	KSA	Avoid excessive displays of knowledge (e.g., excessive displays of expertise as an end in itself).

Table 8.7   Principle 7: Effective Summary Tasks

Item ID		Statement
1	KSA	Summarize the distinctive intelligence value added.
2	KSA	Ensure value added stand outs.
3	KSA	Tailor each summary to the circumstances of the individual assignment
4	KSA	Craft a summary that clearly described new information and its relative importance.
5	KSA	Justify/assure the intelligence consumer of the value of report.
6	KSA	Highlight the value added to ensure that busy readers will read the report.
7	KSA	Support value added with distinctive expertise.
8	KSA	Highlight the value added and expertise through an introductory textbox.
9	KSA	Utilize textbox to serve the needs of peripherally engaged intelligence consumers.
10	KSA	Place technical findings needed to ensure value added for audience in a textbox.
11	KSA	Highlight policy implications on a controversial issue in a textbox.
12	KSA	Utilize a preface to supplement a summary.
13	KSA	Use a preface to explain the precise policy challenges the assessment seeks to clarify.
14	KSA	Use a preface to augment intelligence credibility.
15	KSA	Conform the summary to the text and vice versa. Retrofit any new insights and values into the text.

(Continued)

Table 8.7 (Continued)   Principle 7: Effective Summary Tasks

Item ID	KSA	Statement
16	KSA	Break up the typography to make report "user unfriendly."
17	KSA	Use short paragraphs, bullets and sub-bullets, bold face, and italics to break up the space.
18	KSA	Fit the writing style to audience and purpose.
19	KSA	Concentrate on the new and important.
20	KSA	Use the allotted space to concentrate on content that will make a difference.
21	KSA	Utilize the summary to explain why a busy policy official should spend time on the report.
22	KSA	Make the summary actionable.
23	KSA	Role-play key members of the targeted audience to decide about content.
24	KSA	Make fewer points, but make them well.
25	KSA	If the assessment makes predictive judgment, refer to the key assumptions.
26	KSA	If the assessment conveys important findings, cover the reliability of the sourcing and methodology.

Table 8.8   Principle 8: Implementation Analysis Tasks

Item ID	KSA	Statement
1	KSA	Provide decision makers with an assessment of tactical alternatives for pursuing opportunities.
2	KSA	Identify and evaluate alternatives for implementing objectives.
3	KSA	Illustrative hypothetical cases.
4	KSA	Support policy makers in identifying and assessing opportunities and dangers.
5	KSA	Use implementation analysis to bring important value added to policy makers.
6	KSA	Provide expertise in working with foreign cultures, including risk analysis and negotiating style.
7	KSA	Identify strengths and vulnerabilities of target countries and organizations.
8	KSA	Provide detached analysis separate from departmental bureaucratic pressures.
9	KSA	Provide objectivity in examining tactical alternatives.
10	KSA	Help intelligence maintain effective policy ties on politically charged issues.
11	KSA	Send the message that the intelligence team understands the challenges that the policy team faces.
12	KSA	Develop close lines of communication in delivering implementation analysis.
13	KSA	Advertise intelligence capability and solicit requests for analysis as appropriate.
14	KSA	Execute a briefing or memoranda for one or a handful of principal policy officials.
15	KSA	Perform regularly scheduled repeat briefings or memoranda.
16	KSA	Monitor increases in the circle of recipients.

(Continued)

Table 8.8 (Continued)   Principle 8: Implementation Analysis Tasks

Item ID	KSA	Statement
17	KSA	Incorporate a given analysis into policy planning documents.
18	KSA	Redefine an intelligence issue in the policymakers.
19	KSA	Recognize the policymakers' role as "action officers" charged with getting things started or stopped.
20	KSA	Recognize the policy officials' propensity at times to take risk for gain.
21	KSA	Concentrate on what it takes to achieve the operational goal before doing the analysis.
22	KSA	Present alternatives without crossing the line between analysis and prescription.
23	KSA	Encourage divergent thinking by setting aside mainstream interpretations.
24	KSA	Focus on the full range of plausible alternative interpretations and outcomes.
25	KSA	Do brainstorming, role playing, and "thinking backward."
26	KSA	Provide policymakers with an assessment of the least unpromising tactical alternatives.
27	KSA	Explore alternatives to help the policymaker develop the most sensible game plan, win or lose.
28	KSA	Know how to make an inventory of US means for executing foreign policy.
29	KSA	Present the results of the analytic process in a professional way.
30	KSA	Present and rank alternatives via a matrix leaving the actual choosing to the policymakers.
31	KSA	Engage colleagues and managers early on in the process of defining the issue and selecting alternatives.

Table 8.9 Principle 9: Conclusions Tasks

Item ID	KSA	Statement
1	KSA	Provide findings based on organizing, evaluating, and interpreting the all-source information.
2	KSA	Be precise in conveying the level of confidence in conclusions.
3	KSA	Take appropriate account of the prospect of deception and other sources of uncertainty.
4	KSA	Keep track of facts, fictions, and trivia.
5	KSA	Identify the important event from among the ordinary.
6	KSA	Assemble the underlying patterns from seemingly unrelated pieces of information.
7	KSA	Distinguish reliable sources from the self-serving.
8	KSA	Derive findings from the collective databases of a multidisciplinary team.
9	KSA	Depict the political context for a foreign country's policy.
10	KSA	When available information is incomplete or susceptible to deception share reasonable doubts.
11	KSA	Be prepared to conclude that you do not know.
12	KSA	Avoid projecting thin information as a conclusion.
13	KSA	Attribute ambiguous conclusions to the source.
14	KSA	Ensure the solidity of the individual and collective expertise.

(Continued)

Table 8.9 (Continued)   Principle 9: Conclusions Tasks

Item ID	KSA	Statement
15	KSA	Ensure precision in stating levels of confidence in findings.
16	KSA	Firm conclusions on complex issues need to be stated forcefully.
17	KSA	The credentials and indicators that lie behind the findings must be spelled out.
18	KSA	To minimize confusion, replace adverbial descriptors with a statement of rough numerical odds.
19	KSA	When the quality of available information requires either reserving judgment or multiple plausible interpretations, itemize gaps.
20	KSA	Lay out findings in some detail in a textbox.
21	KSA	Explain any major shift in conclusions from previous assessments.
22	KSA	When appropriate, use chronologies, matrices, and other graphics to supplement the text.
23	KSA	Remember that conclusions are the bedrock foundation for estimative judgments.

Table 8.10 Principle 10: Tradecraft and Counterintelligence Tasks

Item ID	KSA	Statement
1	KSA	Counter deception operations aimed at distorting conclusions and judgments.
2	KSA	Counter espionage by helping to identify secrets foreign intelligence services are most interested in.
3	KSA	Support efforts to manipulate foreign intelligence operations to US advantage.
4	KSA	Prepare denial measures to protect secrets through concealment, camouflage, and other activities.
5	KSA	Execute disinformation operations through appropriate intelligence channels.
6	KSA	Respect deceiver's ability to manipulate perceptions and judgments by compromising collection systems.
7	KSA	Respect deceiver's ability to manipulate perceptions and judgments by planting disinformation.
8	KSA	Adjust balance between speed and care in producing assessments.
9	KSA	Tie the effort as closely as possible to the normal processes analysts use to expand expertise.
10	KSA	Know the warning signs that a deception operation may be underway.
11	KSA	Be skeptical about the reliability of all information.
12	KSA	Prepare to challenge and test even well-established assumptions.
13	KSA	Understand that all countries have well-practiced means to deceive.

(Continued)

Table 8.10 (Continued)   Principle 10: Tradecraft and Counterintelligence Tasks

Item ID	KSA	Statement
14	KSA	Become an expert on foreign intelligence practices.
15	KSA	Where the collection systems or platforms have been countered, be aware of information distortion.
16	KSA	Understand the reach and the vulnerabilities of collection systems.
17	KSA	Where a motive to deceive is present, assume denial and disinformation operations.
18	KSA	Respond to and address suspicious gaps in collection.
19	KSA	Critically examine information that signals an inexplicable change.
20	KSA	Challenge suspicious or coincidental confirmations.
21	KSA	Weigh the costs of deception against the opportunity costs of increased care.
22	KSA	Where there is no reason to suspect, organize the key information by writing it down.
23	KSA	Examine information critically for warning signs of deception.
24	KSA	Question the authenticity of all-sources will occasionally.
25	KSA	Play Devil's Advocate and develop a hypothetical argument for the case for deception.
26	KSA	Determine to what extent the information lends support to the case for deception operation.
27	KSA	Look for "hits and misses" that raise or diminish the likelihood of an elaborate deception effort.

(Continued)

Table 8.10 (Continued)   Principle 10: Tradecraft and Counterintelligence Tasks

Item ID	KSA	Statement
28	KSA	Where there is reason to suspect deception, undertake a more elaborate defense of the analysis.
29	KSA	Employ an extended defense on sensitive issues.
30	KSA	Prepare a case for the possibility that a deception operation is impacting conclusions and estimates.
31	KSA	Prepare a justification for the defense of the assurance case.
32	KSA	Assessment of integrity should convey the way deception has been taken seriously.
33	KSA	Assessment of integrity should use analytic tests to determine the likelihood of deception.
34	KSA	Any reasonable doubts must be forthrightly reported.
35	KSA	Know the ability of the country to engage in deception.
36	KSA	Know about incentives to do so.
37	KSA	Know the reliability and integrity of the sources and collection platforms.
38	KSA	Know what can be said about the availability and consistency of information.
39	KSA	Use tradecraft tests to evaluate the authenticity of the information used to reach key conclusions.
40	KSA	Itemize the means employed to know you are not being deceived.

Implementing the Collect and Operate and Analyze Areas

The capabilities that are described in the collect and operate and analysis knowledge areas are necessary for the decision-making process because all policy makers face complex challenges, which analysts can help them to understand and manage. Analysts provide the necessary expertise in background knowledge, situational assessment, and organization of all-source material. They also bring tradecraft knowledge to the table. None of this is an anything that a top-level decision maker would be expected to do. Thus, the collect and operate and analyze areas are critical to the overall functioning of the nation and every major corporation in the country.

As you can see from the tasks in the last section, the collect and operate and analyze roles all involve the gathering, analyzing, and presentation of information and arguments to support executive decision making in the big picture strategic areas such as policy and warfighting. The tasks themselves are all basically oriented toward managing the processing of disparate raw information into actionable intelligence. The terms "organization," "analysis," and "processing" all are used to describe the process of connecting the inherent set of dots.

Piecing together the intelligence puzzle involves consolidating and evaluating disaggregate sources of information, then distributing the finished intelligence product to various intelligence consumers. At the beginning of that chain, intelligence operatives gather pertinent information without specific reference to a plan or roadmap. Because the intelligence is coming from a number of unrelated sources, the same discrete information item might be rolled into a variety of reports and analyses. These reports and analyses may address different issues at different levels of criticality, with different customers and time scales. But the underlying information is common.

The content of the collect and operate and analyze domains is meant to serve the specific decision-making requirements of policy makers. The analyst does not make the decision. The analyst provides all necessary actionable intelligence as a means of decision support. Therefore, the analyst's first duty is to get assessments in front of those decision makes in a manner that is both timely and effective within their decision cycle. Those assessments encompasses any intelligence information that can help decision makers better understand whatever challenge they are facing. The essence of the challenge of all of the roles in collect and operate and analyze is to sort out the relevant information from the increasing volume of ambiguous and contradictory data that are acquired through open source and clandestine means.

Analysts have to get past the concealment and deception that all of our major adversaries and also our friends adopt in order to mislead rival intelligence services. That requirement implies the need to adopt and follow a well-defined process for the study and presentation of a feasible range of alternate scenarios and likely intelligence outcomes. That method should provide a way to ensure that analysts have considered every aspect of the question. And that they do not dismiss any of the range of potentially relevant situations and intelligence facts that might provide an enhanced appreciation of a threat.

The problem is that analysts are human. Therefore, it is natural for analytic or cognitive bias to creep into their mental processes. That bias can color assessments of fact. It would be a serious error for an analyst to see what they expected in the intelligence. Therefore, it is necessary to also adopt a continuous, careful approach to minimizing the effects of perceptual predispositions. Consequently, the first rule in intelligence work is to make working assumptions explicit and to challenge them forcefully.

Analysts have to consider their internal mind-set in order to utilize any method properly. In simple terms, analysts have to fully understand their orientation to the problem before using structured analytic techniques. Analysts also have to employ "out-of-the-box" thinking in the examination of all feasible alternatives, because even low-probability alternatives might produce the actual desirable outcome.

Specifically, analysts have to have command of the mental models they will employ and the key assumptions that they will adopt in the analytic process. The aim is to optimally organize all of the factors and elements of the analysis, while at the same time making the analytic arguments transparent to both colleagues and also the consumers of the eventual outcome of that process. This is always done by articulating every argument and working with fellow analysts to test each for validity.

Finally, the analyst is always instructed to consider each and every one of the relevant indicators of change. These indicators are called "signposts" in the trade. The objective of that consideration is to take all of the steps necessary to reduce the chance of surprises. For estimation type analyses, this requires focus on the seemingly less likely outcomes in order to present the range of options that decision makers might consider. For action analysis, this implies the identification and assessment of all of the viable alternatives, leaving the decisions to the consumers of the intelligence.

Incorporating findings derived from a critical thinking approach also serves the decision makers in that potential changes that might alter important estimates or forecasts are more likely to be identified. In addition, all of the applicable assumptions, uncertainties, intelligence gaps, and disagreements can also be highlighted. Any of these decision elements might comprise a risk or an additional cost that can be linked to the decision's impact. Because there is more than analysis involved here, the exploration of alternative consequences for a given set of policy actions should be considered to be a partnership process, in that the analyst and the decision maker work together in order to achieve the best possible result.

Performing Collection and Operations and Analysis Work

If the collection and operation and the analysis process is executed as planned it is possible to seize the initiative over an adversary. There are five fundamental activities that characterize and describe the collection and operations and analysis specialty areas. These are (CIA, 1997)

1. *Observation*: Become aware of a threat or opportunity
2. *Orientation*: Put the observation into the context of other information
3. *Decision*: Make the best possible and timeliest action plan
4. *Action*: Carry out the plan
5. *After action*: The actor observes to see the effects of the action

The identification of assumptions and the mind-set that underlies the assumptions you carry into the project is an essential first step in observation. Analysts often rely on stated and unstated assumptions to perform basic analytic work. An assumption is any hypothesis that analysts have accepted to be true and which forms the basis of the assessment. The aim is to identify and articulate a reasonable set of key assumptions and logical outcomes.

Explicitly identifying working assumptions during the initiation of an analytic project helps the analyst to better explain the logic of the analytic argument and expose any faulty logic. It can also help to stimulate thinking about the aspects of an issue as well as enhance the analysts understanding of key factors that shape an issue. Finally, an exercise in self-criticism can help the analyst uncover hidden relationships and links between key factors as well as identify potential changed circumstances that could lead to unpleasant surprises.

The recognition and subsequent evaluation of the implications of any set of biases about observations that are carried into the project can be one of the most difficult challenges in the work. The problem is that by definition a mind-set is innate. Innate bias is very hard to factor into a decision process because it is hard for a person to recognize their own prejudices. Therefore, biases are seldom questioned and almost never directly challenged.

The goal is not to undermine or abandon key assumptions. Rather, it is to make them explicit and identify what information or developments would demand rethinking them. The examination and evaluation of assumptions and their outcomes or directions can dramatically impact the assessment. Tracking where the assumptions eventually led is also a valuable exercise in lessons learned. It is also valuable to validate the logic chain prior to the reporting stage. The aim is to insure that the eventual report does not incorporate faulty premises or reasoning.

Some intelligence disciplines, especially technical ones, will analyze the information in diverse ways, for triangulation purposes. This is particularly the case with empirically collected data. For example, NSA might record all the electromagnetic signals it received from an antenna pointed to a particular target at a particular time and then process it for different considerations such as the type of transmitter, the content of the message, the underlying delivery technology and even the native language of the information. This information can lead in different directions. It can also support various types of analysis, for different intelligence targets. But triangulation is an important part of the process of assuring a valid conclusion.

The Intelligence Process

All of the roles in the collect and operate and analyze knowledge areas involve the application of individual and collective cognitive methods to weigh data and test hypotheses within an essentially clandestine context. Intelligence involves estimation and uncertainty. Thus, intelligence reports are normally referred to as estimates rather than actual fact. Consequently, the reported findings typically express the level of confidence and the reliability of the estimate, rather than certainty.

This is not an electronic endeavor per se. The cornerstone of these areas of intelligence work is the human mind. Its ability to distinguish meaningful patterns and extract meaning from an infinite flood of correct, incorrect, and sometimes deliberately misleading information can be like finding a needle in a haystack. The aim is to provide actionable understanding of the situation while avoiding intelligence errors. Intelligence errors are factual inaccuracies in analysis resulting from poor or missing data. Intelligence failure is systemic organizational surprise resulting from incorrect, missing, discarded, or inadequate hypotheses (CIA, 2009).

The data for these reports are generally organized into a commonly accessible handbook, which analysts can then open and retrieve as needed. There also can be topical handbooks where the same intelligence might be organized around critical issues such as cyberattacks on the US infrastructure. An analyst or a team normally uses these handbooks for every aspect of the intelligence project work.

Each handbook normally specifies the all-source information by source, type, and date as well as the historical trustworthiness of the source. They also categorize the process by which the data were validated, because the analyst will always want as much background information on the relative trustworthiness of the data as is feasible in order to do a proper analysis.

Knowing the circumstances in which the data that are contained in the handbook was obtained is often critical to understanding its validity. With the data in hand, analysts can then (CIA, 2009)

1. Systematically review all sources for accuracy
2. Identify information sources that appear most critical or compelling
3. Check for sufficient and strong corroboration of critical reporting
4. Reexamine earlier dismissed information in light of new facts or circumstances

5. Ensure that analysis based on recalled reporting is reviewed
6. Consider whether ambiguous information has been interpreted properly
7. Indicate a level of confidence that analysts can place in sources, which are likely to figure in future analytic assessments

Generally, in this day and age these handbooks are kept virtually rather than as actual reference books and they are often kept Web accessible.

Commonly accessible information is essential for authorized individuals to do intelligence work. Nevertheless, the problem is that increased accessibility adds another layer when it comes to ensuring the relative security of those repositories and their attendant devices, like computers and networks. Thus, the overall security of the repository and its access control is probably the single most important concern in the application and use of automated and Web-enabled reference resources for intelligence.

A formally organized intelligence process encompasses a set of well-defined standard steps, which are employed to deliver intelligence support to policy and other types of decision makers. The related field of counterintelligence, which is the other part of the collect and operate knowledge area, simply focuses on the reverse side of the intelligence coin. Counterintelligence seeks to obstruct the collection, operational and analytic efforts of other entities and actors both state and non-state. A typical intelligence process consists of the following five well-defined stages:

1. Strategy and planning
2. Information capture and data collection
3. Information processing and exploitation analysis
4. Intelligence assessment and the subsequent production of the report
5. Dissemination and integration with relevant decision processes

The intelligence that is captured and analyzed in these stages can be factored into eight distinct generic categories. Each of these categories is likely to be a consideration in the intelligence work. These categories are (CIA, 2009) as follows:

1. Biographic intelligence
2. Economic intelligence
3. Sociological intelligence
4. Transportation and telecommunications intelligence
5. Military geographical intelligence
6. Armed forces intelligence
7. Political intelligence
8. Scientific and technical intelligence

The routine execution of the intelligence process is called the "intelligence cycle." The general aim of the conduct of an intelligence cycle is to capture and analyze disparate pieces of data on a target of interest. And then convert the collected data into actionable intelligence, which can then be made available to the appropriate set of selected clients.

Planning and Direction

As we said, the intelligence cycle comprises five phases. The first of those is planning and direction. The aim of the planning and direction phase is to decide on the target for focused monitoring and analysis. In intelligence usage, the customary actions in this phase involve determination of the intelligence requirements, the development of an appropriate intelligence architecture in which to collect and analyze the data, the preparation of a collection and analysis plan, and the issuance of explicit orders and requests to the various information collection agencies involved.

The identification and prioritization of intelligence requirements revolves around the definition of a concept of operations for the intelligence mission, which is followed by the design of appropriate architectures to underwrite the mission. The actual identification of the most-effective intelligence services to undertake the actual collection of intelligence data and to analyze and foster the necessary decision support is more difficult than it sounds, because there are a plethora of agencies that collect intelligence data. And too much data or the wrong kind of data can often be worse than not having data at all.

Thus, formal requests to agencies to initiate the collection, integration, and production of all-source intelligence have to be carefully thought through prior to making them. The consumers of intelligence have to communicate their specific intelligence objectives and requirements to the applicable agency. In many respects, this activity embodies the goals of the first three principles for intelligence work: addressing US interests, access and credibility, and clarification of assumptions.

Information Capture and Data Collection

The intelligence gathering process is based on the guidance provided by designated decision makers. For instance, the president or major departments and agencies of government request intelligence information as they need it to guide long-term policy decisions. When a request is made the appropriate contact people in the agency requested interact with the people on the requester side to specifically define all core concerns and intelligence requirements. The outcome of this interaction is a strategy to guide the actual collection approach and the analysis and presentation of suitable intelligence products.

The long-term goal is to deliver the right intelligence product to the consumer. It involves drawing up specific collection requirements leading to the finished intelligence product. The purpose of most intelligence work is to support the operational needs of the requesting agency. The intelligence requirements themselves are determined by the appropriate decision maker. These requirements, which are termed "essential elements of intelligence (EEIs)," initiate the intelligence cycle. Operational and tactical intelligence requirements should always define the information required to help the decision maker make the right decision.

Intelligence estimates develop forecasts of prospective actions or recommended responses. These forecasts are normally given to decision or policy makers. The estimates are based on all existing information obtained from all available sources both overt and covert. These intelligence estimates are created in response to specific decision-making needs of the intelligence consumer. Estimates are based on information obtained from any one of the following collection sources:

1. Human source (HUMINT)
2. Electronic source (ELINT)
3. Imagery (IMINT)
4. Open source (OSINT)

Each intelligence source has different characteristics that can be combined in different ways to support the intelligence mission. Nevertheless, because the collection process is different there are also limitations involved in the utility of these sources. The most common limitations are timing, environmental, or operational phenomena that might impact the availability of the source data.

Clandestine HUMINT collection entails many more risks than the technical collection disciplines. Therefore, how and when it is used must be highly selective, responding to carefully screened and the highest priority requirements. It cannot be kept "on the shelf" and called upon whenever needed. There must be some minimal ongoing capability that can be expanded in response to consumer needs. This has become increasingly difficult for clandestine services, such as diplomats, in response to budget pressures, and has reduced its presence that could otherwise provide official cover.

Also, in some operational cases, intelligence might be too sensitive to be of use. For instance, if it exposed the methods or persons providing such intelligence. For example, the ability of the British to crack the Enigma cypher may have been one of the deciding factors in World War II. However, the use of intelligence derived from Enigma sources would have immediately revealed to the Germans that their encryption had been cracked and they would have stopped using that device.

Information Processing and Exploitation Analysis

The analyst uses any or all of these potential resources to reciprocally substantiate the validity of the information collected. Then the intelligence estimate or forecast is prepared. The process of preparing that estimate is called analysis or processing. The steps involved in processing the information that is obtained from disparate sources are not sequential. In reality, they take place as a set of parallel activities.

This is an action-oriented step that spirals in on an answer rather than marching directly to it. Intelligence analysis is by its policy support nature oriented toward the future. The aim is to inform next steps by policy makers. Thus, the actual intelligence itself is in effect uncertain.

As we can see above, there are a range of key factors that impact an intelligence estimate. Analysts have to make stated and unstated assumptions about all relevant factors in order to conduct their analysis. The goal is not to undermine or abandon key assumptions; rather, it is to make them explicit and identify what information or developments would demand rethinking them. Essential steps in doing that include the following:

1. Examine the logic of the analytic argument.
2. Eliminate any unsupported assumptions or faulty logic.
3. Identify and characterize key factors.
4. Always practice "out-of-the-box" thinking.
5. Seek to identify any hidden linkages between key factors.
6. Identify any change in conditions that would abandon an assumption.
7. Anticipate surprises due to changed conditions.

A standard activity that is termed "collection planning" matches specific collection requirements with the collection capabilities of multiple organizations. This matching process can be targeted at many types of intelligence needs, for example, economic, military, scientific, political, or sociological. Collection planning is a continuous process that organizes and combines the efforts of all relevant units and agencies in the data capture process. Long-term collection planning helps to identify collection gaps and redundant coverage in a timely manner. The aim of this type of activity is to optimize how the available collection capabilities are utilized.

Intelligence Assessment and Reporting

Intelligence analysts use structured analytic techniques to draw explicit conclusions as well as characterize their key assumptions. The aim of these techniques is to

1. Organize and systematically structure the analytic process
2. Articulate and challenge all key assumptions
3. Motivate creative thinking in defining alternative outcomes
4. Identify signposts that can reduce the chances of covert action
5. Emphasize changes in conditions that would alter key assessments or predictions
6. Identify uncertainties, intelligence gaps, and disagreements that impact decisions
7. Explore alternative outcomes that might arise

An assumption is any fact that analysts have accepted to be true and which forms the basis of an intelligence estimate. For example, an economic analysis may identify a set of key business and market factors and "assume" that these factors will be operated in the way they have always been executed.

Nevertheless, if an exercise in "out-of-the-box" thinking is conducted about conditions or factors a dramatic change in the estimate might result. For instance, "What would happen if a major refinery was blown up?" If that were the case the analyst might arrive at very different conclusions about market outcomes. Likewise, political analysts might assume that oil prices will remain constant. If the refinery was destroyed that would have a key impact on economic performance and perhaps even social unrest.

The reliability of the data utilized in the analysis is the key factor in assigning the level of confidence that the analyst can put into analytic judgments. Thus, the validation of the data that will be utilized in the estimation process is the primary consideration. Data validation is ongoing and continuous because new information will arrive as the project is ongoing. The primary concern is that there are normally multiple sources for data on an issue. The key is to be able to say with a high level of confidence that the dataset has been thoroughly examined and found to be valid. In addition, analysts need to occasionally validate the data against their analytic judgments in order to ensure that their basis is robustly supported by valid data.

Data quality is often a team exercise. Analysts should collectively review the correctness and accuracy of their information and confirm their understanding of its strengths and weaknesses. The aim is to always understand the context and conditions under which critical information has been collected and to establish a confidence level it. Such a thorough review of information sources is aimed at understanding "what we know" and "what we do not know." It is also an opportunity to confirm that sources have been cited accurately.

In the case of HUMINT, this will require extensive review of the sources' background information and access as well as his or her motivation for providing the information. Similarly, reviewing technical sourcing can sometimes reveal inadvertent errors in processing, translation, or interpretation that otherwise might have gone unnoticed. In addition, a quality of information check can be valuable because it can aid in the detection of possible deception and denial strategies by an adversary. It can also identify key intelligence gaps and new requirements for collectors. Finally a review can assist policy makers in understanding how much confidence analysts are placing on analytic judgments.

From a reporting standpoint, it is important to maintain a balance between reports designed to provide current targeted intelligence and long-term estimates. In general, the culture of the intelligence community, in particular that of the CIA, has always favored the estimate approach. This is an understandable holdover from the cold war where there were only a few major players, which is definitely not true today. Therefore, the problem with long-term analysis is that the information that is being processed is often collected under existing assumptions and times change.

So in many respects the analyst's estimate is not better than the estimates of their counterparts in academia and the private sector.

Also, many routine estimates are likely to be less relevant to busy policy makers, who have immediate problems. If long-term estimates are produced, it is important that they be concise, that ownership of the report is taken, and that sources justifying conclusions be shown as they would in any academic work. If the project is a group effort, it is particularly important that differences among participants be clarified and acknowledged. While it is valuable to point out consensus, it is more important that areas of dispute be highlighted. This is particularly important in communicating views of complex issues. If there is pressure for consensus, it is likely that the conclusions in the report will represent a lowest common denominator.

Every conclusion in that estimate should be accompanied by a statement of the analyst's confidence in it. The intelligence estimate is then communicated to the consumer and disseminated as appropriate based on the specific classification level specified in the intelligence request.

Dissemination and Integration

Intelligence work is the proactive aspect of national security. That is particularly true where counterintelligence is involved. Where the concern that motivated the intelligence estimate is unmistakably clear and there are options for taking direct action to intervene, which is termed an "intervention," there is a need to identify specific targets as part of the dissemination process. This action is target-centric in nature.

The target for intervention action, must be explicitly identified and efforts are made to determine the appropriate nature and extent of a subsequent intervention. The aim is to optimize the benefit of action. The intervention is planned in the same fashion as a military operation. Actions are designated and alternatives are identified. Just like aiming a rifle, once the decision to intervene is made the target is "fixed" and an estimate is made that the target can be successfully hit under current conditions. During the operation itself, monitoring and assessment of real-time actions take place. The aim is to always understand the probability of success and be able to respond to any contingencies that might impact the situation.

An exploitation analysis might be conducted once the intervention is completed. The aim is to further exploit any successes as well as to refine the intervention process for similar action against related targets. Information gathered from the exploitation analysis may lead to further refinement as well as being recorded to be used in future intelligence assessment activities. Once the intelligence effort has been executed, the intelligence information has to be disseminated to the appropriate consumer. Intelligence agencies are normally tasked to provide specific types of intelligence inputs to a given set of decision makers. It is in the delivery of that intelligence that the effectiveness of the process sometimes breaks down.

Thus, the first step in dissemination is to identify who and in what priority the intelligence information is to be delivered. The collection process itself is either "pull" or "push" depending on the model. The United States normally utilizes a push approach. North Atlantic Treaty Organization (NATO) and other related organizations use a pull process. Pull processes are initiated by a request for information (RFI). The initiator of the RFI is normally the consumer. These RFIs normally flow through the chain of command at the requesting agency.

The push process involves continuous intelligence analysis aimed at providing information on all current items of interest to decision makers. In the push approach, the decision maker receives intelligence information in the form of routine briefings, summaries, reports, and other intelligence estimates.

These can also be tailored to convey critical information of interest to the decision maker, although tailored reports tend to lack explanatory context. Thus, even though the material presented gives key information and recommendations it is not always easy for the decision maker to determine policy directions without constant interaction with the intelligence analysts. Finally, at the highest level of decision making, which is the formulation of rational policies, the effects of personalities, and partisan culture can shape the outcomes of the intelligence services. This is obviously a no–no, but it is a fact of life in a political society.

Upper managers may need intelligence inputs for specific targets on a long-term basis. Long-term monitoring of a target is especially easy and important for technical data collection. But long-term monitoring requires resources and there are never enough of those. So it is always necessary to prioritize the means of collection. This is typically done on a budgetary basis. The budget that is assigned to a given project, over another one, serves to provide effective prioritization of the intelligence efforts of one service versus another. This is also true for projects within services.

Not only must resources be prioritized but it is critical that the analysts know where to begin in assessing mountains of disaggregate information. Thus, collection priorities must not only direct analysts to those subjects that are policy relevant but they must also ensure that intelligence efforts are focused on obtaining information that the intelligence community is most uniquely positioned to ascertain.

Prioritization also acts to prevent politicizing the intelligence services. This is a real danger in all societies, be they democratic or totalitarian. The reason why politicization is dangerous is that it will lead the intelligence community to distort information or judgment in order to please political authorities. Moreover, the danger can never be eliminated if intelligence analysts are involved in any aspect of the political process. Analysts always have to be objective. So the challenge is to develop reasonable safeguards in the intelligence planning while giving intelligence workers the ability to interact to achieve rational policy goals.

The bulk of US intelligence efforts overseas are devoted to traditional national security concerns. Major foreign policy problems or obstructions of ongoing intelligence and diplomatic work can result if the national security focus is ignored.

The problem is that law enforcement agencies also operate in the intelligence sphere. And the pursuit of evidence or individuals for prosecution in a criminal matter has a different set of rules from intelligence work.

In an era of transnational terrorism and organized crime, there may not be clean distinctions between domestic and foreign activities. Therefore, interagency coordination and cooperation is required to ensure that the pursuit of criminals overseas does not impinge on any of the national security considerations. Likewise, the opposite is true in internal security matters except under specific authorization. This is to preserve the civil liberties of American citizens at home. Nevertheless, there are times when intelligence agencies might provide law enforcement agencies with information on US citizens.

When it comes to economic intelligence, private interests are as likely to be involved in the capture and analysis process as public agencies. The private sector may actually have better information on trade policy, resources, foreign exchange, and other economic factors. This intelligence may not be "open source" in the sense that it is often a commodity. Multinational corporations typically utilize intelligence information as part of core business. Nevertheless, private sector intelligence needs can become especially problematic when private organizations utilize their intelligence capabilities for their own benefit.

Intelligence work often involves clandestine human intelligence and covert activities. Those types of activities might require the intelligence service that is involved to break foreign laws, often on a routine basis. It has to be noted in conclusion that each of the five main components of the intelligence process have failed in different countries and at different times. These historic failures represent both the challenge and also the cautionary aspect of intelligence work. However, the proper exercise of the well-defined concepts, principles, and best practices of this fundamentally valuable critical thinking activity will lead to a much more secure nation.

Chapter Summary

Knowledge area 5, collect and operate and knowledge area 6, analyze are combined here. This combination is necessary because unlike the other five areas of the NICE framework, the collect and operate and the analyze knowledge areas encompass the domains of intelligence work, and the job roles, tasks, and KSAs for those areas have not been explicitly defined.

Domain 5, the collect and operate knowledge area entails job roles that perform any type of formally defined work that is meant to inhibit or prevent an act of electronic espionage. Specialty areas in the domain also carry out deception operations aimed at giving an adversary false information that might deceive them into drawing incorrect conclusions or taking faulty actions against an organization's information. While at the same time, operate and maintain collects and interprets electronic information that it uses to produce desired intelligence outcomes. In generic circles, this type of activity is normally termed "counterintelligence."

The three job roles within the collect and operate specialty area typically perform the classic spy versus spy role that is most frequently associated with counterintelligence work. Thus, the specialty areas within collect and operate—collect, process, analyze, and present to decision makers all relevant information obtained from adversarial sources.

The aim of these roles is to be proactive as much as reactive. The work is designed to ensure that no harm can come to the organization's people, resources, or mission. Thus, in essence the overall goal of the specialty areas within this domain is to ensure that our adversaries are unable to read our mail, which is not simply a national defense objective. It can also embrace any item of information in any business that might be subject to attack by hackers, criminals, saboteurs, and industrial spies.

Domain 6, analyze, focuses on classic intelligence work and in that respect its appearance in a cybersecurity body of knowledge reflects the growing role of intelligence in the global fight to keep our systems secure. This area seeks to gather the intelligence information required to ensure against attack or exploitation by any foreign or domestic adversary.

It is the emphasis on active gathering of any pertinent information that might be useful against an adversary in any form that primarily differentiates analyze from collect and operate. Fundamentally, analyze does the information gathering and preparatory work that lets an organization to understand another entity's secrets and plans in order to ensure that the organization can take active steps to make itself safe from attack. Like the classic intelligence function, the analyze knowledge area encompasses those job roles that are responsible for direct, usually covert operations against potential adversaries. It collects and interprets information that lets the organization anticipate and get in front of potential attacks.

The specialty areas in this domain perform all of the activities necessary to obtain actionable intelligence about all relevant adversarial targets. This knowledge area directly corresponds with the general body of knowledge of the intelligence community. Given that the methods and techniques that are required to carry out the necessary espionage practices that are needed to carry out the work.

The following are three specialty areas in the collect and operate areas.

Collection operations. This is classic tradecraft. It is a creative process rather than a linear process. It involves the integration of pieces of information that are collected from diverse sources. And then piecing those bits of the puzzle together into an actionable picture.

Cyber operations. This is counterespionage tradecraft. This category also explicitly embraces the actions associated with cyberwarfare. This specialty area specifically supports the overall intelligence operation. Its focus is on, counterespionage from either electronic or human intelligence sources.

Cyber operations planning. This is the long-term strategy area for the collect and operate knowledge area. This specialty area performs all of the detailed strategic planning for the cyber operations function.

As we saw in the Chapter 1, there are four specialty areas in the analyze knowledge area, as follows:

Threat analysis. All intelligence is based around threat detection. This specialty area fulfills that function. Its general purpose is to identify all meaningful threats, collect the information required in order to be able to judge the capabilities of the relevant threats in the adversarial spectrum. Targets might include every type of threat from local criminal to nation state operations.

All-source intelligence. The purpose of the all-source intelligence specialty area is to amalgamate disaggregated threat information from all relevant sources across the intelligence gathering function.

Exploitation analysis. This is sometimes called "pen-testing." The exploitation analyst collects all information necessary to identify vulnerabilities and potential for exploitation. The tasks and KSAs in this function involve the specific identification of weaknesses and vulnerabilities that are likely targets for exploitation. In effect, this specialty area underwrites the prioritization process that is necessary for good strategic and operational planning.

Targets. This is a diffuse area because it amalgamates the knowledge gained from the impact and risk analysis with the knowledge that is required to understand in detail the nuances of a particular area under scrutiny, or of an adversary of interest. For instance, in order to decide about potential targets for proactive action in some part of the world, the analyst has to have up-to-date knowledge of the region and the countries, non-state entities, and/or technologies that reside there.

The Body of Knowledge for Collect and Operate and Analyze

The NICE framework defines nothing below the specialty areas for these two areas. Therefore, it is necessary to turn to other sources to more completely understand the body of knowledge for this area. Fortunately such a body of knowledge is available in the Tradecraft Notes prepared by the CIA (1997, 2009). There are 10 general principles that underlie and guide these activities (all from CIA, 1997).

Addressing US Interests in Assessments

This first principle makes the essential link between intelligence work and policy making. In essence, it ensures proper focus of the effort. It also directly states that the intelligence community is guided by an agenda set at the policy level not vice versa.

Access and Credibility

This second principle highlights the need for access, credibility, and trust between the intelligence worker and key consumers. It is the principle that demands that close attention must be paid to validating facts and sourcing of intelligence as well as the assumptions that underlie the work. The aim is to maintain credibility in an environment of uncertainty.

Articulation of Assumptions

This third principle simply states that critical thinking is required. In essence, all underlying assumptions about the intelligence mission must be clarified prior to doing the work. That includes the necessity to identify, challenge, and justify all of the key variables involved and think through all of the assumptions that underlie those drivers.

Outlook

This fourth principle requires a little fortune telling. The worker must lay out the probable development and outcomes of the mission going forward. The likeliest courses as well as any probable alternative outcomes all have to be considered in doing the intelligence work. The aim is to have contingency plans in place for all reasonable alternatives. Their likelihood can range from plausible to remote possibilities.

Facts and Sourcing

This fifth principle is the meat and potatoes of intelligence work. Being able to concretely establish the facts and their basis is central to the credibility of the intelligence mission.

Analytic Expertise

This sixth principle is the other side of facts and sourcing. It is also a critical requirement. It simply states that the analysts must have sufficient knowledge and capability to address the issue under examination.

Effective Summary

This seventh principle highlights the need to be able to create an efficient and clear summary of findings for actionable purposes. An effective summary has to convey evidence of the underlying analysis as well as key findings and judgments.

Implementation Analysis

This eighth principle is practical. It requires the intelligence worker to prepare an assessment of tactical alternatives to that decision makers can adopt to address a given threat or weakness.

Conclusions

This ninth principle goes hand-in-hand with the effective summary principle. It requires the intelligence worker to provide an estimate of their level of trust in their conclusions. Intelligence work is by definition speculative.

Tradecraft and Counterintelligence

This tenth principle has to do with the fact that adversaries utilize deception in their own tradecraft. Thus, the information contained in the facts and sourcing and conclusions areas has to be examined in order to test for deception or other forms of tradecraft on the adversary's part.

Collect and operate and analyze roles all involve the gathering, analyzing, and presentation of information and arguments to support executive decision making in the big picture strategic areas such as policy and warfighting. The tasks themselves are all basically oriented toward managing the processing of disparate raw information into actionable intelligence. The terms "organization," "analysis," and "processing" all are used to describe the process of connecting the inherent set of dots.

Piecing together the intelligence puzzle involves consolidating and evaluating disaggregate sources of information, then distributing the finished intelligence product to various intelligence consumers.

At the beginning of that chain, intelligence operatives gather pertinent information without specific reference to a plan or roadmap. Because the intelligence is coming from a number of unrelated sources, the same discrete information item might be rolled into a variety of reports and analyses. These reports and analyses may address different issues at different levels of criticality, with different customers and time scales. But the underlying information is common.

The analyst does not make the decision. The analyst provides all necessary actionable intelligence as a means of decision support. Therefore, the analyst's first duty is to get assessments in front of those decision makes in a manner that is both timely and effective within their decision cycle. Those assessments encompass any intelligence information that can help decision makers better understand whatever challenge they are facing. The essence of the challenge of all of the roles in collect and operate and analyze is to sort out the relevant information from the increasing volume of ambiguous and contradictory data that are acquired through open source and clandestine means.

Analysts have to get past the concealment and deception that all of our major adversaries and also our friends adopt in order to mislead rival intelligence services. That requirement implies the need to adopt and follow a well-defined process for the study and presentation of a feasible range of alternate scenarios and likely intelligence outcomes. That method should provide a way to ensure that analysts have considered every aspect of the question. And that they do not dismiss any of the range of potentially relevant situations and intelligence facts that might provide an enhanced appreciation of a threat.

If the collection and operation and the analysis processes are executed as planned, it is possible to seize the initiative over an adversary. The following are five fundamental activities that characterize and describe the collection and operations and analysis specialty areas (CIA, 1997):

1. *Observation*: Become aware of a threat or opportunity.
2. *Orientation*: Put the observation into the context of other information.
3. *Decision*: Make the best possible plan that can be carried out in a timely manner.
4. *Action*: Carry out the plan.
5. *After action*: The actor observes to see the effects of the action.

The Intelligence Process

Intelligence analysis is the application of individual and collective cognitive methods to weigh data and test hypotheses within an essentially clandestine context. The human mind is the cornerstone for intelligence work. Its ability to distinguish meaningful patterns and extract meaning from an infinite flood of correct, incorrect, and sometimes deliberately misleading information can be like finding a needle in a haystack.

Intelligence involves estimation and uncertainty. Thus, intelligence reports are normally referred to as estimates rather than actual fact. Consequently, the reported findings typically express the level of confidence and the reliability of the estimate, rather than certainty. The aim is to provide actionable understanding of the situation while avoiding intelligence errors. Intelligence errors are factual inaccuracies in analysis resulting from poor or missing data. Intelligence failure is systemic organizational surprise resulting from incorrect, missing, discarded, or inadequate hypotheses (CIA, 2009).

The data for these reports are generally organized into a commonly accessible handbook, which analysts can then open and retrieve as needed. There also can be topical handbooks where the same intelligence might be organized around critical issues such as cyberattacks on the US infrastructure. An analyst or a team normally uses these handbooks for every aspect of the intelligence project work.

Knowing the circumstances in which the data that are contained in the handbook was obtained is often critical to understanding its validity. With the data in hand, analysts can then (CIA, 2009)

1. Systematically review all sources for accuracy
2. Identify information sources that appear most critical or compelling
3. Check for sufficient and strong corroboration of critical reporting
4. Reexamine previously dismissed information in light of new facts
5. Ensure any recalled reporting is identified and properly flagged for other analysts
6. Consider whether ambiguous information has been interpreted properly
7. Indicate a level of confidence that analysts can place in sources

Generally, in this day and age these handbooks are kept virtually rather than as actual reference books and they are often kept Web accessible.

A formally organized intelligence process encompasses a set of well-defined standard steps, which are employed to deliver intelligence support to policy and other types of decision makers. The related field of counterintelligence, which is the other part of the collect and operate knowledge area, simply focuses on the reverse side of the intelligence coin. Counterintelligence seeks to obstruct the collection, operational, and analytic efforts of other entities and actors both state and non-state. A typical intelligence process consists of five well-defined stages:

1. Strategy and planning
2. Information capture and data collection
3. Information processing and exploitation analysis
4. Intelligence assessment and the subsequent production of the report
5. Dissemination and integration with relevant decision processes

The intelligence that is captured and analyzed in these stages can be factored into eight distinct generic categories. Each of these categories is likely to be a consideration in the intelligence work. These categories are (CIA, 2009) as follows:

1. Biographic intelligence
2. Economic intelligence
3. Sociological intelligence
4. Transportation and telecommunications intelligence
5. Military geographical intelligence
6. Armed forces intelligence
7. Political intelligence
8. Scientific and technical intelligence

Key Terms

Actionable Intelligence: The general goal of intelligence analysis is to generate advice that can be acted on by a decision maker.

All-Source Intelligence: Information gathered from a range of activities including human, electronic, and social.

Analyst: A NICE framework role primarily responsible for the development of intelligence estimates using all-source data.

Connect-the-Dots: The act of associating disparate items of information in such a way that a rationally justifiable conclusion can be drawn.

Consumer of Intelligence: The designated decision maker being served by that specific intelligence function.

Counterintelligence: The act of deceiving an adversary or of detecting deception on an adversary's part.

Covert (or Covert Operations): Activities that are designed to take place undetected by the intelligence target.

Critical Thinking: The basic thought process of decomposing a problem into components that are subjected to understanding and actionable resolution and then building the solution out of the components.

Cyber Operations: A Specialty area of the NICE framework as well as the general approach to planning and executing an intelligent exploit in cyberspace.

Data Capture: The process of generating all-source intelligence from a range of sources.

Decision-Making Model: The cognitive and behavioral approach that a decision maker(s) adopt in order to come to a specific action oriented conclusion.

ELINT: Electronic intelligence captured by classic electronic means.

Exploitation (Analyst or Analysis): The attempt to identify any gaps or holes in a defense that an adversary can use to infiltrate an asset.

HUMINT: Human intelligence captured by classic people based, behavioral means.

Intelligence Assessment: A specific judgment made by the analyst regarding a specific target. This is often passed to the consumer of intelligence.

Intelligence Target: Generally an adversary, but it can be any specific point of focus of an intelligence operation.

Mind-set: The innate bias that an analyst carries into a project must be recognized.

OPSEC: A specialized aspect of counterintelligence devoted to deception involving military or national security information.

OSINT: Open-source information that is generally available to any consumer.

Processing: Assembling and organizing intelligence from all sources so that it can be analyzed.

Role: A generic area of security work, delineated by a common set of skills and functional purposes.

Strategic Intelligence Planning: Long-term targeting and resourcing undertaken to achieve policy goals set by decision makers.

References

Central Intelligence Agency (CIA). 1997. *A Compendium of Analytic Tradecraft Notes* (Volume I, Notes 1–10). Directorate of Intelligence. Reprinted with a new Foreword by the Deputy Director for Intelligence.

Central Intelligence Agency (CIA). 2009. *A Tradecraft Primer: Structured Analytic Techniques for Improving Intelligence Analysis.* Prepared by the US Government.

National Institute of Standards and Technology (NIST). 2014. *National Cybersecurity Workforce Framework.* Gaithersburg, MD: NIST.

Chapter 9

Oversee and Govern

Chapter Objectives

At the conclusion of this chapter, the reader will understand:

- The focus and purpose of the oversee and govern general knowledge area
- The seven specialty area knowledge, skills, and abilities (KSAs) of the oversee and govern general knowledge area
- The underlying tasks of each specialty area within the oversee and govern general knowledge area
- The relationship between each specialty area and the cybersecurity framework (CSF)

Introduction

Cybersecurity is a significant business issue that if breached, can dramatically impact the entire organization's relationship with its customers, profitability, and reputation. Employee negligence and noncompliance with information technology (IT) security policies are increasingly cited as a key security problem within organizations. If users do not comply with IT security policies, security measures are ineffective and may be very costly to the organization. To address this concern, proper oversight of an enterprise-wide information assurance (IA) program is critical. Technology has become so embedded into the fabric of organizations that managing cybersecurity risks can no longer be delegated to a person or the IT department—it must be the responsibility of leadership and management at all levels of the organization.

The oversee and govern general knowledge area is responsible for providing leadership, management, direction, or development and advocacy so the organization

Oversee and govern

Specialty areas responsible for providing leadership, management, direction, or development and advocacy so the organization may effectively conduct cybersecurity work.

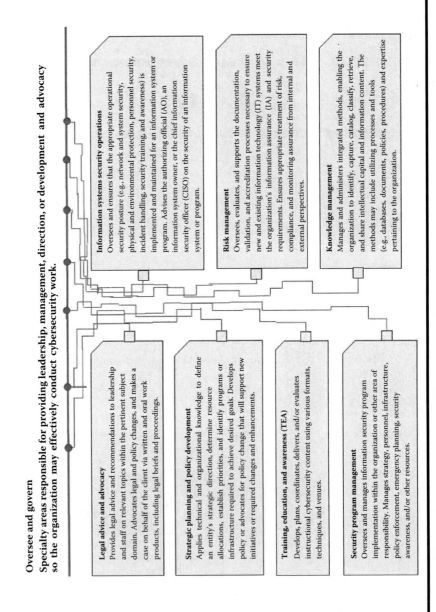

Information systems security operations
Oversees and ensures that the appropriate operational security posture (e.g., network and system security, physical and environmental protection, personnel security, incident handling, security training, and awareness) is implemented and maintained for an information system or program. Advises the authorizing official (AO), an information system owner, or the chief information security officer (CISO) on the security of an information system or program.

Risk management
Oversees, evaluates, and supports the documentation, validation, and accreditation processes necessary to ensure new and existing information technology (IT) systems meet the organization's information assurance (IA) and security requirements. Ensures appropriate treatment of risk, compliance, and monitoring assurance from internal and external perspectives.

Knowledge management
Manages and administers integrated methods, enabling the organization to identify, capture, catalog, classify, retrieve, and share intellectual capital and information content. The methods may include utilizing processes and tools (e.g., databases, documents, policies, procedures) and expertise pertaining to the organization.

Legal advice and advocacy
Provides legal advice and recommendations to leadership and staff on relevant topics within the pertinent subject domain. Advocates legal and policy changes, and makes a case on behalf of the client via written and oral work products, including legal briefs and proceedings.

Strategic planning and policy development
Applies technical and organizational knowledge to define an entity's strategic direction, determine resource allocations, establish priorities, and identify programs or infrastructure required to achieve desired goals. Develops policy or advocates for policy change that will support new initiatives or required changes and enhancements.

Training, education, and awareness (TEA)
Develops, plans, coordinates, delivers, and/or evaluates instructional cybersecurity content using various formats, techniques, and venues.

Security program management
Oversees and manages information security program implementation within the organization or other area of responsibility. Manages strategy, personnel, infrastructure, policy enforcement, emergency planning, security awareness, and/or other resources.

Figure 9.1   Oversee and govern general specialty area overview.

may effectively conduct cybersecurity work (National Institute of Standards and Technology [NIST], 2014). As shown in Figure 9.1, the oversee and govern knowledge area contains seven specialty areas. These are legal advice and advocacy; strategic planning and policy development; training, education, and awareness (TEA); information systems security operations; security program management; risk management; and knowledge management.

In many organizations, intellectual capital has become *the* business and as Peter Drucker stated over a decade ago, "Knowledge is fast becoming the sole factor of productivity, sidelining both capital and labor." (Drucker, 1993) The reliance on information and the systems that process, transmit, and store it has become truly pervasive. Reported breaches of information security (IS) are rising annually by 50% and the term "cyber fatality" no longer just refers to a Mortal Kombat Cyber Sub-Zero fatality, but can now be applied to mean a digital breach that puts a company out of business.

As information assets and other intangibles increasingly comprise more of the value of a typical organization, the rise in spending on security and assurance-related functions as well as governmental regulations continue to rise. Examples of ensuring patient privacy in the healthcare industry, which was once handled by Human Resources is now regulated by the federal Health Insurance Portability and Accountability Act of 1996 (known as HIPAA). Once managed by the finance department, the Sarbanes–Oxley Act of 2002 (known as SOX) is the legislation passed that was designed to enhance corporate responsibility, enhance financial disclosures, and deter corporate and accounting fraud. These various regulated functions all have different reporting structures, use specialized jargon, and have evolved into specialized assurance functions that promote their specialty. Unfortunately, this has created a divide between what should be a unified organization-wide IA process.

The job roles within oversee and govern are diverse and include: legal advisor/staff judge advocate (SJA); paralegal; chief information officer (CIO); chief information security officer (CISO); IS policy manager and analyst; policy writer and strategist; cyber trainer; IS trainer; contracting officer (CO); IA manager; cybersecurity officer; IT director; risk executive; auditor; systems analyst; business analyst; information manager; knowledge manager. It is important to note the tendency of these assurance functions to become fragmented into vertical "stovepipes" despite the fact that all of these serve one common purpose: to preserve the organization to continue to operate and generate revenue. The solution lies in ensuring that IS governance is conducted at the highest levels of the organization.

Increasing predictability and reducing uncertainty of business operations by lowering risk to definable and acceptable levels as well as improving trust in customer relationships and protecting the organization's reputation are significant benefits of good governance. As senior managers are considered ultimately responsible and legally liable for losses due to cybersecurity breaches, it is vital that they understand the significance of and implement effective IS governance. It is also critical that a security governance framework is utilized to ensure that all aspects of IS be coordinated and are tightly aligned with the strategic business objectives.

Specialty Area 1: Legal Advice and Advocacy

The specialty area of legal advice and advocacy "provides legal advice and recommendations to leadership and staff on relevant topics within the pertinent subject domain" (NIST, 2014). Organizations hire legal advisors as part of their risk management strategies. Quality legal advice is fact-specific and the more the legal advocate knows about the organization, the better the legal advice. A well-rounded legal advisor will have the combination of legal knowledge and business experience in order to help the organization avoid unnecessary liability. It is advantageous when the organization can hire its own in-house corporate counsel or a regular external business attorney because the focus on corporate legal matters will be all they do—they will not be handling personal injury cases or working on divorce cases. The focus on business issues will allow them to become more intimately familiar with the operations of the organization thus allowing them to provide targeted legal advice specific to the organization's business needs.

A trusted legal advisor is often called upon to assist with important business decisions and strategic business planning and is often viewed as an employee or executive manager in the organization with intimate knowledge of the business. The direct and continuous contact with internal corporate counsel may identify and focus on issues that management may never have brought to the attention of outside counsel or not until the expense is clearly justified. Traditional attorneys are trained and incentivized to bill as many hours as possible to meet their firm's hourly rate requirements or to generate more income. Employing hourly rate counsel directly affects the cost of legal services and may impact the kinds of questions in which an organization is willing to ask. This can be troublesome and potentially more expensive in the long run in the event management waits until there is critical mass before seeking legal advice.

Factoring Legal Advice and Advocacy Workforce Tasks into the Cybersecurity Framework Categories

As shown in Figure 9.2, the majority of the legal advice and advocacy tasks that are specified by the NICE framework lie in the CSF functional area of "identify." Once an event has been detected and legal action is required, the remaining tasks then fall under the function of "respond."

Identify Tasks

US cybercrime law encompasses 52 distinct sets of laws—the federal system plus the 50 states and the District of Columbia. Legal advocates must acquire and maintain a working knowledge of relevant laws, regulations, policies, standards, or

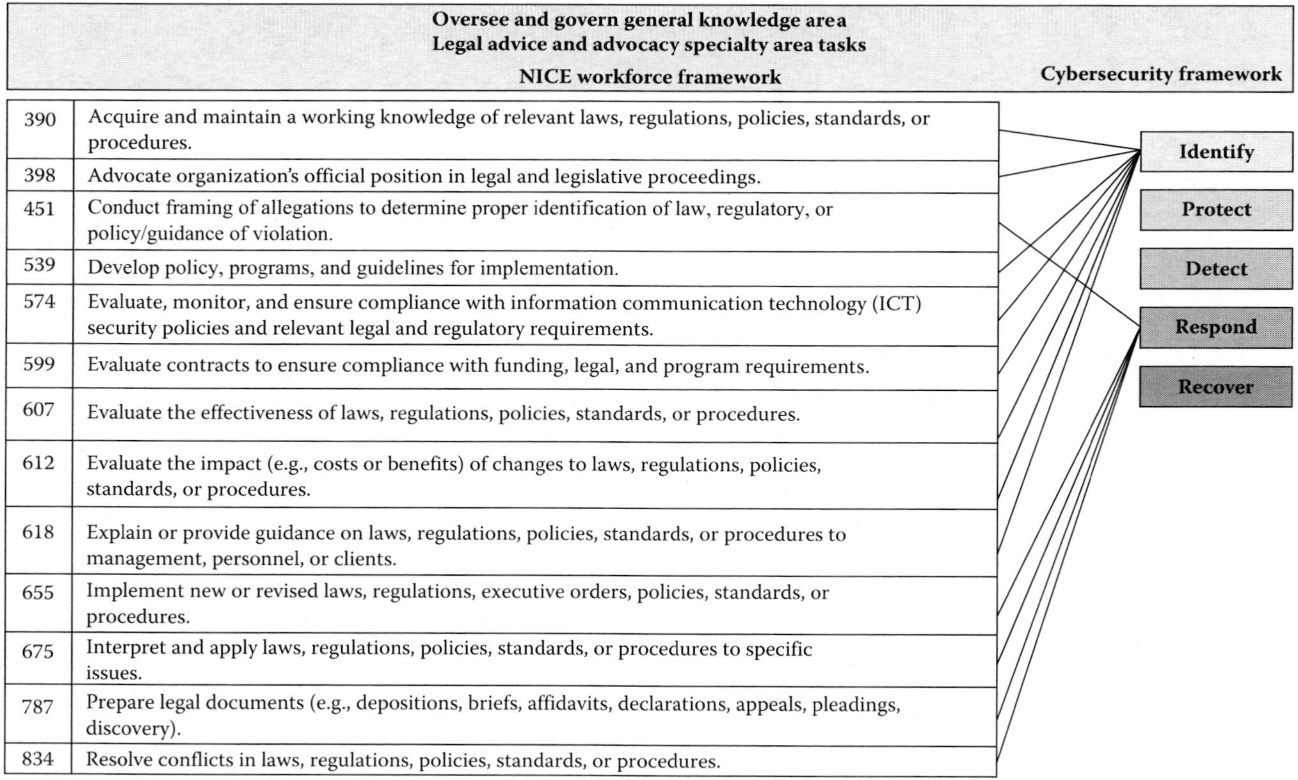

Oversee and govern general knowledge area Legal advice and advocacy specialty area tasks NICE workforce framework	Cybersecurity framework
	Identify · Protect · Detect · Respond · Recover
390	Acquire and maintain a working knowledge of relevant laws, regulations, policies, standards, or procedures.
398	Advocate organization's official position in legal and legislative proceedings.
451	Conduct framing of allegations to determine proper identification of law, regulatory, or policy/guidance of violation.
539	Develop policy, programs, and guidelines for implementation.
574	Evaluate, monitor, and ensure compliance with information communication technology (ICT) security policies and relevant legal and regulatory requirements.
599	Evaluate contracts to ensure compliance with funding, legal, and program requirements.
607	Evaluate the effectiveness of laws, regulations, policies, standards, or procedures.
612	Evaluate the impact (e.g., costs or benefits) of changes to laws, regulations, policies, standards, or procedures.
618	Explain or provide guidance on laws, regulations, policies, standards, or procedures to management, personnel, or clients.
655	Implement new or revised laws, regulations, executive orders, policies, standards, or procedures.
675	Interpret and apply laws, regulations, policies, standards, or procedures to specific issues.
787	Prepare legal documents (e.g., depositions, briefs, affidavits, declarations, appeals, pleadings, discovery).
834	Resolve conflicts in laws, regulations, policies, standards, or procedures.

Figure 9.2 **Legal advice and specialty area tasks mapped to the cybersecurity framework (CSF).**

procedures in order to provide adequate legal advice and recommendations. This knowledge is required in the development of policy, programs, and guidelines for implementation.

Specific knowledge of applicable laws, such as the Electronic Communication Privacy Act of 1986, Foreign Intelligence Surveillance Act of 1978, Protect America Act of 2007, search and seizure laws, civil liberties and privacy laws, and so on, is required to provide adequate legal advice and recommendations. A lack of knowledge or a solid legal strategy in the handling of incidents, for example, may cause forensic evidence to be excluded, potentially losing the case.

With the significant increase of organizations conducting business on a global scale, the nature of business and technology drove the need for standards and regulations designed to govern how organizations will work together and share information. Collaborative partnerships such as the International Organization of Standardization (ISO), the World Trade Organization (WTO), the International Electrotechnical Commission (IEC), and the International Telecommunication Union (ITU) have evolved to promote global trading for all countries. However, national interests, industry concerns, and corporate jockeying create strong political drivers. And the concern each have about confidentiality, integrity, and availability of their information may be addressed by standards and legislation. With this in mind, legal advocates are tasked with developing policy, programs, and guidelines for implementation of systems that may be used in various parts of the globe. And the complexity of international law elevates the requirements of legal advocates to possess the knowledge to evaluate the impact (e.g., cost or benefits) of changes to laws, regulations, polices, standards, and procedures.

Legal contracts with potential strategic business partners, prospective customers, bank covenants, and the like all require familiarity with contract law in order to evaluate and ensure compliance with any funding, legal, and program requirements. Working as internal corporate counsel or a regular business attorney, it is expected that the legal advisor be able to explain and provide guidance on laws, regulations, policies, standards or procedures to management and personnel (during policy development in the "identify" function), and clients (after a violation warrants legal action in the "recover" function).

The trend toward more governmental regulation will also continue and knowledge of intelligence reporting principles, policies, procedures including report formats, criteria, and legal authorities and restrictions is critical.

Respond Tasks

Once an incident has been detected and the organization is in the "respond" function of the CSF, there are five tasks that apply here. Depending upon the nature of the incident, it may be necessary for legal to conduct framing of the allegations to determine proper identification of law, regulatory, or policy/guidance of the violation. Here is where the interpretation and the application of laws, regulations, policies, standards, and procedures to the specific issues is analyzed and addressed. The legal advocate is responsible to then prepare any legal documents that may apply such as depositions, briefs, affidavits, declarations, appeals, pleadings, and discovery. This also includes advocating the organization's official position in legal and legislative proceedings.

In some cases or situations, it is necessary for legal advocates to lobby lawmakers in an attempt to resolve conflicts in laws, regulations, policies, standards, or procedures. Successful legal advocates working to resolve conflicts in laws require persuasive abilities to promote the interests of the organization they represent, a solid network of regional, federal, and international governing agencies, and excellent research skills to know current and pending legislation.

Underlying Knowledge, Skill, and Ability Requirements for Legal Advice and Advocacy Specialty Area

Along with a detailed set of tasks, the NICE workforce framework also provides a distinctive set of KSA specifications for each specialty area as shown in Table 9.1.

Each KSA is also categorized into a specific competency as shown in Figure 9.3. In addition to legal competencies such as legal, government, and jurisprudence, criminal law, reasoning, and contracting/procurement, the legal advisor must also demonstrate competencies in organizational awareness, vulnerabilities assessment, technology awareness, and cryptography.

Skills in tracking and analyzing technical and legal trends will allow legal advisors to provide up-to-date legal advice regarding specific legal issues that arise in cases as well as how particular judges have ruled in similar cases. The ability to determine the impact of technology trend data and knowledge of important cases could lead to precedent-setting decisions and possible policy changes.

Legal advisors also require awareness of technology such as knowledge of new and emerging cybersecurity technologies and the emerging computer-based technology that has potential for exploitation by adversaries. Due to the nature of cybersecurity threats and significant potential for loss, technical knowledge of system and application security threats and vulnerabilities such as buffer overflows, mobile code, cross-site scripting, structured query language (SQL) injections will allow legal advisors to help minimize the risk of data breaches. Technical knowledge could allow legal advisors to assist organizations in determining the source and scope of the breach, assess regulatory compliance requirements, manage notifications with external entities, and effective handle civil litigation that increasingly follows data breaches.

Table 9.1   Legal Advice and Advocacy Knowledge, Skills, and Abilities (KSAs)

Item ID	KSA	Statement	Competency
27	KSA	Knowledge of cryptography and cryptographic key management concepts.	Cryptography
88	KSA	Knowledge of new and emerging information technology (IT) and cyber security technologies.	Technology awareness
105	KSA	Knowledge of system and application security threats and vulnerabilities (e.g., buffer overflow, mobile code, cross-site scripting, procedural language/structured query language [PL/SQL] and injections, race conditions, covert channel, replay, return-oriented attacks, malicious code).	Vulnerabilities assessment
282	KSA	Knowledge of emerging computer-based technology that has potential for exploitation by adversaries.	Technology awareness
297	KSA	Knowledge of key industry indicators that are useful for identifying technology trends.	Technology awareness
300	KSA	Knowledge of intelligence reporting principles, policies, procedures, and vehicles, including report formats, reportable criteria (requirements and priorities), dissemination practices, and legal authorities and restrictions.	Organizational awareness
338	KSA	Knowledge of the principal methods, procedures, and techniques of gathering information and producing, reporting, and sharing intelligence.	Reasoning

(Continued)

Table 9.1 (Continued) Legal Advice and Advocacy Knowledge, Skills, and Abilities (KSAs)

Item ID	KSA	Statement	Competency
339	KSA	Knowledge of the structure and intent of business or military operation plans, concept operation plans, orders, policies, and standing rules of engagement.	Organizational awareness
377	KSA	Skill in tracking and analyzing technical and legal trends that will impact cyber activities.	Legal, government, and jurisprudence
954	KSA	Knowledge of import/export control regulations and responsible agencies for the purposes of reducing supply chain risk.	Contracting/procurement
981	KSA	Knowledge of International Traffic in Arms Regulation (ITARs) and relevance to cybersecurity.	Criminal law
1036	KSA	Knowledge of applicable laws (e.g., Electronic Communications Privacy Act, Foreign Intelligence Surveillance Act, Protect America Act, search and seizure laws, civil liberties and privacy laws), US Statutes (e.g., Titles 10,18, 32, 50 in US Code), Presidential Directives, executive branch guidelines, and/or administrative/criminal legal guidelines and procedures relevant to work performed.	Criminal law
1070	KSA	Ability to determine impact of technology trend data on laws, regulations, and/or policies.	Legal, government, and jurisprudence

Figure 9.3   Competency areas for legal advice and advocacy.

Businesses that have been victimized by a cyberattack also must determine when and how to cooperate with government agencies during the investigation of an attack therefore knowledge of intelligence reporting principles, policies, procedures, including formats and required criteria is essential. Government investigations that require businesses to provide information about their customers and subscribers may force them into situations where conflicting legal obligations arise due to the multiple privacy and security laws worldwide. Knowledge of how to engage with the Federal Bureau of Investigation (FBI), National Security Agency (NSA), Department of Homeland Security (DHS), the Department of Justice (DOJ), as well as state, local, and foreign agencies is required to provide legal advice with compliance and foreign government demands for information.

Specialty Area 2: Strategic Planning and Policy Development

The specialty area of strategic planning and policy development "applies technical and organizational knowledge to define an entity's direction, determine resource allocations, establish priorities, and identify programs or infrastructure required to achieve desired goals. Develops policy or advocates for policy changes that will support new initiatives or required changes and enhancements" (NIST, 2014).

IT security is by definition technology-centric and related to the specific technology deployed within the boundaries of the technology domain. However, from a business and management perspective, IS goes beyond the security related to the technology deployed and is concerned with the broader issues of payload (essential data) and information *safety*. Critical information can be spoken, written, printed, electronic, or stored on a variety of mediums such as magnetic tape, audio recorders, hard drives, paper documents, and microfiche. And whether this information is being transported, created, viewed, stored, or destroyed all falls within the larger scope of IS.

Organizations are reporting that cyberattacks are increasing in both frequency and impact. In 60% of cases, attackers are able to compromise an organization within minutes (Verizon, 2015). Many organizations do not even know whether they have been exploited by a large-scale threat such as stolen user credentials or corporate assets hijacked for botnet use. And if organizations do not know of their security vulnerabilities, they are unlikely to have created a mitigation strategy for them.

The loss of sensitive and protected information due to insider (current and former employees) crime has become the most-cited culprits of cybercrime (PricewaterhouseCoopers [PwC], 2014). In the majority of cases, employees inadvertently compromise the organization's data security through the loss of mobile devices and targeted phishing campaigns. Social engineering incidents such as phishing campaigns using e-mail are used to encourage recipients to immediately open the post and/or to click on a malicious attachment. Hackers do not have to wait long, 50% of users open e-mails and click on phishing links within the first hour of receipt (Verizon, 2015). This does not give the organization much time to detect and react to phishing incidents. In many cases, attackers are looking to establish persistence on user devices, set up camp, and continue their stealthy exploration inside the network. Without security policy guidance to employees, successful phishing attacks will persist.

In a 2014 cybercrime survey, 32% of respondents reported that damage caused by insider attacks were more damaging than outsider attacks (PricewaterhouseCoopers [PwC], 2014). Eighty-two percent of incidents by insiders were unintentional exposure of private or sensitive information, 76% of insider incidents were stolen or compromised confidential records, 71% were from compromised or stolen customer records, and 63% were from compromised or stolen employee records (PricewaterhouseCoopers [PwC], 2014). In another study, the top action, comprised 55% of incidents, was from *privilege abuse*—employees/end users abusing the access they have been given by their organization (Verizon, 2015). Financial gain and convenience were the primary motivators (40% of incidents) (Verizon, 2015). Employees may have planned to sell the stolen data for financial gain or use it to directly compete against their former employer. The motive of convenience is using an unapproved workaround to speed things up or make it easier for the end user.

Surprisingly, many organizations do not have insider-threat programs in place to prevent, detect, and respond to internal threats. Additionally 75% of respondents to the cybercrime survey noted that they did not involve law enforcement or bring legal action against the insider perpetrators. One may argue that by not making publically known the compromises committed by these individuals, future employers could be at risk.

As the concern about privacy and identity theft increases, customers are demanding the security of their information. Organizations that provide mutual network and information access to their business partners, suppliers, and vendors are also requiring security of their information. Therefore to meet these stakeholder requirements, to achieve business objectives, and to maintain compliance with all relevant regulatory entities, effective IS planning, policy development, and governance are essential. The NICE framework specifies 27 tasks for the execution of strategic planning and policy development.

Factoring Strategic Planning Workforce Tasks into the Cybersecurity Framework Categories

As shown in Figure 9.4, all but two tasks fall into the "identify" function of the CSF. The function of "identify" focuses on governance; understanding the business environment to inform cybersecurity roles, responsibilities, and risk management decisions; asset management; and risk management.

With the goal of providing strategic direction, ensuring that business objectives are achieved, managing risk appropriately, and ensuring the organization's resources are used responsibly, the board and executive management are responsible to develop and practice corporate governance. IS governance is a subset of corporate governance and the most fundamental purpose of IS is to help ensure the preservation of the organization and its ability to operate by developing and implementing an IT security strategy to increasingly integrate assurance functions, improve security, reduce losses, and lower costs. In a properly governed organization, IA activities support the organizational goals and objectives while identifying and managing risk at acceptable levels.

To exercise effective IT governance, boards of directors, and executive management must have a clear understanding of what to expect from their enterprise's IS program.

Effective IS governance should result in six outcomes to include (Information Systems Audit and Control Association [ISACA], 2013):

1. *Strategic alignment*: Security activities must be aligned with the business strategy to support the organization objectives. Security solutions take into account the governance style, organizational culture, technology deployed, and the structure of the organization.

Oversee and govern general knowledge area Strategic planning and policy development specialty area tasks	Cybersecurity framework
NICE workforce framework	**Identify**
	Protect
	Detect
	Respond
	Recover

410	Analyze organizational information security policy.
424	Assess policy needs and collaborate with stakeholders to develop policies to govern information technology (IT) activities.
485	Define current and future business environments.
492	Design a cybersecurity strategy that outlines the vision, mission, and goals that align with the organization's strategic plan.
524	Develop and maintain strategic plans.
539	Develop policy, programs, and guidelines for implementation.
565	Draft and publish security policy.
594	Establish and maintain communication channels with stakeholders.
629	Identify and address IT workforce planning and management issues, such as recruitment, retention, and training.
720	Monitor the rigorous application of information security/information assurance (IA) policies, principles, and practices in the delivery of planning and management services
724	Obtain consensus on proposed policy change from stakeholders.
812	Provide policy guidance to IT management, staff, and users.
838	Review existing and proposed policies with stakeholders.
840	Review or conduct audits of IT programs and projects.

Figure 9.4 Strategic planning specialty area tasks mapped to the CSF.   *(Continued)*

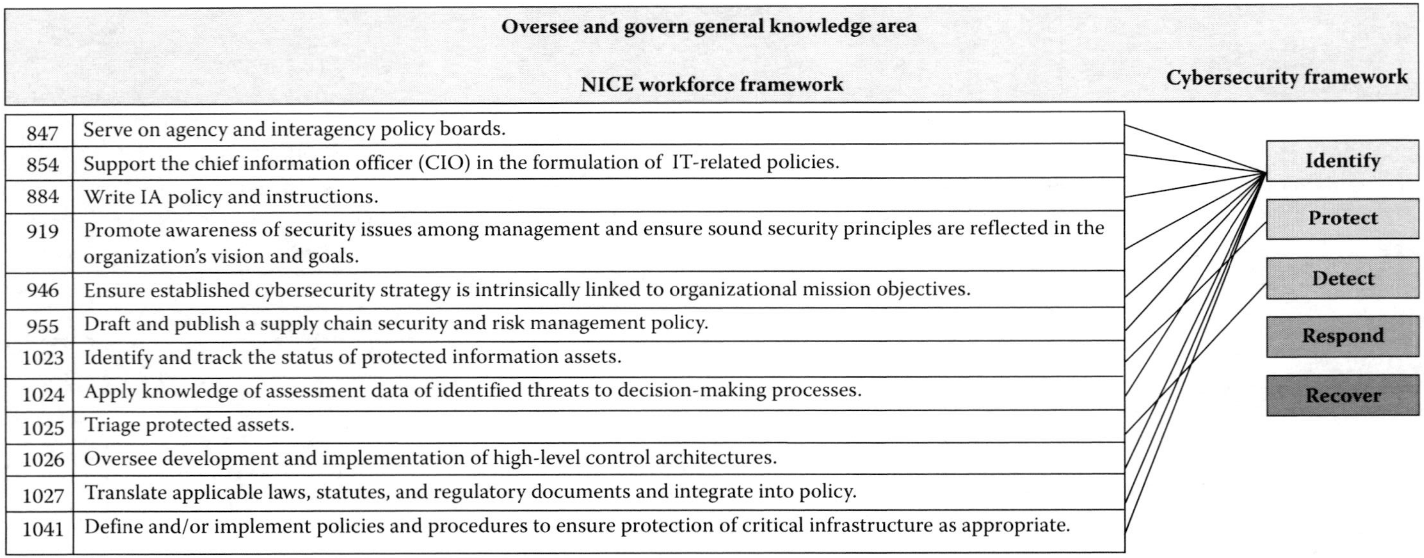

	Oversee and govern general knowledge area	Cybersecurity framework
	NICE workforce framework	Identify / Protect / Detect / Respond / Recover
847	Serve on agency and interagency policy boards.	
854	Support the chief information officer (CIO) in the formulation of IT-related policies.	
884	Write IA policy and instructions.	
919	Promote awareness of security issues among management and ensure sound security principles are reflected in the organization's vision and goals.	
946	Ensure established cybersecurity strategy is intrinsically linked to organizational mission objectives.	
955	Draft and publish a supply chain security and risk management policy.	
1023	Identify and track the status of protected information assets.	
1024	Apply knowledge of assessment data of identified threats to decision-making processes.	
1025	Triage protected assets.	
1026	Oversee development and implementation of high-level control architectures.	
1027	Translate applicable laws, statutes, and regulatory documents and integrate into policy.	
1041	Define and/or implement policies and procedures to ensure protection of critical infrastructure as appropriate.	

Figure 9.4 (Continued) Strategic planning specialty area tasks mapped to the CSF.

2. *Risk management*: Risk mitigation based on the organization's risk profile, acceptable levels of risk, understanding of risk exposure, and the potential impact/consequences of residual risk.
3. *Business process management/value delivery*: This includes the integration of all relevant IA processes and practices to maximize the effectiveness and efficiency of security activities.
4. *Resource management*: Efficient and effective use of IS knowledge and infrastructure to ensure knowledge is captured and available to develop and document security processes and practices.
5. *Performance management*: Develop a measurement process, aligned with strategic objectives, to aid in effective decision making. This includes continuous monitoring and reporting of IS processes and independent external assessments and audits.
6. *Integration*: Ensure that processes function as intended from end to end.

Roles and Responsibilities

IS governance requires strategic direction and commitment and as such members of the board need to be involved in setting and approving policy, appropriate resource allocation, and assigning responsibility for IS management. The organization's executive management team is then responsible for ensuring the needed infrastructure, resources, and organizational functions are made available to carry out the directives of the board and any governmental regulatory agency that is required. Often it is the legal and regulatory requirements that drive the efforts to achieve some level of compliance and is approached with the attitude of doing the absolute minimum necessary to save on expenses.

The level of visibility and involvement from senior managers sets the tone for compliance of the IS program within the organization. Without senior management buy-in and support for security activities, it can be difficult or nearly impossible to achieve the level of security required to adequately address and mitigate risks. IS managers are often outranked in the organizational structure and may run into resistance by higher-ranking individuals throughout the organization who may not have an incentive to support the security program. As such, executive awareness training by IT security managers may help in effectively communicating the security risks and benefits of an effective security governance to garner support for security activities. Many organizations have created the position of CISO and have given it the responsibility and authority over the full scope and breadth of IS activities. The CISO develops, oversees, and manages the IS program and initiatives to include strategic, personnel, infrastructure, policy enforcement, emergency planning, security training, and awareness. The CISO also leads the evaluation and assessment of the security program to ensure that all aspects are in compliance with security requirements.

Security affects all aspects of the organization and to be effective it must be pervasive throughout the organization. Ideally, IS will be managed in such a way as to create an organizational security culture. Many organizations form a steering committee to ensure all stakeholders' concerns are addressed and assist in the prioritization of initiatives that align with the business objectives. The participants of the steering committee are senior managers in both the operational and administrative functions within the organization. The benefits of gathering invaluable organizational intelligence from all areas such as HR, finance, legal, and marketing can help in identifying and mitigating current and potential risk. Another benefit is the wide dissemination of security-related information in order to aid in the continuous improvement of the security program.

An important function to ensure that organizations can substantiate adherence to the security policies is the role of audit executives. Auditors evaluate and report on the degree of alignment to the security policy, corporate risk management practices and results, efficiency of resource management, and report on the effectiveness of assurance processes performed by all areas of the organization.

Security Frameworks

Planning for IS is a demanding process due to the advent of Web-enabled technologies, outsourcing, distributed networking, and changes to embrace an open-business model. Managing and protecting the organization's information has become increasingly complex and the expectation to deliver secure IT solutions can be costly. Like any undertaking, strategic planning is enhanced by approaching it with a methodology that systematically addresses each challenge an organization may face. The scope and responsibilities of an IS program includes the following:

- Development of a security policy that includes agreed-upon levels of acceptable risk the organization is willing to tolerate and data collection philosophy that will drive digital forensics in the event of an incident.
- Conduct an annual evaluation of the security program and report out to the executive management and the board of directors.
- Development of a risk management plan to include risk identification, asset identification and value assessment, data classification and management, threat and vulnerability identification, risk assessment, and risk control strategies.
- Development of contingency planning to include a business impact analysis, incident response plan, disaster recovery plan, and a business continuity plan/business resumption plan.
- Conduct regular assessment of risks, threats, vulnerabilities, and business impact analysis.
- Establish a security management structure to assign roles, responsibilities, authority, and accountability.

- Develop and implement security controls and procedures based on risk assessment to secure information assets.
- Conduct periodic testing and evaluation of security procedures and controls
- Integration of IS into all organizational processes.
- Establish effective access control management for all users and providers of information.
- Extensive and regular implementation of security TEA.
- Conduct thorough and periodic testing of incident response plans, disaster recovery plan, business continuity, and resumption plan.
- Development of meaningful metrics to track progress and evaluate the effectiveness of the security program.

With so many areas to address, it is highly recommended that organizations think critically and adopt a security framework to provide a structure to guide them through the efforts to implement and maintain an effective security program. The use of a proven security framework can strengthen security posture and ensure required compliance with any governmental regulatory agencies. Several widely used security frameworks include ISO/IEC, NIST, Control Objectives for Information and Related Technology (COBIT), IT Infrastructure Library (ITIL), Committee of Sponsoring Organizations (COSO), CSF, Payment Card Industry Data Security Standard (PCI-DSS), and the SANS Institute.

ISO is an independent, nongovernmental membership organization and is the international standard that describes best practices for an IS management system. The latest version (ISO/IEC 27001:2013) was jointly published in 2013 with the IEC and focuses on measuring and evaluating how well the organization's security program is performing, adding a section on outsourcing and cloud computing.

NIST has created standards and controls for numerous disciplines most notably the Special Publication 800-53 *Security and Privacy Controls*. The SP 800-53 provides a catalog of security and privacy controls and a process for selecting controls to protect organizational operations, assets, and individuals from hostile cyberattacks, natural disasters, structural failures, and human errors.

The IT Governance Institute (ITGI) was formed by the ISACA as a nonprofit, independent research entity to advance international thinking on governance and management of enterprise IT. ITGI developed COBIT, the foremost internationally recognized framework for IT governance and control. COBIT 5 provides a comprehensive framework that focuses on program and management functions to guide organizations to effectively maximize IT investments.

Originally called the IT Infrastructure Library, the ITIL as it is now called, is organized around a service life cycle, which includes service strategy, service design, service transition, service operation, and continual service improvement. Updated in 2011, ITIL V3 can be adapted and used in conjunction with other frameworks such as COBIT and ISO 27000.

Five private accounting organizations created the COSO and funded the National Commission on Fraudulent Financial Reporting, also known as the Treadway Commission. COSO is credited with formalizing the concepts of internal control and framework. This framework emphasizes the importance of identifying and managing risks across the enterprise. COSO introduced application controls and general controls for IT to include IT management, infrastructure, security management, software acquisition, development, maintenance.

Executive Order 13636, entitled the framework for Improving Critical Infrastructure Cybersecurity (CSF), was created as a voluntary framework based on existing standards, guidelines, and practices for reducing cyber risks to critical infrastructure. The framework is a risk-based approach to applying the principles and best practices of risk management regardless of size, degree of cybersecurity risk, or the level of sophistication existing within the organization.

Originally five separate programs essentially working to accomplish the same thing, the PCI-DSS is an IS standard for organizations that use credit cards from the major card companies such as Visa, MasterCard, American Express, Discover, and Japan Credit Bureau (JCB). This standard of policies and procedures were created to protect cardholders against misuse of their personal information and secure credit, debit, and cash card transactions.

The SANS Institute was founded as a private research and education organization that specializes in training IS professionals on a variety of topics to include cyber and network defenses, incident response, digital forensics, penetration testing, and audit. The SANS Institute readily makes available numerous CIS security configuration benchmarks, assessment tools, and security metrics definitions. Although not a technically framework, they are well known for their top 20 list of critical security controls for effective cyber defense, which are updated and derived from the most common attack patterns and assessed by a broad community to include government, industry, and academia.

Resources to accomplish the initiatives set out in a security program are always limited. The effective use of a governance framework, coupled with a well-developed strategy, can be very beneficial in helping senior managers understand the need for the appropriate number resources to adequately implement and maintain a security program. Processes to assess resource allocation can ensure that those resources will be related to actual risks, impacts, and recovery efforts.

Often in organizations, the roles and responsibilities are not clearly defined. This lack of clarity and accountability can often create a culture of blame in which mistakes are not used to learn from but as a basis for punishments. Developing a culture of security necessitates creating an environment that supports sharing knowledge of incidents, dialoguing in after-action reviews of incident handling, and mobilizing the energies and abilities throughout the organization to create a learning organizational culture. The use of frameworks can be helpful in making the intent and expectations of management explicit, clearly defining the roles and responsibilities, and establishing processes to engage all stakeholders to construc-tively provide feedback and recommendations on performance.

Risk Management

A subset of a security program is risk management, which involves identifying and controlling the risks to an organization's information assets. Managers of every functional area are expected to actively participate in the development of a risk management plan. Often, the CISO will lead the initiative and form a team to include the risk/vulnerability auditor, IA manager, security control assessor, and systems analyst. More information about risk management will be covered in the section Specialty Area 6: Risk Management of this chapter.

Information Assurance Policy and Security Control Libraries

There are several tasks in the NICE workforce framework that refer to controls, policies, and procedures. They are as follows:

- Write IA policy and instructions.
- Assess policy needs and collaborate with stakeholders to develop policies to govern IT activities.
- Oversee development and implementation of high-level control architectures.
- Define and/or implement policies and procedures to ensure protection of critical infrastructure as appropriate.
- Monitor the rigorous application of IS/IA policies, principles, and practices in the delivery of planning and management services.

An enterprise IS/IA policy shapes the philosophy of IS within the organization. The philosophy is based on the mission, vision, and the organization's strategic plan and is developed with the purpose to define the strategic direction, scope, constraints, and applicability for all security initiatives. The enterprise policy defines the objectives/requirements to be met by the IS program and is reviewed with the stakeholders. Additionally, the enterprise policy document does not usually require continuous modification unless there is a change in the strategic mission of the organization.

After the overarching enterprise policy is completed, guidelines are needed to instruct employees, vendors, suppliers, and all other stakeholders on protecting organizational information assets. These issue-specific security guidelines/policies are referred to by a variety of names. Depending on which framework is used, the framework may refer to the individual controls as objectives, requirements, poli-cies, principles, procedures, and/or standards. For each framework, the developers have created and defined their own set of security control objectives/requirements based on best practices. For example, Table 9.2 shows the SANS Institute 20 Critical

Table 9.2 SANS Institute 20 Critical Security Controls Mapped to CSF, NIST, ISO, and PCI-DSS Framework Security Controls

Critical security control (SANS)		Description	CSF	NIST 800-53 Rev 4	ISO 27002: 2013	PCI DSS 3.0
1	Inventory of authorized and unauthorized devices	Actively manage all hardware, giving access to only authorized devices	ID.AM-1 ID.AM-3 PR.DS-3	CA-7, CM-8, IA-3, SA-4, SC-17, SI-4, PM-5	A.8.1.1 A.9.1.2 A.13.1.1	2.4
2	Inventory of authorized and unauthorized software	Actively manage all software so that only authorized software is installed and can execute	ID.AM-2 PR.DS-6	CA-7, CM-2, CM-8, CM-10, CM-11, SA-4, SC-18, SC-34, SI-4, PM-5	A.12.5.1 A.12.6.2	
3	Secure configurations for hardware and software	Establish, implement, and actively manage the security configuration of laptops, servers, and workstations	PR.IP-1	CA-7, CM-2, CM-3, CM-5-9, CM-11, MA-4, RA-5, SA-4, SC-14,34, SI-2, SI-4	A.14.2.4 A.14.2.8 A.18.2.3	2.2, 2.3. 6.2, 11.5
4	Continuous vulnerability assessment and remediation	Continuously acquire, assess, and take action on new information in order to identify vulnerabilities, remediate, and minimize	ID.RA-1,2 PR.IP-12 DE.CM-8 RS.MI-3	CA-2, CA-7, RA-5, SC-34, SI-4, SI-7	A.12.6.1 A.14.2.8	6.1, 6.2, 11.2

(Continued)

Table 9.2 (Continued)   SANS Institute 20 Critical Security Controls Mapped to CSF, NIST, ISO, and PCI-DSS Framework Security Controls

	Critical security control (SANS)	Description	CSF	NIST 800-53 Rev 4	ISO 27002: 2013	PCI DSS 3.0
5	Malware defenses	Control the installation, spread, and execution of malicious code at multiple points in the enterprise	PR.PT-2 DE.CM-4 DE.CM-5	CA-7, SC-39, SC-44, SI-3, SI-4, SI-8	A.8.3.1 A.12.2.1 A.13.2.3	5.1–5.4
6	Application software security	Manage the security lifecycle of all in-house developed and acquired software	PR.DS-7	SA-13, 15, 16, 17, 20, 21, SC-39, SI-10, 11, 15, 16	A.9.4.5 A.12.1.4 A.14.2.1 A.14.2.6-8	6.3, 6.5–6.7
7	Wireless access control	The processes and tools used to track, control, prevent, and correct the security use of wireless devices		AC-18, 19, CA-3, 7, CM-2, IA-3, SC-8, SC-17, SC-40, SI-4	A.10.1.1 A.12.4.1 A.12.7.1	4.3, 11.1

(Continued)

Table 9.2 (Continued) SANS Institute 20 Critical Security Controls Mapped to CSF, NIST, ISO, and PCI-DSS Framework Security Controls

Critical security control (SANS)	Description	CSF	NIST 800-53 Rev 4	ISO 27002: 2013	PCI DSS 3.0
8	Data recovery capability	The processes and tools used to properly back up critical information with a proven methodology for timely recovery	PR.IP-4	CP-9, CP-10, MP-4	A.10.1.1 A.12.3.1	4.3, 9.5–9.7
9	Security skills assessment and appropriate training to fill gaps	Identify the specific knowledge, skills, and abilities needed to support defense for all functional roles in the enterprise	PR.AT-1-5	AT-1-4, SA-11, 16, PM-13, 14, 16	A.7.2.2	12.6
10	Secure configurations for network devices	Establish, implement, and actively manage the security configuration of network infrastructure devices	PR.AC-5 PR.IP-1 PR.PT-4	AC-4, CA-3, 7, 9, CM-2, 3, 5, 6, 8, MA-4, SC-24, SI-4	A.9.1.2 A.13.1.1 A.13.1.3	1.1, 1.2, 2.2, 6.2

(Continued)

Table 9.2 (Continued) SANS Institute 20 Critical Security Controls Mapped to CSF, NIST, ISO, and PCI-DSS Framework Security Controls

	Critical security control (SANS)	Description	CSF	NIST 800-53 Rev 4	ISO 27002: 2013	PCI DSS 3.0
11	Limitation and control of network ports	Manage the ongoing operational use of ports, protocols, and services on networked devices	PR.AC-5 DE.AE-1	AC-4, CA-7, 9, CM-2, 6, 8, SC-20-22, SC-24, SI-4	A.9.1.2 A.13.1.1, 2 A.14.1.2	1.4
12	Controlled use of administrative privileges	The processes and tools used to tract, control, prevent, and correct the use, assignment, and configuration of administrative privileges	PR.AC-4 PR.AT-2 PR.MA-2 PR.PT-3	AC-2, 6, 17, 19, CA-7, IA-2, 4, 5, SI-4	A.9.1.1 A.9.2.2-6 A.9.3.1 A.9.4.1-4	2.1, 7.1-3, 8.1-3, 8.7
13	Boundary defense	Detect, protect, and correct the flow of information transferring networks of different trust levels	PR.AC-3 PR.AC-5 PR.MA-2 DE.AE-1	AC-4, 17, 20, CA-7, 9, CM-2, SA-9, SC-7, 8, SI-4	A.9.1.2, A.12.4.1 A.12.7.1 A.13.1.1, 3 A.13.2.3	1.1-3, 8.3, 10.8, 11.4

(Continued)

Table 9.2 (Continued) SANS Institute 20 Critical Security Controls Mapped to CSF, NIST, ISO, and PCI-DSS Framework Security Controls

Critical security control (SANS)		Description	CSF	NIST 800-53 Rev 4	ISO 27002: 2013	PCI DSS 3.0
14	Maintenance, monitoring, and analysis of audit logs	Collect, manage, and analyze audit logs that could help recover from an attack	PR.PT-1 DE.AE-3 DE.DP-1-5	AC-23, AU-2-14, CA-7, IA.10, SI-4	A.12.4.1-4 A.12.7.1	10.1-7
15	Controlled access based on the need to know	The processes and tools used to track, control, prevent, correct secure access to critical assets	PR.AC-4, 5 PR.DS-1, 2 PR.PT-2, 3	AC-1-3, AC-6 AC-24, CA-7, MP-3, RA-2, SC-16, SI-4	A.8.3.1 A.9.1.1 A.10.1.1	1.3, 4 4.3, 7.1-3, 8.7
16	Account monitoring and control	Actively manage the life-cycle of system and application accounts	PR.AC-1 PR.AC-4 PR.PT-3	AC-2, 3, 7, 11, 12 CA-7, IA-5, 10 SC-17, 23, SI-4	A.9.1.1 A.9.2.1-6 A.9.3.1 A.9.4.1-3 A.11.2.8	7.1-3, 8.7, 8
17	Data protection	The processes and tools used to prevent data exfiltration	PR.AC-5 PR.DS-2, 5 PR.PT-2	AC-3, 4, 23, CA-7, 9, IR-9, MP-5, SA-18, SC-8, 28, 31, 41, SI-4	A.8.3.1 A.10.1.1-2 A.13.2.3 A.18.1.5	3.6 4.1-3

(Continued)

Table 9.2 (Continued) SANS Institute 20 Critical Security Controls Mapped to CSF, NIST, ISO, and PCI-DSS Framework Security Controls

	Critical security control (SANS)	Description	CSF	NIST 800-53 Rev 4	ISO 27002: 2013	PCI DSS 3.0
18	Incident response and management	Protect the organization's information and reputation by developing and implementing an incident response infrastructure	PR.IP-10, DE.AE-2,4, 5, DE.CM-1-7, RS.RP- 1, RS.CO-1-5, RS.AN-1-4, RS.MI-1-2, RS.IM-1-2, RC.RP-1, RC.IM-1-2, RC.CO-1-3	IR-1-8, 10	A.6.1.3 A.7.2.1 A.16.1.2 A.16.1.4-7	12.10
19	Secure network engineering	Make security an inherent attribute of the enterprise	PR.AC-5	AC-4, CA-3,9, SA-8, SC-20-22, 32, 37	A.13.1.3 A.14.2.5	
20	Penetration tests and Red Team exercises	Test the overall strength of an organization's defenses		CA-2, 5, 6, 8 RA-6, SI-6, PM-6, 14	A.14.2.8 A.18.2.1, 3	11.3

Source: SANS Institute, Critical Security Controls for Effective Cyber Defense—Version 5, 2014. https://www.sans.org/media/critical-security-controls/fall-2014-poster.pdf.

Security Controls for Effective Cyber Defense mapped to the CSF; NIST SP 800-53, Rev 4; ISO 27002:2013; and PCI-DSS, Version 3.0 framework security controls.

As listed in the four columns from the right of the table, each framework has a different naming convention and numbering scheme for their security "controls." For example in the first row of the table, in the CSF, ID.AM-1 refers to the asset management category that is a part of the identify function. In the NIST SP 800-53 framework, CA-7 refers to the continuous monitoring control within the security assessment and authorization family of controls. In the ISO 27002:2013 framework, A.8.1.1 refers to the inventory of assets control under the asset management family of controls. And in the PCI-DSS framework, the 2.4 refers to the requirement to maintain an inventory of system components that are in the scope for PCI-DSS. This framework refers to their procedures as requirements as opposed to controls. There is no one correct set of security controls that address all organization security concerns in all situations.

The individual control policies and procedures are living documents that must be managed to be kept relevant and current. They must be properly distributed, read, understood, and agreed to that requires extensive TEA, which will be covered in more detail in specialty area 3.

Underlying Knowledge, Skill, and Ability Requirements for Strategic Planning and Policy Development Specialty Area

The author of the enterprise IS/IA policy, typically the CISO, must have knowledge of the organization's core business/mission processes and an understanding of the strategic management plan. This is fundamental information in order to craft the philosophy and map out the requirements for an effective IS program. Knowledge of applicable laws and governmental agency requirements are necessary to ensure compliance and to set a baseline of acceptable levels of organizational risk tolerance. An organization may consider to be at a low-, medium-, or high-risk baseline, which will determine how rigorous the IS program is designed and implemented. Selecting the most appropriate framework and set of controls for specific situations require the following KSAs:

- A thorough understanding of organizational mission, strategic direction, and objectives
- The strategy and business functions the information systems will support
- The environments of operation where the systems will reside
- Knowledge of specialized system requirements (e.g., critical infrastructure systems that may not use standard IT) for safety, performance, and reliability
- Knowledge of relevant laws, policies, procedures, or governance related to work impacting critical infrastructure

Knowledge of examining, documenting, and assessing the security posture of the organization to identify the risks as well as applying controls to mitigate the risks to the organization's information is all part of risk management and fundamental to the function of the CISO. Table 9.3 shows the KSAs for this area.

Specialty Area 3: Training, Education, and Awareness

The specialty area of TEA "develops plans, coordinates, delivers, and/or evaluates instructional cybersecurity content using various formats, techniques, and venues" (NIST, 2014). Everyone has a role in the success of a security training and awareness program; however, the IS trainer, security training coordinator, IT security program manager, and ultimately the CISO have key responsibilities to ensure that an effective training program is established and successfully maintained organization wide. The scope and content of the program must be in line with the organization's strategic direction, mission, and business objectives. The IT security program policy must be developed with clear requirements for a security training and awareness program. The scope of the training program will also require an understanding of the budget, resource allocation, organization size, and geographic dispersion of the employees.

The fundamental difference between education and training is that an educational experience has a formative effect on the way one thinks, feels, and behaves as a result of new knowledge. Training involves teaching with specific goals in mind of improving an individual's performance and productivity. It does not necessarily involve the encouragement of critical thinking, questioning extant theory, or developing new theories to add to the body of knowledge in a particular discipline. Often, training programs focus on a specialized area with the goal of developing and modifying behaviors to achieve a greater goal. Examples of focused training objectives include on-the-job training to be able to perform in a vocation, physical training to develop stamina to run a marathon, and military training to survive in combat. The aim of a comprehensive IT cybersecurity program should include elements of both training and education.

It is very challenging to protect the confidentiality, integrity, and availability of information in a highly networked system environment without ensuring that all individuals using and managing IT are involved. It is often stated that people are an organization's most important asset; however, the "people factor" happens to be the weakest link in the attempt to secure systems and infrastructure. All users must understand the organization's IT security policy, procedures, and practices. They also must understand their roles and responsibilities related to the organizational mission. All users must be able to demonstrate adequate knowledge of the various security controls/policies/standards that are required and published to protect the IT resources for which they are responsible. A robust and organizational-wide TEA program is critical to ensuring that people understand their IT security roles, responsibilities, and how to properly use and protect the IT resources entrusted to them.

Table 9.3 **Strategic Planning and Policy Development Specialty Area KSAs**

Item ID	KSA	Statement	Competency
19	KSA	Knowledge of cyber defense mitigation techniques and vulnerability assessment tools, including open source tools, and their capabilities.	Computer network defense
63	KSA	Knowledge of information assurance (1A) principles and organizational requirements to protect confidentiality, integrity, availability, authenticity, and nonrepudiation of information and data.	Information assurance
88	KSA	Knowledge of new and emerging information technology (IT) and cyber security technologies.	Technology awareness
105	KSA	Knowledge of system and application security threats and vulnerabilities (e.g., buffer overflow, mobile code, cross-site scripting, procedural language/structured query language [PL/SQL] and injections, race conditions, covert channel, replay, return-oriented attacks, malicious code).	Vulnerabilities assessment
244	KSA	Ability to determine the validity of technology trend data.	Technology awareness
282	KSA	Knowledge of emerging computer-based technology that has potential for exploitation by adversaries.	Technology awareness
297	KSA	Knowledge of key industry indicators that are useful for identifying technology trends.	Technology awareness
320	KSA	Knowledge of external organizations and academic institutions dealing with cybersecurity issues.	External awareness
336	KSA	Knowledge of the nature and function of the relevant information structure (e.g., National Information Infrastructure [NII]).	Telecommunications

(Continued)

Table 9.3 (Continued)   Strategic Planning and Policy Development Specialty Area KSAs

Item ID	KSA	Statement	Competency
377	KSA	Skill in tracking and analyzing technical and legal trends that will impact cyber activities.	Legal, government, and jurisprudence
942	KSA	Knowledge of the organization's core business/mission processes.	Organizational awareness
954	KSA	Knowledge of import/export control regulations and responsible agencies for the purposes of reducing supply chain risk.	Contracting/ procurement
1021	KSA	Knowledge of risk threat assessment.	Risk management
1022	KSA	Knowledge of the nature and function of the relevant information structure.	Enterprise architecture
1036	KSA	Knowledge of applicable laws (e.g, Electronic Communications Privacy Act, Foreign Intelligence Surveillance Act, Protect America Act, search and seizure laws, civil liberties and privacy laws), US Statutes (e.g., Titles 10,18, 32, 50 in US Code), Presidential Directives, executive branch guidelines, and/or administrative/criminal legal guidelines and procedures relevant to work performed.	Criminal law
1037	KSA	Knowledge of IT supply chain security and risk management policies, requirements, and procedures.	Risk management
1038	KSA	Knowledge of local specialized system requirements (e.g., critical infrastructure systems that may not use standard IT) for safety, performance, and reliability.	Infrastructure design
1040	KSA	Knowledge of relevant laws, policies, procedures, or governance related to work impacting critical infrastructure.	Criminal law
1141	KSA	Knowledge of an organization's information classification program and procedures for level information loss.	Information management

Factoring Training, Education, and Awareness Workforce Tasks into the Cybersecurity Framework Categories

Some of the most effective cyberattacks exploit user behavior. IT security TEA should focus on the entire user population of the organization to help reduce unintentional errors or failures. This includes on-site and telecommuting employees, visitors, guests, outsourcing partners, supply chain partners, procurement vendors, consultants, and any collaborators or associates requiring access. Access is not limited to IT systems but also includes physical access to any site in which an outsider may come in contact with printed or physical materials that encompass protected information.

The tasks for this specialty area can be organized into five distinct areas that build upon one another and should be conducted in the sequence as listed:

1. Conduct an organizational-wide needs assessment.
2. Develop a TEA strategic plan.
3. Develop course learning modules and course materials.
4. Develop an implementation plan.
5. Postimplementation evaluation, monitoring compliance, feedback, continuous improvement.

Each of these distinct areas is required to ensure that the TEA program is effective and sustainable. In order to achieve support and commitment of necessary resources, the overall program must be fully explained. This explanation should include the benefits to the organization, expected results of the program, and expectations of all stakeholders throughout the organization.

All tasks identified for this specialty area in the NICE framework map to the "protect" function of the CSF as shown below in Figure 9.5.

The IT security training and awareness program is designed to communicate security requirements across the entire organization and aimed at all levels including senior and executive managers. It is very important that senior and executive managers set the example for following the IT security program within the organization. Senior level managers and above who exempt themselves from following the same policies and practices as the rest of the organization undermine and can defeat an otherwise effective IT security program.

Accountability for adhering to the security TEA program must include sanctions imposed due to noncompliance. Sanctions must be fair and applied consistently at all levels of the organization in order for them to be relevant and just. Users should be first informed of the expectations before any sanctions are imposed.

Oversee and govern general knowledge area
Training, education, and awareness specialty area tasks

NICE workforce framework | Cybersecurity framework

	Identify	Protect	Detect	Respond	Recover

Code	Task					
453	Conduct interactive training exercises to create an effective learning environment.					
479	Correlate business or mission requirements to training.					
490	Deliver training courses tailored to the audience and physical environment.					
491	Demonstrate concepts, procedures, software, equipment, technology applications to coworkers, subordinates, or others.					
504	Design training curriculum and course content.					
510	Determine training requirements (e.g., subject matter, format, location).					
538	Develop new or identify existing awareness and training materials that are appropriate for intended audiences.					
551	Develop the goals and objectives for cybersecurity training, education, or awareness.					
567	Educate customers in established procedures and processes to ensure professional media standards are met.					
606	Evaluate the effectiveness and comprehensiveness of existing training programs.					
624	Guide employees through relevant development and training choices.					
778	Plan classroom techniques and formats (e.g., lectures, demonstrations, interactive exercises, multimedia presentations) for most effective learning environment.					
779	Plan nonclassroom educational techniques and formats (e.g., video courses, personal coaching, web-based courses).					
841	Review training documentation (e.g., course content documents [CCD], lesson plans, student texts, examinations, schedules of instruction [SOI], and course descriptions).					
842	Revise curriculum end course content based on feedback from previous training sessions.					
845	Serve as an internal consultant and advisor in own area of expertise (e.g, technical, copyright, print media, electronic media, cartography).					
855	Support the design and execution of exercise scenarios.					
885	Write instructional materials (e.g., standard operating procedures, production manual) to provide detailed guidance to relevant portion of the workforce.					
953	Coordinate with human resources to ensure job announcements are written to reflect required training, education, and/or experience.					

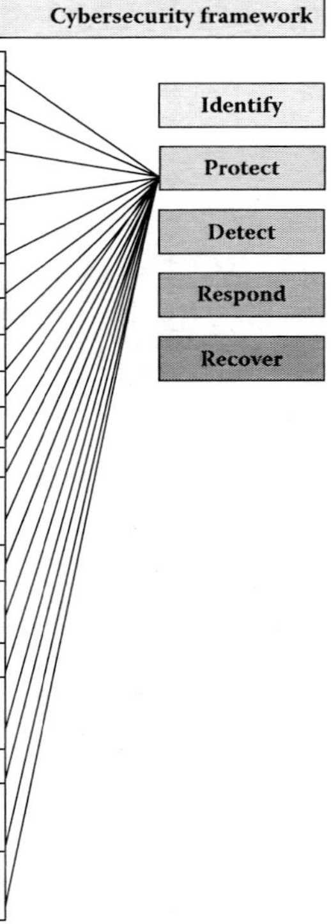

Figure 9.5   Training, education, and awareness specialty area tasks mapped to the CSF.

Awareness

Learning can be thought of as being on an incremental process along a continuum—it starts with awareness, builds into training, and evolves into education. Security awareness is not training and its purpose is to direct attention to security with the aim of reinforcing appropriate security practices or changing behavior. Security awareness involves reaching broad audiences with interesting, attention-getting facts to provide current security information. In the development of the materials, the broad question of "What behavior do we want to reinforce?" should be kept in mind so that the information conveyed will allow users to integrate the content into their everyday work environments. The message in which the security awareness material sends should be explained clearly enough so that there is no margin for misunderstanding or uncertainty.

Topics for security awareness training can be gleaned from internal audits, program reviews, self-assessments, and spot-checks. Ideally, developing materials so that security topics are weaved into personal life experiences such as identity theft, hacking of financial data, and unauthorized access to personal health records helps to reinforce the concepts and may prevent users from "tuning out" of mandatory security awareness sessions. Topics suitable for security awareness fact sheet materials and presentations are as follows:

- *Social engineering.* Sharing passwords, clicking on malicious e-mails, responding to baiting scenarios, introduction of malware via removable media.
- *Incident response.* "What do I do now?"
- *Web usage.* What is acceptable versus prohibited; monitoring of user activity?
- Unknown e-mail attachments.
- Password usage and management to include frequency of changes, creation, and protection (please, no sticky notes with your password attached to your monitor!).
- Bring your own device (BYOD) policy to include what happens if you lose your phone.
- Visitor control and physical access to work areas to include reporting any unusual activity and challenging strangers in the building or on the premise.
- Policy to include consequences for noncompliance.
- *Virus protection.* Updating definitions.
- *Individual accountability.* Communicate how the organization defines this.
- Protecting confidential information before it is destroyed (paper, archived, backups).
- Personal software and devices used on company systems—what is allowed.
- Portable device security and personal responsibility.

Training

Training is more involved than awareness initiatives and is designed to produce needed skills and competencies. The skills acquired in any given training session are built upon the foundation of awareness and should aim to first instill all users with knowledge of security basics. Training can be designed with differing levels such as beginning, intermediate, and advanced to target proficiencies and allow users to gain higher levels of knowledge and skills over time. Training can also include professional development through certification programs to ensure that users possess the required level of knowledge and competencies for their job roles. There is an increase in organizations desiring IT security professionals with certifications. By providing training for technical certifications focusing on security issues related to the specific platforms, operating systems, and software products used within the organization can not only boost employee competencies but help recruit high performers interested in keeping their skills current.

Education

To reach advanced levels of IT and cybersecurity professional positions, completion of formal education in the field is often required. Organizations who do not have the internal resources to develop IT security curriculum may want to consider partnering with a local university to meet their IT security needs. Advanced materials are available through centers of academic excellence with subject matter experts who develop and deliver the training course material. These programs are more characteristic of education than training in that the curriculum integrates several functional specialties into a common body of knowledge and aims to produce IT security specialists and professionals capable of proactive recommendations and adeptness in handling complex cyberattacks.

Security TEA programs must be designed in alignment with the organizational mission, business needs of the organization, and reflect the organization's culture and IT infrastructure. It is important for users to feel that the subject matter and issues presented are relevant to their own work environments.

Needs Assessment

Security training material should be developed based on the participant's position within the organization and the knowledge and security skills required for that position. For those individuals with significant IT security responsibilities, it is recommended to conduct a needs assessment in order to assess their functions and identify their training needs. The results of a needs assessment can be used to provide justification to allocation adequate resources to meet the identified TEA needs.

Techniques for conducting a needs assessment can include an analysis of new and emerging IT and cybersecurity technologies; review of current training programs; review of audit findings; review when changes to the technical infrastructure is made or new technology is adopted; interviews with key departments and functions; and survey instruments.

Training, Education, and Awareness Strategic Plan

Once a needs assessment has been completed and analyzed, the organization can begin to develop a strategy for developing, implementing, and maintaining its IT security awareness and training program. A comprehensive strategic plan should address and include the following:

- Scope of the TEA plan.
- Develop the goals and objectives for the IT security program.
- Roles and responsibilities for those individuals who will be providing day-to-day oversight and program maintenance of the design, development, distribution, course delivery, and maintenance of the material.
- Management of appropriate users to include defining the target audience for each learning module, what material is mandatory versus optional, how the completion of modules will be tracked and used in performance evaluations, and frequency in which each target audience should be provided and expected to complete the learning modules.
- Laws and policy requirements to ensure compliance with governmental regulatory agencies.
- Topics, user requirements, and learning objectives for each course module.
- Delivery methods and formats (classroom and non-classroom) for most effective learning environment.
- Assessment of learning and metrics to determine effectiveness of learning goals and objectives.
- Analysis of performance metrics as well as feedback from learning participants to improve any aspect of the learning modules and materials.

Once a needs assessment and a strategic plan have been completed, any gaps in the current training can be evaluated. Upon completion of a gap analysis, the IT security TEA course material can be developed.

Curriculum and Course Learning Module Development

Organizations must first identify the job functions, roles, and responsibilities for every area in the organization. It is important to also note the individuals who have significant IT and cybersecurity responsibilities within the organization. Due to their positions, these individuals can have the most significant impact, whether positive or negative, on the confidentiality, integrity, and/or availability of information. It is important that these individuals understand that cybersecurity is an integral part of their job and of the organizational expectations of their position.

Some job functions may have more technical responsibility and less management responsibility. Some job functions may have more acquisition-related responsibilities and fewer technical or management ones. And job functions may change over time as individuals assume more management, acquisition, and oversight responsibilities. Keeping the various responsibilities in mind, a flexible training program will need to be created.

Training is generally more structured and formal with the goal of building knowledge and skills to enrich job performance. Training and the development of course materials should focus on the skills and abilities necessary to support the job responsibilities of individuals throughout the organization. A good place to start is with foundational cybersecurity concepts and principles such as

- Intrusion detection and prevention systems (IDPS): network, host, and application based systems
- Intrusion techniques, types of intruders, and motivation
- Network infrastructure design and computer system security vulnerabilities
- Social engineering and its implications to cybersecurity
- Common attack mechanisms, their consequences, and motivation for use
- The technical underpinnings of cybersecurity and its terminology
- Security design principles and their role in limiting points of vulnerability
- Cryptographic algorithms and the different types
- Risk management and the risk posture of the organization
- Incident response and handling

Training can be developing using two different methodologies: topic based and role based. Topic-based training is generally developed for larger and diverse audiences who fill a number of different roles within the organization. These individuals will most likely have differing levels of competencies as well. Topic-based training must be carefully thought out so as to not be too general and deemed unhelpful yet provide enough details to be beneficial. Role-based training differs in that the recipient is trained to learn what s/he needs to know and implement based on their job role and function. The training may cover fewer topics in each module but is more specific and covers the topics in a far greater depth. The complexity of the learning materials should be commensurate with the job role and needs of the learner. For a complex issue such as cybersecurity training, role-based training is required to meet the competency needs of individuals with roles primarily focused on protecting information assets.

Course development best practices include

- Consider the delivery method and its impact on course design.
- Plan classroom educational techniques and formats (lectures, demonstrations, interactive exercises, multimedia presentations).

- Plan non-classroom educational techniques and formats (video courses, personal coaching, and online course offerings).
- Create individual modules for major topics.
- Plan the progression through each learning module and the order in which they should be taken.
- Provide an overview of the expected core skills to be learned for each module, this includes what participants can expect as they progress through the modules/material.
- Develop learning objectives that are in alignment to the organizational business objectives.
- Create individual lessons and assignments for each of the learning objectives.
- Integrate visual elements such as videos, narrated presentations, graphics, and other visual tools to reinforce important concepts.
- Create meaningful assessment tools to determine effectiveness and comprehensiveness of learning modules.

Implementation Plan

After all training course development is completed, an implementation plan includes the organization-wide communication of the TEA plan. This communication includes the benefits as well as the expected results of the program to the organization. Funding issues must all be address and all organizational departments must be informed as to if or how the cost of the training will impact their budgets.

Once the IT security program strategic plan has been communicated and accepted, the implementation can begin. There are a variety of ways that security awareness material and training can be disseminated throughout the organization. Dissemination techniques include

- Messages on awareness tools such as pens, bookmarks, coffee cups, clocks, and so on.
- Screensavers with warning banners/messages.
- Posters and signage.
- Inclusion in the new employee orientation materials; ensure job announcements are written to reflect required training, education, and/or experience.
- Newsletters.

Evaluating the Training, Education, and Awareness Program

Training is expensive and spending resources on training that does not achieve the desired outcomes can reinforce rather than dispel the perception of security as being an obstacle to productivity. Training is cost-effective and meaningful only when it meets the needs of both the participants and the organization. Therefore, evaluation is an essential component of an IT security training, education, and assessment program. It is critical to the evaluation process that the feedback obtained is looped back into the training material for continuous improvement. An example of the development of metrics to determine the effectiveness learning modules can include the measurement of the following:

- The value of the training delivered, compared with other options, to measure *program effectiveness*
- The pattern of individual behavior following a specific awareness initiative or training module to measure *teaching effectiveness*
- An assessment of what participants learned from an awareness initiative or specific course module to measure *learning objectives and effectiveness*

Evaluations can be difficult to quantify and may involve more than surveys to collect meaningful data. Participant evaluations and/or assessment tools are often used to solicit feedback and collect data to evaluate a variety of measures such as:

- A reduction in the gap analysis of current skills and abilities and training needs
- The quality of instructional design and course materials
- The quality of instructor performance and ability to clearly convey concepts and tools that enhance learning
- On-the-job performance of participants before and after completion of the learning modules
- Participant satisfaction and if they are able to apply the material to their jobs
- Completion rates and use statistics
- A reduction in incidents of human error or failure
- Levels of attendance to mandatory awareness and/or training initiatives
- Compliance and consistent practice of adherence to security controls by all levels in the organization

Underlying Knowledge, Skill, and Ability Requirements for Training, Education, and Awareness Specialty Area

The KSAs of the training, education, and assessment specialty area are targeted toward the job roles of cyber trainer, IS trainer, and the security training coordinator. Whether these individuals are internal or external to the organization, they are key players in an IT security TEA program. Table 9.4 shows the KSAs for this area.

Table 9.4 Training, Education, and Awareness Specialty Area KSAs

Item ID	KSA	Statement	Competency
19	KSA	Knowledge of cyber defense mitigation techniques and vulnerability assessment tools, including open source tools, and their capabilities.	Computer network defense
81	KSA	Knowledge of network protocols (e.g., Transmission Critical Protocol/Internet Protocol [TCP/IP], Dynamic Host Configuration Protocol [DHCP]), and directory services (e.g., Domain Name System [DNS]).	Infrastructure design
88	KSA	Knowledge of new and emerging information technology (IT) and cyber security technologies.	Technology awareness
90	KSA	Knowledge of operating systems.	Operating systems
246	KSA	Knowledge and experience in the Instructional system design (ISD) methodology.	Multimedia technologies
252	KSA	Knowledge of and experience in insider threat investigations, reporting, investigative tools and laws/regulations.	Computer network defense
264	KSA	Knowledge of basic physical computer components and architectures, including the functions of various components and peripherals (e.g., central processing units [CPUs], network interface cards [NICs], data storage).	Computers and electronics
282	KSA	Knowledge of emerging computer-based technology that has potential for exploitation by adversaries.	Technology awareness
314	KSA	Knowledge of multiple cognitive domains and appropriate tools and methods for learning in each domain.	Teaching others

(Continued)

Table 9.4 (Continued) Training, Education, and Awareness Specialty Area KSAs

Item ID	KSA	Statement	Competency
332	KSA	Ability to develop curriculum that speaks to the topic at the appropriate level for the target audience.	Teaching others
344	KSA	Knowledge of virtualization technologies and virtual machine development and maintenance.	Operating systems
359	KSA	Skill in developing and executing technical training programs and curricula.	Computer forensics
363	KSA	Skill in identifying gaps in technical capabilities.	Teaching others
376	KSA	Skill in talking to others to convey information effectively.	Oral communication
918	KSA	Ability to prepare and deliver education and awareness briefings to ensure that systems, network, and data users are aware of and adhere to systems security policies and procedures.	Teaching others
942	KSA	Knowledge of the organization's core business/mission processes.	Organizational awareness
952	KSA	Knowledge of emerging security issues, risks, and vulnerabilities.	Technology awareness
1072	KSA	Knowledge of network security architecture concepts, including topology, protocols, components, and principles (e.g., application of defense-in-depth).	Information systems/ network security
1141	KSA	Knowledge of an organization's information classification program and procedures for level information loss.	Information management

The majority of the KSA requirements for the TEA specialty area can be arranged into four distinct competency areas of application.

1. *Organizational awareness*: Knowledge of the organization's core business and mission process are instrumental in developing awareness and training materials that are in alignment with the organization's business objectives.
2. *Technology awareness*: Knowledge of emerging security issues, risks, and vulnerabilities are instrumental in the creation of the strategic plan.
3. *Computer network defense, information systems/network security*: Knowledge of cyber defense mitigation techniques, vulnerability assessment tools, experience in threat investigations, laws/regulations, reporting, and network security architecture concepts will provide expert knowledge for the development of relevant and current learning modules.
4. *Teaching others and oral communication*: Knowledge of multiple cognitive domains, appropriate tools and methods for learning, curriculum development, and skill in talking with others to convey information effectively are instrument in the development, maintenance, and effectiveness of the IT security program.

All of these competencies are required in order to ensure that the process of developing, communicating, delivering, and evaluating an effective IT security program is both effective and sustainable.

Specialty Area 4: Information Systems and Security Operations

The specialty area of information systems and security operations "oversees and ensures that the appropriate operational security posture (e.g., network and system security, physical and environmental protection, personnel security, incident handling, security training and awareness) is implemented and maintained for an information system or program. Advises the Authorizing Official (AO), an information system owner, or the Chief Information Security Officer (CISO) on the security of an information system or program" (NIST, 2014). With the ever increasing demand for IT services, the growing complexity in the design of networks and infrastructure, and a constantly changing security threat environment, IT security has become a mission critical function. As mentioned previously, an IT security program is an essential component of IT security governance and without an operational plan, the organization has no understanding of the risks they may face or rules to enforce. An effective IT operational security plan identifies, controls, and mitigates threats and risks to its information and IT systems. An effective IT security operational plan includes the following:

■ A risk assessment that identifies the organization's assets, the threats and vulnerabilities of those assets, and the magnitude of impact that could result from unauthorized access, use, disruption, modification or destruction of information systems.

- Determine the level of risk that is acceptable to meet the business objectives and comply with all governmental regulatory agencies while controlling for costs.
- Establish boundaries to determine the scope of protection for organization-wide information systems.
- Develop a classification scheme to identify the systems in the inventory that are considered mission critical, essential, or general support systems.
- Identify, define, develop, and implement the applicable security controls to ensure protection of critical infrastructure as appropriate.
- Determine adequate resources allocations required to securely operate and maintain the organization's IA requirements.
- Conduct periodic testing and evaluation of the effectiveness of the IT security controls, policies, procedures, and practices based on risk level tolerance.
- Develop a plan for remedial actions to address any deficiencies in the IT security controls, policies, procedures, and practices of the organization.
- Collect and maintain data needed to meet system IA reporting.

Factoring Information Systems and Security Operations Workforce Tasks into the Cybersecurity Framework Categories

As shown in Figure 9.6, there are 21 tasks in the information systems and security operations specialty area and are mapped to the following 3 functions of the CSF:

1. Tasks that involve participation in the IT security risk assessment; participation in the identification, development or modification of security program plans and requirements; the preparation, distribution of maintenance plans, instructions, guidance, and standard operating procedures concerning the security of network system operations; ensuring plans of actions or remediation plans are in place; and support necessary compliance activities are mapped to the "identify" function (risk assessment category) of the CSF.
2. Tasks that involve collecting and maintaining data; creating and evaluating a baseline configuration; communicating changes in the security posture; integrating requirements into the planning; coordinating inspections, tests, and reviews of the network environment; preparing, distributing, and maintaining plans, and so on are mapped to the "protect" function (information protection processes and procedures category) of the CSF.
3. Tasks that involve recognizing possible security violations and taking appropriate action and managing protective measures when an incident or vulnerability is discovered are mapped to the "detect" function (security continuous monitoring category) of the CSF.

Oversee and govern general knowledge area

Information systems and security operations specialty area tasks

NICE workforce framework	Cybersecurity framework
	Identify · Protect · Detect · Respond · Recover
397	Advise appropriate senior leadership or authorizing official of charges affecting the organization's information assurance (IA) posture.
440	Collect and maintain data needed to meet system IA reporting.
584	Ensure that IA inspections, tests, and reviews are coordinated for the network environment.
585	Ensure that IA requirements are integrated into the continuity planning for that system and/or organization(s).
590	Ensure that protection and detection capabilities are acquired or developed using the information system security engineering approach and are consistent with organization-level IA architecture.
598	Evaluate and approve development efforts to ensure that baseline security safeguards are appropriately installed.
600	Evaluate cost-benefit, economic, and risk analysis in decision-making process.
731	Participate in information security risk assessment during the security assessment and authorization (SA&A) process.
733	Participate in the development or modification of the computer environment IA security program plans and requirements.
790	Prepare, distribute, and maintain plans, instructions, guidance, and standard operating procedures concerning the security of network system(s) operations.

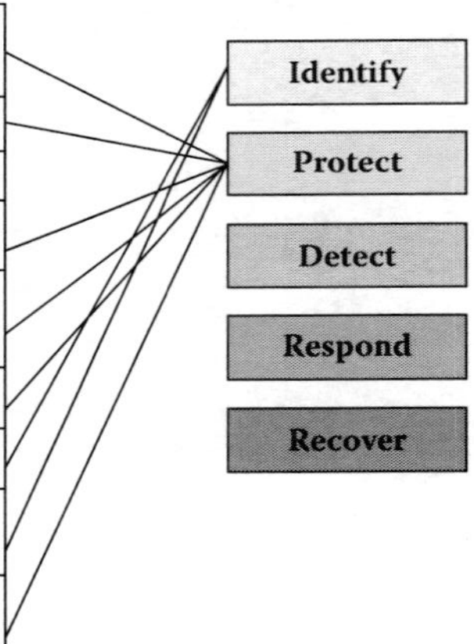

Figure 9.6 Information systems and security operations specialty area mapped to the CSF. *(Continued)*

Oversee and govern general knowledge area

NICE workforce framework	
816	Provide system related input on IA security requirements to be included in statements of work and other appropriate procurement documents.
824	Recognize a possible security violation and take appropriate action to report the incident, as required.
828	Recommend resource allocations required to securely operate and maintain an organization's IA requirements.
852	Supervise or manage protective or corrective measures when an IA incident or vulnerability is discovered.
869	Use federal and organization-specific published documents to manage operations of their computing environment system(s).
962	Identify security requirements specific to an information technology IT system in all phases of the system lifecycle.
963	Ensure plans of actions and milestones or remediation plans are in place for vulnerabilities identified during risk assessments, audits, inspections, and so on.
964	Assure successful implementation and functionality of security requirements and appropriate IT policies and procedures consistent with the organization's mission and goals.
1016	Support necessary compliance activities (e.g., ensure system security configuration guidelines are followed; compliance monitoring occurs).
1017	Participate in the acquisition process as necessary, following appropriate supply chain risk-management practices.
1041	Define and/or implement policies and procedures to ensure protection of critical infrastructure as appropriate.

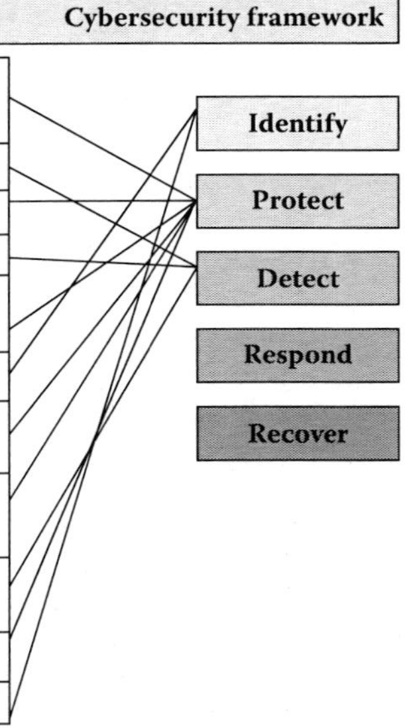

Figure 9.6 (Continued) Information systems and security operations specialty area mapped to the CSF.

Risk Assessment

An effective risk management process requires organizations to plan and deal with risk proactively, identify risk events, develop strategies to deal with them, and then handle them when they arise. Risk assessment activities are a subset of the overall risk management process and are designed to facilitate decision making at all levels of the organization. Risk assessments are not a one-time activity but require ongoing evaluation and change as part of a system development life cycle. Risk assessment activities include the following:

- Identification of potential threat sources and threat events to organizational IT systems and the environments in which they operate
- Identification of vulnerabilities to organizational IT systems and environments in which they operate that may be subject to exploitation
- Identification and estimation of the potential consequences and/or impact if the threats are successful in exploiting any vulnerability
- An estimation of the likelihood that the identified threats are successful in exploiting any vulnerability
- A determination of risk to the operations of the organization (mission, functions, reputation)
- A determination of risk to organization assets, individuals, strategic partners, and so on

Organizations have significant flexibility on how risk assessments are conducted; however, there are risk management life cycles and processes established and available to guide organizations through the process. More information about risk management will be discussed in the sixth specialty area in this chapter.

Risk Tolerance

Management and the board of directors must make informed choices in setting the level of risk they are willing to tolerate or withstand. In an effort to establish organizational risk tolerance levels, a risk assessment identifies the kinds and levels of risk to which the organization may be exposed. The risk assessment also considers both the likelihood and impact of successful breaches. Depending on situations or conditions, organizations can determine their risk tolerance using a low-impact, moderate-impact, or high-impact approach:

- *Low impact.* The unauthorized disclosure of information, destruction of information, or disruption of access that is expected to have a *limited* adverse effect on organizational operations, assets, or individuals. This level of impact may cause only minor financial loss and required only administrative action for correction.

- *Moderate impact.* The unauthorized disclosure of information, destruction of information, or disruption of access that is expected to have a *serious* adverse effect on organizational operations, assets, or individuals. This may include significant financial loss and may require legal action for correction.
- *High impact.* The unauthorized disclosure of information, destruction of information, or disruption of access that is expected to have a *severe or catastrophic* adverse effect on organizational operations, assets, or individuals. This may include major financial loss and require legal action such as imprisonment for correction.

Organizations typically make determinations regarding the level of acceptable risk and the types of acceptable risk taking into consideration their mission, business objectives, priorities, alternatives, and cost. When an identified risk falls within established risk tolerance levels, organizations can then respond (accept, avoid, mitigate, share the risk, transfer the risk, or a combined effort).

Establish Organization Boundaries

One of the most challenging issues for decision makers is identifying appropriate boundaries for organization-wide information systems. Well-defined boundaries establish the scope of what the organization decides and approves to protect to include the systems, technologies, processes, and people that support the organization's mission and business objectives. Before the operational security plan can be developed, the boundaries of information systems and the security classification scheme must be completed. Careful thought must be made to the information system boundaries in that if they are too expansive to include too many system components, it will make the risk management process unwieldy and unnecessarily complex. Boundaries that are too limited unnecessarily increase the amount of information systems that must be managed separately and will drive up the overall costs of providing security.

System Security Classification

Before the security controls can be identified and selected, the business criticality of the information systems that are within the boundaries or scope of what will be protected, must be determined. Mission or business criticality can be defined using the following groupings:

1. *Mission critical*: These are systems, applications, or information resources that if they were to fail, would prevent the organization from accomplishing its core business functions. Mission critical systems may cause immediate business failure if they become compromised and/or become unavailable.

2. *Essential*: Failure of these systems, applications, or information resources would not prevent the organization from accomplishing its core business functions in the short term, but if not resolved within a 4-week window, may negatively impact the business.
3. *Supportive*: Failure of these systems, applications, or information resources may not cause the organization from continuing its core business functions; however, reduced effectiveness of the day-to-day operations would result.

For each system, application, or information resource, it is helpful to identify the system owner, information owner, system users, and who is responsible for managing the resource. Those individuals who are identified as responsible for implementing and managing these resources must participate in addressing the security controls to be applied to their systems.

Security Controls

The purpose of the IT operational security plan is to document the security requirements of the organization and to describe the countermeasures that will be implemented to address those requirements. Complex and evolving technical environments require organizations to adopt a minimum set of security controls to protect their information and IT systems. Security controls are the countermeasures developed and implemented to protect the confidentiality, integrity, and available of IT systems and its information. In the event of a loss of confidentiality, integrity, or availability, the security controls applied to any given information system should be commensurate with the potential impact on the organization-wide assets, operations, and processes.

As noted previously in the specialty area 2, there are several security control libraries which can be adapted for any IT environment. One example of a comprehensive security control library is the NIST SP 800-53 Revision 4 (NIST, 2013). NIST organizes the security controls into *classes* and *families*. The three general classes of security controls are management, operational, and technical. Management controls focus on the management of risk for a system, operational controls address security methods focusing on mechanisms implemented by individuals, and technical controls focus on security controls that are automated and executed by computer systems (NIST, 2013). Table 9.5 shows the 17 NIST SP 800-53 Revision 4 security control families, the classes they belong to, and the 2-digit unique identifier assigned to each control family.

Within each security control family, there are several controls that are related to the security functionality of that family. An example of one security control family (access control in the technical class) with the related security controls for that family is shown in Table 9.6. There are 20 specific controls that are all related to the access control family. For each control, a separate policy document is created

Table 9.5 NIST SP 800-53 Revision 4, Security Control Classes, Families, and Unique Identifiers

Security control class		Security control family	Identifier
1	Management	Certification, accreditation, and security assessments	CA
2	Management	Planning	PL
3	Management	Risk assessment	RA
4	Management	System and services acquisition	SA
5	Operational	Awareness and training	AT
6	Operational	Configuration management	CM
7	Operational	Contingency planning	CP
8	Operational	Incident response	IR
9	Operational	Maintenance	MA
10	Operational	Media protection	MP
11	Operational	Physical and environmental protection	PE
12	Operational	Personnel security	PS
13	Operational	System and information integrity	SI
14	Technical	Access control	AC
15	Technical	Audit and accountability	AU
16	Technical	Identification and authentication	IA
17	Technical	System and communications protection	SC

that provides the details of the control to include, at a minimum, the date created, author, effective date, revision date, policy description, roles and responsibilities, detailed procedures, and who the control applies to.

The individual security control documents are essential for the implementation of the IT operational security plan. They can be used in training and awareness initiatives as well as new employee orientation to ensure that all individuals have access to the appropriate controls, fully read them, and understood the policy, procedures, and consequences of noncompliance. This becomes critical in the event of legal disputes over termination due to policy noncompliance or more significant breaches that result in loss of shareholder value and reputation.

Table 9.6   NIST SP 800-53 Revision 4, Specific Controls Under the Access Control Family of Controls in the Technical Class

Security control number		Access control
1	AC-1	Access control policy and procedures
2	AC-2	Account management
3	AC-3	Access enforcement
4	AC-4	Information flow enforcement
5	AC-5	Separation of duties
6	AC-6	Least privilege
7	AC-7	Unsuccessful login attempts
8	AC-8	System use notification
9	AC-9	Previous logon notification
10	AC-10	Concurrent session control
11	AC-11	Session lock
12	AC-12	Session termination
13	AC-13	Supervision and review—Access control
14	AC-14	Permitted actions without identification or authentication
15	AC-15	Automated marking
16	AC-16	Automated labeling
17	AC-17	Remote access
18	AC-18	Wireless access restrictions
19	AC-19	Access control for portable and mobile devices
20	AC-20	Use of external information systems

Evaluation and Continuous Monitoring

As with any plan, whether it is a disaster recovery, business continuity, or the IT operational security plan, if the plan components are not tested and evaluated, the organization essentially has no plan in place. All implemented security controls must be regularly assessed for effectiveness and it is recommended to implement continuous monitoring mechanisms to collect data at discrete intervals for timely, relevant, and accurate assessments. Newly implemented security controls should be validated and tested to ensure that organization-wide operations remain within acceptable risk levels. Continuous monitoring of implemented security controls can be automated to include support tools such as vulnerability scanning tools and network scanning devices. These tools can make the process of continuous monitoring more efficient and cost-effective. Manual processes for continuous monitoring should be repeatable and verifiable to ensure consistent implementation of the security controls.

Underlying Knowledge, Skill, and Ability Requirements for Information Systems and Security Operations Specialty Area

There is a wide range of competencies and knowledge required to effectively develop, implement, and manage an IT operational security plan. This plan is fundamental to the operations of the organization and requires commitment to appropriately fund and staff members within the organization who are capable of carrying out the requirements. The necessary skills and knowledge for this specialty area can be logically grouped into the following:

1. *Organizational awareness, business processes, and operations*: The CO, IA manager, or IS manager must have a thorough knowledge of the operations and business processes of the organization. This key role requires knowledge of the organization's IT goals and objectives as well as a system life cycle management principles to include software security and usability. The organization of an effective IT operational security plan can be organized around a system life cycle process. Additional knowledge required at this level of the organization is the ability to determine how a security system should work to include its resilience and dependability capabilities, and how changes in the operations and environment will impact the outcomes.

2. *Risk management requirements*: Risk management is a critical functional component of the IT operational security plan and knowledge of all areas of risk management is required. This includes knowledge of applicable laws, strategic goals and objectives, priorities and resource availability, supply chain considerations in order to categorize the information systems. Knowledge of current and emerging threats and structured analysis principles are required to conduct a risk assessment. The ability to communicate and articulate the results of the risk assessment to senior management is required in order to collectively determine the risk tolerance levels for the organization.

3. *Emerging IT and cybersecurity technologies*: Technical knowledge of server administration, operating systems, and critical infrastructure systems is required to understand how to create the boundaries of what will be in scope

as well as creating and ensuring the technical security control policy and procedures are accurate and valid.

4. *Security controls, policies, procedures*: The security control policy and procedure documents are at the heart of an IT operational security plan and knowledge of organizational design standards and frameworks are essential. Attention to detail is a critical skill in creating policies that reflect the system security objectives. Knowledge of relevant laws and governance related to work impacting the critical infrastructure is also required to ensure security controls are created to address mandatory governmental regulatory conformance.

5. *Performance monitoring*: In order to ensure the countermeasures are adequate to support the organizational risk tolerance, knowledge of network systems management principles, models, methods to conduct end-to-end performance monitoring, and all applicable tools are required. Once the plan is operational, it is important to periodically assess the plan; review any changes in system status, functionality or design; and ensure that the plan continues to accurately reflect the right information.

Table 9.7 displays the entire set of general and specialty KSAs for the information systems and security operations specialty area.

Specialty Area 5: Security Program Management

The specialty area for security program management "oversees and manages security program implementation with the organization or other area of responsibility. Manages strategy, personnel, infrastructure, policy enforcement, emergency planning, security awareness, and/or other resources" (NIST, 2014). The group of individuals responsible for planning, designing, implementing, assessing, and monitoring the IT operational security plan typically report to the CISO. It is the CISO's responsibility to organize, evaluate, lead, and oversee a solid IT security program and that everyone in the organization understands their role in all cybersecurity efforts. Much of what the CISO does can be likened to that of a coach. As a coach, the CISO must develop and employ a playbook of strategies. These security strategies must abide by the rules and regulations of the industry and any governmental agencies and must be kept safeguarded and shielded from the organization's opponents.

To successfully execute the elements of the IT security program, the entire organization must be trained to work together and know what is expected. Everyone needs to know the mission and how to consistently execute the plans and procedures that are applicable to their role within the organization. Failure to train and educate the team will produce confusion and noncompliance. To prevent each player from formulating and playing by their own rules, it is critical that everyone knows the consequences for nonconformance. Even if only one player compromises the security of the organization, the entire team loses. And the cost of significant

Table 9.7 **Information Systems and Security Operations KSAs**

Item ID	KSA	Statement	Competency
9	KSA	Knowledge of applicable business processes and operations of customer organizations.	Requirements analysis
37	KSA	Knowledge of disaster recovery and continuity of operations plans.	Incident management
55	KSA	Knowledge of Information assurance (IA) principles used to manage risks related to the use, processing, storage, and transmission of information or data.	Information assurance
58	KSA	Knowledge of known vulnerabilities from alerts, advisories, errata, and bulletins.	Information systems/ network security
62	KSA	Knowledge of industry-standard and organizationally accepted analysis principles and methods.	Logical systems design
69	KSA	Knowledge of risk management framework (RMF) requirements.	Information systems security certification
76	KSA	Knowledge of measures or indicators of system performance and availability.	Information technology performance assessment
77	KSA	Knowledge of current industry methods for evaluating, implementing, and disseminating information technology (IT) security assessment, monitoring, detection, and remediation tools and procedures, utilizing standards-based concepts, and capabilities.	Information systems/ network security
88	KSA	Knowledge of new and emerging IT and cyber security technologies.	Technology awareness
112	KSA	Knowledge of server administration and systems engineering theories, concepts, and methods.	Systems life cycle

(Continued)

Table 9.7 (Continued) Information Systems and Security Operations KSAs.

Item ID	KSA	Statement	Competency
113	KSA	Knowledge of server and client operating systems.	Operating systems
121	KSA	Knowledge of structured analysis principles and methods.	Logical systems design
126	KSA	Knowledge of system software and organizational design standards, policies, and authorized approaches (e.g., International Organization for Standardization [ISO] guidelines) relating to system design.	Requirements analysis
129	KSA	Knowledge of system life cycle management principles, including software security and usability.	Systems life cycle
143	KSA	Knowledge of the organization's enterprise IT goals and objectives.	Enterprise architecture
173	KSA	Skill in creating policies that reflect system security objectives.	Information systems security certification
183	KSA	Skill in determining how a security system should work, including its resilience and dependability capabilities, and how changes in conditions, operations, or the environment will affect these outcomes.	Information assurance
325	KSA	Knowledge of secure acquisitions (e.g., relevant Contracting Officer's Technical Representative [COTR] duties, secure procurement, supply chain risk management).	Contracting/procurement
965	KSA	Knowledge of organization's risk tolerance and/or risk management approach.	Risk management
966	KSA	Knowledge of enterprise incident response program, roles, and responsibilities.	Incident management
967	KSA	Knowledge of current and emerging threats/threat vectors.	Information systems/network security

(Continued)

Table 9.7 (Continued) Information Systems and Security Operations KSAs.

Item ID	KSA	Statement	Competency
1004	KSA	Knowledge of critical IT procurement requirements.	Contracting/procurement
1034	KSA	Knowledge of personally identifiable information (PII) and payment card industry (PCI) data security standards.	Security
1036	KSA	Knowledge of applicable laws (e.g., Electronic Communications Privacy Act, Foreign Intelligence Surveillance Act, Protect America Act, search and seizure laws, civil liberties and privacy laws), US Statutes (e.g., Titles 10,18, 32, 50 in US Code), Presidential Directives, executive branch guidelines, and/or administrative/criminal legal guidelines and procedures relevant to work performed.	Criminal law
1037	KSA	Knowledge of IT supply chain security and risk management policies, requirements, and procedures.	Risk management
1038	KSA	Knowledge of local specialized system requirements (e.g., critical infrastructure systems that may not use standard IT) for safety, performance, and reliability).	Infrastructure design
1039	KSA	Skill in evaluating the trustworthiness of the supplier and/or product.	Contracting/procurement
1040	KSA	Knowledge of relevant laws, policies, procedures, or governance related to work impacting critical infrastructure.	Criminal law
1072	KSA	Knowledge of network security architecture concepts, including topology, protocols, components, and principles (e.g., application of defense-in-depth).	Information systems/network security
1073	KSA	Knowledge of network systems management principles, models, methods (e.g., end-to-end systems performance monitoring), and tools.	Network management

security breaches is not just financial—reputations, careers, and future opportunities may all end up permanently "on the bench."

Factoring Security Program Management Workforce Tasks into the Cybersecurity Framework Categories

As shown in Figure 9.7, there are 35 tasks in the security program management specialty area and are mapped to the following 4 functions of the CSF.

1. Tasks that involve the evaluation of cost–benefit, economic, and risk analyses in the decision-making process; identification of alternative IT security strategies; the identification of implications of new technologies or technology upgrades; the interpretation and approval of security requirements; the management of alignment of IT security priorities with the organization's security strategy are mapped to the identify function (business environment, governance, risk management strategy categories) of the CSF.

2. Tasks that involve acquiring and managing resources to include leadership support, financial resources, and key security personnel to reduce overall organizational risk; acquire the necessary resources to conduct an effective enterprise continuity of operations program; advise senior management on risk levels, security posture, and cost–benefit analysis of the IT security program; communicate the value of the IT security program throughout the organization; collaborate with organizational managers to support the objectives and establish the continuity of operations program, strategy and mission assurance; ensuring that security improvement actions are evaluated, valuated, and implemented, establish the overall IS architecture in alignment with the IT security strategy; oversee the security training and awareness program; and provide leadership and direction to IT personnel are mapped to the "protect" function (awareness and training, information protection processes and procedures categories) of the CSF.

3. Tasks that involve managing and monitoring of IT data sources to maintain organization situational awareness; managing threat or target analysis of an adversary's cyber activity information and production of enterprise threat information; and monitoring and evaluating the effectiveness of the enterprise's IT security safeguards to ensure they provide the intended level of protection are mapped to the "detect" function (security continuous monitoring category) of the CSF.

4. Tasks that involve providing technical documents, incident reports, findings from computer examinations, summaries, and other situational awareness information; recommend policy and coordinate review and approval; and track audit findings and recommendations to ensure appropriate mitigation actions are taken are mapped to the "respond" function (communications, analysis, and improvements categories) of the CSF.

Oversee and govern general knowledge area
Security program management specialty area tasks
NICE workforce framework

Cybersecurity framework

| Identify | Protect | Detect | Respond | Recover |

#	Task
391	Acquire and manage the necessary resources, including leadership support, financial resources, and key security personnel, to support information technology (IT) security goals, and reduce overall organizational risk.
392	Acquire necessary resources, including financial resources, to conduct an effective enterprise continuity of operations program.
395	Advise senior management (e.g., chief information officer [CIO]) on risk levels and security posture.
396	Advise senior management e.g., [CIO] , on cost-benefit analysis of information security programs, policies, processes, systems, and elements.
445	Communicate the value of IT security throughout all levels of the organization's stakeholders.
473	Collaborate with organizational managers to support organizational objectives.
475	Collaborate with stakeholders to establish the enterprise continuity of operations program, strategy, and mission assurance.
578	Ensure security improvement actions are evaluated, validated, and implemented as required.
596	Establish overall enterprise information security architecture (EISA) with the organization's overall security strategy.
600	Evaluate cost-benefit, economic, and risk analysis in decision-making process.
628	Identify alternative information security strategies to address organizational security objective.
640	IT security program implications of new technologies or technology upgrades.
674	Interface and disseminate necessary cyber event information to appropriate external organizations and audiences.
676	Interpret and/or approve security requirements relative to the capabilities of new information technologies.
677	Interpret patterns of non-compliance to determine their impact on the enterprise's levels of risk and/or the information assurance (IA) program's overall effectiveness.
679	Manage alignment of IT security priorities with the organization's security strategy.
680	Lead and oversee information security budget, staffing, and contracting.
705	Manage the monitoring of information security data sources to maintain organizational situational awareness.

Figure 9.7 **Security program management specialty area tasks mapped to the CSF.** *(Continued)*

	Oversee and govern general knowledge area	Cybersecurity framework
	NICE workforce framework	Identify / Protect / Detect / Respond / Recover
706	Publish cyber defense techniques and guidance (e.g., Time Compliance Network Orders [TCNOs], concept of operations, net analyst reports) for the organization.	
707	Manage threat or target analysis of adversary's cyber activity information and production of threat information within the enterprise.	
711	Monitor and evaluate the effectiveness of the enterprise's information assurance (IA) security safeguards to ensure they provide the intended level of protection.	
730	Oversee the information security training and awareness program.	
801	Provide enterprise IA and supply chain risk management guidance for development of the continuity operations Plans.	
810	Provide leadership and direction to IT personnel by ensuring that IA security awareness, basics, literacy, and training are provided to operations personnel commensurate with their responsibilities.	
818	Provide technical documents, incident reports, findings from computer examinations, summaries, and other situational awareness information to higher headquarters.	
848	Recommend policy and coordinate review and approval.	
862	Track audit findings and recommendations to ensure appropriate mitigation actions are taken.	
919	Promote awareness of security issues among management and ensure sound security principles are reflected in the organization's vision and goals.	
947	Oversee policy standards and implementation strategies to ensure procedures and guidelines comply with cybersecurity policies.	
948	Participate in risk governance process to provide security risks, mitigations, and input on other technical risk.	
949	Evaluate the effectiveness of procurement function in addressing information security requirements and supply chain risks through procurement activities and recommend improvement.	
1018	Ensure all acquisitions, procurements, and outsourcing efforts address information security requirements consistent with organization goals.	
1032	Continuously validate the organization against policies/guidelines/procedures/regulations/laws to ensure compliance.	
1035	Forecast ongoing service demands and ensure security assumptions are reviewed as necessary.	
1041	Define and/or implement policies and procedures to ensure protection of critical infrastructure as appropriate.	

Figure 9.7 (Continued) Security program management specialty area tasks mapped to the CSF.

One of the most important roles that security professionals shoulder is that of a leader in personally adhering to all policies and procedures. Personal integrity and conducting everyday business in an ethical manner builds trust within the organization. An organization culture that fosters trust and respect for the IT operational security policies and procedures, albeit sometimes inconvenient and the cause of more work, will often demonstrate higher compliance levels. When senior managers or security administrators operate using a separate playbook to cut corners and bypass IT security controls, employees will not take any of the security countermeasures seriously. Senior leadership should espouse and promote ethical guidelines and standards and set an example by adhering to them. It is not enough to simply compose a list of ethical rules or a code of conduct, all individuals in the organization should use ethics in their everyday lives.

One of the greatest challenges to an organization's cybersecurity efforts is the human element. Organization-wide initiatives of TEA is the most effectual way to lessen the risk of human failure or error. The following lists several common assumptions that end users hold that contribute to noncompliance.

- Users think that looking through other people's systems to obtain information is acceptable. The lines between public and private information has become blurred. Due to a lack of understanding of how to set permissions, especially on social media sites, highly personal information is exposed for all to see. In some cases, users feel they have a legal right to explore this information as a form of free speech or expression.
- Users are often unaware of how much damage their actions may cause. They think that if no one notices or is a minor offense, it will not make any difference and should thus be overlooked.
- Users assume that it is the responsibility of the organization to prevent unauthorized access. If they can easily gain access, it is the organization's fault and not theirs.
- Users who view themselves as activists think that hacking is acceptable for the purposes of the greater good and do not consider they are committing a crime.

If the senior leadership sets a good example and the rest of the organization is aware of how their actions can both damage themselves and the reputation, investment value, and legal liabilities of organization, they may be more willing to work as a team and follow the rules.

Financial Leadership

It is important for the CISO to understand the financial implications of designing, staffing, and conducting an effective enterprise continuity of operations program. To reduce risk, acquiring and managing the necessary resources to support the IT security goals comes at a cost. Frequently changing security requirements and the interconnected global economy creates many opportunities for data theft and organizations struggle with the question of how much security is enough. Complete security is not something that many organizations can afford and requires a careful balancing act between a robust IT security program and appropriate spending. Evaluation of the cost–benefits, economic impact, risk analysis, and alternative strategies are required in the decision-making process and formulation of the IT operational security plan. It is important that the CISO establish strong lines of communication with senior leadership to provide a comprehensive cost–benefit analysis relevant to the risk levels and security posture of the organization.

Enterprise Continuity of Operations Plan

When faced with an interruption of mission critical operations, well-run organizations respond and execute an incident response plan that either leads to a disaster recovery plan or a business continuity of operations plan. The disaster recovery plan is executed when the organization is faced with an incident that allows for normal operations to resume at the primary site. The business continuity plan is executed when critical functions of the operation require the relocation to an alternative site rendering it impossible for the organization to function at the primary site. In many cases, if an organization halts operations due to a disruption, many of them never recover. The planning and development of the disaster recovery and business continuity plans require a specialized team and the CISO is often charged with establishing the enterprise continuity of operations program, strategy, and mission assurance. This includes acquiring all necessary resources, both personnel and financial, to conduct an effective enterprise continuity of operations program. It is important that in addition to developing solid disaster recovery and business continuity plans, they also maintain, update, and test the plans at least annually, and train all stakeholders to execute the continuity plans.

Evaluation and Validation

One critical aspect of the ongoing maintenance of the IT security program includes the evaluation of the policy standards and implementation strategies. Policies and procedures require continuous monitoring and updating to ensure that new information on technologies and known hacking strategies get incorporated into the IT security operational plan and any modifications be made. The CISO is tasked with this continuous evaluation as well as validating that the organization is in compliance with all applicable laws, regulations, and governmental agency requirements. Forecasting ongoing service demands and ensuring that security assumptions and requirements are reviewed is part of the continuous evaluation.

Underlying Knowledge, Skill, and Ability Requirements for Security Program Management Specialty Area

The majority of the KSA requirements for the security program management specialty area can be factored into the following five distinct areas of standard application.

1. *Requirements analysis*: Knowledge of business process, system software and organizational design standards, policies, and authorized approaches (security frameworks and control libraries) are required to formulate a strategy and begin the planning process.
2. *Technical competency*: Knowledge of new and emerging IT and cybersecurity technologies; system administration, network and operating system hardening techniques; infrastructure design to include host and network access control mechanisms, protocols, directory services, encryption algorithms, routing encapsulation, cryptography, network security architecture, and network systems management principles, models and methods is critical in order to effectively create and evaluate all appropriate IT policies and procedures countermeasures. It is the CISO's responsibility to fully understand the heart of the IT operational plan which includes numerous solid security countermeasures that are executable and enforceable.
3. *Vulnerabilities assessment and IA*: Knowledge of key concepts in security management; penetration testing principles, tools, and techniques; network traffic analysis methods; system and application security threats and vulnerabilities is essential in being able to ensure that continuous security monitoring is performed and detection and protection capabilities are fully deployed.
4. *Incident and risk management*: Knowledge of incident response and handling methodologies; disaster recovery and continuity of operations planning, testing, and execution; supply chain security and risk management policies, requirements, and procedures is essential to ensure proactive handling of any detected abnormality. The planning, development, and successful execution of these plans are critical in the event of an attack to keep the organization functioning.
5. *Computer forensics*: Knowledge of IA principles used to manage risks related to the use, processing, storage, and transmission of data; data backups to include types of backups; data recovery concepts and tools; criminal law and relevant laws, policies, procedures, or governance related to work impacting critical infrastructure is essential to ensuring data collection after a detected breach is collected and handled according to proper procedures so as to be admissible in a court of law.

Table 9.8 displays a list of the entire KSAs for the security program management specialty area.

Table 9.8 Security Program Management Specialty Area KSAs

Item ID	KSA	Statement	Competency
9	KSA	Knowledge of applicable business processes and operations of customer organizations.	Requirements analysis
25	KSA	Knowledge of encryption algorithms (e.g., Internet Protocol Security [IPSEC], Advanced Encryption Standard [AES], Generic Routing Encapsulation [GRE], Internet Key Exchange [IKE], Message Digest Algorithm [MD5], Secure Hash Algorithm [SHA], Triple Data Encryption Standard [3DES]).	Cryptography
29	KSA	Knowledge of data backup, types of backups (e.g., full, incremental), and recovery concepts and tools.	Computer forensics
37	KSA	Knowledge of disaster recovery and continuity of operations plans.	Incident management
49	KSA	Knowledge of host and network access control mechanisms (e.g., access control list).	Information systems/ network security
55	KSA	Knowledge of information assurance (IA) principles used to manage risks related to the use, processing, storage, and transmission of information or data.	Information assurance
61	KSA	Knowledge of incident response and handling methodologies.	Incident management
62	KSA	Knowledge of industry-standard and organizationally accepted analysis principles and methods.	Logical systems design
66	KSA	Knowledge of intrusion detection methodologies and techniques for detecting host-and network-based intrusions via intrusion detection technologies.	Computer network defense

(Continued)

Table 9.8 (Continued)   Security Program Management Specialty Area KSAs

Item ID	KSA	Statement	Competency
81	KSA	Knowledge of network protocols (e.g., Transmission Critical Protocol/Internet Protocol [TCP/IP], Dynamic Host Configuration Protocol [DHCPI]), and directory services (e.g., Domain Name System [DNS]).	Infrastructure design
87	KSA	Knowledge of network traffic analysis methods.	Information systems/ network security
88	KSA	Knowledge of new and emerging information technology (IT) and cyber security technologies.	Technology awareness
92	KSA	Knowledge of how traffic flows across the network (e.g., Transmission Control Protocol and Internet Protocol [TCP/IP], Open System Interconnection model [OSI]).	Infrastructure design
95	KSA	Knowledge of penetration testing principles, tools, and techniques (e.g., metasploit, neosploit).	Vulnerabilities assessment
105	KSA	Knowledge of system and application security threats and vulnerabilities (e.g., buffer overflow, mobile code, cross-site scripting, procedural language/structured query language [PL/SQL] and injections, race conditions, covert channel, replay, return-oriented attacks, malicious code).	Vulnerabilities assessment
107	KSA	Knowledge of resource management principles and techniques.	Project management
110	KSA	Knowledge of key concepts in security management (e.g., release management, patch management).	Information assurance
112	KSA	Knowledge of server administration and systems engineering theories, concepts, and methods.	Systems life cycle

(Continued)

Table 9.8 (Continued) Security Program Management Specialty Area KSAs

Item ID	KSA	Statement	Competency
113	KSA	Knowledge of server and client operating systems.	Operating systems
126	KSA	Knowledge of system software and organizational design standards, policies, and authorized approaches (e.g., International Organization for Standardization [ISO] guidelines) relating to system design.	Requirements analysis
129	KSA	Knowledge of system life cycle management principles, including software security and usability.	Systems life cycle
132	KSA	Knowledge of technology integration processes.	Systems integration
150	KSA	Knowledge of what constitutes a network attack and the relationship to both threats and vulnerabilities.	Information systems/ network security
299	KSA	Knowledge of information security program management and project management principles and techniques.	Project management
916	KSA	Skill in deconflicting cyber operations and activities.	Political savvy
1033	KSA	Knowledge of basic system administration, network, and operating system hardening techniques.	Information systems/ network security
1036	KSA	Knowledge of applicable laws (e.g., Electronic Communications Privacy Act, Foreign Intelligence Surveillance Act, Protect America Act, search and seizure laws, civil liberties and privacy laws), US Statutes (e.g., Titles 10,18, 32, 50 in US Code), Presidential Directives, executive branch guidelines, and/or administrative/criminal legal guidelines and procedures relevant to work performed.	Criminal law

(Continued)

Table 9.8 (Continued) Security Program Management Specialty Area KSAs

Item ID	KSA	Statement	Competency
1037	KSA	Knowledge of IT supply chain security and risk management policies, requirements, and procedures.	Risk management
1038	KSA	Knowledge of local specialized system requirements (e.g., critical infrastructure systems that may not use standard IT) for safety, performance, and reliability.	Infrastructure design
1039	KSA	Skill in evaluating the trustworthiness of the supplier and/or product.	Contracting/ procurement
1040	KSA	Knowledge of relevant laws, policies, procedures, or governance related to work impacting critical infrastructure.	Criminal law
1072	KSA	Knowledge of network security architecture concepts, including topology, protocols, components, and principles (e.g., application of defense-in-depth).	Information systems/ network security
1073	KSA	Knowledge of network systems management principles, models, methods (e.g., end-to-end systems performance monitoring), and tools.	Network management
1131	KSA	Knowledge of security architecture concepts and enterprise architecture reference models (e.g., Zackman, Federal Enterprise Architecture [FEA]).	Enterprise architecture
1141	KSA	Knowledge of an organization's information classification program and procedures for level information loss.	Information management

Specialty Area 6: Risk Management

The specialty area for risk management "oversees, evaluates, and supports the documentation, validation, and accreditation process necessary to ensure new and existing information technology (IT) systems meet the organizations' IA and security requirements. Ensures appropriate treatment of risk, compliance, and monitoring assurance from internal and external perspectives" (NIST, 2014). Life is full of uncertainties and there is risk in most everything we do. Cyberattacks on information systems today are increasing in number, breadth, and sophistication; and managing risk requires the involvement of everyone in the organization. Successful attacks can result in significant damage to reputation and finances as demonstrated by the recent attacks on Sony Pictures Entertainment, Anthem, Target, and Home Depot. Well-run organizations are carefully managed and good management endeavors to operate proactively and initiate action that leads the organization to where it needs to go rather than reacting and operating in a constant firefighting mode. Risk management is the process of handling risk in a methodical and choiceful fashion.

Defining risk can be a complex endeavor as it is a combination of the two elements of *likelihood* and *impact*. When risk is viewed from the perspective of likelihood, there is a subject element in the judgment of the individual proposing the level of risk involved. For example, the likelihood of campers encountering mosquitos on a humid evening in Michigan is high; however, the presence of mosquitos is low impact from a risk perspective. Although to the campers they can be quite irritating, they do not pose a serious threat and their presence would hardly be viewed as a significant risk. In defining and describing a risk event, it is important to clarify whether the principle concern is with likelihood and/or impact.

Factoring Risk Management Workforce Tasks into the Cybersecurity Framework Categories

As shown in Figure 9.8, there are 16 tasks in the risk management specialty area and are mapped to the following 3 functions of the CSF.

1. Tasks that develop methods to monitor and measure risk, compliance and assurance efforts; develop specification to ensure risk efforts conform with security requirements; the drafting of statements of preliminary or residual security risks; and the development of an audit process to ensure that operational processes are in compliance with mandatory IA requirements are mapped to "identify" function (risk assessment category) of the CSF.
2. Tasks that maintain IA accreditation materials; manage and approve accreditation packages; recommend new or revised security measures based on results of reviews; confirm that the level of risk is within acceptable limits for each

	Oversee and govern general knowledge area *Risk management specialty area tasks* NICE workforce framework	Cybersecurity framework
		Identify / Protect / Detect / Respond / Recover
537	Develop methods to monitor and measure risk, compliance, and assurance efforts.	
548	Develop specifications to ensure risk, compliance, and assurance efforts conform with security, resilience, and dependability requirements at the software application, system, and network environment level.	
566	Draft statements of preliminary or residual security risks for system operation.	
691	Maintain information systems assurance and accreditation materials.	
696	Manage and approve accreditation packages (e.g., International Organization for Standardization/International electrotechnical Commission [ISO/IEC] 15026-2).	
710	Monitor and evaluate a system's compliance with information technology (IT) security, resilience, and dependability requirements.	
772	Perform validation steps, comparing actual results with expected results and analyze the differences to identify impact and risks.	
775	Plan and conduct security authorization reviews and assurance case development for initial installation of systems and networks.	
798	Provide an accurate technical evaluation of the software application, system, or network, documenting the security posture, capabilities, and vulnerabilities against relevant information assurance (IA) compliances.	
798	Recommend new or revised security, resilience, and dependability measures based on the results of reviews.	
836	Review authorization and assurance documents to confirm that the level of risk is within acceptable limits for each software application, system, and network.	
878	Verify that application software/network/system security postures are implemented as stated, document deviations, and recommend required actions to correct those deviations.	
879	Verify that the software application/network/system accreditation and assurance documentation is current.	
936	Develop security compliance processes and/or audits for external services (e.g., cloud service providers, datacenters).	
937	Inspect continuous monitoring results to confirm that the level of risk is within acceptable limits for the software application, network, or system.	
1146	Develop and Implement IA independent audit processes for application software/networks/systems and oversee ongoing independent audits to ensure that operational processes and procedures are in compliance with organizational and mandatory IA requirements and accurately followed by systems administrators and other cybersecurity staff when performing their day-to-day activities.	

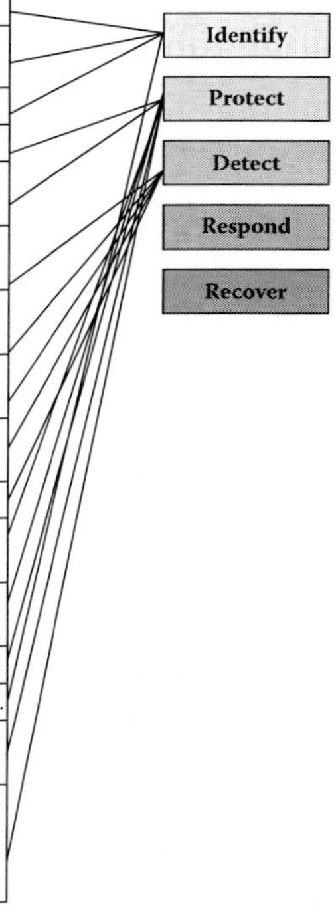

Figure 9.8   Risk management specialty area tasks mapped to the CSF.

application, system and network; verify that security postures are implemented as stated; document deviations and recommend corrective actions; develop security compliance processes; inspect continuous monitoring results; develop and implement audit processes are mapped to "protect" function (information protection processes and procedures category) of the CSF.

3. Tasks that monitor and evaluate a system's compliance with IT security requirements; perform validation steps, comparing actual with expected results and analyze the differences to identify impact and risks; plan and conduct security authorization reviews; and provide a technical evaluation of the software application, system, or network, documenting the security posture, capabilities, and vulnerabilities against relevant IA compliances are mapped to the "detect" function (security continuous monitoring category) of the CSF.

Risk management should be integrated into every aspect of the organization and the use of a framework can ensure that managing IT security risks is in alignment with the organization's mission, business objectives, and risk strategy. A structured framework can also ensure that security specifications and security controls are integrated into the organization's infrastructure and conform to requirements at the software application, system, and network environment level.

There are a number of risk management frameworks that can be adopted to effectively manage information system-related security risks in highly diverse environments. The Project Management Institute (PMI) has developed a risk management framework that outlines six steps (PMBOK, 2013). The following steps, adapted from PMI, are as follows:

1. *Plan risk management*: This is the process of defining how to conduct risk management activities. Planning for risk is an essential element of effective management.
2. *Identify risks*: This process determines which risks may affect the organization-wide IT systems and document their characteristics.
3. *Perform qualitative risk analysis*: This process prioritizes risks by assessing and combining the likelihood of occurrence and impact.
4. *Perform quantitative risk analysis*: This process gathers data and uses modeling techniques to analyze the consequences of identified risks.
5. *Plan risk responses*: This process involves creating a strategy to enhance opportunities and reduce threats.
6. *Control risks*: This process involves implementing the response plans developed in step 5; tracking and monitoring risks; and evaluating the effectiveness of the overall risk management process.

The US DHS has developed the National Infrastructure Protection Plan (NIPP) risk management framework. This is a scalable framework in that it can be adopted for use in organizations of any size. The framework establishes a process to combine consequence, vulnerability, and threat information to produce a comprehensive risk assessment and has the following six elements (NIPP, 2009):

1. *Set security goals and objectives*: Define specific outcomes, conditions, and performance targets that collectively constitute and effective security posture.
2. *Identify assets, systems, networks, and functions*: Develop an inventory to include all locations of the organization; collect information pertinent to risk management that accounts for the fundamental characteristic of each sector.
3. *Assess risks*: Determine risk by combining potential direct and indirect consequences of a breach, known vulnerability, or specific threat information.
4. *Prioritize*: Aggregate and analyze risk assessment results to develop a comprehensive picture; establish priorities based on risk and determine protection and business continuity initiatives that provide the greatest mitigation of risk.
5. *Implement*: Select appropriate protective actions and programs to reduce or manage the identified risk.
6. *Measure effectiveness*: Use metrics to measure progress and assess the effectiveness of the security program.

Integrating IT security requirements into the organization's system development life cycle helps to ensure the development of a more robust infrastructure to reduce risk to the organization's assets and operations. Failure to integrate security requirements may result in significant expense later in the life cycle as the organization reactively works to address security issues that should have been conducted in the initial design phase.

Risk Management Process

The process of developing and implementing risk management tasks will vary from organization to organization and can be applied to the appropriate phases within the system development life cycle. The following comprises a sequential list of risk management tasks and is collectively an overview of the risk management process:

1. Identify all application software, systems, and network infrastructure that will be in scope of the risk assessment and assign a classification category. The identified elements can be categorized into mission critical, important, or supportive as covered in the system security categorization section under specialty area 4.
2. Document each element identified above to include a full description, unique identifier, system owner, location, function, business process supported, types

of information processed, stored, or transmitted, hardware and firmware version, system users, encryption techniques used on data, data flows including inputs and outputs.

3. Conduct a risk assessment to include the identification of threats, vulnerabilities, potential consequences, estimation of likelihood as discussed in the section Specialty Area 6: Risk Assessment. Draft statements of preliminary or residual security risks for system operation.

4. Identify the security controls that will be applied to the identified application software, systems, and network infrastructure. The security controls are selected based on the security categories established.

5. Develop methods to monitor and measure risk, and a continuous monitoring program for the security controls to ensure effectiveness. Implementation of a solid continuous monitoring system allows an organization to understand the state of the system security over time.

6. Implement and document the security controls to include planned inputs, expected behavior, and expect outcomes.

7. Assess the security controls to determine the extent to which the controls are implemented correctly, operating as intended, and producing the desired outcome in meeting the security requirements of the organization. Verify that application software, system, and network security postures are implemented as stated.

8. Determine the risk and if the level of risk is within acceptable limits for each software application, system, and network.

9. Perform validation steps, comparing actual with expected results and analyze the differences to identify impact and risks.

10. Document any deviations and recommend required actions to correct those deviations.

11. Recommend new or revised security, resilience, and dependability measures based on the results of the reviews.

12. Create a security assessment report documenting the issues, findings, and recommendations from the security control assessment.

13. Develop security compliance processes and audits for external services (e.g., cloud service providers, data centers).

14. Develop and implement independent audit processes for ongoing independent audits to ensure that operational processes and procedures are in compliance with all organizational and mandatory IA requirements.

15. Conduct ongoing security control assessments and conduct remediation actions based on those results.

16. Update the IT operational security plan, security assessment report, and plans of action based on the results of the continuous monitoring process.

Security status reporting provides the organization with essential information regarding the state of security and the effectiveness of implemented countermeasures.

The goal is to have efficient ongoing communication conveying key changes to security plans, security assessment reports, and plans of actions. Status reports can be

- Event driven such as when there are changes in the infrastructure or configuration of a system or in the event of a breach
- Time driven such as daily, weekly, monthly, or quarterly

Underlying Knowledge, Skill, and Ability Requirements for Risk Management Specialty Area

The majority of the 23 knowledge skill and ability requirements for the risk management specialty area can be factored into the following distinct areas of standard application.

1. *Organizational awareness, business processes, and operations*: Knowledge of risk management frameworks; supply chain security; and risk management policies, requirements, and procedures is instrumental in efficiently guiding the organization through a structured risk assessment and management process.
2. *Information systems/network security*: Knowledge of known vulnerabilities from alerts, advisories, errata, and bulletins will assist in the risk assessment process.
3. *Infrastructure design*: Knowledge of local specialized system requirements (e.g., critical infrastructure systems that may not use standard IT for safety, performance, and reliability will be necessary for the identification and categorization of systems in the risk management process.
4. *IT performance assessment*: Knowledge of methods for evaluating, implementing, monitoring, detection, and remediation; system diagnostic tools and fault identification techniques; as well as skills in identifying measures or indicators of system performance and the actions needed to improve or correct performance relative to the goals of the system is required to effectively implement and assess if the security controls are operating as intended.

Table 9.9 displays the entire set of KSAs for the risk management specialty area.

Specialty Area 7: Knowledge Management

The specialty area for knowledge management "manages and administers integrated methods, enabling the organization to identify, capture, catalog, classify, retrieve, and share intellectual capital and information content. The methods may include utilizing processes and tools (e.g., databases, documents, policies, procedures) and expertise pertaining to the organization" (NIST, 2014). Unlimited sources of knowledge are readily available due to the rapid global expansion of

Table 9.9   Risk Management KSAs for Risk Management Specialty Area

Item ID	KSA	Statement	Competency
19	KSA	Knowledge of cyber defense mitigation techniques and vulnerability assessment tools, including open source tools, and their capabilities.	Computer network defense
27	KSA	Knowledge of cryptography and cryptographic key management concepts.	Cryptography
58	KSA	Knowledge of known vulnerabilities from alerts, advisories, errata, and bulletins.	Information systems/ network security
63	KSA	Knowledge of information assurance (IA) principles and organizational requirements to protect confidentiality, integrity, availability, authenticity, and nonrepudiation of information and data.	Information assurance
69	KSA	Knowledge of risk management framework (RMF) requirements.	Information systems security certification
77	KSA	Knowledge of current industry methods for evaluating, implementing, and disseminating information technology (IT) security assessment, monitoring, detection, and remediation tools and procedures, utilizing standards-based concepts, and capabilities.	Information systems/ network security
88	KSA	Knowledge of new and emerging IT and cyber security technologies.	Technology awareness
121	KSA	Knowledge of structured analysis principles and methods.	Logical systems design
128	KSA	Knowledge of system diagnostic tools and fault identification techniques.	Systems testing and evaluation

(Continued)

Table 9.9 (Continued)   Risk Management KSAs for Risk Management Specialty Area

Item ID	KSA	Statement	Competency
143	KSA	Knowledge of the organization's enterprise IT goals and objectives.	Enterprise architecture
183	KSA	Skill in determining how a security system should work, including its resilience and dependability capabilities, and how changes in conditions, operations, or the environment will affect these outcomes.	Information assurance
203	KSA	Skill in identifying measures or indicators of system performance and the actions needed to improve or correct performance, relative to the goals of the system.	Information technology performance assessment
942	KSA	Knowledge of the organization's core business/mission processes.	Organizational awareness
1034	KSA	Knowledge of personally identifiable information (PII) and payment card industry (PCI) data security standards.	Security
1036	KSA	Knowledge of applicable laws (e.g., Electronic Communications Privacy Act, Foreign Intelligence Surveillance Act, Protect America Act, search and seizure laws, civil liberties and privacy laws), US Statutes (e.g., Titles 10,18, 32, 50 in US Code), Presidential Directives, executive branch guidelines, and/ or administrative/criminal legal guidelines and procedures relevant to work performed.	Criminal law
1037	KSA	Knowledge of IT supply chain security and risk management policies, requirements, and procedures.	Risk management

(Continued)

Table 9.9 (Continued) Risk Management KSAs for Risk Management Specialty Area

Item ID	KSA	Statement	Competency
1038	KSA	Knowledge of local specialized system requirements (e.g., critical infrastructure systems that may not use standard IT) for safety, performance, and reliability.	Infrastructure design
1039	KSA	Skill in evaluating the trustworthiness of the supplier and/or product.	Contracting/procurement
1040	KSA	Knowledge of relevant laws, policies, procedures, or governance related to work impacting critical infrastructure.	Criminal law
1072	KSA	Knowledge of network security architecture concepts, including topology, protocols, components, and principles (e.g., application of defense-in-depth).	Information systems/ network security
1131	KSA	Knowledge of security architecture concepts and enterprise architecture reference models (e.g., Zackman, Federal Enterprise Architecture [FEA]).	Enterprise architecture
1141	KSA	Knowledge of an organization's information classification program and procedures for level information loss.	Information management
1142	KSA	Knowledge of security models (e.g., Bell–LaPadula model, Biba integrity model, Clark–Wilson integrity model).	Enterprise architecture

transactions traversing the Internet, the consumerization of IT, and the abundance and affordability of hard drive technologies. A workforce capable of managing cross-functional information-based transactions and collaborative technologies is required to fulfill the demands of current work environments.

Institutional memory has been greatly reduced due to downsizing, retirements, and the frequency of people joining and leaving organizations. Undocumented or poorly documented project-based work, in which team members collaborate together until the project is completed and then disburse, hampers the ability to build institutional memory. Additional pressures to manage risk, avoid recreating the wheel, and create innovative processes and new products are challenging organizations to address the growing volume of new knowledge. Organizations have significant amounts of data and information; however, it does not follow that they have meaningful knowledge. Knowledge management is about generating useful, actionable, and meaningful information and disseminating it to the appropriate individuals throughout the organization who can apply it.

Factoring Knowledge Management Workforce Tasks into the Cybersecurity Framework Categories

As shown in Figure 9.9, there are nine tasks in the knowledge management specialty area and are mapped to the following three functions of the CSF:

1. The task that involves developing an understanding of the needs and requirements of information end users is mapped to the "identify" function (business environment category) of the CSF.
2. Tasks that involve administering the indexing/cataloguing, storage, and access of organization documents; construct access paths to suits of information to facilitate access by end users; design, build, implement, and maintain a knowledge management system that provides end-users access to the organization's intellectual capital; develop and implement control procedures into the testing and development of core IT based knowledge management systems; plan and manage the delivery of knowledge management projects; promote sharing through the organization's operational processes and systems by strengthening links between knowledge sharing and IT systems; and provide recommendations on data structures and databases that ensure correct and quality production of reports and management information have been mapped to the "protect" function (awareness and training, information protection processes and procedures, and access control categories) of the CSF.
3. The task that involves monitoring and reporting the usage of knowledge management assets and resources is mapped to the "detect" function (security continuous monitoring category) of the CSF.

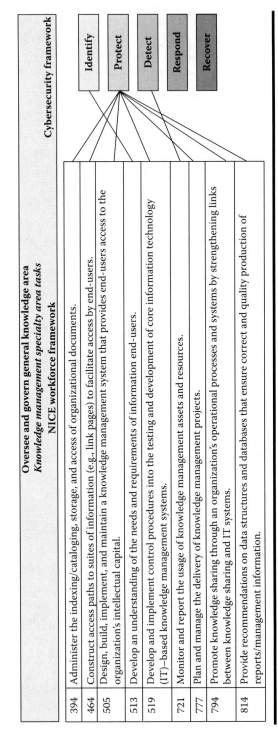

Figure 9.9 Knowledge management specialty area tasks mapped to the CSF.

The core components of knowledge management are people, processes, organizational structure and culture, and technology. Knowledge management is a highly multidisciplinary field and a mixture of strategies, tools, processes, and communities of practice. The wide variety of disciplines that knowledge management draws from include the following:

- Linguistics, corporate storytelling, and communication
- Education and training
- Organizational science, sociology, and anthropology
- Artificial intelligence and cognitive science
- Computer science, intelligent techniques, data mining, expert systems, neural networks, intelligent agents

Knowledge management systems can be grouped into three major types: enterprise-wide, specialized knowledge work systems, and intelligent systems designed to discover patterns and apply knowledge. The variety of knowledge management systems includes the following:

- Enterprise content management systems that have the capabilities to capture, store, retrieve, and distribute knowledge with the goal of assisting organizations in improving their decision making and business processes. These systems are designed to manage both structured and unstructured knowledge and provide portals that include social software such as blogs and wiki's to share research and create and capture new knowledge.
- Workflow systems are designed to manage the process of creating, using, and maintaining knowledge in the form of procedures, processes, and documents within an organization. One feature includes configuration tools that allow for notifications throughout defined processes to inform appropriate individuals of new documents that need review and documents that require approval.
- Groupware are enterprise-wide systems that enable collaboration and sharing of information through tools such as shared online folders, documents, calendars, e-mail, and blogs.
- Learning management systems keep track of employee participation and provide assessment of learning effectiveness for electronic-based modes of instruction and educational content. Publically available massive open online courses (MOOCs) are gaining popularity with organizations to provide online training and education to very large numbers of employees.
- Specialized work systems such as virtual reality systems for simulation and modeling use interactive graphics software that appears so real that they blur the lines between reality and fiction. In some applications, special clothing such as gloves and shoes are used to record the user's movements and transmit this information back to the computer.

- Specialized financial investment work systems integrate both internal and external data to include contact management information, research reports, and historical market data to leverage the knowledge and time of its brokers, traders, and portfolio managers.
- Expert systems are a type of intelligent technology designed to capture the tacit knowledge of skilled employees. They typically perform limited tasks and are organized in the system as a set of rules to follow. These rules are a step-by-step process to solve problems and aid in highly structured decision-making situations.

There are three types of knowledge and differing aspects to each which are important to understand and capture. The three types of knowledge are tacit, structured, and unstructured knowledge. Tacit knowledge is the most challenging to capture in that the knowledge resides only within individual's minds and is usually the most valuable type of knowledge. This type of knowledge can be difficult to articulate and is generally the expertise, accumulated over time, of how to successfully accomplish tasks to produce a final product. One way to capture this knowledge is to conduct after-action reviews or lessons learned upon project completion and document those in the form of reports that can be captured and shared.

Structured knowledge is explicit in nature and exists in tangible formal documents and digital records. However, the majority of knowledge is unstructured and therefore more challenging to capture and catalog. Unstructured knowledge exists in the form of e-mails, text and instant messages, memos, graphics, electronic presentations, videos, podcasts, audio files, proprietary software application files and can be stored on multiple hard drives scattered around the globe.

Laws and regulations require organizations to save and store a variety of documents for many years depending upon the type of record. Hence, organizations should define and document a policy for the retention and proper disposal of all documents and information management. The objective should be the capture and management of authentic, reliable, and retrieval of records capable of supporting business functions and for compliance to all applicable laws. The needs and requirements of information end users and compliance to all applicable laws should drive the contents of the policy. This policy should be periodically reviewed and revised to ensure it reflects the current business needs of the organization. Business continuity planning should ensure that records which are fundamental to the functioning of the organization are identified in the risk analysis process, are fully protected, and retrievable in the event they are needed.

Creating a consistent and appropriate index/classification scheme to organization information into meaningful categories is essential for the purpose of being able to access the data. Each piece of data in which the organization wishes to capture must be consistently tagged or classified for systematic retrieval. Many end users do not want a separate business classification scheme implemented as they view it as too hard to learn, unwieldy, and too difficult to navigate. A more simplified way to code data is to create an index. This is less complex than a classification scheme and should reflect the language of how employees refer to their work. An example of this would be creating an index to search for and retrieve e-mails in a knowledge management system. The self-evident metadata items to index using e-mail are what most users are already familiar with such as: date of e-mail, sender, recipient, CC, BCC, subject, text of the body of the e-mail, and text of any attachments. Understanding how end users envision the words they would use to search for an item is a good way to index information and would be captured during numerous requirements gathering meetings. It is important to develop an understanding of the needs and requirements of information end users and to use the same language they do in their everyday environment to tag data.

Administrators and managers must also develop processes and procedures for the management and dissemination of captured knowledge to the appropriate users. Access control and procedures must be in place so that unauthorized users are prevented from accessing highly sensitive data while allowing other users to access the data they need to productively work. Additionally, it is important to consider the read, write, modify, delete, and print capabilities for each user of the knowledge management system. There may be documents that are read only for some users and have full edit capabilities to others.

Compliance monitoring and internal auditing should conducted be regularly to ensure that the knowledge management systems procedures and processes are implemented according to the organizational policies and user requirements. External auditing may be required to ensure compliance to any governmental regulatory agency or laws. Modifications to the knowledge management system and/ or policies and procedures should be made in the event there are deficiencies or changes to business requirements.

Underlying Knowledge, Skill, and Ability Requirements for Knowledge Management Specialty Area

There are 20 KSAs identified for the knowledge management specialty area and can be factored into the following 5 distinct areas of standard application.

1. *Knowledge management*: The ability to match the appropriate knowledge repository technology for a given application or environment is required to select, configure, and implement the most suitable solution based on user requirements. Skills in using knowledge management technologies, measuring and reporting of intellectual capital, and conducting knowledge mapping can also save time and cost of implementation.

2. *Organizational awareness*: The business analyst requires knowledge of the organization's core business/mission processes in order to be able to gather and document the end-user requirements. Knowledge of all applicable laws and governmental agency compliance requirements is also necessary.

3. *Data management*: Knowledge of the capabilities and functionality for organizing and managing information into databases is critical for the effective retrieval of that information. Effective data management skills are required to be able to properly translate all business requirements and create an appropriate and usable classification/index schema.

4. *Infrastructure design*: Knowledge of use cases related to collaboration and content synchronization across platforms, such as tables, cloud computing services, and mobile devices, is required to create and implement a scalable solution.

5. *Computer network defense*: It is critical that all system administrators, database administrators, and job positions that handle system security ensure the highly sensitive data are secure from unauthorized users. Appropriate permissions must be managed to allow users to access the data they need without compromising the security of the organization.

Table 9.10 displays the entire set of knowledge management specialty area KSAs.

Chapter Summary

The oversee and govern general knowledge area contains seven specialty areas. These are legal advice and advocacy; strategic planning and policy development; TEA; information systems and security operations; security program management; risk management; and knowledge management. All areas collectively focus on planning, developing, testing, and executing the IT security policy, plans, and countermeasures to ensure the organization is protected against malicious attacks or simply human error. Many of the activities in this knowledge area are proactive until an event is detected and requires immediate response.

Due to the widespread use of technology and interconnectivity of systems, IT security oversight and governance is required. Effective security is not just a technical problem but a business issue that includes everyone in the organization. The involvement of the board of directors, executive management, and business process owners is the key to ensure that all stakeholders buy-in and seriously adopt the IT security program. Compliance to all security measures is required at all levels of the organization to build trust and develop an organizational culture that values security and ethically adheres to all countermeasures even when that may mean inconvenience or additional work.

The objective of IS is to ensure information safety—that is, information is kept confidential, available, and protected against unauthorized modification

Table 9.10 Knowledge Management Specialty Area KSAs

Item ID	KSA	Statement	Competency
5	KSA	Ability to match the appropriate knowledge repository technology for a given application or environment.	Knowledge management
19	KSA	Knowledge of cyber defense mitigation techniques and vulnerability assessment tools, including open source tools, and their capabilities.	Computer network defense
77	KSA	Knowledge of current industry methods for evaluating, implementing, and disseminating information technology (IT) security assessment, monitoring, detection, and remediation tools and procedures, utilizing standards-based concepts and capabilities.	Information systems/network security
134	KSA	Knowledge of the capabilities and functionality associated with various content creation technologies (e.g., wikis, social networking, blogs).	Technology awareness
135	KSA	Knowledge of the capabilities and functionality associated with various technologies for organizing and managing information (e.g., databases, bookmarking engines).	Data management
136	KSA	Knowledge of the capabilities and functionality of various collaborative technologies (e.g., groupware, SharePoint).	Technology awareness
163	KSA	Skill in conducting information searches.	Computer skills
164	KSA	Skill in conducting knowledge mapping (e.g., map of knowledge repositories).	Knowledge management
223	KSA	Skill in the measuring and reporting of intellectual capital.	Knowledge management

(Continued)

Table 9.10 (Continued) Knowledge Management Specialty Area KSAs

Item ID	KSA	Statement	Competency
230	KSA	Skill in using knowledge management technologies.	Knowledge management
338	KSA	Knowledge of the principal methods, procedures, and techniques of gathering information and producing, reporting, and sharing intelligence.	Reasoning
907	KSA	Skill in data mining techniques.	Data management
910	KSA	Knowledge of database theory.	Data management
942	KSA	Knowledge of the organization's core business/mission processes.	Organizational awareness
1034	KSA	Knowledge of personally identifiable information (PII) and payment card industry (PCI) data security standards.	Security
1125	KSA	Knowledge of Cloud-based knowledge management technologies and concepts related to security, governance, procurement, and administration.	Distributed systems
1126	KSA	Knowledge of data classification standards and methodologies based on sensitivity and other risk factors.	Data management
1129	KSA	Knowledge of multichannel user access technologies and use cases including mobile technology.	Communications security management
1136	KSA	Knowledge of use cases related to collaboration and content synchronization across platforms (e.g., tables, PC, Cloud, etc.).	Infrastructure design
1141	KSA	Knowledge of an organization's information classification program and procedures for level information loss.	Information management

(integrity). The importance of integrity is especially the key due to the impact that information has on strategy-related decisions. Every organization should identify the roles and responsibilities for those who are charged with the variety of IA activities. To help an organization understand the threats and vulnerabilities, a risk assessment must be completed. This assessment aims to identify the potential threat sources, vulnerabilities, and potential consequences of the threats are successful in exploiting any vulnerability. An estimation of the likelihood of threats coupled with the impact a breach would have on the organization assists managers in understanding and developing risk management strategies to mitigate that risk. Risk assessments are not a one-time activity but require continuous monitoring and testing of the infrastructure and environment for threats and vulnerabilities.

Once a risk assessment has been completed, the organization can determine how much risk they are willing to tolerate or withstand. All applicable laws, legal requirements, and governmental agency requirements must also be factored into the risk tolerance decision. Organizational boundaries around what systems, policies, and technologies to include in the scope of IT security can be next established. Careful thought must be taken to not make the boundaries too wide or too narrow as both will significantly impact the resources needed.

Once the boundaries have been established, the work of classifying each system, process, and technology is needed. Not everything can be restored immediately and a classification system to distinguish between mission critical, important, and general support systems helps in the prioritization of recovery.

Security frameworks can ensure that all areas of IT security are given attention and each framework typically identifies a security control library that is structured into families of more controls. Detailed the policy and procedure documents for each security control is required to ensure compliance and to substantiate that the organization has what is needed in place to secure its information.

One of the greatest challenges to an organization's cybersecurity efforts is the human element. Organization-wide initiatives of awareness, training, and education are the most effectual way to lessen the risk of human failure or error. To effectively develop and deliver training and awareness tools, a needs assessment is recommended in order to assess the knowledge and security skills for each position in the organization. The needs assessment can be used in the development of an organization-wide plan and justify the allocation of adequate resources to meet the training needs. Proactive awareness and training initiatives are essential and could be used for or against an organization during any legal proceedings in the event of a significant security breach.

The complexity of global, interconnected organizations elevates the requirements of understanding the legal requirements, regulations, policies, and standards when forming strategic partnerships. Legal contracts, collaborative partnerships, US cybercrime laws, international laws, and the like require organizations to employ legal experts to help them navigate legal business matters. In the event of a security breach, a legal advisor is needed to interpret law, conduct framing of allegations, and prepare any legal documents that apply. Knowledge of proper legal data collection is critical if the organization's security philosophy is one of collecting data to prosecute intruders.

Key Terms

Awareness: Reaching broad audiences with security information with the aim of reinforcing appropriate security practices or changing behavior.

Classification Scheme: Determining business criticality by distinguishing systems, process, and technologies into differing categories such as mission critical, important, and general support system. The classification scheme determines the priority of restoration in the event of an incident.

Competency: Achievement of a desired outcome based on a given expectation regarding the result.

Continuous Security Monitoring: The consistent use of automated and/or manual tools to detect and respond to any abnormality within the boundaries of the infrastructure and environment.

Framework: A structured guide that can be used to methodically implement and maintain an effective security program.

Governance: Focused activities that provide leadership, oversight, direction, development, and advocacy so that organizations may effectively conduct business.

Incident Response Management: The planning and execution of how an organization effectively responds to incidents.

IT Security Policy: The overarching organization security policy that sets the tone and culture for the organization.

IT Security Operational Plan: The operational security plan that details all security requirements, assessment activities, training, awareness, and education initiatives, and detailed security policy and procedures that all stakeholders must adhere to.

Knowledge Management: Generating, capturing, and classifying useful, actionable, and meaningful information and disseminating it to the appropriate individuals throughout the organization who can apply it.

Legal Advocate: An advisor who is well versed in the business operations and can offer expert legal advice on business matters.

Organization Boundaries: The systems, processes, and technologies that are included within the scope of the IT security plan.

Risk Management: The process of identifying, assessing, prioritizing, and addressing risks.

Risk Tolerance: The amount of risk an organization is willing to accept.

Security Control Library: Internal policy and procedures for the areas of IT systems, processes, and technologies that are covered in an IT security program.

Strategic Planning: The process of defining an organization's mission, an assessment of its current state, and projections of a desired future.

Training: Formal delivery of instruction, guidance, and exercises for the purpose of teaching a particular skill or behavior.

References

Drucker, P. (1993). *Management Challenges for the 21st Century*. New York: Harpers Business.

Information Systems Audit and Control Association (ISACA). 2013. *CISM Review Manual*. Rolling Meadows, IL: ISACA.

National Infrastructure Protection Plan (NIPP), 2009. Partnering to enhance protection and resiliency. Department of Homeland Security, https://www.dhs.gov/xlibrary/assets/NIPP_Plan.pdf.

National Institute of Standards and Technology (NIST). 2013. *Recommended Security Controls for Federal Information Systems Revision 4*. Gaithersburg, MD: NIST.

National Institute of Standards and Technology (NIST). 2014. *NICE Cybersecurity Workforce Framework 2.0*. Gaithersburg, MD: NIST.

PMBOK. 2014. *A Guide to the Project Management Body of Knowledge (PMBOK Guide)*. Newtown Square, PA: Project Management Institute, Inc.

PricewaterhouseCoopers (PwC). 2014. *Managing Cyber Risks in an Interconnected World: Key Findings from the Global State of Information Security Survey 2015*. London, United Kingdom: PwC.

SANS Institute. 2014. *Critical Security Controls for Effective Cyber Defense—Version 5*. https://www.sans.org/media/critical-security-controls/fall-2014-poster.pdf. Accessed May 29, 2015.

Verizon. 2015. *2015 Data Breach Investigations Report*. Basking Ridge, NJ: Verizon Enterprise Solutions.

Chapter 10

Applying the NICE Model to the Real World

Chapter Objectives

At the conclusion of this chapter, the reader will understand:

- The problems associated with practical implementation of security models
- The focus and purpose of a formal implementation process
- The focus and purpose of tailoring
- The link between the National Initiative for Cybersecurity Education (NICE) model and the cybersecurity framework (CSF) in practical implementation
- Recommendations for an implementation process
- The success factors in implementing the NICE framework

Why Cybersecurity Needs a Standard of Practice

In some respects this text is as much about standardization as it is cybersecurity. This chapter presents an overview of the issues associated with implementing a standardized approach. That includes a discussion of why information assets are difficult to protect as well as the putative best practice response needed to create trustworthy cybersecurity processes. We lay out the issues involved in implementing practical day-to-day cybersecurity operations, including the benefits derived from practicing standard-based cybersecurity as well as the potential pitfalls associated with such an approach. We also try to give you an overview of a model implementation process, which is primarily embodied in the tailoring process.

The lesson learned from this chapter is that information and communication technologies (ICTs) and information assets are more difficult to account for and control than conventional physical assets, because information technology (IT) work involves work in a virtual and highly dynamic landscape, which makes it hard to know what to actually secure let alone how to do it. This has been such a universal and pervasive problem for such a long time that the industry's response has been to create a standard that defines the comprehensive basis for cybersecurity assurance.

Three Problems with Cybersecurity

The need for rigorous cyber protections should be self-evident in a world where the exchange of information underwrites global commerce. Nevertheless, that attribute has always been like one of the Ten Commandments, commendable but rather hard to put into day-to-day practice. It is unfortunate because it is also probably true that the fastest and easiest way to bring a postindustrial era business to its knees is to destroy its information.

One element of the problem stems from how we understand, or perhaps the correct term is misunderstand, the concept of information. Generally speaking, when companies undertake to secure their information resources, they apply a very narrow and potentially disastrous definition to the actual asset. Specifically, typical cybersecurity protection schemes are exclusively aimed at assuring the resources maintained in the corporation's electronic repositories. Whereas common sense alone should dictate that any tangible information that adds value to the business should be protected.

Accordingly, an effective cybersecurity scheme needs to assure the integrity of anything of value that is written, formally communicated, or kept in any format. For example, it is a fact (Privacy Resources Clearinghouse [PRC], 2014) that 71% of the breaches of cybersecurity in the year 2013 resulted from human factors and physical theft. That statistic illustrates that no matter how many double lock boxes the electronic encryption scheme implements, there is no practical assurance unless the workforce understands what the form and consequences of a security violation.

The second aspect of the problem lies in the fact that although everybody agrees that cybersecurity is a good thing, nobody has the slightest idea what it entails. The chief executive officers (CEOs) of every information-intensive organization in the world should be able to assure themselves that they are fully protected against every conceivable source of mischief to their information assets.

That is not the case in most instances, since the actual mechanisms for cybersecurity protection security are deployed in an undisciplined and totally unsystematic way. Or in simple terms, they are neither well defined nor well documented. There are a lot of nuances involved in securing the information resource and failure to embody the appropriate defense in any of those cases can open the door to unthinkable disaster.

To make it worse, if these defenses have been prepared by the IT department itself, one can practically guarantee that there will be significant holes related to the business side of the operation. Simply put, IT managers are experts in technology concerns, not security, and most business security experts are specialists in physical security. It means that they are as clueless about the fundamentals of assuring virtual ICT functioning as ICT managers are about enabling business security.

Thus, there is almost always a serious disconnect between the three functional areas of the organization represented by its virtual information, physical IT assets (e.g., those aspects of IT work that are tangible such as the personnel, work space, and machinery), the actual program inventory, and the general business operation itself.

Any security arrangement that does not provide a concrete solution for every aspect of the unique concerns that each of these areas raise is going to be incomplete and, by implication, ineffective. Thus, an itemization of the security requirements for all three legs of the stool is a necessary adjunct to establishing complete security protection for the organization.

To confound this problem further, the responsibility for information assurance is located in an understandable, but totally dysfunctional place in the organization. Figure 10.1 illustrates this.

Essentially the units responsible for achieving the purposes of the business use the corporate information resources to attain those goals. These units in turn are overseen and directed by the board of directors and executive officers of the company. The ICT function supports this through its standard development, operations, and maintenance functions. The flow of information is back and forth from the working units to the IT function as information resources are developed and utilized.

However, the problem lies in the direction of the assignment of responsibility for the assurance of the resource. If the purpose of corporate information is to accomplish the ends of the business, then the responsibility for protecting that asset lies at least with the functional unit managers who use it and, by implication, with the board, not with the management of the IT function.

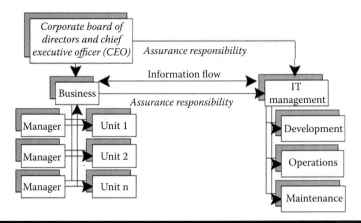

Figure 10.1   Flow of responsibility for information assurance.

At a minimum, the consequence of this illogical placement is that the responsibility for assuring the basis on which the sheer survival of the corporation might rest lies with the group that by definition is the most disconnected from its generation and use. Furthermore, this is a technical group, not one either well versed or interested in the nuances of the business operation. The outcome is inevitably and quite understandably going to be a narrow technical solution, which will not come close to confronting all the myriad of threats faced by a modern, multinational corporation.

The final unique assurance problem stems from the basic purpose of IT itself, which is to enhance communication. In the world of physical security it is easy to account for assets because they are tangible and can be kept in an identified place. The problem with IT assets is that they have to be dispersed as part of their basic function, that is, the whole point of the Internet is to provide remote access from a myriad of sources. So in order to be useful IT assets are by definition difficult to secure.

For example, candidates for security control include such asset categories as "hardware and system software," "applications," "information and data," and "organizational interfaces." None of these is easily assured because they are either intangible or dynamic. The fact is that organizations can rarely account for the exact status of their system and applications software, information and data assets, or events occurring on the organizational interfaces (think Internet transactions, for instance). Yet all of these constitute the asset base that must be accounted for.

Thus, a precondition to the establishment of security assurance is the existence of an explicit mechanism, which can serve as the basis for making ICT work concrete by specifying it. In addition, there must be a formal device that allows for the specification of the rules for management control as well as how the ongoing assessment of status will be conducted. And since security involves coordinating a range of functions as well as communication and cooperation among and between organizations, it would also be helpful if that framework was commonly understood and accepted across the industry.

Requirement for Best Practice Advice

The goal of this book is to explain how standard-based best practice, in the form of the NICE workforce framework, can be used to ensure complete security protection over IT assets and information resources. Simply put, it would be nice if organizations could find a way to underwrite trust in their integrity on a standard basis. Obviously, what is required is a good old-fashioned framework, which will dictate the right set of best practices in sufficient detail to give everybody involved confidence that they are doing the right thing.

The key notion here is "total protection." It ought to be obvious that all of the potential security risks must be identified, assessed, and responded to at every level of the organization in order for it to be able to consider itself adequately protected.

This is problematic since the average business manager cannot be expected to be able to identify every potential threat, let alone devise a foolproof method to respond to them. Unfortunately, however, a security scheme with even one hole is a potential business catastrophe just waiting to happen, particularly, given the level of sophistication of most of our adversaries.

The expedient of an organization basing its security approach on a single commonly accepted standard for cybersecurity protection is an important topic because, competitive advantage and cost efficiency has created a growing dependence on ICT systems. At the same time, business customers want to be assured that their business transactions are protected and safe. Consequently, progressively more trustworthy security approaches are required as organizations grow and diversify.

For that reason there is a corresponding requirement to establish and maintain a suitable stable point of reference that can be used by every practitioner to structure a complete and correct security response. Moreover, given the fact that the technology is constantly undergoing rapid and dynamic change, this also implies that body of knowledge must be comprehensive, carefully researched and constructed, publicized, updated, and maintained.

Nevertheless, the underlying issue here is not just security. It is also a question of how to get the most assurance out of the organization's resources. Obviously, anything can be secured if enough money is thrown at it. But, no organization has the wherewithal to effectively put a cop on every street corner. So, managers must weigh and balance the deployment of their responses against the potential likelihood and material consequences of the threat.

In day-to-day operation this means that a decision has to be made about the level of acceptable risk for every identified weakness. That is hard to do with security assurance because of the complexity of the threat environment particularly when the decision about acceptable risk is weighted against the possible cost of failure.

Therefore, a coherent set of best practice recommendations, which let decision makers benchmark existing and planned security measures against the most expert advice available is an important strategic planning mechanism for any organization. In essence, from a practical standpoint, the organization's approach to security has to be consistent in order to ensure that there are no significant gaps that can be exploited. And logically, in order to ensure that consistency the organization needs to approach the planning and deployment of the security scheme as an across-the-board strategic exercise.

Best Practice and Strategy

Whether they are universally standard or documented, every enterprise is governed by its best practices. This is also true for ICT. Best practices in ICT characterize and communicate how those functions will support the objectives of the business. They ensure that the enterprise's information resources are deployed for maximum effectives and that any threats to the performance of the IT function are managed appropriately.

Obviously, these practices can also form the basis for defining standard operating procedure both to assure the ICT process and to realize its benefits. Operationally, ICT activities can be benchmarked against these recommendations and subsequent controls can be set to ensure that what the organization does reflects best practice.

The direct and qualitative link can only be established by an explicit specification of how each individual information protection activity will be carried out and how it is expected to impact information and ICT resources. It implies the need for a clear statement or plan for how that will happen. These plans are nothing more than a specification of the desired result or outcome of a given set of procedures that are carried out within a particular process. A complete and correct set of these specifications will establish and maintain ICT systems and information resources at an optimum best practice level of functioning. Moreover, this will ensure that the security response is tangible enough to be audited to support overall organizational management aims.

As we have seen in this text, the currently understood set of complete and correct practices for performance of cybersecurity work is specified by the tasks and knowledge, skills, and abilities (KSAs) of the National Institute for Standards and Technology's (NIST), NICE Workforce Model (2.0). The NIST–NICE workforce framework works in conjunction with the NIST CSF.

Each of these large strategic models has a slightly different purpose and application. But both of these models combined provide a comprehensive and specific "expert" approach to practical cybersecurity. Together the actions specified in these two models serve to ensure the "effectiveness," "efficiency," "confidentiality," "integrity," "availability," "compliance," and "reliability" of IT and information assets.

They are both based on the definition of explicit actions to be taken in a given situation, which includes the specification of the tasks, competencies, and the knowledge requirements (NICE), and the standard security functions required to achieve comprehensive security functioning (CSF). Properly thought through and specified this explicit advice ensures that due diligence is exercised by all individuals involved in the management, use, design, development, maintenance, or operation of cybersecurity systems.

Applying the NICE Workforce Framework (v2.0) to the Real World

The purpose of the NICE framework is to provide a common benchmark for best security practice. It is designed to enable IT managers and corporate end users to leverage their levels of security assurance to higher states. It allows companies to identify gaps in their security management infrastructure. It also allows companies of all sizes to demonstrate the effectiveness of their cybersecurity management to prospective trading partners. The framework provides common ground for companies wishing to trade with each other, assuring them that they are operating at a common level of security.

Besides, this functional advantage of common terminology and practice the framework has many practical benefits. ICT security operations tend to be tactical and reactive by nature, passively waiting for the bad guys to show up to rob the bank. On the other hand, if cybersecurity is based on the deterrent principles defined in the two NICE models, it can be strategy driven, that is, organizations can initiate a full-scale set of proactive measures that will prevent rather than react to security threats.

The most important feature of the framework is probably the fact that it provides a solid and reliable management basis for developing and maintaining security over all aspects of a business's information assets. Its objective is to provide "a common basis to develop, implement, and measure" effective security management practice. It is implemented through risk-based assessment process.

A formal infrastructure of standard practices is the quintessential first step in enacting rational management over any aspect of ICT. It just makes good common sense, because without a process it is particularly difficult to establish and maintain organizational control over an activity that is basically conceptual and abstract by nature.

Comprehensive protection requires a formally engineered process architecture tailored to fit the specific requirements of a given situation. However, since the development of this is more an art than a science, some sort of standard, best practice-based model is always needed to guide and structure the definition process.

The knowledge areas itemized in the NICE model are designed to fit anything from an individual software project to a complex organization-wide network security operation. Consequently, compliance with the recommendations of the NICE model amounts to the performance of a standard complete set of security practices.

The specific processes, activities, and tasks identified in the standard are designed to describe all aspects of security assurance. Thus, the NICE model provides all of the details necessary to install a practical security system, which meets the requirements of currently defined best practice.

Using the NICE model companies can walk through a controlled step-by-step assessment of their current security status and then tailor specific management controls to fit a given situation. In essence, by using the NICE model, it is possible to engineer a top-down operational approach for the security work in each individual organization.

This hierarchical approach creates a complete and rational, tangible security infrastructure. It can be tailored directly out of the elements of the model into precise policies and work instructions that define the organization's individual response. The outcome of this top-down tailoring process is a set of explicit work activities, which become the tangible instantiation of the cybersecurity scheme for any given organization.

In general, the resulting documentation set is most useful to the line manager because it substantiates the recommended standard operating procedure (SOP) for performing day-to-day security functions. It embodies and conveys the exact substance of the assurance tasks to every one of the employees working within the individual process.

Tasks are the explicitly designated set of steps required to fulfill the requirements of a given job role within a particular specialty area of work. Conceptually, these tasks are always unit specific and generally cannot be characterized without tailoring. They represent "the currently accepted" optimum approach to the security requirements for that specialty area of work.

Tailoring a Security Architecture to Fit Each Organizational Need

The NICE framework was created to be generic. Or in simple terms, it is applicable to almost all conceivable security requirements and situations worldwide. It is also proactive in the sense that it prescribes a typical set of actions that should be taken to in order to provide active working security assurance.

The NICE framework was designed to meet the needs of a range of target constituencies and it is applicable to a range of environments from leading edge industries to services. NICE delineates all of the elements of assurance that are necessary to structure a complete workforce solution for any organization. Its knowledge and specialty areas are applicable to the definition of a security solution for a single business or a corporation. It assumes that specific security tasks will always be tailored to the common task and KSA functions specified within the general framework of the model.

This is accomplished in three steps. First, once the threats, vulnerabilities, and weaknesses that the organization faces are assessed and determined, the functional roles and knowledge requirements necessary to respond to those threats are identified. This serves as a foundation for tailoring. Then, the standard task specifications are documented for each of the applicable security roles.

Finally, explicit work instructions and the attendant knowledge specifications are tailored to substantiate the specific activities defined for a particular unit. The result is an explicit set of security tasks, which are based on the requirements of the NICE model that accommodate all known situational constraints.

Steps for Creating a Substantive Security Solution

The framework is structured on one simple and pragmatic assumption. That is, information resources should be overseen and secured using a set of naturally grouped processes. These are the knowledge and specialty areas that are then substantiated by task and KSA specifications. The complete set of these task and KSA specifications is assumed to describe and embody all aspects of security for information and ICT functioning.

By satisfying all of the attendant KSA and task requirements, the manager can ensure that a capable ICT security system is in place for any type of organization and at any level of security desired. Finally, and more importantly, the NICE framework can serve as the basis for a risk assessment approach, which is a way of concretely establishing best security practice in ICT work.

In addition to the specification of the substantive ICT security work, the CSF suggests five key functions that can be used to ensure that the cybersecurity operation is meeting its goals. These come in the form of a set of critical factors, which are intended to characterize the most important management-oriented concerns of cybersecurity. Those are identification of threat, protection scheme, active defense, threat response, and recovery.

Measures can then be defined from these factors that will tell management whether a process is achieving its assured objectives. These critical factors force the organization to address such vital management questions as: "How far should we go to secure something and is the cost justified?" "What are the indicators of good security performance?" "What are risks of not achieving our objectives?" and "What do others do? And how do we compare against best practice?"

For the purposes of implementation, the NICE framework demands that the organization develop and document an explicit statement of the work practices required to address the specific security issues that it identifies. In addition, the framework requires that there be a precise itemization of the threats, vulnerabilities, and weaknesses (which was identified by the risk assessment) that these practices will address. And there must be as a ranking of their relative priority.

The NICE framework also requires the organization to itemize the measures that will be used to monitor and judge good performance. If there are best practice benchmarks involved in the actual determination of this, those also have to be specified and their use clarified in terms of how they will be derived and used.

The practical outcome of the implementation process is a tangible set of work practices, which can be assumed to fully assure the information resource within the area of interest. A specific process can be adopted to develop that assurance. This process is specified in Figure 10.2. It should be noted that this generic methodology can be employed to create a practical instantiation of best practice based on the NICE workforce framework and the documentation that results from the execution of each of these stages is what is referenced by an auditor if an assessment is carried out in order to verify conformance to the principles of best practice.

The diagram describes three different types of documentation elements. The first of these are the inputs to the implementation process itself. These inputs represent contextual issues about which a tailoring decision must be made. Using a standard risk assessment process (for instance, NIST Special Publication 800-39), the organization identifies and prioritizes the threats it faces and the vulnerabilities that those represent.

It bases its decisions about levels of assurance on its understanding of the impact of these vulnerabilities on its information assets. The items in the center part of the

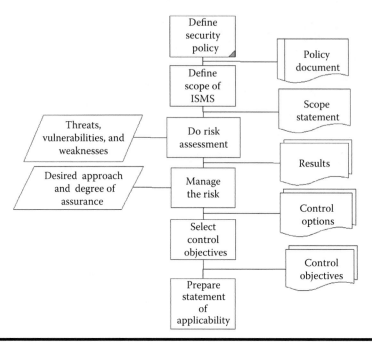

Figure 10.2   Security development process.

diagram represent standard procedures that the organization undertakes during the day-to-day implementation and tailoring of the NICE specifications. Finally, the documentation that is produced (right side of the diagram) drives the activity in subsequent processes as well as documenting the form of the security system for the purposes of management oversight and audit.

As can be seen, this implementation model is executed in six phases, the first two of which involve the establishment of a formal security infrastructure that is based on the definition of comprehensive information security policy and the setting of the boundaries of control. Factors that might enter into this activity include such issues as what is the level of criticality for each of the information assets within the scope of the protection scheme, and what is the degree of assurance required for each? Other infrastructure considerations might embrace any expected strategic initiatives as well as any market, or regulatory influences. The boundary setting element of this is particularly important since there is an obvious direct relationship between the resources required to establish the security level specified and the extent of the territory that must be secured by the process.

Following this, the organization performs a risk assessment. This is the most important element in the process because it identifies the potential threats to the business's information assets. Since a particular threat may not necessarily have much impact within a given situation, vulnerabilities are evaluated on a likelihood and impact basis in order to distinguish only those weaknesses that would create specific and undesirable outcomes.

Once they are all identified, the vulnerabilities are carefully analyzed with respect to the particular organizational situation in order to identify the specific threats that the security work needs to target directly. These weaknesses are prioritized so that the ones with the most critical impacts are dealt with first.

Next, a concomitant set of explicit risk management procedures are formulated from the task specifications of the NICE model. These must address the findings from the risk assessment in the order established by the priorities established in the prior step. And so that these procedures can be monitored and assessed the appropriate set of KSA and competency requirements identified and referenced to each procedure.

Finally, a statement of applicability is prepared and documented for each proposed task. This statement itemizes the asset to be secured along with the reasons for its selection as a target, the measure that will be used to determine whether that objective has been met and the resources necessary to achieve that desired result.

Then the actual security operation can be defined. Practically, the assessment process that creates the operation is based on an assessment of risks and resources available to address them. In general, resulting workforce roles are defined based on the following systematic process. That process is aimed at full implementing the recommendations of the NICE model. Figure 10.3 summarizes the process that an organization would follow to implement the process discussed here.

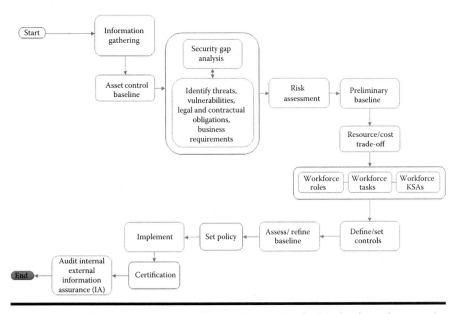

Figure 10.3   Sample process for implementing *National Initiative for Cybersecurity Education* **workforce framework.**

NICE provides a well-defined set of task requirements for establishing, implementing, and documenting an effective CSF scheme. It specifies the specific actions that have to be taken by the organization to meet its security requirements and it establishes the basis of the assessment process that is used to ensure trustworthy long-term security functioning.

The assessment model incorporates an eight-step process. The first step involves information gathering and policy setting. The assets that are meant to fall within the protection perimeter are formally identified and valued and placed into logical control groups, which are also valuated.

Then a formal gap analysis is performed and security requirements are identified using the information obtained from step two. This identifies a particular set of threats and vulnerabilities unique to the organization along with the legal and contractual obligations and the relevant business requirements. In step four, these security requirements are formulated into an individualized organizational baseline; step five performs an assessment of that baseline. That assessment focuses on defining the necessary controls for containing the threats and vulnerabilities identified, and assuring the legal and contractual obligations and business requirements.

A detailed risk assessment is carried out in the sixth step. This involves a formal valuation of the impacts of the threats and vulnerabilities and legal obligations and business requirements, which leads to an explicit calculation of the risk percentages for each factor identified and recommendations for risk reduction. The seventh step amounts to a refinement of the prior six stages. Both the identified baseline and the relevant controls are assessed for the purpose of refining their focus and the effectiveness of their response. The process leading to this is discussed in the following sections.

Information gathering. The first stage logically involves the gathering of all of the pertinent information necessary to define the form of the information asset that will be protected. This establishes a boundary for the protection that balances resources invested against value of the asset. The steps include the identification, labeling, and valuation of all of the assets and the formulation of the complete set into a comprehensive asset control baseline. This baseline is normally valuated and maintained under the dictates of rigorous change control.

Gap analysis. Once all of the organization's information assets have been identified and baselined, the next step is to perform a security gap analysis. The purpose of this is to determine the exact status of the information protection safeguards for each of the individual items in the baseline versus the known threats.

This involves the identification of all of the direct threats, vulnerabilities, and weaknesses for each identified asset as well as specification of any other contextual factors that might impact security such as legal and contractual requirements, or any current or projected business requirements.

Risk assessment decision. This step involves making a decision about the findings of the gap analysis. As we said, this is not a simple matter of plugging holes since it is likely that the gap analysis will find more vulnerabilities than the organization would ever have the resources to properly address. Instead, managers perform a sort of triage identifying and prioritizing the identified security issues such that they can be assured that the organization's critical functions have been adequately addressed by a set of well-defined work instructions.

Preliminary baseline. Once the management team feels like it has got a handle on the security issues it selects a suitable set of tasks from the seven knowledge areas of the NICE model. This includes all of the appropriate worker actions essential to address all of the threats and vulnerabilities identified in the gap analysis as well as to satisfy any other legal, contractual, or business requirements that might have been identified.

Resource trade-off. Once the entire set of controls has been identified, the organization's decision makers perform a rational and explicit trade-off between the inherent cost of addressing the threats and the importance of each of the assets that fall within the preliminary boundaries of the protection scheme.

In simple terms this means that the estimated cost of performing the necessary work is traded-off against the potential impacts of the threat. This process is applied to the identified threats and vulnerabilities as well as the other identified legal, contractual, and business vulnerabilities.

The trade-off that applies here is that the probability of the threat actually happening is balanced against the resources required to address it. The eventual outcome is a sliding scale interpretation called a risk reduction decision—e.g., a partial solution. The final result will range between not dealing with the threat at all, all the way up to deploying the workforce roles required to completely eliminate it.

Selection of workforce actions, refinement of selection, and implementation of the tasks required. The next three steps are really aspects of the same process. Once all of the elements of risk and resources are understood, it is time to select the necessary workforce roles and their attendant tasks and KSAs. This this is actually an iterative selection and validation process.

Over a period the organization decides on and fine-tunes the tasks that it believes are the most effective approach to the assurance of its information assets.

Alterations to this set are based on feedback from lessons learned within the organization itself and normally take time. Once the final set of work practices is installed and provably working as intended they are placed in a baseline configuration. This configuration is maintained under formal, systematic control. This is the final stage in the process.

Chapter Summary

The goal of this book is to explain how standard-based best practice, in the form of the NICE workforce framework, can be used to ensure complete security protection over IT assets and information resources. The key notion here is total protection. It ought to be obvious that all of the potential security risks must be identified, assessed, and responded to at every level of the organization in order for it to be able to consider itself adequately protected. This is problematic since the average business manager cannot be expected to be able to identify every potential threat, let alone devise a foolproof method to respond to them. Unfortunately, however, a security scheme with even one hole is a potential business catastrophe just waiting to happen particularly given the level of sophistication of most of our adversaries.

The expedient of an organization basing its security approach on a single commonly accepted standard for cybersecurity protection is an important topic because competitive advantage and cost-efficiency have created a growing dependence on ICT systems. At the same time, business customers want to be assured that their business transactions are protected and safe. Consequently, progressively more trustworthy security approaches are required as organizations grow and diversify. Accordingly, there is a corresponding requirement to establish and maintain a suitable common point of reference that can be used by practitioners to structure complete and correct security responses. Moreover, given the fact that the technology is constantly undergoing rapid and dynamic change, this also implies that body of knowledge must be comprehensive, carefully researched and constructed, publicized, updated, and maintained.

In day-to-day operation this means that a decision has to be made about the level of acceptable risk for every identified weakness. That is hard to do with security assurance because of the complexity of the threat environment particularly when the decision about acceptable risk is weighted against the possible cost of failure. Therefore, a coherent set of best practice recommendations, which let decision makers benchmark existing and planned security measures against the most expert advice available is an important strategic planning mechanism for any organization.

The direct and qualitative link can only be established by an explicit specification of how each individual information protection activity will be carried out and how it is expected to impact information and ICT resources. It implies the need for a clear statement or plan for how that will happen. These plans are nothing more than a specification of the desired result or outcome of a given set of procedures that are carried out within a particular process. A complete and correct set of these specifications will establish and maintain ICT systems and information resources at an optimum best practice level of functioning. Moreover, this will ensure that the security response is tangible enough to be audited to support overall organizational management aims.

As we have seen in this text, the currently understood set of complete and correct practices for performance of cybersecurity work is specified by the tasks and KSAs of the NIST, NICE Workforce Model (2.0). The NIST–NICE workforce framework works in conjunction with the NIST CSF. Each of these large strategic models has a slightly different purpose and application. But both of these models combined provide a comprehensive and specific set of expert practices for cybersecurity. Together the actions specified in these two models serve to ensure the effectiveness, efficiency, confidentiality, integrity, availability, compliance and reliability of IT and information assets.

These two standards are groundbreaking because they are not just a silver bullet, meaning narrow technological solutions nor do they simply focus on assuring the technology itself. Instead these two models can be used to create a comprehensive and persistent top-down management infrastructure that will allow an organization to maintain effective security over all aspects of its work.

The purpose of the NICE framework is to provide a common benchmark for security best practice. It is designed to enable IT managers and corporate end users to leverage their levels of security assurance to higher states. It allows companies to identify gaps in their security management infrastructure. It also allows companies of all sizes to demonstrate the effectiveness of their cybersecurity management to prospective trading partners. The framework provides common ground for companies wishing to trade with each other, assuring them that they are operating at a common level of security.

A formal infrastructure of standard practices is the quintessential first step in enacting rational management over any aspect of ICT. It just makes good common sense, because without a process it is particularly difficult to establish and maintain organizational control over an activity that is basically conceptual and abstract by nature. Comprehensive protection requires a formally engineered process architecture tailored to fit the specific requirements of a given situation. However, since the development of this is more an art than a science, some sort of standard, best practice-based model is always needed to guide and structure the definition process.

The knowledge areas itemized in the NICE model are designed to fit anything from an individual software project to a complex organization-wide network security operation. Consequently, compliance with the recommendations of the NICE model amounts to the performance of a standard complete set of security practices. The specific processes, activities, and tasks identified in the standard are designed to describe all aspects of security assurance. Thus, the NICE model provides all of the details necessary to install a practical security system, which meets the requirements of currently defined best practice.

Using the NICE model companies can walk through a controlled step-by-step assessment of their current security status and then tailor specific management controls to fit a given situation. In essence, using the NICE model is it possible to engineer a top-down operational approach for the security work in each individual organization.

This hierarchical approach creates a complete and rational, tangible security infrastructure. It can be tailored directly out of the elements of the model into precise policies and work instructions that define the organization's individual response. The outcome of this top-down tailoring process is a set of explicit work activities, which become the tangible instantiation of the cybersecurity scheme for any given organization.

The NICE framework was created to be generic. Or in simple terms, it is applicable to almost all conceivable security requirements and situations worldwide. It is also proactive in the sense that it prescribes a typical set of actions that should be taken in order to provide active working security assurance.

The framework is structured on one simple and pragmatic assumption, because information resources should be overseen and secured using a set of naturally grouped processes. These are the knowledge and specialty areas that are then substantiated by task and KSA specifications. The complete set of these task and KSA specifications is assumed to describe and embody all aspects of security for information and ICT functioning. By satisfying all of the attendant KSA and task requirements, the manager can ensure that a capable ICT security system is in place for any type of organization and at any level of security desired. Finally, and more importantly, NICE can serve as the basis for a risk assessment approach, which is a way of concretely establishing security best practice in ICT work.

For the purposes of implementation, the NICE framework demands that the organization develop and document an explicit statement of the work practices required to address the specific security issues that it identifies. In addition, the framework requires that there be a precise itemization of the threats, vulnerabilities, and weaknesses (which was identified by the risk assessment) that these practices will address.

There must then be a ranking of the relative priority of each threat. The framework also requires the organization to itemize the measures that will be used to monitor and judge good performance. If there are best practice benchmarks involved in the actual determination of this, those also have to be specified and their use clarified in terms of how they will be derived and used.

The practical outcome of the implementation process is a tangible set of work practices, which can be assumed to fully assure the information resource within the area of interest. A specific process can be adopted to develop that assurance. This process is specified in Figure 10.1. It should be noted that this generic methodology can be employed to create a practical instantiation of best practice based on the NICE model and the documentation that results from the execution of each of these stages is what is referenced by an auditor if an assessment is carried out in order to verify conformance to the principles of best practice.

The implementation model is executed in six phases, the first two of which involve the establishment of a formal security infrastructure that is based on the definition of comprehensive information security policy and the setting of the boundaries of control. Factors that might enter into this activity include such issues as what is the level of criticality for each of the information assets within the scope of the protection scheme and what is the degree of assurance required for each? Other infrastructure considerations might embrace any expected strategic initiatives as well as any market or regulatory influences.

The boundary setting element of this is particularly important since there is an obvious direct relationship between the resources required to establish the security level specified and the extent of the territory that must be secured by the process.

Following this, the organization performs a risk assessment. This is the most important element in the process because it identifies the potential threats to the business's information assets. Since a particular threat may not necessarily have much impact within a given situation, vulnerabilities are evaluated on a likelihood and impact basis in order to distinguish only those weaknesses that would create specific and undesirable outcomes. Once they are all identified vulnerabilities are carefully analyzed with respect to the particular organizational situation in order to identify the specific threats that the security work needs to target directly. These weaknesses are prioritized so that the ones with the most critical impacts are dealt with first.

Next, a concomitant set of explicit risk management procedures are formulated from the task specifications of the NICE model. These must address the findings from the risk assessment in the order established by the priorities established in the prior step. And so that these procedures can be monitored and assessed the appropriate set of KSA and competency requirements identified and referenced to each procedure.

Finally, a statement of applicability is prepared and documented for each proposed task. This statement itemizes the asset to be secured along with the reasons for its selection as a target, the measure that will be used to determine whether that objective has been met and the resources necessary to achieve that desired result.

Then the actual security operation can be defined. Practically, the assessment process that creates the operation is based on an assessment of risks and resources available to address them. In general resulting workforce roles are defined based on the following systematic process. That process is aimed at full implementing the recommendations of the NICE model. The steps involved are discussed in the following sections.

Information gathering. The first stage logically involves the gathering of all of the pertinent information necessary to define the form of the information asset that will be protected. This establishes a boundary for the protection that balances resources invested against value of the asset. The steps include the identification, labeling, and valuation of all of the assets and the formulation of the complete set into a comprehensive asset control baseline. This baseline is normally valuated and maintained under the dictates of rigorous change control.

Gap analysis. Once all of the organization's information assets have been identified and baselined the next step is to perform a security gap analysis. The purpose of this is to determine the exact status of the information protection safeguards for each of the individual items in the baseline versus the known threats. This involves the identification of all of the direct threats, vulnerabilities, and weaknesses for each identified asset as well as specification of any other contextual factors that might impact security such as legal and contractual requirements, or any current or projected business requirements.

Risk assessment decision. This step involves making a decision about the findings of the gap analysis. As we said, this is not a simple matter of plugging holes since it is likely that the gap analysis will find more vulnerabilities than the organization would ever have the resources to properly address. Instead, managers perform a sort of triage identifying and prioritizing the identified security issues such that they can be assured that the organization's critical functions have been adequately addressed by a set of well-defined work instructions.

Preliminary baseline. Once the management team feels like it has gotten a handle on the security issues it selects a suitable set of tasks from the seven knowledge areas of the NICE model. This includes all of the appropriate worker actions essential to address all of the threats and vulnerabilities identified in the gap analysis as well as to satisfy any other legal, contractual, or business requirements that might have been identified.

Resource trade-off. Once the entire set of controls has been identified the organization's decision makers perform a rational and explicit trade-off between the inherent cost of addressing the threats and the importance of each of the assets that fall within the preliminary boundaries of the protection scheme. In simple terms this means that the estimated cost of performing the necessary work is traded off against the potential impacts of the threat. This process is applied to the identified threats and vulnerabilities as well as the other identified legal, contractual, and business vulnerabilities.

The trade-off that applies here is that the probability of the threat actually happening is balanced against the resources required to address it. The eventual outcome is a sliding scale interpretation called a risk reduction decision—e.g., a partial solution. The final result will range between not dealing with the threat at all, all the way up to deploying the workforce roles required to completely eliminate it.

Selection of workforce actions, refinement of selection, and implementation of the tasks required. The next three steps are really aspects of the same process. Once all of the elements of risk and resources are understood it is time to select the necessary workforce roles and their attendant tasks and KSAs. This this is actually an iterative selection and validation process.

Over a period of time the organization decides on and fine-tunes the tasks that it believes are the most effective approach to the assurance of its information assets. Alterations to this set are based on feedback from lessons learned within the organization itself and normally take time. Once the final set of work practices is installed and provably working as intended they are placed in a baseline configuration. This configuration is maintained under formal, systematic control. This is the final stage in the process.

Key Terms

Decision Making Model: The cognitive and behavioral approach that a decision maker(s) adopt in order to come to a specific action-oriented conclusion.

NICE Workforce Task: A specific area of work practice that can be identified as fitting within a given area of standard security protection.

Risk Analysis: The process of threat identification and assessment.

Risk Assessment: An estimation of the likelihood of occurrence and potential harm of an identified threat.

Role: A generic area of security work, delineated by a common set of skills and functional purposes.

Strategic Planning: Long-term targeting and resourcing undertaken to achieve policy goals set by decision makers.

Top-Down Implementation: The basic thought process of decomposing a problem into components that are subject to understanding and actionable resolution and then building the solution out of the components.

Total Protection: All priority weaknesses are addressed by security practice designed to ensure against exploitation.

Reference

Privacy Resources Clearinghouse. 2014. *Data Breaches 2005–2014*. San Diego, CA: PRC.

Index